INTERNATIONAL CRIME AND JUSTICE

International crime and justice is an emerging field that covers international and transnational crimes that have not been the focus of mainstream criminology or criminal justice. This book examines the field from a global perspective. It provides an introduction to the nature of international and transnational crimes and the theoretical perspectives that assist in understanding the relationship between social change and crime opportunities resulting from globalization, migration, and culture conflicts.

Written by a team of world experts, International Crime and Justice examines the central role of victims' rights in the development of legal frameworks for the prevention and control of transnational and international crimes. It also discusses the challenges in delivering justice and obtaining international cooperation in efforts to deter, detect, and respond to these crimes.

Arranged in nine parts, International Crime and Justice provides readers with an understanding of the main concepts relevant to the topic and the complex nature of the problems.

Mangai Natarajan is a professor in the Department of Criminal Justice at John Jay College of Criminal Justice, The City University of New York. A policy-oriented researcher, she has published widely in drug trafficking, women police, domestic violence, and international criminal justice. She is the founding director of the international criminal justice major at John Jay College.

INTERNATIONAL CRIME AND JUSTICE

Edited by

Mangai Natarajan

John Jay College of Criminal Justice,
The City University of New York

CAMBRIDGE
UNIVERSITY PRESS

CAMBRIDGE UNIVERSITY PRESS
Cambridge, New York, Melbourne, Madrid, Cape Town,
Singapore, São Paulo, Delhi, Tokyo, Mexico City

Cambridge University Press
32 Avenue of the Americas, New York NY 10013-2473, USA

Published in the United States of America by Cambridge University Press, New York

www.cambridge.org
Information on this title: www.cambridge.org/9781107144490

© Cambridge University Press 2011

First published 2011
First paperback edition 2011

A catalogue record for this publication is available from the British Library

Library of Congress Cataloging in Publication data
International crime and justice / [edited by] Mangai Natarajan.
  p. cm.
Includes bibliographical references and index.
ISBN 978-0-521-19619-2
1. Transnational crime. 2. Criminology – Cross cultural studies. 3. Criminal justice,
Administration of – International cooperation. 4. Criminal justice, Administration of –
Cross-cultural studies. I. Natarajan, Mangai.
HV6252.I56 2011
364–dc22   2010033856

ISBN 978-0-521-19619-2 Hardback
ISBN 978-1-107-14449-0 Paperback

Contents

Contents

Contents

Figures and Tables

FIGURES

TABLES

Contributors

Marcelo F. Aebi, University of Lausanne, Switzerland

Jay S. Albanese, Virginia Commonwealth University, USA

George Andreopoulos, John Jay College of Criminal Justice, USA

Xabier Agirre Aranburu, International Criminal Court, Netherlands

Enrique Desmond Arias, John Jay College of Criminal Justice, USA

Alexis A. Aronowitz, University College Utrecht, Netherlands

Jana Arsovska, John Jay College of Criminal Justice, USA

G.S. Bajpai, National Law Institute University, Bhopal, India

Rosemary Barberet, John Jay College of Criminal Justice, USA

Stefan Barriga, Permanent Mission of Liechtenstein to the United Nations

Roberta Belli, John Jay College of Criminal Justice, USA

Gisela Bichler, California State University, San Bernardino, USA

Steven Block, Rutgers, the State University of New Jersey, USA

Alfred Blumstein, Carnegie Mellon University, USA

Conor Brady, Garda Siochana Ombudsman Commission, Ireland

Rick Brown, Evidence Led Solution, UK

Gloria J. Browne-Marshall, John Jay College of Criminal Justice, USA

David Donat Cattin, International Law and Human Rights Programme, The Hague, Netherlands

Steven M. Chermak, Michigan State University, USA

Monica Ciobanu, State University of New York at Plattsburgh, USA

Roger S. Clark, Rutgers, the State University of New Jersey, USA

Ronald V. Clarke, Rutgers, the State University of New Jersey, USA

Harry R. Dammer, University of Scranton, USA

Marcia Esparza, John Jay College of Criminal Justice, USA

Marcus Felson, Rutgers, the State University of New Jersey, USA

James O. Finckenauer, Rutgers, the State University of New Jersey, USA

Joshua D. Freilich, John Jay College of Criminal Justice, USA

Martin Gottschalk, University of North Dakota, USA

Adam Graycar, Australian National University, Australia

Rob T. Guerette, Florida International University, USA

Ni He, College of Criminal Justice, Northeastern University, USA

David C. Hicks, Cardiff University, Wales, UK

Gregory J. Howard, Western Michigan University, USA

Matti Joutsen, Ministry of Justice, Finland

Helen Kapstein, John Jay College of Criminal Justice, USA

Maria Kiriakova, John Jay College of Criminal Justice, USA

Antigona Kukaj, Mississippi Law School, USA

Leona Lee, John Jay College of Criminal Justice, USA

Theodore Leggett, United Nations Office on Drugs and Crime, Vienna, Austria

Andrew Lemieux, Rutgers, the State University of New Jersey, USA

Eric G. Lesneskie, Rutgers, the State University of New Jersey, USA

Michael Levi, Cardiff University, Wales, UK

Richard Lovely, John Jay College of Criminal Justice, USA

Simon Mackenzie, University of Glasgow, Scotland, UK

Ineke Haen Marshall, College of Criminal Justice, Northeastern University, USA

Rob Mawby, University of Gloucestershire, England, UK

Michael G. Maxfield, Rutgers, the State University of New Jersey, USA

William F. McDonald, Georgetown University, USA

José Luis Morín, John Jay College of Criminal Justice, USA

John Myrtle, Griffith University, Queensland, Australia

Mangai Natarajan, John Jay College of Criminal Justice, USA

Graeme R. Newman, The State University of New York at Albany, USA

William S. Parkin, City University of New York Graduate Center and John Jay College of Criminal Justice, USA

Stephan Parmentier, Catholic University of Leuven, Belgium

Carla Reyes, Duke Law School, USA

Vincenzo Ruggiero, Middlesex University, England, UK

Ernesto U. Savona, The Catholic University of Milan, Italy

Jacqueline Schneider, Illinois State University, USA

Phyllis A. Schultze, Rutgers, the State University of New Jersey, USA

Louise Shelley, George Mason University, USA

Bir Pal Singh, National Law Institute University, Bhopal, India

Edward Snajdr, John Jay College of Criminal Justice, USA

Itai Sneh, John Jay College of Criminal Justice, USA

Alexander Sukharenko, Institute of State and Municipal Management, Vladivostok, Russia

Cécile Van de Voorde, John Jay College of Criminal Justice, USA

Jan Van Dijk, University of Tilburg/Intervict, Netherlands

Klaus von Lampe, John Jay College of Criminal Justice, USA

Noah Weisbord, Duke Law School, USA

Elmar Weitekamp, University of Tuebingen, Germany

Jo-Anne Wemmers, Université de Montréal, Canada

Rob White, University of Tasmania, Australia

Richard Wortley, Jill Dando Institute of Crime Science, University College, London, UK

Marco Zanella, The Catholic University of Milan, Italy

Foreword

It is a truism that the world is getting smaller. The advent of the Internet, the ease of international travel, the emergence of multinational institutions, the global awareness of genocide and other crimes against humanity, and the creation of economies that span national boundaries have all brought the people of the world into closer connection. Not surprisingly, the nature of criminal activity has also changed. New and sophisticated forms of transnational crime have emerged, challenging the capabilities of investigative and law enforcement agencies in the private and public sectors. Cybercrimes that are launched in one country with consequences in dozens of other countries raise questions about the proper locus of criminal prosecutions. Genocides and mass killings that generate a global sense of outrage underscore the need for international forums that can adjudicate these horrific criminal events. At the same time, the need for an appropriate response to these crimes has resulted in new arrangements of international cooperation among police agencies, new multilateral agreements regarding prosecution of offenders, and new efforts to prevent these crimes before they occur.

This new global reality has had important consequences for scholars, policymakers, and advocates who think about the challenges of crime and care about the pursuit of justice. As the essays in this path-breaking book highlight, the global community of criminal justice experts is engaged in a fundamental rethinking of long-standing premises that form the core theoretical and practical pillars of the disciplines of criminal justice and criminology. Indeed, this book argues for the creation of a new discipline – one that embraces the challenges of international crime and justice; one that not only bridges national and cultural boundaries that too often limit intellectual inquiry but also bridges a wide variety of academic disciplines.

The range of topics considered by the authors of these chapters is breathtaking. In terms of the international dimensions of crime, the chapters discuss migration and crime, small arms trafficking, maritime crime, terrorism, drug cartels, tourist crime, organized crime, and genocide. In terms of the global response to these crimes, the chapters cover topics such as the International Criminal Court, the role of international treaties, truth and reconciliation commissions, crossborder policing, and the role of the United Nations. In terms of criminological theories and research strategies, the chapters explore the applicability of routine activities theory, international victimology, a criminological analysis of political violence, and the need for standardized victimization surveys and other data collection programs.

The ramifications of this intellectual inquiry in the new global realities of crime and justice are considerable. On a practical level, an improved capacity to deter, detect, and respond appropriately to the crimes described here will redound to the benefit of millions of members of the global village. On a more ephemeral level, the effectiveness of the international structures created to bring offenders to justice will provide assurance to the world that fundamental norms of a civilized society are more than words found in international treaties and national constitutions. Within the academic community, these discussions will test established theories, open doors for important empirical inquiry, and promote an international dimension to the work of the next generation of scholars. And finally, of personal interest to me and my colleagues engaged in the educational enterprise, this new focus on the international dimensions of crime and justice in the curricula of our universities will ensure that the graduates of our institutions are better prepared for the challenges of global citizenships.

It is with particular pride that I note the substantial contributions to this volume by the faculty at John Jay College of Criminal Justice. They, and their colleagues from institutions around the world who have also written chapters in this book, are exploring an exciting new frontier of our field. We share a hope that this global conversation will provide a solid foundation for a new understanding of these emerging challenges – and, even better, new responses that will promote a world that is more safe and more just.

Jeremy Travis,
President
John Jay College of Criminal Justice,
The City University of New York

Preface

"The structure of world peace cannot be the work of one man, or one party, or one nation [....] It cannot be a peace of large nations – or of small nations. It must be a peace which rests on the cooperative effort of the whole world." Franklin Roosevelt, quoted by Barack Obama, the 44th President of the United States in his Address to U.N. General Assembly, September 23, 2009

In furtherance of world peace, many educational institutions are now broadening their curricula to improve understanding of the global realities of the present-day world. Crime undeniably poses a serious threat to the social order and tranquility and it is certain that the rule of law, coupled with an efficient criminal justice system, is fundamental to social and economic progress. This is true of every sovereign state. The disciplines of Criminology and Criminal Justice have a vital role to play in improving the understanding of crimes that threaten the peace and security of nations and in finding the best way to deal with these crimes.

The rapid increase in globalization at the end of the twentieth century led criminologists to study "transnational crimes," or criminal acts that span national borders and that violate the laws of more than one country. This resulted in the creation of a new field of study, "comparative criminology and criminal justice," though it is also known by many other names, including international criminology and criminal justice, global criminology and criminal justice, supranational criminology, and crosscultural criminology. Meanwhile, growing international awareness of the millions of victims of genocide, crimes against humanity, and war crimes in the late twentieth century compelled the international community to pay attention to these "gravest crimes" that threaten the peace, security, and well-being of the world. These crimes were given formal recognition in the Rome Statute of 1998 (now signed by more than half the member states of the United Nations), which established the International Criminal Court to deal with them.

The disaster of September 11, 2001, accelerated the need to study international crime and criminal justice, not just in the United States but all around the world. A new undergraduate major – International Criminal Justice (ICJ) – was established at John Jay College of Criminal Justice in 2001 and subsequently, in 2010, a companion master's ICJ program was also started. Other universities and colleges are now beginning to offer similar programs at the undergraduate and graduate levels. The programs will help to expand the boundaries of criminology and criminal justice and will open up many new career opportunities for students of these fields.

As the founding director of John Jay's undergraduate ICJ program, I realized that there was an urgent need for a student text that would provide concise, up-to-date information on the broad array of topics covered by international crime and justice. This book is based on a book custom-published by McGraw-hill in 2005. It includes revised and updated chapters originally included in the McGraw-hill book and twenty additional chapters covering new topics. The book is by no means a traditional textbook – indeed, I hope it is more than a textbook. The short chapters, specially written by many of the world experts in this new field, are intended to give students an understanding of the main concepts covered by each topic and to sensitize students to the complex nature of the problems. Given the enormous interest in this field, I confidently expect a new edition of the book will be needed within the space of the next few years.

My sincere thanks go to each and every one of the seventy authors for accepting my invitations to write the chapters. Because of their broad expertise, I had to twist the arms of some of them to do more than one chapter. Many of them not only wrote chapters but also helped by reviewing the chapters of other authors. I also thank some other reviewers who are not authors, including Patricia Brantingham, Ko-Lin Chin, Richard Culp, Dinni Gorden, Dennis Kenney, Edward Kleemans, Mahesh Nalla, Phil Reichel, Kim Rossmo, Aiden Sidebottom, Janet Smith, and Nick Tilley. Without the help of all these friends and colleagues, this project would not have been possible. I am fortunate to have such a wonderful group of international experts as friends. It was a pleasure as well as a great learning experience to work with them. I also thank the anonymous reviewers of the book proposal, selected by Cambridge University Press, whose comments helped me to improve the book and gave me confidence that I was on the right track.

I have been blessed by having many hard-working, talented, eager-to-learn students in the ICJ program. Some of them have read the chapters, have given feedback, and have helped to check and proofread the references. Particular thanks to Christian Aulbach, Pavlina Fidlerova, Viola Sze Yuen Har, Devin Jaipersaud, Mary Kwang, Weijian Li, Jvania Robertson-Ward, Isabella Salgado, and Matthew Thomeczek for their assistance.

There is nothing like having the help of mentors in facing the challenges of an academic career. I thank Professor Ronald V. Clarke, my mentor, or rather my guru (!), for teaching me to be rigorous and self-critical ever since my time at Rutgers. I am also grateful for many brainstorming sessions with him that helped shape this book.

I must acknowledge my special thanks to Professor Roger S. Clark, an optimistic human being and inspirational teacher, who has directed me for the past five years or so on the right path toward understanding international criminal law.

Encouragement can work wonders for one's confidence and I thank Professor Graeme Newman, a founding scholar of global crime and justice, for his encouraging comments when I started thinking about a book on international crime and justice. I pinned up his e-mail by my desk: "Mangai, a very ambitious and impressive book outline. If you can pull it off, there will be nothing else like it anywhere."

Two other people of great importance in my career are Professors Gerhard Mueller and Freda Adler. In 2005, before his death, Professor Mueller paid me the honor of writing the foreword for the earlier, custom edition of this book published by McGraw-Hill.

There are many other people who contributed to the development of the book. First, I would like to thank ex-Provost Basil Wilson, who conceived the idea of an ICJ major at John Jay and who asked me to run the program. Thanks also to Provost Jane Bowers and Dean Jim Levine for their constant and continued support and thanks to the colleagues in my department for their patience with this preoccupied colleague. In particular, my sincere thanks to Dr. Rosemary Barberet for her help with the ICJ major – I wish her success in directing the ICJ master's at John Jay.

I would also like to thank Ed Parsons, Jason Przybylski, Robert Dreesen, J. Neil Otte (copy editor), and Vijayalakshmi Natarajan (Vijee – Production Manager) of Newgen Publishing and Data Services of Cambridge University Press for their enthusiasm about the book and for helping me with production issues.

I am truly grateful to Jeremy Travis, President of John Jay, for his unequivocal support for the ICJ major, for me personally, and for agreeing to write the foreword to this book.

Finally, thanks to all my friends – they know who they are – for constantly cheering me up whenever I have begun to droop under the burden of producing the book. Above all, thanks to Jithendranath Vaidyanathan, my best friend, for his unwavering commitment to my professional success.

Ever since I entered the world of criminology, my passion and ambition have been to understand victimization and to help prevent it. I, therefore, dedicate this book to the victims of international and transnational crimes, in the hope it might help in the future to reduce the terrible harms that they suffer.

Mangai Natarajan, Ph.D.
Professor
Department of Criminal Justice
John Jay College of Criminal Justice
The City University of New York

Introduction

Mangai Natarajan

Criminology seeks to explain the nature, extent, causes, and consequences of crime, while the discipline of criminal justice deals with society's response to crime – how this response is conceived, organized, administered, delivered, and evaluated. For most of their histories, these disciplines have focused on lower-class offenders committing street crimes that impact local neighborhoods and cities. They have paid relatively little attention to corporate or white-collar crimes and they have paid even less attention to studying the cross-cultural context of crime and the different national responses to crime.

In the past two decades, scholars have broken out of this mold and have begun to extend the boundaries of criminology and criminal justice. Specifically, they began to study crime patterns and evolving criminal justice practices in other parts of the world, using their own countries as benchmark comparisons. Their pioneering work resulted in "comparative criminology" and "comparative criminal justice" becoming established subfields of the broader disciplines (Mannheim, 1965; Mueller & Wise, 1965, 1975; Clinard & Abbott, 1973; Chang, 1976; Newman, 1976; Shelley, 1981a, 1981b; Terrill, 1982; Adler, 1983; Johnson, 1983; Bayley, 1985). One of the facts exposed by this body of work, increasingly recognized by the United Nations and the World Bank, is that the rule of law is not simply the result of economic and social progress; rather, it is a necessary condition for this progress to be achieved.

The acceleration in globalization that began in the 1990s has made clear that criminologists must take one further step than that made in comparative criminology (Fairchild, 1993; Adler, 1996; Yacoubain, 1998; Reichel, 1999). They must study, not just the crimes and criminal justice systems of other countries, but they must also study "transnational" crimes that span two or more countries. These crimes include cybercrimes, international money laundering, and various forms of trafficking (e.g., in drugs, humans, stolen antiquities, and endangered wildlife), which result from the huge expansion of world trade, the vast increase in migration, the international-ization of currency markets, and the explosions of international travel and electronic communications. While these consequences of globalization have been lauded by economists and others, criminologists, lawyers, and crime policy officials must now grapple with one of globalization's downsides – the opportunities globalization has created, together with the explosion of new technologies, for transnational crimes to emerge or be transformed into more serious forms (Newman, 1999).

No sooner had criminologists and criminal justice scholars awakened to this reality than developments in international relations and international law drew their attention to yet another large and important class of crimes that they had neglected, so-called international crimes (Yacoubain, 2000). These are crimes such as genocide and mass killings that occur within the boundaries of a sovereign State, but which are so horrific in their scale and consequences that they demand an international response. Some criminol-ogists and criminal justice scholars (notably Hagan & Rymond-Richmond, 2009) have recently begun to conduct research on these crimes and it is becoming evident that a whole new field of study – international crime and justice – is being created. This field includes comparative criminology and criminal justice, and its subject matter is transnational crimes, international crimes, and the international responses to these crimes.

As will become apparent from this book, this new field departs in many important respects from traditional criminology and criminal justice. As discussed below, the international dimension of the field requires input from an even wider range of disciplines than those involved in criminol-ogy and criminal justice. Another important change is that moving the focus, first, from local crimes to transnational crimes and then to interna-tional crimes, results in victims becoming increasingly more important. At the local level, the focus is mostly on offenders – explaining their crimes, apprehending them, and treating them. Relatively little attention is paid to the needs of victims for restitution, compensation, and protection. At the international level this relationship is reversed. There is considerably more concern with the harm to victims, and with restitution and compensation. This is because transnational and international crimes often involve multi-ple victims who suffer egregious harms and who have little recourse to jus-tice. The victims are very visible, whereas the offenders are often difficult to identify, and even more difficult to apprehend. Thus, the implication for scholars is that victimology, the Cinderella of traditional criminology (Fattah, 1991), becomes much more important in international crime and justice.

Recognition of the increasing importance of transnational and international crimes led to the establishment of a new undergraduate major in international criminal justice at John Jay College of Criminal Justice in 2001 (Natarajan, 2002; 2008) and subsequently, in 2010, to the establishment of a master's program. Other universities and colleges are beginning to establish similar programs at the undergraduate and graduate levels. This book is intended to serve the needs of the students in these programs for concise, up-to-date information on the broad array of topics covered by international crime and justice. Later sections of this introductory chapter detail the reasons for studying international criminal justice, lay out the elements of the interdisciplinary approach to the subject, and provide a brief description of the nine parts of the book. The next two sections, however, provide more information about transnational and international crime.

TRANSNATIONAL CRIMES

As mentioned, transnational crimes are criminal acts or transactions that span national borders, thus, violating the laws of more than one country. According to McDonald (1997), an offense is transnational nature if:

1. It is committed in more than one State;
2. It is committed in one State but a substantial part of its preparation, planning, direction, or control takes place in another State;
3. It is committed in one State but involves an organized criminal group that engages in criminal activities in more than one State;
4. It is committed in one State but has substantial effects in another State.

Examples of such crimes include illegal immigration, sea piracy, airliner bombings, and various forms of international trafficking, which include trafficking in drugs, stolen cars, firearms, antiquities and cultural objects, endangered species, human body parts, and women for the sex trade.

Because transnational crimes span the borders of two or more countries, they require action by the specific countries where the laws have been violated. It is the need for cooperation between States, equally interested in protecting their legal values, which makes them willing to assist one another to prevent or prosecute such crimes. Reciprocity is, therefore, a guiding principle (Triffterer, 2006), but some cases where such reciproc-ity is absent require the attention of an international body, in particular the United Nations. An important example is the bombing of Pan Am Flight 103 over Lockerbie, Scotland in 1988, which killed all 259 people onboard and eleven people in the village of Lockerbie. Though the aircraft was American-owned and many of the victims were U.S. citizens, the air-liner was brought down over Scotland. This meant that the case fell squarely under the jurisdiction of Scottish law. Because of the lack of extradition treaties, the Libyan leader Moammar El-Gadhafi refused to hand over the Libyan citizens suspected of the crime. This conflict was resolved by the United Nations' request to the government of Libya to comply by ensuring the appearance in the Netherlands of the two accused for the trial, as well as making available in the Netherlands any witnesses or evidence that might be requested by the court (for details, see Security Council Resolution 1192 (1998) on Lockerbie case). The Libyan leader eventually agreed to the trial being held in a neutral country (i.e., the Netherlands), though under Scottish Law.

INTERNATIONAL CRIMES

The Rome Statute defines international crimes as the gravest crimes that threaten the peace, security, and well-being of the world and are of concern to the international community. This covers the "core crimes" of genocide, war crimes, crimes against humanity, and the crime of aggression (for details, see UN document PCNICC/2000/INF/3/Add.2, on Elements of Crime). At the time of writing, the crime of aggression has not yet been defined, but will be discussed at an upcoming ICC review conference (Clark, 2010). The preamble of the Rome Statute states in paragraph 6 that "it is the duty of every State to exercise its criminal jurisdiction over those responsible for international crimes." While there may be general agreement that the core crimes specified in the Statute are indeed international crimes, there are many other crimes that in some circumstances might also qualify for this designation. Murphy (1999) has argued that international crimes are defined in a two stage process. They are initially defined as crimes in a par-ticular convention or agreement between two or more States. The primary focus of such agreements is the prosecution and punishment of individuals who perpetrate the crimes in question. Subsequently, after the agreement has been ratified by a large number of States and generally accepted even by States that do not become parties to the agreements, the crimes the agree-ment cover may be regarded as crimes under customary international law.

Table I.1. Twenty-four "international crimes"

A. Protection of peace
  1. Aggression
	D. Protection against terror-violence (cont.)
	  14. Taking of civilian hostages
	  15. Attacks upon commercial vessels

B. Humanitarian protection during armed conflicts
  2. War crimes
  3. Unlawful use of weapons
  4. Mercenarism
	E. Protection of social interests
	  16. Drug offenses
	  17. International traffic in obscene publications

C. Protection of fundamental human rights
  5. Genocide
  6. Crimes against humanity
  7. Apartheid
  8. Slavery and related crimes
  9. Torture
  10. Unlawful human experimentation
	F. Protection of cultural interests
	  18. Destruction and/or theft of national treasures
	
	G. Protection of the environment
	  19. Environmental protection
	  20. Theft of nuclear materials

D. Protection against terror-violence
  11. Piracy
  12. Aircraft hijacking and sabotage of aircrafts
  13. Force against internationally protected persons
	H. Protection of communications
	  22. Interference with submarine cables
	
	I. Protection of economic interests
	  23. Falsification and counterfeiting
	  24. Bribery of foreign public officials

Source: Paust et al. (2000); Murphy (1999).

Countries that recognize them can try these crimes, or they can be tried by international criminal courts.

There is no authoritative listing of the acts that qualify, or might qualify, as international crimes, but a survey of conventions that criminalize certain acts produced the list of twenty-four such acts in Table I.1. These acts are categorized under the interests the conventions are designed to protect. The particular circumstances and conditions that might qualify them as international crimes (and thus falling under international jurisdiction) remain unclear. At first sight, many of the crimes would not be punishable under international law because they seem not to pose a threat to values inherent to the international community as a whole, and in particular "the peace, security, and well-being of the world," which includes the sovereignty and independence of each individual State. However, clearer specification and description of the crimes might reveal that in certain circumstances they do indeed constitute a threat to the integrity of the international community. The fact that such vital issues remain unclear reflects the immaturity of the field and the delayed recognition of its importance.

WHY STUDY INTERNATIONAL CRIME AND JUSTICE?

Students sometimes ask me: Why, as Americans, should we concern our-selves with issues such as female genital mutilation and female infanticide that occur in distant lands? They ask: Do we not have enough problems of our own to deal with, and why should we interfere in the cultural practices of other countries? I respond that there are strong reasons supporting why criminal justice scholars should be concerned with victimization and viola-tions of human rights, not just in their own countries, but wherever they occur in the world. In many countries women are sorely oppressed and are subjected to inhumane treatment. Though the authorities in these countries might recognize the problems and develop measures to combat them, the problems tend to be accepted by local people and the measures have little or no impact. Again, one might question how the involvement of foreigners could help with these local problems, but there are some success stories of such intervention. For example, local reformers were only successful in putting an end to "sati," a cultural practice in India that required wives to immolate themselves on their husbands' funeral pyres, when they obtained the backing of the British colonial administration. More might be achieved, however, by raising international awareness about such problems through the United Nations and other international bodies, in the hope that coordi-nated international pressure can work to minimize the harms inflicted.

In the wake of the World Trade Center disaster, the general point is now easier to make that individual countries cannot, on their own, without inter-national help, successfully tackle some crimes. Perhaps the clearest example of this relates to the various bilateral and international agreements now in place to deal with terrorism. In fact, there are many good reasons to study international crime and justice. Twenty such reasons are identified below:

1. International crimes cause harm to millions of innocent people in all parts of the world. It is important to understand the magnitude and extent of this suffering.
2. International crimes are major human rights violations. We must study these violations in order to develop international law and appropriate institutions of justice to prevent and respond to these violations.
3. Victims of State crimes (government crimes against citizens) are not fully protected by international law. It is important to find ways of extending this protection through international treaties and agreements.
4. Differing views are held around the world as to what are appropriate or desirable ways to process offenders in the criminal justice system.

We must examine these differences from a comparative perspective to form some consensus in developing regulatory mechanisms.

5. It is important to understand the role of international relations in providing lawful resolution to atrocities committed around the world.

6. The perpetrators of international crimes are political figures who frequently escape the justice systems of their own countries and obtain sanctuary in other countries. We must try to uncover the political motivations of countries providing asylum to these criminals as a basis for developing more effective extradition treaties.

7. It is important to understand the historical and cultural backgrounds of crimes against humanity, such as slavery and apartheid, so as to find ways to eliminate the roots of these forms of discrimination.

8. Some international crimes are difficult to prosecute due to both political constraints involving State sovereignty issues and the lack of resources of international institutions such as the United Nations. We must find ways around these problems so that an effective international justice system can be developed. It is also important to find ways to improve the effectiveness of regional forces such as "Eurojust."

9. The establishment of the International Criminal Court (ICC) is a major step in international criminal justice. We must find ways to improve the functioning of the court and to make it a force for world peace and justice.

10. Truth commissions are a most encouraging development in the field of international criminal justice. It is important to understand how these commissions came to be established in order to improve their effectiveness in investigating the victimization of indigenous peoples and in rebuilding States.

11. In many parts of the world, women and children are subjected to many forms of violence. They are doubly victimized during times of armed conflict. It is important to find ways to improve the social status of women and children and also ways to develop international guarantees to preserve and protect their rights.

12. Globalization has resulted in the massive migration of people from one part of the world to another in search of better prospects. Local criminal groups often victimize innocent individuals in the process of migration. It is important to find ways of reducing the risks of victimization of migrants.

13. Many local crimes such as car theft span national borders. It is important to understand the factors that contribute to local crimes (including cultural, social, political economic, and environmental conditions), so that effective situational controls can be implemented.

14. The proliferation of organized crime networks, with their extensive resources and sophisticated operations, is a serious threat to world security. We must study the operations of these organized crime networks and learn how they exploit a broad range of criminal opportunities.
15. Law enforcement strategies vary between and among nations. In order to reach some common ground for effective interdiction of international traffickers, it is important to develop international cooperative policing efforts. It is also important to learn how existing resources such as Interpol and Europol can be made more effective.
16. International financial centers have opened doors for many organized crime and terrorist groups to conceal their illegal proceeds. We must learn how to tighten international banking safeguards so as to reduce opportunities for money laundering by these groups.
17. Transnational criminal activities affect all parts of the world, but the literature suggests that they most often originate in developing countries. It is important to understand the impact on crime of global economic development if developing countries are to be helped to combat transnational crimes.
18. Terrorism offers a serious threat to world peace and security. It is important to understand the political, social, economic, and cultural contexts in which terrorists operate if we are to develop effective measures to combat terrorism.
19. Technology has been a powerful force in bringing the world together. By the same token, it has opened new opportunities to commit crimes through the Internet. Traditional criminological explanations do not adequately explain such crimes, which seem little related to deprivation. We need a program of interdisciplinary research in designing out these crimes from the Internet.
20. The mission of criminology and criminal justice has been to train people to assist in dealing with local crime problems. Expanding this mission to train people who are interested in making a career in international criminal justice will enrich both disciplines.

INTERNATIONAL CRIME AND JUSTICE: A COMPREHENSIVE INTERDISCIPLINARY APPROACH

Criminology and criminal justice are both interdisciplinary in nature. They draw upon many other disciplines in developing theories about crime, criminality, and the criminal justice process (including the apprehension, punishment, and treatment of offenders). These disciplines include

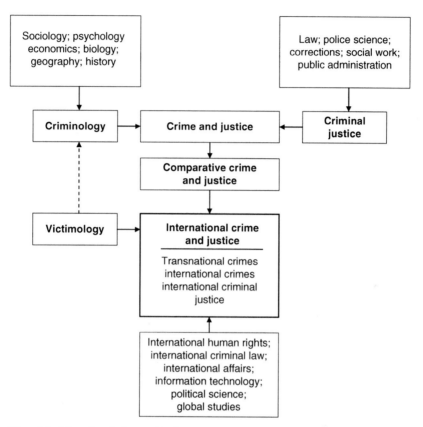

Figure I.1. International crime and justice.

economics, law, human geography, sociology, psychology, corrections, public administration, police science, and social work (see Figure I.1). An even wider range of disciplines must be invoked, however, in the service of understanding and dealing with transnational and international crimes. Victimology has already been mentioned in this context, but there are also important contributions to be made by international criminal law, human rights, international relations, political science, information technology, and global studies (see Figure I.1). Transnational and international crimes are local in origin, but their international reach ratchets up their level of complexity and changes their character in fundamental ways. Thus, once simple frauds have now been transformed by globalization and advances in technology into massive Ponzi and pyramid schemes affecting many thousand of individuals across the world. And the difficulties of identifying offenders, arresting them, and bringing them to justice are multiplied many times when those offenders are engaged in international and transnational crimes. This increased complexity, requiring the contributions of scholars from many disciplines, poses daunting, but exciting challenges to those studying international crime and justice.

ABOUT THE BOOK

As discussed above there are many important reasons for studying international crime and justice, but there has been no single book offering a broad coverage of the many topics in this new field. This book is an attempt to meet this need. It provides an introduction to the nature of international and transnational crimes and to the emerging legal frameworks for their prevention and control. Emphasis is placed on global aspects of the work of different criminal justice agencies and on international structures that have been created for crime prevention, punishment, and control.

The compact and informative chapters presented here make this book suitable for both graduate and undergraduate courses. In many courses, because of the depth and breadth of the book's coverage, it could serve as a main text. In other courses, it might be more suitably used as a supplementary text. Courses that would most likely make use of the book as a course text include: Introduction to International Criminal Justice, Comparative Criminology and Criminal Justice, International Criminology and Global Criminology, International Perspectives on Crime and Justice, and Global Crime and Justice. The book is arranged in nine parts covering the subject matter of international criminal justice.

Part I: International Criminology: This section covers basic explanations of international and transnational crime, including globalization, routine activities, and migration (Chapters 1–3). Chapter 4 provides an example of the criminological analysis of an international crime and Chapter 5 lays out the salient features of international victimology. Chapters 6 and 7 respectively discuss the treatment of children and women in international criminal justice, while Chapter 8 discusses the role of culture in understanding and explaining international and transnational crimes.

Part II: Law, Punishment, and Crime Control Philosophies of the World: This section provides the legal framework for understanding variations in legal systems (Chapter 9). Punishment philosophies, variations in punitiveness, and use of incapacitation around the world are discussed in (Chapters 10–12). Finally, the major approaches to crime prevention that have been adopted around the world are discussed in Chapter 13).

Part III: Transnational Crime: This section includes accounts of some specific and important transnational trafficking crimes. These include: drug trafficking (Chapter 14); trafficking in human beings (Chapter 15); trafficking in stolen vehicles (Chapter 16); trafficking in small arms (Chapter 17); trafficking in art, antiquities, and cultural heritage (Chapter 18); and cigarette smuggling (Chapter 19). Transnational crimes with more general implications are also discussed. These include: cybercrime (Chapter 20); international fraud (Chapter 21); money laundering (Chapter 22) and child pornography (Chapter 23). Other crimes of international concern are also covered, including maritime crimes (Chapter 24), transnational environmental crimes (Chapter 25 includes one of the world's worst industrial disasters due to corporate criminal negligence at Bhopal (Chapter 26), wildlife crimes (Chapter 27) and corruption (Chapter 28). Furthermore, tourist crimes (Chapter 29), which are very local in character but which have international repercussions, are discussed.

Part IV: Organized Crime and Terrorism: This section opens with a discussion of the important reasons for studying transnational organized crime (Chapter 30) and follows up with accounts of organized crime in the Balkans (Chapter 31) and of Russian organized crime (Chapter 32). Chapters follow concerning some of the world's major organized crime groups, including the Italian Mafia (Chapter 33), Asian organized crime groups (Chapter 35), Columbian drug cartels (Chapter 36). It includes a case of the international implications of domestic terrorism (Chapter 37), a chapter on extortion (Chapter 34), and a review of terrorism and practical ways for its prevention (Chapter 38).

Part V: International Crime: This section provides detailed research accounts of some international crimes, beginning with the three core international crimes of genocide, war crimes, and crimes against humanity (Chapter 39). It provides an account of the historical dimensions of genocide (Chapter 40), war crimes, and the humanitarian law, (Chapter 41) as well as apartheid, a crime against humanity (Chapter 42). Finally, in the context of the ICC, Chapter 43 discusses the definition of crimes of aggression when committed by a State's leaders.

Part VI: Delivering International Justice: This section focuses on major developments in international criminal justice including: the role of United Nations in preserving security and peace worldwide (Chapter 44); a discussion of treaties and international criminal law; the workings of major international criminal tribunals; and international hybrid courts established in response to specific international crimes including

Nuremberg, Tokyo, Rwanda, Yugoslavia, and Sierra Leone (Chapters 45 and 46). Chapter 47 focuses on the newly introduced International Criminal Court (ICC) and describes its functioning; Chapter 48 explains how serious international crimes are investigated and how the ICC processes these cases; Chapter 49 discusses the attention paid by the ICC to victims' rights and Chapter 50 discusses the role of NGOs in international criminal justice. Furthermore, Chapters 51–53 describe the development of human rights commissions and the truth commissions in South Africa and Guatemala.

Part VII: *International Cooperation and Criminal Justice*: This part provides an account of law enforcement activities directed against international and transnational crime. It covers worldwide policing systems (Chapter 54); the importance of crossborder patrol (Chapter 55); the development of regional police cooperation and cooperation among the judiciary, specifically in Europe (Chapters 56 and 57); the importance of cooperation in international law enforcement and criminal justice in combating transnational crimes (Chapter 58), and, more specifically, in dealing with money laundering (Chapter 59).

Part VIII: *International Research and Crime Statistics*: Measuring the nature and extent of transnational and international crime is a prerequisite for the scientific discipline of international criminology. Chapters 60 to 63 review the main sources of crime and delinquency data that exist at national and international levels. Chapter 64 discusses the role of qualitative methodology in studying the evolving nature of international and transnational crimes.

Part IX: *International Research Resources*: This last part describes information resources for international crime and justice. Chapter 65 describes the World Criminal Justice Library Network and Chapter 66 gives specific instructions for finding international crime and justice-related information, from journals and databases to the Internet and the mass media.

CONCLUSION

This short introduction has described the scope and coverage of the book. It has explained what is meant by transnational and international crimes and it has drawn attention to the rapid emergence of international crime and justice as an important new subfield of criminology and criminal justice. In particular, it has explained how some pioneering criminologists and criminal justice scholars have responded to the growing realization of the threats to world order posed by international terrorism and transnational organized crime – scourges that have been enabled and facilitated by the acceleration of globalization. It has explained how this new field of study encompasses and enhances previous comparative research and why it demands the contribution of scholars from a wide range of disciplines.

It would be remiss, however, if this introduction closed without exhorting more scholars to follow the example of the pioneers who have expanded their horizons and broadened their focus beyond crimes occurring at the neighborhood and city levels. While these crimes continue to demand attention, the personal and financial harms they cause to their victims pale into insignificance compared with the gross violations of human rights, the suffering of millions, and the vast numbers of violent deaths resulting from international crimes brought daily to our attention in our comfortable homes by newspapers, television, and the Internet. As scholars, we can no longer ignore these crimes, but must find ways to use our disciplinary knowledge and skills in helping to prevent and control them. The chapters in this book point the way and provide a sure foundation for our future efforts.

REFERENCES

Adler, F. (1983). *Nations Not Obsessed with Crime*. Littleton, Colorado: F. B. Rothman.

(1996). A Note on Teaching "International." *Journal of Criminal Justice Education*, 7(2), 323–44.

Chang, H. D. (Ed). (1976). *Criminology: A Cross-Cultural Perspective*. Durham, NC: Carolina Academic Press.

Clark, R. S. (2010). Negotiating Provisions Defining the Crime of Aggression, Its Elements and the Conditions for ICC Exercise of Jurisdiction Over It. *The European Journal of International Law*, 20(4), 1103–15.

Clinard, M. & D. Abbott. (1973). *Crime in Developing Countries: A Comparative Perspective*. New York: John Wiley.

Fairchild, E. S. (1993). *Comparative Criminal Justice Systems*. Belmont, CA: Wadsworth.

Fattah, E. A. (1991). *Understanding Criminal Victimization*. Scarborough, Canada: Prentice Hall.

Hagan, J. & W. Rymond-Richmond. (2009). *Darfur and the Crime of Genocide*. New York: Cambridge University Press.

Johnson, H. E. (1983). *International Handbook of Contemporary Developments in Criminology*. Westport, CT: Greenwood Press.

Mannheim, H. (1965). *Comparative Criminology*. London : Routledge & Kegan Paul.

McDonald, W. (1997). *Crime and Law Enforcement in the Global Village*. Cincinnati, OH: Anderson Publishing.

Mueller, G.O.W. & M. E. Wise. (Eds). (1965). *International Criminal Law*. Publications of the Comparative Criminal Law Project, Vol.2. South Hackensack, NJ: Rothman.

(1975). *Studies in Comparative Criminal Law*. Springfield, IL: Thomas.

Murphy, J. F. (1999). Civil Liability for the Commission of International Crimes as an Alternative to Criminal Prosecution. *Harvard Human Rights Journal*, 12. Retrieved Feb 25, 2010, from http://www.law.harvard.edu/students/orgs/hrj/iss12/murphy.shtml#fn22

Natarajan, M. (2002). International Criminal Justice Education: A Note on Curricular Resources. *Journal of Criminal Justice Education*, 13(2), 479–500.

(2008). John Jay's Bachelor's Degree in International Criminal Justice. In K. Aromaa & Redo, S. (Eds.), *The Rule of Law: Criminal Justice Teaching and Training Across the World*. Helsinki, Finland: The European Institute for Crime Prevention and Control.

Newman, G. (1976). *Comparative Deviance: Perceptions and Law in Six Cultures*. New York: Elsevier.

(Ed.) (1980). *Crime and Deviance: A Comparative Perspective*. Beverly Hills, CA: Sage.

(Ed.) (1999). *Global Report on Crime*. USA: Oxford University Press.

Paust, J., Bassiouni, M., Scharf, M., Gurule, J., Sadat, L., Zagaris, B., & Williams, S. (2000). *International Criminal Law*. Durham, NC: Carolina Academic Press.

Reichel, P. L. (1999). *Comparative Criminal Justice Systems – A Topical Approach*. Upper Saddle River, NJ: Prentice Hall.

Shelley, L. (1981a). *Crime and Modernization. The Impact of Industrialization and Modernization on Crime*. Carbondale, IL: Southern Illinois State University Press

(Ed). (1981b). *Readings in Comparative Criminology*. Carbondale, IL: Southern Illinois University Press.

Terrill, J. R. (1982). Approaches for Teaching Comparative Criminal Justice to Undergraduates. *Criminal Justice Review*, 7(1), 23–7.

Triffterer, O. (2006). Concluding Remarks. In the Austrian Federal Ministry for Foreign Affairs /Salzburg Law School on International Criminal Law, Humanitarian Law and Human Rights Law (Eds.), *The Future of the International Criminal court – Salzburg Retreat*, 25–27 May 2006. (http://www.sbg.ac.at/salzburglawschool/Retreat.pdf)

Yacoubian, G. S. (1998). Underestimating the magnitude of international crime: Implications of genocidal behavior for the discipline of criminology. *The World Bulletin*, 14, 23–36.

(2000). The (In)significance of Genocide Behavior to the Discipline of Criminology. *Crime, Law & Social Change*, 34(1), 7–19.

PART I

INTERNATIONAL CRIMINOLOGY

Decades of study have produced considerable understanding of street crimes and delinquency, but it is unclear whether this knowledge has direct application to transnational and international crimes. Vincenzo Ruggiero (Chapter 4) argues that many standard criminological theories including positivism, functionalism, labeling theory, and conflict theory could be adapted to explain the politically motivated violence of international crimes. On the other hand, these theories, mostly developed through studies of deprived offenders, seem less able to explain transnational organized crimes, particularly their rapid growth. It is more likely that the explanations will be found in the increase of globalization with the attendant huge expansion of world trade and migration and the explosions of new technologies and electronic communications. These changes have opened up new opportunities, not just for legal enterprises, but also for lucrative criminal enterprises to prosper and grow.

Marcus Felson's routine activity theory (Chapter 2), which deals with the relationship between social change and the waxing and waning of crime opportunities, is one criminological theory that can be invoked to explain the effect of these changes. Indeed, as explained by Louise Shelley, in the opening chapter, terrorists and transnational offenders, just like other people, take advantage of increased travel, trade, rapid money movements,

1

telecommunications, and computer links. Globalization undoubtedly helps explain the increasing flow of people from one country to another. Many people flee harsh living conditions in their home countries, or they seek refuge from war crimes and other human rights violations. In other instances, criminal syndicates deceive or kidnap vulnerable individuals and transfer them to host countries to work in servitude or in the commercial sex trade. Migration, therefore, fuels transnational crime and produces the conditions for massive victimization of vulnerable people (see Chapter 3 by Roberta Belli, Joshua Freilich, and Graeme Newman).

If traditional criminology has only little to offer to the study of international and transnational crimes, this is not so for its neglected offspring – victimology. In the criminal law of Western countries, there has been little place for the victims of crime, but the needs of victims is a major preoccupation of the International Criminal Court and other international legal entities (see Chapter 5 by Jan Van Dijk and Jo-Anne Wemmers). Women and children are particularly at risk of victimization, and victimologists have consistently identified them as requiring special protections under international human rights and humanitarian law (see Chapter 6 by Cécile Van de Voorde and Rosemary Barberet). Chapter 7 by Mangai Natarajan and Monica Ciobanu discuss the status of women as offenders, as victims, as subjects of treatment, and as employees in the criminal justice system, and offer suggestions for protecting their status and their rights.

Finally, Edward Snajdr (Chapter 8) reminds us that definitions of crime are conditioned by the prevailing norms and culture of a society, and that any attempt to explain transnational and international crimes will have to address the reality and complexity of cultural variation. Only then can questions be answered, questions such as: Why do genocides occur in some parts of the world but not others? Why does the rest of the world ignore them when they happen? Why is one man's freedom fighter, another man's terrorist? Why are certain countries targeted by international terrorism? Why are women targets for rape and torture during wartime? Why are children used as soldiers? One can hardly think of questions that are more in need of answers.

1 The Globalization of Crime

Louise Shelley

Transnational crime is not a new phenomenon. The Barbary pirates that terrorized the numerous states along the Mediterranean, the trade in coolies from Macao by nineteenth-century Chinese crime groups (Seagrave, 1995), and the international movement and exchanges of Italian mafiosi for the last century illustrate that crime has always been global. Already in the 1930s, Italian organized criminals in the United States were traveling to Kobe, Japan, and Shanghai, China, to buy drugs, and members of U.S. crime gangs took refuge in China in the 1930s to avoid the reach of American law enforcement (Kaplan & Dubro, 2003). Italian organized crime was renewed in the United States by new recruits from Italy, and the postwar resurgence of the Mafia in Italy was facilitated by the arrival of American mafiosi with the U.S. military in Sicily in 1943. An active white slave trade existed between Eastern Europe and Argentina and Brazil in the early decades of the twentieth century (Glickman, 2000; Vincent, 2005).

What has changed from the earlier decades of transnational crime is the speed, the extent, and the diversity of the actors involved. Globalization has increased the opportunities for criminals, and criminals have been among the major beneficiaries of globalization. The criminals' international expansion has been made possible by the increasing movement of people and goods and the increasing ease of communication that have made it possible to hide the illicit among the expanding licit movement of people and goods. More significantly, the control of crime is state-based, whereas nonstate actors such as criminals and terrorists operate transnationally, exploiting the loopholes within state-based legal systems to expand their reach.

Globalization is coupled with an ideology of free markets and free trade, as well as a decline in state intervention. According to advocates of globalization, reducing international regulations and barriers to trade and investment will increase trade and development. Crime groups have exploited the enormous decline in regulations, the lessened border controls, and the greater freedom to expand their activities across borders and into new regions of the world. They travel to regions where they cannot be extradited, base their operations in countries with ineffective or corrupted law enforcement, and launder their money in countries with bank secrecy or few effective controls. By segmenting their operations, they benefit from globalization while simultaneously reducing the risks of operating.

In the 1960s, most of the growth of transnational crime was linked to the rise of drug trafficking in such regions as Asia, Latin America, Africa, and even Italy, the home of the original Mafia. By the late 1980s, the trade in drugs was already equal to that of textiles and steel (United Nations International Drug Control Programme, 1997). Though the drug trade remains the most lucrative aspect of transnational crime, the last few decades have seen an enormous rise in human trafficking and smuggling (Naím, 2006). Yet what all these transnational crimes have in common is that they are conducted primarily by actors based in developing countries who cannot compete in the legitimate economies of the world, which are dominated by multinational corporations based in the most affluent countries. Therefore, the criminals have exploited and developed the demand for illicit commodities such as drugs, people, arms, and endangered species.

Globalization has increased the economic disparities between the citizens of the developed and developing worlds. Marginalization of many rural communities, decline of small-scale agriculture, and problems of enhanced international competition have contributed to the rise of the drug trade as farmers look for valuable crops to support their families. The financial need is exploited by the international crime groups. The same economic and demographic forces have created pressures for emigration, yet barriers to entry into the most affluent societies have increased. Criminals have been able to exploit the demand for people for use as cheap labor and for sexual services, making human smuggling and trafficking grow rapidly.

GLOBALIZATION OF CRIME: FORMS AND METHODS

The drug trade was the first illicit sector to maximize profits in a globalized world. But as the market for drugs became more competitive and the international response to it increased, profits were reduced through competition and enhanced risk. Many other forms of crime have therefore expanded as criminals exploited the possibilities of global trade. These crimes include human trafficking and smuggling; trafficking in arms, endangered species, art, and antiquities; illegal dumping of hazardous waste; and counterfeiting and credit card frauds.

Money laundering has occurred on a mass scale because the financial system can move money rapidly through bank accounts in several countries in a short period. A transaction that might take only one hour to complete and involve banks in three different countries will take law enforcement more than a year to untangle – if they have the full cooperation of law enforcement and banks in each of these countries. With the increase in offshore banking, criminals are able to hide their money in these global safe havens without any fear of law enforcement. Moreover, banks often do not perform more than nominal due diligence (Global Witness, 2009).

Global criminal activity has been facilitated by the possibility of speedy and secure communication. Child pornography has spread because the Internet makes it possible to distribute pornography anonymously through Web sites. Material can be produced in one country and distributed in another by means of the Web, e-mail, and an international financial system that facilitates wire transfers. Drug traffickers can use encryption to provide security for their messages concerning their business operations. Informal financial transfers can be made without a trace, aided by instant messages on computers, and wire transfers made by fax or computer to offshore locales place massive amounts of funds outside of any state regulation.

POLITICAL TRANSITIONS AND GLOBALIZED CRIME

The end of the Cold War has had an enormous impact on the rise of transnational crime. The most important consequences are the political and economic transition under way in the former communist states and the concomitant rise in regional conflicts. With the end of the superpower conflict, the potential for large-scale conflict has diminished, but since the late 1990s there has been a phenomenal rise in the number of regional conflicts. Although regional in nature, these conflicts have entered into the global economy because the arms and the manpower they require have often been paid for by transnational criminal activity. Drugs and diamonds are just two of the commodities that have been entered into the illicit economy to pay for the arms needed to fuel the conflicts (Nordstrom, 2007). In turn, these conflicts have produced unprecedented numbers of refugees and have destroyed the legitimate economies of their regions.

These conflicts decimate the state and divert government energy away from the social welfare of citizens. All efforts are instead devoted to the maintenance of power and the suppression of rebellions. Citizens are left without social protections or a means of financial support. The low priority attached to women and children in conflict regions has made them particularly vulnerable to traffickers in those regions. Psychologically damaged by years of conflict, they have neither the psychological nor the financial means to resist the human traffickers. They are moved along the same global routes used by the human smugglers who exploit men trying to leave economically difficult situations to find employment in more affluent societies.

DECLINE OF BORDER CONTROLS AND GLOBALIZED CRIME

The decline of border controls has proved to be an important facilitator of transnational crime. In some cases, the decline is a consequence of deliberate policy decisions, whereas in other cases it is a result of major political transitions that have followed the end of the Cold War. The introduction of the Schengen Agreement within the European Union and NAFTA in North America permits individuals to travel within a significant part of Western Europe without border checks. This means that criminals can enter Europe at one point and freely move within a significant part of the continent without any passport controls. This has been exploited by Chinese smugglers, who have moved hundreds of thousands of Chinese into France from other entry points in Europe, and by Ukrainian criminals who took advantage of easy access to visas from the German embassy in Kyiv to move large numbers of criminals and traffic women to different parts of Europe.

Border regions in conflict or weakened states experience an absence of effective border controls. In many Asian multiborder areas there is an absence of governmental control, where the crime groups and the smugglers have become the dominant powers. Illustrative of this is the Golden Triangle region in which drugs, women, and children trafficked from Cambodia, Laos, Myanmar, and southern China flow into northern Thailand. In the triborder area of Argentina, Brazil, and Paraguay, crossborder smuggling thrives. But the links between terrorism and crime also flourish in such lawless areas. For example, Hezbollah planned and financially supported its bombing of the Jewish communities in Argentina in the mid-1990s from this region.

The borders of the former Soviet Union are penetrated not only by drug traffickers from Afghanistan. With the collapse of effective controls across the eleven time zones that represent the former USSR, the borders have been rendered indefensible. Across them flow an incredible range of commodities including arms, military technology, nuclear materials, and precious metals; increasingly, there is also an illicit flow of people across these borders.

The porous border areas of Europe, particularly the large seacoasts along the Mediterranean, are the locus of significant smuggling. In Morocco, for example, networks smuggling men to Europe have been adapted for human trafficking, bringing African women into the European sex markets. Large-scale smuggling of illegal migrants is underway from Africa into Spain, and the Italian coast receives Asian immigrants as well as immigrants from North Africa.

A similar dynamic exists along the U.S.–Mexico border, which has large sections that are poorly policed (Andreas, 2000). This border has been the locus of smuggling for more than a century. The Mexican drug cartels have grown dramatically in the last two decades as their proximity to the loosely guarded U.S.–Mexican frontier has given them a competitive advantage over the Colombian cartels. The ever present demand for cheap labor in the United States and the huge economic imbalance between the U.S. and Mexican economies have fueled a huge illicit population flow across the U.S. border.

GLOBALIZATION OF CRIME GROUPS

Crime groups on all continents try to globalize their activities for many of the same reasons as their legitimate counterparts. They seek to exploit valuable international markets, to run internationally integrated businesses, and to reduce risk. They obtain entrée into new markets outside their regions in different ways. When organized crime is closely linked with legitimate business, for example, in the Russian and Japanese cases, the global expansion of legitimate business provides the opportunity for the criminals to globalize. For example, as Japan's large corporations globalized their business, the criminals moved with them, extorting from the corporations' foreign affiliates (Kaplan & Dubro, 2003). Therefore, the illegitimate business follows the patterns of the legitimate business.

Colombian drug organizations have been the most successful in globalizing their business activities. They have far surpassed in profitability the traditional crime groups of Italy and Japan. Their success is based on many of the same principles found in the globalization of large legitimate corporations. They run network-based businesses, not top-down hierarchical structures. They integrate their businesses across continents. The drug cultivation and processing are done at low-cost production sites in Latin America, their products are marketed to the lucrative Western European and American markets, and the profits are laundered at home, in offshore locales such as the Caribbean, and in international financial centers (Thoumi, 2003).

Specialists from different countries are hired to help with transport, money laundering, and the information technology needed to encrypt their communications. Colorful examples of this globalization of Colombian organized crime include the Tarzan case in the United States in which a Russian organized crime figure was prosecuted for working with members of Colombian drug trafficking organizations to purchase Russian submarines and other technology to facilitate their activities. This operation failed. Russian scientists were subsequently imported to Colombia to build a submarine (Lintner, 2002).

SUMMARY AND CONCLUSION

Globalization has contributed to an enormous growth in crime across borders as criminals exploit the ability to move goods and people. Technologies, such as satellite and cell phones, the Internet, and the Web, have been used to facilitate communication among criminals. Although the narcotics trade has been international for a long time yet it has increased significantly with globalization. Globalization has also contributed to an enormous increase in the following categories of crime: human smuggling and trafficking, arms trafficking, trafficking in art, counterfeit goods, credit card fraud, and counterfeiting. Money laundering has increased dramatically in the globalized economy; the illicit funds move along with the licit funds and are frequently hidden in the numerous offshore financial havens that have proliferated in recent decades.

The problems that have caused this globalization of crime are very deep-seated. They result from the enormous disparities in wealth among countries, the rise of regional conflicts, and the increasing movement of goods and people and the increasing speed and facility of communication. States have little capacity to fight this transnational crime because state laws are nation-based but the criminals are operating globally.

REFERENCES

Andreas, P. (2000). *Border Games Policing the U.S.–Mexico Divide.* Ithaca: Cornell University Press.

Glickman, N. (2000). *The Jewish White Slave Trade and the Untold Story of Raquel Liberman.* New York: Garland.

Global Witness. (2009). *Undue Diligence: How Banks Do Business with Corrupt Regimes.* London: Global Witness.

Kaplan, D. E. & A. Dubro (2003). *Yakuza Japan's Criminal Underworld.* Berkeley: University of California Press.

Lintner, B. (2002). *Blood Brothers: The Criminal Underworld of Asia.* New York: Palgrave Macmillan.

Naím, M. (2006) *Illicit: How Smugglers, Traffickers and Copycats Are Hijacking the Global Economy.* New York: Anchor.

Nordstrom, C. (2007). *Global Outlaws: Crime, Money and Power in the Contemporary World.* Berkeley and Los Angeles: University of California.

Seagrave, S. (1995). *Lords of the Rim: The Invisible Empire of the Overseas Chinese.* London and New York: Bantam Press.

Thoumi, F. E. (2003). *Illegal Drugs, Economy and Society in the Andes.* Washington, D.C.: Woodrow Wilson Center Press.

United Nations International Drug Control Programme. (1997). *World Drug Report.* Oxford: Oxford University Press.

Vincent, I. (2005). *Bodies and Souls: The Tragic Plight of Three Jewish Women Forced into Prostitution in the Americas.* New York: William Morrow.

WEB SITES

Terrorism, Transnational Crime and Corruption Center (TraCCC): http://policy-traccc.gmu.edu

United Nations Office on Drugs and Crime: http://www.unodc.org

Nathanson Centre on Transnational Human Rights, Crime and Security www.osgoode.yorku.ca/NathansonBackUp/Publications/nathanso.htm

International Narcotics Control Strategy Report (issued annually): www.state.gov/p/inl/rls/nrcrpt/

International Organization for Migration: www.iom.int

ABOUT THE AUTHOR

Louise Shelley is a professor in the School of Public Policy at George Mason University and the founder and director of the Terrorism, Transnational Crime and Corruption Center. She has just published a book entitled *Human*

Trafficking: A Global Perspective (Cambridge University Press, 2010) and is currently writing one on the relationship of crime, terrorism, and corruption. She is the author of many articles and book chapters on different aspects of transnational crime. She serves on the global agenda council on illicit trade of the World Economic Forum.

2 Routine Activities and Transnational Crime

Marcus Felson

OVERVIEW

All crime is local. That statement seems to be brusque and to conflict with the existence of transnational crime. But in this chapter I will defend the statement and show how emphasizing that crime is local helps us understand transnational crime to a greater extent.

Every criminal act can be disaggregated into a sequence of events. If this chain or sequence includes a border crossing, it is easily classified as transnational. But that classification does not tell the whole story. One or more elements in the sequence has to occur locally (see Levi & Reuter, 2006; van Duyne & Levi, 2005). Indeed, all crime requires a local focus of action at some point, perhaps at most points in its sequence. We expect that most transnational crimes include a chain of local actions that outnumber the border-crossing pieces of the chain. Indeed, local people on both sides of a border are usually involved in local aspects of transnational crimes.

This same argument applies to electronic crimes, which have local requirements in virtually all cases, such as unsupervised computers or local cooperation among offenders. Many criminal acts that eventually affect distant locations nonetheless occur initially in a much more limited setting, perhaps with several additional local requirements.

Transnational crimes are important, but they have not replaced or crowded out traditional crimes, such as direct physical theft and violence carried out in more or less the usual ways. That conclusion also misunderstands ways in which electronic crimes have very local requirements. Thus a cyberoffender needs access to local computer equipment and local ways to hide identity or evade authority. Nor should we assume that the presence of offenders born abroad proves that crime is transnational, since many of these offenders do ordinary things, such as stealing, evading, confounding, invading, attacking, or confusing others.

Although all crimes are sequences of events, some criminal acts have few steps while others have many. These sequences are sometimes inter-related, so the aftermath of one crime becomes the prelude to another. In more and more cases, crimes have transnational outcomes. In some cases something stolen in one nation ends up in another through a sequence of distinct criminal acts by different offenders. Even without the transfer of property, a single criminal act might well transcend national boundaries or use telecommunications not limited to one nation. But at most stages crim-inal acts are local in their onset and early stages.

SEQUENCES AND ROUTINES

Transnational consequences and transnational harm results from a sequence of local crimes. For example, a car stolen here might be resold to someone else, be taken across the border by a person residing near it, then be trans-ported by still another person to a market for stolen cars farther from the border. This is a transnational sequence of local, illegal acts. Although the proceeds of the crime will be drawn in various places, each local offender may be paid locally for his part in the sequence.

To put this in perspective, we should begin with the "routine activity approach" to crime analysis, and then continue with its elaborations (Felson, 2002, 2006). That approach parses crime into three elements: a likely offender, a suitable target, and the absence of a capable guardian against crime. Surprisingly, the offender's characteristics are not so important for understanding the crime or sequence of crimes as the crime targets and guardians against it, and the physical nature of the various illicit transac-tions. An offender considers the target's suitability in terms of how easy it is to overcome, to remove the loot, to hide one's traces, and any other feature of the target that makes it easy for crime.

The phrase "absence of a guardian" normally refers to ordinary citizens out of range and unable to interfere with a crime. The physical placement of people and things is highly important for understanding how everyday routines produce more crime or less. This is because crime finds oppor-tune times and places. In addition, offenders often rely on accomplices who they must find in time and space and verify or vet in one way or another whether these persons are suitable partners in crime.[1] Offenders also need

---

[1] Offenders also need to avoid those who might discourage them from crime, including parents or other family or nonfamily members who interfere with their criminal activity.

a variety of local facilitators, ranging from weapons and tools, to computers and software, keys, and passwords.

An offender must find the target of crime – whether that is a person to attack, property to take, or something or someone to convert to illicit purposes. Crime is historically a physical process, with goods and persons moving about in space and time to provide the convergences needed for crime to occur (Felson, 2006). Offenders historically:

1. moved along physical paths,
2. overcoming barriers,
3. using tools or weapons,
4. converging with
5. the target of crime.

Today, most offenders work along this same sequence of events. But two other paths to crime are found in modern life.

NEWER HISTORICAL PATHS

According to the economic historian, Max Weber, the formal organization developed and spread in Western nations mostly in the past few centuries. Its key elements included a continuous organization of official functions bound by rules; specialization in each office, with defined spheres of competence; division of labor; a clearly defined hierarchy of offices: a firm system of supervision based on clear levels of authority; rules of conduct; technical qualifications; impersonal, fair, and equal treatment of clients; selection and promotion based on competence; and a strict division between private lives and public responsibilities of office. Yet personal interests do not die. In many cases organizations and professions put people in a good position to do bad things. If they use their official roles inappropriately they often commit crimes. Sometimes these offenses are internal to the organization and other times external. Sometimes these are white-collar crimes, but blue-collar workers can do likewise. These can be called "crimes of specialized access," because people are positioned to carry out these offenses. Although organizations are often transnational, their local outposts provide entry points for illicit action. The organizational path to crime starts locally, and its most important barriers and tools are probably local. The target of crime is sometimes transnational, but local processes remain central for organizational crime and its analysis.

Especially in the last decade, telecommunications systems have opened up tremendous additional crime opportunities. The electronic path to crime includes both electronic hardware and software, by which people send and receive information. Offenders often divert these processes for criminal purposes (Newman & Clarke, 2003). The electronic pathway helps us classify a growing variety of criminal convergences using coaxial cable, conventional telephones, cell phones, microwaves, radios, satellites, televisions, and the Internet. These media provide a means to reach crime targets beyond face-to-face contact, but also take advantage of routine activities (Williams, 2004).

More than any other, the electronic path to crime opens up a larger world to offenders. But that opening does not tell us crime is no longer local. Offenders need local access to computers and networks. Offenders need local passwords (often stolen from offices), and manuals (often found in dumpsters). Offenders need to ask local people for information and accomplices can find one another online and in different nations. But local setups from these activities are more important for defining and carrying out illicit acts, as well as for them, setting them up, and making them possible. The harm is extralocal, but not the behavior itself. The offender must escape local notice and interference first.

Indeed, the question concerning cybercrime is: Do computers and computer networks enable criminals to cover their tracks, or do they only help expose criminals?" In either case, these criminal acts occur in specific times and places by people who must get others out of their way or get others to help them, however inadvertently. By thinking globally, crime experts divert attention from central features of the crimes in question. Even if computer crime spills out into other places, it often depends on such mundane local processes as failing to conceal passwords, whether on desks or within computer files. Media coverage of clever and ingenious offenders diverts attention from the vast majority who are not so clever. Most criminal acts are rather simple. Most crime prevention is simple, too, requiring strategies and tactics that are tangible at least in time, if not in space (Felson, 2002; Felson & Clarke, 1997; Felson & Peiser, 1998). Most of these actions against crime occur locally. Even crimes with transnational components have sufficient local components to be vulnerable to local impediments.

PUBLIC AND PRIVATE ACCESS AND CRIME

Oscar Newman (1972), a famous architect and intellectual, distinguished:

1. public space,
2. semipublic,

3. semiprivate, and
4. private.

These distinctions do not concern ownership alone. A shopping mall might be privately owned, but it allows public access at high rates. That makes it highly vulnerable to criminal action. A local school might be publicly owned, but it usually privatizes its space – not allowing others to enter unless they are supposed to be there.

The scale reflects the relative degree of control over space. An open street is public because it is easy to enter. A sidewalk is semipublic since it is easy to enter, but nearby residents might look over it to some extent. An apartment hallway or stairwell might be semiprivate, but the apartments themselves are private places. Metropolitan areas have a crime problem because so much metropolitan space is public. Crime is prevented by environmental designs that increase the share of space that is private and semiprivate in access.

Oscar Newman's concepts can be transferred to the study of electronic crime. The problem with computer systems is that they have moved from being almost totally private to totally public in a very short time. Originally, computers were not linked to the Internet at all. Later some computers were linked, but only for expert users. In time, most computers became linked through the Internet, and hence became vulnerable to intrusion. After that, offenders moved in quickly to extend their local reach well beyond their local setting. Transnational crime became locally possible.

With the intrusions of viruses and other invasions of privacy, computer users learned to devise local barriers to intrusion. Experts developed programs and other shields to stop viruses. Vendors sold these programs. In time, many universities and companies inserted such controls into their systems. More cybernetic space became private and semiprivate. Crime risk was reduced accordingly.

Of course, offenders often learn to overcome controls. Paul Ekblom of the British Home Office (1997, 1999, 2000) explains that crime contends against crime prevention in a never-ending arms race, with move and countermove driven by accelerating technological and social change. Offenders misappropriate, mistreat, or misuse new products, services, and systems as they emerge. The purpose of Ekblom's explanation is not to discourage crime prevention, but rather to encourage more foresight among those seeking to prevent crime. His point, combined with that of Oscar Newman, leads us to another conclusion, too. New technology opened up new crime opportunities by creating new public space, that is, new unsupervised areas that offenders could attack with no guardians present. Cyberspace appears to be nonphysical, but that is only part of the story. New physical space is also involved – computer labs, university computer centers, libraries, homes, schools, and other places where supervision is weak.

Yet barriers can be erected in both physical and cyberspace. Enclosures are the most significant barriers to crime access. The locks on university computers are examples, but passwords and firewalls also enclose and privatize parts of cyberspace. Not all barriers enclose fully. Impediments are often placed in paths to slow down intrusions, not to prevent them entirely. Doors and stairwells lessen outside access to company computers and information about how to use them. Many offices and homes are constructed to give a moderate sense of localism, impeding illegal access to cyberspace through physical means. Computer systems also include partial barriers to entry, some of which operate by increasing the probability that outsiders will simply get lost. Thus, they require a lot of effort to abuse the system. Only those with lots of time or expertise can do so. That is why inside knowledge is so important for illegal action using computers. Inside knowledge is extremely local – strengthening my argument that electronic crimes should be considered local rather than transnational, despite their wide consequences.

In general, the access to broad computer networks is highly local, requiring physical entry into local systems that, in turn, lead offenders beyond their local environment. Local systems can have requirements, barriers, and supervision. We are in a transition period during which these barriers are in the process of development, with offenders sometimes ahead of preventers. Those preventing electronic crime are, in effect, seeking to relocalize network usage and to isolate suitable crime targets from promiscuous incursions. This means shifting cyberspace from public and semipublic dominance toward semiprivate and private locations. It includes making public usage privately evident. It includes, also, the reduction of unsupervised public, physical locations that offenders can abuse for illicit purposes. We should think of cybercrime as requiring physical paths toward electronic paths.

CONCLUSION

Reducing unsupervised and anonymous public entry is the essential strategy for crime control. In the process, we will, of course, see conflicts between security and several other considerations: privacy of some parties, free or low-cost usage, simplicity, and more. But we will probably discover, too, that a more secure electronic world can be devised with minimal loss of privacy, except for those who wish to take it away from others.

REFERENCES

Ekblom, P. (1997). Gearing up Against Crime: A Dynamic Framework to Help Designers Keep Up with the Adaptive Criminal in a Changing World. *International Journal of Risk, Security and Crime Prevention, 2*(4), 249–65.

(1999). Can We Make Crime Prevention Adaptive by Learning from Other Evolutionary Struggles?, *Studies on Crime and Crime Prevention,* 8(1), 27–51.

(2000, March). Future Crime Prevention – a "Mindset Kit" for the Seriously Foresighted. London: *Policing and Reducing Crime Unit. London: Home Office Research Development and Statistics Directorate.* (www.foresight.gov.uk/Crime%20Prevention/Futire_Crime_Prevention_Mindset_Kit_March_2000. pdf, Accessed June 25, 2010.)

Felson, M. (2002). *Crime and Everyday Life.* Third Edition. Thousand Oaks, CA: Sage and Pine Forge Press.

(2006). *Crime and Nature.* Thousand Oaks, CA: Sage and Pine Forge Press.

Felson, M. & R. V. Clarke (1997). *Business and Crime Prevention.* Monsey, NY: Criminal Justice Press.

Felson, M. & R. Peiser (1998). *Reducing Crime through Real Estate Development and Management.*Washington, D.C.: Urban Land Institute.

Levi, M. & P. Reuter (2006). Money Laundering: A Review of Current Controls and Their Consequences. In M. Tonry (Ed.), *Crime and Justice: An Annual Review of Research,* Vol. 34. Chicago: Chicago University Press.

Newman, G. & R. V. Clarke (2003). *Superhighway Robbery: Preventing E-commerce Crime.* Portland, OR: Willan.

Newman, O. (1972). *Defensible Space: Crime Prevention through Urban Design.* New York: Macmillan.

van Duyne, P. & M. Levi (2005), *Drugs and Money.* London: Routledge

Williams, M. (2004). "Understanding King Punisher and His Order: Vandalism in an Online Community – Motives, Meanings and Possible Solutions." *Internet Journal of Criminology.* Retrieved June 13, 2005, from http://www.internet-journalofcriminology.com

ABOUT THE AUTHOR

Marcus Felson is professor at the Rutgers University School of Criminal Justice. He has served as professor at the University of Southern California and the University of Illinois. He received his Ph.D. from the University of Michigan and his B.A. from the University of Chicago. Professor Felson has been guest lecturer in numerous countries, including Argentina, Australia, Belgium, Canada, Denmark, England, Finland, France, Hungary, Italy, the Netherlands, New Zealand, Norway, Poland, Scotland, South Africa, Spain, Sweden, Switzerland,

and Taiwan. He is author of several books. His first book, *Crime and Everyday Life*, is already in its third edition and his current book, *Crime and Nature*, was published in 2006. Professor Felson is author of over one hundred professional papers, including "Redesigning Hell: Preventing Crime and Disorder at the Port Authority Bus Terminal."

3 Migration and Crime

Roberta Belli, Joshua D. Freilich, and Graeme R. Newman

The relationship between migration and crime is a controversial issue that has received considerable attention from academics, media pundits, and politicians. This chapter discusses the extant literature and summarizes its major research findings. It must be noted though that some matters – in particular measurement related issues – remain unresolved. Researchers must determine, for instance, if they wish to study legal migrants, illegal immigrants, or both. The term "migrant" may be operationalized by researchers and nations as foreign-born (counting naturalized citizens as migrants) or noncitizens (counting native born noncitizens as migrants). These differences may make it difficult to compare studies and arrive at general conclusions, since different measurement decisions could lead to contradictory results.

In this chapter we examine current understandings as to whether migration leads to increases in criminal offending, victimization, or both. Under this conception, migration is the independent variable – the cause and crime is the dependent variable – the effect. We would be remiss, if we did not note that the reverse occurs, unfortunately, all too often. Numerous persons migrate to host countries to flee harsh living conditions, war crimes, and other human rights violations occurring in their country of origin. In other instances, criminal syndicates deceive or kidnap vulnerable individuals and transfer them to the host country to work in servitude or to be sexually abused (Aronowitz, 2009). In these cases, crime is the independent variable – the cause, and migration is the dependent variable – the effect.

MIGRANTS AND OFFENDING

Migration is a social phenomenon that has interested all regions of the world and all periods of history. The concern over the connection between migration and crime, however, has grown exceedingly in recent years. For example, during the 1950s economic boom in Europe, the movement of workers from southern to northern countries was encouraged to compensate labor shortages. Migration was considered a contributing factor to the growing economy. The situation changed, however, when the guest workers, who had been recruited temporarily, became permanent residents and failed to adequately integrate within the host population. As a result, stereotypical images of foreigners and their crime-proneness started to spread (Beutin et al., 2007). Today, in many countries migration issues are often considered matters of criminal justice and homeland security, at the same level of organized crime and terrorism. In this sense, the question researchers have attempted to answer is: What is the relationship between migration and offending?

Some studies suggest that first generation immigrants usually – but not always – commit the same or lower number of crimes than the native population. Their children and grandchildren, however, usually – but not always – commit more crime than nonforeigners – in some cases a lot more (Tonry, 1997). Some cross-national research has found that certain countries with greater diversity – including greater numbers of ethnicities, languages, and religions – have higher rates of violent crime (Howard, Newman, & Freilich, 2002). There are exceptions, however, to these general statements. A study based on a sample of eighth-grade students in Italy found no evidence of a higher level of deviance among young "second generation" immigrants compared to other Italians (Melossi et al., 2009).

Why do second and third generation migrants usually commit more crime than the indigenous population? Numerous answers have been proposed, which can be categorized into two views. One perspective emphasizes endogenous factors – in other words, the migrant's culture and attitudes – whereas the other view focuses on exogenous factors, for example, relative deprivation, and harsh living conditions in the host country.

The first perspective reflects the perception of the foreigner as the "deviant immigrant," an image that has become popular in political and media discourses in most Western countries. As Franko Aas (2007) states, "from violent asylum seekers, cynical smuggling and trafficking networks and Muslim terrorists to Nigerian and East European prostitutes, and ethnic youth gangs, the images of foreign criminals abound" (2007: 78).

A common argument among proponents of this perspective is that migrant groups subscribe to cultural values and beliefs that may encourage criminal behaviors – that is, their original culture is "criminogenic." According to this view, migrants "import" their criminality from their country of origin to the host country. Issues of honor and vengeance, religious and ethnic prejudices, and customary behavior that are legal or accepted in the migrant's home country may be criminalized in the host country.

Recent studies link specific migrant groups to transnational criminal activities, such as drug smuggling, weapons running, trafficking of women and children, corruption, extortion, and so forth. In Italy, foreign ethnic groups (primarily Albanian, Nigerian, Chinese, Russian, and Romanian) retain an almost exclusive monopoly over migrant smuggling operations and women's trafficking for sexual exploitation, although some may cooperate with local Mafia organizations (Savona et al., 2004). Colombian cartels, and more recently Mexican drug traffickers, are responsible for the constant flow of illicit drugs from Latin American countries to more than fifty nations around the world. According to Finckenauer and Voronin (2001), there are two hundred Russian groups that operate in nearly sixty countries worldwide, and have been involved in racketeering, fraud, tax evasion, gambling, drug trafficking, arson, robbery, and murder.

A more extreme version of the importation view claims that groups of migrants emigrate with the intention of undermining the host country's traditions from within and replacing these traditions with their own national values. Due to the terrorist attacks in the United States on September 11, 2001, on Spain March 3, 2004, and elsewhere this view is enjoying increased support. It is claimed that some nations and groups (e.g., Al Qaeda) dispatch migrants to attack and destroy specific host countries from within to further their religious and ideological belief systems.

The second perspective opposes the notion that the migrants' culture favors crime. Migrants are instead viewed as vulnerable individuals who are subsequently corrupted by the cultural and structural arrangements of the host country, which are viewed as conducive to crime. The living arrangements (e.g., poverty and blocked opportunities, lack of social organization, stigmatization of minorities and out-groups, and preexisting criminal subcultures) found in migrant neighborhoods are responsible for the higher migrant crime rate. Relative deprivation can also explain why second and third generation immigrants have higher crime rates compared to first generation ones. While the latter may still hold on to old-country quality of life standards, children of immigrants are more exposed to Western values, and can therefore become more sensitive to their marginalization from mainstream society.

Some allege that host governments unfairly imprison migrants for committing crimes that were caused by the host nation's dysfunctional structural and cultural arrangements. This problem is only compounded when host nations, like the United States, deport illegal migrants after completing their prison sentences back to their countries of origin. On occasion, these deportees subsequently form gangs and commit crimes that they learned in the host nation. Others assert that migrants do *not* commit more crime than the native population. Government statistics that demonstrate such a disparity, according to this view, are flawed. Migrants are arrested and imprisoned at higher rates not because they are committing more crime, but because the wider society in general and the criminal justice system in particular unfairly targets them (Tonry, 1997).

MIGRANTS AND VICTIMIZATION

Criminologists have also studied the victimization of migrants, although to a lesser extent compared to migration and offending. Migrants may be at a greater risk of "regular" street-crime victimization because the deprived environments in which they reside are more conducive to criminal behavior (Clarke, 2002). Migrants may also be at risk of victimization from far-right and racist groups that look upon them as inferiors. A wave of antiforeign attacks, for instance, occurred in Germany during the 1990s and continues in other parts of Europe. Illegal immigration has recently emerged as a major issue in the United States, especially in its Southwest. Complaining that the government has neglected the issue, some citizens have created and joined private paramilitary organizations. One such group, the Minutemen, garnered international attention as it "patrolled" the Mexican border in Arizona to prevent drug smuggling and other crimes. Some claim that vigilantes inspired by these groups have committed hate crimes against illegal migrants.

Some criminologists argue that these anti-immigration tendencies can be explained in the context of the "criminology of the other," a theory formulated by Garland (2001) to explain the crime-control approach adopted in late modern societies (Franko Aas, 2007; Welch, 2007). In this case, the migrant is "the other" – different from "us" because of biological, cultural, religious, or linguistic traits – posing a threat to the safety and integrity of "our" nations. This framework provides the basis for the legitimization of strict immigration policies and the use of punitive approaches, such as the criminalization of undocumented immigration. After 9/11, many countries have passed statutes that limit the rights of noncitizens as part of the global "war on terrorism." Freilich, Opesso, and Newman (2006) found that Australia, Canada, and especially the United States curtailed the rights of many noncitizens to bolster their homeland security. The stereotypical image of the "illegal alien" plays a central role in understanding the resurgence of far-right political movements and racially motivated violence.

Female migrants may face unique issues. The intersection of their national status, gender, and class position makes them vulnerable to victimization in the form of trafficking, exploitation, and abuse. According to the United Nations Population Fund, women make up nearly half of all migrants, an estimated ninety-five million of 191 million leaving their origin country in 2005. Female migrants confront ethnic bias from the wider society as well as patriarchal attitudes from both their own community and the larger social order. Many female migrants are thus unable to escape from or report abusive situations. Language difficulties, cultural barriers, fear of retaliation (especially in the case of abused women), fear of deportation, unfamiliarity with the host nation's law, as well as a suspicion of police (that is sometimes due to abuse the migrant suffered in the country of origin) may cause many not to report their victimizations. Governments must take these factors into account when they implement policies to counter domestic violence (Natarajan, 2005) and must do a better job of encouraging migrant victims in general, and females in particular, to report their victimizations to the government.

Some strategies have been implemented to deal with the problem of migrant victimization. In the United States, situational prevention measures, such as increased border surveillance, have been used to improve border security and monitor smuggling activities (Clarke, 2002). To prevent increased death rates among migrants who attempt to illegally cross the U.S.-Mexico border, harm-reduction strategies have also been implemented, including search and rescue operations by U.S. Border Patrol agents specifically trained in lifesaving techniques (Guerette, 2007). Sweden has decriminalized the provision of sexual services by women and criminalized the purchase of sexual services by men as a means to counter the sexual exploitation of smuggled women. In Italy and the Netherlands, victims of human trafficking are granted access to a variety of services for their protection and safety, including the possibility to obtain a temporary residence permit if they decide to cooperate with public authorities and participate in social reintegration programs. These initiatives highlight the importance of considering the different facets of the migration-crime nexus, which include crime prevention and internal security as well as humanitarian and human rights issues.

SUMMARY

There is a tendency in the public and political discourse to blur "illegal immigrants," "asylum seekers," and "ethnic minorities" under the overarching "migration" umbrella. It is important to recognize the differences existing among various migrant types, to devise better policies for the prevention and prosecution of criminal activities by migrant offenders, as well as the protection of vulnerable subjects, like the victims of human trafficking. Solutions to the many issues of migration and crime depend on governments' willingness to change laws where necessary, to implement programs for cultural socialization and bicultural competence, and to improve the depressed living conditions where many immigrant communities reside.

REFERENCES

Aronowitz, Alexis A. (2009). *Human Trafficking, Human Misery: The Global Trade in Human Beings.* Westport, CT: Praeger.

Beutin, R., M. Canoy, A. Horvath, A. Hubert, F. Lerais, & M. Sochacki, (2007). Reassessing the Link between Public Perception and Migration Policy. *European Journal of Migration & Law,* 9(4), 389–418.

Clarke, R. V. (2002). Protecting Immigrants from Victimization: The Scope for Situational Crime Prevention. In J. D. Freilich, G. Newman, S.G. Shoham, & M. Addad (Eds.), *Migration, Culture Conflict and Crime.* Burlington: Ashgate, pp. 103–19.

Finckenauer, J. & Y. Voronin. The Threat of Russian Organized Crime. Washington DC: U.S. Department of Justice, National Institute of Justice, 2001, NCJ 187085.

Franko Aas, K. (2007). *Globalization & Crime.* London: Sage Publications.

Guerette, R. T. (2007). Immigration Policy, Border Security and Migrant Deaths: An Impact Evaluation of Life Saving Efforts under the Border Safety Initiative. *Criminology & Public Policy,* 6(2), 201–22.

Howard, G. J., G. Newman, & J. D. Freilich (2002). Further Evidence on the Relationship between Population and Diversity and Violent Crime. *International Journal of Comparative and Applied Criminal Justice,* 26(2), 203–29.

Melossi, D., A. De Giorgi, & E. Massa (2009). The "Normality" of "Second Generations" in Italy and the Importance of Legal Status: A Self-Report Delinquency Study. *Sociology of Crime, Law & Deviance,* 13, 47–65.

Natarajan, M. (2005). Dealing with Domestic Violence in India: A Problem Solving Model for Police. In J. D. Freilich and R. Guerette (Eds.), *Migration, Culture Conflict, Crime and Terrorism.* Burlington: Ashgate.

Newman, G., J. D. Freilich, & G. J. Howard (2002). Exporting and Importing Criminality: Incarceration of the Foreign Born. *International Journal of Comparative and Applied Criminal Justice,* 26(2), 143–63.

Freilich, J. D., M. Opesso, & G. Newman (2005). Immigration, Security and Civil Liberties: A Comparison of Post 9/11 Legislative and Policy Responses to Noncitizens in Australia, Canada and the United States. In J. D. Freilich and R. Guerette (Eds.), *Migration, Culture Conflict, Crime and Terrorism*. Burlington: Ashgate.

Tonry, M. (Ed.) (1997). *Ethnicity, Crime, and Immigration: Comparative and Cross-National Perspectives*. Chicago: University of Chicago Press.

Welch, M. (2007). Deadly Consequences: Crime-Control Discourse and Unwelcome Migrants. *Criminology & Public Policy*, 6(2), 275–82.

ABOUT THE AUTHOR

Roberta Belli is a Ph.D. candidate in the criminal justice program of the Graduate Center, City University of New York, and research assistant at John Jay College of Criminal Justice. Her research interests include international criminal justice, human trafficking and migrants smuggling, criminal and terrorist networks, and situational crime prevention.

Joshua D. Freilich is the Deputy Executive Officer of the criminal justice Ph.D. program of the Graduate Center, City University of New York, and a member of the criminal justice department at John Jay College. His research focuses on domestic terrorism and criminological theory, and he is a lead investigator for the National Consortium for the Study of Terrorism and Responses to Terrorism (START), a Center of Excellence of the U.S. Department of Homeland Security.

Graeme R. Newman is Distinguished Teaching Professor at the School of Criminal Justice, University at Albany and has published works in the fields of the history and philosophy of punishment, comparative criminal justice, private security, situational crime prevention, and information technology. Among his authored and co-authored books are: *Super Highway Robbery* (Willan, 2003); *Migration, Culture Conflict and Crime* (Ashgate 2002); *The Global Report on Crime and Justice* (United Nations/Oxford, 1998); *Rational Choice and Situational Crime Prevention* (Dartmouth, 1997); *The Punishment Response*, Second Edition (Harrow and Heston, 1985); and *Comparative Deviance: Law and Perception in Six Cultures* (Elsevier, 1976).

4 Political Violence

A CRIMINOLOGICAL ANALYSIS

Vincenzo Ruggiero

When Cesare Beccaria called for an end to institutional barbarianism, invoking humanity in the treatment of offenders, he implicitly warned governments that, without the reform of penal systems, dangerous forms of "sedition" would soon arise. A few years after this warning, the French Revolution and its "excesses" proved how prophetic Beccaria's call was. Meanwhile, Jeremy Bentham revealed more impatience and less understanding for popular rebellions, which were always described uncomprisingly by him as "crimes against the state."

In brief, the two major thinkers that any criminology text would mention in its opening pages believed that political violence should be included among the issues that the new discipline was slowly identifying. It is, therefore, surprising that contemporary criminology devotes scarce attention to such a topic, leaving it to the analytical efforts of political scientists and, at times, students of social movements. And yet, terrorism, which is a specific form of political violence, has been studied by positivists, functionalists, labeling theorists, conflict theorists, and so on: namely, by most theoreticians belonging to the different schools of thought of which criminology and the sociology of deviance are composed.

A BRIEF OVERVIEW

Let us start with the founding father of "La Scuola Positiva," Cesare Lombroso (1876: 258–59), who describes political offenders as individuals in need of suffering for something grand, a need produced by "an excess of passionate concentration in one single idea." As if hypnotized, political offenders are seen as "monomaniacs" who display the typical "sublime imprudence of nihilists and Christian martyrs," and turn rebellious because they are oversensitive. According to Lombroso, some of these offenders suffer from hysteria, which frequently manifests itself through excessive altruism coupled with excessive egotism; theirs is a form of "moral insanity." This formulation, antiquated though it may sound, returns in contemporary descriptions of leaders of developing countries and armed organizations, who are also connoted with variants of moral insanity.

Functionalist criminology inherits from Durkheim (1951) the notion that, under certain circumstances, "moral rules" may lose their regulatory strength, particularly when political or economic change affect the patterns of individual and group expectations and put the previous division of labor in a new, deregulated, condition. Under such circumstances, needs and desires are freed from moral constraints, so that they lose fixed points of reference. Political violence may be one consequence, as the weakening of moral constraints and the loss of points of reference may lead individuals and groups to attempt the establishment of new rules and, through violent action, to try and build a new social system.

Following Durkheim's logic, we can link criminality, including political violence, to contingent social morality, connecting it to the social structure, rather than to universal moral codes and prohibitions. As is well-known, Durkheim stresses the idea of the "normality of crime," and predicts an increase in deviant behavior as a result of growing social differentiation and individualism. Moreover, he suggests that limited levels of criminality are functional to social conservation, as they reinforce collective feelings and solidarity among law-abiding individuals. Our problem, however, is to establish where, given the normality of crime, Durkheim places the boundary between functional types and degrees of crime, and unacceptable, dysfunctional, forms of political violence. In this respect, his thought becomes clear when, using the metaphor of living organisms, he distinguishes between social acts that trigger innovation and evolution, and social acts that only cause disintegration. Durkheim warns that the former bring vital forces together, whereas the latter cause morbidity, like microbes and cancer. His analysis of the French Revolution provides a precise empirical example of this distinction, a revolution in which Durkheim reads an immense effervescence of ideas, but an inability to bring about deep social change or to create new institutions.

Representatives of the Chicago School of Sociology focus on the concept of social disorganization, which incorporates an element of moral dissent. Thus, political violence is seen as marking the distinctiveness of different social worlds devoid of common understandings and meaningful communicative tools. A possible solution to the dilemmas of exclusion and impotence, political violence, in this perspective, signals the existence of shared beliefs and practices among those who deploy it, and the incapacity to establish bonds with those who are targeted.

Strain theorists would argue that political violence is an inevitable manifestation of the broken promise that everybody can rise from rags to riches. While Chicago School criminology believes that disorganization and crime are embedded predominantly in specific urban areas and affect transient groups of migrants, Merton (1968) warns that the emphasis on status and success may turn every citizen into a deviant. Unlike Durkheimian theorists, who believe that anomic conditions mainly manifest themselves in particular periods of transition, strain theorists attribute to anomie a persistent character in developed societies. The strain experienced by those who prove unable to achieve the prescribed goal of monetary success is resolved through a number of deviant adaptations. The most relevant type, for our purpose, is the adaptation Merton describes as "rebellion," consisting of the overturning of both the official goal of success and the means to attain it. "When the institutional system is regarded as the barrier to the satisfaction of legitimized goals, the stage is set for rebellion as an adaptive response" (Merton, 1968: 210). Political violence, in this view, is a completely new, if illegitimate, means to pursue completely new goals, namely a radically different sociopolitical system.

Political violence can also be analyzed through a variety of "learning" theories, for example, theories recognizing basic differences between cultural norms and values between dominant and subordinate groups in society, along with theories emphasizing how deviant behavior is transmitted in social enclaves and techniques of rationalizations are learned in specific peer settings (Hagan, 1988).

Values and rationalizations relate to the celebrated "techniques of neutralizations" suggested by Sykes and Matza (1957), who argue that delinquents drift into a deviant lifestyle through a process of justification. There are five techniques of neutralization: the denial of responsibility, the denial of injury, the denial of the victim, the condemnation of the condemners, and the appeal to higher loyalties. Among these, the last three could apply to political violence, as political offenders would claim that their victims are wrongdoers, would regard their own as a less injurious conduct than that of those who condemn them, and finally, would elect as sole judge of their acts the political ideology inspiring them and the social class they purport to represent.

Examples of labeling theory applied to political violence are numerous, and appear to be put forward by radical and conservative criminologists alike. See for example the argument of Ferracuti (1982: 130), according to whom definitions of human behavior, including terrorism, are embedded in social and institutional processes, as tentatively exemplified in the following words: "Cynically, but perhaps truly, terrorism could be defined as 'what the other person does'. What we, or the state, do is 'anti- or counter-terrorism', but obviously the positions can be reversed by shifting sides, or simply by the flow of history." This view is perfectly consonant with radical thinkers such as Becker (1963: 9), who posits that deviance is not a quality of the act performed by a person, but rather a consequence of the applications by others of definitions and rules to that person: "Deviant behavior is one to whom that label has successfully been applied; deviant behavior is behavior that people so label."

It could be argued that political violence is generated through systemic, relational processes, and that it is prevalent in contexts where control efforts eschew negotiation or accommodation, and are themselves characterized by violence. In this sense, it is not to be solely understood as violence against the establishment, but also as one of the effects of violence perpetrated by the establishment. In other words, "violence from below" and "violence from above" interact and engage in a process of mutual promotion. In this respect, some of the analytical tools offered by symbolic interactionism may be helpful.

Conflict theories might also be of help, particularly notions that people are fundamentally group-involved beings, and that social life is characterized by permanent confrontation. Individuals are said to produce associations based on common interests and to pursue them through collective action. These associations or groups engage in a permanent struggle to maintain, or to improve, the place they occupy in the interaction with other groups. Conflict is, therefore, regarded as one of the principal and essential processes in the continuous and ongoing functioning of society. The conflict between groups seeking their own interests is particularly visible in legislative politics, where definitions of acceptable and unacceptable conducts are forged. Ultimately, conflict theorists posit that the definition of political activity as criminal results from the challenge to authority through dissent, disobedience, or violence, a challenge that is deemed intolerable by the establishment (Turk, 1982).

Elements of criminological theories are used by Hamm (2007), who relies on Sutherland's notion that criminal behavior is learned through interaction and interpersonal communication. Drawing on classical sociological thought, the author also introduces the variable charisma that he applies to specific characters in the contemporary history of terrorism such as Carlos the Jackal and Osama bin Laden. Charisma, or the power of the gifted, is regarded as a quality that elicits loyalty and unquestioned action. Hamm, however, mainly looks at "terrorism as crime" from a particular angle, as he is less interested in political violence per se than in the crimes committed for the provision of logistical support to that violence. His analysis, therefore, focuses on crimes aimed at providing terrorists with money, training, communication systems, safe havens, and travel opportunities.

Arena and Arrigo (2006: 3) claim that the extant literature "examines the causes of terrorism from within a psychological framework." There is, in effect, an abundance of studies addressing violent political conduct as a function of the individual's psyche, or even attempting to identify specific personality traits "that would compel a person to act violently." Arena and Arrigo suggest that the identity construct is too often deemed a contributing factor in the emergence and maintenance of extremist militant conduct, and while noting that knowledge around identity and terrorism is limited, they propose an alternative social psychological framework grounded in symbolic interactionism. The concepts utilized include symbols, a definition of the situation, roles, socialization, and role-taking.

FROM POLITICAL VIOLENCE TO TERRORISM

While there is some agreement around the definition of political violence, great difficulties are encountered when the definition of terrorism is attempted. Political violence, for example, could be described as any violent action carried out during the course of political struggle, aimed at influencing, conquering, or defending the state power. It should be noted that this definition includes both violence "from below" and violence "from above," namely violent acts carried out by a state against its internal or external enemies. As for terrorism, on the other hand, definitions appear to remain extremely controversial. The belief that a set of human acts can be described as terrorism seems today to find exclusive currency in the official political arena. Therefore, a thematic content analysis of definitions found in the international literature may lead to the conclusion that terrorism can only become a criminological or sociological object of study when filtered through the discourses of politics and the media. In this sense, it is argued, the very concept of terrorism is hollow and unworthy of specialist analytical effort.

Laqueur (1977) observes that consensus on a definition of terrorism is most difficult to be achieved, because the word is used more as an ideological weapon than as an analytical tool. At best, the author argues, terrorism serves the purpose of alluding to some mode or intensity of politically consequential violence other than spontaneous uprisings or rioting. This argument, however, obscures the fact that some groups engaged in politically, thoroughly planned, consequential violence may contest the perception by others of their action as terrorism. Terrorism, they will argue, defines forms of violence that are random and target noncombatant civilians, whereas their violent action targets specific representatives of the political and economic power against which they fight. Terrorism, therefore, is equated to "pure" political violence, namely violence that can be defined by the targets attacked. Terrorism, in this perspective, consists of organized civilians, overtly or covertly, inflicting mass violence on other civilians. Political violence, in brief, becomes terrorism when political organizations using it adopt a concept of collective liability applied to the groups against which they fight (Ruggiero, 2006). Targets are not precise actors whose conduct is deemed wrongful, but general populations defined by nationality, ethnicity, religious, or political creed.

SUMMARY

This chapter argues that political violence has been a central concern for father founders of criminology such as Cesare Beccaria and Jeremy Bentham. The former warned that institutional violence exerted through penal practices would trigger violent political responses by civil society and oppositions. The latter was as aware as Beccaria of this danger, but regarded all responses to institutional practices as crimes against the state. The chapter goes on to analyze the different interpretations of political violence offered by positivism, functionalism, labeling theory, conflict theory, and so on, namely the main schools of thought inspiring criminological analysis and the sociology of deviance. Finally, it focuses on terrorism as a specific form of political violence.

REFERENCES

Arena, M. P. & B. A. Arrigo. (2006), *The Terrorist Identity: Explaining the Terrorist Threat*. New York: New York University Press.

Becker, H. (1963). *Outsiders: Studies in the Sociology of Deviance*. New York: The Free Press.

Durkheim, E. (1951). *The Division of Labour*. New York: The Free Press.

Ferracuti, F. (1982). A Sociopsychiatric Interpretation of Terrorism. *The Annals of the American Academy of Political and Social Science*, 463, 129–40.

Hagan, J. (1988). *Modern Criminology: Crime, Criminal Behaviour, and Its Control*. New York: McGraw-Hill.

Hamm, M. S. (2007). *Terrorism as Crime*, New York: New York University Press.
Laqueur, W. (1977). *Terrorism*. Boston: Little, Brown.
Lombroso, C. (1876). *L'uomo delinquente*. Turin: Bocca.
Merton, R. K. (1968). *Social Theory and Social Structure*. New York: The New Press.
Ruggiero, V. (2006). *Understanding Political Violence*. London: Open University Press.
Sykes, G. & D. Matza. (1957). Techniques of Neutralization: A Theory of Delinquency. *American Sociological Review*, 22, 664–70.
Turk, A. T. (1982). *Political Criminality: The Defiance and Defence of Authority*. London: Sage.

ABOUT THE AUTHOR

Vincenzo Ruggiero is professor of sociology at Middlesex University (UK). He has worked for the United Nations on a number of projects on transnational crime, human trafficking and political corruption. Among his books: *La Roba* (1992), *Eurodrugs* (1995), *European Penal Systems* (1995), *Organized and Corporate Crime in Europe* (1996), *Economie sporche* (1996), *The New European Criminology* (1998), *Crime and Markets* (2000), *Movements in the City* (2001), *Crime in Literature* (2003), *Understanding Political Violence* (2006), *Social Movements: A Reader* (2008), and *Penal Abolitionism* (2010).

5 Victimology

SERVICES AND RIGHTS FOR VICTIMS OF DOMESTIC AND INTERNATIONAL CRIMES

Jan van Dijk and Jo-Anne Wemmers

INTRODUCTION

In modern times there was in Western countries almost no place for the victims of crime in criminal justice. The victim had become the forgotten third party of the criminal trial. Likewise criminologists exclusively focused their studies on offenders and largely ignored the role and problems of victims. The first publications on victims dealt with the role of victims in the causation of crimes. The focus of these studies was on the degree of guilt of the victims for the crime committed against them (e.g., provocative behavior). This early interest in the culpability of victims has later been critiqued as manifestations of "victim blaming." The inclination to blame victims of serious crimes for their misfortune has itself been the subject of social psychological studies. Experiments by Lerner and others have revealed that victims of serious crimes often elicit negative responses from their environment because their situation poses an acute threat to the fundamental belief in a just world. By assuming that the victim bears some responsibility for his or her victimization through irresponsible behavior, others can reassure themselves that they have nothing to fear for themselves.

Around 1970 grassroots organizations discovered the needs of victims of domestic and sexual violence and began to provide services for them such as shelter homes and rape crisis centers. Around the same time some criminologists took up an interest in the situation of crime victims as a special research topic. Victimization surveys revealed not only that many victimizations were never reported to the police (the dark numbers of crime) but also that many reporting victims were dissatisfied with the way their cases were handled by the authorities. A sizeable minority of reporting victims even complained that they had been retraumatized by their treatment by the police and the criminal justice system (secondary victimization). Soon an international movement came into being, lobbying for improved services for victims and for the introduction of victims' rights in criminal procedure (Walklate, 2007; Wemmers, 2003). An important international platform for this reform movement was the World Society of Victimology, founded in Münster, Germany in 1979. A landmark achievement of the victims' movement was the adoption by the General Assembly of the *United Nations of the Declaration on the Basic Principles of Justice for Victims of Crime and Abuse of Power* in 1985 (Groenhuijsen & Letschert, 2008). In recent years victimologists have become more and more interested in the needs of victims of international crimes and violations of human rights, as well as the needs of indirect victims such as family members and witnesses (Wemmers et al., 2010).

Today victimology has developed into an academic discipline, with its own body of knowledge, journals, and professional organizations. It can be defined as the scientific study of:

a. victims, direct and indirect, of domestic and international crime or violations of human rights;
b. the material and immaterial consequences of such victimizations; and
c. the various social and legal interventions to assist victims in coping with these consequences (Goodey, 2004; Walklate, 2007; Wemmers, 2003).

VICTIM VULNERABILITIES

One of the research topics of victimology is the vulnerability of persons to be criminally victimized. According to the results of victimization surveys, risk factors for victimization by violent crime are young age, an outgoing lifestyle, and residence in a large city. Especially at risk are people abusing alcohol or drugs. People suffering from Attention Deficit Hyperactivity Disorder have also been found to be more at risk than others (Boogaerts, 2010). Those who have been victimized once by personal crime run an enhanced risk to be revictimized within the same year (repeat victimization). This is especially true for victims of violence between intimates. But also victims of robberies or household burglaries are at risk to be revictimized soon after a previous victimization. This happens either because their lifestyle or personal characteristics expose them more than others to such risks (homogeneity) or because perpetrators decide to hit the same target again where they have been successful before (event dependency) (Farrell & Pease, 2001). The phenomenon of repeat victimization underlines the importance of prevention advice for victims. More recently, the work by David Finkelhor on the victimization of children and youth has highlighted the importance of what he terms, polyvictimization, which refers to the multiple and diverse victimization of children and youth (Finkelhor et al, 2009).

TRAUMA AND TREATMENT

Victims of serious crime often suffer from the same clinical symptoms as victims of extreme war experiences such as flashbacks of the traumatic incident, nightmares, extreme feelings of fear, and anger attacks. Secondary symptoms are loss of concentration, feelings of guilt, and avoidance of cues that trigger memories of the incident. Estimates of the prevalence of Post-Traumatic Stress Disorder (PTSD) among crime victims vary. National victimization surveys in the United States and in Europe suggest that 20 percent to 30 percent of victims of violence, including sexual violence, develop PTSD (Kilpatrick et al., 1987). Treatment interventions aim to assist victims with their coping strategies. Vitally important for successful coping is the support from family and friends. Professional treatment interventions typically consist of exposure to the painful memories in a secured environment with a view to the extinction of accompanying emotions (NICE, 2005). Encouraging results have been obtained with the special technique of Eye Movement Desensitization and Reprocessing (EMDR) (Winkel, 2007).

According to the 1985 UN Declaration victims of crimes of violence are entitled to receive appropriate social services and treatment as well as compensation for their losses from the perpetrator or from state funds. These principles of justice for victims have been incorporated in the national laws and policies of many individual countries. Moreover, they have been incorporated in several UN conventions such as the Convention against Transnational Organized Crime and the protocol against human trafficking, both ratified by the large majority of UN member states including the United States and all member states of the European Union. For the twenty-seven member states of the European Union, adequate provisions for victim support and state compensation for victims of all types of crime are mandatory according to the EU Framework Decision on the Standing of Victims in Criminal Proceedings of 2001 (Groenhuijsen & Letschert, 2008).

The full incorporation of these international legal norms in the domestic legislation and practices of individual countries remains for the moment a

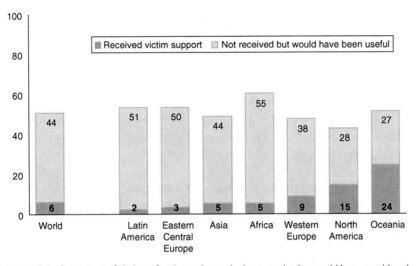

Figure 5.1. Percentage of victims of serious crimes who have received or would have considered useful specialized victim support by world regions.
Source: ICVS, 2005

distant dream. Some European countries including Greece and Italy have introduced neither support organizations nor compensation funds for victims of violent crime. In other countries existing services for victims, however well established, reach just a small part of their potential clients. In Canada, for example, victim compensation is not available across the country (Wemmers, 2003). In the International Crime Victims Survey, 2005, victims of four types of serious crime (burglaries, robberies, sexual offences, threats, and assaults) are asked whether they have received support from a specialized victim support agency. Those who had not received any help were asked whether they would have appreciated help in getting information, or practical or emotional support. Figure 5.1 shows the rates of victims receiving specialized assistance in world regions and the rates of those in need of such services.

The results indicate that the need for help among victims of serious crime is widespread. In developed nations, three or four in ten victims express such needs. In developing countries even more victims would have wanted such help. The comparison between the regional percentages of victims of serious crimes who had received assistance and of those who would have appreciated receiving such assistance indicates a worldwide gap between supply and demand of such services. Even in countries where victim support has become more common, the need for such help is still largely unmet. Victim support was received most often by victims in

Australia/New Zealand (Oceania) and North America (Canada and USA). In Western Europe, 9 percent of victims received help. In other regions including Eastern/Central Europe, a provision of specialized help is still a rare occurrence.

Several of the principles of justice for victims have been incorporated in the legal statute for the International Criminal Court (Wemmers & de Brouwer, 2010). Attached to the ICC is a trust fund that can be accessed at any stage in the trial, including the investigation stage. The Trust Fund for Victims will therefore not only implement reparation awards from the Court, it may also – upon notification to and approval from the Court – implement programs that will assist victims of mass crimes in terms of physical and psychological rehabilitation as well as material support. Indeed, the Trust Fund for Victims has started to implement several activities in Uganda (eighteen projects) and the Democratic Republic of Congo (DRC) (sixteen projects), benefiting an expected total of 380,000 direct and indirect victims. (See ICC Web site, under Structure of the Court/Victims/Trust Fund for Victims/current projects).

VICTIMS' RIGHTS IN CRIMINAL PROCEDURE

The 1985 UN Declaration on principles of justice for victims includes provisions on the procedural role of victims in criminal procedures. Victims are entitled to be treated with compassion and respect for their dignity, to be fully informed about proceedings and outcomes, and to receive legal aid. In addition, the responsiveness to the needs of victims should be facilitated by "Allowing the views and concerns of victims to be presented and considered at appropriate stages of the proceedings where their personal interests are affected." The right to present views has been incorporated into the UN Conventions against Transnational Organized Crime (2000) and Corruption (2002). It is also embodied in the 2001 Framework Decision of the Council of Ministers of the European Union. Article 3 of the said Decision reads as follows: "Each member State shall safeguard the possibility for victims to be heard during proceedings and to supply evidence." In the Rome Statute victims are given, in contrast to their marginal roles in previous war tribunals, the right to participate in criminal justice proceedings through their legal representative as well as the right to request reparation though the court.

Criminal law experts in many countries have expressed concerns that victim participation in trials will result in the imposition of more severe sentences on defendants. Empirical research in the USA and Australia suggests that victim participation does in practice have little impact on sentencing and that its impact does not necessarily result in more severe sentencing (but in a choice for reparation over imprisonment) (Erez, 2000). Research also shows that in many countries existing provisions for victim participation are still not seen as satisfactory by many victims (Hall, 2009; van Dijk, 2009). As is the case with victim services, newly introduced victims' rights seem in most countries to be still in their infancy (Wemmers, 2009).

CONCLUSIONS

Since the adoption in 1985 of the UN Declaration on Victims' Rights, the victims' movement has come a long way. Special services for crime victims have in many countries become more common and the position of victims in criminal proceedings has been enhanced almost universally. In many respects the implementation of international legal norms is still far from satisfactory. The take up rates of victim services remains very low. Even in countries with well-established victim support organizations only a minority of victims in need of assistance is actually reached. Newly introduced procedural rights for crime victims are often only partially implemented and are found wanting by many of the victims. One of the most encouraging developments is the adoption of the Rome Statute and the ensuing jurisprudence by the International Criminal Court. Mass media audiences across the world will soon become acquainted with legal representatives of victims making statements in highly publicized trials in the International Criminal Court in The Hague. The evolving practices of the International Criminal Court will present a useful example to national legislators and courts across the world of how victims ought to be treated in modern systems of criminal justice. Legislators will hopefully start to understand that victims should receive recognition and validation from the criminal justice system, as well as protection from the offender without burdening them with responsibilities.

To promote the implementation of the United Nations Victims' Declaration, the United Nations Office on Drugs and Crime has put together a Handbook on Justice for Victims, available in several world languages (www.worldsocietyofvictimology.org). In addition, the World Society of Victimology has, in collaboration with Tilburg University in the Netherlands, elaborated a draft for a United Nations Convention on Justice and Support for Victims of Crime and Abuse of Power, including a preamble and a section on ways to encourage adoption and implementation (www.universitytilburg.nl/intervict).

REFERENCES

Bogaerts, S. (2010), *Spiegelingen tussen Daders en Slachtoffers*, inaugural lecture, INTERVICT, 23 January.

Erez, E. (2000). *Integrating a Victim Perspective in Criminal Justice through Victim Impact Statements*. In A. Crawford & J. Goodey (Eds.), *Integrating a Victim Perspective within Criminal Justice*. Aldershot, UK: Ashgate, pp. 165–85.

Farrell, G. & K. Pease (2001). *Repeat Victimization. Crime Prevention Studies*, Vol. 12. NY: Monsey: Criminal Justice Press.

Finkelhor, D., R. K. Ormrod, & H. A. Turner (2009). Lifetime Assessment of Poly-Victimization in a National Sample of Children & Youth. *Child Abuse & Neglect*, 33, 403–11.

Goodey, J. (2004). *Victims and Victimology; Research, Policy and Practice*, Harlow: Pearson.

Groenhuijsen, M. & R. Letschert (2008). *Compilation of International Victims' Rights Instruments*. Intervict/Wolf legal Publishers (www.universitytilburg.nl/intervict).

Hall, M. (2009). *Victims of Crime: Policy and Practice in Criminal Justice*. Devon, UK:, Willan Publishers.

International Criminal Court Web site: *(www.icc-cpi.int)*

Kilpatrick, D. G. et al. (1987). Criminal Victimization: Lifetime Prevalence, Reporting to Police, and Psychological Impact. *Crime & Delinquency*, 33, 479–89.

Kirchhoff, G. F. (1994). *Victimology – History and Basic Concepts*. In G. F. Kirchhoff, E. Kosovski & H. J. Schneider (Eds.). *International Debates of Victimology*. Mönchengladbach: WSV Publishing, pp. 1–81.

Lamet, W. & K. Wittebrood. (2009). *Nooit meer Dezelfde, Gevolgen van Misdrijven voor Slachtoffers*. Den Haag Sociaal Cultureel Planbureau.

NICE (2005). Post Traumatic Stress Disorder. The Management of PTSD in Adults and Children in Primary and Secondary Care, by Gaskell and the BPS, online: www.nice.org.uk

Tobolowski, P. (2001). *Crime Victim Rights and Remedies*. Durham: Carolina Academic Press.

van Dijk, J. J. M. (2009). Free the Victim: A Critique of the Western Conception of Victimhood. *International Review of Victimology*, 16, 1–33.

Walklate, S. (2007). *Handbook of Victims and Victimology*. Deon, UK: Willan Publishers.

Wemmers, J. (2003). *Introduction à la victimologie*. Montréal : Les Presses de l'Université de Montréal.

(2010). Where Do They Belong? Giving Victims a Place in the Criminal Justice Process. *Criminal Law Forum*.

Wemmers, J. & A. M. de Brouwer (2010). *Globalisation and Victims' Rights at the International Criminal Court.* In J. J. M. van Dijk & R. Letschert (Eds.), *Globalisation, Human Security and Victims.* Springer.

Winkel, F. W. (2007). *Post Traumatic Anger: Missing Link in the Wheel of Misfortune, Inaugural Lecture.* University of Tilburg/Intervict (www.universitytilburg.nl/ intervict).

ABOUT THE AUTHORS

Jan van Dijk was born in Amsterdam, the Netherlands in 1947. He was director of the Research and Documentation Centre of the Dutch Ministry of Justice and part-time professor of criminology at Leiden University. Between 1998 and 2005 he worked for the United Nations in Vienna and Turin. He acted as president of the World Society of Victimology between 1997 and 2000. In 2008 he received the Sellin-Glueck Award of the American Society of Criminology for his lifelong contribution to international criminology and victimology. He currently holds the Pieter van Vollenhoven chair in victimology and human security at the University of Tilburg (the Netherlands).

Jo-Anne Wemmers obtained her Ph.D. from the University of Leiden (The Netherlands). Presently, she is a professor at the School of Criminology of the Université de Montréal (Canada) as well as head of the Research Group Victimology and Restorative Justice at the International Centre for Comparative Criminology. Professor Wemmers has published many articles and books in the area of victimology, including *Introduction à la victimologie* (Les Presses de l'Université de Montréal) and *Victims in the Criminal Justice System* (Kugler Publications). Former Secretary General of the World Society of Victimology, she is currently Editor of the *International Review of Victimology* as well of the *Journal international de victimologie.*

6 Children and International Criminal Justice

Cécile Van de Voorde and Rosemary Barberet

INTRODUCTION

Insofar as age determines social expectations in our global humanity, we anticipate different behaviors and levels of responsibility from children, adults, and the elderly. Domestic criminal justice systems take account of these age differences in order to provide protection, care, rights, and treatment for children, be they offenders or victims. This chapter examines children as perpetrators, victims, and witnesses within the framework of international criminal justice. It highlights special protections for children as a highly vulnerable population and issues of criminal responsibility under international human rights and humanitarian law. Impunity negatively impacts current and future generations of children by hindering their growth and the development of their identity, values, and beliefs. Similarly, cruel treatment of juvenile offenders is not conducive to their social development. It is, therefore, crucial to study children and international criminal justice as they impact future peace, reconciliation, and stability.

CHILDHOOD AND CRIMINAL JUSTICE

Despite historical support for children's interests in international law and the international consensus on the importance of children's rights, not all nations agree on the definition of childhood. The 1989 Convention on the Rights of the Child defines children as "those under 18 years of age, unless under the law applicable to the child, majority is attained earlier." In some parts of the globe, however, children take on sibling care, work, marriage, and childbearing roles earlier in life than in other parts where such aspects of social life are postponed until near adulthood.

Relevant to this chapter is the age at which children can be held responsible for their offending behavior. Like childhood, this concept is relative. Some nations establish a minimum age for responsibility. Others establish a period for juvenile or youth justice jurisdiction, which typically expires with the passage to adulthood. Even when considered an adult, a youthful offender can benefit from reduced sentencing and treatment based on age. Similarly, domestic legal systems may differentiate between child and adult victims, and punish child victimization more harshly than adult victimization while establishing specific policies and programs for child victims.

NATURE AND TRENDS OF CHILD-SPECIFIC CRIMES

The international community emphasizes protection, care, rights, and treatment for children. Criminologists typically pay more attention to children's offending than victimization. Since the 1990s, the International Self-Report Delinquency Survey has documented the widespread involvement of young people in antisocial and offending behavior. The 2006 United Nations Secretary General's Report on Violence against Children is the most recent report to embrace the wide spectrum of children's suffering in the family, schools, care and justice institutions, the workplace, and the community. UNICEF (2009) reports that between 500 million and 1.5 billion children are experiencing violence annually, 150 million children aged five to fourteen are engaged in child labor worldwide, and more than 250,000 children are associated with armed groups or armed forces today. In addition, 600 to 800,000 people are trafficked each year across international borders and one sixth to one half of these are children.

Violence toward children is underreported and often undetected. It is also gendered: societies with a preference for boys perpetuate such practices as sex-specific abortion or female infanticide, which markedly alters national sex ratios. In most countries, girls are at higher risk for infanticide, sexual abuse, educational and nutritional neglect, and forced prostitution (Krug et al., 2002). Moreover, most of the world's poor are women and children, and 86 percent of the world's children now live in the global South (Beigbeder, 2007).

INTERNATIONAL FRAMEWORK FOR THE PROTECTION OF CHILDREN

The international framework for the protection of children can be traced back to the 1924 Geneva Declaration on the Rights of Child of the League of Nations. After World War II, the UN General Assembly created the United

Nations Children's Fund, now known as UNICEF. Progressively, children's rights came to be enshrined in major human rights instruments: the 1948 Universal Declaration of Human Rights, the 1959 Declaration on the Rights of the Child, the 1966 International Covenant on Civil and Political Rights, and the International Covenant on Economic, Social and Cultural Rights, and the 1979 Convention on the Elimination of All Forms of Discrimination Against Women. A major milestone was the 1989 adoption of the Convention on the Rights of the Child (CRC), a widely ratified treaty that entered into force in 1990. It entitles children to protection by others and the State, and to basic rights: life, health care, education, and protection from harm and exploitation. The Optional Protocol on the Involvement of Children in Armed Conflict establishes eighteen as the minimum age for mandatory recruitment and mandates States to prevent children under the age of eighteen from taking a direct part in armed conflict. The Optional Protocol on the Sale of Children, Child Prostitution and Child Pornography further mandates the criminalization of these activities. The United States and Somalia are the only two countries that have not ratified the CRC.

Like the Committee on the Rights of the Child and UNICEF, the UN Commission on Crime Prevention and Criminal Justice has made strides toward the effective treatment of children as offenders, victims, and witnesses through relevant standards and norms. Moreover, the 2000 Protocol to Prevent, Suppress and Punish Trafficking in Persons, Especially Women and Children, supplementing the UN Convention on Transnational Organized Crime, defines as "trafficking in persons" the recruitment, transportation, harboring, or receipt of a child (understood as someone under eighteen) for exploitation, even if this occurs without force, threat, abduction, fraud, deception, or abuse of power.

JUSTICE FOR CHILDREN AT THE ICC

The International Criminal Court (ICC) was established by the Rome Statute of 1998. As of March 24, 2010 111 countries are States Parties to it. The Statute and accompanying documents include multiple child-related provisions: (1) crimes against children within the jurisdiction of the ICC, (2) special measures to protect children during the investigation and prosecution of cases, and (3) requirements for ICC staff with expertise in children's issues. The ICC has jurisdiction over individuals accused of these crimes, not only those directly responsible but also others who may be liable by aiding, abetting, or assisting with the crime. It has no universal jurisdiction and no jurisdiction over children under eighteen at the time of the alleged commission of the crime. Hence, children can only be victims or witnesses in the ICC process.

Crimes against Children

Children can be victims of any crimes within the ICC jurisdiction. The Rome Statute also includes crimes that can only be committed against children and crimes that are particularly relevant to children (Du Plessis, 2004; No Peace without Justice, 2002).

"Using, conscripting or enlisting children under 15 as soldiers" or using them to participate actively in hostilities is a war crime within the jurisdiction of the ICC. This applies under all conditions: if the child is recruited into national armed forces or armed groups, if the conflict is international or not, and regardless of whether the child was coerced or volunteered. The crime is focused on children who participate directly in hostilities as combatants, but child soldiers also perform tasks as messengers, porters, cooks or spies, and may be exploited for sexual purposes. An example of this can be found in the Lubanga case (*The Prosecutor v. Thomas Lubanga Dyilo*, ICC-01/04–01/06). Mr. Lubanga, a national of the Democratic Republic of the Congo and alleged founder of the Union des Patriotes Congolais (UPC) and Forces Patriotiques pour la Libération du Congo (FPLC), has been on trial at the ICC since January 26, 2009. He is allegedly responsible, as co-perpetrator, of war crimes including enlisting and conscripting children under the age of fifteen into the FPLC and using them to actively participate in hostilities within the context of an international armed conflict and a noninternational armed conflict.

"Forcibly transferring persons under the age of 18," belonging to a national, ethnical, racial or religious group intentionally targeted for whole or partial destruction constitutes genocide. In this context, "forcible" is not limited to physical force but can also include the threat of force or coercion, such as that caused by fear of violence, psychological oppression, or abuse of power.

"Crimes of sexual violence" can be tools or outcomes of war (Harris Rimmer, 2007; Skinnider, 1999). The ICC has jurisdiction over rape, sexual slavery, enforced prostitution, forced pregnancy, enforced sterilization, and other forms of sexual violence of comparable gravity. When such acts are committed during an international or noninternational armed conflict, they are war crimes. If they are committed against civilians as part of a widespread or systematic attack and pursuant to or in furtherance of a State or organizational policy, they can be prosecuted as crimes against humanity, in peacetime or wartime.

"Intentionally attacking schools" is a war crime. The list of protected buildings includes buildings dedicated to education, religion, art, science or charitable purposes, historical monuments, as well as hospitals and other places where the sick and wounded are cared for, provided they are not used for military purposes. Furthermore, "attacks on humanitarian staff and objects" (personnel, installations, material, units or vehicles involved in a humanitarian assistance or peacekeeping mission) can directly affect children and also constitute a war crime.

Children as Victims and Witnesses before the ICC

In most legal systems, special measures and procedures exist to prevent child victims and witnesses from re-experiencing trauma in court. The Rome Statute and the Rules of Procedure and Evidence of the ICC provide for special measures at the request of the Prosecutor, the defense, the victim or witness, and his or her legal representative. The Chamber involved can also, under certain circumstances, order special measures to facilitate the testimony of a traumatized child. One rule directly referring to children states that if a child witness appearing before the ICC is the child of the accused, he or she shall not be required to make any statement that might incriminate the accused parent unless he or she chooses to do so.

The ICC has further implemented a special protection and support scheme, the Victims and Witnesses Unit (VWU), designed to benefit all witnesses and victims who appear before the Court, and to provide appropriate assistance. The VWU is responsible for protection, security, counseling, and other measures. One category of people within its mandate is "others who are at risk on account of testimony given by such witnesses," which may include children at risk of retaliation for testimony given by a parent before the ICC.

SUPPLEMENTARY MECHANISMS OF JUSTICE FOR CHILDREN

Judicial Mechanisms

The International Criminal Tribunal for Rwanda (ICTR) and the International Criminal Tribunal for the former Yugoslavia (ICTY) are ad hoc tribunals created to determine responsibility for crimes committed during armed conflicts under international law. They represent a systematic attempt by the international community to end impunity for wartime crimes against civilians, which was reinforced by the establishment of a permanent international criminal court. Both Tribunals have jurisdiction over natural persons without any reference to age. However, no minor has been indicted or prosecuted for crimes within the jurisdiction of the ICTR or ICTY yet, which may indicate that they find it inappropriate to try children. Children can be used as witnesses and may testify without taking an oath as long as the Chamber believes they are capable of reporting the facts within their knowledge and understanding the duty to tell the truth. Practices sensitive to child victims are also in place in both Tribunals.

When cases involve prosecution in national courts, national legal systems must ensure that children in conflict with the law receive special protection. Children have the right to treatment that takes into consideration their age and special circumstances. Depriving a child of his or her liberty should only be used as a last resort and for the shortest possible time.

Nonjudicial Mechanisms

Human rights abuses can be addressed through truth commissions investigating pervasive human rights violations after armed conflict and within the framework of transitional justice. Truth commissions seek to establish accountability and accurate historical records of atrocities by collecting testimonies and publicly acknowledging previously undisclosed crimes. International child rights and juvenile justice standards guide all proceedings and policies. The South African Truth and Reconciliation Commission has been most efficient at reintegrating children by focusing explicitly on crimes committed against children or adolescents and by organizing separate hearings to encourage children to come forward.

For children who perpetrated atrocities or were victimized during a conflict, traditional justice measures can also complement legal proceedings by providing an alternative system of accountability, as long as they uphold international standards of justice. Traditional justice systems are informal, culture-specific systems based on indigenous or customary practices. Local communities resort to such people-based mechanisms in order to resolve localized disputes and provide safe access to justice to all. Traditional justice for child perpetrators underscores the importance of rehabilitation, reintegration, and respect for the rights of others, as well as reparation to the community that suffered harm (Morss, 2004).

CONCLUSION

Whereas children have received increasing attention from the international community, they often remain invisible, potential but silent political actors in world events. NGOs have actively advocated for the interests of children, and yet children rarely take center stage to share their experiences and concerns. Given their vulnerability and underrepresentation, adults still bear the responsibility of monitoring their protection and safety. Through the creation of the ICC, ad hoc tribunals, and truth commissions, it has become possible to truly promote children's rights. As a result, a culture of accountability for children is now stemming from increased collaboration between all actors and a sound understanding of the role of international criminal justice in regard to the rights of children.

REFERENCES

Beigbeder, Y. (2007). Children. In T. G. Weiss & S. Daws (Eds.), *The Oxford Handbook on the United Nations*. Oxford: Oxford University Press, pp. 511–24.

Du Plessis, M. (2004). Children under International Criminal Law. *African Security Review*, 13(2), 103–11.

Harris Rimmer, S. (2007). "Orphans" or Veterans? Justice for Children Born of War in East Timor. *Texas International Law Journal*, 42, 323–44.

Krug, E. G., L. L. Dahlberg, J. A. Mercy, A. B. Zwi, & R. Lozano. (2002). *World Report on Violence and Health*. Geneva: World Health Organization.

Morss, J. R. (2004). The Status of Child Offenders Under International Criminal Justice: Lessons from Sierra Leone. *Deakin Law Review*, 9(1), 213–25.

No Peace without Justice. (2002). *International Criminal Justice and Children*. Florence, Italy: UNICEF Innocenti Research Centre.

Skinnider, E. (1999). *Violence against Children: International Criminal Justice Norms and Strategies*. Vancouver, Canada: International Centre for Criminal Law Reform.

UNICEF. (2009). *Progress for Children: A Report Card on Child Protection*. New York: UNICEF.

WEB SITES

Child Rights Information Network: http://www.crin.org

Convention on the Rights of the Child: http://www2.ohchr.org/english/law/crc.htm

Save the Children: http://www.savethechildren.org

United Nations Secretary General's Study on Violence against Children: http://www.violencestudy.org

ABOUT THE AUTHORS

Cécile Van de Voorde, L.L.M., Ph.D. is an assistant professor in the Department of Law and Police Science at John Jay College of Criminal Justice. She is a cultural criminologist and documentary photographer whose ethnographic work focuses on genocide, child soldiers, and the use of sexual violence in armed conflict.

Rosemary Barberet, Ph.D. is an associate professor in the Sociology Department at John Jay College of Criminal Justice. Her publications deal with victimology, crime indicators, and comparative methodology. She has received the Herbert Bloch Award of the American Society of Criminology.

7 Women and International Criminal Justice

Mangai Natarajan and Monica Ciobanu

INTRODUCTION

Despite considerable progress made in the past few decades, women in the Western world still suffer discrimination and are not treated equally to men. Consider how much more true this is in the developing world, where the gap between the treatment of men and women is a yawning chasm. These facts illuminate any consideration of women's criminality, the particular nature of their criminal victimization, and their treatment by the criminal justice system. In addition, women's unequal status has repercussions for their employment in the criminal justice system as police officers, prosecution or prison staff, and court judges and magistrates. It even helps to explain the nature of their involvement in transnational and international crimes, whether as offenders or victims. These are the topics explored within this chapter.

WOMEN AS OFFENDERS

Surveys and police records of crime in Western nations show that women still constitute a small minority of offenders, but they are becoming increasingly involved in crime. Women are mostly involved in common crimes – minor thefts and frauds, low-level drug dealing, prostitution, and misdemeanor assaults against their mates or children – and are far less likely than men to be involved in serious crime. At the international level, however, women are becoming more involved in serious crimes of drug trafficking, human trafficking, terrorism, and genocide:

- *Drug trafficking*: Analysis of 1,715 drug traffickers caught smuggling drugs through Heathrow Airport between July 1991 and September

1997 indicate that women take on a high-risk but lower-status role of courier and carry Class A drugs in large quantities (Harper, Harper, & Stockdale, 2002).

- *Human trafficking*: Women make up the largest proportion of traffickers and they are involved in all stages of the trafficking operations, including: recruitment; transportation; escort; provision of forged document; provision of flats; control of victims and cashing (Kangaspunta, 2008).
- *Terrorism*: Women have been participants in terrorist groups in Sri Lanka, Iran, West Germany, Italy, and Japan. They are increasingly involved in many terrorist organizations (in Russia, India, Colombia, Israel, Britain) and in suicide bombing and other attacks (Cunnigham, 2007; de Mel, 2004; Skaine, 2006).
- *Genocide*: A substantial number of women, and even girls, were involved in the slaughter in Rwanda. They inflicted extraordinary cruelty on other women, as well as children and men (Lentin, 1997).

Several competing theories explain why women are increasingly involved in criminal activities:

1. More women are motivated to commit crimes as a result of (a) impoverishment, unemployment, and a lack of educational opportunities and (b) increases in domestic violence, divorce, and separation.
2. Steffensmeier and Allan (1996, 2000) provide an integrated model of female offending intended to assist understanding of gender differences in type and frequency of crime, criminal opportunity, motivation, and the context offending. Their model includes gender norms, moral development and relational concerns, social control, physical strength, aggression, and sexuality.
3. The increase in female crime is a function of the greater emancipation of women in society; as women are liberated and assume more traditional male social roles, they begin to act more like males (Adler, 1975).
4. Cohen and Felson (1979) contend that the most general explanation of crime rate trends is an indicator of the dispersion of activities away from family and household settings. The increased participation of women in work outside the home provides increased opportunities for women to become both victims and criminals just as these opportunities had for men (Anderson & Bennett, 1996).

WOMEN AS VICTIMS OF VIOLENCE

Though women are disproportionally the victims of domestic violence or family violence across societies around the world, there are many specific forms of violence against women that are related to their gender role and that represent the abuse of unequal power relations between women and men at social, cultural, and economic levels. Some of these are presented below.

Culture-specific Violence

1. *Female genital mutilation*: FGM is a social convention that is considered a necessary part of raising a girl properly, and a way to prepare her for adulthood and marriage relating to premarital virginity and marital fidelity. It is primarily practiced in Africa (especially in Somalia, Sudan, Ethiopia, Eritrea, and Cote D'Ivoire), and in some parts of Asia and the Middle East, but also among some immigrant communities in Europe, North America, and Australia.
2. *Honor killings*: These murders are based on the cultural belief that a woman's lack of conformity to sexually prescribed norms severely undermines the honor of her family. When unmarried or married women do not abide by these rules their fathers, husbands, or brothers may kill them to re-establish the family reputation. The majority of these incidents are documented in India, Pakistan, Afghanistan, Egypt, Jordan, Turkey, and Lebanon.
3. *Female infanticide*: This is prevalent in India and among Arabian tribes due to the preference for sons and the low value associated with the birth of females. It is also said to be common among South Asian immigrants in Britain, the United States, and Canada.
4. *Bride burning*: In the Indian subcontinent hundreds of young brides are burned to death every year as result of dowry disputes. The dowry is a customary practice of gift giving by the bride's family to that of groom during and after marriage.
5. *Fatwah*: This is a religious decree practiced against women (relating often to marriage, sexual abuse, and adultery) issued by religious leaders, known as *moulavi* or *moulana* in Bangladesh.
6. *Bonded labor*: In many villages in Sindh and Pakistan some women are virtually imprisoned and forced to labor over many years.
7. *Acid attacks*: In Bangladesh and Pakistan, acid is thrown on women who refuse to marry a man or turn down their sexual advances.

Armed Conflict and Sexual Violence

During wars and other armed conflicts, sexual assaults, enforced prostitution, and many forms of exploitation of women occur. Indeed, systematic violations of women's rights during wars have been the norm around the world, despite the Geneva Convention that codifies the laws of war and conflict. Twenty thousand Muslim women were systematically raped during the 1992 campaign of ethnic cleansing in Bosnia and 15,000 women were raped during the 1994 genocide in Rwanda. Many of the rape victims in Rwanda were infected with AIDS. Sexual violence that routinely involved mutilation, sexual slavery, gang rape, torture before being killed, and disembowelment of pregnant women has been reported in African countries involved in armed conflict between 1987 and 2007 (Bastick, Grimm, & Kunz, 2007).

Transnational Violence against Women

Trafficking of women is common within, as well as across, national borders. Due to vulnerabilities arising from poverty and gender discrimination, trafficking in women flourishes in supplying in many less developed countries. These vulnerabilities are maintained through the collusion of the market, the State, the community, and the family unit. In fact, traditional family structures, which are based on the maintenance of traditional sex roles and the division of labor that derives from such roles (for women, housekeeping, caretaking, and other unpaid or underpaid subsistence labor), frequently support the system of trafficking. According to a CIA report (2000), many women who are trafficked are kept in situations of forced labor through sexual, physical, and psychological abuse. Women are threatened with violence against their families; they are kept in isolation; they are raped and introduced to drugs; and their passports and identity documents are seized.

TREATMENT OF WOMEN IN THE CRIMINAL JUSTICE SYSTEMS

According to the World Prison Brief (2009), in 93 percent of 196 countries less than 10 percent of the prison population consists of female prisoners. This is the reflection of judicial reluctance to impose custodial sentences on women due to the obligations of females in society and also to the lack of facilities to meet the specific needs of female prisoners, such as prenatal and postnatal care. This reluctance has been labeled as "chivalry."

Of particular concern in the international context is that in a number of countries trafficked women who are members of ethnic and racial minorities are held in prison before deportation (United Nations Report, 2000). While in prison these women are confronted not only with linguistic and cultural isolation, but also with racism and xenophobic violence. This is known as secondary victimization. The abuse of women in custody is a particularly urgent matter that requires a more prompt and effective response on the part of prison systems in accordance with international standards and norms.

WOMEN AS JUSTICE PROFESSIONALS

The Tenth UN survey on the representation of women in the criminal justice professions reveals that of the eighty-six countries that provided data, only thirty countries (see Table 7.1) supplied information on all categories of criminal justice professions (police, prosecution, courts, and prisons). Women around the world seem to have the lowest representation among the police (less than one third) and an equal, or more than equal, representation in courts and prosecution. The low representation of women in policing and prisons is related to gender inequality. As shown in Table 7.1, countries that employ few women in the police and prisons are ones that score poorly in the Gender Empowerment Measure (GEM). The GEM measures gender inequality in three basic dimensions of empowerment: economic participation, political participation, and power over economic resources. Additional reasons for the low proportion of women in the police service are the work conditions and the prevailing organizational climate (gender bias, harassment, the military model of policing, and discriminatory practices based on physical differences), which make the job unattractive to women (Natarajan, 2008).

SUMMARY AND CONCLUSION

Seven important points can be drawn from the above discussion of the treatment of women as victims, as offenders, and as employees in criminal justice systems in Western and non-Western countries.

1. There is much wider recognition of the widespread and serious forms of victimization committed against women in many traditional societies. The 1995 UN Convention against the Elimination of All Forms of Discrimination Against Women (CEDAW) requires member states to challenge those cultural beliefs and practices based on gender inequality and to eliminate those forms of victimization against women that are culturally and country specific. National

Table 7.1. Percentages of Women Professionals in the Criminal Justice System and The Gender Empowerment Measure (GEM) Scores for Twenty-Eight Nations

Country	Police	Prosecution	Courts	Prison	GEM
1. Sweden	23	51	48	41	.91
2. Finland	12	37	39	33	.90
3. Germany	15	37	34	21	.85
4. Dominican	10	52	45	45	.79
5. Singapore	17	37	50	24	.79
6. England & Wales	22	54	18	NA	.78
7. Scotland	22	62	16	23	.78
8. Portugal	4	54	49	NA	.75
9. Austria	10	43	44	22	.74
10. Greece	11	58	63	12	.68
11. Estonia	35	71	63	NA	.67
12. Czech Republic	14	55	62	23	.66
13. Latvia	25	61	76	32	.65
14. Slovenia	12	0	75	24	.64
15. Poland	11	53	63	18	.63
16. Lithuania	23	42	54	30	.63
17. Croatia	9	61	65	26	.62
18. Japan	5	12	14	8	.57
19. Mauritius	5	2	54	7	.54
20. Romania	9	48	70	19	.51
21. Nepal	3	1	1	9	.49
22. Ukraine	11	27	NA	25	.46
23. Thailand	6	0	23	19	.45
24. Turkey	3	5	28	8	.38
25. Morocco	3	14	19	13	.32
26. Algeria	NA	9	35	11	.32
27. Liechtenstein	7	29	6	6	.00
28. Monaco	9	75	48	28	.00

Source: UN Tenth Crime Survey

and International efforts are leading to improvements in reporting, recording, and prosecuting crimes against women. The International Criminal Court (ICC) statutes explicitly lay down a number of sexual violence crimes unprecedented in international criminal law. Rape, sexual slavery, enforced prostitution, forced pregnancy, or any other form of sexual violence of comparable gravity are now incorporated as both crimes against humanity and war crimes (see Chapter 47).

2. As more women take their full place in society and more of them make a living outside the home it might be expected that greater proportions of them will fall victim to regular street crimes and to sexual harassment. This is already evident in some societies such as India where "eve teasing" is a widespread problem. An international survey on the victimization of women is therefore an urgent research priority.

3. Women are victimized because they are women. Gender-based violence is most often culturally normalized and socially accepted in most part of the developing world. Understanding and minimizing the harm from such violence requires a more culturally sensitive human rights approach than criminal justice approach. The international agenda should consider ways to empower women to allow them to take charge of their own lives.

4. It is unclear whether the growing emancipation of women in developing countries will result in larger proportions of women becoming involved in crime, as occurred in industrialized and developed countries for the past three decades.

5. If the number of women offenders increase there is likely to be a concomitant increase in the number of women incarcerated. This will have important consequences for the prison system, which has signally failed, even in developed countries, to cater adequately to the special needs of women in custody, including to the need to preserve the relationship with the children and families.

6. Even in developing countries, the growing emancipation of women has resulted in large numbers of them obtaining employment in the criminal justice system in prosecution, the prisons, probation, and courts. One exception is the police where women account for a small minority of officers even within most developed countries. There is a special need to find ways to making policing an attractive job for women, in which their special talents are employed and rewarded.

7. There is a need to develop and to pursue more comparative crosscultural research on women offenders and criminal justice professionals.

The purposes would be to improve treatment of women offenders in the criminal justice system and to find ways to increase the representation of women among criminal justice professionals.

REFERENCES

Adler, F. (1975). *Sisters in Crime: The Rise of the New Criminal*. New York: McGraw-Hill.

Anderson, T. & R. Bennett (1996). Development, Gender and Crime: The Scope of the Routine Activities Approach. *Justice Quarterly*, 19, 499–513.

Bastick, M., K. Grimm, & R. Kunz (2007). *Sexual Violence in Armed Conflict: A Global Overview and Implications for the Security Sector*. Geneva: DCAF.

Cohen, L. & M. Felson (1979). Social Change and Crime Rates. *American Sociological Review*, 44, 588–608.

de Mel, N. (2004). Body Politics: (Re) Cognizing the Female Suicide Bomber in Sri Lanka. *Indian Journal of Gender Studies*, 11(1), 75–93.

Harper, R. L., G. C. Harper, & J. E. Stockdale (2002). The Role and Sentencing of Women in Drug Trafficking. *Legal and Criminological Psychology*, 7, 101–4.

Kangaspunta, K. (2008). *Women Traffickers*. UNODC. http://www.ungift.org/docs/ungift/pdf/vf/traffickerworkshop/women%20traffickers.pdf

Lentin, R. (Ed.) (1997). *Gender and Catastrophe*. London: Zed Books.

Natarajan, M. (2008). *Women Police in a Changing Society: Back Door to Equality*. Aldershot, UK: Ashgate.

Skaine, R. (2006). *Female Suicide Bombers*. Jefferson, NC: McFarland Publishers

Steffensmeier, D. & A. Emilie (1996). Gender and Crime: Toward a Gendered Theory of Female Offending. *Annual Review of Sociology*, 22, 459–87.

United Nations. (2000). Women in the Criminal Justice System. Retrieved Feb 28, 2010 from http://www.uncjin.org/Documents/congr10/12e.pdf

World Prison Brief (2009). Retrieved from http://www.kcl.ac.uk/depsta/law/research/icps/worldbrief/wpb_country.php?country=47

ABOUT THE AUTHORS

Mangai Natarajan, Ph.D. is a professor at John Jay College of Criminal Justice. She has published extensively on women in policing and domestic violence. Her current research includes sexual harassment of women in public places, security, urban design, and burn victims.

Monica Ciobanu, Ph.D. is an assistant professor of sociology in the Department of Sociology and Criminal Justice at Plattsburgh State University of New York. Her current research is focused on issues of memory, truth, and justice in post-communism. Her work appeared in *Europe-Asia Studies, Comparative Sociology, International Journal of Politics, Culture and Society*, and *Nationalities Papers*.

8 Culture and Crime

Edward Snajdr

CULTURE, NORMS, AND TRANSGRESSIONS

This chapter explores the complex relationship between culture and crime. Social scientists define culture as a system of learned, shared ideas and behaviors. All cultural systems include basic ideas of what constitutes proper or improper actions. But not all actions interpreted to be incorrect or immoral by members of one culture may be thought of as such by another group. It is, therefore, important from the perspective of a global criminology to consider how the concept of crime is culturally constructed, that is, how ideas about what is right or wrong vary crossculturally. Describing such variation through ethnographic field research is one of the primary tasks of cultural anthropologists. Understanding how these variations are integrated with broader systems of power, subsistence, and economy is also a major goal for anthropologists.

Anthropologists broadly conceptualize the variety of acceptable and unacceptable behaviors across human societies as norms and transgressions. A norm is essentially what people expect other people to do. Most norms are informal and implicit expectations, which are so widely and consistently followed that there is no need for formal enforcement. For example, words or acts of politeness, such as saying "thank you" or shaking hands, comprise a set of exemplary customs of communication that most everyone performs. Other customs are usually repetitive behaviors, the rules of which are generally passed on orally between generations. For example, the Ju/'hoansi custom of bride service, whereby newly married males in this foraging society in the Kalahari Desert hunt for their bride's parents, is common but not formally codified (Lee, 1993). Many norms, however, are formal, written rules expressed explicitly as laws. In state-level societies, these explicit codes (including statutes, regulations, and local ordinances) are considered to be mandatory and are enforced by representatives of the state. Some rules may be so specialized that they concern only a particular subgroup within a culture. For instance, Federal Aviation Administration regulations provide an intricate set of rules for U.S. commercial airline pilots, of which most laypersons are unaware.

Anthropologists use the term transgression to broadly conceptualize violations of norms. Like norms, transgressions may be explicitly classified and officially enforced or they may be only casually noted by others with a frown or with gossip (Goffman, 1963). For example, in the U.S. there is no formal penalty for rude behavior such as butting in line. Similarly, there are no serious consequences for speaking out of turn in a moot, an informal mediation process practiced by the Kpelle, a tribal community in Liberia (Gibbs, 2001).

A crime is generally understood to be the violation of a law. But not all formal transgressions are labeled as such. In the U.S., transgressions committed against individuals are known as torts, or civil violations, and are usually remedied by the victim herself. Crimes, therefore, are quite specifically characterized in the U.S. as violations against the political system that enacts and maintains the law. Penalties for these types of transgressions are thus pursued not by individual victims, but by people representing the government. Even societies with no formal legal system define many transgressions formally. For example, the Polynesian term *tabu* is a word for a rule that proscribes (or prohibits) certain behaviors in traditional horticultural societies of the Pacific region. A commoner in seventeenth century Hawaii was forbidden to touch or even to look directly at a paramount chief. If this *tabu* were broken the transgressor was forced to pay tribute to the chief as a fine.

Since cultural systems vary widely, what constitutes a transgression in one society may not be the same thing in another. Thus, most anthropologists do not study "crime" per se, but rather, the range and variation of norms and transgressions as constructs of a cultural system.

CULTURAL CONSTRUCTION OF CRIME

Notions of crime are commonly grounded in ideas about the supernatural. For instance, Polynesian *tabus* are reinforced by native cosmology, specifically the concept of *mana* or spirit force. A chief possesses *mana*, an essence that is dangerous to nonroyals and the intricate set of restrictions surrounding communication with the chief supports the spiritual basis of his power.

Crimes in the U.S. such as rape or murder are also thought of as *mala in se* crimes, or inherently evil. Such a label suggests the religious origins of these crime categories, as sacred proscriptions of monotheism. For example, the Christian notion of sin, explicitly expressed in the Ten Commandments (e.g., Thou shalt not kill), corresponds to very serious crimes in the modern legal code (e.g., homicide). Less egregious transgressions are classified as *mala prohibita* crimes that, although not evil, are nevertheless violations of a law or rule.

Transgressive actions may also be shaped by political power structures that reinforce systems of religious or economic stratification. In Hindu India, for example, the caste system includes prohibitions on exogamy, or marrying outside of one's group. Thus, male members of a lower caste may not marry a woman belonging to a higher caste. Untouchables, or people in the lowest caste, are forbidden to interact in many ways with people in the system's upper levels. Other restrictions may also be integrated with notions of gender, class, and race. Sharia or Muslim law dictates certain gender practices, such as public seclusion of females, or lesser degrees of access to inheritances for women (Rosen, 1989). Similarly, upper-class urban residents routinely ignore homeless people, and the state may legally prevent panhandlers from asking for change on the street (Duneier, 2000).

In addition to religion, the way cultures conceptualize kinship also shapes certain rules and violations surrounding sexual relations. For example, incest prohibitions and rules of fidelity, which are found in all cultures, vary depending on marriage practices and descent systems. In most state societies intercourse between kin is forbidden and having more than one spouse is illegal. But cousin marriage and polygyny are common practices among small-scale tribal societies or among some Muslim elites. Divergent gender norms may also influence what types of violent behaviors may be acceptable or discouraged by a culture. Among the Abelam of New Guinea a husband may beat his wife in order to discipline her (Counts, Brown, & Campbell, 1999).

How people are punished for transgressing also varies according to cultural contexts. Many cultures espouse a public approach to punishment, whereby the penalty functions as both a shaming act and a deterrent against future transgression. The Muslim practice of cutting off the foot and hand of a thief, for example, fulfills both of these goals. In a utilitarian system, such as in the U.S., crimes are classified by the type of punishment. For example, minor violations are labeled misdemeanors, restricting imprisonment to less than a year, and more severe crimes requiring more lengthy rehabilitation are known as felonies.

Some nonstate societies believe in supernatural forms of punishment. For example, the Kabana of New Britain, a tribal society in the South Pacific, considers illness or death by sorcery to be a justifiable penalty. Still other cultures may seek collective punishment in cases of transgression. The Kpelle, for instance, penalize not only a husband who mistreated his wife, but also members of the extended family who may have been complicit in the abusive situation.

In cultures with no formal government, punishment may often be improvised. A Ju/'hoansi band once collectively killed a man who had committed the most recent murder in an ongoing blood feud. This rare communal act of homicide essentially ended a chain of lethal violence plaguing this usually peaceful community of foragers.

ETHNOCENTRISM, HUMAN RIGHTS, AND CULTURAL DEFENSE

As members of a culture, people's notions of normality and deviance are reinforced through ethnocentrism, the belief that one's culture is superior to other's and that other cultures should be judged according to one's own standards. While ethnocentrism is a universal human condition, it may be amplified when unequal power relationships exist between different cultures, such as in cases of colonialism, imperialism, and migration. For example, throughout Eurasia, North America, and the Middle East, the Romany Diaspora, more commonly know as the Gypsies, have been popularly labeled as inherently "criminal" by native populations (Fonseca, 1996). Regardless of whether some Gypsies actually engage in explicitly criminal behavior, such as pickpocketing, other Gypsy practices may contribute to their transgressive reputation. For example, Romany customarily share official documents between extended family members and do not have strict notions of personal property. Not surprisingly, when a Gypsy male in a midwestern city used his cousin's social security number to otherwise legally purchase an automobile in a Midwestern city, he was found guilty of a felony and served six months in prison (Sutherland, 2000). Another example of a practice embraced by people but officially criminalized by the government is bride-kidnapping. This Central Asian custom originating among traditionally pastoralist nomads is still followed by some contemporary Kazakhs. Despite the fact that it is against the law, many "kidnappings" are voluntary agreements and public gender performances between future bride and groom, and accepted by both of their kin networks (Werner, 2009).

An area where ethnocentrism presents a special challenge is with the development of a global standard of human rights. In 1946, United Nations member states signed the Universal Declaration of Human Rights, which proposes a set of rights and freedoms that should apply across all cultures. Yet there remains controversy over whether the international community can label any cultural practice as criminal. This debate has recently focused on female circumcision, a rite of passage in many traditional communities ranging from Africa to Asia and even in the U.S. In this rite, girls at puberty undergo genital modification, sometimes by excision of the clitoris or, more extremely, by infibulation of the vagina. In many cases, the practice is performed with the permission of the girls' parents, followed by a public celebration marking the young woman's change in status to adulthood. Human rights organizations are attempting to end this tradition, characterizing the ritual as child abuse. Proponents of the custom argue that they have a right to this practice as it is fundamental to their culture's system of norms (Walley, 1997).

Such an argument also raises the question of whether culture can provide a defensible explanation for criminal behavior in a specific legal system. The "cultural defense" is appearing more frequently in U.S. criminal courts to justify what are perceived by the system to be acts of crime. Levine (2003) finds that this type of defense is attempted in cases of abuse, rape, and other serious crimes. She argues that these areas reflect diverse cultural perspectives on enculturation (child rearing), on sexual and marital norms, as well as on models of healing and health. For example, U.S. authorities have pressed abuse charges against Latin American and Mediterranean immigrants for the traditional treatment of placing a heated cup over a child's open wound. More contentious are cases where defendants use culture-bound interpretations of masculine behavior to justify sexual assault (e.g., *Wisconsin vs. Curbello-Rodriguez* cited in Levine, 2003). Interestingly, culture-based defenses draw on existing legal concepts such as reasonableness, or duress, and have been somewhat successful in U.S. courts, where although defendants are found guilty, juries or judges may reduce their punishment in light of cultural explanations for their unlawful act.

Some transgressive behaviors are part of a larger context of symbolic formations and systems of meaning and thus appear to create a "culture of criminality." For example, gang activity, organized crime, and even white-collar crime often occur within social networks that, regardless of ethnic, religious, or even class affiliations, constitute specific meaning systems. Anthropologists and sociologists have studied how these subcultures develop within larger systems of inequality and domination, and produce fundamental notions of community, belonging, and loyalty. Yet understanding the social aspects of deviance also demands an awareness of how mainstream cultural institutions such as media and government can serve as moral entrepreneurs and gatekeepers who control and disseminate models of standard behavior, and who ultimately sanction deviations from the standard (Ferrell, 1995). Thus a growing subject of research is the culture of law enforcement and social control. Harris (2002) has examined several cases in which cultural misunderstandings have occurred between police officers and people in immigrant communities. What impact does this particular set of institutions and practices have on societies in which the intersections of race, class, and gender are central manifestations of daily life?

Clearly culture plays various roles in shaping notions of crime. Any attempt to formulate universal standards will have to address the reality and complexity of cultural variation.

REFERENCES

Counts, D. A., J. K. Brown, & J. C. Campbell (Eds.) (1999). *To Have and to Hit: Cultural Perspectives on Wife Beating.* Urbana: University of Illinois Press.

Duneier, M. (2000). *Sidewalk.* New York: Farrar, Straus and Giroux.

Ferrell, J. (1995). Culture, Crime and Cultural Criminology. *Journal of Criminal Justice and Popular Culture,* 3(3), 25–42.

Fonseca, I. (1996). *Bury Me Standing: The Gypsies and Their Journey.* New York: Vintage.

Gibbs, J. L. (2001). The Kpelle Moot. In A. Podolefsky & P. J. Brown (Eds.). *Applying Cultural Anthropology.* London: Mayfield Publishing, pp. 234–41.

Goffman, E. (1963). *Behavior in Public Places: Notes on the Social Organization of Gatherings.* New York: Free Press.

Harris, L. (2002). Crime and Culture: Challenges Facing Law Enforcement. *Institute for Criminal Justice Education.* http://www.icje.org/id162.htm, accessed 7-29-2009.

Lee, R. (1993). *The Dobe Ju/'hoansi.* Fort Worth: Harcourt Brace.

Levine, K. L. (2003). Negotiating the Boundaries of Crime and Culture: A Sociolegal Perspective on Cultural Defense Strategies. *Law and Social Inquiry,* 28(1), 39–86.

Rosen, L. (1989). *The Anthropology of Justice: Law as Culture in Islamic Society.* New York: Cambridge University Press.

Sutherland, A. (2000). Cross-Cultural Law: The Case of the Gypsy Offender. In J. Spradley & D. W. McCurdy (Eds.) *Conformity and Conflict: Readings in Cultural Anthropology.* Boston: Allyn and Bacon, pp. 286–93.

Walley, C. J. (1997). Searching for "Voices": Feminism, Anthropology, and the Global Debate over Female Genital Operations. *Cultural Anthropology,*12, 405–38.

Werner, C. (2009). Bride Abduction in Post-Soviet Central Asia. *Journal of the Royal Anthropological Institute.* 15, 314–31.

ABOUT THE AUTHOR

Edward Snajdr, Ph.D. is an associate professor of anthropology at John Jay College of Criminal Justice, CUNY. His research focuses on domestic violence, gender, crime, social justice, and how anthropology can be applied in the fields of criminology and international development. He has conducted ethnographic field research in Eastern Europe, Central Asia, and the U.S. His book, *Nature Protests: The End of Ecology in Slovakia*, was published in 2008. At John Jay, he teaches Cultural Anthropology, Culture and Crime, and Systems of Law.

PART II

LAW, PUNISHMENT, AND CRIME CONTROL PHILOSOPHIES OF THE WORLD

"Nulla crimen sine lege." Like all truisms, "no crime without law" conceals as much as it reveals. In particular, it leaves open the question of how law is defined. It is society, of course, that defines some acts or omissions as crimes, and which acts are considered tolerable or intolerable depends upon the prevailing local culture. Having said that, there are some acts that would receive almost universal condemnation – "almost" because, in every case, small exceptions can be adduced. This section reviews the various legal traditions and philosophies of punishment and crime control. What works for one country may or may not work for others because of deep-rooted cultural beliefs and attitudes. These cultural differences often make it difficult to achieve international agreements in dealing with international and transnational crimes.

There are three major legal traditions that can be found worldwide: civil law, common law, and Islamic law (though some societies follow indigenous traditions where the problems are solved informally without any prescribed codified law). Each legal tradition deals with substantive law (defining crime and specifying punishments) and procedural law (the details of the adjudicatory process and judicial review). Each of these traditions has its own merits in dealing with crime and, in the modern world, most countries incorporate elements of other legal systems into their own laws (see Chapter 9 by Matti Joutsen).

In all legal traditions, punishments for breaking the law vary according to the perceived severity of harm. Two principal punishment philosophies vie with each other – utilitarianism and retributivism – each of which achieves ascendancy in certain situations. The former focuses on deterrence to preserve social order, while the latter focuses on moral order whereby the individuals are held responsible for their crimes (see Chapter 10 by Graeme Newman).

In most countries, the principal punishment reserved for serious offenses has been imprisonment. While a country's rate of imprisonment is often taken as measure of its "punitiveness," there are many components that contribute to a high incarceration rate other than a desire for punishment. These can include more crime, greater police effectiveness in solving crimes, and more aggressive prosecution. Alfred Blumstein shows in Chapter 11 that the recent growth of incarceration in the United States and some other developed countries is largely attributable to changes in the political environment associated with crime. Because of their increased use of incarceration, many of these countries have experienced prison crowding, which exacerbates conditions such as institutional violence, human rights violations, and communicable disease (see Chapter 12 by Harry Dammer).

Partly in response to the enormous costs of imprisonment, some countries are now giving more attention to crime prevention. In Chapter 13, Ronald Clarke discusses the different prevention approaches that vary from measures to reduce opportunities for crime, which can have an immediate effect on crime levels, to longer term measures intended to reduce criminal dispositions, whose benefits are generally longer term.

9 Legal Traditions

Matti Joutsen

LEGAL SYSTEMS AND LEGAL TRADITIONS

A basic distinction is made in comparative law between legal systems and legal traditions. A legal system consists of the set of legal institutions, procedures, and rules that govern the operation of the criminal justice system. A legal tradition is a set of deeply rooted, historically conditioned attitudes about the nature and role of law, about the organization and operation of a legal system, and about how the law is or should be made, applied, studied, perfected, and taught (Merryman, 1985). The criteria that are generally used when classifying which legal tradition a legal system belongs to are its sources of law, the historical background and development of the system, its characteristic mode of thought, and its distinctive institutions, such as the roles of judges and lawyers.

The most common legal traditions are the common law legal tradition, the civil law legal tradition, the Islamic legal tradition, and the indigenous legal tradition. One major legal tradition that is not dealt in this chapter is the socialist legal tradition, which is based on the civil law legal tradition but is politicized law that recognizes the dominance of the Communist Party. It was at one time widespread, primarily in Eastern Europe and the USSR. Today, its influence can be seen for example in aspects of law in China, Cuba, Vietnam, and North Korea.

THE COMMON LAW LEGAL TRADITION

The common law legal tradition emerged in England and is generally associated with judge-made law (as opposed to statutory law) and adversarial procedure (as opposed to inquisitorial procedure). The roots of common law can be traced back to the early Middle Ages (ca. 500 –) when England was a feudal society with a relatively weak king. The "law" that was followed was essentially local folk custom. Disputes were settled in assemblies of free-men in shire and hundred courts. William the Conqueror (1066–87) added a layer of royal courts. These royal courts based their decisions on custom, and often depended on juries to inform them about local custom. Since the members of the jury were part of the same small, tightly-knit community, they were expected to know the people coming before them on trial, and thus have prior knowledge of the case.

A combination of feudal practices, custom, and equity produced a legal tradition that emphasized the grassroots nature of law (and of criminal justice), and the role of the judge in ascertaining custom (the law). Once a judge had established what the custom is in an individual case, the decision served as a guide for other judges in subsequent cases that had similar features; the case became a precedent.

Common law also evolved in an adversarial direction. The most active participants in the trial came to be the lawyers for the two parties (in criminal trials, the defense counsel and the prosecutor), each presenting their client's position. The judge's role was largely a passive one, listening to the arguments of the two sides before deciding the case.

By the time that England began to establish colonies, common law had emerged as a distinct legal tradition. As a result, this legal tradition was spread to English colonies around the world, including, for example, to what are now the United States, Canada, and Australia. Roughly one-fifth of the countries in the world can be classified as belonging to the common law legal tradition. As common law spread, it evolved in different directions. Developments in England were no longer necessarily followed in the colonies, especially after these colonies became independent. In some colonies, the common law legal tradition mixed with other legal traditions. For example, in the case of the early colonies in North America, common law blended here and there with a Puritan emphasis on Biblical law, as well as with an emerging "law merchant" (international trade law). In some North American colonies, Spanish and French law also had an impact. The influence of French law is most clearly visible in North America in the state of Louisiana and the province of Quebec. Although common law originally emerged through decisions made by independent judges, modern common law is based to a large extent on laws passed by legislatures.

THE CIVIL LAW LEGAL TRADITION

The civil law legal tradition (also known as Roman law or Continental law) is often described as being based on laws passed by the legislature (statutory law). (Note: The civil law legal tradition is often referred to simply as "civil law." This term is avoided here, since the same term is widely used to refer to private law – the law of contracts, the law of property, etc. – as opposed to criminal law.)

The roots of the civil law legal tradition in Continental Europe lie in a mixture of Roman law, codification, and Church law. Ancient Rome was highly centralized, and the laws passed by the Roman Senate applied to Roman citizens throughout the Empire – essentially, much of Europe, Northern Africa, and parts of the Middle East.

Roman rule lasted about a thousand years. With time, it became increasingly difficult even for the lawyers to understand how different pieces of legislation enacted at different times fit together. This led to efforts to codify law, to bring all legislation on a certain topic together into one statute. In one important respect, codified law is the opposite of judge-made law. Instead of looking at individual cases, the codifiers try to establish basic principles, and then synthesize a comprehensive set of regulations on this basis.

The fall of the Roman Empire left room for another centralized power structure, the Church, which established a network of courts. These courts did not limit themselves to spiritual or religious matters, but instead took on a wide remit. At a time when nations on the continent of Europe were slowly beginning to coalesce and re-emerge in the aftermath of the fall of Rome, Roman law had largely fallen out of use. As had been the case in England during the Middle Ages, the law that was applied was traditional folk custom. This law was adequate in a static rural society, but could not respond to economic and political developments. During the 1100s, Roman law was rediscovered by jurists and re-introduced into legal practice. This development was supported by the Church and the merchant class, but, more importantly, the re-introduction of Roman law was also supported by the many kings and princes, who saw Roman law as a way of centralizing power into their hands.

Over the next centuries, a mixture of Roman law and Church law came to dominate legal practice throughout Continental Europe. Local folk custom provided regional color, and the kings and princes in the different countries added their own statutes. Thus, for example the law in France became quite different from that in the German states. Beginning with the so-called Napoleonic Code in France in 1804, many countries with a civil law legal tradition codified their law. Each new code replaced previous legislation. Despite the importance of statutory law, however, jurisprudence also in the civil law legal tradition countries began to refer extensively to court cases.

The civil law legal tradition is associated with an inquisitorial process, where the judge is active in fact-finding, for example in collecting evidence, and in questioning the parties or the witnesses during the trial. As was the case with common law, the period of colonization led to the exportation of the civil law legal tradition around the world. Today, roughly one half of all countries apply the civil law legal tradition. In addition to Continental Europe, it is applied in almost all of Central and South America, in most of Africa, and in much of Asia.

THE ISLAMIC LEGAL TRADITION

While the common law and civil law legal traditions are essentially secular, the Islamic legal tradition is decidedly religious. Its basis is the law as revealed by Allah to His Prophet, Muhammad (ca. 570 – 642), written down in the Qur'an. The Qur'an, together with the Sunna (the collected statements and deeds of Muhammad), comprise the Sharia, the "path to follow." Muhammad lived in the Arabian Peninsula, which was then populated by many small tribes worshiping a number of gods. The divine revelations to Muhammad served to restore monotheism and unite the feuding tribes.

Islam, and with it Islamic law, spread very rapidly. Within the space of only a century its influence extended beyond the Arabian Peninsula to northwest India and Central Asia in the east, and to North Africa and the Iberian Peninsula in the west. Subsequently, it spread in particular to many countries in South-East Asia.

The Sharia is more than law; to Muslims, the Sharia is a guide to all facets of life. There is, thus, no distinction between a legal system and other controls on behavior. And since the Qur'an is divinely revealed, it is also immutable. It cannot be amended by the legislator or set aside by the judge.

In order to be able to apply Islam to changing circumstances, two additional sources of Islamic law have evolved: analogical reasoning (*qiyas*) and consensus among jurists (*ijma*). Because *qiyas* and *ijma* vary among the different denominations that have emerged in Islam (the most important of which are Sunni and Shi'a), the way in which Islamic law is applied in practice today varies considerably. Modern Islam also incorporates statutory law, allowing for even more variety from one Islamic country to the next.

During the colonial period, the Islamic legal tradition was eroded by the introduction of the common law or civil law legal traditions. Following independence, Islamic law has resurged in many countries. Today, a distinction can be made between countries where Islam provides the basis for the entire legal system (e.g., Saudi Arabia, Afghanistan, Iran, Iraq, Libya, and Sudan) and countries where Islam is one major source for the legal system, along with elements from, for example, the civil or common law legal traditions (e.g., Indonesia, Malaysia, and Pakistan).

THE INDIGENOUS LEGAL TRADITION

Traditional society has no written law, nor even a sense of law as something apart from proper standards of behavior. When a problem arises in the community, the members gather together to discuss how to resolve it. Using at times ritualized procedures, all those who believe that they can contribute to the discussion are allowed to do so. Village elders might refer to how similar problems have been dealt with before, which helps to guide the discussion and suggests the result. The emphasis is on participation and on restoring harmony within the society.

Despite the spread of the common law, civil law, and Islamic legal traditions, as well as other more developed types of law, this indigenous legal tradition remains in wide use in many areas, alongside the "official" legal system. This is the case in many African countries as well as, for example, Indonesia, Papua New Guinea, and the Philippines. The tradition is also resurging among indigenous people in, for example, the United States, Canada, and New Zealand. Furthermore, many of the elements of the indigenous legal tradition have been used in the development of mediation and restorative justice programs in "mainstream" legal traditions.

MIXTURES OF LEGAL TRADITIONS

The development of the different legal traditions did not take place in a vacuum. Each was influenced by other traditions. To take just one example, the common law legal tradition has taken on some inquisitorial aspects from the civil law legal tradition, and the civil law legal tradition has correspondingly been influenced by common law adversarial procedure.

In some cases, several legal traditions operate alongside one another in the same country. For example, in both Nigeria and Pakistan, common law, Islamic law, and indigenous law are applied in separate court systems. As a result, there are few "pure" examples of a legal tradition. Indeed, according

Table 9.1. Overview of the Main Legal Traditions

	Sources of law	Centralization	Discretion	Features	Examples
Common law	Case law and legislation	Low	Extensive	Jury; rules of evidence; passive role of judge; active role of lawyer	USA, Canada, UK
Civil	Legislation (synthesis; broad principles)	High	Some	Active role of judge	France, Germany, Mexico
Islamic	Shari'a; analogical reasoning; consensus among jurists	Low	Religious interpretation	Law is divinely inspired; immutability of the Shari'a	Saudi Arabia, Iraq, Afghanistan
Indigenous	Local custom; primarily oral sources	Very low	Discretionary; wide use of mediation	Extensive informal control; huge variety; search for community harmony	Tribal courts in the U.S., aboriginal communities in Australia, Maori communities in New Zealand

to one calculation, almost one half of legal systems are hybrids that combine different legal traditions. Historical developments and structural factors help to explain why a country follows a certain legal tradition, but the differences between the traditions are not hard and fast. Table 9.1 provides an overview of the four legal traditions described in this chapter. The differences are not so much of kind, as of degree.

Moreover, there is a lot of variation within legal traditions. Common law countries vary in the extent to which they use codifications, jury trial, and allow judicial activism. Different civil law legal tradition countries have developed different institutions. Examples of such institutions include the investigating magistrate in French-based systems and the role of the victim as a subsidiary prosecutor in some German-based systems.

SUMMARY

The legal traditions may help us to understand the attitudes toward different sources of law, but to a surprising degree there are few major differences between how the legal traditions operate in practice. This can be seen, for example, in how the criminal justice system operates. The way in which each and every society responds to dangerous or harmful conduct such as stealing, fighting, and vandalism is broadly the same. A central authority (usually, a democratically elected legislature, although it can also be, for example, a king, a religious leader, or a council of elders) defines what behavior is prohibited, how to determine whether or not someone has been guilty of such behavior, and what the punishment may be. The broad outlines of the criminal justice process are much the same in every country, with one or more law enforcement agencies charged with the investigation of alleged offences; a prosecutorial service charged with presentation of the cases in court; the court itself, charged with hearing the case and deciding on the outcome; and a separate organization charged with the enforcement of the sentence. The main differences in practice between individual criminal justice systems – and legal traditions – appear to arise not so much from the legal system, but from the political system, and in particular its approach to the question of control.

FURTHER READING

Merryman, J. H. (1985). *The Civil Law Tradition. An Introduction to the Legal Systems of* Europe and Latin America. Chicago: Stanford University Press.
Pakes, F. (2004). *Comparative Criminal Justice*. Portland, OR: Willan Publishing.

Reichel, P. L. (2008). *Comparative Criminal Justice Systems*. Upper Saddle River, NJ: Pearson Prentice Hall.

ABOUT THE AUTHOR

Dr. Matti Joutsen is the director of International Affairs at the Ministry of Justice of Finland. He has served as a criminologist, as a judge, and as Director of the European regional institute in the United Nations network of institutes for crime prevention and criminal justice. He is an active participant in the work of the European Union, the Council of Europe, and the United Nations, and was heavily involved in the drafting of the UN Convention against Transnational Organized Crime. Dr. Joutsen prepared his doctoral dissertation on the role of the victim in European criminal justice systems. He has published and lectured extensively on a variety of topics, including transnational and comparative criminal justice, organized crime, crime trends, and sentencing.

10 Punishment Philosophies and Practices around the World

Graeme R. Newman

INTRODUCTION

While punishment is universal in all criminal justice systems, it varies in the justifications given for its administration, and the kinds of punishments employed. However, comparing or even describing the use of punishments around the world is fraught with many difficulties, as is the comparison of crime (see Chapter 62). By far the most difficult problem is to be sure that when we compare punishment from one country to another we are in fact comparing the same thing.

DEFINING PUNISHMENT

In general, the definition of punishment in criminal justice should include the following elements (Newman, 2008):

- It must result in pain or consequences normally considered unpleasant.
- It must be for an actual or supposed offender for his offence.
- It must be administered for an offence against the law.
- It must be intentionally administered by a legal authority.
- It must be administered by someone other than the offender.

This definition has many problems, but it does serve to establish some boundaries. It eliminates, for example, wanton or indiscriminate violence against others, such as rape in war or death squads in times of insurrection. On the other hand, many countries that have Departments of Corrections aimed at rehabilitation (most do), may claim that the consequences are not intended to be painful, nor are they necessarily experienced as unpleasant.

PHILOSOPHIES OF PUNISHMENT

There are basically two philosophies of punishment – though they are perhaps better termed "justifications" for punishment – offered by governments and societies around the world. These are the utilitarian and the retributive. The modern view of the former, probably the most dominant, holds that, since social order is the supreme necessity of society, any amount of punishment used to deter offenders as an example to the offender and to others is well justified. Thus, the more crime that punishment can deter, the greater the good achieved.

In contrast, the justification based on retribution focuses on a lofty idea of justice: that social order (the utilitarian concern) is secondary to the moral order that is violated when an offender breaks the law. The retributivist holds that since morality is concerned with individual responsibility, the individual offender must be held to account; indeed, it is society's duty to punish him. Thus, the offender deserves to be punished, from which comes the common expression "just desserts." It further follows that the punishment must match the crime as closely as possible in order for the moral balance to be restored. This idea is but a sanitized version of the ancient principle of vengeance, "an eye for an eye." In almost all societies we find elements of both the utilitarian and retributive approaches. Taken to the extreme, there is no limit to the utilitarian use of punishment in order to preserve social order. Retribution provides limits by insisting that the "punishment fit the crime" and no more.

THE FUNCTIONS OF PUNISHMENT

The functions of punishment (often difficult to distinguish from justifications for punishment) are mostly characterized by social theorists as hidden in any given society (Garland, 1993). That is, the obvious functions of punishment such as to deter criminal acts, hide the real functions. These hidden functions gain favor because it is often difficult to demonstrate, in fact, that punishment deters crime. These latent functions of punishment are speculative, and depend, in large part on the detailed analysis of the cultures and histories of particular societies. In general, a short list of the hidden functions of punishment in society advanced by scholars includes: scapegoating ("let he who is without sin cast the first stone"), boundary definition ("they must be bad because they're in prison"), catharsis ("It makes us feel good to see the guilty punished"), enhancing social solidarity ("it's us against them"), and various forms of class or ethnic conflict ("to keep the danger-ous classes in their place") (Newman, 2008).

ADMINISTRATION OF PUNISHMENT

The basic factors that guide the administration of punishment are its: type, intensity, frequency, and duration. For example, whipping (a common pun-ishment in Singapore and other countries) may be administered according to: (1) the intensity with which the lash is brought against the body, which may be a function of the strength of the punisher or the size of the lash; (2) how many strokes are administered in one session; and (3) how often they are administered (e.g., one session a day for two weeks). Depending on the type of punishment, one or another of these administrative elements of punishment may be more dominant. Obviously, for prison, duration is the most dominant feature of the punishment, but cutting off the hand of a thief is an intense punishment of very short duration and low frequency, though its aftereffects are obviously long lasting, as are those of most punishments, including prison.

TYPES OF PUNISHMENT

Any classification of punishments can only be made roughly, since many actual punishments may easily fit into more than one category. The extent to which punishments also express or emphasize retributive or utilitarian philosophies is also sometimes difficult to determine. The preponderance of different types of punishment and their examples described later in this essay are derived from the exhaustive publication *Crime and Punishment Around the World* (Newman, 2010), which surveys crime and punishment in more than 230 countries, dependencies, and territories.

Economic punishments. These are expressed most simply as fines of des-ignated amounts, varying according to the seriousness of the offense and usually, though not always, for property crimes of lesser amounts. However, fines can be complicated because their use is subject to the criticism that they punish unequally those who have the least and are felt less by those who have more. Countries with civil law systems, such as Scandinavia, calculate the amount of a fine according to the daily income of the offender (day fine). This punishment is further complicated if the offender has no income or property. In this case, many legal systems may calculate an equivalent in prison time. For example, in Finland, one day in prison equals three days of fines. In all countries surveyed in *Crime and Punishment around the World*, fines in one form or another were universally applied. The other major form of economic punishment is that of forced labor which may occur in a prison if the crime is a very serious one, but it may also be performed in the community. In common and civil law systems (see Chapter 9) the usual designation given to this economic based punishment is "community service" in which the offender is required to perform tasks in various locations, such as helping in a hospital or charity, sweeping the streets, etc. Finally, a method of economic punishment that responds more to the retributive expression of punishment is the requirement that the offender pay back to the offended the amount that he stole, or at least return the items taken. Many systems will also add a fine on top of this punishment.

Public condemnation. This punishment may take several forms. In many countries the mass media serves to denounce the offender's crimes. In Sweden, the customers of brothels are publicized, and depending on the locality in the USA names of offenders of all kinds will be publicized in local media, and even national media. A more recent and intense form of this punishment (though strictly speaking it is an "after punishment") is the widespread introduction in the USA and other countries of sex offender registries. Customary legal systems are also said to use shaming as a punishment, in which offenders are publicly denounced or shunned. The extreme form of this customary punishment is, of course, stoning to death. In fact, all punishments that are conducted in public assume an element of public condemnation.

Disenfranchisement. Closely related to public denunciation is the disenfranchisement of offenders, most often in the form of removal from public office, or withdrawal of license to practice a profession, such as in law or medicine. These acts of dienfranchisement are widely used throughout countries with developed service economies, and are especially well developed in the criminal codes of civil law countries of Eastern Europe. The crimes for which this punishment is commonly used are corruption and bribery. Banishment or exile, an old form of punishment that mixes disenfranchisement or deprivation of rights, is listed as a punishment in the codes of Uruguay, Maldives, and Haiti, though the extent of its use is unknown. Many countries, however, may deport offenders who are illegal aliens.

Deprivation of liberty. Offenders are deprived of their liberty through the universal application of prison (see Chapter 12). However, there are degrees in deprivation of liberty. For example, the amount of contact allowed inmates with the outside world may vary considerably according to the conditions inside the prison, such as allowing TV or radio access, allowing visitation by family and friends, allowing inmates to work outside of prison in designated businesses or factories, allowing weekend furloughs, etc. Noncustodial deprivation of liberty may take on several forms ranging from house arrest and tracking with ankle bracelets, to probation of various intensities (e.g., reporting to the officer every day or only once every few months). While probation is widely used throughout most countries, it is not universal as is prison. In addition, parole – a probationary period usually applied after release from prison – is not universally applied and tends to be most common in countries with well-established common law or civil law systems. Some critics argue that probation is not painful enough to be classified as a punishment.

Corporal punishments. These commonly include amputation of body parts (e.g., hands and feet), the lash, or caning. Eighty countries or territories use corporal punishment either as a sentence for a crime or as a disciplinary measure within prisons (Newman, 2010). Of these, thirty have Islamic or customary legal systems. Most Islamic legal systems (present in thirty-seven countries or territories around the world) contain corporal punishment as a sentence in their written laws. Where corporal punishment is used in civil and common law systems, it is mostly used as a disciplinary method in prisons, not as a specific sentence for a crime. There are exceptions to this: The Isle of Mann, for example, retains the birch as a punishment, and its system is mostly one of common law.

The death penalty. Seventy-three countries or territories still retain the death penalty. Of these, forty-seven also use corporal punishment. The methods of execution range from lethal injection (USA), firing squad (Ethiopia), shot in the neck (Mongolia), hanging (Sierra Leone), beheading (Saudi Arabia), and stoning to death (Iran). Public executions are still carried out, mainly in Middle Eastern and some African countries.

Restorative punishments. These include actions required of the offender that either compensate the victim or, if possible, reconcile the offender and victim. Customary law, present in at least sixty-two countries or territories around the world, is most commonly identified with this approach to punishment. In many African countries, especially North Africa, customary legal systems (which may be entirely oral, without written law) operate to resolve conflicts that occur between family groups or factions. The solution is usually the payment of compensation by one family group to another for injury or damage done. However, there is a tendency to romanticize these customary legal systems and the logic of reconciliation can take on unexpected forms. For example, in Syria and the Palestine territories, when a girl is raped, the restorative solution is to have her marry her rapist. The argument is that this restores her honor – and it forces the families of the offender and victim to come together. Compensation may also be achieved through "blood money" recognized in some Islamic legal systems where an offender may settle accounts with a victim or, in the case of murder, a victim's family. In these cases, the victim may exert considerable influence over the final punishment of the offender; since, by accepting blood money or other compensation, the offender may escape the death penalty.

MATCHING PUNISHMENTS TO CRIMES

The scale by which punishments are matched to crimes remains a particularly difficult puzzle. Islamic legal systems generally give precedence to retribution in deciding the severity of punishments, but this leads to some difficulties because retribution requires that the punishment match the particular offence and only that offence. Punishing an offender more severely because he has repeated his crime (i.e., deterrence) is not found in the Koran. However, some Islamic scholars have argued that deterrence may be used as a "secondary principle" in punishing offenders, and this has led to the common use of imprisonment (Alizadeh, 2010) in most, if not all, Islamic countries. An additional difficulty is that because Islamic law defines so few crimes compared to civil and common law systems, the small range of punishments available do not lend themselves to establishing a scale of punishments according to their severity. For example, the punishments for rape, murder, robbery, and adultery can all lead to the death penalty under Islamic law. In contrast, in civil and common law countries the degrees of seriousness within each of those crimes are always specified. In fact, in civil law systems, (present in 164 countries and territories of the world) it is typical for there to be a long and exhaustive list of major crimes and their subdivisions, and even subdivisions within these, carefully matched to punishments that are well classified and defined in every detail (see, for example, the codes of Georgia, Czech Republic, Belarus, and Armenia described in Newman, 2010).

The simple conclusion from these observations is that in order to develop and implement a system of punishment that takes into account many fine gradations of seriousness of crimes, one needs a punishment that also can be graded finely. Prison turns out to be the most adaptable punishment for this enterprise, since its frequency and amount can be easily quantified (e.g., days, months, years), as can its intensity (e.g., with or without hard labor, furloughs, conjugal visits, etc.). Among the many explanations put

forward by scholars, this is the simplest and most likely explanation for the
now universal use of prison as a punishment throughout the world.

REFERENCES

Alizadeh, M. S. (2010). Iran. In G. R. Newman (Ed.). *Crime and Punishment Around
   the World.* Volume 1, Africa and Middle East. Santa Barbara: ABC-CLIO.
Beccaria, C. (2009). *On Crimes and Punishments.* Fifth Edition. G. R. Newman &
   P. Marongiu (Eds. and trans.). New Brunswick, NJ: Transaction Publishers.
Garland, D. (1993). *Punishment and Modern Society.* Chicago: University of Chicago
   Press.
Newman, G. R. (2008). *The Punishment Response.* Second Edition. New Brunswick,
   NJ: Transaction Publishers.
   (Ed.) (2010). *Crime and Punishment Around the World.* Four Volumes. New
   Haven, CT: Greenwood Press.
Sellin, T. (1976). *Slavery and the Penal System.* NY: Elsevier.

ABOUT THE AUTHOR

Graeme R. Newman is distinguished teaching professor at the School of Criminal
Justice, University at Albany. Among the recent books he has written or edited
are: *Outsmarting the Terrorists* with Ronald V. Clarke (PSI International 2006),
and a new translation, with Pietro Marongiu, of Cesare Beccaria's classic, *On
Crimes and Punishments* (Transaction Press 2009).

11 Crossnational Measures of Punitiveness

Alfred Blumstein

Incarceration rate, or prisoners per capita, is typically used as the primary measure of a nation's punitiveness. But measuring punitiveness is inherently more complicated. It is possible, for example, that a country developed a high incarceration rate because it has a high crime rate. That might encourage one to measure punitiveness as the incarceration rate per serious crime. But it may be that solving crimes in that country is particularly difficult because police are less competent, or perhaps because the public is less helpful to the police in solving crimes. Thus, one might augment the measures with incarceration rates per arrest. Even this measure will depend on the discretion allowed police in moving cases forward to prosecution. If such constraints are very stringent, then one might turn to the incarceration probability per conviction as a tighter measure of punitiveness. Going still further, a reasonable measure of punitiveness could be the expected time served per crime or per conviction. This last measure would take account of the duration of the sentence as well as the probability of commitment conditional on a crime, an arrest, or a conviction.

This chapter will provide an array of measures that have been explored crossnationally in Blumstein et al. based on crossnational data collected by Farrington and Tonry (2005). The data covers eight countries (UK, Scotland, USA, Australia, Canada, Sweden, Netherlands, and Switzerland) and six crime types (homicide, rape, robbery, vehicle theft, residential burglary, and assault). One limitation is that some crime-type definitions vary across the different countries. For example, some countries include under robbery all thefts while others include only thefts associated with force or threat of force.

MEASURES BY CRIME TYPE

Figures 11.1a, 11.1b, and 11.1c provide different measures of punitiveness for three different crime types: murder, robbery, and burglary. In each figure we present the expected time served per crime and per conviction. For murder (Figure 11.1a), we see that the clearance rate is fairly high in all the countries, and the transition of expected time served from crime to conviction is not very large. That suggests that clearance rates are fairly high (perhaps somewhat lower in the U.S. and Australia), and the expected time served for most of the countries averages about seven years. Switzerland is the least punitive for murder, averaging about 2.5 years per conviction and almost as much per crime, suggesting a very high clearance and conviction rate.

For robbery (Figure 11.1b), we see that the U.S. is the most punitive per conviction (about 2.5 years) and also fairly high, along with Australia, for punitiveness per crime. In contrast to murder, where the two measures are fairly close, there is a much greater discrepancy between the punitiveness per conviction and the punitiveness per crime, largely reflecting much greater failures of arrest and conviction for robbery compared to murder. For burglary (Figure 11.1c), where the probability of commitment per conviction is relatively low, the expected time served is appreciably less, covering a range of about 0.1 years per conviction in Scotland and 0.9 years in the U.S. Here, the difference between expected time served per crime and per conviction is much greater than for robbery, largely reflecting the fact that clearance rates for burglary are very low, and even for those convicted, incarceration is less than likely. While the various countries seem quite comparable in their punitiveness for murder (except, possibly, Switzerland), as we move to the less serious crimes where there is much greater room for discretion, we see mucnh greater variation across the different countries. Here, the U.S. continues to stay on top with the highest expected time served per crime and per conviction.

FACTORS ACCOUNTING FOR THE RISE OF INCARCERATION

The growth of incarceration is attributed largely to changes in the political environment associated with crime. It is possible, however, that other factors, such as an increase in crime, could be contributing, and, if that were the case, then the growth of incarceration would not necessarily be indicative of a growth in punitiveness. Blumstein and Beck (1999 and 2005)

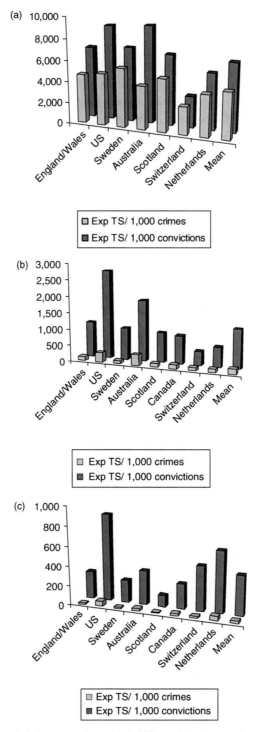

Figure 11.1. Expected time served per (a) 1,000 murder crimes and convictions (years), (b) 1,000 robbery crimes and convictions, (c) 1,000 burglary crimes.

examined this issue in the U.S. by identifying factors that could be contributing to the rise in incarceration from 1980. They examined the growth in incarceration for six crime types (murder, robbery, assault, sexual assault, burglary, and drug offenses), which account for 75–80 percent of prison population. The incarceration rate per hundred thousand adults in the U.S. for each of these crime types over the period 1980–2001 indicates that each of these crime types increases over that period, with the growth of drug offenders in prison being the most dramatic.

Blumstein and Beck then examined for each of these crime types whether the growth was attributable to more crime, to more arrests per crime, to more commitments per arrest, or to longer time served in prison, including time served by parole violators. The basic conclusion was that the entire growth came from more commitments per arrest and from longer time served, the two major policy choices. In the early part of the period (1980–93), these two policy factors contributed about equally to the growth in incarceration, while in the later period (1994–2001), the contribution of time served was about twice that of commitments per arrest. There was no net effect of changes in crimes (some went up and others went down) and there was absolutely no trend in arrests per crime. This lack of an effect of arrests per crime was somewhat surprising, since they anticipated that improvements in policing (e.g., more education, more skillful management, better forensics) would have shown themselves in an increase in arrests per crime, but that did not occur.

The most striking observation is the dramatic ten-fold growth of incarceration for drug offenses. This reflected a response to increasing pressure from the public for the political system to "do something" about the drug problem, and the only response the political system seemed able to find was to increase incarceration. In contrast to many European countries, which saw the drug problem as a public health issue, the U.S. posed it as a moral issue, and so the natural response was incarceration.

Another feature of the political environment surrounding punitiveness in the U.S. is the emergence of what has been called a "prison-industrial complex" (Schlosser, 1998), drawing on the metaphor used by President Eisenhower in his warning of a "military-industrial complex" in his presidential address. When incarceration rates were low and under the control of the criminal justice system, then the politics of those with a stake in incarceration were relatively weak. As incarceration has grown as an economic activity, the influence of those involved in that activity has grown correspondingly. In California, for example, the prison guards' union is known to be the largest contributor to gubernatorial campaigns. In New

York, where prison populations have recently declined, a newly elected governor felt he could find resources to meet the state's other needs by closing some prisons. He was met with vigorous criticism by many of the rural legislators of his state who emphasized the importance of prisons to the economic vitality of their regions, and especially those regions that had lost significant manufacturing industry to other countries (Confessore, 2007). The economic interests of a growing number of stakeholders can thus rally with the always-present public concern about crime and the resulting call for punishment of offenders.

Rallying support for punishment is much easier if the public thinks of the offenders as an identifiable separate group, and especially if they can point to such groups as comprising a different ethnicity. The U.S. is composed of a wide range of ethnic subpopulations. The largest such groups are the African-Americans, who are visually identifiable and who are disproportionately involved in incarceration. Their incarceration rate is about seven times that of whites, although the comparison group of whites includes Hispanics (another significant minority population group that may even be larger than African-Americans) with a higher incarceration rate than non-Hispanic whites. This heterogeneity is, thus, be an important factor affecting a public's interest in accepting a high incarceration rate.

Alesina and Glaeser (2004) have shown that homogeneous societies provide more welfare services and public goods than do the more heterogeneous societies. As it is put by Alesina and La Ferrara (2005), 'altruism does not travel well across ethnic lines.' It is easy to see how such concepts could apply to punitiveness. In a more homogeneous society it is easy to be merciful or "altruistic" to others who are similar but may have offended. To the extent that the sinner is of a different ethnicity, it becomes much easier to bring the differences to mind, to attribute the failings to a group failing, and to treat the offender with greater abstraction and harshness. This phenomena opens an interesting potential area for research. One might examine the ethnic heterogeneity of different states and assess their relationship to the states' punitiveness, considering the differential punitiveness to the majority and minority offenders in each state or nation.

CONCERN ABOUT OTHER COUNTRIES PATTERNING THEIR PUNITIVENESS ON THE U.S. MODEL

Given its role as a leader in entertainment and media generally, and in news media particularly, it seems reasonable to be concerned about the degree to which patterns of punitiveness established in the U.S. are transmitted internationally. As politicians in other democracies see the success of the "tough on crime" rhetoric, it seems reasonable to anticipate that they would be tempted to follow similar patterns. There is already some indication that these trends are working their way internationally from incarceration data maintained by the World Prison Brief at King's College, London. Using these data, Table 11.1 provides information on incarceration rates for industrialized democratic countries in 1992 and 2009. Table 11.1 presents the percentage change over those seventeen years. The groupings are two countries with low rates initially, two countries with high rates, the Scandinavian countries with relatively homogeneous low rates, and a variety of other countries in Europe. Within each group, the countries are ranked by their percentage change.

The first observation from the Table 11.1 is that all of eighteen countries, except Switzerland (with a 4 percent decrease) and Denmark (with no change), had a positive increase over that seventeen-year interval, and all but one (Finland with a 3 percent increase) with double digits. Only one had a decline (although some did have declines within the interval but ended up with a net positive growth). The two countries with very low rates in 1992, Netherlands and Japan, ended up with very high rates of growth; Netherlands' rate grew by 104 percent and Japan's rate grew by 66 percent, and Japan was exceeded only by Turkey (with a growth rate of 85 percent), Spain (grew by 80 percent), and England/Wales (grew by 74 percent). The two countries with very high rates, U.S. and Russia, far exceeded all the others with rates of 723 per hundred thousand for the U.S. and 587 for Russia; however, their growth rates over this interval were relatively modest.

It is clear from this table that incarceration rates are increasing widely, very modestly in some places but rather sharply in others. The sharpest increases seem to be occurring in some places that started with the lowest rates, and those low rates could well have provided the ammunition to the political process for demanding increases. While the table certainly does not indicate that the contagion of the U.S. political process is universal, it does indicate that a good number of European countries, with the likely exception of Scandinavia, do seem to be breaking out of what had previously been a reasonably homeostatic process into a politicized one. Further political analysis of the processes in the individual countries will provide for a sharper assessment of the factors contributing to the rise.

Table 11.1. Trends in incarceration rates in various countries

	1992 Rates	2009 Rates	% Change
Low rates in 1992			
Netherlands	49	100	104%
Japan	38	63	66%
Average	*43.5*	*81.5*	*85%*
High rates in 1992			
USA	505	723	50%
Russia	487	587	27%
Average	*496*	*655*	*39%*
Scandinavia			
Sweden	63	74	17%
Norway	58	70	21%
Finland	65	67	3%
Denmark	66	66	0%
Average	*63*	*69.25*	*10%*
Other European Countries			
Turkey	54	161	198%
Spain	90	162	80%
England/Wales	88	153	74%
Poland	153	224	46%
Scotland	105	148	41%
Germany	71	90	27%
Italy	81	97	20%
France	84	96	14%
Portugal	93	104	12%
Switzerland	79	76	-4%
Average	*89.8*	*131.1*	*51%*

SUMMARY AND CONCLUSIONS

While punitiveness is most often measured by incarceration rates, there can be many components other than a desire for punishment contributing to a high incarceration rate. These can include more crime, greater police effectiveness in solving crimes, and more aggressive prosecution. The most direct effects on incarceration rate as indicators of punitiveness would include longer sentences given by judges and more restriction on release hand resentencing by parole officials. The problem in a democracy, when the public becomes anxious about crime and presses elected officials to "do something" about the crime problem, the response from the very limited repertoire of available responses almost always shows itself as greater punitiveness by sending more people to prison and for a longer time. This has certainly characterized the U.S., which had a stable incarceration rate of 110 per 100,000 population for at least fifty years while punishment was under the control of the criminal justice system, but which now has a rate that is much more influenced by the political environment and is subsequently almost five times higher, making it the world leader in incarceration rate. Because this stance of being "tough on crime" has worked so well for political officials in the U.S., there is considerable concern and some reasonable indications that this model has propagated to other countries. One would hope that fiscal pressures at least would serve to restrain those propagating influences.

Note: This chapter draws heavily on "The Roots of Punitiveness in a Democracy," *Journal of Scandinavian Studies in Criminology and Crime Prevention*, 8, pp. 2–16 (2007), which was based on Blumstein's plenary address upon receiving the 2007 Stockholm Prize in Criminology.

REFERENCES

Alesina, A. & E. La Ferrara (2005). Ethnic Diversity and Economic Performance. *Journal of Economic Literature*, 43(2), 762–800.

Alesina, A. & E. Glaeser (2004). *Fighting Poverty in the US and Europe: A World of Difference*. Oxford: Oxford University Press.

Blumstein, A. & A. J. Beck (2005). Reentry as a Transient State between Liberty and Recommitment. In J. Travis & C. Visher (Eds.), *Prisoner Reentry and Crime in America*. Cambridge: Cambridge University Press, pp. 50–79.

Blumstein, A. & A. J. Beck (1999). Population Growth in U.S. Prisons, 1980–1996. In M. Tonry & J. Petersilia (Eds.), *Crime and Justice*, Vol. 26. Chicago: University of Chicago Press, pp. 17–61.

Blumstein, A., M. Tonry, & A. Van Ness (2005). Criminal Justice Processing as Measures of Punitiveness. In M. Tonry & D. P. Farrington (Eds.), *Crime and Justice: An Annual Review of Research*, Vol. 33. Chicago: University of Chicago Press, pp. 347–76.

Confessore, N. (2007, February 5). "Spitzer Seeks Ways to Find State Prisons He Can Close." *The New York Times*.

Schlosser, E. (1998, December). "The Prison-Industrial Complex." *Atlantic Monthly*.

ABOUT THE AUTHOR

Alfred Blumstein is the J. Erik Jonsson Professor of Urban Systems and Operations Research at Carnegie Mellon University. His research over the past twenty years has covered many aspects of crime and criminal justice including crime measurement, criminal careers, sentencing, deterrence and incapacitation, prison populations, juvenile violence, and drug policy. Among other accolades, he has received the American Society of Criminology's Sutherland Award, the Wolfgang Award for Distinguished Achievement in Criminology, and the 2007 Stockholm Prize in Criminology.

12 Prisons around the World

Harry R. Dammer

This chapter will provide an overview of the key issues related to prisons around the world, including a brief historical overview of prisons, global incarceration numbers, trends, and governance, and the global concern about prison crowding.

HISTORICAL OVERVIEW OF PRISONS

Although the common use of the term "penitentiary" is credited to United States, it is believed that a Benedictine monk named Jean Mabillon in the seventeenth century first coined the phrase. The first institution bearing that moniker appeared in France after the 1790 revolution, while the same year a variation of the penitentiary was being implemented at the Walnut Street Jail in Philadelphia. Nonetheless, philosophical roots of the penitentiary were formed in Europe during the late 1700s through the Age of the Enlightenment and the ideas of Cesare Beccaria, Jeremy Bentham, and John Howard. The penitentiary method was seen as an advance – opposite the retributive view of punishment. It took an optimistic view of human nature and the belief in the possibility of change and reform. Conceived as a place where prisoners would be isolated from the bad influences of society, engaged in productive labor, and made to reflect on past misdeeds, they could be reformed and become "penitent" (sorry) for their sins – hence the term, "penitentiary" (Clear, Cole, & Reisig, 2011).

Although the earliest attempt to institute the penitentiary system failed at the Walnut Street Jail, between 1790 and 1829 numerous other states in America adopted aspects of the system. In 1829, an influential group of Pennsylvania Quakers were eventually able to open two correctional institutions with a system of solitary confinement with labor, silence, and religious instruction in Pittsburgh and Philadelphia called Western and Eastern Penitentiary, respectively. In Auburn, New York a prison opened in 1817, and being influenced by the reported success of the Walnut Street Jail, administrators began to implement the separate and silent Pennsylvania system. But because the Pennsylvania system was found to cause mental and physical problems for the inmates, as well as being very expensive because it called for single cells for all inmates, it was abandoned in 1823. An alternative soon developed called the New York (Auburn) system. Promoted by members of the Calvinist religion, by 1833 this method was adopted by penitentiaries in ten states, the District of Columbia, and in parts of Canada. In the New York (Auburn) system inmates were locked in separate cells at night but allowed to congregate at work and meal times, albeit in silence, during the day. Supporters of the penitentiary hoped that a regime of solitude (i.e., the Pennsylvania system) or of silent, controlled work (the New York/Auburn system) would provide a humane way to bring about a change of disposition and lifestyle in convicted criminals. For decades, the two systems were hotly debated and by 1900 most jurisdictions adopted the New York (the Auburn system) method.

The American experiment rapidly became the focus of reform in other countries as well. The reformative prison spread to Russia in 1863, Brazil in 1834, Japan in 1868, and China in 1905 (Weiss, 2005). The reformative prison was undoubtedly a major topic of discussion at the first International Prison Congress, held in 1872 in London. What is interesting, however, was that the idea of American-style prison continued to grow despite evidence that it did not reform offenders or even provide them with humane conditions of incarceration. The penitentiary movement, launched with high hopes in the late eighteenth century, had not lived up to the expectations of the reformers who conceived it.

By the early twentieth century, it was obvious that prisons were not fulfilling their promise and, in fact, they were generally seen to be as cruel and inhumane as any previous method of punishment. In response, the American Progressive Movement provided a new approach to corrections called rehabilitation. Rehabilitation calls for restoring a convicted offender to a constructive place in society through some form of vocational or educational training or therapy. These methods include probation, parole, therapeutic prison regimes, and separate juvenile justice mechanisms. Until the nineteenth century, many countries, including the United States, did not have separate institutions for males, females, and juveniles. The change to separate the females and juveniles from the adult male offenders was also part of the Progressive Movement.

Table 12.1. Top ten prison population in total numbers and prisoners per 100,000 in 2008

Top ten	Total numbers					Rate per 100,000
1	United States	2,310,984	1	United States		760
2	China	1,565,771	2	St. Kitts & Nevis		660
3	Russian Federation	880,671	3	Russian Federation		622
4	Brazil	469,546	4	Rwanda		593
5	India	373,271	5	Cuba		531
6	Mexico	227,735	6	Virgin Islands (USA)		512
7	Thailand	199,607	7	Virgin Islands (UK)		488
8	South Africa	163,479	8	Palau		478
9	Iran	158,351	9	Belize		476
10	Ukraine	144,380	10	Grenada		430

Source: International Centre for Prison Studies, 2009.

However, in the early 1970s, criminal justice officials throughout the world, especially in the United States, turned to a crime-control model including increased use of incarceration and stricter forms of community supervision. As a result, in the last half of the twentieth century, mandatory sentences, longer sentences, intensive probation supervision, and detention without bail have increased jail and prison populations to record levels throughout the world. Much of the call for increasing severity of sentences has been driven by penal populism, a term used to describe crime policies that are formed by politicians in their attempt to appease the public and their call for punitiveness despite a lack of program efficacy or even a clear understanding of community opinion (Pratt, 2007).

GLOBAL INCARCERATION NUMBERS AND RATES

There are currently more than 9.25 million persons imprisoned throughout the world. Large numbers of those imprisoned are concentrated in a few countries, and about half of them are in the United States, Russia, and China (Walmsley, 2009). Although using incarceration rates (see Table 12.1) is probably superior to the use of absolute numbers for almost any purpose of analysis, they are far from flawless. Many problems exist with the use of rates and absolute numbers in terms of a prisoner and because the meanings of the key terms like "prisoner" and "prison" are not uniform across nations (for more about problems with prison data see Tonry, 2007). Although some nations, especially those in Western Europe, have turned to increasing alternatives to incarceration, such as probation, fines, community service, day fines, and other forms of intermediate sanctions, many others have remained reliant on incarceration and on a general hardening of attitudes toward offenders. According to Walmsley (2009), prison populations have grown in most (more than 70 percent) countries of the world since the 1990s. Here, the total number provided for the prison populations also includes female prisoners. In almost all cases (Thailand is the exceptional case) the number of females consists of less than 10 percent of total inmates incarcerated. The total number of incarcerated juveniles is inconsistently included in the total prison numbers across nations.

PRISON GOVERNANCE

All countries have some form of correctional institution that serves to incarcerate alleged or convicted criminals. In general, prisons serve to incarcerate those who have been convicted of relatively serious crimes, while facilities called jails or remand prisons are used for those awaiting trial, transfer to another institution, and for those serving time for minor offenses.

Prisons have developed classification systems that segregate inmates according to time to be served or seriousness of the offense. In the United States, for example, prisons are classified into levels of security called Minimum, Medium, Maximum, and more recently Super-Maximum or Administrative Maximum. In countries with ample financial resources, some form of rehabilitation is offered to assist offenders. In some countries, institutions called Open Prisons serve to incarcerate inmates during the evening but allow them much freedom to work, attend school, or visit with family during the day. Private prisons, correctional institutions operated by private firms on behalf of governments, are operating in the United States, Puerto Rico, Australia, South Africa, Canada, England, and Wales.

Although many prison systems around the world share similarities, individual nations also have distinctive approaches to prison governance. For example, in England the Independent Monitoring Boards, formerly called the Boards of Visitors or Visiting Committees, represent a way to bring "outsiders" into the prisons to help with problems of administration and discipline. The Boards act as an independent watchdog on the prisons, meeting with inmates and staff to safeguard the well-being and rights of all prisoners. They visit inmates, hear complaints about prison conditions and prison officials, and report back to the prison administration and the national correctional office at the Home Office. The Boards represent a distinctly English way of involving laypersons in the criminal justice process.

In China, the underlying foundation for the correctional system is based on two ancient traditions: Confucianism and legalism. Confucianism holds that social harmony can be secured through moral education that brings out the good nature of all. Formal legal structures are not necessary for this purpose. At the same time legalism, which developed almost two hundred years after Confucianism, held that only a firm application of laws and strict punishments could persuade people who are innately evil not to commit crime. Early in the first millennium AD, these two philosophies began to merge, with Confucianism serving as the primary social control mechanism and formal legalism providing support (Dikotter, 2002). China in the post-1949 Communist era has developed a correctional system that retains remnants of both the Confucian and legalist perspectives, meshing both to placate the Communists' need to reeducate the people in Socialist values. It is important to mention that this article does not specifically address the issue of female or juvenile prisons. While female and juvenile prisons do have some problems that are endemic only to their institutions, the most pressing problem of prison crowding is most often present in all kinds of correctional institutions.

PRISON CROWDING

Prison crowding is the single most pressing problem faced by major prison systems today, not only in Western countries but also in Eastern European and many underdeveloped countries. According to UNAFEI Report (2001), "Factors influencing prison overcrowding may vary from country to country; socioeconomic conditions, crime rates, differences in criminal justice policy, efficiency in on-going practices and functioning in criminal justice systems, public attitudes towards offenders and so on might contribute to modulate the prison population." The most crucial factor contributing to increased incarceration and prison crowding are sentencing decisions made by policy-makers (Kuhn, 1996). Many countries, especially advanced nations with effective media, have greatly politicized crime and this has led to a hardening of penal control. Experts have found that in some poorer countries, like Pakistan, Malaysia, and Kenya, a lack of correctional resources is a major reason for prison crowding, along with a slow and inefficient criminal justice system and a lack of alternatives to incarceration.

Although prison crowding rates may be difficult to determine, the impact of crowding on inmates and staff are painfully clear. Prison crowding can limit the ability of correctional officials, increases the potential for violence and the spread of diseases. For example, communicable diseases such as cholera have contributed to inmate deaths in prisons in Zambia, Malawi, Kenya, and Mozambique. The spread of tuberculosis throughout many prisons, including those of Russia, Brazil, and India, has caused serious health problems. HIV/AIDS has also exacerbated the disease problem, with grossly disproportionate rates of infection in many correctional facilities (Human Rights Watch: Prisons, 2004).

Another problem related to prison crowding is the increasing possibility of human rights violations. Legal challenges to prison conditions and prisoner treatment have become common only in the past thirty years, although they did occur earlier. The legal basis for challenges to prison conditions in the United States comes from the Eighth Amendment to the U.S. Constitution, which states that "excessive bail shall not be required, nor excessive fines imposed, nor cruel and unusual punishments inflicted." In the international community, legal challenges arise from a number of covenants and conventions. The foundation for these documents is rooted in the UN Universal Declaration of Human Rights, which states "no one shall be subjected to torture, or cruel, inhuman or degrading treatment or punishment" (Article 5). The Declaration, originally proposed in 1948 by the United Nations and subsequently ratified by a large number of nations, was the result of the desire to combat the massive violations of human rights that occurred in World War II. Since then, other international organizations have produced documents that support Article 5, such as the European Convention on Human Rights, the African Charter on Human and People's Rights, and the Inter-American Convention on Human Rights (Dammer and Albanese, 2011).

In 1955, the United Nations developed the Standard Minimum Rules for the Treatment of Prisoners address a range of prisoner issues including prison living conditions, amenities and programs, methods of discipline, and the treatment of those that are unconvicted. In December 1990, the United Nations adopted and proclaimed by General Assembly resolution 45/111, which is now called the Basic Principles for the Treatment of Prisoners. The eleven general principles, and ninety-five standards in this convention clearly spell out the minimal treatment that should be present while an offender is incarcerated.

SUMMARY

The purpose and form of prisons has changed considerably throughout history. In the nineteenth century a new prison model emerged called the penitentiary. The penitentiary greatly influenced prison architecture and the treatment of offenders throughout the world. Because the goals of the penitentiary were allusive, other means of dealing with offenders have surfaced such as rehabilitation, and more recently the crime-control model. As a result of increased reliance on incarceration, many countries have experienced prison crowding. Prison crowding has shown to exacerbate factors that erode living conditions such as institutional violence, human rights violations, and communicable disease. International agencies, such as the United Nations, have tried to address treatment issues through the promotion of prison standards and conventions. Although prisons primarily serve to incarcerate criminal offenders, the ways in which this is accomplished vary considerably across the globe.

REFERENCES

Clear, T., G. Cole, & M. Reisig (2011). *American Corrections*. Ninth Edition. Belmont, CA: Wadsworth Cengage Learning.

Dammer, H. & J. Albanese (2011). *Comparative Criminal Justice Systems*. Fourth Edition. Belmont, CA: Wadsworth Cengage Learning.

Dikotter, F. (2002). The Promise of Repentance: Prison Reform in Modern China. *British Journal of Criminology*, 42, 240–49

Human Rights Watch: Prisons. (2004). *Human Rights Abuses against Prisoners*. Retrieved from www.hrw.org/prisons/abuses.html.

Kuhn, A. (1996). Incarceration Rates: Europe Versus the United States. *European Journal on Criminal Policy and Research*, 4(3): 46–73.

Pratt, J. (2007). *Penal Populism*. London: Routledge.

Tonry, M. (2007). Determinates of Penal Policies. In M. Tonry (Ed.), *Crime, Punishment, and Politics in Comparative Perspective*. Chicago: University of Chicago Press, pp. 1–48.

UNAFEI. (September, 2001). *Annual Report for 1999 and Resource Material*, series no. 57. Fuchu, Japan: UNAFEI.

Walmsley, R. (2009). *World Prison Population List*. Eighth Edition. London: International Center for Prison Studies. Retrieved from www.kcl.ac.uk/depsta/law/research/icps/downloads/wppl-8th_41.pdf

Weiss, R. P. (2005). From Anticolonialism to Neocolonialism: A Brief Political-Economic History of Transnational Concern about Corrections. In P. Reichel (Ed.), *Handbook of Transnational Crime and Justice*. Thousand Oaks: Sage Publications, pp. 346–62.

WEB SITES

1. Penal Reform International at www.penalreform.org
2. The treatment of offenders around the world at www.amnesty.org/en/detention

3. International Center for Prison Studies, King's College, London at www.kcl.
ac.uk/depsta/law/research/icps/worldbrief/wpb_stats.php

ABOUT THE AUTHOR

Harry R. Dammer is professor and chair of the Criminal Justice and Sociology at
the University of Scranton. Dr. Dammer received his B.S. and M.S degrees from
the University of Dayton (OH) and his Ph.D. from the Rutgers University School
of Criminal Justice (NJ). He has received two Fulbright Scholar Awards and is
the former Chair of the International Section of the Academy of Criminal Justice
Sciences and has authored or co-authored three books and published numerous
articles, manuals, and professional reports on a variety of criminal justice topics
mainly in the areas of comparative criminal justice, corrections, and the practice
of religion in the correctional environment. He has visited prisons in more than
a dozen countries including throughout Europe and in China, South Africa, and
South Korea.

13 Crime Prevention in an International Context

Ronald V. Clarke

INTRODUCTION

The law and the criminal justice system constitute the modern state's first line of defense against crime. These formal systems of control serve the dual purposes of deterring law breaking among the population at large and of apprehending, punishing, and treating those who offend. Complementing the formal systems of control are society's informal social controls. These include measures taken by parents, by schools, and by religious bodies to (1) instill respect for the law among children and young people, (2) regulate the conduct of people as they go about their daily lives, and (3) afford protection to persons and property by routine precautions and security measures.

The formal and informal systems of control depend upon each other for their effectiveness. Without informal social controls, the criminal justice system would soon be swamped with crime and, without the threat of arrest and punishment provided by the criminal justice system, informal social controls would face a constant challenge to their credibility. As governments have come to recognize the costs and limitations of the formal system of crime control, they have begun to explore more direct ways of improving informal social controls. This activity falls under the general heading of "crime prevention," which can be defined as interventions that seek to promote the security of individuals and communities without resort to formal criminal justice sanctions. It is useful to distinguish among four different general approaches as follows:

1. Child development. Research has documented a variety of risk factors in early childhood associated with later delinquency and crime. Interventions designed to address these factors through improved parenting skills, enriched early education, and improved physical

and mental health could lead to large reductions in future crime and delinquency. Some early efforts focused on delinquency reduction, such as the famous Cambridge-Somerville project and the Head Start program in America, met with little success. However, recent research has begun to identify more promising ways of preventing the development of persistently delinquent personalities (National Crime Prevention, 1999).

2. Community development. Criminologists have long recognized that powerful forces in local communities can promote or inhibit crime. An important strand of preventive work consists of efforts to: strengthen the economic viability and social cohesiveness of local communities; provide more local services and facilities for community enhancement; strengthen resident ties to their local communities; teach young people about the importance of the rule of law; and develop local police-community relations. Sustained efforts along these lines have recently been made in many Western countries, most notably in France (the Bonnemaison initiatives), in Britain ("safer city" programs), in Italy (the anti-Mafia education of young people in Palermo), and in the United States (neighborhood watch and community policing). Unfortunately, there is little hard evidence to date of success. Doubts have also been raised about the meaning of the local community in highly developed, modern societies and about a local community's role in crime prevention.

3. Social development. This is the least advanced of the four approaches, but it is of great interest internationally. It proceeds on the assumption that much crime in developing countries results from poverty, lack of paid employment, poor education, discrimination, and a variety of other social and economic deprivations. It is assumed that social development will remove these "causes" of crime. Unfortunately, there is no direct relationship between social conditions and crime, and crime has even risen in Western countries in times of increased affluence and improved social security. However, these findings may not hold for developing countries and countries in transition, where the general social and economic conditions are much less favorable.

4. Situational crime prevention. Unlike the other forms of crime prevention, all of which seek to reduce the motivation for crime, situational prevention seeks to reduce opportunities for crime. This has been the fastest growing form of crime prevention in the past twenty years. It has come to be associated with the spectacular rise of private policing and the private security industry in Western countries during

the past twenty years (Garland, 1996). In its government-sponsored forms it consists of (i) crime prevention advertising campaigns, (ii) efforts to influence city planning and architectural design to promote a "crime-free" environment, (iii) focused efforts to diagnose and remove opportunities for highly specific forms of crime such as bank robbery or residential burglary, and, more recently, (iv) pressure brought to bear on business and industry to alter criminogenic products and practices.

CURRENT STATUS OF CRIME PREVENTION

It is only during the past thirty years that governments have devoted serious attention to crime prevention and that this prevention has become a subject for concentrated academic study. Even so, remarkable progress has been made, as follows:

1. National crime prevention councils and agencies have been established by governments in many countries, including most of those in Western Europe and in Australia, Canada, and the United States. Numerous national and international meetings have been held to focus public attention on crime prevention and to explore the many issues that surround it.

2. Situational crime prevention has become an established part of government crime policy in many countries and it is also widely practiced by businesses. This has had a direct and visible effect on people's everyday lives. Examples include the adoption of "defensible space" architecture in public housing (which has contributed to the demolition of high rise, public housing buildings), the widespread adoption of closed-circuit television (CCTV) surveillance in streets and town centers in Europe and the wholesale use of antishoplifting technology by retailers.

3. Many community crime prevention programs have been implemented with government support in developed countries. Sometimes this has been in the form of "demonstration" projects such as the "safer cities" initiatives in the United Kingdom, and sometimes in the form of generally available programs such as neighborhood watch in the United States and the "Bonnemaison" community development approach in France (Bousquet, 1996).

4. Criminologists have greatly expanded writing and research on crime prevention during past three decades. Many new concepts assisting

with the design, implementation, and evaluation of crime prevention have been developed. Several specialist journals now exist and numerous textbooks on crime prevention are available (e.g., Tilley, 2009). Many university criminology departments now offer graduate courses on crime prevention. In many countries police training includes an introduction to crime prevention (see www.popcenter.org).

5. Many evaluations, particularly of situational prevention, have been published that show tangible and sometimes dramatic reductions in crime. Already sufficient numbers of evaluations have been reported so that meta-analyses (in which the results of separate evaluations are systematically compared within a common framework) can be undertaken (Sherman et al., 1998). Meta-evaluations provide a methodology for taking account of small inconsistencies among studies to reach the most reliable conclusions about the effectiveness of particular approaches.

6. The International Center for the Prevention of Crime, an organization affiliated to the United Nations, has been established in Montreal with support from a small consortium of countries. It runs a Best Practice Bureau that identifies, compiles, and disseminates information on successful crime prevention (Waller & Welsh, 1999).

NEW CHALLENGES

Despite the considerable progress of the past thirty years, many challenges lie ahead in developing the full potential of crime prevention. These include the following:

1. Even in countries where crime prevention is now an established component of government criminal policy, the resources devoted to it are tiny compared to those devoted to the criminal justice system. Waller (1991) found that the expenditure on prevention was less than one percent of that spent on the criminal justice systems in the United States, the United Kingdom, France, and Canada.

2. Community crime prevention and situational prevention have attracted many more resources than other forms of prevention in the past twenty-five years. More recently, crime prevention through child development has begun to attract research support from governments. The most difficult challenge will be in finding the resources to support research on crime prevention through social development, given that this form of prevention is of greatest interest to developing countries and countries in transition.

3. Crime prevention is primarily a concept recognized in the developed world and it is unclear how technical assistance about crime prevention can be delivered from the more developed to the less developed parts of the world. On the other hand, developed countries have made little effort to learn from the methods of crime prevention already practiced in the less developed world.

4. To date, most crime prevention has been focused on traditional forms of crime comprising the bulk of the official crime statistics – predatory property crimes, assaults and domestic violence, hooliganism, and vandalism. There are many other crimes that have received little preventive attention. These include child pornography, corruption, fraud and economic crimes, hate crimes, and crimes against migrants and tourists. Furthermore, the nature of even the traditional crimes is changing with new technology. For example, in developed countries, the growth in theft seems to involve services (such as telephone and television service) rather than products (such as the telephone or TV equipment). It is unclear whether current preventive models can be adapted to deal with these changes in crime and with new crimes associated with the development of the Internet.

5. It is also unclear whether the preventive approaches developed to date can be applied to transnational crimes – such as drug trafficking, trafficking in humans, and money laundering – that constitute a particular threat to developing countries. These crimes seem likely to increase with increased globalization, and with the associated increase in international trade, the expansion of business and leisure travel, and the greater erosion of political borders (Williams, 1999).

6. Whether or not it operates internationally, nobody knows how to prevent organized crime. It thrives on disadvantage, which means that social development, community development, and child development all have a part to play in prevention. But disadvantage is only part of the explanation for organized crime; equally important is that in every society, developed or not, illegal opportunities abound to make large sums of money. It is these opportunities that permit organized crime to flourish. This being so, considerable preventive potential rests in the situational approach, but this would have to be adapted to deal with the more planned, complex offenses characteristic of organized crime.

7. Implementation difficulties are encountered in every form of crime prevention. In community development, considerable difficulties have been experienced in achieving the necessary coordination

among local agencies to implement agreed measures. Leadership is crucial, and in the United States most of the leadership has fallen on "community" police officers. Several European countries (including France, the Netherlands, and the United Kingdom) have decided, instead, to fund "community safety" or "crime prevention" officers to coordinate local efforts. In social development, implementation difficulties are presently focused on obtaining agreement about the necessity and feasibility of this approach to crime prevention. Subsequently, the issue of obtaining the needed resources will have to be faced. In child development, the controversies focus on resource procurement and the ways in which crime prevention goals should be combined with the other goals of child development. The main obstacle to the implementation of situational prevention is that it is frequently seen as neglecting the social problems giving rise to crime and as a largely repressive approach to crime control (Clarke, 2005).

8. Without evaluation, crime prevention practice cannot be improved. Unfortunately, detailed crime data needed for measuring the outcome of crime prevention measures are frequently not available because statistical record keeping is deficient. There is also a lack of trained personnel competent to undertake evaluative studies, not merely in developing countries and countries in transition, but also in some developed countries without strong traditions of quantification in the social sciences. In particularly short supply is expertise in undertaking cost-benefit evaluations, which attempt to assign a specific monetary value to the outcomes of prevention compared to the cost of implementation. These kinds of evaluations will become increasingly important as businesses assume a greater role in crime prevention.

CONCLUSION

This chapter has reviewed worldwide developments in crime prevention policy during the past thirty years. Crime prevention is now no longer seen as merely a way of avoiding some of the social and economic costs of the criminal justice system, but as a vitally important way to deliver safety and security in a modern democracy. The increased attention being paid by governments to child development is a change of considerable significance. Equally significant is the fact that international bodies, such as the United Nations Organization and the World Bank, are increasingly recognizing that that the rule of law must precede economic and social progress. This could ultimately result in more international resources being channeled into crime prevention through social development. Current debates are focused less on the value of crime prevention than on the merits of different approaches in specific national contexts. Ways are being explored of integrating crime prevention with broader social policy concerns, and of ensuring that ethical and humanitarian values are not compromised. The next thirty years are likely to be as interesting as the previous thirty have been.

REFERENCES

Bousquet, R. (1996). Social Development and Cities. Preventing Crime in France. Paper presented at the International Conference for Crime Prevention Practitioners, March/ April, Vancouver.

Clarke, R. V. (2005). Seven Misconceptions of Situational Crime Prevention. In N. Tilley (Ed.), *Handbook of Crime Prevention and Community Safety*. Cullompton, UK: Willan Publishing.

Garland, D. (1996). *The Limits of the Sovereign State: Strategies of Crime Control in Contemporary Society*. British Journal of Criminology, 36, 445-71.

National Crime Prevention. (1999). *Pathways to Prevention: Developmental and Early Intervention Approaches to Crime in Australia*. Canberra: Attorney General's Department.

Sherman, L. W., D.C. Gottfredson, D. MacKenzie, L. Eck, P. Reuter, & S. D. Bushway, (1998). *Preventing Crime: What Works, What Doesn't, What's Promising*. Washington DC: U.S. Department of Justice.

Tilley, N. (2009). *Crime Prevention*. UK: Willan Publishing.

Waller, I. (1991). *Introductory Report: Putting Crime Prevention on the Map*. Paper presented at the II International Conference on Urban Safety, Drugs and Crime Prevention, November, Paris.

Waller, I. & B. Welsh. (1999). International Trends in Crime Prevention: Cost Effective Ways to Reduce Victimization. In G. Newman (Ed.), *Global Report on Crime and Justice*. United Nations Office for Drug Control and Crime Prevention. New York: Oxford University Press.

Williams, P. (1999). Emerging Issues: Transnational Crime and Its Control. In G. Newman (Ed.), *Global Report on Crime and Justice*. United Nations Office for Drug Control and Crime Prevention. New York: Oxford University Press.

ABOUT THE AUTHOR

Ronald V. Clarke is professor at the School of Criminal Justice, Rutgers University. Trained as a psychologist, he holds an M.A. and Ph.D. from the University of London. Dr. Clarke was employed for nearly twenty years in the British Government's criminology research department, where he had a significant role in the development of situational crime prevention and the British Crime Survey. He is the founding editor of *Crime Prevention Studies* and is author or joint author of some 220 books, monographs, and papers, including, *The Reasoning Criminal* (Springer-Verlag, 1986), *Situational Crime Prevention: Successful Case Studies* (Harrow and Heston, 1997) *Superhighway Robbery* (Willan Publishing, 2003), *Outsmarting the Terrorists* (Praeger 2006) *Become a Problem Solving Crime Analyst* (Jill Dando Institute, 2003), and *Situational Prevention of Organised Crimes* (Willan Publishing 2010).

PART III

TRANSNATIONAL CRIME

Transnational crimes are criminal acts and transactions that span national borders. Globalization and advances in technology have led to a vast increase in these often complex crimes that include cybercrimes, international money laundering, and various forms of trafficking. Drug trafficking is perhaps the preeminent transnational crime. Ever since the Shanghai convention in 1909, the serious threat to human well-being caused by drug abuse has led nations around the world to take action to deal with their drug problems. Indeed, for many decades drug trafficking absorbed most of the United Nations' efforts devoted to the control of transnational crimes. More recently, recognition of the wide-scale violations of human rights resulting from trafficking of humans, especially of women and children for sexual exploitation and servitude, have galvanized international cooperation. But countries whose laws have been violated do not always have an equal interest in stopping transnational crimes. For example, some poorer countries may turn a blind eye to the illegal migration of their nationals seeking employment in wealthier countries. This is because the migrants often remit a large portion of their earnings back home, thus benefiting the local economy.

Transnational crimes involve multiple offenders and often a string of crimes that facilitate trafficking or smuggling operations. For example, money laundering, which involves converting or concealing the financial proceeds of crime, cannot usually be accomplished by a single act. It typically consists of a process of sequential acts that cross the borders of two or more countries. These sequential acts often involve fraud and corruption – notoriously difficult crimes to police. Understanding the factors that promote and facilitate transnational crimes is crucial for developing effective control and prevention strategies. Traditional criminological explanations of transnational crime involve a variety of macrolevel national indicators such as development and modernization, poverty and deprivation, inequality and economic dependency, and discrimination and anomie. However, most transnational crimes are money-making enterprises that require some rudimentary economic understanding of the supply and demand for the goods in question. In fact, the goods and services involved in most transnational crimes are supplied by poorer countries and consumed by the citizens of wealthier ones.

Many examples of the generalizations made above can be found in the chapters collected together in this section, which cover a wide range of transnational crimes, as follows: International Drug Trafficking (Mangai Natarajan); Trafficking in Human Beings (Alexis A. Aronowitz); International Trafficking of Stolen Vehicles (Ronald V. Clarke and Rick Brown); Small Arms Trafficking (Theodore Leggett); Trafficking in Art, Antiquities, and Cultural Heritage (Simon Mackenzie); Cigarette Smuggling (Klaus Von Lampe); Cybercrime (Richard Lovely); International Fraud (Michael Levi); Money Laundering (David Hicks and Adam Graycar); Child Pornography (Richard Wortley); Maritime Crimes (Gisela Bichler); Transnational Environmental Crime (Rob White); The Bhopal Gas Disaster and Corporate Criminal Negligence (G.S. Bajpai and Bir Pal Singh); Wildlife Crimes (Jackie Schneider); Corruption (Adam Graycar); and Tourist Crimes (Andrew Lemieux and Marcus Felson).

14 Drug Trafficking

Mangai Natarajan

INTRODUCTION

Ever since the Shanghai Opium Commission in 1909, many countries around the world have found themselves grappling with problems of drug abuse and many conventions have formulated proposals to reduce the international trade in illicit substances. International collaborative efforts and polices have mostly been geared to obstructing the supply of drugs, while efforts to control demand have been left to national governments. Judged by world seizures, it is clear that various forms of illicit drugs continue to be sold and used at unacceptably high levels in many parts of the world. Moreover, with the advent of globalization, drugs are traveling across borders much more commonly than they once did. Many countries without histories of drug use, particularly developing countries, are now reporting problems of abuse because they have become transit points for international drug trafficking. This has not only become a threat to public health but also to public safety and security.

Because of lucrative profits drug traffickers will always find a way to meet the demand for drugs. Traffickers are opportunistic and can be expected to: market new drugs; seek out new routes to smuggle drugs; seek new partners among organized crime groups in different countries; exploit new manufacturing and communication technologies; recruit vulnerable individuals into the work of trafficking; and find ways to launder the proceedings. This chapter provides a descriptive account of international drug trafficking intended to assist understanding of its complex nature and of the challenges involved in its control.

DEFINITION

Drug trafficking is a crucial link in the chain between illicit drug production and consumption (World Drug Report, 1997: 131) and involves the following sequential stages of distribution:

- Growing or Producing
- Manufacturing
- Importing or Smuggling
- Wholesale Distribution
- Regional Distribution
- Street-level Distribution

Figure 14.1 distinguishes three levels of distribution as follows: Upper-level drug trafficking denotes the movement of drugs in bulk from producing countries to the demand countries; middle-level operations involve the wholesale distribution of the smuggled drugs to different regions; and lower-level distribution involves retail level sales to the consumer markets within the demand countries.

These distinctions provide the framework for understanding the mechanics of drug trafficking operations and also for undertaking international, national, and local level supply reduction strategies.

DRUG SUPPLY

According to 2009 World Drug Report, though the production level of heroin and cocaine has decreased, there is still a large market for these drugs in many parts of the world. The Andes region (Colombia, Peru, and Bolivia) is the major source of supply of cocaine to world markets. (In 2008, 845 metric tons of cocaine was manufactured in this region.) The major producers of opium are Afghanistan, Myanmar, and Lao People's Democratic Republic – countries that are part of the Golden Triangle and Golden Crescent. In 2007, a grand total of 8,890 metric tons of opium were produced around the world. Colombia and Jamaica are now the main source of cannabis for the United Kingdom and the United States, while Morocco and Albania are the main sources for continental Europe. The Netherlands is the main source of amphetamine and "ecstasy" (MDMA) production in Europe, but these substances are also produced in many other countries, including Belgium, Germany, the United Kingdom, Greece, Portugal, the Nordic States, Poland, Estonia, Lithuania, and the Czech Republic. The production of MDMA is also spreading, in particular to Australia, North America, South Africa, China, Southeast Asia (where it is much cheaper to

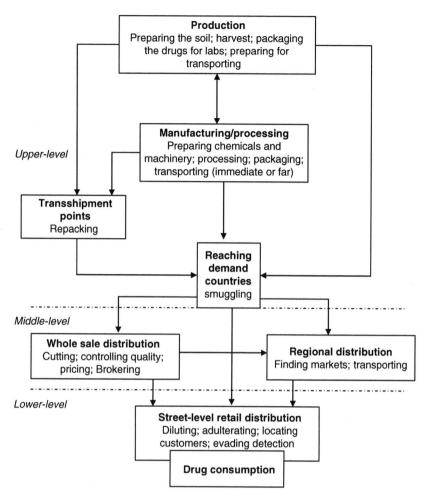

Figure 14.1. Sequential steps in international drug trafficking.

produce than in Europe), and more recently to South America (Europol, 2007). The largest laboratories to date have been reported in Indonesia and Malaysia (UNODC, 2008). UNODC (2009) estimated that in 2007 between 230 and 640 metric tons of amphetamines-group stimulants were manufactured, but only fifty-two metric tons were seized worldwide.

COMPLEXITIES OF INTERNATIONAL DRUG TRAFFICKING

As can be seen from Figure 14.1, drug trafficking involves many stages of operation from production to consumption. Unlike legal international businesses, the illegal drug trade requires clandestine strategies and techniques to move the drugs from producing countries to the consumers. Understanding the ways in which drugs are trafficked (e.g. methods, techniques, and routes) and how the drug trade is organized (e.g. distribution strategies, structure of organizations, and organized crime networks) is important in finding ways to control the flow of drugs.

Variety of Methods and Techniques Used to Transport Drugs

Globalization has greatly increased the volume of containerized trade, the frequency of international flights, the availability of international delivery services, and global access to the Internet. Depending upon the number and proximity of locations, illegal drugs are now finding their ways to consumer nations by air, sea, land, and postal services in the same way as legal commodities. E-trafficking of drugs has also been reported. High-powered motorboats, bulk cargo freighters, and containerized cargo ships remain the most common methods of moving multikilo level quantities of cocaine and heroin. However, any available method may be used. For example, small submersibles are sometimes used in Central America for transporting cocaine, and cannabis resin is transported from Morocco to Spain using goods vehicles, in cars (by ferry) or using small boats. The drugs are then transported overland to France, the United Kingdom, the Netherlands, and other European countries.

Drugs have been swallowed or hidden in body cavities; hidden on the person; packed into luggage or belongings; stashed in cars, boats, or aircraft; and hidden in seemingly legitimate freight. The U.S. Customs and Border Control have listed some of the more unusual methods of concealment:

- Drugs surgically implanted in a man's thigh.
- Contraband hidden in a woman's wig.
- Cocaine surgically implanted in a living dog.
- Marijuana concealed in the hollowed out boards of wooden pallets.
- Cocaine masked in the soles of shoes.
- Marijuana bundles in manmade landscaping stones.
- Drugs stashed in the manifold of an engine.
- A variety of drugs in body cavities and ingested.
- A marijuana load in the floorboard of a trailer hauling two live bears.
- Drugs concealed in new furniture.
- Marijuana hidden in metal cans disguised as food products.

Table 14.1. Drug trafficking routes

Type of drug	Source countries	Routes/transit	Demand countries
Cocaine and cannabis	South American countries	Caribbean islands, Dominican Republic, Haiti, and Puerto Rico	North America and UK
Heroin	Golden crescent Golden triangle	"Northern Balkan Route": To Italy via Greece, Albania, or the former Yugoslav Republic of Macedonia "Southern Balkan Route": Central Asia to Europe. "Silk Route": Through Turkey, Bulgaria, Romania, Hungary, and Austria. India, Pakistan, Nigeria	Europe and the U.S.
Synthetic drugs	China Netherlands	Asia- Pacific rim Belgium, Estonia	Japan and Australia. North America, Middle East, UK, and Western Europe

VARIETY OF ROUTES

Table 14.1 shows some of the routes that traffickers use to transport illegal drugs (WCO, 2004). They choose routes where law enforcement efforts are minimal so that the drugs can be transshipped with least risk of loss. Drug traffickers are constantly looking for new routes that are convenient and safe. In order to increase their profits, the traffickers develop markets for drugs in the transshipping points or countries. This is why there have been surges in drug use among the general population in Nigeria and other African countries as well as in the Indian subcontinent.

Varieties of Trafficking Organizations and Distribution Strategies

Traffickers must develop routine ways of transacting business and the distribution systems that have been developed in some cases are highly complex. Large drug networks are organized with extensive human "trust" contacts between supply and destination points (Decker & Townsend, 2008) and with a distinct hierarchical structure similar to some business corporations. They may be controlled by so-called "king pins" who negotiate transactions with other drug organizations. Within the networks, middle managers oversee operations on behalf of the king pins; couriers transport drugs within and between the demand countries and wholesalers distribute the drugs to retailers (or street dealers) who in turn supply the users (Adler, 1985; Dorn, Levi, & Leslie, 2005; Pearson & Hobbes, 2001).

An example of such a complex distribution system would be that developed by the Colombian or Mexican cartels, which continue to dominate cocaine trafficking in the United States. These cartels have created wholesale distribution and money-laundering networks comprised of distinct cells functioning in a number of major metropolitan areas, including New York City. From these major centers, cocaine is distributed more widely throughout the country for sale in other cities. The cells recruit and employ large numbers of personnel, assign tasks, monitor performance on a daily basis, punish infractions by their operatives, develop corrupt relationships with local law enforcement, maintain records of drug transactions and revenues, and maintain continuous communication with key mangers in Colombia (Fuentes, 1998). They use all available technology, including personal computers, public telephones, cell phones, pagers, and facsimile machines in their daily operations.

The enormous profits available from drug trafficking attract a wide spectrum of participants. These range from individuals working alone to major organized crime syndicates involving a variety of ethnic groups that undertake a variety of tasks. The organized crime groups include: Italian and Sicilian Mafia; Neapolitan Camorra and Calabrian Ndrangheta; Asian Triads and Tongs; Japanese Yakuza; Medellin and Cali cartels; the Cuban and Russian Mafias; and many other criminal groups from the Middle East, the Caribbean, and Europe. They take part in all stages of distribution (from setting up connections with the producers, to transshipping and distributing to the retailers) by networking with one another. The activities of these groups have become a major challenge for law enforcement (Natarajan & Belanger, 1998). In New York City, Natarajan, Zanella, and Yu (2008) studied forty drug trafficking organizations prosecuted in New York City from 1997 to 2007. They found four main kinds of organization – "freelance," "family-based businesses," "communal businesses," and "corporations." A high degree of specialization exists in the tasks performed by some of the trafficking enterprises in order to minimize the risks of detection and arrest (Desroches, 2005).

Global Strategies to Combat the Supply and Demand
of Illegal Drugs

Various international organizations have important roles in controlling drug supplies and the demand for drugs around the world. These include the United Nations International Drug Control Programme, the United Nations Educational Scientific and Cultural Organization (UNESCO), International Narcotics Control Board (INCB), the World Health Organization, Interpol, Europol, and the World Customs Organization (WCO). The United Nations Office on Drugs and Crime (UNODC), which functions as a global leader in this field, has extensive liaison arrangements with these agencies and with regional enforcement authorities in order to develop and strengthen crossborder and regional cooperation in apprehending traffickers and seizing drugs. Despite these global efforts and despite stringent enforcement at the street level, illegal drugs still reach the hands of millions of users.

It is difficult to set in place a unified mechanism to combat the illicit supply of drugs due to variations in legal systems, law enforcement tactics, cultures (languages and cultural practices), financial institutions and banking systems, political and economic conditions, and tolerance levels of drugs and ideologies. However, it is imperative to develop increased international cooperation in apprehending the traffickers and disrupting supplies. There is also an urgent need to develop international regulatory controls with high standards for entry in banking and financial institutions so as to control the money laundering of the proceeds from drug trafficking.

SUMMARY

A recent report by UN General Assembly Special Session (UNGASS) on Global Illicit Drugs Markets (Reuter & Trautmann, 2009) found no evidence that the global drug problem was reduced during the period from 1998 to 2007. Nonetheless, if interdiction efforts were not in place drug supplies might have skyrocketed and so might have the numbers of users. The fundamental economic point is that so long as there is the demand, and the rewards of meeting this demand are sufficiently great, there will be criminal groups willing to supply the drugs. A handful of evaluations show some positive impact of crackdowns on street-level local markets, but hardly any empirical evaluations exist of supply reduction efforts aimed at higher-level markets. This lack of scientific research is due largely to the difficulty of collecting data on the complex and dynamic nature of drug trafficking. Finding a solution to this difficulty presents an urgent challenge to the community of researchers concerned with combating drug trafficking.

REFERENCES

Decker, S. H. & M. Townsend (2008). *Drug Smugglers on Drug Smuggling: Lessons from the Inside*. Philadelphia, Temple University Press.

Desroches, F. (2005). *The Crime that Pays: Drug Trafficking and Organized Crime in Canada*. Toronto: Canadian Scholar's Press.

Dorn, N., M. Levi, & K. Leslie (2005). *Literature Review on Upper Level Drug Trafficking* London, UK: Home Office Report.

European Monitoring Centre for Drugs and Drug Addiction (2006). Annual Report 2006: The State of the Drugs Problem in Europe. Retrieved http://ar2006.emcdda.europa.eu/download/ar2006-en.pdf

Europol. (2007). *Amphetamine-type Stimulants in the European Union 1998–2007*. Retrieved from www.europol.europa.eu/publications/Serious_Crime_Overviews/EuropolUNGASSAssessment.PDF

Fuentes, R. J. (1998). *Life of a Cell: Managerial Practice and Strategy in Colombian Cocaine Distribution in the United States*. (Doctoral Dissertation, City University of New York, 1998).

Natarajan, M. & M. Belanger (1998). Varieties of Upper-Level Drug Dealing Organizations: A Typology of Cases Prosecuted in New York City. *Journal of Drug Issues*, 28 (4), 1005–26.

Natarajan, M., M. Zanella, & C. Yu (2008). *Typology of Drug Trafficking Businesses: Challenges for Law Enforcement*. Paper Presented at The International Conference Justice and Policing in Diverse Societies, June 9–12, 2008, San Juan, Puerto Rico.

Pearson, G. & D. Hobbs (2001). *Middle Market Drug Distribution. London*: Home Office.

Reuter, P & F. Trautmann (2009). *A Report on Global Illicit Drugs Markets 1998–2007*. Netherlands: European Communities.

United Nations International Drug Control Programme. (1997). *World Drug Report*. New York: Oxford University Press.

United Nations Office on Drugs and Crime (UNODC). (2009) World Drug Report 2009, New York: United Nations.

World Customs Organization. (2004). *2003 Customs and Drugs Report. http://wcoweb04.wcoomd.org/ie/En/Press/press.html*

WEB SITES

US Drug Enforcement Administration www.usdoj.gov/dea/major/major.htm
US Custom and Border Protection
www.cbp.gov/xp/cgov/newsroom/news_releases/archives/cbp_press_releases/092003/09122003.xml

www.unodc.org/unodc/en/data-and-analysis/WDR-2009.html
www.homeoffice.gov.uk/rds/pdfs05/rdsolr2205.pdf
United Nations Educational, Scientific and Cultural Organization
www.unesco.org/most/globalisation/drugs_vol2.pdf
International Narcotics Control Board (INCB) www.incb.org

ABOUT THE AUTHOR

Mangai Natarajan Ph.D. is professor at John Jay College of Criminal Justice. She has a long-standing research interest in drug trafficking. Her volume with Prof. Mike Hough of King's College, London, (*Illegal Drug Markets: From Research to Policy*, Monsey, NY: Criminal Justice Press, 2000) is a compilation of research papers on drug dealing, trafficking, and drug use. Using a variety of analyses (including rational choice, network, and crime mapping), she is currently studying the mechanics of wholesale drug dealing enterprises. Her recent publications (2010) include *Drugs of Abuse-The International Scene (Volume 1) Drugs and Crime (Volume 2). Drug Abuse: Prevention and Treatment (Volume 3)*. The Library of Drug Abuse and Crime. (Ashgate, Aldershot, UK).

15 Understanding Trafficking in Human Beings

A HUMAN RIGHTS, PUBLIC HEALTH, AND CRIMINAL JUSTICE ISSUE

Alexis A. Aronowitz

INTRODUCTION

The United States Department of State (2009) has documented trafficking in human beings and their exploitation in 175 countries around the world. Trafficking affects the most vulnerable in the poorest societies, often women and children. With promises of good jobs and salaries, educational opportunities or marriage, unsuspecting victims are lured into virtual slavery often coupled with psychological, physical, and sexual abuse. The International Labour Organization (2005) estimates that 2.45 million people worldwide are in forced labor as a result of trafficking. According to the United Nations, the trafficking industry is estimated to be worth between five to seven billion U.S. dollars annually.

While much attention has been focused on the trafficking of women and children for sexual exploitation, trafficking can occur in any industry in which there is a demand for cheap labor. Trafficking and exploitation have been documented in the construction, brick making, domestic, food service industries, on farms, and on fishing boats. Trafficking also occurs for the purpose of prostitution, sex tourism, child soldiering, forced begging, and organ harvesting. The markets and industries differ across regions and countries and within countries and cities (Aronowitz, 2009).

Human trafficking may occur:

(1) internally, within a country's borders, either within a city or from rural to metropolitan areas, for example, from a rural area or village to the capital city in a country

(2) intraregionally with children and adults being trafficked, for example, throughout West and Central Africa and South-East Asia regions

(3) internationally, for example, from Africa to Europe, or from Russia and Southeast Asia to the United States.

DEFINITIONS, TRENDS, AND STATISTICS

The United Nations Protocol to Suppress and Punish Trafficking in Persons Especially Women and Children 2000 (hereafter referred to as the Trafficking Protocol) defines trafficking in persons as

> ... the recruitment, transportation, transfer, harboring or receipt of persons, by means of the threat or use of force or other forms of coercion, of abduction, of fraud, of deception, of the abuse of power or of a position of vulnerability or of the giving or receiving of payments or benefits to achieve the consent of a person having control over another person, for the purpose of exploitation. Exploitation shall include, at a minimum, the exploitation of the prostitution of others or other forms of sexual exploitation, forced labor or services, slavery or practices similar to slavery, servitude or the removal of organs.

This trafficking definition contains three separate elements: *criminal acts (the recruitment, transportation, transfer, harboring, or reception of persons), the means used to commit these acts (threat or use of force, coercion, abduction, fraud, deception, abuse of power or vulnerability, or giving payments or benefits to a person in control of the victim), and goals (exploitation, including exploiting the prostitution of others, other forms of sexual exploitation, forced labor or services, slavery or similar practices, and the removal of organs).* At least one element from each of these three groups is required before the definition applies.

The consent of a victim of trafficking in persons to the intended exploitation is deemed irrelevant if consent was obtained through threat or use of force, coercion, abduction, fraud, or deception. In the case of children, trafficking can exist in the absence of abduction, coercion, fraud, or deception, and the Trafficking Protocol literally excludes the possibility of consent to trafficking by a person under the age of eighteen.

According to the definition of smuggling of migrants put forth by the UN Protocol against the Smuggling of Migrants, smuggling involves the "... procurement, in order to obtain, directly or indirectly, a financial or other material benefit, of the illegal entry of a person into a State Party of which the person is not a national or a permanent resident." The essential element in smuggling involves bringing persons illegally across national border whereas in trafficking of persons, the essential element is the exploitation of the individual victim.

Due to its clandestine nature, accurate statistics on the magnitude of the problem are elusive and unreliable. This is due to a number of reasons. Foremost is the fact that – out of fear of the police or their traffickers, shame, unwillingness to recognize their victimization or the fact that they may be in love with or dependent upon their traffickers – victims rarely report their victimization. Further, definitions of trafficking may vary, government officials still view trafficked persons as illegal migrants and freelance sex workers, failing to recognize and register victims, and there may be no centralized agency systematically collecting such data. Available statistics range from those measuring the actual number of victims rescued or repatriated (the tip of the iceberg), to estimates of the total number of trafficked victims.

There is a large disparity between the number of known cases and estimates. Estimates are unreliable, often ranging from a high figure many times that of the low estimate; the U.S. Department of State (2008) estimates range from four million to twenty-seven million. The methodology for computing the estimates is rarely given. Reports also often fail to indicate whether estimates are annual figures or cover a period of several years (Makkai, 2003).

The United Nations (2009) reports that for the sixty-one countries on which data on victims were disaggregated into gender and age, 66 percent of the victims were women, 13 percent girls, 9 percent boys, and 12 percent men. The UN warns that the high number of female victims may be due to countries focusing on trafficking for sexual exploitation. Arrests and prosecutions are limited. In 2007, The U.S. Department of State (2009) reported 5,212 prosecutions and only 2,983 convictions for human trafficking worldwide. These low numbers may indicate that trafficking is prosecuted under other legislation or reflect problems in reporting or recording offenses.

FACTORS THAT CONTRIBUTE TO TRAFFICKING

The root causes of trafficking can be explained in terms of "push" and "pull" factors. Push factors include economic, political, and social conditions in the supply (or origin) countries that encourage individuals to migrate in search of a better life elsewhere. Specifically, rapid growth of population, persistent poverty, high unemployment, internal conflicts resulting in widespread violence and civil disorder, oppressive political regimes, and grave violations of human rights, push people from developing and poorer nations to migrate.

Pull factors, or reasons why migration occurs to a particular country, can be attributed to the demand for cheap manual labor and the high demand for paid sex in destination countries. Children and women are targeted for the trade due to their powerlessness and innocence. They are easier to exploit and are less able to claim their rights.

Other factors that facilitate trafficking are the involvement of organized crime groups and corruption in source (origin), transit, and destination (receiving) countries.

ROLE OF ORGANIZED CRIME GROUPS IN FACILITATING HUMAN TRAFFICKING

Trafficking organizations range from single individuals exploiting a single victim, to highly sophisticated organizations that are able to move large numbers of people across numerous countries with the use of fraudulent documentation and the assistance of corrupt border guards. These organizations are then able to place their victims in various brothels, factories, farms, or households. Somewhere in between these two extremes are loose networks of criminals (Aronowitz, 2001, 2009). Depending upon the complexity of the operation, the distance between the source and destination country, the number of people being moved, and the possible use of fraudulent documentation, trafficking units can be divided into several sub-units that specialize in a particular part or sequence of the operation. These sub-units provide various services from recruitment and escort to logistical support (Schloenhardt, 1999).

METHODS OF RECRUITMENT AND OPERATION

Methods of recruitment and the deceit used to lure the victim vary depending upon the source country, age, and gender of victims. False promises of marriage are used to traffic young girls from rural areas in Albania who are later forced into prostitution in Italy and other Western European countries. In Western Africa, children are promised a good education, an internship, a job, or some small token such as a bicycle or radio. The children often leave willingly and are later forced into often life-threatening situations involving harsh manual labor. In Edo State, Nigeria, young female victims reportedly sign contracts promising to repay debts of up to $50,000 prior to their departure for Western European countries where they are forced into prostitution. To ensure repayment, priests use a personal item from the victims to perform a voodoo ritual and thus bind the young women to their traffickers. In the Philippines, women have been known to travel to destinations such as Japan on formal contracts and "entertainer visas" and were then forced into prostitution in clubs. The United States has documented a number of cases in which male migrant workers were lured to the country on false promises of good wages and held in virtual bondage.

HUMAN TRAFFICKING IS MORE THAN JUST A SINGLE CRIMINAL ACT

Human trafficking can be viewed as a process involving three distinct phases: recruitment, transportation (in international trafficking), and exploitation. During each of these phases, numerous crimes ranging from kidnapping, threats of violence, theft of documents to assault, rape, or death can be perpetrated against the individual victims. Violence, both psychological and physical, occurs most often in the last phase. Victims, furthermore, have been forced into committing criminal acts such as the consumption or smuggling of drugs, theft, begging, and other crimes (Aronowitz, 2009).

HARM TO VICTIMS: HUMAN RIGHTS AND PUBLIC HEALTH CONCERNS

Victims of trafficking are almost always subjected to various forms of abuse, including abuses that are physical, sexual and psychological. Adult women forced into prostitution are also frequently coerced into taking drugs and alcohol. Many trafficked victims are subjected to abhorrent working, living, and sanitary conditions (Bales, 1999) during which time their movements are restricted and they are denied food, medical care, and proper shelter. Their documents may be seized and they are often socially isolated and threatened with deportation by the traffickers because of their often illegal status. If they come to the attention of immigration and enforcement officials in many destination countries they are viewed, not as victims of trafficking, but as willing accomplices in smuggling schemes and illegal immigrants. They are subsequently incarcerated and frequently deported without medical or psychological support or protection. Upon return to their countries of origin they are often vulnerable to re-victimization or retaliation if they cooperate with criminal justice authorities.

In addition to these human rights violations, a strong link has been established between trafficking in persons for prostitution and HIV/AIDS infection. Girls and young women are often forced to have unprotected sexual contacts with multiple partners, greatly increasing their risk of contracting sexually transmitted diseases (STDs) including HIV/AIDS. There is also a risk of unwanted pregnancy, early motherhood, and illnesses that might affect future reproductive ability (Zimmerman, 2003).

ENDING HUMAN TRAFFICKING AND VICTIMIZATION

Ending trafficking will require focusing upon the four Ps: prevention, prosecution (of traffickers), protection (of victims), and partnerships – between Governmental and nongovernmental organizations, private industry, and faith-based organizations – at the grass roots, local, national, and international levels. The United Nations Office on Drugs and Crime, together with other international and local partners, has implemented various antitrafficking projects with services around the globe: providing advice on drafting and revising relevant legislation, advice and assistance on establishing and strengthening antitrafficking offices and units, training for law enforcement officers, prosecutors and judges, strengthening victim and witness support, and promoting awareness-raising. The International Organization for Migration, the International Labour Organization, and the United Nations Children's Fund have also been active in providing training to law enforcement, immigration, and judicial officers, in running awareness-raising campaigns targeting the general public and populations at risk, and in providing shelter, rehabilitation, skills training, and microcredit programs to repatriated victims.

A more permanent solution requires changes in social and economic policies, historical and cultural practices, and national-level initiatives to prevent vulnerable persons from falling prey to traffickers. Only long-term sustainable strategies, such as the eradication of poverty and corruption and the provision of education, job, and career opportunities for the most vulnerable populations in the society will truly eradicate trafficking (Aronowitz, 2009).

SUMMARY AND CONCLUSION

According to the U.N. Trafficking Protocol, trafficking in human beings covers a broad range of activities (recruitment, transportation, harboring, and receipt) through the use of force, coercion, or deceit for the purpose of exploitation of a person in prostitution, sexual exploitation, forced labor, slavery-like practices, or the removal of organs. Trafficking must be recognized as a human rights, public health, and criminal justice issue.

Trafficking is a sophisticated crime, almost always involving a degree of organization. It should be dealt with through investigation and prosecution of offenders for trafficking and any other criminal activities in which they engage. Trafficked persons must be seen as victims of crime, and victim support and protection are important humanitarian objectives. Only by protecting victims can governments respect their human rights, restore their dignity, and hope to secure their cooperation in the prosecution of offenders. Failure to secure conviction of offenders and compensation for victims will allow traffickers to thrive on the countless number of those seeking a better future for themselves and their families.

REFERENCES

Aronowitz, A. A. (2009). *Human Trafficking, Human Misery: The Global Trade in Human Beings.* Westport, CT: Praeger Publishers.
  (2001). Smuggling and Trafficking in Human Beings: The Phenomenon, the Markets that Drive It and the Organisations that Promote It. *European Journal on Criminal Policy and Research*, 9,(2), 163–95.
Bales, K. (1999). *Disposable People.* Berkley: University of California Press.
International Labour Organization. (2005). *A Global Alliance Against Forced Labour.* Geneva. Retrieved from www.ilo.org/public/english/standards/relm/ilc93/pdf/rep-i-b.pdf www.ilo.org/wcmsp5/groups/public/ - -ed_norm/ - -declaration/documents/publication/wcms_081882.pdf
Makkai, T. (2003). *Thematic Discussion on Trafficking in Human Beings.* Workshop on Trafficking in Human Beings, Especially Women and Children. (Twelfth Session of the Commission on Crime Prevention and Criminal Justice), Vienna.
Schloenhardt, A. (1999). Organized Crime and the Business of Migrant Trafficking. *Crime, Law and Social Change*, 32, 203–33.
United Nations Office on Drugs and Crime. (2009). UN.GIFT, *Global Report on Trafficking in Persons.* Vienna Retrieved from www.unodc.org/documents/Global_Report_on_TIP.pdf
United States Department of State. (2008 & 2009). *Trafficking in Persons Report 2008 and 2009.* Washington, D.C. Retrieved from www.state.gov/g/tip/rls/tiprpt/2008 and www.state.gov/g/tip/rls/tiprpt/2009
Zimmerman, C. (2003). *The Health Risks and Consequences of Trafficking in Women and Adolescents: Findings from a European Study.* London School of Hygien and Tropical Medicine. London: U.K.

WEB SITES

Anti-Slavery International www.antislaveryinternational.org
International Labour Organization www.ilo.org
International Organization for Migration (IOM) www.iom.int
U.S. Department of State Office to Monitor and Combat Trafficking in Persons www.state.gov/g/tip
United Nations Office on Drugs and Crime www.unodc.org/unodc/en/human-trafficking/what-is-human-trafficking.html

ABOUT THE AUTHOR

Alexis A. Aronowitz is a senior lecturer and academic advisor at the University College Utrecht, the Netherlands. She has served as a staff member and consultant on projects in the field of trafficking in human beings for the United Nations Interregional Crime and Justice Research Institute, the United Nations Office on Drugs and Crime, the United Nations Division for the Advancement of Women, the International Organization for Migration, the Organization for Security and Cooperation in Europe and other international organizations. Her recent book is *Human Trafficking, Human Misery: The Global Trade in Human Beings* by Praeger Publishers (2009).

16 International Trafficking of Stolen Vehicles

Ronald V. Clarke and Rick Brown

INTRODUCTION

For many years, cars stolen in the United States have been exported to countries in South America or the Caribbean using containers and ferries. Others have simply been driven across the border into Mexico. Thefts are sometimes organized on a massive scale, with criminal groups responsible for the trafficking of dozens of vehicles. Other thefts are more opportunistic, often committed by juvenile offenders, who might steal a car in the afternoon and sell it that same evening in Mexico (Resindez, 1998). A recent analysis has found that vehicle theft hot spots in the U.S. are in counties bordering Mexico and those with busy ports (Highway Loss Data Institute, 2008). This pattern has become more pronounced in recent years, suggesting that theft for export might be a growing problem. It might even be the case, as many law enforcement officials believe, that stolen vehicles are being exported to pay for drugs imported from overseas.

Beyond the United States, the demise of the Soviet system resulted in large numbers of cars being stolen in Western Europe and exported to Russia and other countries of Eastern Europe. The emerging market economies in those countries created a demand for cars (especially luxury models) that could not be met by domestic producers, and criminal entrepreneurs moved in to fill the gap. Increasing globalization has created similar conditions in other parts of the world with the result that many other countries have become markets for cars stolen abroad. Thus, the Middle East is now a destination for cars stolen in Europe, West Africa for cars stolen in the U.S. and the U.K., and China for cars stolen in the U.S. and Japan. Regional theft markets have also developed. For example, Bolivia is the destination for cars stolen in Brazil and Argentina, Nepal for ones stolen in Northern

India, Indonesia for ones stolen in Malaysia, Cambodia for cars stolen in Thailand, and other parts of Africa for cars stolen in South Africa. Japan has been a major source of exported stolen vehicles to Indonesia, the Russian Far East, the United Arab Emirates, Nigeria, and even the U.K. (Clarke & Brown, 2003).

No reliable figures exist for the scale of the problem. Combining official estimates from different countries suggests that half a million vehicles are stolen and sold abroad each year, though Clarke and Brown (2003) argue that these estimates are inflated. Most of the trafficked vehicles are cars, exported whole with false identities. There is also a small export trade in stolen commercial vehicles and motorcycles and a large, though poorly measured trade in stolen vehicle parts. Clear differences exist among recipient countries in preferred models. For example, luxury BMWs and Mercedes are in heavy demand in Eastern Europe. African and South American countries prefer jeeps and other 4x4 vehicles that suit the local roads. In Mexico, the models most in demand are ones manufactured in the U.S., but which are also manufactured or marketed in Mexico (Miller, 1987).

Whichever vehicles or countries are involved, the pattern is the same: The principal flow of stolen vehicles is from rich to poorer countries. This mirrors the wider global economy in which manufactured goods move from the developed to the less developed world, but is contrary to most other forms of transnational crime, where the flow is in the other direction.

HOW IS TRAFFICKING IN STOLEN CARS ACCOMPLISHED?

In order to devise countermeasures, more needs to be known about the traffickers' methods. Unfortunately, our understanding is limited by the complexity of the crime, which is due to the following:

1. Each of the three main forms of vehicle trafficking has to be understood in detail. These are: (1) driving stolen cars across national borders or transporting them in ferries; (2) shipping them overseas in sealed containers; and (3) disassembling them and shipping them overseas for sale as spare parts.
2. Trafficking in stolen cars involves a complex sequence of actions, including the following:
   - preferred vehicles are identified and stolen, either to order or "on spec";
   - they may be moved to a safe place and their identities changed;
   - they may be stored, awaiting pick-up for transfer across the border;

- depending on the method of transfer, they may be placed in sealed containers and loaded onto ships, or they may be driven across the border;
- at the destinations they may be handed over to a local contact or collected by such a person from the docks;
- they may be legally registered; and finally
- they may be sold on the open market or to a private buyer.

3. Due to local conditions, many differences exist in methods employed. Thus, in South Africa, where stolen cars are mostly driven to neighboring countries, criminals often acquire the vehicles through carjacking, in other words, at gunpoint from their owners. This method is rarely used in other countries. At the export stage, traffickers use many different routes; Liukkonen (1997) identified six distinct routes in Europe alone. Some routes require only a single bordercrossing, while others require many border crossings, which increases the risks for the criminals involved.

4. The traffickers' methods, the routes they use, and the countries principally involved, all undergo constant change in response to law enforcement initiatives or the changing opportunity structure for their crime. For instance, in the early-1990s, there were many reports of cars being exported from Hong Kong and Japan to China, but by the mid-1990s, the trade in illegal imports to China decreased, partly as a result of actions taken by the Chinese authorities, including banning the import of right hand drive vehicles.

WHAT FACILITATES TRAFFICKING IN STOLEN CARS?

At the most general level, trafficking in stolen cars relies upon a ready supply of attractive vehicles in one country or region, the demand for such vehicles in another, and a ready means of transporting them from origin to destination. These conditions have existed for many years in the Americas and have more recently arisen in Europe with the emergence of free markets in the former countries of the Soviet bloc. Some other specific conditions that facilitate trafficking in stolen cars should be noted because of their potential relevance to policy. These include:

- Vast numbers of cars cross national borders every day. As a result of trade agreements and worldwide increases in tourism, many border controls have been eased or lifted, in order to cope with the huge number of cars traversing national boundaries. Looking for stolen cars among this vast amount of legal traffic is like searching for the proverbial needle in the haystack.

- Huge volumes of containers shipped from many ports in developed countries. Stolen cars and auto parts are frequently shipped in sealed containers to other countries. Many of the cars have been given new identities, but in some cases, they are shipped in containers labeled as "kitchen equipment" or "household goods." Customs officials examine only about 1 percent of containers shipped from U.S. ports, partly because cargo ships work in tight turnarounds.

- A substantial legal trade between countries in used cars. Large volumes of used cars are legally traded between developed countries and undeveloped countries. Criminals involved in trafficking in stolen cars can shelter behind this trade, masking their activities as legitimate business.

- Customs controls focused on arrivals, not departures. This pattern holds worldwide because customs officers are responsible for levying duties on certain goods entering the country and keeping prohibited goods out. In the U.S., this pattern has become more pronounced as fears of terrorism have increased.

- The inhibition of law enforcement activity by the commitment of developing countries to fostering international trade. Many countries encourage the swift export of goods in order increase economic efficiency. This can result in law enforcement organizations needing to justify their actions in searching suspicious containers and may result in fewer checks being undertaken.

- The difficulty many countries have in even controlling the illegal import of cars that have not been stolen. Until countries can control illegal imports, they have little prospect of preventing the import of stolen cars.

- The nonexistence of International standards for vehicle registration and ownership documents. This makes it difficult for officials to detect forged or altered papers. Language barriers make the task even more difficult.

- The great variation and lax enforcement of vehicle registration procedures among countries. Even in some developed countries, such as the U.K., it is not necessary for the registering officer to see the vehicle. In many less developed countries, vehicle registration requirements are very poorly enforced.

- Widespread corruption among officials in undeveloped countries. Prior to the current agreements concerning the recovery of stolen cars, police officers in Mexico could routinely be seen driving around in stolen American cars, sometimes with their U.S. number plates still in place. In South Africa, corruption (and intimidation) of officials in vehicle registration offices is one method of obtaining a new identity for stolen vehicles, many of which are exported to neighboring countries (Ndhlovu, 2002).

- The low priority given by law enforcement to vehicle theft. Developing countries are faced with many more serious crime problems than the import of stolen cars and cannot be expected to give vehicle theft high priority. In developed countries, law enforcement action to reduce the export of stolen vehicles is eclipsed by the need to tackle other forms of organized crime (e.g., drugs importation, human trafficking, etc.).

- The expansion of the number of offenders with the necessary contacts to undertake vehicle trafficking, expanded by substantial migration into developed countries. Available evidence suggests that many of those involved in vehicle trafficking are immigrants, who discover and exploit the opportunities existing for this crime. They may already have the necessary contacts in their home countries and they may avoid prosecution by working in their own language, which may be unfamiliar to the police.

HOW ORGANIZED IS VEHICLE TRAFFICKING?

Recent research has suggested that organized crime is no longer dominated by the traditional "Mafia" of the textbooks. Instead, there are now many more small, loosely structured networks of criminal entrepreneurs, often with specialized knowledge, who come together to exploit specific opportunities for crime, such as credit card fraud or counterfeiting banknotes. It would, therefore, not be surprising if many people engaged in the trafficking of stolen cars were not members of organized crime groups, but were employed in vehicle repair garages, in selling used cars, or in legitimate export businesses. These individuals then discover that they can exploit their knowledge and contacts to make large profits in exporting stolen vehicles. (See Brown and Clarke (2004) for a summary of the differences between traditional organized crime syndicates and more contemporary descriptions of "criminal entrepreneur" networks.)

WHAT IS BEING DONE TO REDUCE THE PROBLEM?

Despite the low priority accorded to vehicle theft by law enforcement authorities, much has been done over the years by the U.S., Interpol, and the United Nations to tackle the problem, including the following:

- The U.S. has developed a model bilateral agreement for the repatriation of stolen vehicles (see United Nations, 1997) and has signed agreements with numerous countries in Latin America. U.S. agents have provided training in ways to identify stolen cars to customs officials in these countries.
- The National Insurance Crime Bureau (which is supported by the American insurance industry) has assisted these efforts by stationing officials in Mexico and other South American countries to assist the process of repatriation.
- X-ray machines are now being routinely used in inspecting sealed containers in U.S. ports. Documentation relating to any car for export must now be presented seventy-two hours prior to loading (General Accounting Office, 1999).
- The U.S. Motor Vehicle Theft and Law Enforcement Act of 1984 requires car manufacturers to mark the major body parts of high-risk models to deter their theft for chopping and for export.
- The stolen vehicle database maintained by the FBI is being opened to other countries. Interpol has developed a similar database of stolen vehicles for access by member states, while EUCARIS, the European Car and Driving License Information System (www.eucaris.net), was established in 1994 in response to increased international trafficking of cars in Europe.
- Many countries have established committees or task forces to study auto theft and to make policy recommendations, including ways to curb the export of stolen vehicles (United Nations, 1997).

Much of this activity has been undertaken to assist the repatriation of stolen cars. Important as this is, it may play only a minor role in deterrence since very small numbers of trafficked cars are detected. Much greater attention should be devoted to the earlier stages of trafficking in an effort to prevent cars leaving the countries of origin.

CONCLUSIONS

Because of improved security on new cars and generally falling crime rates, auto theft in developed countries is declining. Trafficking in stolen cars will probably be immune to this trend because improvements in vehicle security provide little deterrent to professional thieves, who find ways of stealing vehicles with keys – for example, through carjackings or fraudulent rental and lease agreements. Furthermore, the demand for stolen cars in developing countries, fueled by increasing globalization, is unlikely to abate. While the problem may have been exaggerated in the past, there is some evidence that it is now increasing. Research could assist law enforcement efforts by uncovering the methods used by traffickers to circumvent licensing requirements and to avoid detection at customs and border checkpoints.

REFERENCES

Brown, R. & R. V. Clarke (2004). Police Intelligence and Theft of Vehicles for Export: Recent UK Experience. In M. G. Maxwell & R. V. Clarke (Eds.), *Crime Prevention Studies*, Vol. 17. Monsey, NY: Criminal Justice Press.

Clarke, R. V. & R. Brown (2003). International Trafficking in Stolen Vehicles. In M. Tonry, (Ed.), *Crime and Justice. A Review of Research*, Vol. 30. Chicago: University of Chicago Press.

General Accounting Office. (1999). *Efforts to Curtail the Exportation of Stolen Vehicles*. Report to the Chairman, Permanent Subcommittee on Investigations, Committee on Governmental Affairs, U.S. Senate. GAO/OSI. Washington, DC: U.S. General Accounting Office.

Highway Loss Data Institute. (2008). *Insurance Special Report: Theft Losses by County: 1999-2007 Models*. Arlington, VA: The Institute.

Liukkonen, M. (1997). *Motor Vehicle Theft in Europe*. Paper No. 9. Helsinki: HEUNI.

Miller, M. V. (1987). Vehicle Theft Along the Texas-Mexico Border. *Journal of Borderland Studies*, 2, 12–32.

Ndhlovu, F. K. (2002). Organized Crime: A Perspective from Zambia. In J. S. Albanese, D. K. Das, & A.Verma (Eds.) *Organized Crime: World Perspectives*. Upper Saddle River, NJ: Prentice Hall.

Resindez, R. (1998). International Auto Theft: An Exploratory Research of Organization and Organized Crime on the U.S./Mexico Border. *Criminal Organizations*, 12, 25–30.

United Nations. (1997). *International Cooperation in Combating Transnational Crime: Illicit Trafficking in Motor Vehicles*. Commission on Crime Prevention and Criminal Justice. Vienna: United Nations.

ABOUT THE AUTHORS

Ronald V. Clarke-See Chapter 13 on Crime Prevention.

Rick Brown is managing director with Evidence Led Solutions, a research consultancy that specializes in criminal justice and community safety issues. He was previously employed by the British government's criminological research department, where he worked on a range of vehicle crime related subjects. He has published widely on vehicle crime issues.

17 Transnational Firearms Trafficking

GUNS FOR CRIME AND CONFLICT

Theodore Leggett

INTRODUCTION

The trafficking of firearms is unlike many of the other forms of trafficking discussed in this book because firearms are durable goods. Unlike drugs, rhino horn, or counterfeit pharmaceuticals, a well-maintained AK-47 will last indefinitely. As a result, there is little need for a continuous contraband flow. Trafficking tends to be episodic, often from an established stockpile to a region descending into crisis.

In addition, the modern pistol or assault rifle represents a "mature technology," so current weapons holders do not need to regularly update their stock to remain competitive. There has been very little innovation in small arms design in the last fifty years – it appears there are few ways to make small arms more accurate or more deadly than they are today. Consequently, the number of new small arms purchased each year is only about 1 percent of those already in circulation. Even the world's most innovative militaries only update their small arms every second decade or so.

As the global turnover in the licit arms industry is limited, the same is likely true for the illicit arms industry. Many still-functional weapons were distributed in developing countries during the Cold War and thereafter, and since the destruction of weapons has been limited in many parts of the world, there is little need to import new weapons into these regions today. Small Arms Survey, a Geneva-based arms monitoring group, estimated the global authorized trade in firearms has been estimated at approximately US$1.58 billion in 2006, with unrecorded but licit transactions making up another US$100 million or so. The most commonly cited estimate for the size of the illicit market is 10 percent to 20 percent of the licit market, which would be about US$170 million to US$320 million per annum. This may sound like a lot of money, but it appears to be diffused among a large number of small players. It is also small compared to, for example, the value of drug markets, typically estimated to be in the tens of billions of dollars.

There are two primary markets for illicit arms: those who need weapons for criminal purposes, and those who need them for political ones.

GUNS FOR CRIME

For criminals, there are often more immediate sources of firearms than those trafficked internationally. In most cities in the developed world, there is limited use for military-type weapons for street criminals (see Box 1), and so the demand is for concealable handguns. For example, despite availability of a wide range of small arms in the United States, including semiautomatic assault rifles, 88 percent of firearm murders in 2008 were committed with handguns, and earlier studies have found the same for 87 percent of all violent firearms offenses. Firearms used in crime are often diverted from the legal handgun market that exists in many countries. If handgun controls are tight in one country, they may be looser in a neighboring one, and while the transborder movement of these weapons could be considered trafficking, the volumes are rarely big or concentrated enough to be deemed an organized trafficking flow.

For example, it is likely that the largest crossborder movement of firearms for criminal purposes today is the flow from the United States to Mexico's *carteles*. All the available evidence suggests most of this trafficking is done by small groups moving small amounts of weapons very frequently. The Mexican Attorney General's Office asserts, "At the present time, we have not detected in Mexico a criminal organization, domestic or foreign, dedicated to arms trafficking." Docket research by the Violence Policy Center suggests that most of these weapons were purchased legally in the United States, using "straw" purchasers (i.e., people who are paid to buy guns on behalf of others).

To have a sense of the relative value of the market for firearms compared to other forms of contraband, it helps to look at some concrete examples. On November 16, 2009, the Nicaraguan government made what was hailed as "one of the largest seizures of weaponry ever made by the Nicaraguan authorities" – a consignment of arms for the local representatives of the Mexican Sinaloa cartel. The shipment comprised fifty-nine assault rifles, two grenade launchers and ten grenades, eight kilos of TNT, and nearly

---

Box 1. Are military weapons used in street crime?

Handguns have obvious advantages over long arms for use in street crime. They can be concealed and carried constantly; they are easier to use at close quarters; and they are every bit as deadly. But they can be difficult to find in many developing countries, since few can afford them. Criminals wishing to use firearms in poorer countries would have to make use of military arms left over from past conflicts, or somehow access (buy, rent, steal) handguns from the police. Given that most people are unarmed and bullets are expensive, bladed weapons, which may also have agricultural uses, may be more commonly used in crime. For example, according to the South African Police Service, despite the widespread availability of both military and civilian firearms, the majority of murders are still committed with sharp instruments, and less than 30 percent are committed with a gun. In 2007 and 2008, for the first time, docket research indicated that guns had outpaced knives as the most common weapon used in robberies in South Africa.

In states where handguns are accessible, most criminals prefer to use them. Military weapons may be used, however, when criminal conflict becomes tantamount to a low intensity military conflict. Some of the best-known examples include conflicts in the favelas of Brazil and some states in Mexico.

In Brazil, an analysis by a consortium including the local NOG Viva Rio of over 200,000 firearms seized between 1974 and 2004 in the state of Rio de Janeiro found that just under 92 percent were civilian-type arms (68 percent were revolvers, 16 percent pistols, and 8 percent shotguns). Less than 2 percent were assault rifles or submachine guns, and 82 percent were manufactured in Brazil. Some 70 percent of the weapons seized chambered either thirty-eight short or thirty-two short rounds. In other words, in one of the areas best known for the use of military arms, the police far more commonly seized smaller weapons.

An updated study found that assault weapons had indeed increased their share of the weapons seized in crime in the city of Rio de Janeiro after 1992, but only to 4 percent. The share of pistols also increased while the share of revolvers decreased.

In short, even in those few countries where criminals use military weapons, handguns still seem to be preferred for most forms of street crime.

20,000 rounds of ammunition. While this sounds impressive, the total value of this shipment was likely less than US$200,000 at point-of-sale. Three days later, the Nicaraguan navy seized 2.4 tons of cocaine off the Caribbean coast. The value of this shipment was at least four hundred times as much, around US$80 million in U.S. wholesale markets.

GUNS FOR WAR

The second source of demand for illicit weapons – demand from groups whose objectives are political rather than criminal – emerges when a set of militants finds the resources to equip an unauthorized force, or when a state subject to international embargoes attempts to circumvent these controls. Similar to criminals, insurgents may be able to access the weaponry desired from local sources or by stealing, renting, or purchasing weapons from the police and military. In particular, poorly resourced insurgents may have to fall back on whatever is available locally. State actors and some insurgent groups may have state allies willing to shuttle weaponry around the international agreements in what is often referred to as the "gray market." It remains unclear what share of transnational arms trafficking could be considered organized crime, and what share can be attributed to those with political, rather than economic, motivations.

WHAT IS FIREARMS TRAFFICKING?

The Protocol against the Illicit Manufacturing of and Trafficking in Firearms, Their Parts and Components and Ammunition, supplementing the United Nations Convention against Transnational Organized Crime defines a firearm as: "any portable barrelled weapon that expels, is designed to expel or may be readily converted to expel a shot, bullet or projectile by the action of an explosive ...." Firearms are generally deemed a subset of the larger category of "small arms and light weapons," which also includes armaments such as heavy machine guns and grenades. "Firearms" include both handguns (such as pistols and revolvers), as well as long arms (such as rifles, shotguns, and assault rifles). "Craft weapons," produced by amateurs or artisans, are especially important in the developing world and may also be included.

Under the Protocol, "illicit trafficking" is defined as "the import, export, acquisition, sale, delivery, movement or transfer of firearms ... from or across the territory of one State Party to that of another State Party if any one of the States Parties concerned does not authorize it ...." In practice, firearms trafficking is similar in nature to the trafficking of any other ostensibly licit good. Although clandestine crossborder movement does occur, it is often easier to ship the weapons though regular commercial channels, relying on false or fraudulently acquired paperwork and corrupt officials to ensure passage. To get to their final users, a combination of licit shipping and clandestine movement may be required. But, in theory, the "organized crime group" responsible for the trafficking could be as small as one well-placed broker and his conspirators on the receiving end. The rest of the people in the trafficking chain may be comporting themselves entirely within the ambit of the law.

During the Cold War, much of the politically oriented firearms trafficking was conducted by agents of national governments, as antagonists armed their proxies in conflicts around the world. Following the collapse of the Soviet Union, a large number of surplus weapons became available for purchase. While nations continue to use firearms supply for geostrategic purposes, since the 1990s many of the actors have been profit-motivated criminals. However, as many commentators have noted, with the global proliferation of democracy, the number of international conflicts and civil wars has dropped dramatically since the mid-1990s. In short, there appears to have been a drop in demand for illicit military-grade firearms.

Global trends in the criminal acquisition and use of firearms are more difficult to discern. Some prominent countries have seen dramatic reductions in the amount of firearm homicides in recent years, including Colombia, South Africa, and the United States. Others have apparently seen firearms violence levels rise, including the northern triangle of Central America, parts of the Caribbean, and Venezuela. But firearms were already widely available in most of the areas affected by criminal violence, so there has been little apparent increase in demand.

WHY SOME AREAS ARE VULNERABLE TO GUN TRAFFICKING

While overall firearms trafficking may be in decline, the existence of large stockpiles of both military and civilian weapons pose a major source of vulnerability to future trafficking. Destruction of surplus arms is, therefore, both a form of crime prevention and conflict amelioration. Defining "surplus" is controversial, however, and even getting accurate information on firearms holdings can be difficult.

To get a sense of where the stockpiles are most acute in terms of military weapons, estimates of the size of the largest firearms arsenals in the world can be compared to the size of the active military in each country. Where there are many more weapons than there are soldiers to use them, there could be a vulnerability to firearms trafficking. This analysis leaves out reserve personnel. In some countries, reserves actively drill, while in others they exist only on paper. Theoretical reserves can be used to justify firearms surpluses.

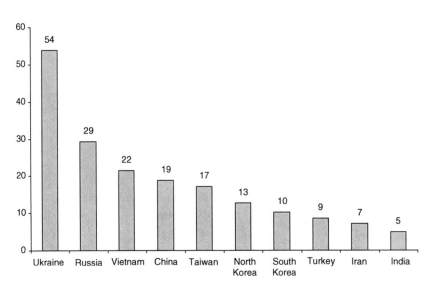

Figure 17.1. Firearms per active duty soldier, top ten largest arsenals.
Source: Elaborated from data from Small Arms Survey and International Institute for Strategic Studies yearbooks.

The Ukraine represents a country that has been plagued by weapons surpluses, including decaying munitions stocks that have accidentally detonated on more than one occasion (see Figure 17.1). The country was allegedly a source of weapons for a number of notorious international firearms traffickers in the past, such as Victor Bout and Leonid Minin. In a transitional economy, there is considerable pressure to realize value for these assets, and recent licit sales to countries like Kenya and Chad appear to have been fed into conflict zones.

When it comes to evaluating crime, however, civilian handgun holdings are more relevant. Small Arms Survey has also made estimates of the number of registered and unregistered civilian firearms in countries around the world. In these estimates, the United States appears to be the clear leader in terms of the number of weapons per capita. One quarter of U.S. citizens own a firearm, and many gun owners own several firearms (See Figure 17.2).

For obvious reasons, criminals in the United States avoid using weapons registered in their names. Research among convicts in the United States shows that some purchased their weapon directly from a licensed dealer, but most acquired it through social networks or from criminal sources. There is a large market in stolen firearms in the U.S.: the FBI received an

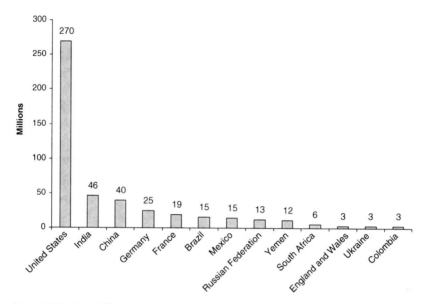

Figure 17.2. Total civilian firearms holdings, selected countries.
Source: Small Arms Survey 2007.

average of over 274,000 reports of stolen firearms per year between 1985 and 1994, most of which were handguns. This represents a large pool of firearms that can be used by criminals without fear of ownership traces. But transnational firearms traffickers may be less concerned about ownership traces, which is why straw purchases seem prevalent in the sourcing of weapons for Mexico's drug wars.

SUMMARY

- As a durable good, firearms do not need to be trafficked in the continuous way consumable contraband, such as drugs, must.
- There are two major sources of demand: political (e.g., insurgents, sanctioned states) and criminal.
- Political demand tends to favor military weapons; criminal demand tends to favor handguns.
- Both sources of demand can often be met without the need for illicit international trafficking.
- As a result, transnational arms trafficking should be regarded as exceptional, and not as a mainstay, of organized crime.

WEB SITES

Small Arms Survey: www.smallarmssurvey.org
Norwegian Initiative on Small Arms Transfers: www.prio.no/nisat
Stockholm International Peace Research Institute: www.sipri.org
Saferworld: www.saferworld.org.uk
Federation of American Scientists Arms Sales Monitoring Project:
www.fas.org/programs/ssp/asmp/index.html

ABOUT THE AUTHOR

Ted Leggett is the research officer in the Studies and Threat Assessment Section of
the United Nations Office on Drugs and Crime in Vienna, where he has been the
author of a series of regional crime assessments. Before joining UNODC, Ted spent
nine years doing field research on crime in Africa, first at the School of Development
Studies at the University of Natal in Durban, and then at the Institute for Security
Studies in Pretoria. His most recent publications concern transnational trafficking
in West Africa, and he is presently working on a global transnational organized
crime threat assessment.

18 Trafficking Antiquities

Simon Mackenzie

INTRODUCTION

Antiquities are old objects of cultural heritage. They can be very valuable, and are often found in museums or private collections. There is still much cultural heritage buried under the ground around the world, or otherwise *in situ* as part of a temple or other heritage structure like a church. Items can be illegally removed from temples or gravesites in one country (the source country) and trafficked internationally for sale in another (the market country). Source countries for antiquities tend to be developing countries, whereas market countries are richer, developed nations. In other words, looted antiquities tend to move from the poor countries where they are found to the rich countries where the buyers are (Mackenzie, 2005; Polk, 2000). Many countries suffer this kind of looting. The most high profile cases of looting have been in countries such as Egypt, Turkey, Greece, China, and in South American countries such as Peru and some South-East Asian countries such as Cambodia and Thailand. Antiquities looting can destroy the archaeological context in which objects are found, diminishing our capacity to record knowledge about past civilizations. Looting and trafficking can also harm the objects themselves, and this is sometimes deliberate, such as when objects are cut or broken into pieces for ease of transport.

MEASUREMENT PROBLEMS

The trafficking of antiquities typically involves clandestine excavation or theft, smuggling in transit, and either private sale or mixing with objects in the legitimate market. It is therefore difficult to arrive at reliable estimates of the size of the illicit market. We do, however, have continuing evidence of sometimes widespread looting in source countries (Brodie, Doole, & Renfrew, 2001; Coggins, 1969), and case studies of specific types of objects have suggested that very high proportions of them have been looted (Gill & Chippindale, 1993). There are recent examples of researchers attempting to develop innovative methods to achieve greater accuracy in estimating the size of the problem, such as by using auction catalogues or import and export records. Conventional crime statistics are generally not revealing in relation to this type of offence. Recording practices for crimes against antiquities vary across jurisdictions, and often these crimes are recorded only in the category of thefts, along with all other such property violations, with some specificity in relation to the way the theft was committed (e.g. "theft by housebreaking" or "robbery") but not in respect of the type of object stolen.

PROVENANCE AND PROVENIENCE

In order to understand how the illicit market in antiquities functions, one must understand two terms. "Provenance" refers to the history of ownership of an object – so where a buyer asks "what is the provenance?" in relation to an ancient artifact or other work of art, they want to know who owned the object previously, for as far back as this is known. "Provenience" is the information about an object's "findspot" – in the case of an archaeological object, provenience refers to the place where it was excavated, by whom, and in what circumstances. Confusingly, buyers in the market tend only to use the word provenance; provenience remains a term used mostly by scholars. So when a buyer of antiquities asks "what's the provenance?" they might be asking about the findspot or about previous owners. Obviously, whether an object has had a prior owner is not always relevant to the question of whether it has been looted. Further, there are different degrees of specificity within the idea of provenance, and information may range from a specific collector's name to a vague reference to prior ownership by, for example, "the collection of a Belgian gentleman." Often, therefore, provenance can obscure an object's history, rather than help to trace its past. There is no accepted international approach to standards of proof in provenance, such as by way of certificates or object passports.

HOW DOES THE INTERNATIONAL MARKET IN ILLICIT ANTIQUITIES FUNCTION?

There are two streams of transnational commodity flow that constitute the illicit market in antiquities. The first stream is made up of artifacts which have been looted but which enter the publicly-visible chain of supply, in the end being sold through shops or auction houses. These antiquities are "laundered" in the sense that once they have managed to enter the apparently legitimate chain of supply, each public sale gives them more of a provenance and provides a point of reference for future buyers to look to in determining whether they are licit objects. Buyers may well suspect that the objects have a dubious past, but they tend to be happy with the formalities of having confirmed an object's provenance; they are interested in protection from legal repercussions rather than from actually having bought looted cultural heritage.

The same is true of export documentation. Some places function as transit ports for art and antiquities. Hong Kong, for example, is a transit port for material illegally coming out of the Far East. In China, as with most source countries, it is generally illegal to dig or export antiquities. However, they are smuggled out to Hong Kong, and then exported to a market nation such as the US or UK, arriving with valid export documents from Hong Kong. Unless a customs officer in the market country has the expertise required to identify them as recently looted from China, and is prepared to seize them on this basis, they will proceed past the customs barrier. They have then entered the legitimate chain of supply with documents to suggest they have been legitimately exported. Educated buyers will know this is a sham, as Hong Kong is not a major source of antiquities other than those in transit.

The second stream of antiquities is what has come to be called "the invisible market." This is constituted by off-the-record or nonpublic sales between individuals, and, as the name suggests, it is very hard to research. Therefore, we have little knowledge of the size or importance of the invisible market, although it is widely believed that a high number of illicit transactions are conducted in this market.

THE LEGAL AND POLICY CONTEXT: HOW THE PROBLEM IS ADDRESSED

International Treaties

Two main treaties provide the framework for international approaches to regulation in the antiquities market: the UNESCO Convention on the Means of Prohibiting and Preventing the Illicit Import, Export and Transfer of Ownership of Cultural Property of 1970 and the UNIDROIT Convention on Stolen or Illegally Exported Cultural Objects of 1995. Of these, the UNIDROIT Convention provides the more stringent guidelines in relation to obligations on buyers of antiquities and rules for the return of looted objects to their rightful owners. Unfortunately only a small fraction of the number of countries that have signed up to the UNESCO Convention have chosen to take on the obligations in the UNIDROIT Convention. None of the major market countries have done so, which currently neutralizes much of the practical value of the 1995 Convention.

Domestic Laws

As well as restricting export, most source countries have passed laws that attempt to combat the problem of looting through vesting ownership in undiscovered antiquities in the state. A finder of an antiquity who keeps it will therefore be guilty of a theft; this is intended to discourage those who deliberately dig to look for objects. It also helps in claims for repatriation of looted artifacts once they have traveled to market countries, and in charging dealers in market countries with crimes involving the handling stolen goods.

Nonlegal Prevention Measures

Registers of stolen objects exist, which allow buyers to check whether what they are being offered has not been stolen. The main ones are the Art Loss Register, and the Interpol database of stolen works of art. Objects will only be listed on these databases, however, if they are known by their owners to have been stolen (and even then the owner might not choose to list the object). Antiquities which are illicitly excavated and which were unknown prior to their finding will not appear on a stolen art database. Other practical prevention measures include improving security at archaeological sites (although it is usually far too costly to effectively guard such sites), and education campaigns aimed at tourists and buyers in market countries (see O'Keefe, 1997 for a review of commonly discussed crime prevention and reduction measures in this field).

FACTORS WHICH FACILITATE ANTIQUITIES TRAFFICKING

Trade Culture

Most antiquities dealers are willing to buy looted antiquities, although as with other stolen goods markets, they use techniques of neutralization to play down their role in creating a market for criminal activity (Mackenzie, 2005). They think, for example, that people would loot antiquities whether or not there are willing buyers, and that they are saving antiquities, preserving them for future generations to enjoy. Other dealers simply do not ask where the objects they buy have come from. This allows them to avoid criminal prosecution, as most laws relating to handling stolen goods require proof of some level of knowledge of wrongdoing.

There are also dealers who are closer to our conventional understanding of criminals. In 2002, prominent New York dealer Fred Schultz was sentenced to thirty-three months in federal prison, with a fine of US$50,000, for his part in a scam to disguise his sale of antiquities looted from Egypt by manufacturing fake provenance for them. In 2009, an appellate court in Italy upheld the conviction of the infamous antiquities trafficker Giacomo Medici who was sentenced to eight years in prison and received a Euro 10 million fine for conspiracy to traffic in antiquities. In 1995, Medici's storage warehouse in Switzerland had been raided by police, revealing looted Italian artifacts and other evidence that led to successful claims for repatriation of objects from major museums worldwide, which had bought some of the looted objects. Medici was also in possession of Polaroid photos of objects *in situ*, suggesting that he would organize the looting of these artifacts on demand once interest was expressed by a buyer.

Limitation Periods

Antiquities that have been in circulation for some time will invariably have been "legitimized" through the operation of statutes of limitation that bar legal action against unchallenged owners of property after a number of years. The timescales for these differ depending on jurisdiction. Often a short timescale (three to five years is usual) is available for a "good faith" buyer. The formal approaches to checking provenance mentioned above are therefore important, as they can support an argument that a purchase was in good faith, and if the object was in fact stolen then only a few years later the buyer will own it, or (depending on the local rules) the original owner will be time-barred from reclaiming it even if the law does not consider the buyer the owner.

Corruption

Antiquities trafficking is made easier by corrupt officials. Sometimes these officials have a direct financial interest in the practice, such as where the military is involved in looting (Thosarat, 2001). Sometimes it is simply customs agents who are bribed so as to avoid inspection of a shipment. Corruption is tied to the relative poverty experienced in many of the countries that are the major sources of antiquities, but there have also been scandals in the antiquities market that show that unethical practice is not limited to officials in source countries. Perhaps the most famous of these scandals was revealed by the journalist Peter Watson, who showed that professionals in a major international auction house were knowingly dealing in looted cultural objects (Watson, 1997).

SUMMARY AND CONCLUSIONS

We can conclude by summarizing the main characteristics of the transnational crime problem of looted and smuggled cultural heritage as follows.

- A crime problem in poorer source countries that provides an income for local populations.
- Ineffective enforcement of local laws in source countries due to resource issues in policing and other public service jobs, and corruption.
- A ready market for looted objects in richer countries providing a driver for the international transportation of looted objects.
- Difficulty in telling illicit objects apart from licit ones once they are mixed together in the chain of supply – compounded by buyers' reluctance to ask too many searching questions about provenance.
- A lackluster law enforcement and policy response to the issue in market countries, since the main harm is perceived to be done to foreign states, and dealers form a reasonably powerful trade lobby group.
- Techniques of neutralization and other rationalizations used by dealers and collectors in the market to justify their continuing participation in a destructive activity.
- High-level international treaties that receive much lip service in international policy circles but do not effectively regulate the problem at hand.
- Criminal laws in market countries that result in the occasional, and quite spectacular, conviction of a prominent art world figure, but again, do not provide much in the way of day-to-day regulation of the market.
- Professional associations who promulgate codes of ethics for their members – but with no real penalties for failing to abide by these codes.

REFERENCES

Brodie, N., J. Doole, & C. Renfrew (Eds.). (2001). *Trade in Illicit Antiquities: The Destruction of the World's Archaeological Heritage*. Cambridge: McDonald Institute for Archaeological Research.

Coggins, C. (1969). Illicit Traffic of Pre-Columbian Antiquities. *Art Journal, Fall*, 94–98.

Gill, D. J. W., & C. Chippindale. (1993). Material and Intellectual Consequences of Esteem for Cycladic Figures. *American Journal of Archaeology*, 97(3), 602–73.

Mackenzie, S. (2005). *Going, Going, Gone: Regulating the Market in Illicit Antiquities*. Leicester: Institute of Art and Law.

O'Keefe, P. J. (1997). *Trade in Antiquities: Reducing Destruction and Theft*. London: Archetype.

Polk, K. (2000). The Antiquities Trade Viewed as a Criminal Market. *Hong Kong Lawyer, September*, 82–92.

Thosarat, R. (2001). The Destruction of the Cultural Heritage of Thailand and Cambodia. In N. Brodie, J. Doole & C. Renfrew (Eds.), *Trade in Illicit Antiquities: The Destruction of the World's Archaeological Heritage*. Cambridge: McDonald Institute for Archaeological Research.

Watson, P. (1997). *Sotheby's: The Inside Story*. London: Bloomsbury.

ABOUT THE AUTHOR

Simon Mackenzie is reader in criminology at the Scottish Centre for Crime and Justice Research, University of Glasgow. Dr. Mackenzie's main research interests are in international criminal markets, white-collar crime, organized crime, and policing. He has published two books on antiquities trafficking and has worked with the UN on crime prevention in this field.

19 The Illegal Cigarette Trade

Klaus von Lampe

INTRODUCTION

The smuggling and illegal distribution of cigarettes is a global phenomenon in a dual sense. It can be observed in some form or other on every continent, and there are some schemes that span the globe, connecting distant places such as a clandestine factory in China producing counterfeit cigarettes with a street corner in London where these cigarettes are eventually sold to consumers.

Cigarettes are essentially a legal good. What makes the trade in cigarettes illegal is the evasion of excise and customs duties. Excise duties are taxes levied on certain goods produced or sold within the country. Customs duties are charged on goods imported from another country. Cigarettes are among the highest taxed commodities and provide a significant source of revenue for governments. While the level of taxation varies across jurisdictions, in many countries taxes account for as much as 70 to 80 percent of the price smokers have to pay for a pack at a legal retail outlet store. Through a number of different schemes, suppliers and customers circumvent the taxation of cigarettes. As a result, cigarettes are being made available at a cost below legal retail prices, providing both lucrative profits for suppliers and significant savings for consumers, while causing substantial losses of revenue to governments, estimated at around forty billion USD globally in 2007, and at the same time undermining public health policies that aim to discourage smokers through high tobacco taxation (Joossens et al., 2009).

The illegal cigarette trade shows similarities but also some notable differences to other illegal markets. Illegal markets are characterized by the exchange of goods or services in violation of the law. Some goods are illegal under all circumstances, such as child pornography, some goods are illegal when they are handled without official permission or license, such as arms and pharmaceutical drugs, and some goods, such as cigarettes and gasoline, are illegal when duties are not paid. The peculiarity of the latter category is that, parallel to the black market, the same commodity is widely available through legal channels. In most countries, the legal market for cigarettes is much larger than the illegal market. It has been estimated that the global illicit cigarette trade accounted for 11.6 percent (or 657 billion cigarettes) of all cigarettes sold worldwide in 2007 (Joossens et al., 2009). In some countries like Libya and Guinea-Bissau, however, allegedly most (around 80 percent) of the cigarettes are sold illegally (United Nations Office on Drugs and Crime, 2009). One consequence of the parallel existence of legal and illegal market seems to be that there is no stigma of illegality attached to the commodity as such and perhaps for that reason the cigarette black market has a higher chance of social acceptance than other illegal markets. Another characteristic of the cigarette black market is the uniformity of the commodity. While there are special kinds of cigarettes deviating from the norm, most cigarettes are similar in shape, size, consistency, and weight, and they are usually packed in packs of twenty sticks and cartons of ten packs (two hundred sticks). This means that the handling of cigarettes poses the same challenges for illegal traders irrespective of place and time. Yet, there are significant variations in the manifestation of the cigarette black market internationally and nationally, and there are, as indicated, differences in the schemes used for procurement and distribution of illegal cigarettes that deserve closer examination.

THE ANATOMY OF THE ILLEGAL CIGARETTE TRADE

The term "illegal cigarette trade" as understood here is broader than the often-used term "cigarette smuggling" and encompasses three levels: the procurement level, an intermediate level where cigarettes are moved in the direction of the consumer, and the level of retail distribution.

Procurement Schemes

Cigarettes are procured for distribution on the black market in different ways, with different degrees of illegality and different levels of complicity of those involved. Three main schemes can be distinguished: bootlegging, large-scale smuggling, and counterfeiting.

Bootlegging

Bootlegging involves the purchase of cigarettes in low-tax countries for resale in high-tax countries, taking advantage of crossborder differentials in legal retail prices. In these cases taxes on cigarettes are paid, though not in the country of consumption (see, e.g., Hornsby & Hobbs, 2007).

Large-Scale Smuggling

Large-scale smuggling takes advantage of the temporary suspension of customs duties, excise, and other taxes on goods destined for export to a third country. Cigarettes destined for markets abroad are not subject to taxation in the country of origin, or any transit country along the way for that matter, as long as certain procedures for storage and transport are followed. These untaxed cigarettes either never leave the country and are directly diverted to the black market, or, far more commonly, they are properly exported and disappear on the black market abroad or are illegally reimported (see, e.g., Joossens & Raw, 2008).

Counterfeiting

While in cases of both bootlegging and large-scale smuggling, cigarettes are procured from originally legitimate sources, counterfeiting involves the production of fake brand cigarettes, including packaging and, on occasion, fiscal marks made by unauthorized manufacturers. In addition to tax evasion, the trade in counterfeit cigarettes constitutes a violation of brand property rights. Most counterfeit cigarettes are said to be produced in illegal factories and tend to differ in every respect from their legal counterparts, including tobacco, paper, filter tips, and packaging. China, also the largest manufacturer of legal cigarettes, is believed to be the main source of counterfeit cigarettes (Shen, Antonopoulos, & von Lampe, 2010).

Other Sources of Black Market Cigarettes

Since 2004, a new phenomenon has begun to shape the cigarette black markets across Europe: cigarettes legally manufactured in Kaliningrad, Russia, and other locations in Eastern Europe under the brand name "Jin Ling." These cigarettes appear to be readily available to smugglers and, indeed, appear to be primarily distributed through black market channels (Candea et al., 2008).

Another facet of the cigarette black market that should not be entirely ignored, although it will probably never reach the significance of the previously described schemes, is the selling of stolen cigarettes.

Smuggling and Wholesale Distribution Schemes

The second major element of the illegal cigarette trade, following the initial procurement of cigarettes for the black market, comprises the smuggling of cigarettes, or their clandestine transport across borders without paying taxes and customs duties. However, the border crossing is only a small part of the overall handling of cigarettes between procurement and retail selling. In fact, there are schemes where the crossing of international borders is not required and all illicit activities take place within one country. In the United States, for example, cigarettes are brought from states with low taxes to states with high taxes. Another pattern pertains to cigarettes destined for export. These untaxed cigarettes may be diverted to the black market without ever leaving the country.

The cigarettes that are procured for illegal distribution may go through similar and, at times, identical channels on the lower levels of the black market, as is true for the illegal crossborder transport of cigarettes. Smuggling modes, it seems, vary not so much according to the source of the cigarettes but rather with the size of the consignments that are being moved. Large loads of about one million sticks and more are typically transported while concealed in or behind legal goods under the guise of legal crossborder commerce.

The smuggling of smaller loads is typically embedded in the flow of noncommercial crossborder traffic, although smuggling across unregulated land and sea borders has also been reported. Common methods include the use of hidden compartments in cars and vans, for example, in the form of false bottoms or modified gas tanks. Another method, connected especially to the illicit sale of cigarettes over the Internet, is the use of parcel post services.

Cigarettes may be passed on directly to consumers. However, in most cases there seems to be a separate pattern of activities linking procurement and retail distribution. On this intermediate level cigarettes may be stored, reconfigured, and typically broken up into a number of smaller consignments which are then passed on to buyers positioned further down in the distribution chain.

RETAIL DISTRIBUTION SCHEMES

A variety of patterns have also emerged by which contraband cigarettes are sold to consumers. These patterns can be grouped into three broad categories by the type of setting: public places, semipublic places, and private settings.

At public places like street corners or flea markets, the opportunity to purchase illegal cigarettes is advertised by vendors to passers-by. In semi-public places like bars and kiosks, the illegal cigarettes can be purchased under the counter as an alternative to legal cigarettes. Sometimes, consumers are defrauded when counterfeit (or stolen) cigarettes are sold as legitimate merchandise. Finally, illegal cigarettes may be passed on to consumers in private settings through social network relations.

Interestingly, the dominant distribution scheme varies geographically within and across countries. One striking example is Germany where street vending of illegal cigarettes has been widespread in the Eastern parts of the country but virtually absent elsewhere (von Lampe, 2006).

WHO IS INVOLVED IN THE ILLEGAL CIGARETTE TRADE?

Criminal Groups and Terrorist Groups

One of the reasons why the illegal cigarette trade provides an interesting object of study is the diversity of the players involved in illicit activities. Three aspects have received particular attention: the level of involvement of criminal groups, and the involvement of terrorist groups, and the complicity of the tobacco industry. It has often been alleged that the illegal cigarette trade is the domain of well-organized criminal groups who have previously been active in other areas of crime like drug trafficking. However, research in Europe has found that the illegal cigarette trade is primarily run not by known criminals but by individuals without a previous criminal record (see, Van Duyne, 2003) . Likewise, the involvement of terrorist groups who trade in illegal cigarettes to raise funds (see Shelley & Melzer, 2008) seems to be the exception rather than the rule.

The Tobacco Industry

The involvement of tobacco manufacturers in the illegal cigarette trade appears to have been a more common occurrence in the past. There are several well-documented cases of complicity between major tobacco companies and cigarette smugglers (e.g., Joossens & Raw, 2008). In other cases, tobacco companies have at least turned a blind eye to the fact that their cigarettes are being funneled into illicit channels, typically through small countries with no significant domestic cigarette market. More recently, however, tobacco companies, under pressure from governments, have significantly reduced or entirely ceased their exports to such countries. This has apparently resulted in a sharp decline in the availability of major brands on the black market (Jossens & Raw, 2008). In fact, the emergence of counterfeit cigarettes and the brand "Jin Ling" may well be connected to stricter sales policies adopted by the large tobacco companies in the early 2000s.

COUNTERMEASURES

There is a heated debate over the best approaches to tackle the illegal trade in cigarettes. While antismoking lobbyists place the major blame on the tobacco industry, the tobacco industry itself argues that the high taxation of tobacco products more or less automatically creates a black market. From the available evidence it seems that, although there would not be an illegal cigarette trade without excise and customs duties, high taxes do not automatically lead to the emergence of a black market of significant size. Black markets for cigarettes are not necessarily most prevalent in high-tax countries and least prevalent in low-tax countries (Joossens & Raw, 2002: 5–6). Likewise, there are substantial regional variations in black market prevalence within particular countries despite uniform tax rates nationwide (von Lampe, 2006). It appears to be at least as important that supply of and demand for untaxed cigarettes are linked up in an efficient way and that illegal transactions can take place in a relatively nonhostile environment. This, in turn, depends on the strength or weakness of law enforcement and civil society in a community. In this context it should be noted that through a number of countermeasures, mirroring efforts against drug trafficking, the illegal cigarette trade has become more risky in recent years. Most notably, through the introduction of stationary and mobile scanners and the use of tobacco sniffing dogs the control of international cargo has been made substantially more effective.

The illegal cigarette trade is essentially a form of tax evasion. Different schemes have developed to circumvent taxation to supply cigarettes to consumers below legal retail prices. Cigarettes are either diverted from legal channels, or they are produced specifically for distribution on the black market.

REFERENCES

Candea, S., D. Campbell, V. Lavrov, & R. Shleynov, (2008, October 19). *Made to Be Smuggled: Russian Contraband Cigarettes 'Flooding' EU*. The Center for Public Integrity. Retrieved February 25, 2009, from www.publicintegrity.org/investigations/tobacco/articles/entry/763

Duyne, P. C. van (2003). Organizing Cigarette Smuggling and Policy Making Ending Up in Smoke. *Crime, Law and Social Change*, 39, 285–317.

Hornsby, R. & D. Hobbs (2007). A Zone of Ambiguity: The Political Economy of Cigarette Bootlegging. *British Journal of Criminology*, 47, 551–71.

Joossens, L., Merriman, D., Ross, H., & Raw, M. (2009). *How Eliminating the Global Illicit Cigarette Trade Would Increase Tax Revenue and Save Lives.* Paris: International Union against Tuberculosis and Lung Disease. Retrieved August 30, 2009, from http://www.fctc.org/dmdocuments/INB3_report_illicit_trade_save_revenue_lives.pdf

Joossens, L. & M. Raw (2002). *Turning Off the Tap: An Update on Cigarette Smuggling in the UK and Sweden, with Recommendations to Control Smuggling.* London: Cancer Research UK.

  (2008). Progress in Combating Cigarette Smuggling: Controlling the Supply Chain. *Tobacco Control*, 17, 399–404.

Shelley, L. & S. Melzer (2008). The Nexus of Organized Crime and Terrorism: Two Case Studies in Cigarette Smuggling. *The International Journal of Comparative and Applied Criminal Justice*, 32, 43–63.

Shen, A., G. Antonopoulos, & K. von Lampe (2010). "The Dragon Breathes Smoke": Cigarette Counterfeiting in the People's Republic of China, *British Journal of Criminology*, 50, 239–258.

United Nations Office on Drugs and Crime. (2009, July). *Transnational Trafficking and the Rule of Law in West Africa: A Threat Assessment.* Vienna: UNODC. Retrieved August 28, 2009, from www.unodc.org/documents/data-and-analysis/Studies/West_Africa_Report_2009.pdf

von Lampe, K. (2006). The Cigarette Black Market in Germany and in the United Kingdom. *Journal of Financial Crime*, 13, 235–54.

WEB SITES

Framework Convention Alliance (for a Framework Convention on Tobacco Control): www.ftct.org

Action on Smoking and Health (Anti-smoking NGO): www.ash.org

The Center for Public Integrity (Investigative Journalists on the "Tobacco Underground"): www.publicintegrity.org

Tobacco Control (Journal): http://tobaccocontrol.bmj.com

Philip Morris International (tobacco manufacturer): www.philipmorrisinternational.com

ABOUT THE AUTHOR

Klaus von Lampe is an assistant professor at John Jay College of Criminal Justice, New York. He has been studying the illegal cigarette trade for more than ten years. His other research interests include drug trafficking, underworld power structures, and strategic crime analysis. Dr. von Lampe is the author, co-author, and co-editor of numerous publications on organized and international crime.

20 Cybercrime

Richard Lovely

Cybercrimes are criminal offenses that involve or occur in cyberspace, the ethereal region created when computers and people connect over electronic networks that gspan the world. Cybercrime's emergence as an international crime and justice problem is a vexing downside to the blending of digital communications technology, especially the Internet, into everyday life and global commerce.

THE NATURE OF CYBERCRIME

Anyone can commit a crime by using the Internet for such offenses as cyberstalking, auction fraud, dating Web site scams, or child pornography. But cybercrime is often seen as the special province of 'hackers' who create and use clever programs to gain illegal access to software, computers, and networks whenever a new technology emerges. In the 1980s the exploits of hackers were mostly a costly nuisance and hackers were even viewed sympathetically by some (Chiesa, Ducci, & Ciappi, 2008; Duff & Gardiner, 1996). An underground subculture of hackers emerged that treated penetrating computers and networks as sport. Successful hacking techniques were packaged into easy to use programs or scripts. This greatly increased the pool of offenders and the costs of time and money to clean up their mischief. The stakes rose when commerce moved to the Internet and hacking took on financial motivations (Grabosky, 2001).

From the earliest days of the Internet, a shadowy vice industry has provided the usual fare: sex, pornography, illicit drugs, and gambling. In some countries doing and offering such things online is a crime, but in others it is not. Likewise, in some countries it is legal for Web sites to use advanced file sharing technology to create virtual flea markets or swap meets that make it easy for ordinary Web users to find and exchange digital contraband. The industries who produce software, music, and movies call this stealing, as do the laws of most countries, but there is overt cultural and legal ambivalence about handcuffing people for taking advantage of state-of-the-art and easily available technology. As well, some Web sites show how to collect and use the products of hackers, such as how to harvest e-mail addresses and send out spam, a practice that cybercrime treaties compel countries to make illegal. When one country outlaws one practice or another, the Web sites move to another where it is legal. Some countries, such as Russia, are suspected of recognizing the economic benefits of offering safe harbor to Web sites that are illegal elsewhere.

The enormous amount of junk e-mail or "spam" sent every day has become a burden on the networks that make up the Internet. Spam, however, is not just a nuisance but also a tool to attract victims. While some spammers may be after a retail sale from a user who opens an e-mail, the goal actually may be covert access to the user's computer in order to install malicious software or "malware." These programs may be able to perform various nefarious tasks such as stealing passwords, logging keystrokes, snooping around files, or ID-theft. As spam filters made it less effective to lure victims through e-mail, the search for victims went elsewhere, such as using social networking sites like MySpace, Facebook, and Twitter. A Facebook user is sent a fake message from a "friend" that invites her to watch a video, which will lead to installing a virus or worm on her computer. Cybercrime depends as much on "social engineering" or the manipulation of users as technically defeating software and hardware.

The most insidious use of malware is to hook a personal computer into a "botnet," a remotely controlled network that can link many, even millions, of computers together to work on a common task. These botnets were intended for useful projects but cybercriminals quickly recognized the profit potential in using other people's computers to run their own networks without cost or the knowledge of the computer users. Illegal botnets are used to broadcast spam, distribute malware, and carry out attacks on given Web sites by sending so many requests for service that host servers crash. Ironically, a user whose computer works as part of a botnet may never know it or experience any harm.

Perhaps the most sophisticated cyber offenses are automated attacks on Internet banking. Malware slipped into a computer can detect and transmit a user's personal banking information in order to facilitate raiding of the user's bank account. Standard encryption safeguards are bypassed because the program is on the user's computer. These programs can even be smart enough to limit the amount withdrawn so as to delay triggering notice as long as possible. The withdrawn funds are sent to the accounts of "mules" who then transfer the money to the cybercrime enterprise running the botnet. The amazing thing about these automated schemes is an offender can be on any continent and never know or care from whom or where the money that appears in his or her own account came.

THE EXTENT OF CYBERCRIME

Cybercrimes are not listed separately in official crime reports but are included in relevant offense categories. However, there are various special independent efforts by government agencies and corporations to keep track of cybercrime. In the U.S., the Internet Crime Complaint Center (IC3) receives complaints from citizens but they represent only a fraction of all cybercrimes. Computer security firms constantly monitor the Internet to keep track of botnets, viruses, worms, and denial-of-service attacks on Web sites. The numbers from these various reports are more useful to assess trends than actual rates of cybercrime. Everywhere, indications are that cybercrime is growing apace with the growth of the Internet throughout the world.

Business interest groups for producers of movies, software, and music also attempt to measure the extent to which their industries are victimized worldwide from stolen or "pirated" intellectual property. The Business Software Alliance found that 41 percent of all commercial software used in the world in 2007 is pirated with rates reaching 95 percent in Georgia and 80 percent in China. The Motion Picture Association estimates that in 2005 losses from movie piracy by movie studios were $6.1 billion dollars with 40 percent of that due to Internet downloads. Movie piracy rates in China were estimated at 90 percent and 79 percent in Russia. An eight nation survey in 2004 suggested a quarter of all Internet users had downloaded movies without paying for them and 70 percent of respondents said they did not think movie piracy was a problem, which suggests digital piracy will continue.

Other businesses suffer great losses and inefficiency due to penetrations of their computer systems. Despite laws to require safeguards, there are frequent incidents of thefts of databases containing sensitive trade information or customer or client data, sometimes putting millions of people at risk of ID-theft. Regular findings from an annual FBI cybercrime survey show the most expensive security incidents suffered by corporations are from financial fraud and dealing with computers controlled by "bots" (automated malicious software). About half of corporations report they are hit by a computer virus in a given year. But the survey shows that insiders are almost as great a threat as cyber attacks from outside the firm. This is a particularly difficult problem for organizations and suggests how difficult cybercrime is to prevent.

Fraud has become a persistent problem of online commerce because of the remote link between the seller and buyer. Many Internet businesses provide no physical address on their Web site. As successful Internet-based business models, such as eBay, have become global, so has the potential to exploit them with untoward intentions. It turns out that much of the merchandise and software sold through eBay is counterfeit. In France, eBay was held liable for hosting these crimes but the U.S. courts held it was not, that the offense lies with the seller of the counterfeit goods and not the Internet host.

Botnets are considered threatening enough to have been on the agenda of leaders of the world at the 2007 World Economic Forum in Davos. Some estimates are that a quarter of all computers that connect to the Internet are part of a botnet, about 250 million computers in 2009. The scale of things to come is boggling. With the breathtaking pace of technological change, the implications of adding another billion more Internet users, just from China and India, on the future of global cybercrime cannot be known.

THE CAUSES OF CYBERCRIME

Criminologists have been challenged to provide explanations of the phenomenon of cybercrime. The most convincing explanation for early hacking behavior may be to look to the behavior itself to appreciate its seductive, even addictive, appeal to youthful offenders (Taylor, 1999). While there are still cyber offenders who fit that model, it is clear that much cybercrime has become financially motivated.

Psychological models have promise for understanding individual cyber offenders, especially pedophiles or those whose behavior reflects addiction. But while social, economic, and personal background factors may affect cybercrime rates just as they do general crime rates, it may be that the very nature of the Internet, namely such characteristics as the sense of anonymity, speed, stealth, safety, and access to unlimited numbers of potential victims or mischief, makes it hard for offenders to resist the temptations of cybercrime (Newman & Clarke, 2003).

At the social level, given the virtual nature of cyber communities, theories that focus on how normative structures affect deviance are fertile explanations of some types of cybercrime. For example, digital piracy rates around the world follow patterns consistent with sociological strain theory as economic globalization has set the stage for predictable widespread pirating of intellectual property. The rub with strain theory is it does not explain the widespread digital piracy within wealthier countries. This behavior is more consistent with the notion that without adequate safeguards people will take advantage of potential illicit gains.

The most ambitious international project to study hackers and their motivations has been the Hackers Profiling Project, a project of the United Nations Interregional Crime and Justice Research Institute, a long-term study that attempts to apply criminal profiling techniques to understanding hacking (Chiesa, Ducci, & Ciappi, 2008). The project has an interesting bias, which is to challenge some of the stereotypes about hackers and to suggest there will be no success in controlling cybercrime unless we understand them.

THE CONTROL OF CYBERCRIME

Although law enforcement agencies handle cybercrimes when probes are necessary, there is a limit to how successful formal social control of cybercrime can be. Effective social control begins with the establishment and enforcement of norms in an informal community context. That traditional social context is lacking in cyberspace. Into this vacuum have stepped various citizen groups that maintain Web sites to combat what they see as undesirable behavior on the Web, such as hate speech or child pornography. These groups may be based anywhere in the world and recruit members worldwide. Some of these civilian groups maintain Web sites to publicize the extent of the problem and to allow reporting of offenses. Other groups have attempted to use "hactivist" techniques to disable child porn or hate sites by using hacking tactics to disrupt the activities of sites to which they object. Of course, in countries that protect freedom of speech these activities themselves may be cybercrimes. Some countries like China are trying to impose online order by controlling access to Web sites and with government mandated filtering software but the controllers' tactics always seem to lag behind the technology and cleverness of users.

Likewise, the recording and software industries have largely taken enforcement of the law into their own hands by suing companies that facilitate file sharing and individual Internet users who illegally download large numbers of files. The first lawsuits were issued by the Recording Industry Association of America (RIAA) in the United States and targeted consumers. In Europe, the International Federation of the Phonographic Industry

(IFPI) has also begun to use lawsuits as a deterrent. These efforts have yielded mixed results and strong opposition. The serious threat of cybercrime to international finance and business has sparked numerous international efforts to study the problem and develop policies, laws, and organizations to respond to the problem but the differences across countries are highly problematic (Koops & Brenner, 2006).

Law enforcement agencies are struggling to gain the technological wherewithal to combat cybercrime. It is becoming common to have specialized police and prosecution units that deal with cybercrime. In India there is even a cybercrime police station in Bangalore. In Europe, Europol, the European Police Office located in The Hague, has created a high tech crime center, and the FBI has created regional digital forensics labs throughout the United States. The transnational nature of cybercrime has prompted more than thirty countries to cooperate in providing immediate response assistance in the investigation of a cybercrime that reaches across borders.

SUMMARY AND CONCLUSION

Cybercrime is a byproduct of the genius of the Internet, which erases the geography between people to create a virtual world in cyberspace. This allows ordinary users to become exposed to the risk of becoming victims of cybercrime by merely Web surfing or tending to e-mail. They also have ready access to a shadowy world of vice many of them would never otherwise visit where they may become victims or offenders. Likewise, the Internet offers financially motivated and technically sophisticated criminals anywhere in the world direct access to an endless supply of potential individual and organizational victims. Investigation of cybercrime requires unprecedented use of technology by law enforcement and transnational cooperation between law enforcement agencies. The contest between criminals who master and use high technology to commit cybercrime and the efforts of social control forces to stop and catch them will be a technological and legal free-for-all.

REFERENCES AND RECOMMENDED READINGS

Chiesa, R., D. Sefania, & C. Silvio (2008). *Profiling Hackers: The Science of Criminal Profiling as Applied to the World of Hacking.* Boca Raton: Auerbach.
Duff, L. & S. Gardiner. (1996). Computer Crime in the Global Village: Strategies for Control and Regulation – In Defence of the Hacker. *International Journal of the Sociology of Law,* 24, 211–28.

Grabosky, P., R. G. Smith, & G. Dempsey. (2001). *Electronic Theft: Unlawful Acquisition in Cyberspace.* Cambridge: Cambridge University Press.

Koops, B. & S. W. Brenner. (Eds.) (2006). *Cybercrime and Jurisdiction: A Global Survey.* The Hague: T.M.C. Asser Press.

Newman, G. & R. V. Clarke. (2003). *Superhighway Robbery: Preventing E-commerce Crime.* Portland: Willan Publishing.

Sofaer, A. & S. E. Goodman. (2001). *The Transnational Dimension of Cyber Crime.* Stanford, CA: Hoover Institution Press.

Taylor, P. (1999). *Hackers: Crime in the Digital Sublime.* London; New York: Routledge.

Wall, D. S. (2007). *Cybercrime: The Transformation of Crime in the Information Age.* Cambridge: Polity.

WEB SITES

Computer Crime and Intellectual Property Section (CCIPS)
of the Criminal Division of the U.S. Department of Justice: www.cybercrime.gov
Computer Crime Research Center: www.crime-research.org
Criminal Justice Resources: CyberCrime: www.lib.msu.edu/harris23/crimjust/cybercri.htm
Center for Democracy and Technology International Issues: Cybercrime: www.cdt.org/international/cybercrime

ABOUT THE AUTHOR

Richard Lovely is director of the graduate Forensic Computing Program at John Jay College of Criminal Justice, The City University of New York, and associate professor of Sociology with a Ph.D. from Yale University. Besides cybercrime, he has done research on serious youth violence, search and seizure, organizational change and innovation, and has developed software for educational research. Prior to his academic career, he was a counterintelligence officer with the U.S. Army and a special agent with the U.S. Secret Service.

21 International Fraud

Michael Levi

INTRODUCTION

In essence, fraud is the obtaining of goods or money by deception. Systematic socioeconomic or organizational status data are available only from research studies rather than from official offender statistics, especially prior to the National Incident–Based Reporting System (Barnett, 2000). However, deception is widespread and can readily be – perhaps even more than theft in practice – committed by the more powerful against the less powerful, as well as by the poor and by professional criminals against those with many assets to lose. Thus, fraud comprises a spectrum of social statuses of offenders and of victims (for a typology of fraud, see Box 1).

Box 1. Types of economic crime

1. Harm government/taxpayer interests
2. Harm *all* corporate as well as social interests: that is, systemic risk frauds that undermine public confidence in the system as a whole; domestic and motor insurance frauds; maritime insurance frauds; payment card and other credit frauds; pyramid selling of money schemes; high-yield investment frauds
3. Harm social and some corporate interests but benefit other "mainly legitimate" ones, such as some cartels, transnational corruption (by companies with business interests in the country paying the bribe)
4. Harm corporate interests but benefit mostly illegitimate ones, such as several forms of Intellectual Property theft – sometimes called "piracy" – especially those using higher quality digital media.

The boundary between fraud, organized crime, and money laundering can be hard to discern. Properly analyzed, money laundering is a subcategory of both fraud and the activities that constitute organized crime, being proceeds of crimes that are saved and perhaps reinvested with its criminal origins concealed (see Hicks, this volume; see Chapter 22; van Duyne & Levi, 2005). Influenced as we are by profound cultural images of the Sicilian Mafia and the Italian-American Mafia that have brought *The Godfather* and *The Sopranos* to our screens, it is difficult not to be seduced by the assumption that this hierarchical, deeply embedded cultural, and family mode of organization is the natural evolution of all serious crime: the general public, criminals, and the police are all subjected to (and sometimes entranced by) these images of power and "threat to society." However, it is dangerous to transplant models derived from the peculiar historical conditions of Italy before the collapse of communism – or even of some North-Eastern U.S. cities – to other countries and regions. As the major scams of the twenty-first century – from Enron to Madoff – demonstrate, fraud and other "white-collar crimes" may be committed as part of a transnational "serious crime community" (Block & Weaver, 2005) who largely outwit the forces of criminal justice control anywhere in the world, but they are capable of functioning unconnected to "organized crime" as commonly conceptualized in intelligence-led policing. (Though gangsters may seek to prey on them as extortionists or as collaborators if they develop sufficient intelligence on the fraudsters' activities.)

What might we mean by international fraud (or international crime generally)? The immediate assumption might be that people in one country are defrauding people in another, but this is only part of the story. One helpful way of thinking about this is by placing fraud within the context of a process map of crime for gain (see Box 2 and Levi, 2007). We may deduce from this that criminal finance, as well as some or all criminal personnel and the "tools of crime," may come from or go to another country at some stage of the planning and aftermath processes, constitute international crime. In the case of fraud, offenders may start with differential access to international resources, but the exploitation of international regulatory and criminal justice asymmetries – for example, different levels of enforcement in the countries in which the fraudsters operate – represents an advantage for the criminal.

We can see from Box 2 one important difference between fraud and most traditional crimes that have victims: At the time when the offence is committed (which, in contrast with other property offenses, may happen over years), the fraudster can be, but does not normally need to be, in the

---

Box 2. The Process of Crime for gain

- Obtain finance
- Find people willing and able to offend (whether specific to the crimes contemplated and/or if already part of a "criminal organization")
- Obtain any tools/data needed to offend
- Neutralize immediate enforcement/operational risks
- Carry out offences in domestic and/or overseas locations with or without physical presence in jurisdiction(s)
- Launder or hide *safely* unspent funds (at home and/or overseas)
- Decide in which country you want to live afterwards, taking into account extradition and proceeds of crime confiscation/civil suit risks

---

same place or even continent as the victims or their property. However, few frauds need to be executed on an international basis, and some fraudsters (like gangsters) have their geographic comfort zones. Fraudsters, like other "organized criminals," may be part of ethnic or national diasporas operating globally, of whom Nigerians are the most prominent, but even here there are problems, for Nigerians have variable family, regional, and religious affiliations and should not be seen as a homogeneous group (Levi, 2008a; Smith, 2008). Since almost all frauds involve some movement across U.S. State lines, or victimize federally insured institutions or the government, they almost all constitute "mail fraud" or "wire fraud," giving rise to Federal jurisdiction within the U.S. However national boundaries – the formal unit for police powers and crime statistics – are poor indicators of travel time and fraud opportunities. For example, it is quicker for a credit card fraudster or telemarketer to fly or drive from New York to Toronto than to do so from New York to Miami or Los Angeles, and that can be important when the rate of fraud upon a stolen or counterfeited card is time-critical. Crossborder frauds generate problems for police jurisdiction everywhere, since even short distances require referral via national mutual legal assistance units, consuming time and financial resource. Fraudsters – and, for that matter, any other criminals – crossing international borders to and from the U.S. with large quantities of cash or monetary instruments (like checks) run the risks of asset forfeiture and of conviction for nondeclaration of funds, but may benefit from there being greater "turf wars" and hassle in international cases than in merely local or national cases.

HOW SIGNIFICANT A PROBLEM IS FRAUD?

There are a number of different dimensions of harm: economic damage (perhaps best seen in terms of the effects on individual and corporate victims' abilities to restore themselves to their precrime economic welfare level), and psychological and health damage (including disruption of expectations about future security and welfare). In standard economic terms, it is generally accepted that high value frauds and contract procurement bribes exceed in costs the total of all other crimes (Barnett, 2000; Pontell et al., 2004), especially when tax evasion is included. However, another dimension of harm is the sense of equal justice and social fairness that is offended by the nonprosecution of serious fraud, especially when committed by social elites.

Following a systematic review of existing studies commissioned by the British Home Office, excluding income tax fraud (which is difficult to estimate) and intellectual property crimes (which are seldom considered fraud), the direct costs of fraud were found to total a conservatively estimated minimum of £12.9 (US$19.2) billion, fairly equally distributed between private and public sectors (Levi & Burrows 2008; Levi et al. 2007), later revised with additional data sources and estimates to £30 (US$44.6) billion (NFA, 2010). People buying counterfeit products almost invariably know that they are fake because of the price and context, though sometimes stores sell counterfeit products as genuine. Comprehensively collated or critically assessed cost information is not available for fraud in the United States (though for some American evidence, see ACFE 2008; Friedrichs 2006; Rosoff, Pontell, & Tillman 2006); however, there is no reason to think that the distribution of costs found in the U.K. will be found elsewhere.

Such studies do not normally examine the international components of those costs, but even when frauds are not international in their execution, they are often international in their storage or laundering (see Box 2). However, this international component increases the social problem of fraud by placing obstacles in the way of enforcement, not just because of problems in assigning jurisdiction (e.g., whose law, if any, applies to this conduct?) but also because law enforcement agencies are more motivated to act when they consider – on their own initiative or under political or media pressure – that the conduct harms the people they are paid to protect. If Canadian "boiler room" stock fraudsters or telemarketers rip off British or American victims from Belgium or Spain, and place the funds in an honest (to depositors) but noncooperative (to foreign authorities) offshore finance

---

Box 3. The Bernie Madoff ponzi scheme

The Madoff investment funds allegedly grew from as much as $7 billion in 2000 to as much as $50 billion by the end of 2005. What had started decades before as a small-time recruiting effort by Madoff agents networking at country clubs had gone global. Major international institutions such as Grupo Santander, Fortis Bank, and Union Bancaire Privée were all funneling billions – sometimes through intermediaries – to Madoff, lured by steady 10 to 12 percent returns. The Abu Dhabi Investment Authority sank tens of millions of dollars into the Ponzi scheme via its investment in one of the big feeder funds. Japanese put money in a Swiss bank account held by a private Scottish bank that sent the money to an offshore firm investing in Madoff through Fairfield Greenwich funds. So did New York University. But no-one really understood how he was producing those returns, and we now know he just robbed Peter to pay Paul.

---

center, who will have sufficient motivation to spend vast sums of money unraveling this crime with an uncertain outcome? U.S. agencies typically have more money to spend and political pressure to exert than their counterparts around the world, especially in the Third World – but parochial interests predominate everywhere.

SOME TYPES OF INTERNATIONAL FRAUD

Fraudulent Investment Schemes

There are many types of investment fraud, varying from the simple "419" frauds (named after the relevant section of the Nigerian Penal Code) that many of us used to receive through the post and nowadays receive mainly via e-mail, offering us the opportunity to share the unclaimed billion-dollar wealth of whichever African kleptocrat has most recently been in the news if only we will give them our bank details, to the sort of high-yield investment fraud detailed in Box 3, committed over many years by Bernie Madoff, or Box 4, prosecuted by the UK Serious Fraud Office, to far more ambiguous schemes in which the victims may never realize that they have been swindled at all but rather think either (a) that their investments have failed legitimately or (b) that they have made less money than they hoped. In some of these schemes, the victims are innocent dupes but in others – like some "419" schemes – they may be viewed as, or even charged as, attempted conspirators in transnational frauds and corruption.

Box 4. US$16 million stolen in high-yield investment fraud

Thomas Pilz, Richard Walker, and Dariusz Maruzsak promoted a high-yield investment scheme that attracted US$16 million. The money was placed in an account at Swepstone Walsh, a London firm of solicitors, investors believing it would be pooled for investment in a lucrative and exclusive banking trading program not available to private investors. However, the money was instead transferred to a New York attorney's account, to the benefit of Pilz and Walker, under the guise of funds to set up a commercial venture in the USA. Pilz and Walker pleaded guilty to theft and were sentenced on October 11, 2002 to terms of imprisonment of four-and-half years and three years, respectively. Pilz was ordered to pay nearly £1.29 million as confiscation of crime proceeds.

The investigation into the consortium led the U.K. authorities to another suspect investment scheme. The five defendants were charged with offenses relating to money laundering of US$11.5 million. The trial opened on October 7, 2003. Part way through the trial, the judge expressed a view that the prosecution case depended heavily on the evidence of a solicitor who had acted for Maruszak's business affairs and who had been prosecuted separately for stealing client funds. After a review, the judge concluded that the SFO case was not sustainable and the defendants were acquitted by order of the court.

In a similar way the international investors were swindled by a scheme based in London that also involved crossnational funds transfers by the fraudsters and the use of American lawyers as unwitting intermediaries. In Enron, senior staff (and potential whistleblowers) were bought off with shares in offshore special purpose entities, abusing accounting rules to artificially boost their profits and spending power (which few of us can do at home!).

Bankruptcy and Other Credit Frauds

A popular enduring theme holds that frauds that do not obtain money directly but rather obtain goods on credit for which they do not pay either (a) disappear altogether, having given false identities or (b) give false explanations for nonpayment and false valuations of assets, sometimes in league with dishonest company liquidators. In some cases, professional fraudsters or gangsters set new businesses up, building up credit with the intention of fraud, but in other cases, they find businesspeople in trouble and either persuade them or threaten them into turning their businesses

into fraudulent ones; and in still others, the business just carries on ordering goods for which there is no reasonable chance of payment, hoping that
"something will turn up" (Levi, 2008b). The Internet has enabled "phishing" and "pharming" of corporate identities, enabling some to simulate the
legitimate businesses when ordering goods or getting financial intelligence
from the public – a corporate form of identity fraud. In the second half
of 2008, there were at least 56,959 phishing attacks worldwide (national
boundaries being irrelevant, as our e-mail in-boxes will testify), a significant
rise even from the first half of that year. An "attack" is defined as a phishing site that targets a specific brand or entity: but one domain name can
host several discrete attacks against different banks (APWG, 2008). Again,
there is no need for these frauds to be international, but some goods usually are ordered from overseas. In a variant, the company may make up
artificial sales of, say, computers, using credit card details taken from elsewhere and defraud the card companies by getting reimbursed for the card
vouchers before the cardholders get their statements and realize they have
been defrauded.

Some individuals and groups may commit credit and loan frauds on an
international basis. Banks may lose hundreds of millions of dollars in "letter
of credit" frauds because of false documentation pretending to have underlying assets. At a lower level, people may hire cars using false documents
and then make them "disappear," sometimes being driven across borders
to be sold.

CONCLUSION

Opportunity reduction takes many forms – social, technological, and targeted on individuals perceived to be particularly high risk. For volume
frauds such as payment card frauds, until everyone adopts PINs with chip
cards to replace magnetic stripes (as in Europe), people in key positions
(hotel receptionists, car hire businesses, stores) may copy card details electronically and send them to their confederates overseas, who may make up
good counterfeits or simply encode them onto unembossed "white plastic"
to defraud the individual or, more commonly since innocent consumers
are reimbursed in most countries, the card issuer. For these credit card and
insurance frauds, aggregated databases for the industry as a whole, plus software that hunts for connections, can help to combat organized fraud. For
telemarketing frauds, transnational cooperation and proactive intervention
by regulators and police is essential, as is better consumer education to get

people to realize that if something sounds as if it is too good to be true, it almost certainly is! However, for the larger frauds committed by elites, vigilance by the media, by internal and external auditors, and by other professionals may be necessary to cut down the scale of frauds as well as to stop them happening. Keeping out "bad people" by bans on directorships and on the sale of financial services will reduce only part of the problem.

In sum, fraud has become democratized in terms of both victims and offenders and, as individuals and corporations expect to trade with transnational businesses, it has become normal for both legitimate trades and scams to be international. This creates significant problems for regulation and criminal justice enforcement mechanisms that are still largely premised upon the nation state and the locality.

REFERENCES

ACFE. (2008). 2008 ACFE Report to the Nation: On Occupational Fraud and Abuse. Retrieved from http://www.acfe.com/documents/2008-rttn.pdf.

APWG, Anti-Phishing Working Group . (2008). Retrieved from http://www.anti-phishing.org/reports/APWG_GlobalPhishingSurvey2H2008.pdf.

Barnett, C. (2000). *The Measurement of White-Collar Crime Using Uniform Crime Reporting (UCR) Data*. Washington, D.C.: US Department of Justice.

Block, A. & W. Constance. (2005). *All Is Clouded by Desire*. New York: Praeger.

Friedrichs, D. (2006). *Trusted Criminals* Third Edition. Belmont, CA: Wadsworth.

Levi, M.(2007). Organised Crime and Terrorism. In M. Maguire, R. Morgan, & R. Reiner (Eds.), *The Oxford Handbook of Criminology* Fourth Edition. Oxford: Oxford University Press.

(2008a). Organised Fraud: Unpacking Research on Networks and Organization, *Criminology and Criminal Justice*, 8(4), 389–420.

(2008b). *The Phantom Capitalists: The Organization and Control of Long-Firm Fraud*, Second Edition. Aldershot: Ashgate.

Levi, M. & J. Burrows. (2008). Measuring the Impact of Fraud: A Conceptual and Empirical Journey, M. Levi and J. Burrows. *British Journal of Criminology*, 48(3), 293–318.

Rosoff, S. M., H. N. Pontell, & R. Tillman. (2006). *Profit without Honor: White-Collar Crime and the Looting of America Fourth Edition*. Upper Saddle River, NJ: Prentice Hall.

Shover, N., S. C. Glenn, & H. Hobbs. (2003). Crime on the Line: Telemarketing and the Changing Nature of Professional Crime. *British Journal of Criminology*, 43, 489–505.

Smith, D. J. (2008). *A Culture of Corruption Everyday Deception and Popular Discontent in Nigeria*. Princeton, NJ: Princeton University Press.

Van Duyne. P. & M. Levi. *Drugs and Money*. New York: Routledge.

ABOUT THE AUTHOR

Dr. Michael Levi holds degrees from Oxford, Cambridge, Southampton and Cardiff and has been professor of criminology at Cardiff University, Wales, UK since 1991. He has researched and published widely on international fraud, money laundering and organized crime, as well as on violent crime and policing. Recent and pending books include Drugs and Money and White-Collar Crime and its Victims. Professor Levi's contribution was funded via ESRC RES-051–27–0208.

22 Money Laundering

David C. Hicks and Adam Graycar

INTRODUCTION

This chapter discusses available knowledge about money laundering and discusses selected definitions of money laundering offences, and available evidence on the size and scope of the problem. Particular emphasis is placed upon evidence concerning the underlying or predicate offending and laundering methods.

The United Nations Convention against Illicit Traffic in Narcotic Drugs and Psychotropic Substances (Vienna Convention, 1988) signaled the beginning of the international drive, and parallel national responses, to target money laundering. Early efforts focused on laundering linked to drugs and designated offences. From the turn of the century, international conventions and much national legislation has expanded the focus to include laundering related to all serious crimes (punishable by four or more years imprisonment) and virtually any interaction with the proceeds of crime.

The responses that have been developed (see Hicks, 2010 for example) are key drivers behind what we know about the money laundering problem. Responses that generate the bulk of our knowledge in this area may be divided into two generic and interactive categories: prevention and enforcement (Levi & Reuter, 2006). Prevention activities focus on knowing your customer policies, the reporting of suspicious and other financial transactions, and the regulation and supervision of financial institutions with various sanctions for noncompliance. Enforcement activities focus on predicate offences that generate the proceeds of crime, investigation, prosecution, punishment, and criminal and civil forfeiture of the proceeds of crime.

DEFINITION

There is a commonsense definition that characterizes efforts to convert or conceal the "financial" proceeds of crime as it constitutes money laundering. This involves turning "dirty money" into "clean money" or hiding the origins of the proceeds of crime – a process which people typically understand as defining money laundering. Contemporary to national definitions explicitly or implicitly include the hiding component; most definitions also include broad laws and regulation which criminalize all forms of interaction with the proceeds of crime.

There are similarities and differences concerning how the offence of money laundering is defined and enforced in various jurisdictions. The Australian Institute of Criminology (2009) outlines the offences in a variety of countries, and reports that the simplest codification is in Hong Kong, where under principal drug-trafficking and organized-crime ordinances (a) knowingly dealing with the proceeds of crime; or (b) having reasonable grounds to suspect the origins of the property, are basic money laundering offences.

In the United Kingdom the offences include (a) concealing, disguising, converting, transferring criminal property, and removing criminal property from the country; (b) entering into or becoming involved in an arrangement known, or suspected, to facilitate the acquisition, retention, use or control of criminal property by another person; and (c) acquiring, using, or possessing criminal property.

In the United States, the three core offences focus on (a) conducting a transaction using the proceeds of crime, with the intent to disguise its origins, avoid a transaction report, or commit another offence; (b) transporting the proceeds of crime into, out of, or through the country with the intent to disguise its origins; and (c) conducting transactions with funds represented as the proceeds of crime. The United States also criminalizes conducting transactions in illicit funds to the value of US$10,000 or more, using a statute commonly known as the "spending statute."

Under the criminal code of Canada, the offence includes the use, transmission, alteration, or disposal of any proceeds (with intent to convert or conceal) that are known to have derived from, or are believed to have derived from an offence in Canada, or an act or omission anywhere that, if it had occurred in Canada, would have constituted a designated offence.

Australia has one of the most complex sets of criteria for the offense, but in essence their definitions revolve around the movement of money or assets known, thought to have been illegally gained, or money that will be used to commit an offence. In addition, if one has failed to exercise a reasonable standard of care to ensure that money or property is not the proceeds of crime, then there is an offence under the code.

Each of these definitions has adopted a broad approach to criminalizing virtually any interaction with the proceeds of crime. Many definitions also focus on the intent to convert or conceal the proceeds of crime. These approaches to definition recognize that money laundering is generally not a single act, but rather it is typically a process. The complexity of that process relates to predicate offender circumstances, in addition to the nature of their interaction with financial and related service providers, and the regulatory and control architecture. This interaction may include self-laundering such as lifestyle spending, acquiring or facilitating the use of the proceeds of crime for themselves and other parties, and any efforts that violate or attempt to violate applicable antilaundering laws and regulations. Individuals may escape liability for money laundering prosecution by exercising due diligence about the source and nature of monies or assets with which they interact, by engaging in fair market value transactions for goods and services, and by reporting suspicions of laundering to competent authorities.

Case Study 1. Three money-laundering convictions in Australia

Defendant A conducted 335 remittance transactions, each valued at less than $10,000, to China and Hong Kong. The total value of the transactions was $3,088,311. Defendant A received a fee for each transaction conducted and collected approximately $30,000 for these activities. The funds were provided to Defendant A by his employer. The court found that Defendant A believed that the funds were remitted overseas in order to avoid paying tax in Australia and were not the proceeds of crime. Defendant A was sentenced to five and a half years imprisonment in 2007. Defendant B, employed in the same business, conducted fifty-nine remittance transactions of less than $10,000 to Hong Kong. The total value of Defendant B's transactions came to $556,400. Defendant B collected less than $3,000 in fees for his role. Unlike Defendant A, the court found that Defendant B was aware that the funds were the result of illegal abalone fishing. Defendant B was sentenced to five years' imprisonment. Both Defendant A and Defendant B were acting on the directions of Defendant C, and neither had an interest in the money they were moving. Defendant C was convicted of laundering more than $3 million and was sentenced to sixteen and a half year imprisonment in March 2008.

Source: Australian Institute of Criminology (2009).

PREDICATE OFFENCES AND LAUNDERING METHODS

In the past few decades, the threat of serious and organized crime has often been presented in estimates on how much money is believed to be involved. The estimates have ranged from US$300 billion in annual global illicit drug proceeds to United Nations estimates of US$1.5 trillion per year in global organized crime earnings. The accounting firm KPMG (2007: 4) argues "estimated money laundering flows are reported to be in excess of US$1 trillion, being laundered every year by drug dealers, arms traffickers, and other criminals."

An often repeated and popular official claim is the International Monetary Fund (IMF) estimate, from its then director in 1988, that two to five percent of global gross domestic product (GDP) represents laundered funds. Unfortunately, the estimates too often rely upon a composite of indirect indicators, guesswork, and the generation of "facts" by repetition. There has been little attention toward constructing systematic evidence based on the size and scope of the "money laundering problem," which continues to impair ability to offer valid and reliable estimates (Levi & Reuter, 2006).

Nevertheless, we do know a fair amount about the predicate offending as well as the methods that are used to launder money. Our knowledge in this area is largely a product of the prevention and enforcement activities noted above as opposed to a systematic data collection process. Where there have been data collection processes the results vary considerably.

Reuter and Truman (2004: 33) have reviewed cases (N=580) drawn from two international typology reports covering the period 1998 to 2004. This work represents the case examples submitted by national enforcement agencies. The largest group of their cases relate to drug trafficking (32 percent), then fraud (22 percent), and then nondrug smuggling (16 percent). Most of the other cases related to terrorism, unknown crimes, and blue-collar crimes such as prostitution and illegal gambling, bribery and corruption, as well as tax evasion. The techniques most used in money laundering were wire transfers, and the use of a front company or organization. Additionally, the use of accountants, financial officers, shell corporations, and the purchase of high value goods as well as the use of money orders and cashiers' checks, offshore accounts, and the purchase of real estate have existed in small measures.

Citing data for the United States over many years, while focusing particularly on the year 1990, Levi and Reuter (2006: 329–31) show that the largest proceeds of criminal activity came from tax evasion (55 percent), then cocaine trafficking (13 percent), fraud (nonarson) (13 percent), heroin trafficking (3 percent), prostitution (3 percent), and loan sharking (3 percent). The remaining 10 percent was spread among ten other crimes. Proceeds from these crimes cannot, of course, be legally deposited into one's bank account, so a process is required to clean the money.

Stamp and Walker (2007) report on a survey (N=39) involving twenty-one overseas financial intelligence units (FIUs), fourteen Australian law enforcement agencies, and four researchers and criminologists. The results revealed that overwhelmingly the largest categories of predicate offence proceeds generated domestically and laundered within or outside Australia were fraud (82 percent) and illicit drugs (11 percent). The authors estimated that of the estimated $2.8 billion laundered in Australia each year, 23 percent ends up in real estate investments; 21 percent in further crime activities; 16 percent in gambling; 15 percent in luxury goods; 12 percent in legitimate business; and 7 percent in professional services. The survey of overseas FIUs also questioned the relative frequencies of suspected offences in suspicious activity or transaction reports. It was found that fraud and tax (or customs) evasion were noted four times as often as drug trafficking.

We should not be surprised to see both similarities and differences between jurisdictions in terms of the proportion of different predicate offences. Offender circumstances, the nature of their predicate offending, and their interaction within a given national context and control framework should impact upon their laundering behavior. Once the proceeds of crime are generated through the course of committing a predicate offence, a common description of the laundering process is as follows:

- "Placement" refers to converting the proceeds of crime into financial instruments such as bank deposits or cashier's checks.
- "Layering" refers to supplementary transactions such as wire transfers to move the funds around and obscure their criminal origins.
- "Integration" refers to the purchase or investment into legal assets such as real estate in order to enjoy the proceeds of crime and give them the appearance of legitimacy.

The case studies included in this article, illustrate offender efforts to attempt to evade the prevention and enforcement mechanisms that have been established to detect and deter money laundering.

Case Study 2. An example of over- and under-Invoicing of goods

---

Company A (a foreign exporter) ships one million widgets worth $2 each, but invoices Company B (a colluding domestic importer) for one million widgets at a price of only $1 each. Company B pays Company A for the goods by sending a wire transfer for $1 million. Company B then sells the widgets on the open market for $2 million and deposits the extra $1 million (the difference between the invoiced price and the "fair market" value) into a bank account to be disbursed according to Company A's instructions.

Alternatively, Company C (a domestic exporter) ships one million widgets worth $2 each, but invoices Company D (a colluding foreign importer) for one million widgets at a price of $3 each. Company D pays Company C for the goods by sending a wire transfer for $3 million. Company C then pays $2 million to its suppliers and deposits the remaining $1 million (the difference between the invoiced price and the "fair market" price) into a bank account to be disbursed according to Company D's instructions.

Source: FATF (2006: 4).

SUMMARY AND CONCLUSION

Money laundering is a truly global business and it is estimated that money laundered by drug dealers, arms traffickers, and other criminals exceeds US$1 trillion every year. Money laundering is a process of turning "dirty money" into "clean money," that is, hiding the origins of the proceeds of crime and any interaction that violates laundering laws and regulation.

There are global treaties that deal with money laundering, and two thrusts inform these activities, prevention and enforcement. Before one can prevent or enforce money laundering, one needs a clear definition of the activity, and while definitions vary from country to country, they generally focus not only on the movement of money, but also on the knowledge that money or assets are obtained through illegal activities and that they may be used for further illegal activities. There is very little survey data on money laundering activity, so no consistent pattern is observable, though most of the known laundering activities derive from a combination of drugs, tax evasion, and fraud.

REFERENCES

Australian Institute of Criminology (2009). "Charges and Offences of Money Laundering" *Transnational Crime Brief*, No 4, Canberra, Australian Institute of Criminology. Retrieved Feb 8, 2010 from: www.aic.gov.au/en/publications/ current percent20series/tcb/1–20/tcb004.aspx

Financial Action Task Force (FATF) (2006). *Trade Based Money Laundering*, www. fatf-gafi.org/dataoecd/60/25/37038272.pdf

Hicks, D. C. (2010). Money Laundering. In F. Brookman, M. Maguire, H. Pierpoint, & T. Bennett (Eds.), *Handbook of Crime*. Cullompton, Devon: Willan.

KPMG. (2007). *Global Anti–Money Laundering Survey 2007 – How Banks are Facing Up to the Challenge* www.kpmg.com.kh/files/Advisory_ AntiMoneyLaundering2007.pdf

Levi, M. & P. Reuter. (2006). Money Laundering. In *M. Tonry* (Ed.), *Crime and Justice: A Review of Research*, Vol. 34. Chicago: Chicago University Press, pp. 289–375.

Reuter, P. & E. M. Truman. (2004). *Chasing Dirty Money: The Fight against Money Laundering*. Washington, D.C.: Institute for International Economics.

Stamp, J. & J. Walker. (2007). Money Laundering in and through Australia, 2004. *Trends and Issues in Crime and Criminal Justice*, No. 342, Canberra, Australian Institute of Criminology. Retrieved on Feb 8, 2010, from www.aic.gov.au/ publications/current percent20series/tandi/341–360/tandi342.aspx

WEB SITES

Egmont Group (provides links to national financial intelligence units): www.egmontgroup.org

Financial Action Task Force: www.fatf-gafi.org

International Monetary Fund: www.imf.org

United Nations International Money Laundering Information Network (IMoLIN): www.imolin.org

United Nations Office of Drugs and Crime (UNODC): www.unodc.org/unodc/en/ money-laundering/index.html

World Bank: www.worldbank.org

ABOUT THE AUTHORS

Prior to joining the staff at the Cardiff University School of Social Sciences, where he is a lecturer in criminology, Dr. David C. Hicks worked with academic, enforcement, intelligence, nongovernment, and government institutions in Canada.

Adam Graycar has worked at senior levels of government, and has also been the director of the Australian Institute of Criminology and Dean of the School of Criminal Justice at Rutgers University, New Jersey. He is now professor at the Australian National University.

23   Child Pornography

Richard Wortley

OVERVIEW OF CHILD PORNOGRAPHY

The treatment of children as sexual objects is as old as humanity, with evidence of child-adult sex practices recorded in societies such as ancient Greece and the Roman Empire (Linz & Imrich, 2001). There has also been a long history of erotic literature and drawings involving children, but pornography in the modern sense began with the invention of the camera in the early nineteenth century. Almost immediately, pornographic images involving children were produced, traded, and collected. Even so, child pornography remained a restricted activity through most of the twentieth century. Images were generally locally produced, of poor quality, expensive, and difficult to obtain (Ferraro & Casey, 2005). However, the advent of the Internet in the 1980s dramatically escalated the problem by increasing the amount of material that was available, the efficiency of its distribution, and the ease by which it could be accessed. The Internet also made child pornography a truly international enterprise.

The idea of protecting children from sexual exploitation is relatively modern. For example, as late as 1880s in the U.S., the age of consent for girls was just ten years old and the use of children in obscene material was not specifically outlawed by the U.S. federal government until 1978 (Wortley & Smallbone, 2006). Today, law enforcement agencies are faced with the challenge of controlling a flood of child pornography generated by an increasingly sophisticated technology. This is a global problem that crosses state and national borders, and requires an international response.

WHAT IS CHILD PORNOGRAPHY?

Legal definitions of both "child" and "pornography" vary considerably among jurisdictions. For example, while in the U.S. a child is defined as a person under the age of eighteen years, whereas in other Western countries the age ranges from sixteen years (e.g., Australia, the United Kingdom, Sweden, Norway, Switzerland, and France) to fourteen years (Germany) (Wortley & Smallbone, 2006). Similarly, the portrayal of sexual acts that are illegal in one country may be lawful in another. For the purpose of this chapter, child pornography is defined as any record of sexual activity involving a prepubescent person. Pornographic records include still photographs, videos, and audio recordings. In terms of content, Taylor, Quayle, and Holland (2001) identified ten levels of image severity, ranging from nonsexualized pictures of children collected from legitimate sources such as magazines, to graphic depictions of children engaging in sexual acts with other children, adults, and even animals.

Child pornography involves three elements: production, distribution, and possession. Sometimes the same people are involved in each stage. The production and distribution of pornographic images may be done professionally, and in these cases it often involves the abuse of children in third world countries. However, more frequently amateurs make records of their own child sexual abuse exploits, which they then make available to others.

TRENDS AND STATISTICS

Today, child pornography invariably involves the Internet. The Internet greatly enhances the capacity of individuals to create, distribute, and access child pornography (Calder, 2004). Electronic recording devices such as digital cameras, Web cameras, and multimedia messaging (MMR) cell phones, permit individuals to create high quality, "homemade" child pornography images, and to upload them to the Internet from anywhere in the world. Once uploaded, these images along with the vast quantities of other pornographic images are instantly available and may be conveniently accessed anonymously and in private, and at any time or place. The pornographic images downloaded from the Internet are inexpensive, do not deteriorate, and can be conveniently stored on the computer's hard drive or on a removable disk (e.g., CD-ROM). The Internet provides for a variety of pornography formats (pictures, videos, sound), as well as the potential for real-time and interactive experiences. If desired, images may be modified to create composite or virtual images (i.e., "morphing"). In addition to providing access to pornography Web sites, the Internet provides for direct communication among users, allowing for the sharing of images and the mutual support of one another's belief systems.

It is difficult to be precise about the extent of Internet child pornography, but all the available evidence points to it being a major and growing problem (Wortley & Smallbone, 2006). There are estimated to be over one million pornographic images of children, with more than two hundred new images posted daily. Offenders have been arrested in possession of more than half a million child pornography images. A single child pornography Web site can receive as many as a million hits in a month. Increasingly, those distributing child pornography are moving away from open areas of the World Wide Web and are being driven to "hidden" levels of the Internet (e.g., newsgroups, chat rooms, etc.) to elude detection.

PROFILE OF USERS

There is no one type of Internet child pornography user, nor is there any easy way to recognize an offender. People can behave very differently on the Internet than they do in other areas of their life. Interacting anonymously with a computer in the safety of one's own home is a disinhibiting experience and encourages people to express hidden thoughts and desires. Offenders may come from all walks of life and show few obvious warning signs. Those arrested for downloading online child pornography have included judges, dentists, soldiers, teachers, rock stars, and police officers. Among the few distinguishing features of offenders are that they are most likely to be white, male, and between the ages of twenty-six and thirty-nine years (Wolak, Finkelhor, & Mitchell, 2005).

The overlap between child pornography use and hands-on sexual offending is unclear but probably less than is often supposed. Smallbone and Wortley (2000) found that less than 10 percent of convicted child sexual abusers reported having used child pornography. Looking from the other direction, estimates of the percentage of child pornography users who sexually abuse children have ranged from 7 percent (Webb et al., 2007) to 40 percent (Wolak et al., 2005). However, these estimates are usually based on research involving convicted offenders, who are probably at the more serious end of the offending spectrum and it would not be surprising if the actual figure was at the lower end of these estimates. A number of studies have found that the two groups of offenders have different demographic and psychological characteristics (Elliott et al., 2008; Sheldon & Howitt,

2007; Webb, Craissati, & Keen, 2007). In general, child pornography users are more likely than child sex abusers to be better educated, to be professionally employed, and to have fewer criminal convictions, but to engage in more pedophilic fantasies.

The effects of pornography on users have been extensively researched but the results are contentious. Some argue that child pornography is sought out by individuals who have an existing sexual attraction to children, and that this attachment to child pornography is part of their pattern of sexual gratification. Others suggest that pornography may have a long-term corrosive effect, and that individuals may become increasingly attracted to child pornography and desensitized to the harm experienced by victims. Still others argue that pornography may have a cathartic effect; that is, it may be the sole outlet for an individual's sexual attraction to children and helps him or her resist engaging in hands-on offending (Wortley & Smallbone, 2006). In all likelihood, the effects of child pornography vary among users, and all of the above relationships may apply depending upon the individual in question. Cooper, Putnam, Planchon, and Boies (1999, in Calder, 2004) suggested the following categories of Internet pornography users in general that may also apply to child pornography users:

1. Recreational users: They access pornography sites on impulse, out of curiosity, or for short-term entertainment. They are not seen to have long-term problems associated with pornography use.
2. At-risk users: They are vulnerable individuals who have developed an interest in pornography, but may not have done so had it not been for the Internet.
3. Sexual compulsive users: They seek out pornography to satisfy existing pathological sexual interests.

INVESTIGATING AND CONTROLLING CHILD PORNOGRAPHY

The structure of the Internet makes control of child pornography very difficult. The Internet is an international communication tool that crosses jurisdictional boundaries. Local citizens may access child pornography images that were produced or are stored on another continent. Different countries have different laws and levels of permissiveness pertaining to child pornography. Moreover, the Internet is a decentralized system with no single controlling agency or storage facility, making it difficult to enforce legislation or to electronically screen content even when there is agreement between jurisdictions. Because it is a network of networks, even if one pathway is blocked there are many alternative pathways that can be taken to reach the same destination. In addition, rapid technological developments such as peer-to-peer networks (connections that allow direct communication between computers and facilitate file sharing), remailers (servers that strip the sender's identity from e-mail), and file encryption (methods of hiding or scrambling data) exacerbate the control problem (Ferraro & Casey, 2003).

Despite the difficulties involved in policing the Internet, computers and their associated services retain a considerable amount of evidence of the uses to which they have been put (Ferraro & Casey, 2003). While determined, computer-savvy offenders may take precautions to cover their tracks, many offenders will have neither the foresight nor the necessary expertise to do so, and will leave a trail of incriminating evidence. The most obvious evidence of pornography use is actual downloaded images on the computer's hard drive. However, there are also more subtle records that specialist forensic technicians can locate during examination of a suspect's computer. For example, files on the computer can reveal when a computer was connected to the Internet and what Web sites were visited. Similarly, servers used to connect a computer to the Internet or to store pornographic images, retain records of customer account details (the Internet Protocol or IP address), which can then be used to identify users.

There have been a number of major interagency and international investigations of Internet child pornography rings in recent years. Perhaps the most famous is the Operation Avalanche investigation into Landslide Productions, a child pornography company run by Thomas and Janice Reedy from Fort Worth in Texas (U.S. Postal Inspection Service, n.d.). Landslide involved a complex network of some 5,700 computer sites around the world, especially in Russia and Indonesia, that stored the child pornography images. The operation at Fort Worth acted as a gateway into the network. Online customers provided credit card details to obtain network access. These credit card numbers were scrambled by Landslide to protect customers' identity. There were over 250,000 subscribers from around the world, generating a monthly turnover of up to $1.4 million. The investigation began in 1999 when the U.S. Postal Inspection Service discovered that Landslide's customers were paying monthly subscription fees into a post office box or via the Internet. A joint investigation between the Postal Inspection Service and the Internet Crimes Against Children Task Force (ICAC), comprising more than forty-five officers, was conducted over two years. Officers cracked the code that scrambled the credit card numbers and then tracked down the owners of cards. Landslide's bank accounts were seized and 160 search warrants were executed that recovered large quantities of graphic child pornography. To date there have been 120 arrests in the U.S., including Thomas and Janice Reedy who were given a life and fourteen-year sentence, respectively. The investigation was expanded to include the U.K. (Operation Ore) where some 7,000 customers were identified, 1,300 people arrested, and 40 children taken into protective custody (Calder, 2004).

Considerable law enforcement resources are now dedicated to tackling the child pornography problem on an ongoing basis, with many police forces establishing dedicated ICAC or similar teams. Many investigations involve "sting" operations in which officers infiltrate pedophile newsgroups and chat rooms. In the U.S. there are around a 1,000 people arrested annually for online child pornography offenses (Wolak et al., 2005). Internet service providers (ISPs) also have a role to play by denying space for child pornography sites and banning the use of key words used in Internet searches (Linz & Imrich, 2001). Since 1996, ISPs have removed more than 20,000 pornographic images of children from the Internet (Calder, 2004).

SUMMARY

The scale of the child pornography problem has increased dramatically with the introduction and rapid growth of the Internet. There are now estimated to be in excess of one million pornographic images of children available online. The Internet has also made the problem of child pornography a truly international one. Almost all investigations that begin in one jurisdiction will need to cross state and even international borders to be effective. As Operation Avalanche demonstrates, perhaps more than any other offense, the fight against child pornography requires international cooperation and coordination among law enforcement bodies and other agencies.

REFERENCES

Calder, M. C. (2004) The Internet: Potential, Problems and Pathways to Hands-On Sexual Offending. In M. C. Calder (Ed.), *Child Sexual Abuse and the Internet: Tackling the New Frontier.* Lyme Regis UK: Russell House Publishing.

Elliott, I. A., Beech, A. R., Manderville-Norden, R., & Hayes, E. (2008). Psychological Profiles of Internet Sexual Offenders. *Sexual Abuse: A Journal of Research and Treatment*, 21, 76–92.

Ferraro, M. M. & E. Casey. (2005). *Investigating Child Exploitation and Pornography: The Internet, the Law and Forensic Science.* San Diego: Elsevier.

Linz, D. & D. Imrich. (2001). Child Pornography. In S. White (Ed.), *Handbook of Youth Justice.* NY: Kluwer Academic Press.

Sheldon, K. & D. Howitt. (2007). *Sex Offenders and the Internet*. Chichester: John Wiley.

Smallbone, S. W., & R. Wortley. (2000). *Child Sexual Abuse in Queensland: Offender Characteristics and Modus Operandi*. (Volume 2 of Project Axis). Brisbane: Queensland Crime Commission.

Taylor, M., E. Quayle, & G. Holland. (2001). Typology of Paedophile Picture Collections. *The Police Journal*, 74, 97–107.

Webb, L., J. Craissati, & S. Keen. (2007). Characteristics Internet Child Pornography Offenders: A Comparison with Child Molestors. *Sexual Abuse: A Journal of Research and Treatment*, 19, 449–65.

Wolak, J., D. Finkelhor, & K. J. Mitchell. (2005). *Child Pornography Possessors Arrested in Internet-Related Crimes. US*. Alexandria, VA: Department of Justice, National Center for Missing and Exploited Children.

Wortley, R. & S. Smallbone. (2006). *Child Pornography on the Internet. Problem-Oriented Guides for Police Series*. Washington DC: U.S. Department of Justice.

WEB SITES

FBI. *Online child pornography. Innocent images national initiative*.
www.fbi.gov/hq/cid/cac/innocent.htm

U.S. Department of Justice, Office of Justice Programs, Office for Victims of Crime. *OVC Bulletin*.
www.ojp.usdoj.gov/ovc/publications/bulletins/internet_2_2001/welcome.html

U.S. Postal Inspection Service. *Operation Avalanche*.
www.usps.com/postalinspectors/avalanch.htm

ABOUT THE AUTHOR

Professor Richard Wortley is Chair of Crime Science at the Jill Dando Institute of Crime Science, University College London. He is a former prison psychologist and a past national chair of the Australian College of Forensic Psychologists. His main research interest is crime prevention, and, in particular, the prevention of sexual offences against children. He has published internationally in this area. Recent books include *Situational Prevention of Sexual Offenses Against Children* (co-edited with Stephen Smallbone), *Child Pornography on the Internet* (written with Stephen Smallbone), and *Preventing Child Sexual Abuse* (written with Stephen Smallbone and William Marshall).

24 Maritime Crime

Gisela Bichler

GENERAL OVERVIEW

Maritime crime refers to a broad class of criminal and quasicriminal behavior that is connected to recreational and commercial transportation involving ships (excluding aircraft). This includes conventional crimes (e.g., murder), special crimes (e.g., piracy), and other quasicriminal acts involving regulatory and public welfare offences under admiralty law (e.g., trade violations). Admiralty law consists of a body of common law rules, precepts, and practices that govern all transactions having a direct relationship with navigation or commerce on water.

Geographically, maritime crime can be divided into: (a) prohibitions involving local, recreational, and commercial sailing on internal waters; (b) illicit activity affecting navigation on the territorial sea; and, (c) illegalities that concern international seafaring on the high seas or foreign waters (see Box 1). This chapter examines maritime crime affecting international commercial seafaring because it involves 80 percent of world trade. Generally, most maritime crime involves the exploitation of legal and legislative weakness in the transportation system.

THE MARITIME TRANSPORTATION SYSTEM

To understand how the system can be exploited it is necessary to consider the legal authority of flag states and enforcement that create opportunities for maritime crime.

Box 1. Maritime jurisdictional zones

Maritime jurisdiction extends up to two hundred nautical miles (nm) from the low water mark of the shoreline (a line drawn along irregular parts of the coastline). Jurisdictional zones include:

Internal waters zone – which extends from the territorial sea baseline landward.

Territorial sea zone – which extends from baseline twelve nm seaward.

Contiguous zone – for which states may take limited enforcement action related to customs, immigration, and pollution twelve to twenty-four nm from the shore.

Exclusive economic zone – which extends from twelve to two hundred nm seaward wherein the state can explore and exploit resources providing that they protect and conserve the marine environment.

Continental shelf zone – which may extend beyond the two hundred nm limit and is subject to the same jurisdiction as the exclusive economic zone.

Beyond these zones are the high seas, which are public waters vessels.

Legal Authority of Flag States

Ships, like people, must have a single, documented nationality in order to call on foreign ports and to travel the high seas. Seagoing vessels acquire a flag or nationality by registering with a country that is then referred to as the "flag state." Registration brings the vessel under the legal authority of the country of registration. To attract a large merchant fleet (and the tax base provided by these ships) countries offer economic incentives (i.e., increased profitability by avoiding labor laws) and administrative conveniences (i.e., rapid registration with few inspection requirements).

A vessel is said to be flying a flag of convenience (FOC registry) when it is registered with a nation that permits foreign owned or controlled vessels to fly its flag when it is convenient and opportune. With no "genuine link" between flag state and vessel operations it is thought that the registry is unable to regulate the administrative, technical, and social matters of its fleet as specified in article 91 of the Law of the Sea (1982). Honduras, Liberia, Malta, Netherlands Antilles, and Panama, are generally considered FOC registries.

Classification societies (comprised of ship owners, builders, and marine underwriters) focus on ensuring the structural integrity of vessels; in exchange for a fee, they issue certificates of compliance following inspection of the hull structure, engine, and other critical components. Large classification societies (e.g., Lloyd's Register of Shipping) locate offices at key ports around the world. This accessibility leads nations to "hire" classification societies to inspect vessels, thereby delegating statutory responsibility to private interests to ensure that the fleet is in compliance.

Competition enables owners to "shop around" to find the cheapest classification society willing to certify the vessel, and typically this is the one that enforces the least stringent standards. With a certificate of compliance, the vessel may be insured by underwriters. Distributing liability amongst multiple insurance agents reduces the risk for loss and increases the opportunity for operators to run substandard ships.

Maritime Law Enforcement

Law enforcement on the world's waterways is a challenging endeavor for all coast guard fleets. Generally, jurisdiction is related to three factors:

1. the nationality of the vessel in question (flag states have full jurisdiction over their own vessels);
2. the physical location of a foreign vessel in question (if the vessel is within the territorial sea there are internationally sanctioned boarding and inspection rights);
3. the status of the vessel in question (i.e., a warship can be used to board a vessel when there are reasonable grounds to suspect that a foreign vessel is engaged in piracy, engaged in the slave trade, or if the ship refuses to show its flag).

Coast guard fleets have the combined functions of a state highway patrol and customs and border inspection; as such, it is responsible for vessel safety inspection, waterways management, enforcement of immigration law, drug trafficking interdiction, and homeland security in ports, harbors, and along the coastline. The immense area (about six million square miles with 9,500 miles of coastline containing hundreds of ports) of the Marine Transportation System (MTS) falling within the United States Coast Guard's (USCG) jurisdiction exemplifies the geographic challenges facing all coast guard operations.

Due to the size and complexity of the global MTS, much of the system remains a self-policing environment with economic incentives not to comply with shipping conventions. The International Maritime Organization (IMO) is the only international body that negotiates with flag states to set shipping standards – standards that include antipiracy equipment, crew training, and vessel integrity. The IMO relies on flag nations to enforce standards, and flag nations may, in turn, rely on classifications societies. Generally, coast guard fleets are expected to police all activity within territorial waters, but not all fleets are equally equipped to handle this daunting task. It is these system weaknesses that are exploited by maritime criminals.

MARITIME CRIMES

Trafficking

Maritime trafficking involves the illicit transport of legal goods, illicit substances, and people from origin nations to land-based distribution networks located in transitory or primary consuming countries. Materials and humans can be smuggled in a variety of ways:

- hidden in shipping containers, goods, or vessel compartments;
- transferred at sea from "mother ships" to smaller accomplice vessels (i.e., trawlers); or,
- dropped from airplanes to small boats.

Human Smuggling. A report by the IMO states that between 1999 and 2008, member countries investigated 1,667 maritime incidents involving 61,413 illegal migrants. Given the poor mechanisms for developing a global figure, this number is thought to grossly underestimate the magnitude of the human smuggling problem. For instance, in 2008, the USCG interdicted nearly 5,000 undocumented migrants attempting to illegally enter via sea routes.

Until recently, seafaring human smuggling operations into the US were generally associated with the Florida Straits, where boats and rafts loaded with immigrants bound for Florida are interdicted from Cuba, Haiti, and the Dominican Republic. With tightening land borders, smugglers are increasing their use of Pacific routes and the Gulf Coast of Texas.

Access to Western Europe is often gained through Italy's 7,600-kilometer coastline. Launched from Libya, many of these small vessels, painted blue to avoid detection by searchlights, are unable to safely cross 660 miles to the coast; estimates suggest that more than 20,000 people have drowned en route as many attempt the crossing in small fishing vessels ill-equipped for the voyage.

Drug Smuggling. The estimated volume of the illicit drug trade is staggering; to illustrate, the European Commission projects that the total revenue in Western Europe, the U.S., and Oceania for cannabis in 2005 was almost ninety-five billion dollars (USD). Much of this trade moves through the MTS. For example, over the last decade the USCG detained 495 vessels, arresting 2,432 people and seizing tons of illicit drugs with a street value exceeding of fifty billion (USD).

Creativity increases in response to tightening border controls on land. Recently, cocaine was found: dissolved in diesel fuel; loaded in self-propelled, semisubmersible (SPSS) vessels; and, strapped, unbeknown to the vessels' crew, to the hulls of commercial ships (this practice is called "torpedoing").

To combat illicit trafficking, many Coast Guard operations are working to secure funds to modernize their fleets. In addition, many join forces with the Navy to supplement patrol resources. For example, through the Posse Comitatus Act (18 USC 1385) and provisions under 10 USC 371–78, the USCG can use Navy vessels to board and inspect ships. This joint action has been useful in combating the flow of illicit goods and illegal migration.

Piracy and Armed Robbery

Piracy and armed robbery have plagued maritime transportation for centuries. The legal distinction between these crimes is geographically based. "Piracy" refers to international crimes involving acts of violence, vessel detention, or depredation by the crew or passengers of a private ship on international waters against another ship, persons, or property aboard. When the same actions occur within the jurisdiction of the flag state – in other words, while the vessel is at the home port – then the crime is labeled an armed robbery.

Currently, pirates are most active around Somalia, in the Gulf of Aden, and on the waters west of Somalia. Political and social crisis have exacerbated piracy levels in these regions. For example, of the 240 reported cases between January and June in 2009, 41.7 percent occurred in the Gulf of Aden and 18.3 percent occurred near Somalia. These crimes are more likely to involve hostage situations where the crew and ship are held for ransom. Bulk carriers, containerships, general cargo ships, and tankers are most frequently besieged. Most of these vessels are registered with Panama, Liberia, or the Marshall Islands.

Statistics collected by the IMB suggest that 50 percent of attacks on merchant vessels occur when the vessel is anchored in port or is berthed, and that the other half of attacks occur when vessels are underway. This marks a notable shift in attack status: previously most vessels were attacked while berthed. Pirates typically fire automatic weapons and rocket propelled grenades (RPGs) in their effort to board and hijack vessels. In some situations, pirates hijack fishing vessels and other ocean going vessels, monitor radio frequencies and launch attacks on steaming vessels. Once hijacked many vessels are sailed toward the Somalian port of Eyl.

The underreporting problem makes it difficult to ascertain the full extent of this crime. Manufacturers that own the cargo (shippers), companies that own the vessels (carriers), and the insurers of the vessels and cargo (underwriters) all have a vested interest in preventing piracy and armed robbery; however, as with other forms of business victimization, many corporate interests often decide not to report incidents, electing to absorb losses rather than face increased insurance costs for placing claims or incurring investigation related delays (i.e., operators can lose thousands of dollars each day in port costs). It is likely that the actual costs are in the billions annually.

To combat piracy some carriers employ armed guards while others turn to technological enhancements such as nonlethal electrified fences to deter boarding attempts, and satellite ship-tracking systems with emergency silent alarm buttons to automatically alert owners and authorities of attack. The IMO regulation SOLAS (the International Convention for Safety of Life at Sea) XI-2/6 adopted in December of 2002 requires all vessels weighing more than five hundred gross tons to be equipped with silent alarm systems by July 2004.

Cooperative military action between Southeast Asian nations has improved the situation in recent years. Since February 2009, an Internationally Recognized Transit Corridor (IRTC) has been established; strategic deployment of military assets (naval and air) along this corridor have augmented the private security precautions many shipmasters must adopt to secure transport through these areas.

BUILDING LAW ENFORCEMENT CAPACITY OF PORT STATES

Despite significant efforts on the part of the IMO and classification societies to establish shipping standards, as well as flag states to police their fleets through coast guard operations, there is a critical need for multinational, cooperative law enforcement efforts. Enhancing port state control of maritime traffic is probably the most effective method of improving law enforcement capacity to combat many forms of fraud, illegal immigration, drug trafficking, and piracy. This is likely the case because all ships must dock to both unload cargo and take on supplies.

Proponents of "harmonized inspection" programs argue that cooperative enforcement strengthens international conventions; vessels failing to adhere to international standards or to carry the necessary documentation face a blanket ban from all ports in the region. Inspections check for compliance with various IMO conventions such as the International Convention for the Safety of Life at Sea (SOLAS 74/78/88). Vessels are targeted when they enter a port for the first time or after an extended absence, if its flag state has a high detention rate, or if the vessel carries dangerous or polluting goods.

When detained, all costs incurred by the port state are charged to the owner or operator of the ship. Detentions are not lifted until payment is made in full. Of the five regional organizations, Paris MOU is the oldest (originated in 1982). Member nations inspect at least 25 percent of the foreign merchant ships entering their ports and share the information that produces a regional coverage averaging between 85 and 95 percent. Democratic People's Republic of Korea, Bolivia, Albania, Moldova, and Dominica are the poorest performing flags.

Consolidated inspection information is publicly available; it typically includes access to an inspection database, access to a list of flag states with consistently poor safety records, names ships with poor safety records, lists ships with multiple detentions, provides details about banned ships, and contains detailed reports of "rust buckets."

CONCLUSIONS

Commercial operations span the globe and while every nation has the right to maintain a merchant fleet, the MTS cannot adequately monitor all vessels.

(1) Legal authority does not rest with a single body; rather, law enforcement relies upon a mosaic of coast guard operations with varying capacities and resources, voluntary compliance with international conventions set, and the vigilance of flag nations.
(2) The self-policing apparatus of the maritime transportation industry developed various circular spheres of influence.
(3) Economic incentives to violate international shipping conventions, violate laws, and "cheat" the system are abundant, particularly given the disjointed nature of operations spanning across several nations and thousands of miles.
(4) Geographic and resource challenges impact on the ability of coast guard operations to effectively patrol and control ship movement.

Harmonized port inspection programs, in conjunction with joint enforcement efforts of navy and coast guard operations, can strengthen enforcement efforts aimed at suppressing maritime crime. If met with similar efforts by private interests – shippers (manufacturers that own the cargo), carriers (vessel owners and operators), and insurers – to harden soft targets, inroads can be made to improve the safety and efficiency of the MTS while reducing crime.

REFERENCES

ICC International Maritime Bureau (2009, July). *Piracy and Armed Robbery against Ships, Report for the Period 1 January – 30 June 2009.* London, UK: International Chamber of Commerce.
ICC International Maritime Bureau (IMB) . http://www.icc-ccs.org
International Maritime Organization (IMO) . http://www.imo.org
International Transport Workers' Federation (ITF). http://www.itfglobal.org/index.cfm
Paris MOU is the model cooperative Port State inspection program. http://www.parismou.org
USCG (2009). *Coast Guard 2009 Snapshot.* http://www.uscg.mil/top/about/overview.asp
World Maritime News. http://www.worldmaritimenews.com

ABOUT THE AUTHOR

Gisela Bichler Ph.D. is an associate professor at California State University, San Bernardino. She is also the co-director of the Center for Criminal Justice Research. Her interest in maritime crime stems from her doctoral research on commercial passenger ship casualties. Recently, Dr. Bichler has become heavily involved in various research initiatives integrating geographic information system technology with social network analytic techniques in the study of crime trends and patterns, both on land and on the water.

25 Transnational Environmental Crime

Rob White

INTRODUCTION

Transnational environmental crime is one of the many reasons why our planet is in peril. Such crimes include the dumping of toxic waste, the pollution of land, air, and water, and the illegal trade of plants and animals, in ways that cross borders and, in many instances, have a global dimension. A more expansive definition of transnational environmental crime also extends to "harms." These include:

- transgressions that are harmful to humans, environments, and non-human animals, regardless of legality per se (i.e., harm occurs whether or not the activity is legal or illegal); and
- environment-related harms that are facilitated by the state, corporations, and other powerful actors, insofar as these institutions have the capacity to shape official definitions of environmental crime in ways that allow or condone environmentally harmful practices.

The definition of transnational environmental crime is, therefore, contentious and ambiguous. This depends upon who is defining the harm, and to what criteria – for example, legal versus ecological, criminal justice versus environmental justice – is used in determining the nature of the harms so described (see Beirne & South, 2007; White, 2008).

The post–World War II period has seen major growth in the internationalization of treaties, agreements, protocols, and conventions in relation to environmental protection, and with respect to the securing of environmental resources. In recent years, nation-states have been more interested in taking governmental action on environmental matters, since these matters pertain to national economic interests. Moreover, the transboundary nature of environmental harm is evident in a variety of international protocols and conventions that deal with such matters as: the illegal trade in ozone-depleting substances, the dumping and illegal transport of hazardous waste, trade in chemicals such as persistent organic pollutants, and illegal dumping of oil and other wastes in oceans (Hayman & Brack, 2002). A major concern today is the proliferation of "e-waste" generated by the disposal of tens of thousands of computers and other (electronic) equipment.

The examination of transnational environmental harm needs to take into account geographical locations of varying environmentally harmful practices. This includes analyzing production (toxic materials), transit points (illegal trade – at sea, on land, and in particular regions), and end points (waste dumping). A global mapping of harmful practices can provide useful insights into how harm is transferred around the planet, and who or what is ultimately responsible for which kinds of harm.

Simultaneously, the combined effects of human transformations of nature are having repercussions well beyond the local and regional level. Thus, "as a result of the growing competition and demand for global resources, the world's population has reached a stage where the amount of resources needed to sustain it exceeds what is available … humanity's footprint is 21.9 ha/person, while the Earth's biological capacity is, on average, only 15.7 ha/person, with the ultimate result that there is net environmental degradation and loss" (UNEP, 2007: 202/Box 6.1). For criminologists, this kind of ecological observation ought to be of major concern, not least of all because if the problems are to be addressed they will require new categorizations of environmental harms as criminal. This will also require enhanced crime prevention, law enforcement, prosecution, sentencing, and restoration strategies in this area.

The bottom line is that, regardless of legal status, action has to be taken immediately to prevent harms associated with global warming, further pollution and waste generation, and threats to biodiversity. The imperative is ecological, not legal, and the outcome, ultimately, is human survival. Thus, analysis of transnational environmental harm needs to incorporate different notions of harm within the broad overarching perspective of green criminology (see Box 1).

Differing conceptions of harm, therefore, will give rise to different understandings and interpretations of the nature and dynamics of transnational environmental crime.

Box 1. Concepts of environmental harm

Laws, rules, and international conventions inform legal conceptions of harm. The key issue is one of legality, and the division of activities into legal and illegal categories. Examples include the illegal taking of flora and fauna (e.g., illegal fishing), pollution offenses (e.g., air, water, and land pollution associated with industry) and the transportation of banned substances (e.g., the illegal transfer of radioactive waste).

Ecological well-being and holistic understandings of harm are informed by the interrelationship between species and environments. The key issue is that of ecological sustainability and the division of social practices into two categories: benign and destructive. Examples include the problem of climate change (those activities that contribute to global warming), the problem of waste and pollution (those activities that defile the environment, leading to things such as the diminishment of clean water), and the problem of biodiversity (i.e., issues relating to species extinction).

Conceptions of harm are informed by notions of human and animal rights, as well as ecological and egalitarian concerns. It is important that different kinds of harm and violates of rights be adjudicated within the context of an eco-justice framework. Important aspects of such a framework include a concern with environment rights and environmental justice (e.g., practices that deny some groups adequate access to safe, nontoxic environments), ecological citizenship and ecological justice (e.g., preserving complex ecosystems that should be preserved for their own sake), and animal rights and species justice (e.g., preventing animal abuse).

DIFFERENT TYPES OF TRANSNATIONAL ENVIRONMENTAL CRIME

Transnational environmental crime can be viewed from the perspective of four intertwined social processes that are affecting world ecology (see White, 2008, 2009; UNEP, 2007). These perspectives relate to varied forms of extraction and exploitation of nature, generally for purposes of private profit. They include the following:

- Resource depletion – extraction of nonrenewable minerals and energy without development of proper alternatives, and overharvesting of renewable resources such as fish and forest timbers.
- Disposal problems – waste generated in production, distribution, and consumption processes, and pollution associated with transformations of nature, burning of fossil fuels, and using up of consumables.

- Corporate colonization of nature – genetic changes in food crops, use of plantation forestry that diminishes biodiversity, preference for large-scale, technology-dependent, and high-yield agricultural and aquacultural methods that degrade land and oceans and affect species' development and well-being, as well as bio-piracy of indigenous knowledge, lands, and techniques.
- Species decline – destruction of habitats, privileging of certain species of grains and vegetables over others for market purposes, and super-exploitation of specific plants and animals, due to presumed consumer taste and mass markets.

Crimes Related to Disposal of Toxic and Other Hazardous Wastes

More specific studies uncover particular kinds of problems and the peculiarities of these problems. For example, the waste management area presents numerous opportunities for crime (Van Daele et al., 2007). This is evidenced by the illegitimate international trade and transportation of hazardous wastes, the role of organized criminal syndicates in waste management, and the illegal dumping of waste by legitimate corporations. What is meant by the term "hazardous waste" is itself subject to much ambiguity and debate. It is notable in this regard that in November 2008 the European Union enacted a new Waste Framework Directive, with several articles and an appendix dealing specifically with hazardous waste, and the properties of waste that render it hazardous. The definition of hazardous waste, and the link of disposal of hazardous waste to specifically criminal activity, warrants close scrutiny. Certainly from a criminological perspective, in many countries there is little knowledge of the scale of the problem, the types of criminality involved, or the precise nature of the disposal (e.g., illegal dumping, combining illegal with legal waste, and illegal export).

Crimes Related to Global Processes

One consequence of global trends related to climate change is an expected upsurge in social conflict (Smith & Vivekananda, 2007). The conflicts include those pertaining to diminished environmental resources, to the impacts of global warming, to differential access and use of nature, and to friction stemming from the crossborder transference of harm. To take one example, Inuit populations in the eastern Canadian Arctic and Greenland have the highest exposures to persistent organic pollutants and mercury from traditional diets of populations from among anywhere in the world.

They have had no choice in the matter, since the problem actually originates outside of their territory. "Scientific assessments have detected persistent organic pollutants (POPs) and heavy metals in all components of the Arctic ecosystem, including in people. The majority of these substances are present in the ecosystems and diets of Arctic peoples as a result of choices (such as using the insecticide toxaphene on cotton fields) by industrial societies elsewhere. Contaminants reach the Arctic from all over the world through wind, air, and water currents, and enter the food chain" (UNEP, 2007: 20). Specific practices that are deemed to be good and productive for the global, political economy have dire consequences for environments, humans, and nonhuman animals throughout the world.

Crimes Related to Specific Geographical Regions

While there are broad similarities in the types of environmental crimes that traverse borders – such as pollution, the international transfer of hazardous wastes, and the illegal trade in wildlife – it is still necessary to examine such crimes in the context of their immediate geographical and criminal specificity. The export of e-waste to Southeast Asia and to Africa, for example, has the same general drivers but different specific dynamics from the export of hazards, especially related to agriculture and mining, to Latin America. Illegal fishing varies greatly depending upon location, and particular types of illegal fishing, such as abalone (Australia), lobster (Canada), and toothfish (Southern Ocean), show great variation in motives, techniques, local cultures, and scales of operation. Elephant poaching in Africa is very different to bio-prospecting in South America, while the taking of "bush meat" is a distinctive African phenomenon very different in character to illegal fishing by Indonesian fishers off the coast of Australia (Cifuentes & Frumkin, 2007; Lemieux & Clarke, 2009; UNEP, 2007; White, 2008).

Different regions of the world share overlapping problems, such as those related to climate change and those involving international transfers of harmful products. Albeit at the same time, it is vital that criminologists be aware of distinct local and regional variations in the kinds of harms that are evident, and in the specific forces at play within each region. For example, the response to climate change in the USA, New Zealand, and Indonesia may mean greater reliance upon and production of crops for biofuels, which in turn affects food consumption in places such as Mexico and, in some instances, involves the forcing of indigenous people off of their land in countries such as Brazil.

TRANSNATIONAL ENVIRONMENTAL HARM AND ECO-GLOBAL CRIMINOLOGY

The question of scale of analysis is one that ranges from the local to the global and is at the heart of contemporary efforts to study transnational environmental crime (Gibbs et al., 2010; White, 2008). "Eco-global criminology" refers to a criminological approach that is informed by ecological considerations and by a critical analysis that is worldwide in its scale and perspective. It is based upon eco-justice conceptions of harm that include consideration of transgressions against environments, nonhuman species, and humans (White, 2009). This new sort of criminology occupies that space between the traditional concerns of criminology (with its fixation on working class criminality and conventional street crimes) and the vision of an egalitarian, ecologically sustainable future (where the concern is with ecological citizenship, precautionary social practices, and inter- and intragenerational equity).

The barriers to and prospects of a more ecologically balanced world are interwoven with powerful social interests and the contestation of what matters when it comes to change and transformation. The differences in conceptualizations of environmental harm to some degree reflect differences in social position and lived experience (i.e., issues of class, gender, indigeneity, ethnicity, and age). They are also mired in quite radically different paradigmatic understandings of nature and human interests (e.g., ecology-centered versus human centered). An adequate policy response to transnational environmental crime will require both ongoing dialogue about the nature and definition of such harms, and the cooperation of environmental law enforcement officials across different jurisdictions.

For the eco-global criminologist the biggest threat to environmental rights, ecological justice, and nonhuman animal well-being are system-level structures and pressures that: commodify all aspects of social existence; are based upon the exploitation of humans, nonhuman animals, and natural resources; and privilege powerful minority interests over the vast majority. Those who determine and shape the law are very often those whose activities ought to be criminalized. Dealing with transnational environmental crime will always be fraught with controversy and conflict to the extent that fundamental interests clash and questions of justice come to the fore. However, for the sake of planetary well-being, criminologists must take on the task of researching transnational environmental crime regardless of the politics and hurdles to such work.

REFERENCES

Beirne, P. & N. South. (Eds.) (2007). *Issues in Green Criminology: Confronting Harms Against Environments, Humanity and Other Animals*. Devon: Willan.

Cifuentes, E. & H. Frumkin. (2007). Environmental Injustice: Case Studies from the South, *Environmental Research Letters*, 2, 1–9.

Dorn, N., S. Van Daele, & T. Beken. (2007). Reducing Vulnerabilities to Crime of the European Waste Management Industry: The Research Base and the Prospects for Policy, *European Journal of Crime, Criminal Law and Criminal Justice*, 15(1), 23–36.

Gibbs, C., M. Gore, E. McGarrell, & L. Rivers III. (2010). Introducing Conservation Criminology: Towards Interdisciplinary Scholarship on Environmental Crimes and Risks. *British Journal of Criminology*, 50(1), 124–44.

Hayman, G. & D. Brack. (2002). *International Environmental Crime: The Nature and Control of Environmental Black Markets*. London: Sustainable Development Programme, Royal Institute of International Affairs.

Lemieux, A. & R. Clarke. (2009). The International Ban on Ivory Sales and Its Effects on Elephant Poaching in Africa. *British Journal of Criminology*, 49(4), 451–71.

Smith, D. & J. Vivekananda. (2007). *A Climate of Conflict: The Links Between Climate Change, Peace and War*. London: International Alert.

United Nations Environment Programme. (2007). *Global Environment Outlook*. New York: UNEP.

White, R. (2008). *Crimes Against Nature: Environmental Criminology and Ecological Justice*. Devon: Willan Press.

White, R. (2009). Climate Change and Social Conflict: Toward an Eco-Global Research Agenda. In K. Kangaspunta & I. Marshall (Eds.), *Eco-Crime and Justice: Essays on Environmental Crime*. Turin, Italy: United Nations Interregional Crime Research Institute [UNICRI].

ABOUT THE AUTHOR

Rob White is a professor of criminology in the School of Sociology and Social Work at the University of Tasmania, Australia. He has published extensively in the areas of youth studies and criminology. Among his recent books are *Crimes Against Nature: Environmental Criminology and Ecological Justice* and *Global Environmental Harm: Criminological Perspectives*.

26 The Bhopal Gas Disaster and Corporate Criminal Negligence

G. S. Bajpai and Bir Pal Singh

INTRODUCTION

Bhopal, the capital of the state of Madhya Pradesh in India, is known throughout the world for the huge industrial disaster, affecting millions of people, that occurred at a Union Carbide pesticide plant on the night of December 3, 1984. The Union Carbide Corporation technical team reports that a large volume of water was introduced into the Methyl Isocyanate tank and triggered a reaction (MIC) that resulted in the gas release (Lapierre & Moro, 1997).

In 1969, the Union Carbide Corporation (UCC), a U.S. company, set up a plant in Bhopal in a joint venture with the Indian government. The plant was intended to produce pesticides for use in India's huge agricultural sector. The decision to manufacture the pesticide in India, as opposed to relying on imports, was based on India's goal of preserving foreign exchange and its policy of industrialization (Cassels, 1994). The site was chosen for several reasons. Bhopal is centrally located in India, with good railway connections. There are many nearby lakes to provide water. It has sufficient supplies of both electricity and labor needed to sustain a large industrial plant.

FACTORS CAUSING LEAKAGE OF GASES

It is puzzling that such a massive accident could occur in a plant that was supposed to meet international standards of safety. Many factors have been blamed for the leakage of gas in official and independent probes. The first factor relates to the huge and unsafe storage of lethal chemical tanks. The UCC was invariably storing more than the permitted quantities.

In the interests of economy, several vital safety arrangements were also reported to have been compromised. Some NGOs accused the UCC of having double standards for safety when planning factories in developing countries (Chouhan et al, 1994; Ecikerman, 2003). The most serious allegations of negligence were the weaker safety measures and environmental standards in the Indian plant as compared to a similar plant located in West Virginia in the United States. The parent plant had computerized warning and monitoring system while the Indian plant relied on manual gauges and the human senses to detect gas leaks. The capacities of storage tanks, gas scrubbers, and flare towers were also greater at the parent plant in the U.S.

The location of the Bhopal plant near a very densely populated area, which was devoid of any effective systems of health care and disaster management, aggravated the impact of the catastrophe. In fact, an alternative location had been suggested to the UCC by the local administration, but it was not agreed mainly because of infrastructural conveniences. In addition, the staffing policy in the UCC also smacked of gross carelessness. The operators, in most cases, were insufficiently trained to handle the sensitive task of maintaining the storage and upkeep of a plant that used lethal materials. The management as a whole did not understand the true measures of safety and monitoring that were essential. This is evident from the fact that between 1974 and 1984 several minor incidences of leakage and other malfunctions were brought to the notice of management, but without any serious action resulting. It was also found that the gas scrubber designed to neutralize any escaping MIC had been shut off for maintenance. Even had it been operative, postdisaster inquiries revealed that the maximum pressure it could handle was only one quarter of that actually reached in the accident (Weir, 1987). The UCC itself admitted that most of the safety systems were not functioning on the night of December 3, 1984.

MAGNITUDE OF CALAMITY

The gas leakage was so intensive and engulfing that it took a massive toll of lives of people who were sleeping in their dwellings in a radius of about 10 kilometers and beyond. The exact number of casualties is unknown due to mass burials, cremations, and conflicting medical opinions. In the beginning, the death toll was said to be 2,259. By 1987, it was reported as about 3,500 and by 1992, it was more than 4,000. Victims' organizations placed the figure many thousands higher. In addition, 30,000 to 40,000 people were maimed and seriously injured, and 200,000 were otherwise affected through minor injury, death of a family member, and economic and social dislocation (Cassels, 1994). It is now widely believed that more than 7,000 people died within a few days with a further 15,000 deaths in the following years. Around 100,000 people are suffering chronic and debilitating illnesses that cannot be effectively treated.

The catastrophe stunned the world and posed fundamental questions about corporate and government responsibility for industrial accidents that wreak enormous damage to human life and the environment.

OTHER HEALTH-RELATED CONSEQUENCES

The true impact of the tragedy cannot be measured just by the number of deaths. There was also a toll in serious physiological disorders, which emerged either immediately after the incident, or developed even after many weeks. The range of disorders was extremely crippling. In the longer term, the majority of survivors developed chronic respiratory illness. Several surveys found the prevalence of respiratory disorders to the extent of 96 percent among those exposed to gases. A survey by the Indian Council of Medical Research (ICMR) found the gases caused serious eye irritations, corneal erosions, and cataracts, a phenomenon termed the "Bhopal eye syndrome." According to the Madhya Pradesh Gas Relief and Rehabilitation Department, the gas leak also caused damage to the immune system. Nearly twenty-five years after exposure, severely exposed people were four times more likely to suffer from common illnesses, five times more likely to suffer from lung ailments, three times more likely to suffer from eye problems, and more than twice as likely to suffer from stomach ailments. Autopsies revealed changes not only in the lungs but also cerebral oedema, tubular necrosis of the kidneys, fatty generation of the liver, and necrotizing enteritis.

The gases had a particularly severe impact on women and children. It is estimated that children born in Bhopal after the disaster face twice the risk of dying as do children elsewhere, partly because parents cannot care for them adequately. As early as March 1985, two studies revealed a large number of gynecological disorders in women who were exposed to gases. Chief among the symptoms were excessive vaginal discharge and abnormal uterine bleeding. It was also reported that many women who were pregnant at the time of the gas leak suffered miscarriages. According to the ICMR, of 2,566 pregnant women, 373 had "spontaneous abortions." Rates of miscarriage decreased sharply from severely exposed to less exposed areas. In severely exposed areas, the rate was more than 50 percent in 1984.

The ICMR reported that 10 to 12 percent of patients who visited clinics had "psychological symptoms." According to data from ten satellite government clinics in moderately and severely affected areas, 22 percent of 855 patients had psychiatric problems. Newspapers have reported increased cervical and breast cancers among women.

The location of the plant aggravated the effects of the leakage. Apart from the fact that there were a large number of settlements in proximity to the plant where mostly laborers and other underprivileged groups were living, the wind direction on that night meant that the gas leak disproportionately affected the poorest in the city. As confirmed by ICMR studies, 68 to 86 percent of the population in the severely affected area belonged to a "very depressed socio-economic class."

ENVIRONMENTAL HARMS

A report produced by The Indian Council of Agricultural Research on damage to crops, vegetables, animals, and fish from the accident stated that as many as 4,000 cattle as well as dogs, cats, and birds were killed. Plant life was also severely damaged by exposure to the gas. There was also widespread defoliation of trees, especially in low-lying areas.

Legal Action

The Chairman and CEO of Union Carbide, Warren Anderson, was arrested and released on bail by the Madhya Pradesh Police in Bhopal on December 7, 1984. In 1987, the Indian government summoned Warren Anderson, eight other executives and two company affiliates to appear on homicide charges in an Indian court. Union Carbide resisted this on grounds of jurisdiction. Warren Anderson was charged in 1991 with manslaughter, a crime that carries a maximum penalty of ten years of imprisonment, by a local court in Bhopal. The Government of India sought Anderson's extradition from the United States, with whom India had an extradition treaty in place, but repeated attempts did not succeed. Meanwhile, very paltry sums of money from the settlement reached the survivors, and people in the area felt betrayed not only by Union Carbide, but also by their own politicians. On the anniversary of the tragedy, effigies of Anderson and politicians are regularly burned.

To provide greater protection of victim rights, the Government of India enacted the Bhopal Gas Leak Disaster (Processing of Claims) Act in March 1985. The act was amended in 1992 and authorizes the Government of

India, as *parens patriate* exclusively to represent the Bhopal Gas victims so that interests of those victims of the disaster are fully protected, and that claims for compensation are pursued speedily, effectively, equitably, and to the best advantage of the claimants.

In July 2004, the Indian Supreme Court ordered the Indian government to release any remaining settlement funds to victims. The fund is believed to amount to $500 million after earning interest "from money remaining after all claims had been paid." August 2006 saw the Second Circuit Court of Appeals in New York City uphold the dismissal of remaining claims in the case of *Bano versus Union Carbide Corporation*. This move blocked plaintiffs' motions for class certification and claims for property damages and remediation. In the view of Union Carbide, "the ruling reaffirms UCC's long-held positions and finally puts to rest – both procedurally and substantively – the issues raised in the class action complaint first filed against Union Carbide in 1999." In September 2006, the Welfare Commission for Bhopal Gas Victims announced that all original compensation claims and revised petitions have been "cleared."

Criminal charges are proceeding against former senior officers of Union Carbide India Limited and Federal class action litigation (*Sahu vs. Union Carbide et al.*) is presently pending on appeal before the Second Circuit Court of Appeals in New York. The litigation seeks damages for personal injury, medical monitoring, and injunctive relief in the form of cleanup of the drinking water supplies for residential areas near the Bhopal plant. A related complaint seeking similar relief for property damage claimants is stayed, pending the outcome of the Sahu appeal before the federal district court in the Southern District of New York. In February 2009, U.S. Federal Court in New York declined to declare mediation in the Sahu case. Thus, litigation of the Bhopal Gas Disaster has become an ever-increasing process and, ultimately, has only given more pain to the living of the affected people. This painful, lengthy legal process adds to the list of basic human rights violation. A fair and speedy trial is now *sin qua non* of Article 21; it is implicit in the broad sweep and content of Article 21. (*Hussainara Khatoon vs. Home Secretary*, State of Bihar. AIR 1979 SC1360).

On June 7, 2010, after twenty-three years of the occurrence of Bhopal accident, a local court in Bhopal convicted former Union Carbide India Chairman Keshub Mahindra and seven others in the Bhopal Gas tragedy case and awarded them a maximum of two years imprisonment for acting rashly and negligently. This has triggered countrywide outrage. The main controversy is that the punishment is disproportionate to the enormity of their offense. Looking at the massive protests and huge campaigning across the country, the Madhya Pradesh Government has decided to move the Supreme Court to reopen the case. The jurists and lawyers are divided on this point as the reopening of case is generally not admissible. The investigations and archives are under scanner to spot the culpability of political leaders, bureaucrats, and others who allegedly played crucial role in effecting the safe exit of Mr. Anderson, the prime accused in the case.

Present Condition of the Site

The disaster site is becoming further contaminated owing to the massive chemical vestiges that remain on the UCC site because the area around the plant was used as a dumping ground area for hazardous chemicals. Between 1969 and 1977, all effluents were dumped in an open pit. From then on, neutralization with hydrochloric acid was undertaken. The effluents went to two evaporation ponds. In the rainy season, the effluents used to overflow. By 1982, tube wells near the UCC factory had to be abandoned. In 1991, the municipal authorities declared water from more than one hundred tube wells to be unfit for drinking.

Studies made by Greenpeace and others of soil, groundwater, well water, and vegetables from the residential areas around UCIL and from the UCIL factory area show contamination with a range of toxic heavy metals and chemical compounds. A sample of drinking water from a well near the site had levels of contamination five hundred times higher than the maximum limits recommended by the World Health Organization. Some areas are reportedly so polluted that anyone entering the area for more than ten minutes is likely to lose consciousness. Rainfall causes run-off, polluting local wells, and boreholes. Surveys of local residents, with a control population in a similarly poor area away from the plant, are reported to reveal higher levels of various diseases around the plant. Cleanup operations on the site could not make any headway mainly due to the sale of company and the indifference of authorities.

SUMMARY AND CONCLUSION

The Bhopal incident was not only an industrial disaster but was also a fundamental violation of human rights. It is the leading example of a corporate violation of human rights. It is also a classical example of reckless negligence constituting what could be termed as "corporate deviance." Such views find mention in the Amnesty Report (2004: 2): "Governments have the primary responsibility for protecting the human rights of communities endangered by the activities of corporations, such as those employing hazardous technology. However, as the influence and reach of companies have grown, there has been a developing consensus that they must be brought within the framework of international human rights standards."

REFERENCES

Amnesty International. (2004). *Clouds of Injustice – Bhopal Disaster 20 Years On.* Retrieved from *www.amnesty.org/en/library/info/ASA20/015/2004.*

Cassels, J. (1994). *The Uncertain Promise of Law – Lessons from Bhopal.* Toronto: University of Toronto Press.

Chouhan, T. R. (1994). *Bhopal: The Inside Story – Carbide Workers Speak Out on the World's Worst Industrial Disaster.* New York: Apex Press.

Indian Council for Medical Research (ICMR). (1994). Health Effects of the Toxic Gas Leak from the Union Carbide Methyl Isocyanate Plant in Bhopal.

Lapierre, D. & J. Moro. (1997). *Five Past Midnight in Bhopal: The Epic Story of the World's Deadliest Industrial Disaster.* New York: Simon & Schuster.

UN Norms on the Responsibilities of Transnational Corporations and Other Business Enterprises with Regard to Human Rights, UN Doc. E/CN.4/Sub.2/2003/12/Rev.1 (2003).

Weir, D. (1987). *The Bhopal Syndrome: Pesticides, Environment, and Health.* San Francisco: Sierra Club Books.

ABOUT THE AUTHOR

Prof. G. S. Bajpai serves as Chairperson at the Centre for Civil & Criminal Justice Administration, National Law Institute University, Bhopal (M.P.), India. His areas of interests include criminology, criminal justice, victimology, and research methods. He has held several international assignments including the Commonwealth Academic Staff Fellowship in the U.K., and visits under cultural exchange programs for undertaking advanced research in France, Japan, and the Netherlands.

Dr. Bir Pal Singh is presently working as assistant professor at the National Law Institute University, Bhopal (M.P.), India. His teaching and research interests include sociology, sociology of law, rural sociology, social-cultural anthropology, tribal and customary laws, legal anthropology, conflict management, democratic decentralization in rural India, and empowerment of weaker sections.

27 Endangered Species Markets

A FOCUS FOR CRIMINOLOGY?

Jacqueline Schneider

THE TRANSNATIONAL CRIME OF ILLEGAL TRAFFICKING IN ENDANGERED SPECIES

Approximately 50,000 species of wild fauna and flora become extinct each day. In large part, they reach this status because of human being's illegal activities. In addition to habitat destruction, species are illegally hunted, harvested, and transported for sale, either for personal consumption or for profit in international illegal market structures. These illegal activities are partly due to the extreme scarcity of food in some areas; therefore, endangered fauna and flora, including those protected by international conventions, are sacrificed for human survival. Illicit markets have increased the speed at which various species reach such critically low numbers. The loss of species has long-term, negative consequences on ecosystems worldwide. We must keep in mind that it is not just the plight of the majestic tiger or magnificent elephants about which action is necessary; rather, there are less well-known species, including the rarely considered algae that are critically endangered due to human activity and whose demise has negative effects on other plant and animal populations. We must keep in mind that the elimination of a given fish species can have devastating effects – for example, if particular algae-eating fish become extinct, the fate of an entire coral reef could very easily come into question. Some of the end effects of the various ecosystem-chain reactions are simply yet to be known.

Historically, conservation agency reports have provided much of what we know about the plight of endangered wild animals and plants. Despite the illegal nature of the activity, the topic has not been one of particular importance or interest to traditional criminologists. Given the consequences associated with endangered species markets, criminologists seem negligent in their lack of attention. Reasons for this disregard are complicated. Perhaps because poaching is seen to take place in faraway lands, it seems irrelevant to those so far removed. Or perhaps it is because competing areas of study, such terrorism or human trafficking, are seen as far more important or prestigious to pursue. Furthermore, criminologists seem to be rooted firmly in their own country's domestic crime issues, and most are reluctant to enter into the realm of international criminology, thus leaving widespread international crime to spread without fear of intervention. It has been suggested that the lack of attention is attributable to the criminology community believing that the subject is best suited to conservationists or ecologists. However, as illicit international markets orchestrate a more sinister scenario in the demise of endangered fauna and flora, criminologists have a unique and critical perspective to contribute.

THE PRACTICES AND ESTIMATED COSTS

According to Cook et al. (2002), there are five types of illegal activities related to the illegal trade in protected fauna and flora. These are illegal timber trade; caviar trafficking; related activities with drug trafficking; skins, fur, and traditional Asian medicines (TAMs); and specialist species collection. There is some discrepancy as to how the markets operate. A study by Cook et al. (2002) states that each of the five activities has its own unique, highly organized set of practices and markets, while Cowdrey (2002) claims that all the trade routes run parallel with, not only one another, but other illegal markets. Zimmerman (2003) reports that endangered species trade is linked to organized crime activities, such as weapons and drugs trafficking. This raises the need for criminological research on how illegal endangered species markets operate and then on how to reduce their existence.

In the most rudimentary terms, species are taken from their natural habitat, or range state, to the final consumer, who can literally be thousands of miles away or right next-door. What happens between capture, kill, harvest, and purchase is relatively arcane. For example, with animals we know that either two things can occur: (1) They can be kept alive for sale through illicit markets as either pets or beasts of burden or (2) they can be slaughtered, dissected, and sold (again through illegal markets) for their most valuable parts – either to be ingested or cherished. How and when these activities take place are not known; we simply remain in the dark about these processes.

Perhaps the most widely known example of the effects of the endangered species trade is that of the tiger. The tiger is one of the most recognized and regal of all land mammals and it is also among the most endangered. There is no exact census of wild tigers, but research estimates that all subspecies combined total under 4,000 – globally. All nine subspecies of tiger are listed in Appendix 1 of the Red List of Threatened Species; moreover, three are extinct, one is functionally extinct in the wild, one is critically endangered, and four have recently been upgraded from critically endangered to endangered. These animals are killed mainly for use in TAMs, as the tiger is thought to be of value for its curative powers along with its magical powers, but its skins are coveted for their beauty and the status they bestow. Appendix 1 contains species most seriously threatened with extinction and no commercial trade of species in this category is permissible.

Criminologists can longer ignore crimes that bring species close to extinction, ruin communities, and destroy ecosystems. Research shows that profits generated from illicit trafficking in endangered species are only second to that of the illegal drug trade (Zimmerman, 2003). Estimating profits produced by black markets is extraordinarily difficult. Cooke et al. (2002) calculate profits at US$159 billion based on values of declared imports; whereas the Wildlife Unit of the London Metropolitan Police approximate the amount generated by the illegal trade to be US$25 billion. Cowdrey (2002) measures the illegal trade in caviar from the UAE alone to be worth US$25 million. These are simply a few examples of estimates, which are no doubt undercalculated due to the underground nature of the trade. Currently, there is no central agency that collects data in a uniform manner that would result perhaps in more consistent calculations and more accurate estimates (see Schneider, 2008).

The crime of trading in endangered species does indeed have the potential to generate enormous illicit profits. The laws of supply and demand dictate that the more scarce the commodity, the higher the purchase price. The rarer the demanded species is, the harder it is to locate, hunt, dissect, and transport, which will increase costs at every link in the illegal market chain. Because of its invisibility to authorities, a favorable risk-to-reward ratio for offenders is created. These two conditions combined set the stage for extreme profits (see Cook et al., 2002; Schneider, 2008; Lemieux & Clarke, 2009).

RELEVANT AGENCIES AND LEGISLATION

Endangered species are protected via international and domestic legislation that aims to control the trade in certain wild animals and plants in order to ensure the viability of those specifically threatened with extinction. While each country has responsibilities to these ends, there are a number of international organizations that take charge with protecting endangered species globally. The organizations are nongovernmental organizations (NGOs) or quasigovernmental agencies whose remit is to conserve species and to help countries organize national efforts to do so.

Agencies

The UN Office of Drugs and Crime (UNODC) is responsible for crime prevention, justice, and legal reform. The major foci within UNODC are transnational and organized crime, corruption, and terrorism. These stem from the UN Convention Against Transnational and Organized Crime and its protocols (in force September 2003), which focus on several areas including: firearms, protection of wild fauna and flora, cultural items, vulnerable persons (women and children), smuggling of migrants, and smuggling human organs (see UN 2001, 2004).

The UN Environmental Programme (UNEP) is responsible for the implementation of the Convention on the International Trade in Endangered Species of Wild Fauna and Flora (CITES), which is considered to be the most successful and long-standing international agreement pertaining to the protection of wild endangered species. The CITES Secretariat is administered by UNEP and is the coordinating and advisory body for CITES – providing assistance to the signatories on all aspects of the implementation of it.

CITES Secretariat works closely with: the International Union for Conservation of Nature and Natural Resources (IUCN); TRAFFIC; and the UNEP-World Conservation Monitoring Centre (UNEP-WCMC). IUCN is a network of government representatives, NGOs, and individual scientists working in sixty offices worldwide. The mission of IUCN is to encourage and help countries put conservation and sustainable use and development at the forefront of their efforts. IUCN actively helps countries and related NGOs to develop laws, policies, and best practices regarding conservation and preservation. IUCN also produces the Red List of Threatened Species, which catalogues those species that warrant protection and sets standards for recording species status. Currently, there are more than 30,000 species on the Red List, which classifies species as either: extinct, extinct in the wild, critically endangered, endangered, vulnerable, near threatened, least concern, data deficient, and not evaluated. The determination as to what category a species belongs is an extremely complicated process (see IUCN, 2001 for further details).

TRAFFIC is an international organization that monitors wildlife trade worldwide. Their primary aim is to ensure that wild fauna and flora remain at viable and sustainable levels; they also work to expose illegal trade activities. Through active research, they help communities identify ways to bolster their economies in alternative ways so as to preserve the integrity levels of wildlife.

UNEP-WCMC also provides input and guidance on species conservation in addition to offering information about CITES, the European Union's Wildlife Trade Regulations, the Convention on Migratory Species, and the Convention on Biological Diversity. The main responsibility of UNEP-WCMC is to provide analyses and information on conservation, sustainable use to those countries and NGOs who are involved in the initiative.

International Legislation

There is a rich history of national and international legislation that has afforded the requisite level of protection to those specific species deemed in danger of extinction; most have been species-specific, enacted by conservationists, and short-lived. For example, in 1781, a convention aimed at protecting forests and game fowl was agreed between the King of France and Prince-Bishop of Basel. The agreement, however, was formed on the basis of economic protections for each signatory. The London Convention of 1933 for the protection of African Wildlife transformed how protection of fauna and flora was approached. Rather than just focusing on those species that transcend national borders, it was decided that domestically located animals and plants deserved legal protections. The paradigm shift was significant because nations suddenly became responsible for all species that lived within their borders and it was acknowledged that each nation's responsibility had global implications, thus bringing to light the "notion of common heritage" (van Heijnsbergen, 1997: 7).

Today, the most significant international agreement for protecting wild endangered species is CITES, which went into force in 1975. The aim of CITES is to monitor and regulate the trade in certain wild species in order to ensure they do not reach extinct or critically endangered status. CITES requires each signatory to establish a scientific authority, which advises on classifications, and a management authority, which deals with policy issues. Signatory parties agree to the tenets of CITES voluntarily, but the convention is legally binding. By signing on to CITES, nations simply agree to design national legislation that supports the mission of the Convention.

CITES established a permit system that regulates the import and export of regulated wild fauna and flora. Three CITES appendices categorize wild animals and plants based on the level of protection needed, which in turn dictate the level of trade permitted. Appendix 1 contains species threatened with extinction and holds that trade is therefore permitted only in extraordinary circumstances. Appendix 2 species are not yet threatened with extinction, but in order to stop the further decline in the species' number, trade is extremely restricted. Animals and plants listed in Appendix 3 are not currently under extreme threat; however, at least one country seeks to protect the species within their borders and is calling on other countries to assist in their efforts.

Enforcement

Each signatory party to CITES is required to implement national legislation that enables each country to protect its natural resources. Unfortunately, enforcement of these laws is the weakest link in the chain of efforts aimed at protecting our most rare resources, including endangered fauna and flora. Efforts around the globe are largely geared toward detecting offenders. Even in countries with wealthy economies, policing wildlife crimes is a challenge. For example, in the United Kingdom, the National Wildlife Crime Unit has only one dedicated full-time officer, with others contributing as time and workloads allow. Other range countries have instituted antipoaching patrols that do arrest offenders, but it seems implausible to think these units are the answer. Many patrol areas are national parks whose areas exceed hundreds of thousands of square miles. Enforcement funding is extremely limited and will never fully provide adequate coverage to actively patrol these areas for motivated offenders. An alternative is needed to supplement these efforts. The market reduction approach is an innovative crime reduction strategy that aims to reduce market-level wildlife crimes by making it more risky for all those in the market chain to engage in the illicit activities (see Schneider, 2008).

SUMMARY AND CONCLUSION

Reducing the illicit trade of endangered species is an extremely low priority among traditional criminologists. The crime has dangerous consequences not only for the targeted species and their ecosystems, but also for the collateral damage inflicted on those on the periphery of the trade. The trade is extremely structured and has links to other organized criminal activities, such as the international drug and weapons trades. The practice of hunting, harvesting, transporting, and selling protected wild fauna and flora is invisible, which makes it extremely difficult to reduce. The crime is under-enforced and underfunded, thus complicating efforts to stop the illegal killing and trading of species.

Several international legal foundations and agencies are committed to protecting endangered species. CITES is the most significant agreement between countries that makes mandatory efforts to conserve species threatened with extinction. The treaty is considered to be the most successful international treaty in existence.

1. What is the Red List and how does it help conservation efforts?
2. What are the main legal tools to help regulate endangered species trade?
3. Why is it important to look at the crime of illegally trading protected species?
4. What part does the United Nations play in reducing the illegal trade in endangered species?

REFERENCES

Convention on International Trade in Endangered Species of Wild Fauna and Flora (CITES) www.cites.org. Retrieved July 28, 2009.

Cook, D., M. Roberts, & J. Lowther. (2002). *The International Wildlife Trade and Organized Crime: A Review of the Evidence and the Role of the UK.* Wolverhampton, UK: WWF-UK.

Cowdrey, D. (2002). *Switching Channels: Wildlife Trade Routes into Europe and the UK.* A WWF/TRAFFIC report. Wolverhampton, UK: University of Wolverhampton.

International Union for Conservation of Nature: www.iucn.org. Retrieved July 28, 2009.

Lemieux, A. & R. V. Clarke. (2009). The International Ban on Ivory Sales and Its Effects on Elephant Poaching in Africa. *British Journal of Criminology,* 49, 451–71.

Schneider, J. L. (2008). Reducing the Illicit Trade in Endangered Species. *Journal of Contemporary Criminal Justice,* 24(3), 274–95.

United Nations. (2001,2004). *UN Convention Against Transnational Organized Crime.* New York: United Nations Office on Drugs and Crime.

van Heijnsbergen, P. (1997). *International Legal Protection of Wild Fauna and Flora.* Amsterdam, The Netherlands: IOS Press.

Zimmerman, M. E. (2003). The Black Market for Wildlife: Combating Transnational Organized Crime in the Illegal Wildlife Trade. *Vanderbilt Journal of Transnational Law,* 36, 1657–1689.

WEB SITES

Interpol Environmental Crime Unit: www.interpol.int/public/environmentalcrime/
    wildlife
International Union for Conservation of Nature: www.iucn.org
Metropolitan Police (UK): www.met.police.uk/wildlife
TRAFFIC: www.traffic.org

ABOUT THE AUTHOR

Dr. Jacqueline Schneider is an associate professor and chair of the Department of Criminal Justice Sciences at Illinois State University. For six years, she taught and conducted research in England. She was the first recipient of the UK Home Office's Innovative Research Challenge Grant. She authored articles and book chapters on gangs, stolen goods markets, and endangered species, a topic on which she is currently writing a book.

28 Corruption

Adam Graycar

INTRODUCTION: A GENERAL OVERVIEW OF THE TOPIC

Corruption is not always criminal. Like criminal behavior, corruption hurts people and it causes outrage to victims and those who value civil society. Like criminal behavior, corruption is unethical. Corruption does not feature prominently in the criminal justice literature, and to learn about it students turn to literature in development economics, public administration, law, political science, and business studies. The criminal nature of corruption should be studied so that offender, opportunity, and target can be understood, in order that controls can be put in place.

Corruption can and does occur in all spheres of activity, and in all countries. In many countries the criminal justice system is badly corrupted. In others, criminal justice activities are at the forefront of dealing with corruption. Corruption is costly and devastating. The World Economic Forum has estimated that the cost of corruption equals more than 5 percent of global GDP (about US $2.6 trillion). The World Bank has estimated that about $1 trillion per year is paid in bribes; whereas about $40 billion per year is looted by corrupt political leaders.

BACKGROUND: DEFINITIONS, TRENDS, AND STATISTICS

Definitions of corruption abound, but certain behaviors are broadly agreed to be corrupt, and these include bribery, theft, embezzlement, and fraud by an individual whose position or employment provides access or opportunity; extortion, again by virtue of position, abuse of discretion, creating or exploiting conflict of interest, nepotism, clientelism, and favoritism.

The common characteristic in all these instances is the abuse of a formal position that involves a situation of trust.

Transparency International, the world's leading anticorruption NGO, defines corruption as "the misuse of entrusted power for private gain" (TI, 2008).

The abuse of position for personal gain has occurred throughout history, and has often been tied into culture and relationships. In ancient market societies, being allowed to have a stall in the bazaar depended on whether one was favorably viewed by the ruler. In modern societies if one wants to operate a stall in a market, one buys a permit from an authority or pays an agreed rent. There are rules and procedures and the process is usually regulated, orderly and simple. However, there are occasions when buying the permit might involve currying favor with an official, or giving a gift, or paying a consideration to achieve an inexpensive permit to carry out a routine activity.

Corruption can be grand or petty. Grand corruption involves those at the highest level of government who loot the treasury and improperly and dishonestly manipulate and control the institutions of power. "Grand corruption" describes the activities of former presidents like Suharto of Indonesia, Marcos of the Philippines, Mobutu of Zaire, Milosevic of Yugoslavia, all of whom were reported to have looted billions while in power. Grand corruption also describes "state capture," the manipulation by those not formally in power, and of the institutions of the state and its economic direction.

Petty corruption involves relatively small amounts of money changing hands to obtain some basic service or a permit, or to prevent something like a small fine or a parking or speeding ticket. It also covers a lot of contracts and purchases in procurement and in development aid programs, everything from medical equipment, bribes for medical services, purchase of textbooks in educational programs, and licenses for land clearing.

The corrupt behavior may be active or passive – one party actively offers a bribe or inducement, the other passively receives it. This can be complicated if the passive recipient solicits the bribe.

In some countries where corruption is all pervasive and endemic, combating corruption is a monumental and overwhelming task. It goes to the very heart of the culture and relationships, and involves a major change in the way people do business.

There are a number of behaviors that everyone would agree are corrupt behaviors. They include bribery, where money changes hands to obtain or to facilitate a satisfactory outcome that might not have happened without the money, or might not have happened as quickly. The inducement might be in cash, but it could also be in the form of inside information, meals and entertainment, holidays, employment, sexual favors, etc. It can involve getting somebody to do, or not to do something, or to overlook something. It can flow in either direction. It can be offered by the principal, or it can be solicited by the agent.

Extortion involves the use of force or other forms of intimidation to extract payments.

Theft and fraud have a place in corruption studies when they involve entrusted power. This can be on a huge scale, as evidenced in the case of the aforementioned kleptocrats, or can involve an official selling food from a relief aid shipment, or medical supplies that find their way into private practice when they have been donated for community health programs.

Abuse of discretion is very common. It happens in issuing of permits and licences, procurement, real estate developments, and often in the judicial system in some countries.

Self-dealing involves hiring one's own company, or the company belonging to close associates or relatives, to provide public services.

Patronage, nepotism, or favoritism occurs when one hires somebody because of who they are related to or who they are, rather than what they can do. It may provide benefits to somebody in the family or a close associate. There are also numerous examples of creating "no show" jobs – a corrupt pay-off where salaries are paid for people who never or rarely turn up.

Conflict of interest occurs when somebody is in a position to make a decision, and when they have an interest (real or perceived) that could benefit from that decision. There may be no actual impropriety, but the appearance of a conflict can undermine confidence. This is the subject of considerable debate, as very different standards are often brought to bear.

Political corruption and campaign financing irregularities are huge fields that strike at the very heart of democratic activities. Each of these phenomena and more, occur in different activities and different sectors of any society. Most commonly these apply in buying things – procurement processes, issuing contracts; in appointing personnel, or delivering programs or services; making things – road construction, major capital works, housing developments; controlling activities, such as licensing, regulation, or the issuing of permits etc.; and many forms of administering, such as the administration of justice, or health, or environmental services.

MEASURING CORRUPTION

Unlike many crimes, corruption does not lend itself easily to measurement. What we measure depends on how we describe the specific activity, and how it is defined, if it is, in criminal codes. Even where the activity is codified, asking, "how much corruption is there in a society" does not yield a clear and unambiguous number.

While it might be good to measure types of corruption, occurrence of corrupt behavior, or costs and effects, the most common measurement is of perceptions of corruption.

Transparency International publishes an annual corruption perception index in which it ranks 163 nations, as well as a "bribe payers index" of thirty countries. The methodology is explained in each publication, and one criticism of this approach is that it is not a measure of how much there is, or what effect it has, but rather what a group of well-placed experts thinks is the state of play.

The normal empirical tools of measurement are not always useful, as significant transactions are hidden and not reported, and any survey is unlikely to elicit a valid and reliable response. ("Do you take bribes? From whom? How often? What is the value? What do you have to do in return?")

Those studying corruption do often undertake desk reviews, surveys, focus groups, case studies, field observations, and professional assessments. Of course, these will yield results that may be applicable in a specific study rather than an overall assessment.

DISCUSSION OF MAJOR CONCEPTS

In some countries it is said that corruption is a response to need. Civil service salaries may be so very low that in order to survive people working in government offices depend on bribes as part of their income. Those who have dealings with the public, such as police officers, customs officials, tax collectors, and health or building inspectors can extort money from those with whom they are dealing by threatening not to allow a transaction, or prohibiting an import or closing down a business or activity if no extortion payment is forthcoming.

Need is no excuse for illegal or corrupt behavior. More often, however, the motivating factor is greed. For those so inclined, greed drives people in official positions to undertake activities that are both unprofessional and illegal.

Several strategies for combating corruption can be implemented.

Criminalization, Investigation, Prosecution, Sanctions

In many countries corruption has been criminalized – that is, it is basically illegal for a public official to solicit or accept a bribe or behave corruptly. However, investigation, enforcement, prosecution, and imposing sanctions can be challenging. These may not always be pursued with sufficient independence, nor be sufficiently resourced, or be rigorously implemented.

Anticorruption Agencies

Many countries also have anticorruption agencies, and some work wonderfully well, such as those in Singapore and Hong Kong, while in some other countries they have become part of the problem rather than the solution.

Structural Reform

Solutions sometimes lay in structural reform – making the civil service more accountable, merit based, formally organized, and very importantly, better paid. This needs to occur within a context of strong institutions of integrity – a legislature and executive that has and is seen to have integrity, a clean and functioning judiciary, an auditor general, watchdog agencies like an ombudsman, or an anticorruption agency, whistleblower protection, etc.

Education, Integrity Building Mobilization of the Public

A strong civic culture, vocal advocacy groups, civic education, information and education campaigns aimed at young children, an open media, and mobilization of the public are all factors that contribute to this set of strategies.

THE UNITED NATIONS CONVENTION AGAINST CORRUPTION

The most comprehensive response is the United Nations Convention Against Corruption. This is a global response to a global problem. So far 131 countries have ratified this treaty, which came into effect at the end of 2005.

The Convention introduces an extensive set of standards, measures, and rules that all countries can apply in order to strengthen their legal and regulatory regimes to fight corruption. It calls for preventive measures and the criminalization of the most prevalent forms of corruption in both public and private sectors. And it makes a major breakthrough by requiring member states to return assets obtained through corruption, to the country from which they were stolen.

As Kofi Annan, the former UN Secretary General said when introducing the convention "corrupt officials will in future find fewer ways to hide their illicit gains."

The convention commits signatory countries to developing preventive anticorruption policies and practices, which reflect the rule of law, integrity, transparency accountability, and properly manage public affairs and public property. States are to establish anticorruption bodies, and disseminate knowledge about the prevention of corruption.

The big task in the Convention is to strengthen the public sector by having open systems of recruiting, hiring, retention, and promotion of civil servants, as well as decent pay and education programs. There are to be codes of conduct for public servants, proper systems for public procurement and management of public finances, as well as open public reporting. The judiciary and prosecution services are to follow standards of integrity, and the public is to have access to information. In addition, there are to be measures for prevent money laundering.

To develop specific mechanisms to combat corruption it is necessary to identify available opportunities that facilitate corrupt behavior. Opportunities for corruption occur in societies and organizations where there is:

- a lack of a culture of integrity, especially among leaders,
- a lack of ethical codes or a lack of enforcement,
- the acceptance of patronage and nepotism,
- complexity of regulations or complexity of systems,
- weak financial controls, and
- weak institutions of governance.

In specific and localized activities, opportunities for corruption occur where:

- supervision and oversight is not taken seriously, or is remote from the activity (e.g., a police officer patrolling a highway);
- specialized knowledge and high discretion both operate;
- decisions affect costs and benefits of activities;
- there is no capable guardian;
- there is low decision monitoring;
- there is a silencing of whistleblowers;
- there is low risk of being caught.

Although there are no quick fixes, one way forward may be to examine some of the crime prevention approaches elsewhere in this volume, and work creatively to apply them to the control of corruption.

SUMMARY

- Corruption occurs in rich and poor countries alike. It is sometimes a response to need, sometimes a response to greed.
- Corruption can be classified as grand corruption or petty corruption.
- Defining corruption leads to long and convoluted debates, but defining the component parts (e.g., bribery, self-dealing, extortion, etc.) can be useful.
- The impacts of corruption disproportionally affect the poorest and most vulnerable in any society, and when widespread, corruption deters investment and weakens economic growth. If system integrity is dubious then the rule of law cannot be maintained.
- Combating corruption has had mixed success. Criminalization has not always worked. Global approaches include the United Nations Convention against Corruption, while local approaches include statutes, codes of conduct, investigation, and prosecution.
- Another likely approach is to develop situational responses in response to opportunities that may arise for corruption behavior. The first step here is to understand the opportunity structure for corruption.

REFERENCES

Transparency International (TI). (2008). *Frequently Asked Questions About Corruption*. Retrieved May, 16, 2009, from www.transparency.org/news_room/faq/corruption_faq#faqcorr1

WEB SITES

Transparency International: www.transparency.org
World Bank Institute: Anti-Corruption Program: www.worldbank.org/wbi/governance
United Nations Office on Drugs and Crime: www.unodc.org/unodc/en/corruption/index.html
United Nations Convention against Corruption www.unodc.org/pdf/corruption/publications_unodc_convention-e.pdf
OECD Fighting Corruption: www.oecd.org/corruption
Council of Europe GRECO (Group of States against Corruption): www.coe.int/t/dghl/monitoring/greco/default_en.asp

Internet Center for Corruption Research: www.icgg.org
U4 Anti-Corruption Resource Center: www.U4.no
USAID Anti-Corruption Resources: www.usaid.gov/our_work/democracy_and_
    governance/technical_areas/anti-corruption

ABOUT THE AUTHOR

Adam Graycar has worked at senior levels of government, and has also been the
director of the Australian Institute of Criminology and dean of the School of
Criminal Justice at Rutgers, the State University on New Jersey. He is now a professor at the Australian National University.

Andrew Lemieux and Marcus Felson

Many nations depend on tourism for their prosperity, yet tourists are very vulnerable to crime. This chapter puts tourist crime in a larger visitor perspective with concepts that can apply within and between nations, for those who travel both long and short distances from home. This chapter delineates tourist crime as part of a larger category, "visitor crime." Not only do visitors fall victim to crime but they also often participate in other ways, such as committing offenses when they visit. In addition, many people work or engage in recreation outside their residential area, even if they return home in the evening. Visitors are a diverse population, including (a) seasonal visitors, (b) overnight visitors, (c) day visitors, and (d) night visitors. Overnight visitors include foreign tourists, tourists within nations, and short-term visitors for pleasure and business purposes. Each of these subpopulations contributes to crime opportunity in their own way. We present a typology of visitor crime to assist officials and researchers who study crime events that involve one or more visitors.

TOURISTS AND VISITORS

Visitors are often crime victims. For example, Chesney-Lind and Lind (1986) studied mean annual crime rates per 100,000 in Honolulu, finding that robbery rates were 256 for visitors and 157 for residents. In Barbados, de Albuquerque and McElroy (1999) report burglary rates in 1989 of 2,173 for visitors compared to only 847 for residents. Visitors were four times as victimized as residents. Although these ratios were somewhat lower in subsequent years, the same general conclusion remains. Stangeland (1995) investigated tourist victimization in an interesting way, interviewing tourists in the Malaga, Spain, airport as they waited to leave the country. Despite visiting only a week or so, a very high percentage of visitors had been victimized.

In the studies just cited, the words "visitor" and "tourist" are used synonymously. Taking a deeper look, many visitors are not tourists in the normal sense. Residents of surrounding towns and suburbs visit a city for recreation and work. Some people visit overnight and others just for the day. For this reason we define "visitor crime" as the larger category, then treats "tourist crime" as one part of visitor crime. We further distinguish the different roles that tourists play in crime. However, much of our discussion is about tourist crime rather than other forms of visitor crime. Our main purpose in using the larger category here is to make readers aware of the theoretical link to a larger literature than the tourist crime literature alone. Indeed, the purpose of this paper is to embed tourist crime within a larger body of information about visitors – who are more likely to be offenders or victims and less likely to be guardians against crime.

We do not assume that visitors are only victims, since some visitors commit crimes and others witness crimes in which they are neither victim nor offender. When offender and victim come from different nations, this can create tensions between those nations or interfere with the tourist industries. It can also create local hostility toward outsiders. Within nations, visitor crime involvement can raise internal tensions and interfere with industries that depend on visitors.

PUBLIC OPINION AND TOURIST-RELATED CRIME

The economic dependence on tourism provides an incentive to hide or deny tourist crime. Such evasions may lead to a failure to face up to crime's realities and the need to change them. On the other hand, some people blame their crime on outsiders without considering the contribution of locals – a point to which we will return in a moment.

We do not assume that tourist crime is significant everywhere. To quote John M. Knox's 2004 study of tourist crime in Hawaii, "The relationship between serious crime and tourism varies from place to place and time to time. It is a matter of local circumstances." Yet in some places, tourist crime is a very serious component of the crime situation. A vast influx of tourists can enhance the crime rate of a given city or region. That influx often adds numbers to the numerator, without being included in the denominator. As a consequence, tourist crime appears even greater than its reality, creating an image problem for the area into which tourists flow. Information about tourist victimization can generate bad publicity, impairing future tourism, and, as a result, harm local and regional economies. Even false reports and media exaggerations of tourist crime can have major economic consequences. In addition, as offenders tourists or victims can generate new conflicts or enhance old conflicts among nations involved.

Exaggeration of tourist crime can also have negative consequences by giving the false impression that local crime is not locally generated. When tourists are victimized, local residents are still participants in many of these crimes. When tourists join with local residents in crime, the latter are not necessarily innocent parties. We can argue whether the local prostitutes or the tourist customers are more at fault, but the fact remains that the influx of tourists contributes to a local problem of social control.

THEORETICAL IMPORTANCE OF TOURIST-RELATED CRIME

Social control reminds us that tourist and visitor crime have theoretical importance. During the period 1920–40, the "Chicago school of sociology" conceptualized urban life (including crime) as influenced by the mix of locals and strangers. At the very foundation of crime theory, cities were seen as generating the anonymity that facilitated crime. Visitors could engage in activities that would be disapproved on their home turf, avoiding recognition. In addition, normative obligations are sometimes relaxed when strangers meet. At the very heart of urban theory and urban studies is the notion that a city assembles large numbers of people who are, in some sense, visitors. This point was central in the work of Robert Ezra Park, Ernest W. Burgess, Roderick D. McKenzie, and other participants and followers of the "Chicago School." Arguably, the mixture of populations brings with it more opportunity for crime than either population would produce alone.

Brantingham and Brantingham (1993) distinguish between crime attractors and crime generators. A given place can generate crime because its local routines afford sufficient crime opportunities. In time a place rich in crime opportunities can become a crime attractor, where offenders go with crime in mind before they depart their prior locations. If a tourist location builds up a reputation for illicit behavior, it may in time attract offenders with that in mind. An established crime attractor may draw tourists from abroad and internally, as well as routine crime participants from within. Thus, some nations have developed a widespread reputation for prostitution or even child prostitution, drawing their own citizens to provide services and consumers from elsewhere.

Some criminal acts are very simple: A tourist arrives; someone steals his wallet and uses the money. Others are more complex: A tourist arrives, buys illicit drugs, representing the endpoint of a chain of illicit events, including the production and transport of those drugs. Many hands may be involved. In addition, a local economy can become dependent or at least reliant upon a chain of illicit activities, with tourists from abroad playing a part in fueling the entire system. In addition, some visitors purchase drugs to take home, thus linking two or more sets of illicit complexity. Moreover, tourists are but one type of visitor whose presence can be linked to crime.

TYPES OF VISITOR CRIME

Once we have dichotomized visitors and locals, we have seven types of crime combination (with examples):

1. VISITOR AGAINST LOCAL: A visitor steals something from a local person.
2. LOCAL AGAINST VISITOR: A local person robs a visitor.
3. VISITOR AGAINST VISITOR: A visitor assaults another visitor.
4. LOCAL AGAINST LOCAL: A local person steals from another local person.
5. VISITOR WITH LOCAL: A visitor joins a local in exchanging illegal drugs or sex.
6. VISITOR WITH VISITOR: One visitor sells illicit drugs to another visitor.
7. LOCAL WITH LOCAL: A local person purchases illicit sex from another local person.

By distinguishing foreign visitors from domestic visitors, and by allowing more complex combinations of offenders, these categories are easily extended. For example, some crimes involve mixes of localities and foreigners, and some involve offender networks across several nations.

Tourism is especially interesting because some offenders pose as tourists when their real purposes are to carry out illicit activities, not tourism. A strong influx of tourists makes possible the entry and exits of people with crime in mind. A vast population crossing borders provides camouflage for illicit activities. And so on many dimensions tourism is linked to transnational crime.

TOURISM, VISITOR CRIME, AND ROUTINE ACTIVITIES

Understanding tourist crime requires us to consider how tourism alters or clashes with the routine activities of the receiving nation, region, or city. Tourists often arrive in particular seasons, producing major shifts in activities. Those dependent on tourism for their livelihood prosper most during the tourist season and they spend more money at that time. In addition, tourism may produce an influx of workers to serve the tourists. Thus, tourism produces a multiplier of community activity beyond the number of tourists. This multiplier further enhances the impact of tourism upon the volume of crime in the area.

The significance of tourist crime also brings situational prevention to the fore. Better prevention related to tourist areas and activities can have a major payoff for crime control in general and the security of the tourist industry in particular. Tourist areas can be given extra policing, and pose a challenge for problem-oriented policing. Yet improved design of environmental settings used by tourists and better management of the public places they frequent offer potential for low-cost crime reduction without depending on arrests. Hotel security and situational prevention within hotels play an important role in reducing tourist crime. Bar and tavern management and design are especially likely to assist in reducing crime involving tourists.

Tourist activities have a major impact on the nighttime economy, both leisure and work activities. Indeed, tourism has a major impact upon the distribution of crime over the hours of day, days of week, and month of year. Moreover, the ebb and flow of tourist volume from year to year is significant for local crime rates. Tourist crimes not only impact local areas that receive tourists, but tourist acquisition of illicit substances away from home allows import of those substances to their local area. Therefore, tourist crime is linked to local crime in the areas from which tourists originate. We can readily see that tourist crime is a tale of localism as well as transnationalism, helping us understand how crime grows and flows in space and time.

In addition, visitor crime involving nontourists is dependent on commuting to work, weekend visits, leisure activities outside of one's own area of residence, and more. We can readily see that visitor crime is a very complex topic, indeed. Tourist participation in crime is just one part of this larger field of inquiry. This larger field has theoretical and empirical significance. In general, nonlocal participation in crime is part of a system of events and relationships that will require future research and theoretical effort to understand and assimilate.

REFERENCES

de Albuquerque, K. & J. L. McElroy. (1999). Tourism and Crime in the Caribbean. *Annals of Tourism Research,* 26(4), 968–84.

Brantingham, P. & P. Brantingham. (1993). Nodes, Paths and Edges: Considerations on the Complexity of Crime and Physical Environment. *Journal of Environmental Psychology,* 13, 3–28

Chesney-Lind, M., & I. Y. Lind. (1986). Visitors as Victims: Crimes Against Tourists in Hawaii. *Annals of Tourism Research*, 13,167–91.

Knox, M. J. (2004). *Socio-cultural Impacts of Tourism in Hawaii (General Population). Part IV of Planning for Sustainable Tourism*. Prepared for Hawaii State Dept. of Business, Economic Development, & Tourism. John M. Knox & Associates, Inc.

Robert, E. P., E. W. Burgess, & R. D. McKenzie. (1925). *The City: Suggestions for the Study of Human Nature in the Urban Environment*. Chicago: University of Chicago Press.

Stangeland, P. (1995). The Crime Puzzle: Crime Patterns and Crime Displacement in Southern Span. Malaga, Spain: Instituo Andaluz Interunversario de Criminologia and Miguel Gómez Ediciones.

ABOUT THE AUTHORS

Andrew Lemieux is a Ph.D. candidate at Rutgers University. He is a graduate of the University of Arizona. Trained originally as a biochemist, he is now studying risk of violence. His dissertation considers how various routine activities expose people to differential risk of violent victimization, taking into account the amount of time people spend in different activities.

Marcus Felson is a crime theorist and specialist in crime trends and cycles. He is currently studying how co-offending is generated by routine activities of youths. His book, *Crime and Everyday Life*, is now entering its fourth edition. His book, *Crime and Nature*, considers how crime depends on noncriminal activities. Professor Felson is author of over one hundred professional papers, including "Redesigning Hell: Preventing Crime and Disorder at the Port Authority Bus Terminal."

PART IV

ORGANIZED CRIME AND TERRORISM

Organized crime is usually thought of as being committed by highly organized, professional criminals exemplified by the Italian Mafia (see Vincenzo Ruggiero's description of the Italian Mafia in Chapter 33). Chapters in this section provide a wealth of information about similar criminal organizations from the various regions of the world, including Balkan organized crime groups (Chapter 31 by Jana Arsvoska), Russian organized crime groups (Chapter 32 by Jim Finkenauer, Alexander Sukharenko and Eric Lesneskie), Asian organized crime groups (Chapter 35 by Leona Lee), and Columbian drug enterprises (Chapter 36 by Desmond Arias). In many ways, terrorist groups are similarly organized and this section contains two chapters on terrorism (Chapter 37 by William Parkin, Joshua Freilich, and Steven Chermak and Chapter 38 by Graeme Newman and Ronald Clarke). Organized crime groups, like the Italian Mafia, are generally portrayed as being involved in a wide variety of different criminal enterprises, such as drug dealing, smuggling, extortion (see Chapter 34 by Ernesto Savona and Marco Zanella), prostitution, and so forth. It is widely assumed that if police operations close off any of these sources of income, the organization switches resources to one of its other enterprises, or finds a new avenue for illegal profit. This is why police have tried to take out these organizations and why the United Nations has devoted so much effort to coordinating international efforts to eradicate these groups. The UN work culminated in 2000 with the adoption of the Palermo Convention, which formalized international agreements to deal with transnational crime syndicates and to harmonize the necessary legal requirements.

However, recent research is putting forward a quite different view of organized crime. Instead of consisting of a few, highly structured, semi-permanent organizations formed to conduct criminal business, researchers are now suggesting that organized crime consists of a much larger number of small, criminal enterprises, often transitory in nature, that develop to exploit particular opportunities for illegal profit. This new picture of organized crime is reinforced by the results of research on transnational crime, including money laundering, trafficking in women and stolen cars, and counterfeiting of currency and high value products. Consistent with routine activity theory, these new forms of organized crime have emerged in response to new opportunities for criminal profit resulting from increased globalization and technological development. Globalization has led to increased migration, legal and illegal, which in turn has increased the opportunities for transnational crimes. Recent immigrants still have ties in their home countries, which enable them to find the partners needed for transnational crime. Thus, connectivity is a key factor leading directly to increased opportunity for transnational organized crime (see Chapter 30 by Jay Albanese).

But it is unclear which kinds of organizations are most dominant, the hierarchical Mafia-type or loosely linked criminal entrepreneurs. The recent definitions of organized crime promulgated by the UN and EU, which require that only two or three offenders are acting in concert, have complicated the issue. If accepted, almost by definition, or at least by the laws of statistics, these definitions would mean that the vast majority of organized crime groups are small groups of criminal entrepreneurs. On the other hand, a survey of forty organized crime groups in sixteen countries conducted in 2000 by the UN Office on Drugs and Crime gives a quite different picture. It found that two thirds of the groups had a classical, hierarchical structure, while one third of them were more loosely organized.

Furthermore, most of the groups were of moderate size (twenty to fifty members), engaged in only one primary criminal activity, but operated in several countries. The effort needed to sort out this apparent confusion about the nature of organized crime and the organizations involved is beyond the scope of these chapters, but it does provide an important challenge for future research.

30 Transnational Organized Crime

Jay S. Albanese

Twenty-one persons were indicted after a three-year investigation of distribution of large quantities of cocaine and heroin. The drugs were concealed inside operable car batteries, and couriers smuggled the batteries across the Mexican border into Texas, redistributing the cocaine and heroin to automobile dealers and auto parts stores in the Washington, D.C. area. The defendants were also charged with using drug proceeds to purchase vehicles for export to Guatemala and smuggling bulk amounts of currency to Texas, Mexico, and Guatemala. In another case, kilograms of cocaine were concealed inside multiple foreign shipments of children's Lego toy boxes. The drug proceeds were brought regularly to a check-cashing business where wire transfers were sent to associates offshore (U.S. Fed News, 2005; U.S. Drug Enforcement Administration, 2008).

These scenarios appear to be classic examples of transnational organized crime where some of the victims and offenders are outside the United States, but what are the essential elements?

WHAT IS ORGANIZED CRIME?

"Organized crime is a continuing criminal enterprise that rationally works to profit from illicit activities that are often in great public demand. Its continuing existence is maintained through the use of force, threats, monopoly control, and /or the corruption of public officials" (Albanese, 2007). It is distinguished from other forms of criminal behavior in four primary ways: (1) It emanates from a continuing enterprise, (2) its crimes are rationally planned, (3) it requires force, threats, monopoly control, or corruption, to insulate itself from prosecution, and (4) it often caters to public demand for illicit goods and services. Given important and sweeping social, political, economic, and technological changes over the last twenty-five years, organized crime has become a sophisticated international venture, involving connections among individuals and groups across borders. Therefore, transnational organized crime consists of activities that correspond to the definition above, but also involves two or more countries to complete the criminal conspiracy. Different nationalities are not required, nor are the crossborder transportation of illicit goods or services. The transnational aspect of organized crime may lie in money laundering profits across national borders, smuggling goods or people systematically across borders, taking illegal bets internationally, selling illicit goods to those in another country, or similar types of transnational criminal conspiracies.

TYPES OF ACTIVITIES OF ORGANIZED CRIME

Organized crime involves two general types of activity: provision of illicit goods and services and infiltration of legitimate business or government (see Table 30.1).

The provision of illicit goods and services involves consensual activities between the organized crime group and the customer, involving no inherent violence in the activity itself, although economic harm is produced to legitimate society. On the other hand, the infiltration of legitimate business and government is inherently nonconsensual, because organized crime elements push the business or government agency from their lawful purposes by (a) forcing themselves on legal businesses or government entities to illegally extort funds or obtain unjust financial advantage or (b) criminally motivated business or government insiders misuse their positions to exploit the business or government agency for criminal purposes.

Because agreements to provide illegal products cannot be enforced in court, organized crime groups must enforce agreements on their own with threats and sometimes actual violence. The use or threat of violence has several objectives. It intimidates outsiders, terrorizes would-be informers, discourages competition, and encourages quick settlement of disputes. Therefore, threats and violence enforce contracts, and also perform symbolic functions, similar to the use of force by legal governments in discouraging undesirable behaviors in conventional society.

Table 30.1 also illustrates how the manifestations of these basic forms of organized crime have changed in recent years. There has been an evolution from fencing stolen televisions and stereos to theft of intellectual property, such as software codes and pirated copies of movies. A shift has occurred from traditional prostitution to trafficking in human beings, where victims are moved using fraud or coercion to force them into sexual slavery.

Table 30.1. Typology of organized crime activities

Type of activity	Traditional nature of activity	Examples of more contemporary forms	Harm
Provision of illicit goods and services	Gambling, lending money, sex, narcotics, stolen property	• Theft of intellectual property • Illicit arms trafficking • Money laundering • Trafficking in persons	• Consensual activities • No inherent violence in the activity itself • Economic harm
Infiltration of legitimate business or government	Coercive use of legal businesses or government agencies (from the inside or from the outside) for purposes of exploitation	• Business and consumer fraud • Extortion by computer • Corruption using intimidation	• Usually non-consensual activities • Threats, violence, extortion • Economic harm

In analogous fashion, simple business scams have moved toward more sophisticated (and harder to detect) frauds. In 2008, for example, a member of a mafia group was charged with supervising others (including his son) in a racketeering enterprise involving theft of credit card information, fraudulent magazine subscriptions, and deceptive real estate transactions. These traditionally white-collar crimes of fraud illustrate the movement of traditional organized crime groups into new kinds of crime in the hope of maintaining illicit income while reducing the risk of detection.

TYPES OF ORGANIZED CRIME GROUPS

A United Nations survey of sixteen countries identified five types of organized crime groups:

- Rigid hierarchy – single boss with strong internal discipline within several divisions.
- Devolved hierarchy – regional structures, each with its own hierarchy and degree of autonomy.
- Hierarchical conglomerate – a loose or umbrella association of otherwise separate organized crime groups.
- Core criminal group – a horizontal structure of core individuals who describe themselves as working for the same organization.
- Organized criminal network – individuals engage in criminal activity in shifting alliances, not necessarily affiliated with any crime group, but according to skills they possess to carry out the illicit activity.

Table 30.2. Typology of organized crime groups

Type of group or network	Nature of activity	Examples
1. Ethnic or culturally based groups that associate in both criminal and noncriminal social activity	Group performs social functions apart from just criminal activity. Group defines relationships among members, inspires loyalty, and has an ongoing structure.	Mafia groups in Italy and the USA, Yakuza in Japan.
2. Groups or networks that emerge to exploit a specific criminal opportunity	Group acts as a network where members come together because of access, connections, or expertise needed to carry out a particular criminal scheme, but there is no ongoing group structure.	Smaller networks involved in specific enterprises, such as human trafficking, counterfeiting, or fraud, as seen in recent cases emanating from Eastern Europe, Asia, and Africa.

These groups range from the highly organized to the least structured. It was found that group members in the forty organized crime groups included were usually unrelated to one another but were drawn from similar social backgrounds (United Nations, 2002). Most significant is that two-thirds of the groups identified were active in three or more countries, illustrating the significance of transnational organized crime, and that the criminal networks are more common than hierarchical groups.

A study based on interviews with people involved in organizing and transporting Chinese nationals to the United States found that the smuggling rings are comprised of "decentralized associations of criminals of diverse backgrounds, and the relationships among core members mostly horizontal." They are small, ad hoc, and highly organized with a limited hierarchy and limited group cohesiveness. No connection was found between these smuggling groups ("Snakeheads") and traditional Chinese criminal groups (e.g., Triads, Tongs) (Zhang, 2008). It can be seen that transnational organized crime often involves different networks and groups of different sizes and types, making classification difficult.

Organized crime groups exist in all cultures and nations, and are interethnic in nature (Albanese, 2007). They are two types: social/cultural groups that preexist their criminal activity and those that form around specific criminal opportunities (see Table 30.2).

Mafia and Yakuza groups are good examples of organized crime of the first type; they each have ongoing hierarchical structures from "bosses" to "soldiers," and they also socialize as a group and engage in neighborhood life together apart from crime. Their criminal activities are often long-standing due to their influence in a local area. The second type is more entrepreneurial and less structured than "traditional" groups like Mafia or Yakuza, characterized by more fluid networks where partners are taken on when needed to carry out a criminal activity, nonethnic partners are often involved, and there is no hierarchy that exists independent of the crime. (Finckenauer & Waring, 2001; Glenny, 2009).

THE SCOPE AND FUTURE OF TRANSNATIONAL ORGANIZED CRIME

Organized crime was originally a local or regional phenomenon, but it has become an international problem for reasons that include the globalization, opening of borders to more trade and travel, and a growing ease of communication via the Internet, worldwide e-mail, and mobile phones. These changes have been promoted by the collapse of the Soviet Union, increased migration worldwide, and advances in technology that facilitate the movement of illegal goods, services, money, and people. These global changes have had the effect of "shrinking" the world, making possible the shift from local, neighborhood enterprises to national and international schemes linking illicit supply with illicit demand. The time lag between the supply and consumption of illegal goods has decreased as they can now be moved very quickly from source to destination.

Table 30.3 illustrates how organized crime has changed in nature in recent years. Intervention and prevention efforts must keep pace, reducing the opportunities for organized crime networks to form and be successful.

What were once localized organized crime problems have become manifestations of transnational organized crime, as criminal networks exploit suppliers and markets for the provision and consumption of illicit goods and services. This has resulted in international concern and action, culminating in the United Nations Convention against Transnational Organized Crime. The Convention provides model law, policies, enforcement techniques, and prevention strategies against transnational criminal groups, money laundering, witness protection, and shielding organized crime figures. The Convention had to be ratified by forty countries in order to become binding, which occurred in 2003, and as of this writing, 153 of the 192 countries of the United Nations have ratified this agreement, representing 80 percent of the world's nations. Countries that are party to the Convention must adopt laws that prohibit participation in organized criminal groups, money laundering, corruption, and obstruction of justice. The Convention directs participating countries to engage in mutual

Table 30.3. Traditional organized crime versus modern transnational organized crime

Traditional OC	Modern transnational OC
Local numbers gambling	Internet gambling (at international websites)
Heroin, cocaine trafficking	Synthetic drugs (e.g., methamphetamine and Ecstasy – less vulnerable to interruption of supply; multiple shipment points/methods)
Street prostitution	Internet-based prostitution and trafficking in human beings
Extortion of local businesses for "protection"	Extortion of multinational corporations, and ransom kidnapping of executives
Loansharking (usury)	Money laundering in cash, precious stones, commodities
Fencing stolen property	Theft of intellectual property, forgery of CDs, software, DVDs

legal assistance, training, extradition agreements, joint investigations, and witness protection. Three separate protocols were added for countries to ratify on the related issues of trafficking in persons, smuggling of migrants, and illicit manufacture and trafficking in firearms – each of which direct countries to criminalize these behaviors, take affirmative steps to investigate and prosecute suspects, and devote resources to training and prevention efforts. The UN efforts are important because they demonstrate that a multinational response is required to effectively address the problem of transnational organized crime. Efforts in a single country cannot succeed due to the nature of criminal market, because producers, transporters, sellers, and buyers now often cross national boundaries.

A recent U.S. Department of Justice report (2008) states that like traditional organized crime, international networks still "have economic gain as their primary goal," but "international organized criminals have evolved towards loose network structures and away from traditional hierarchical structures." This international focus is necessary since the prosecution success in the U.S. against domestic organized crime has opened greater opportunities for other groups (Albanese, 2008).

CONCLUSIONS

It remains to be seen whether nations can reduce their high demand for illicit products and services, secure their borders from those interested in trafficking in these products, and successfully prosecute those organized crime networks already present. The long-term solution to transnational organized crime will be a reduction in demand for the products and services that fund transnational organized crime but in the short-term greater efforts toward detection and prosecution are necessary to disrupt organized crime operations. Also, crime prevention efforts are needed to reduce the supply of vulnerable victims and available markets through pressures placed on motivated offenders and their products (Felson, 2006), as well as greater economic development and anticorruption efforts to reduce the temptations of illicit organized criminal activity around the world.

REFERENCES

Albanese, J. (2007). *Organized Crime in our Times*. Fifth Edition. Lexis/Nexis/ Anderson.
    (2008). Family Fortunes – The Cosa Nostra in the US: Identifying Short-Term and Long-Term Prospects. *Jane's Intelligence Review*, vol. 20 (November, 2008).
Felson, M. (2006). *The Ecosystem for Organized Crime*. Helsinki: European Institute for Crime Prevention and Control.
Finckenauer, J. O. & E. J. Waring. (2001). *Russian Mafia in America: Immigration, Culture and Crime*. Boston: Northeastern University Press.
Glenny, M. (2009). *McMafia: A Journey Through the Global Criminal Underworld*. New York: Vintage.
United Nations Centre for International Crime Prevention. (2002). *Assessing Transnational Organized Crime: Results of a Pilot Survey of 40 Selected Organized Criminal Groups in 16 Countries*. www.unodc.org/pdf/crime/ publications/Pilot_survey.pdf
U.S. Department of Justice. (2008). *Overview of the Law Enforcement Strategy to Combat International Organized Crime*. www.usdoj.gov/criminal/icitap/press/ room/2008/apr/04–23–08combat-intl-crime-overview.pdf
U.S. Drug Enforcement Administration. (2008, September 23). *Cocaine Hidden in Kiddie Toys*. www.usdoj.gov/dea
U.S. Fed News. (2005, February 16). 21 Men Indicted in International Organized Crime Drug Trafficking Conspiracy. *U.S. Fed News*.
Zhang, S. X. (2008). *Chinese Human Smuggling Organizations: Families, Social Networks, and Cultural Imperatives*. Palo Alto, CA: Stanford University Press.

ABOUT THE AUTHOR

Jay S. Albanese is professor in the Wilder School of Government & Public Affairs at Virginia Commonwealth University. He served as chief of the International Center at the National Institute of Justice, the research arm of the U.S. Department of Justice, from 2002 to 2006. His recent books include *Criminal Justice* (Fourth Edition., Allyn & Bacon, 2008), *Organized Crime in Our Times* (Fifth Edition., Lexis.Nexis, 2007), *Professional Ethics in Criminal Justice* (Second Edition, Allyn & Bacon, 2008) and *Combating Piracy: Intellectual Property Theft and Fraud* (Ed., Transaction, 2009). Dr. Albanese has served as executive director of the International Association for the Study of Organized Crime and is past president of the Academy of Criminal Justice Sciences (ACJS).

31 The Rise of Balkan Organized Crime

Jana Arsovska

After the end of the Cold War, organized crime became a subject of grave concern for the European Union (EU). No longer was it perceived as an American or Italian phenomenon only. In 2000, Javier Solana, the Secretary General of the Council of the EU stated: "It is an enemy we must defeat, or it will defeat us." In particular, organized crime groups from Southeast Europe (SEE) – frequently referred to as Balkan organized crime groups – attracted enormous international attention during the 1990s. One reason for their dramatic rise was the way the postcommunist transition was initiated in SEE, compared to Central Europe or the Baltic states. In SEE, the reform process was neither smooth nor peaceful; it was marked by the violent dissolution of Yugoslavia.

Moreover, the emerging accommodations between corrupt SEE authorities and organized crime groups during the creation of new states fostered the development of crime-permeated societies. Balkan organized crime groups often enjoyed political support and profited from the 90s' lawlessness. They were labeled "highly dangerous," posing a serious threat to Western societies (European Council, 2003; UNODC, 2008). For the purpose of this chapter, the term "Balkan organized crime" refers to organized crime groups whose members originate mainly from Albania, Kosovo, Bosnia and Herzegovina, Bulgaria, Croatia Macedonia, Montenegro, Romania, and Serbia. This chapter discusses the nature, structure(s), and activities of these groups.

THE EU DEFINITION OF ORGANIZED CRIME

In 2001, the European Commission and Europol tried to operationalize their broad 1998 organized crime definition in order to ensure coherent action among their member states. They developed a working definition according to which eleven characteristics of criminal organizations are associated with the term "organized crime." The EU definition requires the presence of a minimum of four mandatory and two optional criteria.

The EU Organized Crime Definition

Mandatory: (1) Collaboration among more than two people; (2) Extending over a prolonged or indefinite period; (3) Suspected of committing serious criminal offences, punishable by imprisonment of at least four years or more; and (4) The central goal of profit and power.

Optional: (5) Specialized division of labor among participants; (6) Exercising measures of discipline and control; (7) Employing violence or other means of intimidation; (8) Employing commercial business-like structures; (9) Participating in money laundering; (10) Operational across national borders; and (11) Exerting influence over legitimate social institutions.

However, in developing international definitions there is always a tension between those who want an all-encompassing legislation and those who want the law to be tightly drawn. Although the term "organized crime" is used to distinguish more sophisticated forms of illicit enterprise from conventional criminality, the line between the two is not clear. Organized crime encompasses a wide range of profit-motivated criminal activities, such as transnational smuggling. It can also, however, have a domestic focus, profiting from protection rackets or fraudulent acquisition of state funds.

KEY ACTIVITIES AND OPERATIONAL METHODS

From Peripheral Actors to Central Players

Until 1997, Balkan organized crime groups were regarded as peripheral actors, lacking capital to invest in high-level, criminal businesses. Initially, they were mainly involved in extortion, kidnappings, protection rackets, prostitution, and burglaries – all high-risk criminal activities – and often worked as service providers for established organized crime groups. Some were working as *scafisti*, or boatmen, for Italian criminal organizations, smuggling people from Albania to Italy. In order for an Italian mafiosi to gain foothold in Albania and take advantage of the Balkan criminal markets, they often allowed Albanian groups to regulate the prostitution market in southern Italy. In the 90s, Balkan criminals also acted as drug

couriers and contract killers for Italian and Turkish drug trafficking and
loan sharking organizations. However, the balance shifted as circumstances
brought Balkan organized crime groups into a position of greater influence.
Following the conflict in Kosovo (1998–9) and the collapse of the pyramid
schemes in Albania (1997), many of these groups gained power and grew
more international.

Since 2003 – having established themselves as prominent criminal actors
in Europe and elsewhere, partly through their reputation for being violent –
Balkan organized crime groups have kept a lower profile. They have ties
to legitimate businesses and acquire a position of central players in international criminal networks. They still engage, however, in a full range of
criminal activities, such as, arms, drugs, and human trafficking; racketeering and extortions; fraud; money laundering; and organized theft.

Transnational Smuggling

TRADE IN ARMS

One of the international community's first reactions to the Yugoslav wars
(1991–99) was the arms embargo imposed on Bosnia and Herzegovina,
Croatia, Macedonia, Montenegro, Serbia (including Kosovo), and Slovenia
in 1992. The UN embargo had little effect on Serbia, which maintained the
control of the Yugoslav army, but it affected the smaller Yugoslav republics.
In order to push forward for their independence, Bosnia and Herzegovina,
Croatia, and Kosovo established networks with foreign actors for the
importation of weapons (Arsovska & Kostakos, 2008). Initially, the illegal arms trade was organized at the state level. Later, it ended up in the
hands of local organized crime groups. Former secret security agents
who had the "know-how" of arms trading also took part in the business
(Huisman, 2004).

For forty-five years Albania was under the communist regime of Enver
Hoxha (1944–85) who placed enormous emphasis on weapon supplies. The
breakdown of the Albanian government in 1997, however, resulted in the
looting of more than 550,000 small arms, 839 million rounds of ammunition, and sixteen million explosive devices from army stockpiles, in a
response to a failed pyramid savings scheme (Khakee & Florquin, 2003).
These weapons become available on the European black markets. Many
ended up in the hands of the Kosovo Liberation Army (KLA), a militant
group fighting for the independence of Kosovo, and Albanian rebel groups
in Macedonia. Since the Yugoslav wars, the Balkan region has been viewed
as the predominant source of Europe's illegal gun trade.

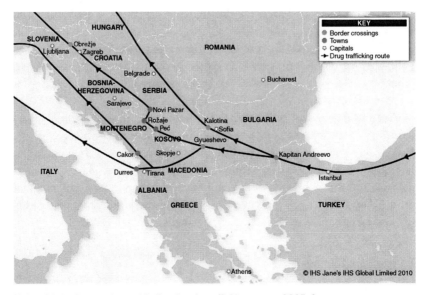

Figure 31.1. Commonly used Balkan heroin trafficking routes, 2005-9.
Source: Arsovska (2009) © IHS Jane's IHS Global Limited 2010.

DRUG TRAFFICKING

Prior to the Yugoslav wars, most of the heroin destined for Europe went through the Balkan route (via Serbia and Croatia). The 1992–95 wars redirected the trade through Macedonia, Kosovo, and Albania. This strengthened the position of ethnic Albanian (particularly Kosovo-Albanian) organized crime groups. For the purpose of arming the KLA, Kosovo-Albanians established connections with relatives in Europe and the USA – some known for drug trafficking (Hajdinjak, 2002).

During the last five years, ethnic Albanian traffickers have expanded their activities to the USA, Canada, and Australia, establishing direct links with suppliers in drug production areas (e.g., heroin in Turkey, cocaine in South America, and ecstasy in Belgium). Heroin trafficking remains their core activity. The heroin, frequently transported by trucks, often travels from Turkey to Italy via Bulgaria-Macedonia-Albania or Kosovo-Montenegro-Serbia-Bosnia and Herzegovina (Figure 31.1). According to the 2008 UN World Drug Report, close to 60 percent of all heroin seizures (in 2006) were made in countries located along the western Balkan route. More frequently, Balkan organized crime groups also use women and people from their diaspora who hold legal EU or U.S. documents, as drug curriers, since they attract less police attention.

As trafficking routes are changing due to stricter antitrafficking measures, the Balkan countries are increasingly being used for the transit of cocaine from South America. Balkan groups are gaining a prominent role in this profitable business. In January 2008, the Macedonian police seized half a ton of cocaine – hidden in cans filled with rubber-tree paint and imported by a legal company. The cocaine, from Venezuela, was offloaded at a port in Montenegro. It was intended for transportation to Greece by truck, via Serbia, Kosovo, and Macedonia.

HUMAN TRAFFICKING

Balkan organized crime groups are also active in facilitating illegal migration. During the 90s, many people lost their jobs when hundreds of factories closed down. Extortions and kidnappings became common realities for ordinary citizens. This resulted in a massive exodus of refugees to Greece, Italy, and other Western destinations (UNODC, 2008: 45–6). At first, the emigration flows were spontaneous. However, stricter police measures made ad hoc border crossing difficult. As a result, Balkan crime groups saw an opportunity to make money quickly by servicing the emigration demand.

From 2000 onward, many Balkan organized crime groups became part of international networks, smuggling Kurds, Chinese, and Pakistani nationals. Clients were provided with forged travel documents, or were hidden in trucks. In a 2001 confidential report, one *scafist* reported: "The border police is paid to smuggle clandestines into Albania. Then taxis drive them to Vlore. The taxi drivers have a budget to pay the traffic police. The clandestines are put in hotels managed by the scafisti. The facilitator comes back later with the ferry."

Balkan criminals, particularly ethnic Albanians, are known for being notorious traffickers of women for sexual exploitation (Limanowska, 2005). They have been trafficking Albanian, Romanian, Moldovan, Ukrainian, and Bulgarian women to Western Europe via Albania and Italy. Traditionally, they recruited their victims using a "lover boy" method whereby a man seduces a girl by promising her marriage and, once abroad, either sells her or forces her into prostitution. Kidnapping, violence, and threats are also common recruitment methods (Arsovska, 2008).

From 2000 onward, some Balkan countries turned out to be major points of destination for trafficking victims. The highly paid international staff (UN, NATO, NGOs) present in the Balkans due to the regional conflicts, has also affected the local prostitution markets by keeping the business profitable (Stefanova, 2004).

VULNERABILITY TO ORGANIZED CRIME

Many factors contributed to the rise of Balkan organized crime. First, the transition from communism to democracy led to (1) a diminished capacity of law enforcement agencies undergoing reform to impose order, (2) new criminal opportunities due to changes in the regulation of economic activity, and (3) sociocultural confusion, a product of globalization and rapid social change. When the social control weakened in postcommunist Europe, many people found themselves lost in a multiloyalty system. Drifting between tradition and modernity, socialism and capitalism, many – driven by the "American Dream" – fled their homeland. There was a false romanticism about "making it" in "the West." Traditional values lost importance. Being wealthy became the most cherished cultural goal; no emphasis was placed on the legitimate means to achieve such goal.

Second, conflict situations contribute to the rise of organized crime, too. In a war zone, social controls are loosened and criminals operate without a hindrance. Throughout the war, Balkan organized crime groups profited by selling "protection" to their co-ethnics. Irregular combat groups in turn protected and exploited their own communities (UNODC, 2008: 50). Smuggling was also seen as necessary for survival, enabling smugglers to enrich themselves. Conflicts are associated with deteriorating economy, inequalities, and a lack of legitimate opportunities as well, all leading to crime increase.

Third, the strategic location of the Balkan Peninsula has been historically an important factor for trade between the powers of the East and the West. SEE was destined to become a transit zone for a range of criminal goods since, for instance, it is placed between the world's main supply of heroin and its most lucrative destination market.

The fourth factor is the criminal-political nexus that has been flourishing in SEE since communist times. Communist leaders tolerated organized crime to: (1) earn extra money for the state, (2) supply the consumer needs unmet by the official economy, and (3) destabilize capitalist societies (e.g., growing and producing illegal narcotics and selling them in Western countries to "poison" capitalist societies) (UNODC, 2008: 48). After the fall of communism, the criminal-political ties strengthened. Members of the former communist elite that were awarded state-owned companies "teamed their clandestine skills with their criminal contacts to create … shady multinational conglomerates" (UNODC, 2008: 49). As former Interior Minister of Bulgaria, Bogomil Bonev stated, "One of the reasons our criminal

groups became so powerful is that they were organized by the state itself"
(Huisman, 2004).

CRIMINAL STRUCTURE

Balkan organized crime groups are characterized by strong family ties. It
is, however, too simplistic to describe them as kinship-based organizations with well-defined boundaries. Each core group is often composed
of three to ten members from the same clan or ethnic background. It
represents a smaller, criminal subunit that is part of a larger multiethnic
criminal network with strong ties to legal businesses and political structures. In order to engage in transnational organized crime, the different
subunits communicate with one another. Advanced groups cooperate with
foreign groups in order to expand their opportunities. Local subunits stay
in contact with "trustworthy outsiders" from Turkey, Italy, Greece, China,
Columbia, Germany, and other countries. Intelligence reports show that
kinship ties remain strong at the leadership level of each subunit, particularly if the members are ethnic Albanians. At the periphery, the number of
family members is decreasing.

CONCLUSION

Balkan organized crime groups grew rapidly over the years, partially due to
the transitional and postconflict dynamics present in postcommunist SEE.
Smuggling routes established to supply arms to militant factions, and escape
routes for economic and political migrants became used for trafficking illicit
commodities. These routes brought Balkan organized crime groups into
contact with foreign groups, such as the Italian Mafia, and as their influence spread, they became important partners for Turkish and Colombian
crime groups. The links with political leaders formed during communist
times and times of conflict left a legacy of criminal-political symbiosis.
Nowadays, Balkan organized crime is an evolving phenomenon, which
does not necessarily bear the hallmarks of violence and homogeneity of the
90s. Instead, many Balkan organized crime groups have wide connections
and use legal companies as a front for their criminal activities.

REFERENCES

Arsovska, J. (2008). Decline, Change or Denial: Human Trafficking and EU
    Responses in the Balkan Triangle. *Policing: A Journal of Policy and Practice*,
    2(1), 50–63.

Arsovska, J. (2009). Networking Sites: Criminal Group Expands Across the Balkans, *Jane's Intelligence Review*, 22(1), 44–47.

Arsovska, J. & P. Kostakos. (2008). Illicit Arms Trafficking and the Limits of Rational Choice Theory: The Case of the Balkans. *Trends in Organized Crime*, 11(4), 352–87.

European Council (2003). *A Secure Europe in a Better World.* France: EU Institute for Security Studies.

Hajdinjak, M. (2002). *Smuggling in Southeast Europe: The Yugoslav Wars and the Development of Regional Criminal Networks in the Balkans.* Sofia: CSD.

Huisman, S. (2004). Public Administration, Police and Security Services, Corruption and Organised Crime in Albania. Paper presented at CIROC Conference, Amsterdam, June 9.

Khakee A. & N. Florquin (2003). *Kosovo and the Gun.* Geneva: Small Arms Survey.

Limanowska, B. (2005). *Trafficking in Human Beings in South Eastern Europe.* Sarajevo: UNDP.

Stefanova, R. (2004). Fighting Organised Crime in a UN protectorate: Difficult, Possible, Necessary, *Southeast European and Black Sea Studies*, 4(2), 257–79.

UNODC (2008). *Crime and Its Impact on the Balkans.* Vienna: UNODC.

WEB SITES

Center for the Study of Democracy www.csd.bg
Balkan Investigative Reporting Network www.birn.eu.com
IOM Tirana www.iomtirana.org.al
RiskMonitor www.riskmonitor.bg

ABOUT THE AUTHOR

Jana Arsovska is an assistant professor at the Sociology Department at John Jay College of Criminal Justice. She holds a Ph.D. degree in criminology from the Catholic University of Leuven where she studied ethnic Albanian organized crime. Dr. Arsovska acted as a consultant for the World Bank and underwent training at Interpol. She has published widely on Balkan criminality.

32 Russian Organized Crime

James O. Finckenauer, Alexander Sukharenko,
and Eric G. Lesneskie

INTRODUCTION

Organized crime today inflicts serious harm on Russia's economic and political development. The old Soviet Union provided fertile ground for the growth of organized crime, but the demise of the USSR in 1991 has seemingly provided even more opportunities for organized criminal networks. These latter day Russian groups are more sophisticated than their predecessors, and have extended their spheres of influence worldwide. In the U.S., for example, Russian crime groups are involved in a host of criminal operations that are causing a significant degree of harm.

In this discussion we want to do several things. The first is to explain which groups are defined as being Russian organized crime (ROC). Next, we will provide an historical account of ROC – a history that lays the foundation for the current organized crime situation in Russia, the U.S., and elsewhere. Thirdly, we will discuss some of the methods used to combat organized criminal networks and make a few policy recommendations.

DEFINING ROC

In order to begin to have an understanding of ROC, we must be clear about what groups are encompassed by the term "Russian." A popular misconception is that all criminal groups which are classified as being "Russian" are actually from Russia. In fact, this label has been applied broadly to groups of criminals from any of the fifteen former republics that made up the Soviet Union, including Armenia, Georgia, Ukraine, Moldova, and others

(Finckenauer & Waring, 1998). Essentially, what is often called Russian organized crime is not strictly Russian.

HISTORY OF RUSSIAN ORGANIZED CRIME

Organized crime has been present in Russia for more than four hundred years, but the form of organized crime that we see today was mostly shaped by the seventy-five-year Soviet regime that collapsed in 1991. During the 1960s, there existed a three-tiered hierarchical pyramid of organized crime in the USSR (Finckenauer & Voronin, 2001). The first and top tier was composed of communist party and state officials. These corrupt government officials, through the abuse of their power and authority, facilitated the existence of illegal markets and other criminal ventures. The middle tier was made up of black marketers and shadow economy operators. In most instances, organized crime arises to meet market demands for goods and services that are illegal, regulated, or in short supply. The shortage of goods during Soviet times encouraged the emergence of a shadow economy and a black market to make up for these shortages. The shadow economy produced legal goods outside the state-mandated production quotas, which were then sold or bartered illegally. The black market dealt with the sale of illegal goods, such as prohibited items from the west and drugs. The bottom tier of the pyramid was composed of professional criminals, which included the so-called *vory v zakone* or "thieves-in-law." The *vory* were products of the old Soviet prison system or *gulag*, and they lived by a rigid set of criminal rules, dedicated their life to crime, and rejected involvement with the legitimate world.

The integration of these three tiers reflected the high level of corruption that existed in the USSR at that time. The corrupt party and state officials received bribes in order to protect the illegal ventures of the black marketers, the shadow economy operators, and the professional criminals. This level of corruption and illegal activity was only heightened when private enterprise was encouraged by the Soviet leadership beginning in the late 1980s (Finckenauer & Voronin, 2001). Criminal groups were best positioned to exploit the opportunities when state properties and assets began to be sold to private owners – a process known as privatization. Organized crime groups and corrupt officials bought these properties and assets at low prices because they had insider-trading information. Corruption during the final years of Soviet power was so pervasive that it contributed to lawlessness, and to the creation of new forms of organized crime (Finckenauer & Voronin).

CURRENT ISSUES

Organized Crime in Russia

Following the collapse of the former Soviet Union, there has been a rapid growth in economic crime. As a new government began grappling with the problems of developing laws and regulations to govern private business and economic activities, organized criminal groups exploited the opportunities that became available. This wave of criminal activity has been a destabilizing influence as Russia struggles to achieve economic and political reform. It thwarts foreign investment, widens the gap between rich and poor, and ultimately undermines confidence in the government.

ROC represents a new level of professional group crime. This is reflected not only in its high level of criminal sophistication and the well developed network of corruption, but also by the broad scale of activities and influence exerted over a considerable portion of the economy. The Russian Ministry of Internal Affairs (MIA) estimates that 249 organized criminal groups with 11,622 active members are currently operating in Russia. Most are interregional and heavily linked with corruption. About one in five groups has an ethnic base, with the most dangerous being the Chechens, Georgians, Azerbaijanis, and Armenians.

The organizational structure of these organized crime groups ranges from those with a defined leadership and subordinate roles to those that are small and loosely structured, with no set hierarchy. The size also varies from organization to organization. The most established groups are headed by individuals of *vory*. The *vory* usually do not commit crimes, but instead provide social support for their members, maintain criminal traditions, and arbitrate disputes. An important responsibility of a *vory* is maintaining an illegal fund called the *obshchak* that is used to carry out new crimes, support imprisoned members, and bribe public officials. It is estimated that there are 149 *vory* operating in Russia and another ninety-two *vory* are currently serving prison sentences.

Criminal networks in Russia commit a wide range of crimes, including fraud, extortion, robbery, car theft, prostitution, drug trafficking, and murder. Annually, about 30,000 crimes are committed by the various criminal groups. Since 1991, the MIA estimates that the number of such crimes has increased more than eight times. Organized crime has gained control of a significant share of the economy. The lack of laws, lax regulation, corruption, and violence have enabled criminal groups to make substantial inroads into several lucrative economic sectors, including energy, metallurgy, construction, banking, fishery, retail trade, and transportation. The MIA estimates that activities of major organized crime groups fund more than 3,000 enterprises of different ownership forms, with almost 2,000 enterprises falling under their direct control (Annual Report of the MIA, 2008). Organized groups not only commit various economic crimes, but they then transfer money through shell (fictitious) companies, including many located offshore. About 70 percent of criminal proceeds are believed to be laundered through legitimate commercial enterprises.

The Russian Central Bank estimated that between 1991 and 2008, pure outflow of private capital has generated nearly two trillion dollars, half of which has been illegally wire transferred. Some of this money was returned to Russia at very favorable exchange rates, where it was invested in other criminal schemes or used to purchase real estate, privatized enterprises, and banks. As a result, organized crime bosses make up a significant proportion of the new wealthy class in Russia. Their economic activities are closely intertwined with those of legitimate businessmen.

ROC in the U.S.

Having already established a strong foothold in Russia, the most powerful criminal organizations have expanded their activities overseas. The MIA estimates that there are three hundred criminals that have ties to forty-four countries, including the U.S.

The first indications of ROC in the U.S. actually date back to the 1980s, when a significant number of Soviet émigrés arrived. According to the U.S. Immigration and Naturalization Service (now ICE), approximately 200,000 Soviet citizens entered the U.S. during the 1970s and 1980s. Among these émigrés were a few professional criminals who took advantage of the new environment and set up criminal organizations. Thus, it was during the 1990s that Russian criminal activity increased in the U.S., mostly centered in Brighton Beach area of New York, and much of that involving Ukrainians.

Although the actual number is not well documented, it is estimated that there are some twenty Russian criminal groups operating in the U.S. and are mostly concentrated on the east and west coasts, generally where there is a significant Russian-speaking population (U.S. Department of Justice, 2004). U.S. authorities suggest that there are two main types of criminal enterprises comprised of individuals from the former Soviet Union: (1) loosely structured criminal networks that are composed of various ethnic combinations and (2) cells of foreign-based criminal organizations.

The first type is formed for a variety of criminal purposes. Unlike some of the traditional, ethnically-based organized crime groups such as *La Cosa Nostra*, these Russian criminal groups do not have permanent hierarchical structures. They operate mainly as organized criminal networks. In such networks, individuals engage in criminal activity in shifting alliances, but are not necessarily affiliated with any crime group in particular. Instead, they shift according to the skills needed to carry out particular crimes. The networks vary in their size, scope, and in the degree of their affiliation with other criminal groups. They are deeply involved in large-scale white-collar crimes, such as health care (false medical claims) or insurance (staged auto accidents) frauds. Some networks are violent and engage in traditional racketeering activity, such as murder, extortion, prostitution, and drugs. Some operate autonomously, while others have loose ties to networks of fraudsters.

The foreign-based organized crime enterprises, such as the powerful Russian Solntsevskaya, Tambovskaya, or Uralmash criminal organizations, are involved in a wide variety of criminal activities including trafficking in women for prostitution, and trafficking drugs, firearms, and stolen vehicles. Their main activity inside the U.S. appears to be the laundering of illicit proceeds from overseas operations through U.S. financial institutions. In recent years, ROC groups have also been active in cybercrimes like identity theft, online auction and investment frauds, the production and distribution of child pornography, and dating scams.

To date, ROC groups in the U.S. have shown an ability to cooperate closely with other established criminal organizations, including *La Cosa Nostra* families, and the Colombian and Mexican drug trafficking organizations. There is no evidence, however, of a central "commission" overseeing the various criminal activities. Russian organized crime groups have also not established monopoly control over any of their criminal operations (Finckenauer & Waring, 2001). And they have not (yet) made the necessary political contacts to facilitate the use of corruption. Russian organized criminal groups have shown a willingness to use violence to achieve their goals, and their criminal activity clearly causes considerable economic harm.

COMBATING ROC

The first set of tools for confronting organized crime are those at the national level. Among the tools that are regarded as effective organized crime control methods are laws, such as the U.S. Racketeer Influenced and Corrupt

Organizations (RICO) statute. RICO enables the prosecution of all individuals associated with a continuing criminal enterprise, irrespective of their direct and personal involvement in a particular crime. This form of group prosecution permits reaching into the highest levels of a criminal organization. A second tool is the use of informants and undercover investigators to penetrate the inner sanctums of organized crime groups. Finally, electronic surveillance (wiretapping and eavesdropping) is another method that is important for penetrating criminal organizations. Russia does not have a RICO-type law; however, there are Russian federal laws on plea-bargaining and the punishment of "thieves-in-laws" who have been charged with organizing criminal groups. Furthermore, there has been recent legislation passed that will ensure safety of victims, witnesses, and other participants in criminal proceedings.

Some of the most effective international cooperation has been achieved under mutual legal assistance treaties (MLATs) where each country is obliged to assist the other in the investigation, prosecution, and other proceedings related to criminal matters. Under the U.S.-Russia MLAT (1999), eight areas of cooperation are guaranteed: assistance with taking testimony and statements; obtaining documents and records; serving documents; locating and identifying persons and items; executing requests for searches and seizures; transferring persons in custody; locating and immobilizing assets for purposes of forfeiture, restitution, or collecting fines; and, any other assistance not prohibited by the requested state's law. MLATs have been particularly useful with complex investigations.

POLICY RECOMMENDATIONS

Currently, there are a small number of collaborative working groups involving various countries to fight transnational organized crime. One example is the Eurasian Organized Crime Working Group that deals with transnational organized crime committed by offenders from the former Soviet Union or Central Europe. Working groups are effective mechanisms to coordinate and implement joint practical measures to combat global organized crime. It is suggested that ad hoc working groups be formed to investigate specific criminal cases. The use of ad hoc working groups between law enforcement agencies from both Russia and the U.S. to investigate criminal cases would improve the effectiveness of combating ROC.

Since there is no extradition treaty between the U.S. and Russia, there also must be greater cooperation between law enforcement authorities in both countries to avoid the risk of fugitives finding safe havens. To date, there are about seventy Russian criminals hiding in the U.S. due this lack of cooperation. This collaboration could include investigations and prosecutions of the respective country's own citizens accused or suspected of committing crimes in the requesting country or elsewhere.

SUMMARY AND CONCLUSION

ROC is a problem for many countries, including the U.S. The collapse of the Soviet Union and the privatization process that ensued created opportunities for exploitation and corruption by organized crime networks. These ROC groups have engaged in numerous illegal ventures that generate enormous sums of money – money that is in turn laundered through legitimate businesses. ROC groups have increased in the sophistication and breadth of their criminal ventures. This has lead to criminals in Russia having ties in other countries, mostly in Europe and North America. ROC groups in the U.S. are not as "organized" as their Russian-based counterparts; however, they do pose a significant threat and are capable of considerable harm. Combating ROC is a difficult and lengthy process. In order to more effectively control organized crime both in the U.S. and Russia, it is recommended that ad hoc working groups be created specifically to deal with organized crime and to increase cooperation between the two countries.

REFERENCES

Finckenauer, J. O. & Y. A. Voronin. (2001). *The Threat of Russian Organized Crime*. Washington, DC: U.S. Department of Justice.

Finckenauer, J. O. & E. Waring. (1998*). Russian Mafia in America*. Boston: Northeastern University Press.

(2001). Challenging the Russian Mafia Mystique. *National Institute of Justice Journal, April*, 2–7.

Ministry of Internal Affairs. (2008). *Annual Report of the Russian Ministry of Internal Affairs*. Russia.

U.S. Department of Justice. (2004) Fiscal Year Performance Report. Washington, D.C.

ABOUT THE AUTHORS

James O. Finckenauer is Professor II at the Rutgers University School of Criminal Justice in Newark, NJ. From 1998 to 2002, he was director of the International Center at the National Institute of Justice in Washington D.C. He is past editor of Trends in Organized Crime and past President of the Academy of Criminal Justice

Sciences. He is the author or editor of nine books, as well as numerous articles, chapters and reports on comparative criminal justice and organized crime.

Alexander Sukharenko is the director of the New Challenges and Threats Study Center of Primorsky Institute of State and Municipal Management (Vladivostok, Russia). He is the author of numerous publications on transnational organized crime and corruption.

Eric G. Lesneskie is a doctoral student at the Rutgers University School of Criminal Justice in Newark, NJ. His current research interests include street gangs, co-offending, and juvenile delinquency.

33 The Italian Mafia

Vincenzo Ruggiero

INTRODUCTION

It is widely known that the Italian Mafia, which is more appropriately termed the Sicilian Mafia, is a very specific form of organized crime; a criminal organization that may share some characteristics with its counterparts operating in other countries, while retaining some peculiar traits making it somewhat unique. In order to highlight this uniqueness, a crucial preliminary distinction should be made. According to Block (1980), there are two main types of criminal syndicate. One is the "enterprise syndicate," which operates exclusively in the arena of illicit businesses such as prostitution, gambling, contraband, and drugs. The second he calls the "power syndicate," which is predominantly engaged in extortion as a form of territorial control rather than enterprise. Territorial control is certainly one of the central objectives of the Sicilian Mafia, making it an organization of the second type in Block's classification. Its overriding aim appears to be the control over territory and the people who are part of it (Catanzaro, 1988).

THE MILITARY MAFIA

The history of the Italian Mafia runs parallel with the history of the unitary Italian state, and though predating 1860 (the date of the unification of Italy), the Mafia is best understood against the background of the political and economic events occurring in the country in the last century and a half or so. Historians have shown that landowners in Sicily employed groups affiliated to the so-called military Mafia as their private law enforcers, entrusting them with the collection of rents, taxes, and agricultural produce. This private army also played a political role, in that it acted as a violent deterrent power against the rural labor force and its attempts to organize collective bargaining through associations of mutual aid and trade unions.

In 1876, member of parliament Leopoldo Franchetti wrote what is perhaps the most important report ever published on the Mafia. He described it as a form of political crime promoted by sectors of the ruling class, namely, official political actors and businessmen. Sectors of the elite were said to employ members of this "military Mafia" and to use them as an illegal resource in their economic or political activity. The violence of the Mafia, in other words, was granted the role of discouraging economic competitors and intimidating political opponents. The management of the violent aspects of political and economic competition was, therefore, delegated to groups specializing in violence, while these groups, in exchange, were granted a relative freedom to operate in other illegal activities (mainly protection rackets and contraband). Franchetti's report, which could easily apply to the current situation, was sidelined and long neglected, and an analysis of the Italian Mafia slowly prevailed describing the organization as a glamorous group of affiliates sharing traditional cultural traits and characterized by an archaic anthropological makeup. In a recent rewriting of the history of the Mafia, however, a number of crucial events appear to corroborate the views of that old, groundbreaking, report.

In 1893 Emanuele Notarbartolo, ex-mayor of Palermo and director of a leading Sicilian bank, was assassinated. Investigators discovered that the murder was the consequence of Notarbartolo's refusal to establish partnerships with fellow businessmen and politicians connected to them. Similar assassinations took place until fascism gained political power. During the twenty years of the fascist regime, Prefect Mori, also known as the "Iron Prefect," was entrusted with waging the "definitive" war against the Mafia, but he only managed to hit some elements of the military Mafia" while failing to unveil their connections with the economic and political interests they served.

After World War II the Italian Mafia was unexpectedly reinvigorated. Italy became an important strategic country in world politics because of its strong socialist party and the massive popularity of its communist party, the most powerful in the Western world. The Cold War indirectly gave the Mafia a prominent function in fighting the Soviet scare. In 1948, the very year in which the Italian constitution was promulgated, the U.S. National Security Council warned that "the US must use all its political, economic and, if necessary, military power to help prevent Italy falling under the influence of the USSR"(Scarpinato, 2004: 266). In this climate, the military Mafia was again strategically used by employers and conservative politicians against opponents and competitors. In the most infamous episode of this strategy, a political rally was attacked by a Mafia gang with machine guns in Portella della Ginestra, a name which is also a scar in Italian history. The political elections held on April 20 and 21, 1947 gave the left a significant relative majority over the Christian Democrats, the party supported by the USA. Amid growing fear of the ascent of socialism, on May Day 1947, while rural workers and their families were taking part in the traditional workers' parade, a gang led by Salvatore Giuliano opened fire, killing twelve people and injuring and twenty-seven. Giuliano was hired by an alliance of conservative politicians and fearful entrepreneurs, who thought that such violent actions were part of fighting communism. Some of his associates, after being arrested, were not given a chance to denounce the officials on behalf of whom they had acted, because they were found dead in their prison cells.

The Italian Mafia has never stopped acting as a military organization, as proven by the long list of "excellent victims" of its violent action. These victims include judges, law enforcers, politicians, and intellectuals who have rebelled against the specific form of political and economic power the Mafia represents. This power system is based on a coalescence of conventional, economic, and political crime that students of the Mafia have tried to unravel in a number of different ways.

INTERPRETATIONS AND PERSPECTIVES

In order to identify the different interpretations of the Mafia it is useful to refer to the concept of social organization. This concept relates to the variety of social relations which give rise to two types of networks. First, social organization can be viewed as an association, a network of relations among individuals who form some sort of culturally homogenous group. Second, social organization can be seen as a series of transactions and a network of relations among individuals involved in a common activity, whether or not they belong to the same association, or in other words, whether or not they are socially and culturally homogenous. Transactions range from brief encounters to elaborate, rigid, and highly coordinated undertakings. If we view social organization in terms of association, we emphasize the structure and internal cohesiveness of groups. On the contrary, if we view social organization in terms of transactions we emphasize the structure and modality of joint activities.

Some students of the Italian Mafia choose the first analytical route, thus describing the organization as a separate entity constituted by cohesive groups, and characterized by specific cultural codes. Others opt for the second route, focusing therefore on the links the Mafia establishes with external, mainly official actors with whom the organization carries out joint activities. Arlacchi (1983), for example, looks at the Italian Mafia as an enterprise, viewing its criminal activity as incorporating the attributes of licit business. These attributes include an emphasis on innovativation, an element of rational calculation, and an irrational and aggressive "animal spirit" incorporated in any economic enterprise. Santino and La Fiura (1990) emphasize the "power" aspect of the organization, which is said to be guided by economic interest and, simultaneously, by the ambition to control and govern the territories in which it operates. The attempts made by the Mafia to establish forms of alliance with representatives of the local church can be regarded as part of this territorial power building (Dino, 2008). Gambetta (1992) studies the Mafia merely as a service-providing organization. Among the goods provided, trust and protection are singled out as paramount. Trust and protection, which should be supplied by the state, may under certain circumstances become the preserve of private entrepreneurs, including organized crime. This type of crime is therefore an industry for the supply of private protection and the distribution of trust to economic actors who would otherwise be unable to interact safely. In the case of the Sicilian Mafia, for example, its strength as an industry for the supply of protection and trust is deemed a consequence of the traditional popular distrust of the official agencies.

Other contributions highlight the capacity of the Italian Mafia to polarize markets through the use of violence, thus implying that the "military Mafia" is far from having exhausted its function (Catanzaro, 1988). Finally, observing the alliances and partnerships between organized crime and the official economic and political world, the suggestion has been made that the Italian Mafia combines forms of conventional crime with a variety of white-collar offences. This happens, in particular, when proceeds from illicit activities are invested in the official economy, where members of the Italian Mafia are said to "learn" the techniques and the rationalization of their white-collar counterparts. It has also been hypothesized that organized crime and the official world establish an exchange of services and engage in mutual entrepreneurial promotion. For example, in activities such as the trafficking in weapons and the disposal of toxic waste, the Mafia offers illegal transportation (or dumping) services to legitimate entrepreneurs. On the other hand, the official economy offers organized crime the opportunity to launder its profits or to invest them in some legitimate enterprise (Ruggiero, 1996). This analysis echoes recent assessments of the Italian Mafia's current activities. It has been argued that the "military Mafia" is declining, as proven by the dramatic reduction in killings and all forms of violent intimidation in Sicily. After the outrage of the 1990s, with the killings of high-profile judges such as Giovanni Falcone, the Mafia is now keeping a low profile, and violent conflict has been replaced by persuasion and cooperation. Alliances and partnerships are preferred to harsh competition leading to violence. This appears to be happening in the domain of conventional crime, in which the Mafia is still involved, as well as in the area of legitimate economic activity. The Italian Mafia, for example, has established good working relationships with other groups engaged in protection rackets and drugs trafficking, but also with politicians who distribute resources at the local level (Sciarrone, 2004). The Sicilian Mafia operates with its own companies in the area of public work and service contracting, where partnerships with other legitimate companies are increasingly frequent. In this respect, it might be appropriate to talk about criminal networks, as Mafia-owned companies link with other economic actors in markets where unorthodox practices and illegal behavior are widespread (Ruggiero, 2002). Criminal networks imply the existence of interdependent units linked by a wide-ranging variety of ties, including kinship, ethnicity, cultural homogeneity, social proximity, or simply business partnership. The Italian Mafia may well be evolving in one such licit-illicit network (Lodato & Scarpinato, 2008).

The question has often arisen: To what extent is the Italian Mafia capable of expanding beyond its regional and national confines? While it is obvious that the power of the Sicilian organization can be perceived in other Italian regions and, at times, at the national level, it is controversial whether such power can transcend the national borders and affirm itself internationally. Cases such as the "pizza connection" (international heroin trafficking) seem to prove that the Italian Mafia can establish effective working relationships with large and established communities of Sicilians resident in the USA, but may find it difficult to do the same in other contexts. In this respect, other criminal organizations (e.g., the Calabrian 'Ndrangheta and the Neapolitan Camorra) seem to be more prone to establish international links than the Sicilian Mafia. The international connections of the Mafia, it would appear, are the result of specific, individual initiatives of members of families setting up criminal partnerships with associates abroad, rather than a strategy driving the organization as a whole toward international expansion.

SUMMARY

This chapter provides an account of the Italian Mafia as an organization accompanying the history of united Italy, from 1860 to the present. Its uniqueness is highlighted among other forms of organized crime. The military force of the Mafia is analyzed and the paper focuses on the use of this force by the ruling groups in the country, as an ancillary reservoir of power. After discussing different hypotheses on the role of the Mafia in the economy and its relationship with the official political apparatus, the chapter suggests that the organization is now evolving into a licit-illicit network.

REFERENCES

Arlacchi, P. (1983). *La Mafia imprenditrice*. Bologna: Il Mulino.
Block, A. (1980). *East Side – West Side: Organizing Crime in New York*. Cardiff: University of Cardiff Press.
Catanzaro, R. (1988). *Il delitto come impresa. Storia sociale della Mafia*. Padua: Liviana.
Dino, A. (2008), La Mafia devota. Chiesa, religione, Cosa Noistra, Rome/Bari: Laterza.
Lodato, S. & R. Scarpinato. (2008), Il ritorno del principe. La criminalità dei potenti in Italia, Milan: Charelettere.
Ruggiero, V. (1996). *Organized and Corporate Crime in Europe*. Aldershot: Dartmouth.
   (2002). Fuzzy Criminal Actors. In V. Ruggiero (Ed.), *Is White Collar Crime Organised Crime?*, 37, 177–90.
   (2002). Fuzzy Criminal Actors. *Crime Law and Social Change*. 37(3), 177–90.
Santino, U. & G. La Fiura. (1990). *L'impresa mafiosa*. Milan: Franco Angeli.
Scarpinato, R. (2004). La storia: Italia mafiosa e Italia civile. *Micro Mega*, 5, 259–86.
Sciarrone, R. (Ed). (2004). *La Mafia esiste ancora*. Rome: l'Unità.

ABOUT THE AUTHOR

Vincenzo Ruggiero is a professor of sociology at Middlesex University (UK) and at the University of Pisa (Italy). He has worked for the United Nations on a number of projects on transnational crime, human trafficking, and political corruption. Among his books are: *La Roba* (1992), *Eurodrugs* (1995), *European Penal Systems* (1995), *Organized and Corporate Crime in Europe* (1996), *Economie sporche* (1996), *The New European Criminology* (1998), *Crime and Markets* (2000), *Movements in the City* (2001), *Crime in Literature* (2003), *Understanding Political Violence* (2006), *Social Movements: A Reader (2008), and Penal Abolitionism: Acelebration (2010).*

34 Extortion and Organized Crime

Ernesto U. Savona and Marco Zanella

INTRODUCTION

Extortion is "the obtaining of property from another, with his consent, induced by wrongful use of actual or threatened force, violence, or fear, or under color of official right" (The United States Code 18 U.S.C. § 1951(b)(2)). The legal definitions of extortion in other countries are similar to the US. definition.

When extortion is committed on a regular basis, it turns into racketeering: "an institutionalized practice whereby tribute is collected on behalf of a criminal group that, in exchange, claims to offer [...] protection" (Volkov, 2002: 1).

This chapter deals with extortion, racketeering, and organized crime in Europe. The overall argument is that market opportunities for extortion driven by lack of trust in market dynamics and variations in the characteristics of organized criminal groups may give rise to two different types of extortion racketeering: systemic and casual. Extortion racketeering is systemic when it is deeply rooted and extends across a territory since it is a core part of organized crime groups' activities. Extortion racketeering is casual when it is not extended across a territory since criminal organizations do not routinely engage in such a criminal activity. These types of extortion racketeering are shaped by four interrelated variables: 1. market opportunities; 2. the organizational structure of criminal groups; 3. their presence at local level and 4. the victim/offender relationship. Put another way: on the one hand, the more organized criminal groups focus their activity on the local territory because of market opportunities, the more they develop a monopolistic position and a consequential hierarchical structure, and the more they establish parasitical and symbiotic relationships with their extortion victims, the more extortion racketeering becomes systemic (i.e., widespread and continuous). On the other hand, the more criminal market opportunities are open to transnational activities, the more criminal groups are organized in networks, and the more they establish predatory relationships with their extortion victims, the more casual extortion racketeering becomes.

Four variable and their interrelations can help us understand the nature of extortion and organized crime.

Market Opportunities

Extortion is an old and simple crime committed by organized crime when the risks are low and the benefits are high. It occurs in contexts where (1) victims do not report the crime and (2) are willing to pay the protection tax. These two conditions often arise within close-knit ethnic communities (e.g., among Italians at the beginning of the century in New York City, or among Chinese communities in the U.S. or in Europe). If the risk is low because of this ethnic homogeneity and the consequent control of the territory, the benefits are high only in relation to possible criminal market opportunities. Extortion is systemic when other criminal alternatives are not available or cannot be adopted because of the low expertise of the group and its organization.

Organizational Structure of Criminal Groups

Although there is no direct relationship between the organizational structure of criminal groups and extortion, the literature and the data show that where extortion is practiced on a large scale, and is systemic, the groups that engage in it are organized hierarchically. Where extortion is more casual, their structure is more flexible (taking the form of a network).

Owing to their structure, which enables a lasting presence in a given territory, hierarchical criminal groups gain in reputation and may exercise effective threats of contingent violence against their victims. Moreover, these threats are reinforced by the fact that those threatened believe that these criminal groups "can corrupt legitimate authority or in some other way ensure that they avoid apprehension" (Reuter, 1994: 95) and can act as an industry which produces and sells private protection (Gambetta, 1992).

These elements of reputation – in other words, the ability to neutralize law enforcement by means of corruption, and the production and sale of protection – are closely related to the type of organized criminal group. Criminal groups with network structures "are not interested in, or capable of, exercising such a quasi-political power" (Paoli & Fijnaut, 2004: 608). They are too small and ephemeral to be able to carry out systemic extortion racketeering. Only in few cases are they involved in casual extortion racketeering practices. Networks may openly use violence to heighten their capacity to commit extortion, but they tend to be short-lived because they lack the necessary structure and expertise.

In sum, although it is not automatic, the relationship between hierarchical structure and systemic extortion, on the one hand, and flexible structure and casual extortion on the other, can be explained by means of the other variables that shape extortion: the local dimension of the organized crime action, its control over the territory, and the victim/offender relationship.

Operations at Local Level

Why does extortion proliferate when organized crime operates at a local level? And why is control of the territory so important? The explanation resides in the relationships between organized crime groups and local politicians, administrators, and businesses. The local level is the dimension where collusion with organized crime is easier and reciprocal exchange more profitable. Extortion racketeering is used to finance the criminal organization and its criminal activities, and to consolidate its capacity to control local resources such as property, markets, services, and votes.

Criminal groups that exercise intense control over the local territory tend to commit systemic extortion racketeering within legal markets and in the underworld. As far as the legal markets are concerned, extortion racketeering is often viewed as the key "to infiltration and baronial domination of sections of the legitimate economy" (Bell, 2000: 183). In regard to the underworld, it has been noted (Landesco, 1968) that extortion racketeering is often used to "protect" criminal markets. By collecting extortion money from criminals, organized criminal groups establish a form of tax levying system which facilitates the establishment of monopolistic areas and creates barriers to entry that make criminal offences less attractive.

The Victim/Offender Relationship

When analyzing the victim/offender relationship in extortion racketeering cases, it should be considered that "the boundaries between victim and accomplice are often [...] blurred" (Blok, 2008: 8). These boundaries account for the difference between systemic and casual extortion racketeering.

When networks are involved in extortion racketeering, they establish predatory relationships with their victims. Unable to establish lasting relationships with their victims, they consequently act with the "aim or effect to destroy or bleed to death" (Passas, 2002: 21) their victims, exacting considerable extortive payments in a short period. This is typical of casual extortion racketeering.

By contrast, hierarchical criminal groups benefiting from their reputation and durability may establish parasitical or symbiotic relationships with their victims. This contributes to making extortion racketeering systemic.

The relationship is "parasitical when the aim is to preserve the viability of the target, such that illegal benefits can be extorted on a more or less regular basis" (Passas, 2002: 21). By establishing a lasting relationship with the victim, the offender "harms the host a little at a time, without killing it, or only kills it in slow motion" (Felson, 2006: 196). In other cases, the relationship may be symbiotic in nature, so that the victim becomes a "friend" of the extorter. The victim thus gains an advantage that is not "simply that of avoiding the likely damages that would otherwise ensue, but can extend to assistance in disposing of competitors, or protection against the threat of isolated bandits, and against the risk of being cheated in the course of business transactions" (Gambetta, 2000, p. 166).

SYSTEMIC AND CASUAL EXTORTION RACKETEERING: THE EUROPEAN CASE

The link between the presence of casual or systemic extortion racketeering and the variables indicated above has been recently investigated in a study on extortion and organized crime in the twenty-seven European Union Member States (Transcrime, 2009). This study analyzed the complex variety of criminal organizations present in the twenty-seven EU Member States, the criminal market opportunities they exploit, differences in their organizational structures (some are hierarchical, some take the form of a network, some are permanent, some are more ephemeral), together with their differing criminal activities and control over the territory, and the various relationships that they establish with their victims.

The study has explained that extortion racketeering is casual in most of the European Union Member States (EUMS). The only exceptions are the Eastern EUMS (Bulgaria, Czech Republic, Estonia, Hungary, Latvia, Lithuania, Poland, Romania, Slovakia, Slovenia) and some EUMS in the south of Europe, namely Spain and Italy.

When the geographical locations of the twenty-seven EU MS are divided into four regions, the following patterns emerge (see Caneppele, Gosetti, & Zanella, 2009: 253–4):

1. **North Europe** (Denmark, Estonia, Finland, Latvia, Lithuania, Sweden). Owing to the prevalence of smuggling activities in this

region, extortion racketeering is casual in Denmark, Finland, and Sweden. In fact, these countries are distinguished by the presence of criminal organizations that do not exercise control over the territory because they are transnational in their smuggling activities. Proximity to Russia and the Caucasian countries and the presence of hierarchical criminal groups have generated systemic extortion racketeering in Estonia, Latvia, and Lithuania.

2. **West Europe** (Austria, Belgium, France, Germany, Ireland, Luxembourg, the Netherlands, United Kingdom). Owing to the structure of the organized criminal groups operating in this area and to their transnational activities, extortion racketeering is casual. Most of the countries in this area suffer from extortions carried out within close-knit ethnic communities. This is the case, for example, of Austria, Belgium, France, Germany, Luxembourg, and the United Kingdom.

3. **Central/East Europe** (Bulgaria, Czech Republic, Hungary, Poland, Slovakia, Slovenia, Romania). Because of its proximity to the Balkans, this region is an important transit area for criminal goods and services, and in particular for smuggling and trafficking activities. However, the likely hierarchical structure of the criminal organizations operating in this area, together with their strong presence at local level, make extortion racketeering systemic in countries such as Bulgaria, Czech Republic, Hungary, Poland, Romania, Slovenia, Slovakia.

4. **South Europe** (Cyprus, Greece, Italy, Malta, Portugal, Spain). The region is highly heterogeneous. Differences outweigh similarities in the structure of organized crime groups operating in these countries, and this is also reflected in the different ways in which extortion racketeering is conducted. Extortion racketeering is casual in most of the countries belonging to this cluster. In two countries – Italy and Spain – extortion racketeering is systemic. In Spain, it is systematic because it is carried out by terrorist groups belonging to ETA, which are well-structured and rooted in the territory (see Transcrime, 2009, Spain country profile). In Italy the phenomenon is mainly linked to Mafia-like organized crime, for which extortion racketeering plays a fundamental role in terms of both exercising control over the territory and financing criminal activities.

CONCLUSION

This chapter has dealt with extortion and organized crime in Europe. Its analysis has been based on the observation that market opportunities and variations in the characteristics of organized criminal groups may give rise to two different types of extortion racketeering: systemic and casual. Four variables explain this process: 1. market opportunities, 2. the organizational structure of criminal groups; 3. their presence at the local level; and 4. the victim/offender relationship. Each of these variables interrelates with the others and continues to shae the ways in which well-established criminal groups perpetrate this old and vicious crime.

Box 1. Definitions

Extortion racketeering: An institutionalized practice whereby tributes are collected by organized criminal groups with the intent to control legal and illegal markets and to establish territorial sovereignty.

Systemic extortion racketeering: Extortion is deeply rooted and extends across a territory. Criminal organizations routinely engage in extortion, and extortion racketeering is a core part of criminal business.

Casual extortion racketeering: Extortion is episodic and not extended across a territory. Criminal organizations do not routinely engage in extortion.

Intraethnic extortions racketeering: When, in a particular country, foreign organized criminal groups are involved in extortion racketeering and, by operating within close ethnic communities, victimize their own people.

Hierarchical structures: A group with a hierarchical structure is "characterized by a single leader and a relatively clearly defined hierarchy. Systems of internal discipline are strict. Strong social or ethnic identities can be present, although this is not always the case. There is a relatively clear allocation of tasks and often some form of internal code of conduct, although this may be implicit and not 'officially' recorded"

Network structures: A group with a network structure "is defined by the activities of key individuals who engage in illicit activity in often shifting alliances. Such individuals may not regard themselves as being members of a criminal group, and may not be regarded as being a criminal group by outsiders. Nevertheless they coalesce around a series of criminal projects. [...] Networks usually consist of relatively manageable numbers of individuals [...]" (UNODC, 2002: 34-5, 41).

Victim/offender relationships:
Predatory: When a considerable extortive payment is demanded only once.
Parasitical: When the perpetrator demands small payments over a long period of time.
Symbiotic: When the perpetrators and the victims establish a prolonged relationship that produces illicit benefits for each of them.

REFERENCES

Bell, D. (2000). *The End of Ideology. On the Exhaustion of Political Ideas in the Fifties.* Harvard: Harvard University Press.

Blok, A. (2008). Reflections on the Sicilian Mafia: Peripheries and Their Impact on Centers. In D. Siegel & A. Nelen (Eds.). *Organized Crime: Culture, Markets and Policies,* Dordrecht: Springer.

Felson, M. (2006). *Crime and Nature.* London: SAGE publications.

Gambetta, D. (1993). *The Sicilian Mafia: The Business of Private Protection.* Harvard: Harvard University Press.

(2000). Mafia: The Price of Distrust. In D. Gambetta (Ed.). *Trust: Making and Breaking Cooperative Relations.* Oxford: Oxford University Press. 158-210.

Landesco, J. (1968). *Organized Crime in Chicago. Part III of The Illinois Crime Survey 1929.* Chicago: The University of Chicago Press.

Paoli, L. & C. Fijnaut. (2004). *Organised Crime in Europe. Concepts, Patterns, Control Policies in the European Union and Beyond.* Dordrecht: Springer.

Passas, N. (2002). Cross-Border Crime and the Interface Between Legal and Illegal Actors. In P. Van Duyne, K. Von Lampe, & N. Passas (Eds.), *Upper World and Underworld in Cross-Border Crime.* The Netherlands: Wolf Legal Publishers, pp. 11–43.

Reuter, P. (1994). Research on American Organized Crime. In R. J. Kelly, K. Chin, & R. Schatzberg (Eds.). *Handbook of Organized Crime in the United States* Santa Barbara: Greenwood Press. 91–120.

Transcrime (2009). *Study on Extortion Racketeering the Need for an Instrument to Combat Activities of Organized Crime.* Final Report prepared for the European Commission. Bruxelles (unpublished).

Volkov, V. (2002). *Violent Entrepreneurs. The Use of Force in the Making of Russian Capitalism.* London: Cornell University Press.

UNODC (2002). *Results of a Pilot Survey of Forty Selected Organized Criminal Groups in Sixteen Countries.* Vienna: UNODC.

ABOUT THE AUTHORS

Ernesto U. Savona is a professor of criminology at the Catholic University of Milan (Italy) and director of Transcrime, Joint Research Centre on Transnational Crime–Università Cattolica del Sacro Cuore (Italy)-Università degli Studi di Trento.

Marco Zanella, Ph.D. is a candidate of the international Ph.D. in criminology at the Catholic University of Milan (Italy).

35 Organized Crime in Asia

Leona Lee

INTRODUCTION

Triads and bryokudan are two major kinds of criminal organizations in Asia. Triads originated in China but have spread to many major Southeast Asian countries, such as Hong Kong, Taiwan, Singapore, Malaysia, and Indonesia. Boryokudan are criminal organizations in Japan. Their members, boryoku-danin, are informally referred to as yakuza. In recent decades, triads and boryokudan have established bases in the United States and Europe. This chapter provides an account of the origin and modern-day operation of triads and boryokudan, and a description of the context that supports the growth of these organizations.

THE ORIGIN OF THE TRIADS

Triads initially emerged to fill a need in society, providing services and protection that were unavailable or hard to obtain from the government. Members of these groups occupied a marginal status in society. They were often outcasts or lost their social status due to changes in the social system. Gradually, they expanded and began to "sell" protection to others who needed it. Lacking legitimate means, they resorted to violence and intimidation to protect themselves and their customers. Due to the nature of their business, triads have many opportunities to engage in illegal activities. Criminal activities are also a good source of power and profits to sustain these organizations.

The word "triad" is often understood to symbolize a triangle formed by three entities: heaven, earth, and man. Thus, it is synonymous with Tiandihui (Heaven and Earth Society). This interpretation, however, was absent from the early literature and documents on triads (Chu, 2000). A popular legend traces the origin of the triad as a political organization with roots in the Shoalin (meaning, "a young forest") Temple of China. The Ching emperor persecuted the Shoalin monks after they helped the government quell a rebellion. The Shaolin monks responded by forming the triad with the goal of overthrowing the Ching dynasty and restoring the Ming dynasty (1368–44), which was overthrown when the Manchus invaded China and established the Ching Dynasty. After the downfall of the Ching dynasty in 1911, the triads abandoned their political mission and turned increasingly to criminal activities (Chu, 2000).

Recent studies indicate that the Tiandihui, or Triad, emerged in 1674 as a mutual aid organization. It helped mediate socioeconomic conflicts among subethnic groups in the Fujian area, provided protection to frequent travelers, and engaged in criminal activities (Chu, 2000: 12). As the Fujiannese migrated to other parts of Southeast Asia (including Hong Kong and Taiwan), triads established branches in these areas (Chu, 2000). During their early days in Hong Kong, triads engaged in salt and opium smuggling, robbery, assault, and piracy (Sinn, 1989). They also organized migrant laborers. Many laborers joined or paid the triads to protect their job opportunities. Nontriad laborers also organized and formed their own triads to protect their interests. As a result, the number of triads burgeoned. When China fell to the communists, the various triads in Hong Kong consolidated into four main groups: Chiu Chow/Hoklo, 14K, Wo, and Luen (Chu, 2000: 39–40).

A typical traditional triad consists of a chief (mountain master) at the top. The second tier consists of a deputy chief, an incense master (who officiates during initiation and promotion rites), and a vanguard (responsible for recruitment and assisting in ceremonies). The next tier consists of red poles (fighters), white paper fans (for general administration), and straw sandals (liaison officers). Beneath them are the ordinary members.

THE OPERATION OF TRIADS IN THE PRESENT DAY

Today, triads in Hong Kong are involved in legal and illegal businesses. According to official statistics published by the Hong Kong Police, more than 2,000 triad-related crimes were committed each year between 2006 and 2008, constituting about three percent of all crimes (Hong Kong Police Force, 2009). The Wo Shing Wo, Sun Yee On, and 14K are the most powerful groups (Booth, 1990). Many legal businesses prefer to rely on triads for protection and seek their help to resolve disputes and collect bad debts.

According to Chu (2000), cinemas, nightclubs, restaurants, and massage parlors often engage triad members as business partners, security guards, or bouncers for protection. These businesses are easily victimized by gang members or customers who cause trouble by making a scene, interfering with other customers, or refusing to pay. On the other hand, triads also engage in extortion by deliberately causing trouble in a new business and then offering peace in exchange for protection fees. Reporting these crimes to the police is not a solution, because police response can be slow and ineffective. Furthermore, making headlines in the media will only taint the company's reputation and drive away customers. Therefore, many businesses comply with the triads' demands.

Businesses also seek the help of triads to collect bad debts. The Commercial Crime Bureau of Hong Kong only investigates commercial fraud involving at least five million Hong Kong dollars (about US $640,000) (Chu, 2000). For smaller claims, one may opt to hire triad members to track down the debtor and settle the claim. Some credit card and financial companies routinely hire triad members to harass customers that are delinquent in their payments.

Triads also actively "market" their protection services to construction companies and film production companies (Chu, 2000). Many residential and commercial building construction sites are located in isolated areas. A commonly used tactic to secure protection fees from construction companies is to damage or threaten to damage expensive equipment at the construction site. Triads also allege that outdoor filming for movie production negatively affects the feng shui (the harmony of the environment) of an area and demand compensation. Failure to appease the triads will result in disruption during filming. The triads may damage sets, props and equipment, throw objects at the crew, and make loud noises during the filming. In one incident, a film crew was bombed when they refused to pay. Some triads are also in the movie production business, where they intimidate popular actors so that the actor will appear in the triad's films at a reduced salary (Chu, 2000). In the 90s, during the real estate boom in Hong Kong, potential condominium buyers often camped outside the sales office days before the first day of sales to secure an opportunity to purchase an apartment. Triads attempted to corner the market on popular housing developments by harassing potential buyers. In one incident, a triad held a press conference and shamelessly defended their offenses after a few hundred of their members were arrested by the police for disrupting the queue outside a condo sales office.

Triads are also heavily involved in drug trafficking, illegal gambling and prostitution. They may have control of local markets but are too provincial and often lack the capital and expertise to manage international operations (Chin, 1990; Chu, 2000). International drug kingpins are entrepreneurs, such as import/export businessmen with substantial capital, expertise, and connections. The smuggling of illegal aliens to the United States and Europe has attracted widespread attention in recent years. The Fuk Ching gang from China is alleged to be especially active in human smuggling to the United States. But human smuggling is not monopolized by gangs and triads. Businesses with connections to the tourist industry, such as travel agencies and counterfeit travel documents syndicates, run these lucrative operations (Chu, 2000; Zhang & Chin, 2003).

Since Hong Kong returned to Chinese control in 1997, many Hong Kong triads have expanded their businesses to the north where they were originally quite welcome. China's minister of public security declared in 1993 that as long as triad members were committed to maintaining the prosperity of Hong Kong, they should be respected. As the Chinese economy evolves from a planned economy to a market economy allowing ownership of private property, opportunities arise for legal and illegal businesses. Coupled with the increase in wealth is the rising demand for consumer goods and services that cannot be adequately met through legitimate channels. Through corruption and bribery, many triads in Hong Kong cultivate ties with government officials in China. In return, they obtain "free passes" to conduct illegal businesses. Triads and businessmen seized the opportunities arising from the rapidly expanding Chinese economy to develop legal (e.g., hotels, restaurants, nightclubs) and illegal (e.g., casinos, prostitution rings) businesses in China. In Hong Kong, some triads operating parking lots routinely steal expensive cars and sell them in China. Some also smuggle women from China to Hong Kong to work as prostitutes.

THE ORIGIN OF THE YAKUZA

The word "yakuza" means hooligan or gambler. Boryokudan, meaning "violent groups," is the official term used to describe criminal organizations and gangs in Japan (Huang & Vaughn, 1992). Boryokudan can be traced to twelfth century feudal Japan, where there was a lord (shogun) and vassal system with a distinct hierarchy that cultivated the way of the warrior (Sansom, 1943). The samurai or warriors, served the shogun and occupied a high status, followed by farmers and merchants. The demise of the samurai occurred during the Meiji Restoration (1868–1912), when the Japanese society changed from a feudal system to a business economy. Merchants' social status rose while samurai's stipends and privileges declined. In order to survive, many masterless samurai began working for the merchants as assassins and thieves (Hill, 2003). The displaced samurai were the origin of yakuza. Like the triads, yakuza offer protection to those vulnerable to victimization.

In addition to the samurai, Bakuto (gamblers), Gurentai (gangsters or hoodlums), and Tekiya (peddlers) were also outcasts in the early Meiji era. These groups developed their own criminal subculture. Gurentai mainly use force and violence to control the operation of small cafes and entertainment establishments. Tekiya are peddlers who cheat their customers, intimidate other street vendors, and collect protection fees and rents from them. Bakuto originated as professional gamblers working for the government during the Tokugawa era (1600–1867). Many became casino owners and are involved in loan sharking.

Burakumin and Japanese-born Koreans are two other groups of outcasts that formed or joined criminal organizations. Burakumin were originally the descendants of Hinin Pariahs (i.e., butchers, hide tanners, and grave diggers), occupying the lowest rank in society during the Tokugawa era. Japanese-born Koreans are denied citizenship and some operate pachinko (gaming parlors) that are fronts for illegal gambling.

THE OPERATION OF BORYOKUDAN IN THE PRESENT DAY

National Police reported that there are about 85,000 yakuza members in Japan (National Police Agency of Japan, 2008). Associate membership of yakuza has been on the rise in recent years, surpassing regular membership, which has been declining (National Police Agency of Japan, 2008). Crimes committed by associate yakuza members are outnumbering those by regular members. Of the more than twenty boryokudan groups, the three major ones are Yamaguchi-gumi, Inagawa-kai, and Sumiyoshi-kai, with total membership exceeding 60,000.

The modern boryokudan is close-knit. Members form strong bonds with one another, practicing ancient rituals and traditional ceremonies dating back to the samurai times. Strict demands for loyalty and obedience to authority are maintained through violence. A typical boryokudan is headed by a kumi-cho (boss), followed by saiko-kanbu (senior executives), kanbu (executives), kumi-in (soldiers), and jun-kosei-in (trainees) (Hill, 2003). Every member in the boryokudan has a position and a role, similar to the father-child relationship. The kobun (subordinate/child) must obey the oyabun (leader/father). As an extreme act of loyalty, lower-level boryoku-danin sometimes confess to crimes and go to jail for crimes committed by higher-ranking members (Hill, 2003). Disobedience and disloyalty are punishable by excommunication, severing of relations (and fingers), fines, even death. Kaplan and Dubro (1986) reported that more than 40 percent of yakuza members had their fingers chopped off.

Like the triads, boryokudan engage in legitimate and illegitimate businesses. Many Japanese corporations do not want to reveal the details of their operations to shareholders. Thus corporate officials hire boryokudanin to intimidate shareholders during company meetings to prevent them from asking too many questions. Yakuza sometimes end up infiltrating these companies and blackmailing the officers (Huang and Vaughn, 1992). Some boryokudan also operate as soukaiya (meeting goers), disrupting and blackmailing corporations. The most common arrests for boryokudan members are crimes involving stimulants, followed by bodily injury, larceny, extortion, and fraud (National Police Agency Organized Crime Department, 2005). In addition, boryokudan engage in loan sharking, gambling, pornography, and accident and bankruptcy scams. Some boryokudan have joined forces with criminal organizations in other countries and are involved in international money laundering, drug and firearms trafficking, and importing women from nearby Asian countries to work as prostitutes (Huang & Vaughn, 1992; Shikata, 2006).

An interesting note is the symbiotic relationship between the police and boryokudan (Huang & Vaughn, 1992). Boryokudan are considered a necessary evil. They maintain order in decrepit and disorganized neighborhoods, relieving the police of the unpleasant duties of patrolling them. While illegal businesses thrive, the neighborhood is relatively safe thanks to the presence of boryokudanin. Furthermore, police officers, government officials, and businessmen often rely on boryokudan to protect their business and power (Curtis, 1983).

CONCLUSION: CONTROLLING ORGANIZED CRIME

In their study of the Sicilian and New York Mafia and Tongs in the United States, Fiorentini and Peltzman (1995) found that these groups flourish under three conditions. First, when businesses need to operate in areas deemed illegal by the government, there will be incentives for criminal organizations to emerge and establish local monopolies. Second, when fiscal and regulatory pressure makes it too cumbersome to conduct business in a legal manner, people will search for ways to circumvent such regulations and operate illegally, thus fostering organized crime. Third, the crackdown on criminal enterprises can backfire, leading to more violence and corruption as a means for survival.

Triads and boryokudan are two major century-old criminal organizations originating in China and Japan, respectively. Both have adapted to changes in modern society, seizing upon new opportunities to become actively involved in local, international, and transnational crimes in other Asian countries, Europe, and the United States. When examining the triads and boryokudan, one can see that similar factors led to their emergence and supported their growth. Members of triads or boryokudan are disenfranchised or of marginal status. As business and trade flourish, many merchants and businesses become vulnerable to victimization. Since the protection provided by the government is usually inadequate, criminal organizations create a monopoly by offering protection and generate demands for their services through intimidation and extortion (Hill, 2003).

Policies aimed at controlling criminal organizations should be based on the factors that led to their emergence and survival. Chu (2000) suggested three ways to curb the power of triads. First, businesses can change their way of operation and eliminate opportunities for triad involvement. For example, triad involvement in the Hong Kong housing market was eliminated when potential buyers were awarded their buying opportunity based on a lottery system rather than on a first come, first served basis. Second, if government protection is swift and effective, businessmen will be less inclined to seek the help of triads. Third, the legalization or decriminalization of certain trades and activities will eliminate the need for black markets and allow people to seek help from the police rather than the triads.

REFERENCES

Booth, M. (1990). *The Triads: The Chinese Criminal Fraternity*. London: Grafton Books.

Chin, K. L. (1990). *Chinese Subculture and Criminality: Non-traditional Crime Groups in* America. New York: Greenwood Press.

Chu, Y. K. (2000). *The Triads as Business*. London: Routledge.

Curtis, G. (1983). *Election Campaigning Japanese Style*. Tokyo: Kodansha.

Fiorentini, G. & Peltzman, S. (Eds.). (1995). The *Economics of Organized Crime*. Cambridge: Cambridge University Press.

Hill, P. (2003). *The Japanese Mafia: Yakuza, Law and the State*. New York: Oxford University Press.

Hong Kong Police Force. (2009). Crime Statistics. Retrieved from www.police.gov/hkp-home/english/statistics/index.htm.

Huang, F. & M. Vaughn. (1992). A Descriptive Analysis of Japanese Organized Crime: The Boryokudan from 1945 to 1988. *International Criminal Justice Review*, 2, 19–57.

Kaplan, D. & A. Dubro. (1986). *Yakuza – The Explosive Account of Japan's Criminal Underworld*. Reading, MA: Addison-Wesley.

National Police Agency of Japan. (2008). Retrieved from www.npa.go.jp/toukei/keiji36/PDF/ H19_ALL.pdf

National Police Agency Organized Crime Department. (2005). *The Situation of Violent Groups in 2004*. Tokyo: National Police Agency.

Sansom, G. (1943). *Japan: A Short Cultural History*. New York: Appleton-Century-Crofts.

Shikata, K. (2006). Yakuza-Organized Crime in Japan. *Journal of Money Laundering Control*, 9, 416–21.

Sinn, E. (1989). *Power and Charity: The Early History of the Tung Wah Hospital, Hong Kong*. Hong Kong: Oxford University Press.

Zhang, S. & Chin, K. L. (2003). The Declining Significance of Triad Societies in Transnational Illegal Activities: A Structural Deficiency Perspective. *British Journal of Criminology*, 43, 469–88.

WEB SITES

National Police Agency of Japan: www.npa.go.jp/english/index.htm
Hong Kong Police Force: www.police.gov/hkp-home/english/statistics

ABOUT THE AUTHOR

Leona Lee is a faculty member with the Sociology Department of John Jay College of Criminal Justice. She received her Ph.D. in criminal justice from Rutgers University and her master's in philosophy from Cambridge University, England. Her research interests are in juvenile delinquency, juvenile justice, biosocial theories of crime, sentencing, and comparative studies of these topics. She has published in the *Journal of Criminal Justice, Journal of Crime and Justice, Juvenile and Family Court Journal*, and *Youth and Society*.

36   Drug Cartels

NEITHER HOLY, NOR ROMAN, NOR AN EMPIRE

Enrique Desmond Arias

In the 1980s the term "cartel" became shorthand for powerful Colombian criminal syndicates that exported narcotics as a result of the way that it dovetailed with the wider political discourse of the war on drugs (Kenney, 2007: 235–34). The two most prominent groups were based in the cities of Medellin and Cali. The Colombian groups, which achieved immense notoriety and political power, became the targets of vigorous repression efforts on the part of the U.S. and Colombian governments that resulted in their destruction during the 1990s. These successes have had the effect of decentralizing the Colombian drug trade and shifting control of trafficking in the region to Mexican organizations. I will begin this chapter with a historical and political background of these groups, looking at how they operated, examining them from a theoretical perspective to understand why the term "cartel" is inappropriate, and will conclude with a comparison of Colombian and similarly named Mexican trafficking groups operating today.

BACKGROUND

During the nineteenth century Colombia experienced several civil wars culminating in the Thousand Days War. Conflict again erupted in 1948 with assassination of Jorge Gaitan, the leader of a reformist faction of the Liberal Party (Crandall, 2002: 55; Bowden, 2002: 7–14). His supporters rioted for days and unrest spread to the countryside where an amorphous civil war known as *La Violencia* erupted. The conflict lasted until 1957 and resulted in the deaths of between one thousand and three hundred thousand Colombians. A pact to end the conflict did not resolve the rancorous national tensions over social justice that motivated many combatants

(Crandall, 2002: 57). As a result, in the 1960s a new civil war began between groups influenced by Marxist-Leninism and the government.

The Andes Mountains are the natural home of the coca plant which indigenous groups have long consumed to help with the back breaking work of high altitude farming as well as for medicinal and ritual purposes. In 1859 a German scientist developed a process to extract the active chemicals in coca to create cocaine hydrochloride. Over the next twenty years the drug became popularized for pharmaceutical and recreational purposes (Friman, 1999: 84). Cocaine was legal in the U.S. and sold in pharmacies around the country until 1914 when the federal government passed narcotics controls (Spillane, 1999: 25).

North American and European demand increased in the 1960s. Colombia became a player in the drug market in the late 1960s when U.S. marijuana merchants encouraged small farmers to grow the plant after a crackdown on Mexican marijuana growing. While U.S. citizens dominated trafficking during this period, Colombians saw the economic potential and developed the international connections to engage in large-scale narcotics trafficking. Until the early 1970s Chile was the leader of the international cocaine trade. In 1973, however, a military coup took place and the new government destroyed the local drug gangs (Thoumi, 1995: 130).

Colombia's cocaine trade exploded after 1978. In that year, the television show "60 Minutes" broadcast an alarming report that the Carter Administration had internal documents proving connections between high-ranking Colombian officials, including presidential candidate Julio Cesar Turbay, and marijuana traffickers. Turbay was elected and, to shore up his relationship with the U.S., unleashed the Colombian military on marijuana growers (Chepesiuk, 2003: 60). This pushed Colombian criminals into cocaine since it was easier to grow and harder to interdict.

COLOMBIA'S CARTELS

Colombia and its people are divided by large rivers, high mountain ridges, and dense jungles. Economically this has led to small groups of local elites dominating business through regional conglomerates. These practices ensured the diversified regional economies at the expense of national consolidation.

The cartels built the narcotics trade on the same principals. The result was the emergence of two prominent trafficking organizations based around groups of criminals from Medellin and Cali, the country's second and third largest cities. Colombia's approximately one hundred to two hundred trafficking organizations generally affiliated with one of these groups.

The Medellin Cartel, led by Pablo Escobar, Carlos Lehder, and the Ochoa brothers, played a major role in the early commercialization of cocaine in the U.S. Strategically, the Medellin traffickers enjoyed the advantage that a large proportion of the Colombian emigrants to the U.S. came from Medellin, providing them with a potential distribution network (Roldan, 1999: 166). With Carlos Lehder's purchase of Norman Cay, an island in the Bahamas, Medellin traffickers shifted the cocaine trade away from smuggling small amounts of drugs through *mulas* (mules) who carried the contraband on their persons, to large-scale shipments by small airplane and boat (Thoumi, 1995: 143).

Medellin criminals enjoyed notoriety and sought public acceptance (Roldan, 1999: 169). This group was violent and freely used cash and threats to buy off state officials. Its leaders' aspirations to political power and popular acclaim led them to provide social services in areas where they had special connections. Pablo Escobar, for example, lavished money on his native town of Envigado and was elected an alternate representative to the Colombian legislature. Carlos Lehder provided social services in his home city of Armenia where he founded a right-wing nationalist political party (Thoumi, 1995: 141). These efforts had the effect of buying their leaders a certain amount of popular support and protection.

The Cali Cartel had a different reputation. Led by Jose Santacruz Londoño, Gilberto and Miguel Rodriguez-Orejuela, and Helmer Herrero Buitrago, this group kept a lower profile (Clawson & Lee, 1996: 55). Its leaders frowned on overt violence against government officials and cooperated in state efforts to bring the Medellin Cartel to justice (Chepesiuk, 2003: 21). Cali traffickers put less emphasis on providing social services, instead reinvesting their money in the local economy to build support among the well-off. As Clawson and Lee (1996: 58–9) write, "[i]n general, Cali's protection strategy has relied on establishing good relations with the power elite, not in cultivating a following among the poor."

In principal the two major cartels divided control over export markets with Medellin controlling Miami and Cali controlling New York, but often found themselves during the 1980s in turf conflicts. As the decade wore on drug violence became a major concern in New York and Miami. The U.S. government began to pressure the Colombian government to accept an extradition treaty that would allow traffickers to be sent to the U.S. to stand trial. The traffickers opposed this with extensive violence and terror. Luis Carlos Galan, a charismatic presidential candidate, and Rodrigo

Lara Bonilla, a young attorney general, were killed, and, among count-less other violent acts, a jet with 133 passengers was blown up. In 1993 Colombian police, operating with US agents, killed Escobar. Colombian law-enforcement agents also summarily executed 209 alleged members of the Medellin Cartel and arrested many more. These efforts effectively elimi-nated the cartel by the mid-1990s (Clawson & Lee, 1996: 54).

Law enforcement resources only began to focus on the Cali Cartel in ear-nest in 1994. During the elections that year the U.S. Embassy received strong evidence that traffickers had donated $3.5 million to Ernesto Samper's pres-idential campaign. Samper, nonetheless, won the election. To mollify U.S. sentiments and, in an ultimately failed attempt to avoid decertification as an ally of the United States in the war on drugs, Samper pursued a vigorous campaign against the Cali Cartel by forming a military unit of 6,000 elite troops and appointing a general supported by the United States to head the Colombian National Police. During Samper's administration most of the important members of the Cali Cartel were brought to justice.

In the years since the collapse of the major cartels, Colombia's drug trade has become more fluid. Many different criminal gangs, often specialized in particular illegal activities, operate in the country. Over the past decade Colombia has been wracked by a civil war that has pitted the Colombian military, allied with violent paramilitaries originally funded by traffickers, against leftist guerilla groups that make money by protecting drug growers. While various criminal organizations manage elements of the drug trade, trafficking today in Colombia involves active participation from leftist gue-rillas and paramilitaries, corrupt police and military officers, and common criminals.

DYNAMICS OF CARTELS

From a technical perspective, a cartel is a group of economic actors who use their collective market power to fix prices at levels favorable to them. Two prominent examples of cartels stand out. The first is the Organization of Petroleum Exporting States (OPEC) whose members jointly set production quotas in order to reduce oil supply and artificially inflate prices. A second cartel operating today is DeBeers, a South African company that manages the world diamond trade on behalf of major producers by setting produc-tion quotas, purchasing stones, and limiting wholesale distribution. By controlling supply, the company dramatically inflates world diamond prices.

Colombian criminals never had any interest in reducing the supply of cocaine since government repression more than did its part to reduce supply and ensure high profits. Rather, the cartels operated more along the lines of export syndicates by bringing together a variety of criminals to collectively overcome economic and political barriers to exporting drugs (Thoumi, 1995: 93–108).

The two major criminal groups independently pooled their resources for political lobbying through bribes and violence. In these efforts the Cali Cartel preferred bribes, whereas the Medellin group was given to high profile violence.

The Cali and Medellin Cartels also worked separately to protect the interests of their own organizations. Both shared intelligence among members. After the kidnapping of the sister of a Medellin trafficker, the cartels agreed not to pay ransom and jointly formed *Muerte a los Sequestradores* (Death to Kidnappers). This organization assassinated several members of the guerilla group that organized the kidnapping and secured the victim's release (Chepesiuk, 2003: 64).

The cartels also developed the *apuntada* system in which traffickers built relationships with wealthy people without criminal records, allowing them to buy into shipments of cocaine through proxies. This permitted wealthy members of Colombian society to profit from the cocaine trade without dirtying their hands and gave cartel members access to larger pools of cash (Thoumi, 2003: 96).

Finally, the cartels separately aggregated the resources of traffickers to negotiate agreements with powerful international criminal organizations. The Cali Cartel, for example, established transshipment deals with Mexican traffickers (Clawson & Lee, 1996: 41). The Medellin Cartel made an agreement with Manuel Noriega, Panama's strongman in the 1980s, for free passage of cocaine through that country.

All of these efforts, however, occur in relative secrecy. If legitimate law-enforcement officers were to become aware of these arrangements they could easily destroy the organization. As a result, Colombian drug traffickers operate through clandestine networks that enable criminals to work together based on personal knowledge and relationships (Kenney, 2007: 241–2).

MEXICAN CARTELS

In recent years commentators have also applied the term "cartel" to Mexican drug trafficking organizations. These are large hierarchical criminal organizations that dominate the transit of cocaine and heroin into the United States through their control of territory around Mexican transportation arteries, links into the Mexican political system, and connection with gangs in the United States (Cook, 2007: 4–6, 9–10). While these groups concentrate many different types of criminal activity including drugs commercialization and transshipment as well as money laundering, they also employ specialized criminal gangs such as the Zetas and the Negros to undertake military operations within Mexico (Cook, 2007: 6–9). The principal objective of these activities is fighting ongoing wars with competing cartels. The organizations also engage in violence against security forces, government officials, journalists, and citizens opposed to their activities. Politically, the Mexican organized crime groups are making a clear effort to use violence to influence political decisions at the local, state, and national levels. In this sense the wide array of violent acts reflects the appropriation of some terrorist tactics in promoting their political agenda in ways similar to the failed violent efforts of Pablo Escobar and other Medellín traffickers in the 1980s and 1990s as they sought to convince the Colombian government not to use extradition proceedings to send them to the United States.

There is little evidence that these organizations are cartels. These groups control ninety percent of the cocaine traffic into the United States and could use this market leverage to work collaboratively to raise prices for consumers and lower prices paid to producers earlier in the production chain. These groups compete intensely with one another and, at least in terms of supplying the United States' market, have no reason to work to raise prices since antidrug efforts here are effective in setting extremely high prices.

CONCLUSION

Given governments' efforts to repress illegal activities, criminals have little reason to act as a cartel. Around the world other types of criminal organizations operate in different political and structural environments. Nevertheless, there is almost no evidence that these organizations collude to reduce the supplies of illegal commodities to drive up prices. Rather, these groups derive profits from undermining state imposed scarcity of illicit goods and services.

Readers of this chapter should take away two lessons. First, the word "cartel" is a misnomer. These groups are not collectives of firms that aggregated market strength to control price. Rather, they operate as networked syndicates to cooperatively assist criminal activities. Second, the Colombian cartel's vertical integration attracted governmental attention, resulting in the destruction of these organizations, and their replacement with a looser set of gangs that have had just as much success delivering cocaine into North America and Europe.

REFERENCES

Bowden, M. (2002). *Killing Pablo: The Hunt for the World's Greatest Outlaw*. New York: Penguin Books.

Chepesiuk, R. (2003). *The Bullet or the Bribe: Taking Down Colombia's Cali Drug Cartel*. Westport: Preager Publishers.

Clawson, P. & R. Lee III (1996). *The Anderan Cocaine Industry*. New York: St. Martin's Gryphon.

Cook, C. W. (2007, 16 October). "Mexico's Drug Cartel, CRS Report for Congress: Foreign Affairs, Defence and Trade Division," Retrieved from www.fas.org/sgp/crs/row/RL34215.pdf

Crandall, R. (2002). *Driven by Drugs: U.S. Policy Toward Colombia*. Boulder. Lynne Rienner Publishers.

Kenney, M. (2007). *The Architecture of Drug Trafficking: Network Forms of Organization in the Colombian Cocaine Trade*. Global Crime, 8(3), 233–59.

Friman, H. R. (1999). Germany and the Transformations of Cocaine, 1960–1920. In P. Gootenberg (Ed.), *Cocaine: Global Histories*. London: Routledge, pp. 83–104.

Roldan, M. (1999). Cocaine and the "Miracle" or Modernity in Medellín. In P. Gootenberg (Ed.), *Cocaine: Global Histories*. London: Routledge, pp. 165–81.

Spillane, J. F. (1999). Making a Modern Drug: The Manufacture, Sale, and Control of Cocaine in the United States, 1880–1920. In P. Gootenberg (Ed.), *Cocaine: Global Histories*. London: Routledge, pp. 21–45.

Thoumi, F. (1995). *Political Economy and Illegal Drugs in Colombia*. Boulder: Lynne Rienner Publishers.

  (2003). *Illegal Drugs, Economy, and Society in the Andes*. Washington D.C., Woodrow Wilson Center Press.

ABOUT THE AUTHOR

Enrique Desmond Arias is an associate professor in the Department of Political Science at the John Jay College of Criminal Justice and a member of the doctoral faculty in Criminal Justice at CUNY. He is the author of *Drugs and Democracy in Rio de Janeiro: Trafficking, Social Networks, and Security* (UNC, 2006). He has published articles in the Journal of Latin American Studies, Latin American Politics and Society, Qualitative Sociology, and Comparative Politics.

37 The International Implications of Domestic Terrorism in the United States

William S. Parkin, Joshua D. Freilich, and Steven M. Chermak

INTRODUCTION

On February 25, 1994, Baruch Goldstein entered the mosque at the Tomb of the Patriarchs in Hebron in the West Bank and opened fire on a group of Muslims as they began their morning prayers. More than thirty people, including Goldstein, died that day. Years earlier, when living in Brooklyn, New York, Goldstein was a founding member of the Jewish Defense League, an organization linked to terrorist acts and extremist ideologies in the United States (Firestone, 1994). In October of 1998, James Kopp, an antiabortion extremist, shot and killed Dr. Barnett Slepian in the state of New York. Kopp fled the United States, hiding out in Mexico, Ireland, and France before being caught by law enforcement three years later. Convicted of the crime, Kopp was sentenced to life in federal prison. In addition, Kopp was linked to four other shootings in New York and Canada (Staba, 2007).

This chapter discusses the international implications of domestic terrorism within the United States. With globalization, the separation of peoples through cultural and geographic distance has decreased and in some cases disappeared entirely. In the United States, the proverbial melting pot of religions, ideologies, and cultures, the international implications of domestic terrorism can be far reaching. Extremist beliefs, which were once restricted by the geography of where one lived, can now be broadcast around the globe in seconds. Similarly, individuals willing to commit acts of violence in the name of a fringe ideology can travel anywhere in the world in a matter of days if not hours. This potential for the dissemination of extremist ideologies, the ability for transnational collaboration between terrorists, as well as an increased audience to whom to preach their beliefs, creates unique challenges for law enforcement and intelligence agencies who must share information and work together to make sure that home-grown threats in one country do not turn into an international terrorist incident in another.

DOMESTIC VERSUS INTERNATIONAL TERRORISM

Domestic terrorism is an act where (1) the terrorists, (2) the victims, and (3) the location of the act are international, that is, they originate from and occur within the same country. For a terrorist act to be considered international, only one of those three criteria needs to originate from or occur within a country different from the other two. For example, Timothy McVeigh was an American who targeted both United States citizens and a government building on U.S. soil. This is an act of domestic terrorism. The World Trade Center bombing in 1993 was conducted on American soil, by terrorists who were not U.S. citizens, against individuals who were primarily U.S. citizens. This act is considered one of international terrorism.

In the United States, although acts of international terrorism have taken more lives over the last thirty years, incidents of domestic terrorism are more prevalent. Public awareness regarding the threat of domestic terrorism is limited, however, because the attention of the media and policy makers has primarily been focused on international terrorist threats against American interests or domestic terrorism in other countries. With one notable exception, the bombing of the Alfred P. Murrah Federal Building on April 19, 1995 by Timothy McVeigh, the public is primarily concerned about terrorism threats from abroad. Most recently, the deadly terrorist acts of September 11, 2001, have made the international threat even more poignant in the minds of American citizens. This focus, however, on the threat of international terrorism is shortsighted. In fact, LaFree, Dugan, Scott, and Fogg's (2006) analysis of global terrorism found that acts of domestic terrorism usually outnumber acts of international terrorism by seven to one in a typical year. Although threats of violent terror attacks from transnational organizations, such as Al Qaeda, are real and immediate, they are only one piece of a much larger puzzle related to the national security goals of American law enforcement and intelligence agencies. In the United States, the threat of domestic terrorism has many policy and safety implications for American citizens, but it also has the potential to gravely threaten the safety of the international community.

TERRORISM IN THE UNITED STATES

More than 3,000 terrorist incidents occurred in the United States between 1954 and 2001. These attacks are unique to America in two ways, the first being a marked diversity in ideologies that motivate individuals to commit violence and second, an even greater division of individuals and groups within those ideologies (Hewitt, 2003). Researching violent incidents that occurred between 1980 and 1989 and which resulted in federal charges, Smith (1994) classifies domestic terrorists as falling under the following typologies: Puerto Rican terrorism, Jewish terrorism, left-wing terrorism, right-wing terrorism, and special interest or single-issue terrorism. Left-wing groups during this time period were primarily Marxist, operated in urban areas, and chose symbolic targets of capitalism and government. Right-wing groups were formed around religion, such as the Christian Identity movement, operated out of rural areas, and attacked law enforcement targets and groups that represented opposing ideologies. Single-issue terrorist organizations were represented by the antiabortion movement and environmental groups, such as the Earth Liberation Front and Animal Liberation Front (Smith, 1994).

From those six typologies, only one included terrorists or terrorist groups that would be defined as international. Although Puerto Rican and Jewish terrorist groups have, for the most part, become inactive over the last twenty years, the far-right, far-left, and single-issue terrorist groups have not. According to Freilich and Chermak (2009), there have been at least 122 ideologically motivated homicide incidents in the United States since 1990 that were performed by suspects adhering to far-right ideology. In addition, groups such as the Earth Liberation Front and the Animal Liberation Front continue to attack targets that they identify with as representing companies and interests that threaten the environment (Smith & Damphousse, 2009).

Domestic terrorism in the United States, however, infrequently expands outside of the country. Historically, extremist ideologies developed abroad were transferred to the United States through immigration or the more recent spread of technology and information. Therefore, extremist ideologies specific to the United States are rare; more common would be the import of extremism, such as occurred with the Christian Identity Movement. This religious and political ideology argues the Aryan race is descendant from the lost tribes of Israel and supreme to all other races and religions. The Christian Identity Movement, although most prevalent in America, originated from British Israelism and was transported to the United States in the late nineteenth century (Barkun, 1997). Its importation and subsequent repackaging does not make it unique to the United States. The antiabortion movement, however, has its roots in the United States and acts of violence related to the ideology have almost exclusively occurred in America, against Americans, and have been perpetrated by Americans. The reference to James Kopp's murder of a Canadian abortion doctor at the onset of this chapter is one of very few examples where an extremist ideology with roots in the United States spread to another country.

This low rate of occurrence, however, is not one that should be ignored by policy makers, law enforcements officials, intelligence agencies, or their counterparts in other countries. The spread of extremist ideologies and hate speech across national borders, whether those unique to America or not, has become infinitely easier over the last fifteen years. The advent of the information age allows individuals to share their thoughts and ideas, whether extreme or not, with others across the globe. This information sharing presents unique challenges for law enforcement officials who not only must worry about criminal acts motivated by ideologies native to their countries, but extremist ideas from anywhere in the world.

INTERNATIONAL COLLABORATION

The idea of collaboration between terrorist organizations is a serious consideration that law enforcement agencies must address. Several types of collaboration could occur that might turn a domestic or intranational terrorist organization into an international one. In one instance, a domestic group might collaborate with an international group on American soil. For example, an American white supremacist that meets with an Islamic extremist who emigrated from Afghanistan. In another instance, a domestic group might reach out to a terrorist organization with a similar ideology in a foreign country. This might entail an American white supremacist group such as the Aryan Brotherhood attempting to make connections with a racist far-right group based in Germany or Italy. Chermak, Freilich, and Simone (2010) note that in a survey of state police agencies, two agencies stated there was evidence of collaboration between the domestic far-right and Islamic extremists to commit crimes in their states. Importantly, the authors also uncovered at least two additional cases of such cooperation through their examination of open sources.

Collaboration is not reserved for the terrorists alone. As new technologies make it easier for extremist ideologies to perforate national borders, they also make it easier for law enforcement and intelligence agencies to share information that will help track and stop terrorists from committing acts of violence. For domestic and intranational terrorism, the mechanisms are already in place for the dissemination of such information. Federal, state, and local agencies can collaborate through centralized information sharing organizations, such as Fusion Centers. Although the effectiveness of such organizations has not been evaluated and there are reasons to suspect that there are significant obstacles to full cooperation across agency, a framework for information sharing has been put into place. Unfortunately, very few formal channels of communication exist on an international level. Interpol, the International Criminal Police Organization, acts as an information clearinghouse and is able to share information with its member countries regarding terroristic threats. Treaties and alliances through cooperative agreements can also mandate the sharing of intelligence, although it limits the flow of information between specific countries.

Nation states, however, have an interest in protecting information and selectively sharing it with international agencies, and the United States is no different. To collaborate with other countries so that domestic terrorist threats unique to the United States do not spread abroad can be difficult, as the sharing of information must be done in a way that does not weaken American national security. Lacking specifics that can be shared through collaboration, law enforcement and intelligence agencies can share general knowledge on how such domestic terrorist groups behaved in the United States so that international organizations can plan for similar group behaviors if those ideologies spread to their countries. Although it is not clear if this occurred, when members of the Jewish Defense League left the United States and moved to Israel, ideally American agencies would have shared information with Israeli agencies on group behaviors and past violent activities so that the Israeli government could plan accordingly based on prior acts. In addition, countries that are beginning to see the creations of anti-abortion movements, might want to look at how the movement not only originated in the United States, but at what point and in what situations those who adhered to its ideology moved from simple protest to violent action.

CONCLUSION

Domestic terrorism in the United States does outnumber acts of international terrorism, but the extremist ideologies that originated in America have been slow to spread outside of its borders. With the advent of instant global communication, however, the opportunities for domestic terrorists to not only spread their messages of hate, but also collaborate with groups and individuals of similar ideologies, will increase exponentially. Law enforcement and intelligence agencies are not at a disadvantage as the same technologies are also at their disposal. Collaboration between countries, however, will be imperative to stop similar acts of violence from occurring abroad. This collaboration must be based on the sharing of information and lessons learned from decades of studying, countering, and responding to acts of domestic terrorism in the United States so that the international community will be prepared for terroristic threats that have been historically unique to America.

REFERENCES

Barkun, M. (1997). *Religion and the Racist Right: The Origins of the Christian Identity Movement.* Chapel Hill: The University of North Carolina Press.

Chermak, S. M., J. D. Freilich, & J. Simone. (2010). *Surveying American State Police Agencies About Lone Wolves, Far-Right Criminality, and Far-Right and Islamic Jihadist Criminal Collaboration. Studies in Conflict & Terrorism.* Forthcoming.

Firestone, D. (1994, February 27). West Bank Massacre; Seed Planted in Brooklyn Blooms as Violence. *The New York Times.* p. A1.

Freilich, J. D. & S. M. Chermak. (2009). United States Extremist Crime Database (ECDB), 1990–2008: Preliminary Results. *2009 DHS Summit Archives.* Retrieved from http://www.orau.gov/DHSSummi/2009/materials.htm

Hewitt, C. (2003). *Understanding Terrorism in America: From the Klan to Al Qaeda.* New York: Routledge.

LaFree, G., L. Dugan, H. V. Fogg, & J. Scott, (2006). Building a Global Terrorism Database. NCJ 214260, National Institute of Justice. Retrieved from www.ncjrs.gov/pdffiles1/nij/grants/214260.pdf

Smith, B. L. (1994). *Terrorism in America: Pipe Bombs and Pipe Dreams.* Albany: State University of New York.

Smith, B. L. & K. R. Damphousse, (2009). Patterns of Precursor Behaviors in the Life Span of a U.S. Environmental Terrorism Group. *Criminology and Public Policy,* 8(3): 475–96.

Staba, D. (2007, June 20). Life Term for Killer of Buffalo-Area Abortion Provider. *The New York Times.* p. B7.

ABOUT THE AUTHORS

William Parkin is a doctoral student in criminal justice at the Graduate Center CUNY and a researcher at John Jay College of Criminal Justice. His research interests include media, terrorism, and victims of extremist crime in the United States.

Joshua D. Freilich is the deputy director of the criminal justice Ph.D. program and a professor in the Criminal Justice Department at John Jay College, the City University of New York. He is a lead investigator for the National Consortium for the Study of Terrorism and Responses to Terrorism (START), a Center for Excellence of the U.S. Department of Homeland Security (DHS), as well as a member of the Terrorism Research and Analysis Project (TRAP).

Steven Chermak is a professor of criminal justice at Michigan State University. His research focuses on domestic terrorism, intelligence practices, and media coverage of crime and justice. He is also a lead investigator for the National Consortium for the Study of Terrorism and Responses to Terrorism (START), a Center of Excellence of the U.S. Department of Homeland Security.

38 Terrorism

Graeme R. Newman and Ronald V. Clarke

Criminology and criminal justice programs were late in recognizing the relevance of terrorism to international criminology because it was thought that terrorism was completely different from crime, the province of political scientists. But it was also because the traditional approaches of criminology have remained preoccupied with root causes of crime and have been only secondarily interested in how to prevent it. The 9/11 attack demanded immediate action to make sure that nothing like it ever happened again. Applying the perspective of situational crime prevention, this chapter will demonstrate that it is possible to explain terrorism and develop a systematic way to prevent it without necessarily studying its "root causes."

DEFINING TERRORISM

There have been many attempts to define terrorism and here are two notable examples:

1. Terrorism is the use or threatened use of force designed to bring about political change (Brian Jenkins, Rand Corporation).
2. Terrorism is the unlawful use of force or violence against persons or property to intimidate or coerce a government, the civilian population, or any segment thereof, in furtherance of political or social objectives (FBI).

The first definition makes no mention of illegality, thus leaving open the possibility that the acts of the terrorists may be legitimate. The FBI definition states clearly that terrorism is unlawful, but of course, this leaves open the problem of "freedom fighters" acting against an unlawful government. Both of the definitions make force and violence central to a description of terrorism. While the majority of terrorist attacks are obviously violent (some are not, such as cyberterrorism), focusing on the violence itself ignores the conditions and behaviors that make for the successful completion of terrorist attacks. These are the opportunities of which terrorists take advantage. Research in situational crime prevention has shown that offenders develop many techniques and procedures as they carry out different kinds of crimes from car theft to credit card fraud. It is necessary to identify these crime specific conditions and environmental situations in which they occur in order to identify points of intervention. Generally, these conditions reveal the opportunities that make criminal behavior possible.

In applying this approach to terrorism, the precise definition of terrorism becomes of secondary importance and we may simply say that terrorism is crime with a political motive. This is also an unsatisfactory definition, not because it calls terrorism crime, but because both those words, "terrorism" and "crime" are very abstract terms hiding vastly different kinds of acts. For example, successfully carrying out a suicide bombing in a restaurant requires a completely different sequence of acts (in terms of preparation, planning, and operations) than hijacking an airliner and holding the passengers and crew for ransom. And each act requires that a completely different set of actions be taken to prevent them. This is the central lesson also of decades of research on the situational prevention of crime.

In sum, from a situational crime prevention point of view, there is no essential difference between crime and terrorism. As with crime, in order to design ways to prevent terrorism we need to identify the opportunities in society and the physical environment that terrorists exploit in order to carry out the specific kinds of attacks they are planning, whether these are airliner hijackings, political assassinations, suicide bombings, bombings of buildings, mass shooting of civilians, roadside bombs, etc. This approach addresses squarely the immediate and urgent need of taking steps to prevent terrorist attacks like the 9/11 attack from happening again. It focuses on reducing opportunities by manipulating or altering the conditions that surround the immediate environment in which the terrorist operates. The path or journey taken by the offender to the completion of his or her terrorist act is blocked or even removed. In other words, we ask not *why* do they do it, but *how* do they do it.

THE "ROOT CAUSES" OF TERRORISM

Critics of situational prevention insist that one cannot prevent terrorism unless one eradicates its root causes. They argue terrorists are different from criminals because terrorists are motivated by a "higher cause." Terrorists are motivated by their ideology, while criminals are motivated by greed or some other base human trait. That Islamic extremists, far-right militias, or Marxist guerillas inflict violence in the service of their "higher" cause, is better seen as (a) justifications or excuses (rather than explanations) for what they do and (b) expressions of their belief that violence is the most effective means of achieving their distant goal, which is usually toppling a government, or forcing an opponent to stop what it is doing (e.g., get the U.S. to leave Iraq, or get researchers to stop using animals for experimentation).

It is also apparent that ideology does not predict which targets will be attacked. Routine suicide bombing attacks in the Palestine territories, for example, do not primarily target synagogues or places of worship, but rather restaurants and places where many people gather. When places of worship are attacked, this is usually for tactical or strategic reasons (e.g., to inflame interethnic violence in Iraq) rather than ideological ones.

One characteristic of terrorism that both sets terrorism apart from other kinds of crime and increases the risk of terrorism is that most terrorists depend on publicity to magnify the impact of their attacks. This means that they must make their attacks a media affair but at the same time keep their organizations and actions secret. Even though the publicity of terrorist acts is usually accompanied by ideological justifications, it is essentially tactical since it makes up for terrorists' lack of firepower compared to the usual overwhelming weaponry possessed by any given government that may be its enemy (hence the concept of "asymmetrical warfare").

In sum, the operational demands of terrorists to maximize the successful completion of their attacks will almost always trump whatever ideologies they say are the reasons for their attacks.

INTERNATIONAL AND DOMESTIC TERRORISM

Terrorism is generally divided into two kinds: domestic and international. However globalization continues to blur the boundaries between domestic and international because:

- globalization makes it much easier for terrorist groups, domestic or foreign, to purchase weapons;
- international drug dealing and human trafficking, which always have a domestic source and destination, is a ready source of finance to terrorists;
- terrorist groups that are well established within particular countries depend on foreign sources for financial and other kinds of support.

The IRA in Northern Ireland is a typical example. Before 9/11 it received financial support from sympathizers in the United States, and was able to purchase Semtex explosives from Mohamar Khadafi of Libya. These kinds of supply chains have made it possible for groups such as the IRA and the various terrorist groups in Palestine (e.g., Hamas) to conduct frequent attacks within countries on a routine basis.

In the United States, domestic terrorism has been mostly limited to acts by single issue terrorists such as the right-to-life or environmentalist extremists, or isolated hate crimes by individuals or militia groups. Vastly more attacks carried out against the United States occur not on U.S. soil, but on U.S. embassies and other establishments in foreign countries. The explanation for this is simple: Terrorists find it operationally much easier to carry out attacks in locations close to home (the same goes for burglars). Iraq is much closer to home for Al Qaeda than the North American continent. Thus, the presence of many U.S. personnel and structures in the Middle East makes them the most attractive and easiest targets compared to the extensive organizational demands needed to carry out similar attacks in the continental United States. This is why there have been no suicide bombings in New York City's restaurants.

HOW MUCH TERRORISM IS THERE?

Counting terrorist acts is very difficult, not least because of definitional problems but also because many of these acts take place in countries that are not accustomed to maintaining good statistical records. Probably the best way to count terrorist acts is through newspaper and media reports. This method is used by the Global Terrorism Database (GTD), which shows that worldwide, terrorist incidents rose from less than two hundred in 1970, to a peak of some five thousand in the early 1990s, falling off to almost three thousand in 2007. While the global number of terrorist incidents has decreased in recent years, their lethality has increased greatly, with dramatic increases in injuries and a noticeable increase in deaths. This is no doubt because of the ready availability throughout the world of greatly enhanced conventional weapons of many kinds, including easy-to-use plastic explosives such as Semtex.

PREVENTING TERRORISM

Given their commitment to violence, terrorists will do what is, generally speaking, the easiest. This means that terrorists will survey the immediate environment in which they operate, taking advantage of opportunities that will make their job easier. These opportunities may be classified into four kinds:

1. *Targets.* Targets differ widely in their attractiveness: how easy they are to reach, how much impact their destruction will bring, whether they are occupied by many people, whether government or businesses, whether their destruction would be symbolic of victory.

2. *Weapons.* The range of weapons available and how appropriate they are for reaching the target are important considerations. Suicide bombers are used, not because of some fanatical Islamic ideology, but because they offer clear advantages such as removing the necessity of planning an escape route, increasing the chances of reaching the specific target, or even a substitute target if thwarted. Semtex explosive is used because it is small and easy to conceal under clothing. Terrorists, in fact, prefer weapons they know. Thus, they prefer conventional weapons, not weapons of mass destruction.

3. *Tools available for conducting the mission.* These are tangible products that are used in the course of an attack. Among these important and essential (depending on the mission) products for conducting terrorism are: vehicles, rented or stolen; cell phones, cash and credit cards (it is difficult to rent a car in most places without a credit card, and buying a plane ticket with cash is viewed as suspicious); false documents such as passports, driving licenses; and information about targets such as maps, timetables, and schedules). All these tools that terrorists use are also tools that ordinary offenders use: stolen cars, stolen cell phones, false or stolen identities.

4. *Facilitating conditions.* These are the social and physical arrangements of modern society that make specific acts of terrorism possible. Conditions that facilitate terrorist acts include:
   - a local community that is sympathetic to the terrorists, or that can be used as cover by foreign terrorists;
   - an accessible arms market;
   - banking and market conditions that permit money laundering for obtaining financial support for terrorist operations;
   - lax or nonexistent security procedures by government agencies or businesses.

Situational crime prevention research developed four principles of crime prevention that are aimed at making the successful completion of crime difficult for offenders. These are: increase the effort, increase the risks, reduce the rewards, and reduce provocations and excuses for the offender. If we put

Table 38.1. Four principles of situational prevention and the four pillars of opportunity for terrorism

	Targets	Weapons	Tools	Facilitating conditions
Increase the effort	Prioritize targets for protection; close streets, build walls and barriers	Restrict sale of weapons; hold contractors liable for stolen explosives	Eliminate high value bank notes; make banks liable for money laundering	High tech passports, visas, driving licenses; National ID cards
Increase the risks	Strengthen surveillance through CCTV, citizen vigilance, hot lines	RFIDs to track weapons; increase Internet surveillance of terrorist groups	Make cars more difficult to steal, parts marking on all tools	Tighten identity authentication procedures; tighten border controls
Reduce the rewards	Bomb proof buildings, Kevlar vests; swift cleanup of attack site	Locks and immobilizers to make weapons difficult to use	Make cell phones and other tools unusable without ID to unlock.	Publicity to portray hypocrisy and cruelty of terrorist acts
Reduce provocations and excuses	Unobtrusive public buildings at home and abroad	Avoid use of controversial weapons such as phosphorous bombs	Maintain positive relations with local communities	Avoid maltreatment of prisoners; clear rules for interrogation

these together with the four pillars of opportunity, a quick guide to planning prevention and protection against terrorist attacks may be constructed as in Table 38.1.

COLLECTING INTELLIGENCE

The popular view of almost all law enforcement approaches to terrorism is that intelligence is needed in order to identify, arrest, or otherwise "take out" the terrorists. While important, the take-them-out approach cannot provide all the protection that society needs because there are many other individuals ready to take the places of the terrorists arrested or killed. Instead, the collection of intelligence should be informed by the four main sources of terrorist opportunity and the four techniques of situational crime prevention as depicted in the table. Local police are in the best position to collect such intelligence. They must know their communities better than the terrorists who depend on local knowledge to search out targets, gain access, and resources. It also follows that the interrogation of suspects should be focused on finding out how they carry out their acts rather than trying to extract names of other terrorists through coercive interrogation. The latter rests on an often mistaken preconception that all terrorist acts are the result of some highly organized terrorist group with tentacles stretching around the world. Generally, this is not supported, even in the case of Al Qaeda.

SUMMARY AND CONCLUSION

Approaching terrorism from the point of view of situational crime prevention reveals many practical and policy choices that will help to prevent future terrorist attacks and to protect targets within communities. Identifying the specific opportunities within the four pillars of terrorist opportunity available for terrorists is the first step, followed by identifying and protecting potential targets and collecting intelligence at the local level. Finally, responses to terrorism must be forward-looking, applying interventions that aim at making life harder for terrorists: increasing the efforts they must make, increasing their risks, reducing their rewards, and reducing provocations and excuses for their attacks.

REFERENCES

Clarke, R. V. & G. R. Newman (2005). *Outsmarting the Terrorists*. CT: Praeger Security International.

Freilich, J. & G. R. Newman (Eds.) (2009). *Reducing Terrorism through Situational Crime Prevention*. Crime Prevention Studies. No.25. NY: Criminal Justice Press.

National Consortium for the Study of Terrorism and the Responses to Terrorism. Global Terrorism Database (GTD). http://www.start.umd.edu/start

Newman, G. R. & R. V. Clarke (2008). *Policing Terrorism; an Executive's Guide*. Washington. D.C. Office of Community Oriented Police Services.

ABOUT THE AUTHORS

Graeme R. Newman is distinguished teaching professor at the School of Criminal Justice, University at Albany and Ronald V. Clarke is university professor at the School of Criminal Justice, Rutgers University. They have a long history of working together. Their most recent joint books are *Policing Terrorism: An Executive's Guide* (US Department of Justice, 2008), *Outsmarting the Terrorists* (Praeger 2005), *Designing out Crime from Products and Systems* (Criminal Justice Press, 2005), and *Superhighway Robbery* (Willan, 2003).

PART V

INTERNATIONAL CRIME

After decades of deliberation, agreement was reached among the countries signing the Rome Statute in 1998 on the definition of international crimes that would fall under the jurisdiction of the International Criminal Court. These were considered to be the gravest crimes that threaten the peace, security, and well-being of the world. This definition covers specific crimes yet to be agreed upon, but it includes the following four core crimes: (1) the crime of genocide; (2) crimes against humanity; (3) war crimes; and (4) the crime of aggression. At the date of writing, more than half of the countries of the United Nations have now signed the Rome Statute and have begun to incorporate the crimes that it identifies into domestic legislation. This section provides brief descriptions of the four core crimes as a background to understanding the challenges in enforcing the Rome Statute.

The concepts of genocide, war crimes, and crimes against humanity have undergone considerable transformation since the end of World War II. Whether one examines the main elements of each crime, or the context in which they occur (wartime or peacetime, whether they are international or not), there is a discernible trend toward strengthening the protection of individuals and groups at the expense of state-centric interpretations of legal obligations (see Chapter 39 by George Andreopolous).

In respect of the four core crimes, however, there are many difficult questions to be resolved. For genocide, two of the important questions are

"At what point do individual killings amount to genocide?" and "Does the crime of genocide always require it to be demonstrated that there was the intention to eradicate a particular ethnic or racial group?" Chapter 40 by Itai Sneh grapples with these and other questions while reviewing the history of genocide and considers recent advocacy and policy guidelines that are influencing emerging international law concerning intervention in acts of genocide.

According to the Rome Statute, crimes against humanity involve degradation of human dignity and the infliction of violence in the course of a widespread or systematic attack intentionally directed against a civilian population. In 1976, the UN General Assembly recognized the South African's government policy of apartheid as a crime against humanity. In Chapter 41, Helen Capstein describes the systematic persecution of black South Africans under apartheid and shows that this fits the definition of a crime against humanity.

War crimes are violations of a special body of criminal law triggered by an armed conflict. They were comprehensively addressed in the Geneva Conventions of 1949, which are still considered the cornerstone of contemporary international humanitarian law. They define as war crimes a wide variety of inhumane acts including the following examples: A Congolese warlord fighting for control of diamond mines in Ituri forces local children into his army as cannon fodder; Al Qaeda operatives crash airplanes into buildings in New York City with the intention of killing innocent civilians; and American guards sexually humiliate detainees in Iraq. Weisbord and Reyes in Chapter 42 discuss why these acts fall under the Geneva Conventions and, at least on their face, qualify as war crimes.

What constitutes the crime of aggression (the "supreme international crime") is still under discussion. In Chapter 43, Stefan Barriga seeks to clarify the definition by considering questions such as: Which instances of the use of force would qualify, by their character, gravity, and scale, as manifest violations of the UN Charter? Does criminal responsibility for the crime of aggression rest with leaders only? Why should it be possible to hold an individual soldier accountable for war crimes, but not the state for which he or she is fighting?

39 Genocide, War Crimes, and Crimes against Humanity

George Andreopoulos

INTRODUCTION

The atrocities that have been associated with genocide, war crimes, and crimes against humanity have been witnessed throughout human history. Whether in times of war, or in times of peace, human wrongs have been committed against fellow human beings, often in a systematic or widespread manner, irrespective of existing moral and legal restraints. While each of these concepts has followed its own trajectory, there are considerable overlaps among them; overlaps which progressive codification and evolving jurisprudence have both confirmed and reaffirmed in an effort to prevent and punish the commission of such acts.

WAR CRIMES

"War crimes" refers to serious violations of treaty and customary rules applicable in situations of international and noninternational armed conflict. The body of rules and customs that address issues pertaining to armed conflict situations is known as the laws of war, or international humanitarian law (IHL). The term IHL, although increasingly used by many analysts and commentators, is resisted by others because it is viewed as reflecting the influence of human rights law on the laws of war and as privileging one section of the laws of war, known as "Geneva law," over the other, known as "Hague law." The latter section of IHL ("Hague law") includes the set of rules and regulations found in The Hague Conventions that cover the various categories of lawful combatants and issues relating to the means and methods of warfare, as well as to the treatment of those who do not take part in hostilities (civilians) or are *hors de combat* (wounded and sick, prisoners of war). The former section ("Geneva law") refers to the set of rules found in the 1949 Geneva Conventions and the 1977 Additional Protocols (I and II), and cover issues that relate to the treatment of those who do not, or no longer, take part in hostilities (Cassesse 2003). Having said that, it should be noted that the distinction between Hague and Geneva law is less relevant today because more recent instruments (like the 1977 Additional Protocol I) contain provisions relating both to the means and methods of warfare, as well as to protected persons.

The changing nature of many modern-day conflicts and the evolving jurisprudence of international tribunals have contributed to some interesting developments in IHL. Due to space limitations, two of these will be highlighted here: (1) the erosion of the distinction between international and noninternational armed conflicts, and (2) the reinterpretation and further development of certain basic IHL concepts in light of the experiences drawn from said conflicts. Concerning the former, traditionally the rules and regulations covering international armed conflicts (i.e., conflicts between two or more states, or between one or more states and a national liberation movement) were more fully developed, and perpetrators of abusive conduct could, and sometimes would, incur criminal responsibility. By contrast, the rules and regulations covering noninternational armed conflicts were much less developed and violations committed in the course of such conflicts were not criminalized. Clearly, from a human rights or humanitarian perspective this did not make sense; why would the same type of offenses against human beings receive different responses in accordance with the type of conflict (international, noninternational) in which they occurred? Part of the reason for this reconsideration is the sheer brutality exhibited in many modern-day conflicts, in which the primary target of combatants is the civilian population as opposed to their armed opponents (Kaldor, 1999). In this context, the international criminalization of internal atrocities, as exemplified in the 1995 appeals chamber decision of the International Criminal Tribunal for the former Yugoslavia (ICTY) in the *Tadic* case, does constitute a promising development (Meron, 1998). More recently, the decade-long ICRC study on customary international humanitarian law concluded, "that many rules of customary international law apply in both international and non-international armed conflicts" (Henckaerts & Doswald-Beck, 2005). Concerning the latter, the evolving jurisprudence of the ad hoc tribunals, and in particular of the ICTY on key concepts like that of protected persons, has demonstrated the ability of international courts to maintain conceptual relevance in light of the changing context of warfare. In particular, in the Celebici case, the appeals chamber of the ICTY relied on a broad and purposive interpretation of the Geneva Conventions to rule that, given the nature of the conflict, nationality should not be the defining criterion for the protected status of persons; thus Bosnian Serbs, detained in the camp by Bosnian Muslims, should be regarded as "having been in the hands of a party to the conflict [...] of which they were not nationals," and, therefore, as protected persons.

Crimes against Humanity

Crimes against humanity refer to acts that violate fundamental tenets of human dignity (e.g., murder, extermination, enslavement, deportation); are committed as part of a widespread or systematic attack against (primarily, but not exclusively) any civilian population, which is instigated, condoned, or tolerated by a state or nonstate authority; and can be committed during war or peace (Cassesse, 2003). Crimes against humanity are usually divided into two categories: "murder type" offenses that can be perpetrated against any civilian population, and more targeted "persecution type" offenses which can be perpetrated against any collectivity on "political, racial, national, ethnic, cultural, religious, gender [...] or other grounds that are universally recognized as impermissible under international law" as stipulated in the statute of the International Criminal Court (ICC). The crime of genocide is an offspring of "persecution type" offenses.

Since its appearance in the charter of the Nuremberg Tribunal, the concept has undergone a considerable evolution. In the charter, the concept was anchored to the other two crimes in the indictment, namely crimes against the peace and war crimes. This meant that only those crimes against humanity that resulted from interstate aggression would be punishable, what came to be known as the "war nexus requirement" (Van Schaack, 1999). Genocide, as noted below, was the first crime against humanity to be de-linked from the war nexus requirement. Recent jurisprudential developments indicate that such de-linking now applies to all crimes against humanity. As the ICTY appeals chamber noted in the Tadic case, "it is by now a settled rule of customary international law that crimes against humanity do not require a connection to international armed conflict [...] customary international law may not require a connection between crimes against humanity and any conflict at all." Moreover, the term "any" in reference to civilian population means that crimes against humanity could be committed against any civilians irrespective of their defining characteristics. As the ICTY trial chamber noted in the *Vasiljevic* and *Kunarac* cases, a crime against humanity could "in principle be committed against a state's own population if that state participates in the attack" (Mettraux, 2006). Last, but not least, in discussing the policy element in the commission of crimes against humanity, the ICTY ruled in the *Tadic* case that state policy does not constitute any more a requirement for their commission: "In this regard the law in relation to crimes against humanity has developed to take into account forces which, although not those of the legitimate government, have de facto control over, or are able to move freely within, defined territory." Thus, crimes against humanity could be committed by nonstate entities.

GENOCIDE

Genocide is the most heinous crime against humanity. According to the 1948 Convention on the Prevention and Punishment of the Crime of Genocide, genocide refers to "any of the following acts committed with intent to destroy, in whole or in part, a national, ethnical, racial or religious group, as such: (a) Killing members of the group; (b) Causing serious bodily or mental harm to members of the group; (c) Deliberately inflicting on the group conditions of life calculated to bring about its physical destruction in whole or in part; (d) Imposing measures intended to prevent births within the group; (e) Forcibly transferring children of the group to another group." In addition to the commission of genocide, the convention also made conspiracy, incitement, attempt, and complicity in genocide punishable under international law.

What primarily distinguishes genocide from other crimes against humanity is intentionality (Andreopoulos, 1994). Intentionality indicates, in addition to the criminal intent that accompanies the underlying offense (e.g., killing), the existence of an aggravated criminal intention (*dolus specialis*) to commit this offense in order to destroy the targeted group as such (Cassesse, 2003). This definition was included, without changes, in the statute of the ICC.

The Genocide Convention has certain noticeable strengths and weaknesses. Among its strengths (this list is by no means exhaustive) are: first, the delinking of this crime against humanity from the war nexus requirement. In its very first article, the Convention characterizes genocide as a crime under international law, "whether committed in time of peace or in time of war." Second, the provision for the international criminal responsibility of all individuals for the commission of this crime, irrespective of their status (i.e. whether rulers, public officials, or private individuals); and, third, the prospect for the use of force under international auspices for the prevention and suppression of acts of genocide. Concerning the last issue, it is worth noting that, with article VIII of the Convention, member states "may call upon the competent organs of the United Nations to take such action under the Charter [...] as they consider appropriate" to deal with situations involving genocide. Since one of these "competent organs" is the Security Council, the international community had at its disposal, ever since the entering into force of the Convention, the option of authorizing coercive measures, including, if necessary, the use of force for humanitarian purposes (prevention and suppression of genocide) (Andreopoulos, 2002). Among its weaknesses (again the list is not exhaustive) are: (1) the exclusion of certain groups from the list of those groups whose persecution would constitute the crime of genocide (in particular, social and political groups); and (2) its enforcement provisions. Concerning the latter, according to article VI of the Convention, those responsible for the commission of genocide "shall be tried by a competent tribunal of the State in the territory of which the act was committed," or by an international penal tribunal. This meant that, for a long period of time, there was no credible forum for judicial enforcement. Until the creation of the ICC, the only possible legal venue would have been the courts of the country in which the crime was committed; thus, unless a regime responsible for the commission of genocide were to be overthrown and the successor regime were to embark on legal proceedings against the perpetrators of the predecessor regime (a remote possibility indeed) nothing could be done to punish those responsible for the commission of such acts.

The Genocide Convention was first used in international proceedings in 1993, when the Republic of Bosnia and Herzegovina (RBH) instituted proceedings against the then Federal Republic of Yugoslavia (FRY) before the International Court of Justice (ICJ). The Republic of Bosnia and Herzegovina argued that former members of the Yugoslav Peoples' Army together with Serb military and paramilitary forces had engaged, with the assistance of FRY, in acts that amounted to breaches of the Genocide Convention. This petition was followed by RBH requests for provisional measures that would enable RBH to exercise its inherent right of individual or collective self-defense. After almost fourteen years of proceedings, the ICJ eventually rendered its judgment in February 2007. In a decision that stirred great controversy, the Court found that Serbia had not committed genocide, had not conspired to commit genocide, and had not been complicit in genocide, in violation of its obligations under the Convention; however, it also ruled that Serbia had violated the obligation to prevent genocide in respect of the genocide that had occurred in Srebrenica, and had violated its obligations under the Convention by having failed to fully cooperate with the International Criminal Tribunal for the Former Yugoslavia (ICTY).

With the establishment of the two ad hoc tribunals for the Former Yugoslavia (ICTY) and Rwanda (ICTR), the Genocide Convention was finally invoked before international criminal proceedings. The evolving jurisprudence of these two tribunals has been instrumental in the clarification of key elements of the crime of genocide. Concerning "the intent to destroy," for example, the ICTY ruled in the *Krstic* case that the targeting of Bosnian men of military age in Srebrenica constituted such intent, since "this selective destruction of the group would have a lasting impact upon the entire group." Moreover, the issue of "direct and public incitement to commit genocide" has received considerable attention in both tribunals due to the role of the media. The media, in both the Yugoslav and Rwandan conflicts, engaged in a variety of actions (e.g., in the spreading of messages of ethnic hatred, in the issuing of calls to violence) that contributed to the legitimization of mass killings (Mettraux, 2006). In particular, the trial Chamber (ICTR) in the *Nahimana* case noted the power of the media to both create and destroy important human values; this power, the Court stated "comes with great responsibility. Those who control such media are accountable for its consequences" (Mettraux, 2006). Last, but not least, concerning the act of "complicity in genocide," both courts have ruled that an accomplice, to be considered as such, must provide the type of support which has a "substantial effect on the perpetration of the crime" (*Furundzija* case; Mettraux, 2006).

CONCLUSION

There is no doubt that the concepts of genocide, war crimes, and crimes against humanity have undergone considerable transformation since the end of World War II. Whether one examines our understanding of the main elements of each crime, or of the context in which they occur (whether in times of international or noninternation war or peace), there is a noticeable trend toward strengthening the protection of individuals and groups at the expense of state-centric interpretations of legal obligations. However, these normative developments also pose the challenge of relevance: namely, the extent to which state practice as manifested during the conduct of hostilities, as opposed to declarations before international fora or during treaty deliberations and the signing of agreements, corresponds to the relevant treaty provisions and the interpretation of these provisions by judicial organs. What is urgently needed at this stage is not further standard-setting (although this remains an important task), but better implementation of already existing standards.

REFERENCES

Andreopoulos, G. J. (Ed.) (1994). *Genocide: Conceptual and Historical Dimensions.* Philadelphia: University of Pennsylvania Press.
Andreopoulos, G. J. (2002). On the Prevention of Genocide. Humanitarian Intervention and the Role of the United Nations. In G. J. Andreopoulos (Ed.), *Concepts and Strategies in International Human Rights.* New York: Peter Lang.
Cassesse, A. (2003). *International Criminal Law.* New York: Oxford.
Henckaerts, J-M. & L. Doswald-Beck. (2005). *Customary International Humanitarian Law.* Volume I: Rules. Cambridge: Cambridge University Press.
International Court of Justice. (2007). Application *of the Convention on the Prevention and Punishment of the Crime of Genocide (Bosnia and Herzegovina Versus Serbia and Montenegro)* Judgment.
Kaldor, M. (1999). *New & Old Wars. Organized Violence in a Global Era.* Stanford: Stanford University Press.
Meron, T. (1998). *War Crimes Law Comes of Age.* New York: Oxford University Press.
Mettraux, G. (2006). *International Crimes and the Ad Hoc Tribunals.* New York: Oxford University Press.
Prosecutor v. Tadic, IT-94-1, Appeals Chamber (1995). *Decision on the Defense Motion for Interlocutory Appeal on Jurisdiction.*
Prosecutor v. Anto Furundzija, IT-95–17/1-T (1998). Judgement. Prosecutor v. Krstic, IT-98–33-T (2001). Judgment.
Prosecutor v. Dragoljub Kunarac, Radomir Kovac and Zoran Vukovic, IT-96–23-T & IT-96–23/1-T (2001). Judgment.
Prosecutor v. Zejnil Delalic, Zdravko Mucic (aka. "Pavo"), Hazim Delic and Esad Landzo (aka. "Zenga"). Celebici Case. IT-96–21-A (2001).
Prosecutor v. Mitar Vasiljevic, IT-98–32-T (2002). Judgment.
The Prosecutor v. Ferdinand Nahimana, Jean-Bosco Barayagwiza, **and** Hassan Ngeze, ICTR-99–52-T (2003). Judgement and Sentence.
Van Schaack, B. (1999). The Definition of Crimes Against Humanity: Resolving the Incoherence. *Columbia Journal of Transnational Law,* 37(3), 787–850.

ABOUT THE AUTHOR

George Andreopoulos is a professor of political science at John Jay College of Criminal Justice and the Graduate Center, City University of New York. He has written extensively on international organizations, international human rights, and humanitarian law issues. He is currently completing a book on humanitarian intervention.

40 History of Genocide

Itai Sneh

INTRODUCTION

"Genocide," is an attempt to destroy a group of people. Genocide mixes the Greek *genos* (race or kind) and the Latin *cide* (kill). It was coined by Raphael Lemkin (1900–59), a Polish Jew, in his 1944 book *Axis Rule in Occupied Europe* to describe Nazi Germany's extermination policy, later called the Holocaust.

Historical studies on the background, scope, prevention, and punishment of genocide explain how racism, politics, and hatred trigger genocide by addressing ideological, psychological, social, gender, class, security, territorial, economic, diplomatic, and cultural problems. Tracing the history of genocide, recent advocacy and policy guidelines focus on how to prevent genocide by identifying and addressing such issues, then treating them. This chapter covers the definition and history of genocide, developments in researching the field, and its popular culture presentations.

GENOCIDE: HISTORICAL BACKGROUND

Earlier Genocides

Acts of genocide reoccurred, carried out especially by empires craving territories and obedience. Examples include the Assyrians who destroyed and exiled the Arameans and the Israelites between the ninth to seventh centuries BCE. The Babylonians perpetrated genocide in the seventh and sixth centuries BCE against the Phoenicians and the Judeans.

The Greeks and the Romans, from the fourth century BCE until the fifth century CE, created, expanded, and preserved their empires – among other policy, military, and cultural tools – by committing acts of genocide against ethnic and religious groups. For example, the Dacians lost their identity and became known as Romanians.

In medieval times, Muslims committed acts of genocide against non-believers. European Christians reacted in kind with the Crusades, the Inquisitions, and the "Reconquista" of Spain. The Mongols led by Genghis Khan perpetrated acts of genocide against multiple populations in Eurasia.

Colonial European empires such as the Spanish, the French, the British, the Portuguese, and the Belgians committed acts of genocide since the sixteenth century against indigenous populations in Africa, in the Americas, in the Asia-Pacific, and even in Ireland. Victims included the Carib, the Incas, the Seminoles, the Sioux, the Mohawks, the Cherokee, the Congolese, the San (Bushmen), the Maoris, the Tasmanians, and the Aboriginals.

TWENTIETH-CENTURY GENOCIDES

Approximate death numbers:

- Germans of Herreros and the Namaqua in Southwest Africa, 1904–05: 70,000.
- Turk Ottomans of Armenians, 1914–18: 1.2 million.
- Stalin of farmers and Ukrainians, 1932–35: seven million.
- Japanese of Chinese, especially the Rape of Nanking, 1931–38: 300,000.
- German's Holocaust of the Jews, 1938–45: six million.
- Khmer Rouge Communists in Cambodia killing teachers, 1975–78: two million.
- Mostly Serbs of Croats, and of Muslims in Bosnia-Herzegovina: 1991–95: 200,000.
- Rwanda, 1994, mostly by Hutus of Tootsies: 800,000.

In 1904–05, the Germans perpetrated genocide against the Herreros and the Namaqua in Southwest Africa. That conflict followed the 1899–1902 Boer War between the British and Dutch settlers in neighboring South Africa. Both sides, but especially the British, committed acts of genocide.

The Ottoman Turks suspected Armenians of supporting Russia in previous conflicts. During World War I, the Ottoman perpetrated genocide against the Armenians. Whatsoever, genocide is in no way whatsoever justified by these suspicions (that had valid sources).

While the promise of "nevermore" was still reverberating after the Holocaust of World War II, genocides occurred in Cambodia, the Balkans, and throughout Africa.

CONTEMPORARY ISSUES

In the twenty-first century, the focus is on African regions such as Darfur and the Great Lakes, where inhabitants suffer from territorial, religious, and ethnic conflicts heightened by divisive colonial heritage. The emerging international law's duty to prevent genocide and stop actions is an advocacy goal.

The rise in exploring social, gender, race, and class issues leads sophisticated researchers to expand their interests from organizational structures, political leaders, and military elites, to common people, the methods used to demonize opponents, and sexual assaults. This new perspective highlights the motives, roles, and reactions of victims, foot soldiers, and ordinary people that murdered, helped, warned against, resisted, or escaped acts of genocide, and responses.

THE 1948 GENOCIDE CONVENTION

After the Holocaust, the United Nations held the 1948 Convention on the Prevention and Punishment of the Crime of Genocide. The definition the UN proposed included the destruction of national, ethnical, racial, and religious groups, but not politics or social classes. The definitions strength is in the pioneering recognition of genocide as a crime in international law, but its scope betrays inadequacy. As a superpower, the Soviets used their leverage to exclude atrocities like purges. Thus, Stalin's extermination of independent farmers (*Kulaks*), Hitler's murder of homosexuals, or slavery worldwide, were ineligible.

Perpetrators excuse genocide by asserting their group rights to sovereignty, ideology, or security. Official and dehumanizing terms used to justify genocide include "vigilante justice," "counter-insurgency," "transfer," "ethnic cleansing," "purification," and "decolonization." Activists, diplomats, scholars, and judges ask how many must die violently for "humanitarian tragedy," "mass murders," "massacres," and "atrocities," to become legally-charged "war crimes," and "crimes against humanity," then "genocide"?

The UN Security Council examines and confronts acts of genocide. The authoritarian states of China and Russia; former colonial empires with residual interests, namely the French and the British; and America, with a dubious past toward natives and slaves, may wield veto power if they or their allies are culprits. This veto power indeed is detrimental to intervention not only by the UN, but also by regional powers or continental associations nongovernmental organizations (NGOs), especially Genocide Watch,

Human Rights Watch, Amnesty International, and Human Rights First, as well as being detrimental to research efforts and advocates for preventing and stopping genocide.

RESEARCH AGENDA

The academic understanding of genocide is growing worldwide. Books, articles, exhibitions, museums, workshops, conferences, lectures, courses, programs, majors, and centers are rising in quantity and in quality.

Scholars confront ethical choices by translating the absolutes of good and bad with addressing moral relativity of politics or prescribing rehabilitation and reconstruction. Conceptual questions include: When genocide occurs, does crime always indicate intention? When do individual killings amount to genocide?

The history of genocide incorporates existing geographic designations (such as Europe), national or ethnic studies (such as Jewish), functional disciplines (such as law, sociology, forensic and clinical psychology, medicine, criminology, criminal justice, ethnography, cultural anthropology, gender studies, education, media and communications, political science, international relations, strategic studies, comparative literature, theology, philosophy, economics, demographics, and, regrettably, genetics, biology, and anatomy), together with emerging fields (such as human rights, transnational justice, conflict resolution, and genealogy).

Holocaust scholars reconstruct acts of genocide by analyzing personal testaments and written submissions by eyewitnesses to understand the context, probing for details, names, and numbers. They aim for humanity's collective memory, justice for dead and living victims, shaming of the culprits, warning of the potential for future atrocities, and encouragement of preventive activism.

Their studies addressed Jewish and gentile homes; personal, family, social, and communal lives; relations with neighbors; means of survival; and paths of resistance. Inquiries expanded to other victims such as homosexuals, the Roma ("Gypsies"), blacks, and individuals with mental or physical problems. Revelations included sexual slavery in German concentration camps and of "Comfort Women" in Japanese army garrisons.

Research explored the plight of refugees, displaced persons, and their descendants. The role of Nazi allies such as Ukrainians and collaborators among the French and the Dutch were more closely scrutinized.

In 1994, building on the cinematic success of *Schindler's List*, its director, Steven Spielberg, established the California-based Survivors of the Shoah

Visual History Foundation. It educates about the Holocaust through collecting testimonials, providing open access through vast archives available on the Internet. This initiative complements its fellow California-based Simon Wiesenthal Institute, created in 1977.

Probing the behavior of German corporations has dispelled false but widely held depictions of their involvement, images inspired by self-presentation, by providing detailed assessments of their industrial and financial complicity in German acts of genocide, revealing the forced work of prisoners of war, and the looting of Jewish accounts. Simultaneously, the willing institutional support of churches, foreign governments, and international organizations is now more evident thanks to archival and oral research.

The collective memory and the political agenda of groups such as Native Americans, descendants of African slaves, and other forcibly removed indigenous peoples in Australia and Latin America, demand exposure and cries for justice.

Consistent coverage, with ample photos of death and destruction, by the international media of the wars and massacres in Yugoslavia, Rwanda, Central America, and East Timor, increased public awareness worldwide. Documentation focused on the mass killings. Research considers the role, or the silence, of the international community through the United Nations and its related agencies, or regional associations like the African Union and the European Union, and particular foreign countries such as the United States or France, in preventing or helping acts of genocide.

The study of European imperialism highlighted the brutality of the British and the Germans. In particular, the Belgian subjugation of Congo in the nineteenth century murdered many in Congo, and led to acts of genocide in neighboring Rwanda in the twentieth century.

The influences of modernity, colonialism, and environmental changes on human brutality are ambivalent. The combination of nationalist ideology; scientific justification of racism; available technology, communication, and transportation; and the scarcity of land and resources are thrust upon pre-existing conflicts, and make mass murders easier.

Scholarship had focused on states during international or civil wars in the twentieth century. Three major trends inform contemporary genocide studies. One trend stresses the stages of genocide, the responsibility to educate and advocate for a duty to prevent. It focuses on sensitizing the international community to escalating bias, racism, hatred, sedition, and harassment that deteriorates into sporadic attacks, organized violence, and then genocide. A dilemma for activists, diplomats, scholars, and judges is how to allow freedoms of speech and expression without jeopardizing vulnerable groups.

Secondly, another trend is the increased discussion of the aftermath of genocide, and how to reconstruct, rehabilitate, and heal societies.

Historians reevaluate the 1945–49 trials in Nuremberg and 1946–48 in Tokyo. The guilt of the political and military elites of Germany and Japan is tainted by criticism of these proceedings as "victor's revenge" or as "victims' justice."

Focus on leaders and death camps shielded Emperor Hirohito, the Japanese Unit 731 that conducted human experiments, and German middle- and lower-level army officers and bureaucrats. Such omissions legitimized traditional institutions, and aided experts in business, civil service, and scientific fields in reconstructing West Germany and Japan as pro-American, while inaccurately dismissing Nazism and militarism as moral aberrations.

Postconflict resolution studies commend comprehensive truth and reconciliation commissions that facilitate transitional justice in countries such South Africa and Argentina. Commissions move from exclusively trying prominent decision-makers, and focus on collective suffering, with the goal of documenting individual accounts and rehabilitating societies.

Thirdly, the dimensions and lessons of the Holocaust are debated while understanding its planning, execution, and consequences by weaving Jewish history, German culture, European politics, and international relations.

This trend asks: Is its legacy Jewish or universal? Do Holocaust deniers have any legitimacy, or are they thinly-disguised anti-Semites and anti-Zionists? Is Israel entitled to represent the victims as a part of its raison d'être? What is the liability of the Swiss who helped German finances and suppressed Jewish ownership, or the French whose Vichy regime had its own fascist agenda? Were the Ukrainian agents for the Germans or anti-Communists?

Early books on the Holocaust were personal testimonials. *The Diary of Anne Frank* who hid in Amsterdam, was issued posthumously by her father in 1947. It was followed by potent memoirs of Auschwitz survivors: in 1947. Primo Levi authored *If This Is a Man*, translated as *Survival in Auschwitz*, and in 1955 Elie Wiesel published *Night*. These volumes were analyzed by scholars, are often assigned in courses, and are widely performed.

Recently, personal stories and memoirs by and of family members highlight the horrors witnessed by their kin and the multiple consequences of genocides. Books include Grigoris Balakia's *Armenian Golgotha*, Daniel Mendelsohn's *The Lost: A Search for Six of Six Million*, and Louise Mushikiwabo and Jack Kramer's *Rwanda Means the Universe: A Native's Memoir of Blood and Bloodlines*.

Popular movies on genocide blend reality with fiction, pain with absurdity. In 1984, *The Killing Fields* addressed Cambodia. In 1993, *Schindler's List* comforted audiences with the saving of select Jews by a German industrialist during the Holocaust. In 1997, *Life is Beautiful* humorously celebrated survival over surrender by an Italian Jew. In 1999, *The Specialist*, on Adolph Eichman's trial in Jerusalem, caused controversy by enhancing Hannah Arendt's "banality of evil" or "cog in the machine" paradigm that arguably exculpate bureaucrats and soldiers alike. In 2004, *Hotel Rwanda* realistically portrayed survival amid the horror. In 2004, the Austrian-German *Downfall* presented the Nazis' final days in a humane way. In 2008, *Valkyrie* presented elite Nazis in an anti-Hitler, positive light, and *The Reader* arguably did so for common perpetrators. In 2009, *Inglorious Basterds* used fantasy to allow Jews revenge.

CONCLUSION

The danger of additional acts of genocide, and the need to draw lessons from history persists. Historians and NGOs analyze past and ongoing acts of genocide. The duty to prevent or intervene during acts of genocide is emerging in international law. Growing genocide scholarship blends prevention, punishing perpetrators, and acknowledging heroism. Studies have advanced beyond describing graphic details into exploring contexts and consequences.

RECOMMENDED READINGS

Bartov, O. (2003). *Germany's War and the Holocaust: Disputed Histories.* Ithaca and London: Cornell University Press.

Bloxham, D. (2001). *Genocide on Trial: War Crimes Trials and the Formation of Holocaust History and Memory.* Oxford: Oxford University Press.

Gellately, R. & B. Kiernan, (Eds.). (2003). *The Specter of Genocide: Mass Murder in Historical Perspective.* Cambridge: Cambridge University Press.

Heberer, P & M. Jürgen. (Eds.). (2008). *Atrocities on Trial: Historical Perspectives on the Politics of Prosecuting War Crimes.* Published in association with the United States Holocaust Memorial Museum. Lincoln, Nebraska: Lincoln University of Nebraska Press.

Hornstein, S. &, J. Florence. (Eds.). (2003). *Image and Remembrance: Representation and the Holocaust.* Bloomington: Indiana University Press.

Powers, S. (2002). *A Problem from Hell: America and the Age of Genocide,* NY: Basic Books, 2002.

Stanton, Gregory. "The Eight Stages of Genocide," www.tamilnation.org/indictment/eight_stages_of_genocide.htm

ABOUT THE AUTHOR

Tenured at the department of history in John Jay College of Criminal Justice of the City University of New York, Associate Professor Itai Sneh completed his doctorate at Columbia University. He holds a law degree and a master's in Eastern European Jewish History from McGill University in Montreal, Canada, and a B.A. in Jewish History (with minors in International Relations, Biblical Studies, and Yiddish Language and Culture) from Hebrew University in Jerusalem, Israel. His research interests, presentations, and publications include books, articles, and lectures on the history of human rights, American presidential, diplomatic, legal, and political history, international law, terrorism, genocide, and the Middle East. He serves as a peer reviewer in the *Interdisciplinary Journal of Human Rights Law*, the *Journal of American History*, and *Peace & Change*.

41 Apartheid

A CRIME AGAINST HUMANITY

Helen Kapstein

INTRODUCTION

South Africa's racist apartheid regime was officially inaugurated in 1948 with the victory of the Afrikaner[1] National Party and technically ended in 1994 with the country's first nonracial election resulting in a government led by the opposition African National Congress (ANC) and former political prisoner Nelson Mandela. However, these dates cannot be considered the actual start and end points of apartheid, since a long history of discrimination and segregation predates the official policy of apartheid, and a deeply embedded legacy of inequality persists today.

Apartheid, from the Afrikaans[2] for apartness, was a system of multiple laws, rules, and regulations designed to keep South Africans physically, economically, and culturally apart in order to consolidate power and wealth in the hands of the white minority. Using discredited social and scientific theories to claim differences of culture and nature, South African authorities classified people as white, black, "colored,"[3] or Indian, and endowed these groups with unequal rights and degrees of mobility and opportunity. A highly institutionalized structure, apartheid governed every aspect of South African life, determining everything from whether one could vote and where one could live to what sort of education one was entitled to and with whom one could interact.

This chapter offers a synopsis of South Africa's history of official discrimination, apartheid, and its aftermath. It concentrates on the ways in

---

[1] Afrikaners, also known as Boers or Voortrekkers, are South Africans of Dutch descent.
[2] Afrikaans, a Dutch-derived language spoken only in South Africa.
[3] The term "colored" is the vernacular for mixed-race South Africans, often descendents of former slaves.

which apartheid criminalized certain groups and behaviors and on how apartheid itself amounted to a humanitarian crime against the citizens of South Africa.

HISTORICAL BACKGROUND

South Africa's culture of segregation dates back to its earliest days as a contact zone. In 1658, only a handful of years after the arrival of the first Dutch settlers, two shipments of slaves were imported (Thompson, 2000: 36), introducing codes and practices of discrimination that would shape the area's history. Tensions over race relations marked interactions between Dutch and British settlers, who arrived to colonize in the early 1800s. After the Afrikaner loss of the Anglo-Boer War (1899–1902), the Union of South Africa (1910) amalgamated the country for the first time, but only because of compromises over racial policy. Unity initiated the institutionalization of racial discrimination, with the 1913 Natives Land Act forcing hundreds of thousands of Africans off of land they occupied. It also spurred the growth of opposition parties, including what would become the ANC, and the parallel development of the National Party, a response to Afrikaner penury and to a perceived threat from black Africans (Omond, 1985: 15–16). With the 1948 election of the National Party, de facto racial boundaries, beliefs, and attitudes swiftly became systematized. This legislation reinforced inequities and increased the government's power to control and classify the population. It infiltrated the most personal aspects of people's lives and it restructured society in the broadest possible ways, creating, for instance, geographical divisions that designated certain areas for certain racial groups.

What these laws amounted to in the everyday lives of individuals cannot be overstated. To mention only a few: the Population Registration Act (1950) designated the racial categories of all South Africans. The Bantu Education Act (1953) gave the government control of African education to prepare blacks for "certain forms of labor," in the words of former Prime Minister Hendrik Verwoerd. The Group Areas Act (1950) divided zones for living and working by race. The Promotion of Bantu Self-Government Act (1959) created homelands, allegedly independent nations within South Africa's borders, not internationally recognized. A slew of pass laws required identification of South Africans of color, granting them permission to live or work in certain areas and limiting freedom of movement. The Prohibition of Mixed Marriages (1949) and the Immorality Act (1950) enforced color lines in private life. From every side, South Africans were pushed and pulled into obedience to the inequitable laws of the land.

THE LANGUAGE OF APARTHEID

Apartheid terminology was replete with euphemism, used highly cynically by the authorities to provide the thinnest veneer of justification for
their policies, as in the case of the term homeland, where the government
performed the successful prestidigitation of appearing to exchange South
African citizenship for independence but in fact leaving people with no real
power. Here, the appellation "home" seems like a brutal irony when applied
to the remote and unusable fragments of land designated as homelands for
which residents had little or no previous affiliation. Similarly, the concept of
group areas cements the idea that racial groups empirically exist and that,
therefore, policy built around them makes sense.

Such policies tried to petrify apartheid's racial identities as timeless,
pure, and physically isolated qualities when they were really the source of
constant displacement and rootlessness. The invented geography of homelands and group areas made the majority of South Africans into foreigners
in their own country. Reimported as strictly controlled labor units, they
now came from places that prior to forced removals they had never been. In
other words, apartheid relied on the illusion of fixity while operating under
the need for mobility. Mobility and access were thus granted unevenly and
only at the whim of the authorities. It is important to note that, considering
curbs on freedom of speech, publication, and gatherings, discursive mobility was as much at stake as physical mobility.

APARTHEID'S APPARATUSES

As a strategy for control, apartheid can be read a number of ways. As a
geographic strategy, even before homelands were created various legislative
acts had redistributed land into the hands of whites, leaving millions fenced
in by artificial borders which they needed permission to move across, or
across which they were unwillingly moved. As a primarily economic ploy,
apartheid took advantage of those geographic boundaries to concentrate
the vast wealth of a resource-rich land in the hands of a few and position
the rest of society at their service. Apartheid depended on the production of
specifically placed laboring bodies and on the regulation of their movement
so that the laboring population was both carefully contained and also available for work. Everything was organized toward this end, from the specific
mechanisms that controlled mobility such as pass laws and influx control,
to the state's investment in education as a workforce tool, calibrating the
dispensation of education to suit different groups to different vocations. It
would be a mistake, however, to read apartheid as a singular strategy and,

therefore, to overlook the ways in which South Africans were radically positioned by race, class, gender, and geography simultaneously.

In order to accomplish this extreme social manipulation, the regime applied legalities illegally and immorally. That is, apartheid criminalized the legal system by developing it to support crimes committed in the name of apartheid. Among these were forced removals, detention without trial, torture, treason trials, arrests, banning, and censorship. Infamous examples of removals include Sophiatown, a township[4] near Johannesburg emptied of its black inhabitants in 1955 and rezoned for whites under the mocking moniker Triomf (Afrikaans for triumph), and District Six in Cape Town, a "colored" community razed to the ground starting in the late 1960s. Legal grounds for the removals came from a dozen and more laws on the books. By declaring the nation under threat from a "total onslaught" of black radical and communist forces, the government allocated to itself the power of detention without trial and the right to declare states of emergency. These powers were invoked in 1960 (not for the last time) after the police massacre of pass law protesters in Sharpeville.

These spectacularly violent forms of coercion, layered over the swaddling of everyday experience in apartheid divisions, expose the difficulties of enforcing the system. Despite the extremes of separation under apartheid, the ambiguities and complexities of keeping people segregated become apparent in such seeming contradictions as the police officer of color or the use of Afrikaans (widely perceived as the language of the oppressor) as the mother tongue of the Cape Colored community. Apartheid produced powerful resistance movements, notably led by labor unions and student groups, which engaged millions of people and made the townships ungovernable. This resistance in turn produced a proliferation of draconian laws. In hindsight, the ultimate unsustainability of the system is evident in this snarled and to some extent unenforceable (and expensive) mass of restrictions. In the face of ever-more organized domestic resistance – school boycotts, strikes, sabotage – and increasing international disdain – widespread decolonization, United Nations embargos – a series of states of emergency were declared in the 1980s, illustrating the anxiety about a loss of control on the part of the authorities.

THE CRIME OF APARTHEID

Apartheid resulted in the saturation of South African life and culture by the normalization of criminality and violence. A glance at the cultural

[4] Townships, black urban settlements adjacent to white cities.

production of apartheid shows the structuring force of crime and the persistence of the problem. The literature (e.g., Nadine Gordimer's postapartheid novel *The House Gun* (1999)) shows the intrusion of a culture of violence into the privileged lives of those shielded from it under apartheid. The films (e.g., *Mapantsula* (1988)) reveal the intersections of public and personal crime. Nonfiction sources, such as prison memoirs, newspaper articles, and the truth and reconciliation commission (TRC)[5] reports, headline the human rights violations, war crimes, and everyday acts of violence that characterized apartheid's modus operandi. None of these texts exaggerates and many of them underestimate the reach and result of the crimes of apartheid: Apartheid-era South Africa's high crime rate probably correlated to increasing state violence, and there has been a well-documented rise in violent crime in apartheid's aftermath, attended by a growing perception of the threat of violence. Although there is clearly a split between representations of criminality and illegality during and after apartheid, there is also a great deal of continuity since apartheid leaves behind a legacy of brutality and social disarray. The system imposed illegality on black South Africa and left habits of crime as its inheritance. In order to survive under apartheid, black South Africans inevitably had to break the law, which was constructed so as to trap them in a maze of restrictions and controls that governed every aspect of behavior. By the official end of apartheid in 1994, crime was no longer the sole burden of the oppressed, but the obsession of a society unanchored from its familiar chains.

Beyond the crimes perpetrated under apartheid, beyond the postapartheid rise in violent crime, apartheid itself was a crime against the majority of the South African population for almost fifty years, as the ANC has charged (ANC, 1987). The UN's Office of the High Commissioner of Human Rights concurs, declaring in 1973 that apartheid is a crime against humanity and that "the term 'the crime of apartheid,' which shall include similar policies and practices of racial segregation and discrimination as practiced in southern Africa, shall apply to [...] inhuman acts committed for the purpose of establishing and maintaining domination by one racial group of persons over any other racial group of persons and systematically oppressing them." In 1977, Additional Protocol 1 to the Geneva Convention called apartheid a war crime (UNHCHR, 1073). And we have seen in this overview the built-in contradictions of a legal system enforcing systemic crimes against its own people.

---

[5] The Truth and Reconciliation Commission (TRC) was a postapartheid mechanism for addressing apartheid-era human rights violations, amnesty, and reparations. Operating from 1995 to 1998, it conducted amnesty hearings on crimes by all parties.

SUMMARY AND CONCLUSION

To use a now slightly tired phrase, the "new South Africa" does not face particularly new issues of crime and justice. Under apartheid, while Africans comprised the majority of the population, whites were allotted the bulk of urban, and thus profitable, land, and were afforded the jobs and education systemically denied the other groups. Since huge social inequities persist, there has been a continuity of crime and its causes in the post-apartheid era, including police aggression, vigilantism, and gang violence. Although the TRC attempted with all good intentions in the years after 1994 to address and redress crimes committed under apartheid, it fell far short of gaining proportionate reparations and met with criticism for its undefined notion of truth, its suggestion of a break with the past, and its risk of promoting forgiving and forgetting over remembering. Regardless, the TRC alone was always going to be an insufficient mechanism to deal with apartheid's fallout. To make South Africa new, the nation needs a radical, ongoing restructuring of social and economic opportunities to follow its transition to democratic politics.

Apartheid officially began in 1948, but it had a long prehistory in the racially inequitable settler and colonial years of the country. Apartheid, as a policy, crystallized those inequalities, and built up over the decades a total system of control, treating black South Africans as criminals in their own nation. Nevertheless, between internal resistance from the ANC among other organizations, and outside pressure, such as international sanctions, the apartheid regime eventually conceded defeat and bowed out to make way for the country's first democratically elected government in 1994. Post-apartheid society faces a legacy of apartheid's crimes with a radical imbalance between the haves and the have-nots, and the inevitable crime and violence that go along with it.

REFERENCES

African National Congress (ANC). (1987, December 1–4). *The Illegitimacy of the Apartheid Regime, the Right to Struggle Against It, and the Status of the African National Congress.* Statement from the ANC Arusha Conference. Retrieved June 15, 2005, from www.anc.org.za/ancdocs/history/acrime.html
Omond, R. (1985). *The Apartheid Handbook.* Middlesex: Penguin.
Thompson, L. (2000). *A History of South Africa.* Third Edition. New Haven: Yale UP.
UNHCHR. (1973, November, 30). *International Convention on the Suppression and Punishment of the Crime of Apartheid.* Retrieved June 15, 2005, from www.unhchr.ch/html/menu3/b/11.html

WEB SITES

ANC Web site www.anc.org.za
BBC country profile for South Africa http://news.bbc.co.uk/2/hi/africa/country_
    profiles/1071886.stm
Center for the Study of Violence and Reconciliation www.csvr.org.za
Mail & Guardian newspaper www.mg.co.za
TRC Web site www.doj.gov.za/trc/index.html

ABOUT THE AUTHOR

Helen Kapstein is a tenured professor in the English Department at John Jay
College of Criminal Justice, The City University of New York. She earned her M.A
and Ph.D. in the Department of English and Comparative Literature at Columbia
University. Her academic areas of interest include postcolonial and modern British
literatures, cultural and media studies, and southern African literature and culture.
Her work has appeared in *Safundi* and *The Journal of Literary Studies*, among other
places, and she is currently working on a book project about tourism in postcolonial literature and society.

42 War Crimes

Noah Weisbord and Carla Reyes

INTRODUCTION

War crimes are violations of a special body of criminal law triggered by an armed conflict. The most serious violations of the patchwork of international treaties and customs that make up the laws of war – violations such as torture, rape, and pillage during wartime – have been criminalized and offenders can be prosecuted in national or international courts with jurisdiction. Humanitarian lawyers, lawyers who specialize in the laws of war, attempt to deploy laws to moderate the behavior of fighters and their leaders and to reduce human suffering. This, at least, is the ideal. The notion that law can and should permeate war is, however, intensely problematic.

Humanitarian law, which at first appears to be a principled constraint on war, is intricately entwined with it. The involvement of law and lawyers with the dominating, destructive, and coercive aims of war lends war making the legitimacy of the law and this has on-the-ground implications. Humanitarian law's contradictions and ambiguities, meanwhile, create opportunities for strategic lawyering. Consequently, humanitarian law exists as a humanizing influence on warfare, but also as an important zone of contestation where the courtroom, a multilateral treaty negotiation, or the media become the battlefield.

THE LAW OF WAR: AN INTRODUCTORY HISTORICAL OVERVIEW

Ancient History

The laws and traditions of war in ancient times are an early lesson about the moral dangers – and strategic possibilities – of entwining law and war. The

Code of Manu (350–283 BC), the Hindu text that became the basis of the Indian caste system, contained rules that might be described as concerned with war crimes. For example, it instructs that noncombatants and warriors who surrender must never be killed. According to the German philosopher Friedrich Nietzsche, writing two thousand years later, The Code of Manu was a positive manifestation of the will to power based on the "Holy Lie" of religious authority. (Nietzsche, 1988: 239) Even today, it is difficult to know whether the law of war moderates violence, increases its efficiency, or both.

Eighteenth and Nineteenth Century Precursors

The modern war crimes regime is often traced to the 1859 Battle of Solferino and the legal innovation of the Swiss businessman Henry Dunant, who witnessed the carnage. In *A Memory of Solferino* (1862), Dunant proposed an international congress where sovereigns would agree to a war convention with shared rules applicable to all parties. This innovation brought the battle, metaphorically, to the halls of Geneva and The Hague, where diplomatic delegations vied to draft humanitarian rules that would offer them a military advantage over their adversaries.

As Dunant labored to finish his book, Francis Leiber, an American professor, was drafting General Orders No. 100, another precursor to the modern war crimes regime. The Leiber Code, as General Orders No. 100 came to be known, was intended to limit the destruction wrought by the armies of the United States to acts deemed strictly necessary to accomplish military goals. Confederate Secretary of War James Seddon, however, denounced the code as a tool of "military despotism [allowing] a barbarous system of warfare under the pretext of military necessity." "It is in this code of military necessity," argued Seddon, "that the acts of atrocity and violence which have been committed by the officers of the United States and have shocked the moral sense of civilized nations are to find an apology and defense" (Seddon, 1863: 123).

Birth of the Modern War Crimes Regime

The proposal for the first Hague Convention in 1899, where the modern international laws of war were born, came from Russian Czar Nicholas II, who called for a legal regime "insuring to all peoples the benefits of a real and durable peace, and, above all putting an end to the progressive development of armaments." Other European leaders at the time suspected that

the proposal was a "ruse to enlist public opinion to support measures that would help Russia overcome its military weakness" (Jochnick & Normand, 1994: 69–70).

World War I broke out in 1914 and tested the law of war with new forms of weaponry and tactics. The war's end galvanized a fresh round of humanitarian law conventions addressing gas and bacteriological warfare, protection for the wounded and the sick, and the treatment of prisoners of war. These inter-war agreements required states to enact national legislation through which individual offenders would be punished, while holding states accountable in the international realm for failure to prevent or punish violations by individuals.

The Nuremberg Trial

International humanitarian law survived the industrialized barbarity of World War II, in large part, through the judgment of the International Military Tribunal at Nuremberg. Following the Allied victory, the German leaders were held criminally accountable and punished for violations of The Hague and Geneva Conventions with the Nuremberg court famously holding, "crimes against international law are committed by men, not by abstract entities." This decision began a transformative shift in the subject of international law of war from the state to the individual that only culminated at the end of the Cold War.

Cold War–Era Lawfare

Cold War era (1945–91) international law was shaped by the epochal conflict between American and Soviet superpowers to determine the ideological basis of the international system, liberal or communist. The Soviets and the Americans each supported international laws of war that, first and foremost, advanced their geostrategic agendas.

The Soviet Union, which aimed to escalate wars of national liberation and thereby loosen the grip of the West (i.e., the United States and its allies) on its colonies, challenged the legitimacy of the Hague Conventions, asking,

> … can we confine a sacred people's war against an aggressor and enslaver, a heroic struggle of millions of people for their country's independence, for its national culture, for its right to exist, can we confine this war with the strict bounds of the Hague rules, which were calculated for wars of a different type and for a totally different international situation? (Ginsburgs, 1964: 934–5)

U.S. President Ronald Reagan, for his part, refused to send Protocol I of the 1977 Geneva Conventions to the Senate for ratification, arguing that it "would give special status to 'wars of national liberation' [....] [W]e must not, and need not, give recognition and protection to terrorist groups as a price for progress in humanitarian law" (Message to Senate, 1987).

The Post–Cold War Moment

The 1990s was a period punctuated by internal armed conflicts occurring in the power vacuum left by the Soviet Union and not yet filled by the Western liberal democracies. Instead of preventing the massive violations of international humanitarian law arising out of sectarian conflicts in the former Yugoslavia, Rwanda, and elsewhere, the liberal democracies, through the UN Security Council, established a number of ad hoc international war crimes tribunals to punish them. When diplomatic delegations met in Rome in 1998 to create a permanent international criminal court with global reach, many of the great powers – Russia, China, India, the United States – chose not to subject themselves to its jurisdiction. Nonetheless, the statute establishing the International Criminal Court was adopted and the majority of the world's states have now ratified it.

The Challenge of 9/11 to the Laws of War

Debates raged in the United States and abroad over the characterization of the 9/11 attacks under the laws of war and the bounds of the legally justified response. Politicians, pundits, and legal scholars debated the legal status of Al Qaeda fighters (Did they qualify for the protections offered by the Geneva Conventions?), the most appropriate forum for prosecuting terror suspects (International, military, or domestic tribunal?), and the relevance of the laws of war generally in the age of terror (Were they obsolete?).

MAJOR CONCEPTS: CATEGORIES OF WAR CRIMES

War crimes are conventionally divided into four categories: use of prohibited weapons, engaging in prohibited means of combat, altering the status of particular civilians, and targeting crimes. The first category of war crimes aims to protect both combatants and noncombatants by prohibiting the use of weapons that "are of a nature to cause superfluous injury or unnecessary suffering or which are inherently indiscriminate." The ICC Statute, for example, bans poisoned weapons, asphyxiating gases, and bullets that expand when they hit.

As to the second category, the ICC Statute contains a hodgepodge list of prohibited means of combat. These proscribed means include, but are not limited to, killing or wounding a combatant who has laid down his arms, pillaging, sexual violence and, using civilians as human shields.

The third category of war crimes, altering the status of particular civilians during war, developed to prevent warring parties from using tactics that "are capable of destroying the fabric of particular nations or communities" (Bantekas & Nash, 2007: 120). It is a war crime, for example, to compel civilians of the enemy nation to take part in hostilities against their own country.

Targeting crimes involve violations of the principle that participants in armed conflict may only lawfully target military combatants and objects, and must refrain from targeting civilians and civilian objects. The law regulating targeting crimes is intricately linked to another key concept: collateral damage (discussed below).

Trends

SEXUAL VIOLENCE AS A WAR CRIME

Until the 1990s, rape was often explicitly absent from international war crimes treaties. According to Theodore Meron, former President of the International Criminal Tribunal for the former Yugoslavia, the "abuse of thousands of women in the territory of former Yugoslavia was needed to shock the international community into re-thinking the prohibition of rape as a crime under the laws of war" (1993: 425). The ICTY, in the *Celevici*, *Furundzija*, and *Kunarac* cases, found that because rape and other sexual violence constitute torture, it amounts to a grave breach of the Geneva Conventions and is punishable as a war crime and as a crime against humanity. Although these decisions have been applauded as a step forward in international gender jurisprudence, they have also been criticized for identifying women, first and foremost, as victims of war and stripping them of political agency (Engle, 2005: 812).

LAWFARE

U.S. Airforce General Charles J. Dunlap Jr. (2001) defines lawfare as "the use of law as a weapon of war," and describes it as "the newest feature of 21st century combat." He warns that, "there is disturbing evidence that the

rule of law is being hijacked into just another way of fighting (lawfare), to
the detriment of humanitarian values as well as the law itself" (p. 2). When
insurgents in Iraq use human shields to deter law-abiding American soldiers from firing upon them, or hide weapons in mosques that are protected
under the laws of war, they are using the law as a strategic weapon. The
challenge to humanitarians is to protect law from being hijacked by warring
parties for strategic ends and, ultimately, to ensure that it mitigates harm to
civilians rather than exacerbating it.

COLLATERAL DAMAGE (NECESSITY, PROPORTIONALITY, AND DISTINCTION)

The United States Department of Defense defines collateral damage as
"[u]nintentional or incidental injury or damage to persons or objects that
would not be lawful military targets in the circumstances ruling at the
time." The term collateral damage derives from the IHL principles of necessity, proportionality, and distinction, summed up by ICC Prosecutor Luis
Moreno Ocampo in his 2006 open letter responding to allegations of war
crimes in Iraq,

> [T]he death of civilians during an armed conflict, no matter how grave
> and regrettable, does not in itself constitute a war crime. International
> humanitarian law and the Rome Statute permit belligerents to carry out
> proportionate attacks against military objectives, even when it is known
> that some civilian deaths or injuries will occur. A crime occurs if there is
> an intentional attack directed against civilians (principle of distinction)
> [...] or an attack is launched on a military objective in the knowledge that
> the incidental civilian injuries would be clearly excessive in relation to the
> anticipated military advantage (principle of proportionality). (pp. 4–5)

Legal arguments over the characterization of civilian deaths as collateral
damage or war crimes arise because the terms "necessity" and "proportionality" are dynamic, changing throughout an armed conflict. The malle-
ability of these principles creates opportunities for strategic lawyering and
lawfare and recalls Confederate Secretary of War James Seddon's warning
that the Leiber Code has served as "an apology and defense" for acts of
atrocity.

CONCLUSIONS

The history of international humanitarian law might be – and has been
(Bassiouni, 2008: 269–80) – told as a story of barbarity to civilization
whereby enlightened individuals recognize the awfulness of war and,

against adversity, manage to curtail it with law. This history has also been presented as a tragedy where reason struggles to control violence and fails. (Provost, 2002) This chapter, by contrast, has attempted to identify the tensions between proscription and prescription, humanitarianism and patriotism, and law and politics, which have run deep through the field of humanitarian law from its early inception. The following chapter questions are an opportunity to consider these historic tensions in relation to current events.

REFERENCES

Bantekas, I. & S. Nash. (2007). *International Criminal Law*, Third Edition. London: Routledge- Cavendish.

Bassiouni, M. C. (2008). *International Criminal Law: Sources, Subjects & Contents*, Third Edition. Leiden, The Netherlands: Martinus Nijhoff Publishers.

Dunlap Jr., C. J. (2001). *Law and Military Interventions: Preserving Humanitarian Values in 21st conflicts.* Humanitarian Challenges in Military Intervention Conference. Washington D.C.: Carr Center for Human Rights Policy, Kennedy School of Government, Harvard University.

Engle, K. (2005). Feminism and Its (Dis)contents: Criminalizing Wartime Rape in Bosnia and Herzegovina. *American Journal of International Law*, 99, 779–815.

Ginsburgs, G. (1964) Wars of National Liberation and the Modern Law of Nations: The Soviet Thesis. *Law and Contemporary Problems*, 29, 910–42.

International Criminal Court Office of the Prosecutor, Open Letter from Chief Prosecutor Luis Moreno Ocampo (2006). Retrieved from: http://www2.icc-cpi.int/NR/rdonlyres/- F596D08D-D810–43A2–99BB-B899B9C5BCD2/277422/OTP_letter_to_senders_re- _Iraq_9_February_2006.pdf.

Jochnick, C. & R. Normand. (1994). The Legitimization of Violence: A Critical History of the Laws of War. *Harvard International Law Journal*, 35(1), 49–96.

Letter from James A. Seddon. Confederate Secretary of War, to Ould, denouncing the General Orders, No. 100 (June 24, 1863). Reprinted in Hartigan R. S.

Letter from James A. Seddon. (1983). *Lieber's Code and the Law of War*. Chicago: Precedent Publishing, Inc.

Meron, T. (1993). Rape as a Crime Under International Humanitarian Law. *American Journal of International Law*, 87(3) 424–428.

Nietzche, F. Der Anitchirst. In G. Colli, & M. Montinari, (Eds.) (1988) *Kritische Studienausgabe*.

Office of the President. (Jan. 29, 1987). *Message to the Senate Transmitting a Protocol to the 1949 Geneva Conventions*. Retrieved from: www.reagan.utexas.edu/archives/speeches/1987/012987B.htm.

Provost, R. (2002). *International Human Rights and Humanitarian Law*. Cambridge: Cambridge University Press.

ABOUT THE AUTHORS

Noah Weisbord, B.Sc., B.S.W., LL.B., B.C.L., M.S.W. (McGill), LL.M., S.J.D. Candidate (Harvard) is an assistant professor at Florida International University's College of Law. Professor Weisbord was an independent expert on the working group that defined the crime of aggression and added it to the ICC Statute. He was law clerk to ICC Chief Prosecutor Luis Moreno Ocampo in The Hague and, prior to that, traveled to Rwanda to study gacaca – community-based genocide trials inspired by an indigenous justice tradition.

Carla Reyes, J.D., LL.M, M.P.P., is currently a public interest fellow with the Volunteer Advocates for Immigrant Justice. She was formerly editor in chief of the *Duke Journal of Comparative and International Law*.

43 The Crime of Aggression

Stefan Barriga

INTRODUCTION

The crime of aggression, or crime against peace, has been famously labeled as the "supreme international crime" by Robert H. Jackson, the Chief American Prosecutor at the Nuremberg trials. Of the twenty-two former Nazi leaders tried in Nuremberg, twelve were convicted for crimes against peace. The International Military Tribunal for the Far East (the "Tokyo Tribunal") had an even stronger focus on aggression. It prosecuted only those military and political leaders whose crimes included aggression. Twenty-four of them were convicted of this crime.

The crime of aggression is, in essence, the crime of waging an illegal war, in order words, a war in contravention of the United Nations Charter. It is, thus, the criminal law corollary to state responsibility for the most serious cases of illegal use of armed force. The Charter prohibits the threat or use of force except in the case of self-defense or when authorized by the Security Council. But while there have been many instances of such illegal use of force since the founding of the United Nations, no international (or domestic) trials for a crime of aggression have been conducted during the last six decades. This is due to two basic reasons: a longstanding controversy over a legally binding definition of aggression, and the lack of an international court effectively empowered to prosecute aggression. Both of these issues, however, have recently been resolved for the purpose of the Rome Statute of the International Criminal Court (ICC): In June 2010, a Review Conference held in Kampala, Uganda, adopted amendments to the Rome Statute on the crime of aggression by a consensus decision. The amendments contain a legally binding definition of the crime and the precise conditions under which the ICC will be empowered to prosecute those responsible for crimes of aggression committed no earlier than 2017. Already prior to the Review Conference, it was generally accepted that the crime of aggression was indeed an existing crime under international law. In 2006, this view was confirmed by the British House of Lords. Furthermore, some two dozen countries worldwide (including Germany and the Russian Federation) have incorporated the crime of aggression into their domestic criminal codes.

The notion of "crime" of aggression must be distinguished from the "act" of aggression. The former refers to the conduct of the individual leader who bears criminal responsibility for the state's use of force, typically without even actively participating on the battlefield. The latter refers to the act of the state, such as one state army's invasion of a neighbor state's territory.

A crime of aggression and war crimes often go hand in hand, though conceptually they are very different. War crimes are serious violations of the rules applicable in armed conflict (*ius in bello*), whereas a crime of aggression constitutes a serious violation of the rules that govern the use of force by a state (*ius ad bellum*). War crimes can be committed by individual soldiers on the field, whereas a crime of aggression can only be committed by a state's leadership. War crimes can be committed in both international and noninternational armed conflicts, whereas a crime of aggression is by definition of international character, as it always involves at least two states.

DEFINING THE CRIME OF AGGRESSION

While the drafters of the United Nations Charter could not agree on a definition of aggression, the 1945 London Charter of the International Military Tribunal in Nuremberg referred to crimes against peace as the "planning, preparation, initiation or waging of a war of aggression, or a war in violation of international treaties, agreements or assurances, or participation in a common plan or conspiracy for the accomplishment of any of the foregoing." That rather vague definition of aggression was subsequently endorsed by the International Law Commission as part of the 1950 Nuremberg Principles.

In 1974, following decades of negotiations, the UN General Assembly agreed on a much more detailed "Definition of Aggression," contained in resolution 3314 (XXIX). Article 1 defines aggression as "the use of armed force by a State against the sovereignty, territorial integrity or political independence of another State, or in any other manner inconsistent with the Charter of the United Nations, as set out in this Definition," and Article 3 contains an illustrative list of acts that qualify as aggression, such as an "invasion or attack by the armed forces of a State of the territory of another

State, or any military occupation, however temporary, resulting from such invasion or attack." The major drawback of that definition, however, was its nonbinding nature. Its primary purpose was to guide the Security Council in the determination of state acts of aggression, and it was not intended to serve as the basis for individual criminal proceedings.

At the 1998 Rome Conference establishing the ICC, there was no agreement on how to define aggression for the purpose of individual criminal justice. While the ICC Statute includes aggression as one of the crimes under the jurisdiction of the Court, the Court's active exercise of jurisdiction over the crime was deferred until a provision was adopted defining the crime and setting out any further conditions for that exercise of jurisdiction, such as possibly an authorization by the UN Security Council. In February 2009, a Special Working Group on the Crime of Aggression submitted its proposal for a definition of aggression, thereby concluding an important phase of the negotiations. The Working Group's proposal incorporates the definition contained in resolution 3314, but seeks to exclude some acts from the Court's jurisdiction. Only an act of aggression – as defined in resolution 3314 – "which, by its character, gravity and scale, constitutes a manifest violation of the Charter of the United Nations" would qualify. A minor border skirmish, for example, would thus not trigger the ICC's jurisdiction. Similarly, a use of armed force whose illegal character is debatable rather than "manifest" would not end up before the ICC – arguably to protect the Court from entering highly controversial political terrain.

The 2010 Review Conference decided to include the above-mentioned definition in the Rome Statute as a new article 8 bis. In addition, the Conference adopted a number of "understandings" that should guide the interpretation of the definition. One such understanding states that "aggression is the most serious and dangerous form of the illegal use of force," thereby re-confirming that not every illegal use of force constitutes aggression.

Under the amended Rome Statute, criminal responsibility for crimes of aggression will be limited to those in charge of the aggressor state's policies. Such leaders are defined as persons "in a position effectively to exercise control over or to direct the political or military action of a State." This leadership clause could refer to more than one single person and include, for example, cabinet-level officials or military leaders. It would, however, clearly exclude individual soldiers from criminal responsibility for aggression. The proposal does not suggest to criminalize the "participation in a common plan or conspiracy" for the accomplishment of aggression, as Nuremberg did, but it incorporates the Rome Statute's general rules on modes of participation. Secondary modes of participation, such as aiding and abetting, do therefore give rise to criminal responsibility – provided that the perpetrator fulfills the leadership requirement.

Rome statute definition of the crime of aggression (excerpt)

ARTICLE 8 BIS CRIME OF AGGRESSION

1. For the purpose of this Statute, "crime of aggression" means the planning, preparation, initiation or execution, by a person in a position effectively to exercise control over or to direct the political or military action of a State, of an act of aggression which, by its character, gravity and scale, constitutes a manifest violation of the Charter of the United Nations.
2. For the purpose of paragraph 1, "act of aggression" means the use of armed force by a State against the sovereignty, territorial integrity or political independence of another State, or in any other manner inconsistent with the Charter of the United Nations. Any of the following acts, regardless of a declaration of war, shall, in accordance with United Nations General Assembly resolution 3314 (XXIX) of 14 December 1974, qualify as an act of aggression:
   a) The invasion or attack by the armed forces of a State of the territory of another State, or any military occupation, however temporary, resulting from such invasion or attack, or any annexation by the use of force of the territory of another State or part thereof;
   b) Bombardment by the armed forces of a State against the territory of another State or the use of any weapons by a State against the territory of another State;
   c) The blockade of the ports or coasts of a State by the armed forces of another State;
   d) An attack by the armed forces of a State on the land, sea or air forces, or marine and air fleets of another State;
   e) The use of armed forces of one State which are within the territory of another State with the agreement of the receiving State, in contravention of the conditions provided for in the agreement or any extension of their presence in such territory beyond the termination of the agreement;
   f) The action of a State in allowing its territory, which it has placed at the disposal of another State, to be used by that other State for perpetrating an act of aggression against a third State;
   g) The sending by or on behalf of a State of armed bands, groups, irregulars or mercenaries, which carry out acts of armed force against another State of such gravity as to amount to the acts listed above, or its substantial involvement therein.

CONCLUSIONS: A COMPROMISE ON THE ROLE OF THE SECURITY COUNCIL

While the Special Working Group was successful in approaching an agreeable definition of aggression, it could not overcome a deep division over the equally important issue of the "conditions for the exercise of jurisdiction." The central question here was whether the UN Security Council should act as a gatekeeper for the Court's exercise of jurisdiction, given the Council's primary responsibility for the maintenance of international peace and security under the Charter. Some countries argued that the ICC should only be allowed to proceed with investigations into crimes of aggression if so authorized by the Security Council, in order to prevent the Court from interfering unduly with the Council's business. Others considered such a role as incompatible with the concept of equality before the law, as it would allow any single permanent member of the Security Council to shield individuals from prosecution.

The 2010 Review Conference found a compromise on this issue. First, it deferred the "activation" of the Court's exercise of jurisdiction to a decision to be taken by ICC states parties no earlier than 2017, and second, it agreed on a differentiated jurisdictional regime, based on different trigger mechanisms, through the inclusion of two new articles 15 *bis* and 15 *ter*.

Article 15 *ter* will empower the Court to investigate and prosecute crimes of aggression based on a referral by the Security Council – even where the act of aggression involves a nonstate party to the Rome Statute. Based on such a referral, the Court could investigate a crime of aggression even in the absence of an explicit Security Council determination that an act of aggression has occurred. In any event, the Court would not be bound by such a determination, in order to preserve the due process rights of the accused.

Furthermore, a new article 15 *bis* was added regarding *proprio motu* investigations and state referrals. When acting on the basis of these two trigger mechanisms, the Court's jurisdiction will be limited to crimes of aggression arising from acts of aggression committed among states parties to the Rome Statute. The only way for the Court to be able to deal with acts of aggression committed by or against nonstates parties will thus be on the basis of a referral by the Security Council (article 15 *ter*), but not on the Prosecutor's own initiative or based on a state party referral under article 15 *bis*. In addition, states parties will be allowed to prospectively opt-out of that provision. The Court's investigation and prosecution under article 15 *bis* will thus be based on the prior consent of the states concerned. In recognition of the Security Council's primary responsibility for the maintenance of international peace and security, however, article 15 *bis* instructs the Court to await a determination of aggression by the Security Council for up to six months, after which the Court may proceed even in the absence of such a determination.

In conclusion, the scope of the Court's jurisdiction over the crime of aggression will be limited when compared to the other crimes, due to the special nature of the crime of aggression and its unique placement in the Rome Statute. Except where the Security Council takes the initiative to refer a situation that may involve a crime of aggression, the jurisdictional regime will be consent-based. Given its effects, this aspect of the jurisdictional regime resembles a voluntary pact of nonaggression among states parties whose enforcement by way of individual criminal justice will be entrusted to the ICC.

REFERENCES

Background Materials on Aggression by the Coalition for the International Criminal Court, available at www.iccnow.org/?mod=aggression.

Barriga, S., W. Danspeckgruber, & C. Wenaweser. (2009). *The Princeton Process on the Crime of Aggression – Materials of the Special Working Group on the Crime of Aggression 2003–09*. Princeton: Lynne Rienner Publishers.

Ferencz, B. (1975). *Defining International Aggression – The Search for World Peace: A Documentary History and Analysis*. Dobbs Ferry, New York: Oceana Publishers.

ICC Working Group on the Crime of Aggression: www.icc-cpi.int/Menus/ASP/Crime+of+Aggression/

Solera, O. (2007). *Defining the Crime of Aggression*. London: Cameron & May.

United Nations Office of Legal Affairs: Historical Review of Developments Relating to Aggression, 2003 (available at www.ods.un.org as Doc. Nr. PCNICC/2002/WGCA/L.1)

United Kingdom House of Lords: *R. v. Jones et al.*, [2006] UKHL 16, available at www.publications.parliament.uk/pa/ld200506/ldjudgmt/jd060329/jones.pdf

ABOUT THE AUTHOR

Stefan Barriga is the Deputy Permanent Representative of Liechtenstein to the United Nations in New York. He acted as legal adviser to the Chairman of the Special Working Group on the Crime of Aggression between 2003 and 2009 and continued to advise the chief negotiators on the crime of aggression up to the successful conclusion of this process at the Review Conference 2010. Since 2002, he has represented Liechtenstein in numerous negotiations on legal issues, in particular in the context of the Sixth Committee (legal) of the UN General Assembly and the ICC Assembly of States Parties. Mr. Barriga holds a doctoral degree in law from University of Vienna (Austria) and an L.L.M. from Columbia University.

PART VI

DELIVERING INTERNATIONAL JUSTICE

As explained in the introductory chapter, the Rome Statute defines international crimes as the gravest crimes that threaten the peace, security, and well-being of the world. Because these crimes are of such gravity, the Statute declares "it is the duty of every State to exercise its criminal jurisdiction over those responsible for international crimes." This provides the foundation for international criminal law and for the institutions required to uphold and deliver that law. This section of the book is concerned with the various legal instruments, international treaties (see Chapter 45 by Gloria Brown Marshall), charters, protocols, and understandings that have contributed to the development of international criminal law and it deals with the criminal tribunals, commissions, and courts that are playing a part in administering the law. It describes the important role of the United Nations in these developments and it provides several chapters describing the International Criminal Court (ICC), the court's short history, and key aspects of the court's work.

The United Nations has long been concerned with the development of international laws and standards. This work falls into two basic categories: (1) the formation of international obligations by treaty to criminalize, at the national and international level, activities of fundamental concern to the international community; and (2) the development of norms and standards in criminal justice, which are desirable or even obligatory practices (see Chapter 44 by Roger Clark).

The Rome Statute led to the creation of the permanent ICC. The statute sought the commitment of signatory nations to apply and enforce the rule of law in their own territory, but also their commitment to support the work of the ICC in processing the cases brought to its attention. This marks the beginning of truly global criminal justice (see Chapter 47 by Mangai Natarajan and Antigona Kukaj). Since its inception in 2002, the ICC has handled four major "situations." One of these situations, referred by the Security Council, concerns Darfur, Sudan, a nonstate party to the ICC. The account of this situation in Chapter 48 by Xabier Agirre Aranburu and Roberta Belli exposes the complexities inherent in the investigation of international crimes where the primary purpose may be to restore a sense of justice to victims and bring international condemnation of the suffering inflicted upon them. In fact, the proceedings of the ICC include an unprecedented role for victims' rights in three important respects: 1) protection, 2) participation, and 3) reparations (see Chapter 49 by David Donat Cattin).

In addition to the ICC, ad hoc international criminal tribunals have been created for prosecuting individuals responsible for the grossest violations of international humanitarian law (see Chapter 46 by Gloria Browne-Marshall). Nonjudicial forums have also been established that allow victims to seek resolution and redress. These include regional and global human rights commissions (see Chapter 51 by Jose Morin) and the remarkable truth commissions that have sought to promote reconciliation in South Africa (See Chapter 52 by Stevan Parmentier and Elmar Weitecamp), and in Guatemala (Chapter 53 by Marcia Esparza). Truth commissions are especially important when societies are in transition – moving from an autocratic regime toward more democratic forms of government. Finally, nongovernmental organizations play an important role in the delivery of international criminal justice, both through their relationship with the United Nations and as grassroots movements that are promoting social change with the goals of achieving global peace, justice, and security (see Chapter 50 by Rosemary Barberet).

44 The Role of the United Nations

Roger S. Clark

UN work in the area of International Crime and Justice is rooted in the UN Charter. In the preamble to that treaty, "we the peoples of the United Nations" are said to be "determined to save succeeding generations from the scourge of war, which twice in our lifetime has brought untold sorrow to mankind." The Charter contemplates not only coercive power against aggressors but also efforts to build a just world to secure peace. Thus, Article 55 of the Charter exhorts the organization (especially through the General Assembly and the Economic and Social Council) to promote:

a. higher standards of living, full employment, and conditions of economic and social progress and development;
b. solutions of international economic, social, health, and related problems; and international cultural and educational cooperation; and
c. universal respect for and observance of, human rights and fundamental freedoms for all without distinction as to race, sex, language, or religion.

The UN has no standing body with criminal jurisdiction over particular crimes. Its court, the International Court of Justice, deals with states and international organizations, not individuals. Occasionally, on an ad hoc basis, the UN has taken on some features of a law enforcement agency, as in the Security Council's creation of the International Tribunals for Former Yugoslavia and Rwanda. Those Tribunals are designed to enforce international law relating to genocide, crimes against humanity and war crimes against individual perpetrators in the particular instances of former Yugoslavia and Rwanda. But the Security Council chose not to create international tribunals for situations that were arguably as egregious. The UN

337

was, however, involved in the creation of several "hybrid" courts, having a mixture of local and foreign judges. These were formed in, for example, Cambodia, Sierra Leone, Timor-Leste, and Lebanon.

Against this backdrop of selectivity, the UN provided the forum for negotiations to create the International Criminal Court (ICC) at a diplomatic conference in 1998. The ICC is a separate legal entity from the UN but has a close working relationship with it. Proponents of the ICC hope that in due course it will have power to deal with the most egregious of international crimes in all countries of the globe where the states most closely involved are unwilling or unable to prosecute. It already has potential jurisdiction over acts occurring on the territory of, or perpetrated by the nationals of the 111 states that are currently parties to the Rome Statute of 1998, the treaty setting up the Court. In 2009, the ICC began its first trial, that of Mr. Lubanga Dyilo. He is charged with recruiting child soldiers (less than fifteen years of age) and sending them into battle in the Congo.

These concrete efforts at law enforcement are exceptional. Mostly, the UN's work on international crime and international justice has been concerned with the development of international laws and standards. This work falls into two basic categories: (1) the formation of international obligations by treaty to criminalize, at the national and international level, activities of fundamental concern to the international community, and (2) the development of "norms and standards" in criminal justice, desirable or even obligatory practices.

THE OBLIGATION TO MAKE CERTAIN ACTIVITIES CRIMINAL

The UN first used the treaty suppression approach in the 1948 Genocide Convention. State parties to that treaty undertake to make it criminal to take part in genocide on their territory. This model was expanded in later instances, notably in the areas of terrorism, torture, trafficking in drugs, transnational organized crime, and, most recently, corruption. In treaties of this kind, states promise to make the actions in question criminal under their domestic laws. The object of the treaties is to get as many states as possible with power to prosecute (not only the territorial state where the events occurred or the state of which the accused is a national). This reduces the odds that there will be "safe havens." The trend is for states to agree by treaty either to prosecute suspects who come on their territory (regardless of where the crime occurred or whose citizens they are) or to extradite them to someone else who will undertake a genuine prosecution (such as the state where an aircraft was registered, or from where it began its journey).

This is known as *aut dedere aut judicare* (extradite or bring before a legal process – see also Podgor, & Clark, 2009).

The success of these law-making efforts relies on painstaking treaty negotiation followed by ratification or acceptance – state by state. The UN General Assembly, where most of these treaties gained approval, has never been regarded as a legislator in this. It is merely the midwife who makes the process happen. After the events of September 11, 2001, however, the Security Council (as opposed to the General Assembly) entered into new waters in SC Resolution 1373. The Council, purporting to act under its compulsory powers in Chapter VII of the UN Charter dealing with the maintenance of international peace and security, required states to give effect to obligations which track those in the 1999 Convention Against Terrorist Financing, even for states not party to that treaty. It created a Council Committee to ensure that states take appropriate action. The Council thus began acting as a legislator and making efforts to see that its legislation is enforced. Whether the Council has power to do this is only just beginning to be discussed in the literature on international relations and international law.

PROMULGATION OF UN NORMS AND STANDARDS IN CRIMINAL JUSTICE

Formulating standards in criminal justice has occurred in two main parts of the UN structure: that part dealing with the broad field of human rights (operating primarily through the office of the United Nations High Commissioner for Human Rights in Geneva and the Human Rights Council which was created by the General Assembly in 2006) and that dealing specifically with Crime Prevention and Criminal Justice (operating primarily through the Office of Drugs and Crime in Vienna ("UNODC")). The Vienna office, the most significant part of the UN system for this chapter, combines longstanding programs in crime prevention and criminal justice and in drug control with more recent efforts to combat terrorism and corruption. Standards dealing with crime prevention have been developed primarily under the auspices of the Commission on Crime Prevention and Criminal Justice and the UN "Congresses" (see infra). In the drug area, the Commission on Narcotic Drugs and the International Narcotic Control Board are the significant focal points for what the General Assembly has designated as the "UN International Drug Control Program" ("UNDCP"). The work of the UNODC is augmented by a network of criminal justice institutes loosely affiliated in the International Scientific and Professional Advisory Council for the program ("ISPAC"). Notable among the institutes are the United Nations Interregional Crime and Justice Research Institute ("UNICRI"), Turin, Italy, the European Institute for Crime Prevention and Control ("HEUNI"), Helsinki, Finland, the National Institute of Justice ("NIJ"), Washington, D.C., and the International Centre for Criminal Law Reform and Criminal Justice Policy ("ICCLR&CJP"), Vancouver, Canada.

A feature of the UN program specific to criminal justice has, since 1955, been the holding of five yearly Congresses on Crime Prevention and Criminal Justice, attended by most states, by individual experts and by numerous representatives of civil society. Numerous instruments setting forth criminal justice standards and model treaties were finalized at the congresses up to 1990 and then endorsed by ECOSOC or the General Assembly (Clark, 1994).

Space constraints preclude detailed discussion of these documents, but a brief mention of the most significant will suggest what has seemed important internationally. The First Congress in 1955 adopted the Standard Minimum Rules for the Treatment of Prisoners. The 1975 Congress produced the Declaration on the Protection of All Persons from Being Subjected to Torture and Other Cruel, Inhuman or Degrading Treatment or Punishment. In 1982, the General Assembly followed up the Torture Declaration by adopting Principles of Medical Ethics designed to preclude doctors from assisting torture. The 1985 Congress produced, notably, the Declaration of Basic Principles of Justice for Victims of Crime and Abuse of Power, the Beijing Rules for the Administration of Juvenile Justice, a Model Agreement on the Transfer of Foreign Prisoners and a very important statement on judicial integrity, the Basic Principles on the Independence of the Judiciary. The 1990 Havana Congress added several standards about human rights in the administration of justice.

Since the 1990s, partly in response to criticisms of the sheer volume of material being produced, standard-setting has taken place mainly under the auspices of the Commission on Crime Prevention and Criminal Justice rather than the Congresses. As before, final endorsement comes either from ECOSOC or the General Assembly.

While some of the criminal justice provisions are in treaties like the Covenant on Civil and Political Rights, most of the instruments are in the form of recommendations to states. Neither the General Assembly nor ECOSOC is given a direct power to "legislate" under the Charter. It is widely accepted, however, that such resolutions may contribute to the development of general international law, by codifying past developments, by providing an authoritative interpretation of treaty obligations, or by providing a basis for new (customary) law. For customary law to develop there must be both some relevant state practice and some *opinio juris*, a notion that what is done is done from a sense of legal obligation. In modern international law both the practice and the *opinio juris* may be inferred from what states do in international organizations. The strongest candidates for international law are resolutions called "Declarations." Note that the Universal Declaration of Human Rights and the 1975 instrument on torture, for example, are in form General Assembly Declarations. On the other hand, the titles and adopting language of many of the others are peppered with words like "guidelines," "standards," and "principles" which suggest something much softer and aspirational rather than "legal."

The soft nature of such standards and norms does not mean that most states, as members of the United Nations club, do not feel some obligation to make an effort to comply – or to rationalize reasons for not complying. Nor does it mean that the organization is powerless to try to encourage the implementation of the instruments, starting with disseminating the material as widely as possible. Particularly by asking for reports of what states are doing and making some effort to discuss responses, the UN seeks to invoke the principles in the abstract if not in concrete cases. In the human rights part of the system there are also several "treaty bodies" such as the Human Rights Committee established under the Covenant on Civil and Political Rights. These bodies try to give effect to the specific treaty materials. Increasingly, they have been referring to the Standard Minimum Rules for the Treatment of Prisoners and to other nontreaty instruments as a way to interpret the general provisions of the treaties. A number of "theme mechanisms" such as Special Rapporteurs and Committees have been put in place in particular areas to encourage states, sometimes quietly, sometimes by shaming in the glare of publicity, to give effect to the material. Examples of such mechanisms are those dealing with torture, extrajudicial killings and the independence of lawyers and judges.

Moreover, nontreaty material has a habit of creeping into later treaties. Much of the material in the Universal Declaration Human Rights found itself in the two 1966 Covenants on Human Rights. Substantial parts of the 1985 Declaration concerning victims appear in the Rome Statute of the International Criminal Court and the Convention Against Transnational Organized Crime.

There is a very large body of norms and standards covering all the basic fields of criminal justice. The challenge now is to make it operational on a global basis.

SUMMARY

Generally, the UN is not a law enforcement agency. Its main function in criminal justice is to formulate international laws and standards. They are twofold: those creating international treaty obligations to make certain heinous activities criminal under the criminal justice system of nation-states; and those developing "norms and standards" – desirable and sometimes obligatory practices that are applicable domestically within states and internationally when the UN itself or some other international organization operates.

REFERENCES

Clark, R. S. (1994). *The United Nations Crime Prevention and Criminal Justice Program: Formulation of Standards and Efforts at Their Implementation.* (Vol. 20). Philadelphia: University of Pennsylvania.

Podgor, E.S., & R. S. Clark, (2009). *International Criminal Law: Cases and Materials, Third Edition.* Newark: LexisNexis.

United Nations. (2006). *Compendium of United Nations Standards and Norms in Crime Prevention and Criminal Justice.* New York: United Nations. Available at: www.unodc.org/pdf/compendium/compendium_2006_cover.pdf

WEB SITES

United Nations Office on Drugs and Crime: www.unodc.org
Office of United Nations High Commissioner for Human Rights: www.ohchr.org
International Scientific and Professional Advisory Council of the UN
Crime Prevention and Criminal Justice Programme ("ISPAC"): www.ispac-italy.org

ABOUT THE AUTHOR

Roger S. Clark is Board of Governors Professor of International Law and Criminal Law at Rutgers University School of Law in Camden, New Jersey. He holds advanced doctorates in law from Victoria University of Wellington in New Zealand and from Columbia Law School in New York. Between 1986 and 1990, he was a member of the United Nations Committee on Crime Prevention and Control, a group of independent experts elected by the Economic and Social Council ("ECOSOC"). The Committee supervised the criminal justice work of the United Nations. (It has since been replaced by the Commission on Crime Prevention and Criminal Justice, which is composed of representatives of states.) Since 1995, he has represented the government of Samoa in negotiations in the 1990s to create the International Criminal Court and more recently in efforts to extend the Court's jurisdictional reach to the crime of aggression.

45 Treaties and International Law

Gloria J. Browne-Marshall

INTRODUCTION

In 1815, the Treaty of Vienna, a multilateral treaty, banished Napoleon Bonaparte after his brutal invasion of Europe. This treaty was a sanction as well as a preventive measure against future aggression, and acted as precedent for the treatment of another sovereign, Wilhelm II of Hohenzollarne, the Kaiser of Germany (1859–1941), who was accused of committing horrific acts against civilians during World War I (Romano, Nollkaemper, & Kleffner, 2004). The Treaty of Versailles, signed in 1919, established a tribunal guided by international policy and international morality of that era to try Wilhelm II for crimes against the laws and customs of war. Kaiser Wilhelm argued that he was a victim of *ex post facto* or acts made criminal after the fact, and fled. The Netherlands, where he took refuge, refused to extradite Wilhelm (Jorgenson, 1999). Despite the failure to directly punish Kaiser Wilhelm, The Treaty of Versailles was evidence that under certain circumstances the world community would place limits on national sovereignty by international agreement or treaty.

The 1969 Vienna Convention defines a treaty as "an international agreement concluded between States in written form and governed by international law, whether embodied in a single instrument or in two or more related instruments and whatever its particular designation." The 1986 Vienna Convention extends the definition of treaties to include international agreements involving international organizations as parties. Treaties are binding bilateral agreements, as between two States or multilateral agreements, as between several States. These agreements represent one area within the complex system of courts, agreements, customs, principles, and national laws that comprise international law. International criminal law involves agreements between States to criminalize certain conduct with an internationally accepted response even if that conduct is outside of a particular State's jurisdiction or national authority. States entering as signatories to an agreement are not bound by its terms until the government of that State ratifies the treaty. The State may limit the application of certain terms prior to ratification by adding reservations or declarations to clarify the manner in which the treaty will be applied in that State. Once ratified, enforcement of treaty terms is defined by the compliance provisions within the particular treaty. This chapter examines the characteristic features of international treaties and international law, including multilateral, bilateral, interpretation, enforcement, and comparison with customary international law.

INTERNATIONAL CRIMINAL LAW AND SCOPE OF TREATIES

One can best understand international criminal law by examining the development of treaties with criminal law implications and the values a treaty is meant to protect. Criminal law covers a myriad of crimes and may be addressed by treaty, national law, or the United Nations. States may enter into bilateral or multilateral treaties covering specific crimes unique to that region. The treaty may set forth extradition, the place of trial, and due process rights. The United Nations Office on Drugs and Crime Programme (UNODC) focuses on combating transnational organized crime such as drug trafficking, money laundering, and the illicit trafficking of human beings. Regional counterterrorism treaties drafted by entities such as League of Arab States and North Atlantic Treaty Organization as well as national laws against terrorism assist in the international effort to address acts of terrorism. Under the Convention of the Protection of the Environment through Criminal Law, each State member of the Council must adopt domestic laws that criminalize offences against the environment.

Therefore, a treaty has a specific scope. International law has jurisdictional limits. Jurisdiction may be the territorial boundaries of a State or in international criminal law it is the authority to prosecute. A treaty may provide the terms for jurisdiction over a person participating in a criminal activity, the criminal activity itself, or the persons victimized by the crime such as in cases of human trafficking. Extraterritorial crimes involve criminal activity outside of State borders that may be prosecuted under the jurisdiction of national laws because the crimes affect that State such as drug trafficking.

The League of Nations and International Law

The initial laws governing war crimes were enforceable only by the national government. After the devastating magnitude World War I, national leaders created a society of States called "The League of Nations." The League of Nations had as its mandate the codification of international values, the resolution of disputes, and above all, the prevention of war (Kittichaisaree, 2001). The League of Nations was the first truly international forum. Formed by Covenant, or constitution, in 1919, "to promote international cooperation and to achieve peace and security," the original members of the League of Nations were the victors of World War I. Twenty-eight countries were permanent members of the League. More than thirty nations joined and withdrew during its existence. The United States never ratified the Treaty of Versailles to join the League of Nations (Paust et al., 2000). Although the League of Nations failed to prevent World War II, it provided the basis for a forum in which States could work out their differences peacefully and create legal contracts and consequences for international disputes. With little international support and limited resources, this historic institution dissolved itself in 1946. That same year, the League's Geneva property was transferred to a new organization – the United Nations (Paust et al., 2000). Many of the treaties ratified by members of the League of Nations remained enforceable international law under the United Nations.

U.N. Security Council, the organ of the United Nations charged with the maintenance of international peace and security, is instrumental to the fight against breaches of international criminal law. The Council has fifteen members, five of whom are permanent members and ten are elected by the General Assembly for two-year terms. The Security Council may undertake an investigation and mediation of nations. The Council can issue ceasefire directives, sanctions, or send peacekeeping forces to help reduce tensions in troubled regions (Weissbrodt, Fitzpatrick, & Newman, 2009). The Council may authorize regional organizations such as the North Atlantic Treaty Organization (NATO), the Economic Community of West African States or coalitions of willing countries to implement certain peacekeeping or peace enforcement functions. Most important to this analysis is that the U.N. Security Council can establish international criminal tribunals to adjudicate international crimes following war or armed conflict.

The need for international criminal law to address drug trafficking was recognized as early as 1908. The International Opium Convention of 1912 resulted in a treaty to control the distribution of narcotics, internationally. The United Nations adopted the Convention against Illicit Traffic in

Narcotic Drugs and Psychotropic Substances in 1988. In 2000, the United Nations developed a Protocol to Prevent, Suppress and Punish Trafficking in Persons Especially Women and Children, supplementing the United Nations Convention against Transnational Organized Crime. The United Nations Convention against Transnational Organized Crime and its Protocols to stem the laundering of illicit funds from drugs, prostitution, or governmental corruption.

Suppression Treaties

Treaties may be created to suppress or limit the actions of another State. During the Atlantic Slave Trade, millions of persons were kidnapped from Africa, forced onto ships and enslaved in far regions of the world. After centuries of involvement in the slave trade, England, France, Russia, Austria, and Prussia abolished slavery and entered into the Quintuple Treaty of 1841 intended to suppress the continued slave trade among other European nations by seizing their ships on the high seas (Browne-Marshall, 2007). Modern suppression treaties include the Treaty on the Non-Proliferation of Nuclear Weapons that attempts to contain the spread of nuclear weapons among States. States in possession of nuclear weapons agree not to transfer nuclear weapons and non-nuclear weapon States agree not to receive nuclear weapons. Suppression treaties are often created to reach international crimes. Treaties to limit the manufacture or trade in illicit drugs represent an agreement intended to suppress criminal activity such as growing and transporting opium plants from which the narcotic drug heroin is manufactured.

Extradition Treaties

"Extradition refers to the delivery of a person, who is suspected or has been convicted of a crime, by a country or other jurisdiction where the person has taken refuge to the country or jurisdiction that asserts legal authority over said person" (Deflem & Irwin, 2006: 352). State's refusal to extradite, or surrender, an alleged violator of international law is an obstacle to international justice. Extradition is controlled by treaty or custom between States (Podgor & Clark, 2008). Law enforcement agencies can be stymied by a lack of cooperation between States (Crashaw, Cullen, & Williamson, 2007). Extradition of suspects depends on the cooperation of national governments while enforcement of international law relies on cooperation and international clearinghouses of informational resources. International law has evolved into treaties of mutual assistance. The effectiveness of which depends upon mutual goals of peace, productivity, and security.

Humanitarian Treaties

International humanitarian law arose from the horrific treatment of wounded soldiers during the battle of Solferino (1859) chronicled by Henry Dunant. The Geneva Convention of 1864 was the first multilateral humanitarian treaty as well as the Convention for the Amelioration of the Condition of the Wounded in Armies in the Field of 1865 and The International Red Cross. Humanitarian laws restricted the type of warfare as well as the proximity of battle to civilian residences, places of worship, hospitals, and other nonstrategic buildings. The Geneva Convention of 1949 provides the legal standards for the treatment of prisoners of war or armed conflict.

The League of Nations of 1919 provided the basis for the United Nations where States could resolve differences through treaties and international cooperation. In 1948, members of the United Nations adopted the Convention on the Prevention and Punishment of the Crime of Genocide. This treaty can be enforced by either an international tribunal or a national court within the State committing the breach (Sands, 2003). The Universal Declaration of Human Rights adopted in 1948 is not a treaty; however, it is an agreement that forms the basis of international human rights law (Weissbrodt, Fitzpatrick, & Newman, 2009). International human rights law recognizes the basic rights of people as set forth in the Universal Declaration. As the world community recognized the need to protect human rights, the need to punish crimes against humanity evolved as well. The U.N. Security Council, charged with maintenance of international peace and security, is instrumental in the fight against crimes against humanity and thus breaches of international criminal law. The Council investigates, issues cease-fire directives, sanctions and can send peacekeeping forces to help reduce tensions in troubled regions (Weissbrodt, Fitzpatrick, & Newman, 2009). The U.N. Security Council can establish international criminal tribunals to adjudicate international crimes following war or armed conflict. Tribunals are ad hoc or temporary with limited jurisdiction, venue, and scope (Paust et al., 2000).

The Rome Treaty

The tribunals created by the U.N. Security Council led to treaty creating the international criminal court. In 1993, the U. N. Security Council established the International Criminal Tribunal for the former Yugoslavia (ICTY) for the Prosecution of Persons Responsible for Serious Violations of International Humanitarian Law Committed in the Territory of the former Yugoslavia and in 1994, the International Criminal Tribunal for Rwanda (ICTR) , for the Prosecution of Persons Responsible for Genocide or Other Serious Violations of International Humanitarian Law Committed in the Territory of Rwanda, and Rwandan Citizens Responsible for Genocide and Other Such Violations Committed in the Territory of Neighboring States, (Weissbrodt, Fitzpatrick, & Newman, 2009). However, these tribunals and others that followed are limited in jurisdiction and scope.

The United Nations Diplomatic Conference of Plenipotentiaries convened in Rome, Italy, from June 15 to July 17, 1998, to finalize a draft statute for the establishment of the International Criminal Court. In 2002, the Rome Treaty established the International Criminal Court. It became the first permanent international criminal court with the jurisdiction to adjudicate crimes of genocide, crimes against humanity, crimes of aggression, and war crimes; its jurisdiction is complementary to national criminal courts. The creation of the International Criminal Court provides the international community, both military and civilian, with a legal standard for moral conduct during war and civil conflict (Weissbrodt, Fitzpatrick, & Newman, 2009). The International Criminal Court is adjudicating criminal allegations from countries around the world. Only States that have ratified the Rome Treaty are bound by the jurisdiction of the International Criminal Court.

SUMMARY AND CONCLUSION

Treaties may be bilateral, as between two States or multilateral, as between several States. These agreements represent one area within the complex system of courts, agreements, customs, principles, and national laws that comprise international law. Suppression treaties may be created to limit the criminal trafficking within or between States. International criminal law covers a myriad of crimes and may be addressed by treaty, national law, or the United Nations. States may enter into bilateral or multilateral treaties covering specific crimes unique to that region. Although controlled by extradition treaty or custom, a State's refusal to extradite, or surrender, an alleged violator of international law is an obstacle to international justice. As the world community recognized the need to protect human rights, the need to punish crimes against humanity evolved, as well. The Rome Treaty established the International Criminal Court. The application and interpretation of the Rome Statute presents the next phase in the development of international criminal law. Treaties of mutual assistance, extradition and the sharing of information between States will assist in the effectiveness of international criminal laws.

REFERENCES

Browne-Marshall, G. (2007). *Race, Law, and American Society: 1607 to Present.* New York: Routledge.

Crawshaw, R., S. Cullen, & T. Williamson. (2007). *Human Rights and Policing, Second Edition.* Leiden, The Netherlands: Martinus Nijhoff.

Deflem, M. and K. Irwin. (2006). Extradition, International. In O. H. Stephens, Jr., J. M. Scheb II, & K. E. Stooksbury (Eds.). *Encyclopedia of American Civil Rights and Liberties.* Westport, CT: Greenwood Press. 352–54.

Dunant, H. (1937). *A Memory of Solferino.* Washington, D.C.: American Red Cross. (Original work published 1864).

Jorgensen, N.H.B. (2000). *The Responsibility of States for International Crimes.* New York: Oxford University Press.

Podgor, E. & Clark, R. (2008) *Understanding International Criminal Law, Second Edition.* Newark: LexisNexis.

Romano, C.P.R., A. Nollkaemper, & J. Kleffner. (2004). *Internationalized Criminal Courts and Tribunals.* New York: Oxford University Press.

Sands, P. (Ed.). (2003). *From Nuremberg to The Hague: The Future of International Criminal Justice.* Cambridge: University of Cambridge Press.

Weissbrodt, D., J. Fitzpatrick, & F. Newman. (2009) *International Human Rights: Law, Policy, and Process.* New York: LexisNexis.

WEB SITE

NTI: http://www.nti.org/index.php (Retrieved February 24, 2010)

United Nations Treaty Collection: http://treaties.un.org/Pages/Home.aspx?lang=en (Retrieved February 25, 2010)

ABOUT THE AUTHOR

Gloria J. Browne-Marshall, JD., M.A., is an associate professor at John Jay College of Criminal Justice and founder and director of The Law and Policy Group, Inc. Professor Browne-Marshall's publications include *Race, Law, and American Society: 1607 to Present* and *The Constitution: Major Cases and Conflicts* as well as several articles and book chapters. She has chaired both the International Human Rights Committee and the Civil Rights Committee of the American Bar Association.

46 International Criminal Tribunals and Hybrid Courts

Gloria J. Browne-Marshall

INTRODUCTION

International criminal tribunals were created for prosecuting individuals responsible for the grossest violations of international humanitarian law embodied in the Universal Declaration of Human Rights, the International Covenant on Civil and Political Rights, the Hague Conventions, Geneva Conventions, the Genocide Convention, and the Convention against Torture and Cruel, Inhuman and Degrading Treatment and Punishment. This chapter examines the continued development of international tribunals from the Nuremberg and Tokyo Trials to Criminal Tribunal for the former Yugoslavia, Criminal Tribunal for Rwanda, and the hybrid courts including East Timor, Sierra Leone Special Court, and the Cambodian Extraordinary Chambers.

THE NUREMBERG TRIBUNAL

More than sixty million persons, primarily civilians, lost their lives during World War II. The German military was accused of the premeditated murder of civilian populations. After the war, leaders of the Allied nations – United States, France, Great Britain, and the USSR – drafted the Nuremberg Charter creating the International Military Tribunal for the "just and prompt trial and punishment of the major war criminals of the European Axis" powers (Ball, 1999). The Chief Prosecutor was Robert H. Jackson, Associate Justice of the United States Supreme Court. The trial was conducted in Nuremberg, Germany.

The Tribunal had jurisdiction or authority to adjudicate crimes against peace, war crimes, and crimes against humanity (Podgor & Clark, 2008).

Jurisdiction is the scope of authority or extent of power over a person, subject area, or thing. Crimes against humanity are massive acts of cruelty and destruction taking place during war or strife, usually against civilians. Acts of genocide were subsumed within crimes against humanity. The defendants were provided counsel, due process rights, and translators. They argued that their actions were not crimes and, alternatively, that they were following the orders of the government; thus, individual soldiers should not be held responsible for war crimes. The Nuremberg Tribunal established *in personam* jurisdiction or jurisdiction over the person leading to the indictment of twenty-four individuals (Best, 2002). Sentences ranged from imprisonment to death by hanging.

The Nuremberg Tribunal remains an important part of international criminal law because it established limits to State sovereignty and established the principle of individual responsibility for barbaric military acts during wartime.

THE TOKYO TRIBUNAL

Japan was accused of brutally murdering civilians, torturing prisoners, and utilizing the bubonic plague against Chinese cities during World War II. Japanese wartime terror campaigns called for soldiers to "kill all, burn all, destroy all." In 1946, the Tokyo Tribunal was created for the "just and prompt trial and punishment of the major war criminal in the Far East" (Best, 2002).

Defendants were represented by counsel, given translators, and provided due process rights. Prime Minister, Tojo Hideki, was indicted. However, the Emperor of Japan, Hirohito, was not charged with any crimes. Arguments of nonresponsibility similar to those of the Nuremberg defendants were defeated in similar fashion. Upon convictions, sentences ranged from imprisonment to execution. Although verdicts of the Nuremberg and Tokyo Tribunals were condemned by some as "victor's justice" the creation of these historic tribunals drew attention to the need for a permanent court to address crimes of massive brutality taking place during times of war and peace.

In 1948, the United Nations adopted the Convention on the Prevention and Punishment of the Crime of Genocide. The Charter of the United Nations gives the UN Security Council the power and responsibility to take collective action to maintain international peace and security when a war torn national's infrastructure and court system makes it unable to provide proper adjudication of accused war criminals.

AD HOC INTERNATIONAL CRIMINAL TRIBUNALS AND COURTS

International Criminal Tribunal for the Former Yugoslavia (ICTY)

Yugoslavia was a federation (Croatia, Bosnia, and Herzegovina) comprised of different ethnic and religious groups, generally, Croats, Serbs, and Muslims. In 1991, systemic acts of government-led violence by Serbs against Muslims and Croats led to the deaths of hundreds of thousands of persons and the displacement of millions. Civil war ensued with vicious exchanges of violence. An investigation revealed violations of the Geneva Convention and humanitarian laws with allegations of mass graves, concentration camps, torture, rape, and genocide.

In 1993, the UN Security Council established the International Criminal Tribunal for the former Yugoslavia (ICTY) in response to Serious Violations of International Humanitarian Law Committed in the Territory of the former Yugoslavia) since 1991. This is the first international war crimes tribunal since the Nuremberg and Tokyo Tribunals. Located in The Hague, the Netherlands, the ICTY is financed with contributions from the UN and UN Member States. It is expected to complete all cases including appeals by 2010.

The ICTY is significant because it recognizes rape as a war crime and a crime of genocide. Military as well as governmental leaders can be found individually liable for war crimes committed against civilian populations. ICTY established enslavement as a crime against humanity. Working with domestic courts of the region, defendants are provided counsel and due process while thousands of victims have been provided the opportunity to testify. The death penalty is prohibited. International humanitarian law and international criminal have been expanded by the work of the ICTY (Schaba, 2006).

International Criminal Tribunal for Rwanda (ICTR)

Long-simmering animosities between Rwanda's majority Hutu and minority Tutsi rose to the surface in 1994. Between April and July, more than 800,000 Tutsis were murdered by Hutu civilians and military personnel. The Hutu led government is accused of inciting Hutu civilians to rape, torture, murder, and utilize biological warfare in the form of HIV patients against Tutsi civilians. In 1994, the Security Council of the United Nations established the International Criminal Tribunal for Rwanda (ICTR).

Located in Arusha, Tanzania, the ICTR is an ad hoc tribunal for the Prosecution of Persons Responsible for Genocide or Other Serious Violations of International Humanitarian Law Committed in the Territory of Rwanda and Rwandan Citizens Responsible for Genocide and Other Such Violations Committed in the Territory of Neighboring States, Between 1 January 1994 and 31 December 1994. Unlike the ICTY, the Rwandan Tribunal violations are not war-related. Significantly, the ICTR has the authority to prosecute and adjudicate charges of genocide, crimes against humanity, and breaches of Common Article 3 of the Geneva Conventions. This tribunal became operational in 1996. Unlike the ICTY, a defendant may receive a prison term or a capital sentence. The ICTR recognizes rape as both a war crime and as genocide.

The ICTR is based largely on the ICTY sharing Appeals Chamber and the Chief Prosecutor with the ICTY. Unlike the ICTY, tens of thousands of civilians committed brutal acts led by members of the military. Those military defendants are tried separately. Civilians may be tried in tribunals by an appointed panel of respected members of the community or prosecuted in official courtrooms. The ICTR is financed through the UN General Assembly, which requests voluntary contributions from member UN States in the form of financial support, services and supplies. In sum, despite obstacles, the ICTR plays a very important role in the evolution of international criminal law in that it established international standards of conduct for the military as well as civilians who commit such crimes during civil unrest.

HYBRID COURTS

The Hybrid Courts are significant in that there is shared jurisdiction, funding, and staff with the United Nations and the domestic courts of the State wherein the criminal acts occurred. The Hybrid Courts allow the State to have more input in the development of cases and the outcome. However, these courts have also come under criticism due to the influence States have over the legal process, selection of witnesses, pursuit of defendants, and the application of law. A hybrid of international law and domestic law is applied in these cases.

East Timor Special Panels

In 2000, the United Nations Security Council established the UN Transitional Authority for East Timor (UNTAET) to adjudicate crimes against humanity in the form of murder, rape, property loss, and displacement following election results in East Timor in 1999. UNTAET has jurisdiction over genocide, war crimes, crimes against humanity, murder, rape, and torture committed in East Timor between January 1 and October 25, 1999. Primarily, low-level military personnel have been prosecuted (Cohen, 2002). The obstacles to justice in East Timor are underfunded court system, lack of cooperation by the government, well-funded defense, and lack of witness protection. Indonesia's lack of cooperation plays a key role in the events of East Timor. High-level officials and witnesses with important evidence concerning the crimes are located in Indonesian. Their refusal to testify continues to undermine justice in East Timor.

The Special Court for Sierra Leone

In 1991, an attempted coup supported by paramilitary forces from Liberia led to attacks on civilians and soldiers who supported the standing government in Sierra Leone. Crimes of murder, torture, mutilation, and burned villages were committed against tens of thousands of civilians during this civil war. In 2002, the United Nations assisted in the creation of the Special Court for Sierra Leone to adjudicate crimes against humanity taking place in Sierra Leone from 1996. Significantly, in addition to violations against humanity, violations under Common Article 3 of the Geneva Conventions and Additional Protocol II, the Special Court for Sierra Leone will adjudicate crimes against peacekeepers, the crime of recruitment of child as soldiers as well as violations of local Sierra Leone laws (Sands, 2003). Rape does not fall within its jurisdiction. A defendant may receive a prison sentence or the death penalty for participating in crimes against humanity for reasons of political expediency and revenge allegedly fomented by former President Charles Taylor. Financed through voluntary contributions raised by a Management Committee of the United Nations, obstacles include a lack of infrastructure, resources, and trained personnel. Despite these obstacles, Charles Taylor is in custody and awaiting trial by the Special Court for Sierra Leone.

Extraordinary Chambers in the Courts of Cambodia

During the final battles of the Vietnam War, the Khmer Rouge, a political and military movement rose to power in Cambodia. Led by Pol Pot, the Khmer Rouge executed elites, intellectuals, and certain ethnic groups using murder, scientific experimentation, forced labor, and torture. Between 1975 and 1978, more than one million lives were lost and millions were displaced. Evidence of these crimes against humanity was received as early as 1979. Decades passed. Given the lapse of time, there was uncertainty as to whether the Khmer Rouge would ever be brought to justice. Pol Pot was finally tried by a national court and condemned to death. Pol Pot was sentenced to life in prison after a subsequent trial that was viewed by many as procedurally flawed, thus renewing efforts for an international tribunal (Romano, Nollkaemper, & Kleffner, 2004).

In 2003, after years of negotiation, the United Nations and Cambodia signed an agreement establishing the Extraordinary Chambers in the Courts of Cambodia for Prosecution of Crimes Committed during the Period of Democratic Kampuchea. The Extraordinary Chambers is a national tribunal financed by pledges from UN Members States placed in a Trust Fund. Due process is based on the Cambodian system, which has a death penalty. In 2009, the Extraordinary Chambers with Cambodian and U.N. justices began trials of senior personal accused of genocide. The effectiveness of this tribunal largely depends on the abilities of the Cambodian jurists, prosecutors, and investigators, as well as the cooperation of the Cambodian government. Cambodia's policy of reconciliation with former members of the Khmer Rouge, may undermine the necessary governmental cooperation required to fully adjudicate high level officials and others who participated in war crimes against civilians.

Special Tribunal for Lebanon

A special tribunal has been established by the United Nations for Lebanon. It is the Special Tribunal for Lebanon to prosecute person responsible for the attack of February 14, 2005 resulting in the death of former Lebanese Prime Minister Rafiz Hariri and in the death or injury of twenty-two other persons. Although the Tribunal is located in the Netherlands, members of the Special Tribunal seek to create a dialogue and high level of cooperation with Lebanese civil society as trial preparation proceeds.

SUMMARY AND CONCLUSION

The Nuremberg Tribunal was created in 1945 to address premeditated crimes against civilian populations by the German military during World War II. Created in 1946, the Tokyo Tribunal adjudicated war crimes and crimes against humanity committed by Japanese soldiers during World War II. In 1993, the UN Security Council formed ICTY to adjudicate crimes against humanity within the Former Yugoslavia in the 1990s. In 1994, the Security Council created the ICTR to adjudicate crimes by the Rwandan

government and Hutu civilians against Tutsi civilians. The hybrid courts
of Cambodia, East Timor, Sierra Leone, and Lebanon provide States with
shared jurisdiction resulting in possible political influence and delays.

Each international criminal tribunal, or special court, plays a significant
role in the evolution of international criminal law. From a tribunal following international warfare for military personnel accused of crimes against
civilians to hybrid courts using both domestic and international law established to adjudicate cases involving military, governmental, and civilians
accused of an expanding range of crimes committed during wartime and
civil unrest, victims are gaining justice.

REFERENCES

Best, G. (2002). *War and Law: Since 1945.* New York: Oxford University Press.
Cohen, D. (2002). *Seeking Justice on the Cheap: Is the East Timor Tribunal Really a Model for the Future?* Asia-Pacific Issues No. 61. Honolulu: East-West Center.
Podgor, E. & R. Clark (2008) *Understanding International Criminal Law.* Second Edition. Newark: LexisNexis.
Romano, C. P. R., A. Nollkaemper, & J. Kleffner. (2004). *Internationalized Criminal Courts and Tribunals.* New York: Oxford University Press.
Sands, P. (Ed.). (2003) *From Nuremberg to The Hague: The Future of International Criminal Justice,* Cambridge: University of Cambridge Press.
Schaba, W.A. (2006) The UN International Criminal Tribunals: The Former Yugoslavia, Rwanda and Sierra Leone Cambrige: Cambridge University Press.

WEB SITES

International Criminal Tribunal for former Yugoslavia: www.icty.org
International Criminal Tribunal for Rwanda: www.ictr.org
www.sc-sl.org
East Timor Hybrid Court: www.eastwestcenter.org/stored/pdfs/api061.pdf
Special Tribunal for Lebanon: www.stl-tsl.org/action/home

ABOUT THE AUTHOR

Gloria J. Browne-Marshall, J.D., M.A., is an associate professor at John Jay College of Criminal Justice and founder and director of The Law and Policy Group, Inc. Professor Browne-Marshall's publications include *Race, Law, and American Society: 1607 to Present* and *The Constitution: Major Cases and Conflicts* as well as several articles and book chapters. She has chaired both the International Human Rights Committee and the Civil Rights Committee of the American Bar Association.

47 The International Criminal Court

Mangai Natarajan and Antigona Kukaj

"In the prospect of an international criminal court lies the promise of universal justice."

– Kofi Annan, United Nations Secretary-General

For many years, the United Nations held a series of meetings to establish an independent and permanent structure – the International Criminal Court (ICC) – to deal with the gravest international crimes and gross violations of international humanitarian law. This dream became a reality in July, 17, 1998, when the Rome Statute was agreed upon by 120 nations. Some four years later, on July 1, 2002, the ICC was established and of 2010, 111 have ratified the Rome Statue. ICC is thus a product of a multilateral treaty whereas the ad hoc International Criminal Tribunal of Yugoslavia (ICTY) and the International Criminal Tribunal of Rwanda (ICTR) were created by decision of the Security Council.

The ICC, a permanent entity situated in The Hague, Netherlands, offers a new paradigm of accountability, equality and justice in dealing with the most serious crimes of concern to the international community. This chapter provides a brief account of its structure and functioning, of its ongoing investigations and trials, as well as the challenges inherent in executing the mission of Rome Statue.

THE ROME STATUTE IS THE ICC

The Rome Statute is a unique legal apparatus that takes in to account of both the adversarial and inquisitorial models of criminal procedure in seeking to provide protection for all global citizens (Kress, 2003). It directs and governs the ICC which has jurisdiction over the following: international crimes, genocide (art. 6), crimes against humanity (art. 7) and war crimes

357

(art. 8). It was also intended to cover the crime of aggression (art. 5), but this has not yet been brought into effect due to the lack of consensus about its definition. A review conference in 2010 will discuss and further clarify the crime of aggression (for details see chapter on Crimes of Aggression).

Under the Rome Statute, the ICC can act only when a country is "unwilling" to or "unable" to take up the case. In essence, domestic and national courts have supremacy over the jurisdiction of cases before they are referred to the ICC. This complementary nature of the Statute is a symbol of a symbiotic relationship between national and international judiciaries in dealing with the gravest crimes of the world order.

Since there is no international police force or enforcement mechanism to apprehend war criminals, states must cooperate with the court in the investigation, arrest, and transfer of suspects. The maximum term of imprisonment is thirty years, but if the crime is of extreme gravity then life imprisonment can be imposed. In addition to imprisonment fines can also be imposed. The prisoner serves the sentence at a volunteering State party or otherwise in the Netherlands. ICC has its detention center located in Scheveningen, a suburb of The Hague.

The ICC has jurisdiction over crimes committed only after July 1, 2002; in other words, the Court can only address crimes committed after the entry into force of the Statute and the establishment of the court.

STRUCTURE OF THE ICC

The ICC is comprised of four main parts: presidency, judiciary, office of the prosecutor, and registry.

The presidency manages all administrative concerns of the court, with the exception of the prosecutor's office. It makes decisions regarding the full-time status of the judges (Sadat, 2002).

The judiciary consists of pretrial, trial, and appeals divisions made up of eighteen judges.

The pretrial division is a unique element of the Court in that it maintains oversight over the activities of the prosecutor. As expressed in the Rome Statute, the trial chamber must adopt all the necessary procedures to ensure that a trial is fair and expeditious, while fully respecting the rights of the accused with consideration for the protection of victims and witnesses. The Appeals chamber may decide to reverse or amend a decision, judgment, or sentence and may also order a new trial.

The office of the prosecutor (OTP) "acts independently as a separate organ of the court" (art. 42(1)) and is responsible for receiving and investigating referrals made to the ICC. In June 2003, Mr. Luis Moreno-Ocampo of Argentina was appointed as the first Prosecutor of the court. As per Article 53 (initiation of an investigation), the prosecutor shall initiate an investigation unless he or she determines that there is no reasonable basis to proceed under this Statute.

The registry handles nonjudicial matters, such as maintaining the ICC's records and serving as a depository of notifications and providing channel for communication with states. The registry is also responsible for the development and operation of the Victims and Witness Unit, as well as for supervising and facilitating the assignment of a defense counsel. The Registry is headed by the Registrar, who is the principal administrative officer of the court.

As of January 2009, 285 women and 302 men work for the ICC from more than eighty-five states.

FUNCTIONING OF THE ICC

The referral of a case to the prosecutor of the ICC may occur under the following circumstances:

1. A state that has ratified the Rome Statute can refer the case if crimes within the jurisdiction of the court appear to have been committed.
2. The UN Security Council can refer the case by acting under Chapter VII of the UN Charter. Under these circumstances, no state consent is required.
3. The prosecutor can initiate investigations *proprio motu* on his or her own behalf.

Except where the Security Council makes the reference, the "preconditions" to the court's jurisdiction require that the accused must be a national of a state party or that the alleged crime was committed on the territory of a state party. A country may also voluntarily accept the ICC's jurisdiction over a crime by formal agreement.

In order for ICC to function effectively two things must be in place: the necessary finance to pursue the case and the cooperation of affected nations. Article 116 stipulates that the ICC is permitted to receive and make use of any voluntary contributions from governments, international organizations, individuals, corporations, and other entities. It also requires that member states to the Assembly of State Parties (ASP), the body responsible for adopting the Financial Regulations and Rules must match their political commitment with the financial resources necessary for the operation of the Court.

The estimated ICC budget for 2010 is a total of €102.98 million ($147.52 million) which is just a fraction of the proposed US Judiciary budget of $7.04 billion for 2010 – itself only a small fraction of the total US criminal justice budget which is probably close to $200 billion.

ICC CASE PROCESSING

To proceed with an investigation, the OTP must establish (1) jurisdiction; (2) admissibility (including complementarity and gravity); and (3) the interests of justice. In the course of its investigation and prosecution, the OTP must protect the rights and interests of victims and the rights of the accused, including investigation of exonerating circumstances. The prosecutor targets the main leaders and the main criminals (Wouters, Verhoeven, & Demeyere, 2008). See Box 1 for steps in case processing.

Since July 2002, the prosecutor's office has received more than 8,000 communications from more than 132 countries, most of which come from individuals in the United States of America, the United Kingdom, Germany, Russia, and France. To date, three state parties to the Rome Statute – Uganda, the Democratic Republic of the Congo, and the Central African Republic – have referred situations occurring in their territories to the Court. In addition, the Security Council has referred the situation in Darfur, Sudan – a nonstate party. The following cases are being heard by the pretrial and trial chambers:

- Thomas Lubanga and Bosco Ntaganda (Democratic Republic of Congo) for recruiting child soldiers and transforming them into killers.
- Joseph Kony and other leaders of the LRA (Uganda) for killing entire communities, raping and abducting children, and transforming them into sexual slaves and killers, and Germain Katanga and Matthew Ngudjolo for killing and raping civilians.
- Jean-Pierre Bemba (Central African Republic), for a massive campaign of rape and pillage.
- Ahmed Harun and Ali Kushayb (Darfur, SUDAN) for widespread killings, rapes, and torture of civilians. The Court has also requested an arrest warrant for Omar Al Bashir for genocide, crimes against humanity and war crimes.

At the time of writing, six other situations on four continents were under preliminary analysis by the Office of the Prosecutor, including those in Afghanistan, Colombia, Côte d'Ivoire, Georgia, Kenya (for crimes

---

Box 1. Steps in ICC case processing

INVESTIGATION *(PROSECUTION)*

- Preliminary analysis of the situation; Investigation of situation; Collating evidence for seeking arrest warrant for cases

PRETRIAL *(PRETRIAL CHAMBER)*

- Evaluation of evidence for executing the arrest warrant
- Authorization to bring the named individuals before the court
- First appearance of suspects before the Pretrial chamber for public hearing
- Confirmation of charges and detention

ADJUDICATION *(TRIAL CHAMBER)*

- Trial begins
- Determination of the innocence or guilt of the accused
- Sentencing - imprisonment and or fine; monetary compensation, restitution or rehabilitation for victims

POSTTRIAL *(APPEALS DIVISION)*

- Appeal by prosecutor or convicted persons
- Revision of sentences
- Review of sentence after the person has served two thirds of the sentence

---

allegedly committed in relation to the postelection violence of 2007–8), and Palestine. Two further cases on Iraq and Venezuela were dismissed (Jacobs & Arajärvi, 2008).

SPECIAL FEATURES OF THE ICC

Deterrence

In principle, the ICC has enormous power to deter the gravest crimes against world peace, law, and order. It is too early yet to determine whether the ICC serves that deterrent function, but this should be a research priority when it has been in existence for a sufficient period of time.

Victim Rights and Support

According to the Rome Statute, victims can intervene before the pretrial chamber when the prosecutor is seeking authorization to proceed with an investigation. Victims can also intervene at the trial stage and may be represented by counsel in the presentation of their views and concerns. This confirms that the ICC Statute and Rules of Procedure and Evidence offer important protections for victims and witnesses, particularly those who suffered sexual or gender violence. This provides avenues for scholars of victimology to undertake empirical and policy research concerning the Rome Statute and victim concerns.

Checks and Balances

The prosecutor must seek authorization from the pretrial chamber to initiate an investigation. If the prosecutor is not given this authorization, the appeals division can overrule the pretrial chamber in order to allow the prosecutor to proceed. The interaction of these chambers exemplifies the court's system of checks and balances where the pretrial division has oversight over the prosecutor, and the decisions of the pretrial and trial chambers are subject to checks by the appeals division.

Gender Sensitive Justice

The ICC statute governs a number of sexual violence crimes unprecedented in international criminal law. For the first time, rape, sexual slavery, enforced prostitution, forced pregnancy, enforced sterilization, or any other form of sexual violence are explicitly incorporated as both crimes against humanity and war crimes. Sexual violence crimes can also be prosecuted under the crime against humanity of persecution based on gender (Pillay, 2008).

Role of Nongovernmental Organizations (NGOs)

The ICC is supported by the Coalition for the International Criminal Court, comprised of 2500 NGOs from 150 countries. These serve (1) to ensure that the ICC is fair, effective, and independent; (2) to make justice both visible and universal; and (3) to advance stronger national laws that deliver justice to victims of international crimes.

Opportunity for Jobs, Internships, and Visiting Professionals

The ICC seeks to raise awareness about the role of the Court through internships, employment opportunities, and visiting programmes. These provide avenues for many young people and scholars to contribute to research and to develop professional careers in dealing with international crimes.

CHALLENGES

One of the major political challenges is that the United States, China, and India, all major powers, are not parties to the ICC, although the United Kingdom, France, Germany, and Japan are. The United States played a leading role in the establishment of the Rome Statute, but it strongly opposes the ICC on grounds that it will be used as a tool for politically motivated trials against America (Bradley, 2002). The lack of endorsement by the United States and other major powers has important repercussions on the substantive law that dictates the procedures of ICC.

The lack of international police and prisons poses a major problem for the ICC because it has to depend on volunteering state parties to supply the criminal justice services in executing the arrest warrants and imprisoning the prisoners. The need to negotiate these services contributes significantly to delays.

There is a danger that the state parties that provide a disproportionate amount of funding for the ICC might expect to have a commensurate influence in its proceedings.

While the ICC makes strenuous and real efforts to involve victims in the proceedings and to provide them with assistance in terms of counseling and financial help, it is impossible for ICC to recover their lives and heal their wounds. Ways must be found of retaining and strengthening the focus on victims without leading them to expect unrealistic outcomes.

More needs to be done to educate state parties and the public about the unavoidable reasons for the lengthy investigations and trial processes so as to forestall criticism of the court.

The fact that all of the cases so far under trial relate to countries in Africa might suggest that ICC is only able to intervene in cases where governments are weak or disorganized.

SUMMARY AND CONCLUSIONS

Despite the many obstacles confronting the ICC, its establishment represents the dawning of a new era in international criminal justice. Its key purpose is to ensure that war criminals are subject to individual criminal liability in cases of serious human rights violations. As one of the first permanent international institutions to challenge threats to international order, the ICC is intended to contribute to the prevention and deterrence of the Rome Statute's core crimes. As stated by Clark (2005), what is important is "getting the best possible judges and Prosecutor and making proper provision for the defense; legislative implementation at the national level; fostering a culture of boldness on the part of States Parties and civil society in bringing well-documented situations to the attention of the Prosecutor; making operational the Statute's many provisions dealing with victims; responding to the chilling effect of the United States' efforts, in the Security Council and through a complicated series of bilateral negotiations, to chip away at the edges of the Statutory regime; and finally, the unfinished business of Rome and the Preparatory Commission, the crime of aggression."

REFERENCES

Bradley, C. A. (2002, May). *U.S. Announces Intent Not to Ratify International Criminal Court Treaty.* The American Society of International Law *Insights.* Retrieved from www.asil.org/insights/insigh87.htm

Chung, C. H. (2008). Victims' Participation at the International Criminal Court: Are Concessions of the Court Clouding the Promise? *Journal of International Human Rights,* 6(3), 459–545.

Clark, R. (2005). Challenges Confronting the Assembly of States Parties of the International Criminal Court. In E. Vetere. & David P. (Eds.), *Victims of Crime and Abuse of Power: Festschrift in Honour of Irene Melup* 141. Bangkok: 11th UN Congress on Crime Prevention and Criminal Justice.

Jacobs, D. & N. Arajärvi. (2008). The International Criminal Court. *The Law and Practice of International Courts and Tribunals,*7 (1),115–60.

Pillay, N. (2008). *Gender Justice at the ICC.* Plenary Speech at the John Jays' Eighth International Conference, Puerto Rico.

Sadat, L. (2002). *The International Criminal Court And The Transformation of International Law: Justice For The New Millennium.* New York: Transnational Publishers, Inc.

Schabas, A. W. (2007). *An Introduction to the International Criminal Court.* Cambridge University Press.

Shah, A (2005). United States and the International Criminal Court. *Global Issue.* Retrieved on 04 Jan. 2010, from http://www.globalissues.org/article/490/united-states-and-the-icc

Wouters, J., S. Verhoeven, and B. Demeyere, (2008). The International Criminal Court's Office of the Prosecutor: Navigating Between Independence and Accountability?, *International Criminal Law Review,* 8(1/2), 273–317.

WEB SITES

International Criminal Court
www.icc-cpi.int/iccdocs/asp_docs/ASP8/OR/OR-ASP8-Vol.II-ENG-Part.A.pdf
ICC Preparatory commission work:
www.un.org/law/icc/prepcomm/prepfra.htm or at www.jus.unitn.it/icct82/home.
    html
Coalition for the ICC: www.iccnow.org

ABOUT THE AUTHORS

Mangai Natarajan Ph.D. is a professor at John Jay College of Criminal Justice and the founding director of the International Criminal Justice Major. She played a leading role in designing and implementing the ICJ Major in which she teaches the following courses: Introduction to International Criminal Justice, Capstone Seminar in International Criminal Justice, and International Criminology. In April 2009, she visited the International Criminal Court at The Hague, for her research on the ICC.

Antigona Kukaj, an ICJ graduate of John Jay College, holds a M.A. degree in Human Rights Studies (with a concentration in genocide studies and transitional justice) from the Columbia University Graduate School of Arts & Sciences. She has participated in many United Nations activities relating to the International Criminal Court and the work of international courts and tribunals. She is currently is pursuing her legal studies at the Mississippi College School of Law.

48 The ICC and the Darfur Investigation

PROGRESS AND CHALLENGES[1]

Xabier Agirre Aranburu and Roberta Belli

INTRODUCTION

The investigation in the Darfur region of Sudan, where one of the worst humanitarian crises in the world is still unfolding, has been especially challenging for the newly founded International Criminal Court. The Prosecutor of the ICC has succeeded in completing the investigation of three cases against senior leaders in Darfur, in spite of the huge and complex nature of the crimes, lack of cooperation, security threats, and open armed conflict. This chapter will provide a brief introduction on the Darfur investigation with a timeline of legal precedents, and focus on the cases brought before the ICC judges, the methods and evidence utilized for this investigation, and the issues that still need be resolved to ensure prospects of justice for the victims of Darfur.

BACKGROUND

In February 2003, fighting erupted between Sudanese military troops and Darfur rebels, who were accusing the government of purposefully marginalizing the western region of Darfur from the economic and political agenda, and of discriminating against the local tribes of the Fur, Zaghawa, and Masalit. The government responded with a brutal counterinsurgency campaign (assisted by the *Janjaweeds*, militias from Arab tribes) that quickly escalated to widespread and indiscriminate violence. A large part of the civilian population fled to eastern Chad, and hundreds of thousands of civilians were internally displaced within Sudan (Prunier, 2005).

---

[1] The views contained in this chapters are those of the authors and do not represent necessarily the views of the Office of the Prosecutor of the International Criminal Court.

In July 2004, the U.S. State Department, in cooperation with the U.S. Agency for International Development's Office of Transitional Initiatives (USAID OTI) and the Coalition for International Justice (CIJ), established the "Darfur Atrocities Documentation Team" (ADT), a multinational team of investigators who traveled along the Chad/Sudanese border to interview refugees and collect data on the magnitude of the crisis. Based on the results of this survey, on September 9, 2004, U.S. Secretary of State Colin Powell declared that the violence perpetrated in Darfur amounted to genocide. This was the first time in history that a sovereign nation accused another one of genocide during an ongoing conflict (Totten and Markusen, 2006).

The U.S. government referred the matter to the UN Security Council, who passed Resolution 1564 on September 18, 2004, establishing a "Commission of Inquiry," composed of five prominent international justice and human rights experts, to investigate the genocide allegations. In January 2005, the UN Commission of Inquiry released its final report concluding that several violations of international humanitarian law had been committed in Darfur, including crimes against humanity and war crimes. The Commission of Inquiry additionally recommended that the situation be referred to the International Criminal Court for a proper criminal investigation.

On March 31, 2005, the UN Security Council passed Resolution 1593, which referred the situation in Darfur to the ICC, with eleven votes in favor of the Resolution and four abstentions (the United States, Algeria, Brazil, and China). The ICC Office of the Prosecutor (OTP) received several thousands of evidence items collected by the Commission and other organizations, including statements from victims and experts, pictures, videos, documents, maps, and forensic reports. On June 6, 2005, the Chief Prosecutor Luis Moreno-Ocampo publicly announced his decision to start an official investigation into the atrocities committed in Darfur after determining there was sufficient evidence to proceed.

CASES UNDER INVESTIGATION

Between 2005 and 2008, the ICC-OTP completed the investigation of three cases comprising six individuals who were identified as bearing the greatest responsibility for crimes committed in Darfur.

On February 27, 2007, the Prosecutor filed an Application for a Warrant of Arrest (AWA) against Ahmed Harun and Ali Kushayb for war crimes and crimes against humanity committed mainly in West Darfur. The corresponding Warrants of Arrests were issued by the Pre-Trial Chamber I on May 2, 2007. The evidence gathered by the Prosecutor showed that the Sudanese government launched a counterinsurgency campaign starting in 2003 against the areas of activity of the Darfur rebel groups. While counterinsurgency warfare as such is not a crime under international law, the Sudanese forces conducted their campaign in full disregard of the principle of distinction (the duty under International Humanitarian Law to distinguish between civilians and military), and systematically destroyed hundreds of villages throughout the three states of Darfur (North, South, and West Darfur), with the result of tens of thousands of civilians killed, raped and tortured, and hundreds of thousands forcibly expelled. Unable to target the elusive guerrilla units, the government decided to punish and destroy the civilian fabric from which the rebels were gathering their recruits and supplies. The military operations were planned from the top level of the government in Khartoum and they were carried out jointly by the military, air force, police, intelligence, and the local *Janjaweed* militias.

Multiple documents and witnesses identified Ahmed Harun, a devoted member of the ruling National Congress Party, as the senior officer in the Ministry of Interior who was in charge of financing, mobilizing and coordinating operations with the *Janjaweed*. In 2003–4, at the height of the military campaign, Harun traveled in numerous occasions from Khartoum to Darfur to transmit instructions and to deliver money and weapons to the militias that carried out the most murderous attacks. This kind of senior civilian bureaucrat is typically used by the top level of authority to develop a shorter and more secretive chain of command that may be more suitable than the conventional army for clandestine criminal operations. His profile resembles that of Jovica Stanisic, the senior civilian officer that worked directly for Milosevic in mobilizing Serbian paramilitary groups to carry out massive ethnic cleansing in former Yugoslavia in the 1990s. Ali Kushayb was identified as the militia leader that acted as field commander in a series of deadly attacks on villages in West Darfur in 2002–03.

The second case was a progression from the first one, focusing on the same scenario of violence but covering the whole geographical scope, a longer period up to 2008, charges of genocide in addition to war crimes, and crimes against humanity and the highest authority of the President of the Republic Omar Hassan Ahmad Al Bashir. The Prosecutor filed the AWA against Bashir on July 14, 2008, and Pre-Trial Chamber I issued the corresponding Warrant of Arrest on March 4, 2009. The evidence gathered by the Prosecutor showed that, because the Republic of Sudan is a presidential system, President Bashir directed all branches of the State that were involved in the criminal campaign against the civilians of Darfur. The Statute of the

ICC establishes that "official capacity as a Head of State or Government [...] shall in no case exempt a person from criminal responsibility under this Statute" (Article 27.1). Bashir joined the list of heads of State prosecuted for crimes under international law, alongside Pinochet (Chile), Habre (Chad), Milosevic (Serbia), Mengistu (Ethiopia), and Taylor (Liberia) .

The third case deals with an attack and destruction by a rebel group against an African Union peacekeeping base in Haskanita in September 2007, in which twelve peacekeepers were killed. The Prosecutor considered the attack particularly grave because of the broader impact on the civilian population that benefited from the protection of the peacekeepers, and filed charges of war crimes against three rebel commanders. Further to the Prosecutor's application, on May 7, 2009, Pre-Trial Chamber I issued a Summons to Appear for Bahr Idriss Abu Garda, the leader of the United Resistance Front and former commander of the Justice and Equality Movement.

THE ICC INVESTIGATIVE STRATEGY

According to the Rome Statute, the ICC Warrants of Arrest or Summons to Appear are based on the evidence collected by the Office of the Prosecutor and reviewed independently by the judges of the Pre-Trial Chamber. Investigating Darfur was particularly challenging because of the ongoing armed conflict in the areas of the crime and the lack of access to the scene of the crime (unlike the precedents of international investigations in Yugoslavia or Rwanda).

The Prosecutor overcame these difficulties with a creative investigative strategy that included the following: (1) recruiting investigators and analysts with field experience in Darfur; (2) interviewing victims in third countries that had received them as refugees around the world; (3) interviewing qualified international observers who gained an overview of the violence and interacted with key leaders; (4) conducting systematic open-source searches, including video records and public statements by the suspects; (5) using satellite imagery and remote sensing data; (6) analyzing military and other official documents provided by the Sudanese government and the African Union; and (7) using the evidence collected by the UN Commission of Inquiry.

From an early stage of the investigation, the OTP Analysis Unit developed a crime database to integrate multiple sources of evidence and analyze the patterns of violence, including their geographical and chronological distribution (e.g., to find "hot spots" and "peaks" of crime), statistics and correlations with key actions of the suspects and their military forces. The results of the investigative strategy persuaded the judges, who confirmed charges against all of the six leading individuals requested by the Prosecutor, as well as the UN Security Council, which has received progress reports from the Prosecutor every six months since the opening of the investigation as part of the referral procedure.

PROCEDURAL AND INVESTIGATIVE ISSUES

The Darfur investigations have been innovative for international criminal justice in a number of ways. For example, in the case against Abu Garda, the ICC judges issued for the first time a Summons to Appear, under article 58 of the ICC Statute, instead of a Warrant of Arrest. Upon suggestion from the Prosecutor, the judges found that the arrest of Abu Garda was not necessary because he had cooperated with the Court and committed himself to appear before the judges. The required conditions were not met by the other two commanders indicted together with Abu Garda, and therefore Warrants of Arrest were issued against them. Mr. Abu Garda honored his commitment and had his first appearance before the ICC judges on May 18, 2009. His collaboration stands in sharp contrast with the others accused in Darfur and it should serve as an example to promote further cooperation by individuals subject to international investigations.

Whether genocide was committed in Darfur has been the subject of controversy. In the first Darfur case, the evidence collected by the Prosecutor sufficed to obtain Warrants of Arrest for multiple war crimes and crimes against humanity, including murder, rape and expulsions at a massive scale. In the second case, against President Bashir, the AWA included additional charges of genocide because a holistic understanding of the case, and in its full geographical extent and chronological duration, convinced the Prosecutor that such massive mortality and destruction must have followed from the specific intent of Bashir to destroy the ethnic groups perceived as harboring the rebellion. The judges confirmed unanimously the charge of extermination as a crime against humanity (Article 7-1-b of the Rome Statute), which is an extraordinarily grave charge, but they were divided in their assessment of the genocide allegations because of the very strict requirements to establish the mental element for this crime under the ICC Statute. The issue rests currently before the Appeals Chamber (as of October 2009).

Quantitative estimates about mortality in armed conflicts are often controversial because of problems of data quality and sampling over areas and periods with sharp pattern variations. Since 2005, social scientists and activists have engaged in a controversy about the figures of mortality in Darfur, with estimates ranging from some 10,000 (as alleged by the government of Sudan) up to 400,000 (as reported by some NGOs; see also Hagan and Rymond-Richmond, 2009). Such wide-ranging discrepancies have even led the U.S. Government Accountability Office (GAO) to take the unusual step of conducting an expert review of the statistical estimates produced by different agencies. The ICC Prosecutor avoided this controversy, focusing on the consensus among all reliable sources about the massive scale of the violence and quoting conservative estimates of 30,000 direct killings, a larger number of deaths caused by the hardship of the expulsions and destruction, and up to two million civilians forcibly displaced.

Finally, the ICC Statute does not allow trials *in absentia*, so that the development of actual prosecutions depends on the arrest of the accused (with the exception of the Abu Garda case). The ICC does not have the resources to carry out the arrests, which must be trusted to the cooperation of national and international authorities. Additionally, the Sudanese government has so far refused to cooperate with the Court. Despite these problems, the ICC Prosecutor continues monitoring the activities of the accused and is actively engaged in seeking the necessary cooperation so that international fugitives are brought to justice. Interpol is contributing to the enforcement of the ICC arrest warrants, and the international cooperation has so far led to the arrest of four ICC accused from other situations and their transfer to the Detention Unit in Scheveningen (The Hague, the Netherlands), where they should be soon joined by those responsible for the crimes in Darfur.

CONCLUSION

The mission of the ICC to put an end to impunity for the perpetrators of the gravest crimes of concern to the international community is as paramount and crucial as it is hard to achieve. The Darfur investigation provides an example of the many problems and obstacles an international prosecutor must deal with compared to a national prosecutor. Despite the many challenges, however, significant steps have been made, and the international justice system can greatly benefit from the efforts of the ICC investigators.

REFERENCES

Flint, J. & A. De Waal (2008). *Darfur: A New History of a Long War.* London: Zed Books.

Grzb, A. (Ed.) (2009). *The World and Darfur: International Response to Crimes Against Humanity in Western Sudan.* Montreal: McGill-Queen's University Press.

Hagan, J. & W. Rymond-Richmond. (2009). *Darfur and the Crime of Genocide*. New York: Cambridge University Press.

International Criminal Court, Pre-Trial Chamber I (April 27, 2007). Warrants of Arrest for Ahmad Muhammad Harun ("Ahmad Harun"). Retrieved October 25, 2009, from ICC Situations and Cases: www2.icc-cpi.int/iccdocs/doc/doc279813.PDF

International Criminal Court, Pre-Trial Chamber I (April 27, 2007). Warrants of Arrest for Ali Muhammad Al Abd-Al-Rahman ("Au Kushayb"). Retrieved October 25, 2009, from ICC Situations and Cases: www.icc-cpi.int/iccdocs/doc/doc279858.PDF.

International Criminal Court, Pre-Trial Chamber I (March 4, 2009). Warrants of Arrest for Omar Hassan Ahmad Al Bashir ("Omar Al Bashir"). Retrieved October 25, 2009, from ICC Situations and Cases: http://www.icc-cpi.int/iccdocs/doc/doc639078.pdf.

International Criminal Court, Pre-Trial Chamber I (May 7, 2009). Decision on the Prosecutor's Application under Article 58 for Abu Garda. Retrieved October 25, 2009, from ICC Situations and Cases: www.icc-cpi.int/iccdocs/doc/doc689342.pdf.

Prunier, G. (2005). *Darfur: The Ambiguous Genocide*. Ithaca, NY: Cornell University Press.

Totten, S. & E. Markusen (2006). *Genocide in Darfur: Investigating the Atrocities in the Sudan*. New York: Routledge.

U.S. Government Accountability Office (November, 2006). *Darfur Crisis. Death Estimates Demonstrate Severity of Crisis, but Their Accuracy and Credibility Could Be Enhanced*. (Publication No. GAO-07-24). Retrieved October 25, 2009, from GAO Reports: www.gao.gov/new.items/d0724.pdf.

ABOUT THE AUTHORS

Xabier Agirre Aranburu is a senior analyst at the Office of the Prosecutor of the ICC (International Criminal Court) since 2004, when he joined the first team that established the Office. For the last twelve years he has worked in the investigation of international crimes (war crimes, crimes against humanity, genocide) as well as the training of Prosecutors and judges around the world with the UN ICTY (United Nations International Criminal Tribunal for the former Yugoslavia), ICRC (International Committee of the Red Cross), UN OHCHR (UN Office of the High Commissioner for Human Rights), ICTJ (International Center for Transitional Justice), and several universities and NGOs.

Roberta Belli is a Ph.D. candidate in the Criminal Justice doctoral program of the Graduate Center, City University of New York, and research assistant at John Jay College of Criminal Justice. Before moving to New York City, she was a law clerk in the Office of the Prosecutor at the ICC (International Criminal Court). Her research interests include international and comparative criminal justice, criminal and terrorist networks, human trafficking, and situational crime prevention.

49 Victims' Rights in the International Criminal Court (ICC)

David Donat Cattin

INTRODUCTION: GOALS OF THE ICC

The unprecedented role for victims in the International Criminal Court (ICC) proceedings is an important feature of the ICC, a judicial institution that should fulfill – at the same time – the criminal justice goals of prevention and retribution as well as truth-telling and reparation. Hence, it is very important to understand that such goals are present in the innovative legal framework of the ICC, which is the first international penal jurisdiction where victims' rights are recognized and enforced. This chapter provides an introduction on victims' rights in the current and future ICC practice and identifies core principles in three areas of victims' rights: (1) protection, (2) participation, and (3) reparations. These are crosscutting elements in the ICC procedural law, and are regulated by principles that serve one another and may not be separated when defining the elements of the victim's right to justice, which is an inalienable human right attributed to victims of crime or abuse of power under international law.

THE CORE PRINCIPLES OF VICTIMS' RIGHTS

Protection

To protect victims and witnesses is an absolute duty for all the organs of the Court that may not be derogated even if there is express consent of the relevant victim(s) or witness(es). Such a legal principle, which is present throughout the entire Statute and the Rules of Procedure and Evidence (the Rules), is expressly defined at article 68, paragraph 1 and entails the unconditioned right to be protected for victim(s) and witness(es) relevant to the

ICC at any stage of its proceedings. The extreme consequence of this principle is that in case the production of a certain piece of evidence in Court, or outside Court, would cause risks for a given victim or witness, and those risks could not be effectively minimized by measures of protection available to the ICC or States Parties to the Statute, the relevant Chamber and the Prosecutor shall abstain from admitting or producing such evidence. The reasoning behind the principle is to be found in the doctrine against secondary victimization (retraumatization), which does not occur as a direct result of the criminal act but is caused by the response of institutions or individuals to the victim's demand to access to justice (UNODC, 1999). In no way shall criminal proceedings before the ICC or complementary national jurisdictions result in the secondary-victimization of a victim or the victimization of a witness. Protective measures taken by all appropriate ICC organs and by relevant organs and agencies of States must be targeted to the prevention of this phenomenon.

Participation

"Justice must be done and must be seen to be done." This appeared to be the favorite motto of victims' rights advocates before, during and after the Rome Diplomatic Conference. But how can justice be seen to be done if victims are not entitled to access to the justice process and contribute, in a way or another, to its effective and fair development? This question finds its ICC-related answer in article 68, paragraph 3 of the Statute, which mirrors section 6(b) of the Declaration of Basic Principles of Justice for Victims of Crime and Abuse of Power (UNGA Res. 40/35 1985). Victims are entitled to participate in ICC proceedings and to express their views and concerns at appropriate stages of the proceedings to be identified by the relevant Chamber. Victims' interventions shall be appropriate vis-à-vis the rights of the accused and the "fair and impartial trial." Such interventions may, therefore, appropriately be done through a third person (a legal representative) who has the legal skills to interact with the judges and the parties in open Court and *ex parte*, within the complex framework of principles, rules, and regulations of international criminal jurisdiction.

Victims who decide to participate in ICC trials may take the courageous decision to expose themselves to the public scrutiny and to the potential retaliation of the accused and his or her accomplices, who may still be at-large (e.g., under an ICC or a national arrest warrant, not yet executed) or may have been spared from prosecution by the selective practice of the

ICC Office of the Prosecutor[1] and by the failure of States' authorities to effectively exercise their complementary national jurisdiction. Even though protective measures may be put in place for these victims, the fact that they formally participate in ICC public hearings make them known to the accused and, in one way or another, to the wider public. However, it has been demonstrated that in several circumstances the best way to be "protected" is to go public and openly declare one's personal status. Protective measures shall be tailored to such victims without frustrating their aspiration to intervene in ICC proceeding when they believe that this is best way to give effect to their "right to justice."

Reparations

Remedying wrongs is always difficult when such wrongs entail the violation of criminal law(s). Redress for victims of ordinary crimes is often not available in national legal orders. It is, therefore, even more difficult to provide redress for victims of crimes under international law in the ICC system, which consists of the complementary jurisdictions of State Parties and of the ICC itself.

An important attempt in the right direction is made in articles 75 and 79 of the Statute and related-provisions in the Rules, which affirm the right of victims to obtain reparations on the basis of "principles relating to reparation" that shall be established by the Court in each and every case before it. Other important features of the discipline of reparations in the ICC framework will not be commented here. Appropriate reparations will have to be tailored to the individual case as a result of the assessment of concrete victimization of individuals and groups of individuals. The jurisprudence will, thus, play a crucial role in applying and shaping the development of standards fulfilling the victims' right to see their wrongs remedied to a degree that, while aiming at restoring the situation(s) preexisting the

---

[1] It is of particular concern for this author that the ICC prosecutor has so far followed a policy to restrict its prosecutions to very few individuals (fourteen in seven years of operations), namely, those allegedly "bearing the greatest responsibility for the most serious crimes" of concern to the international community as a whole (www.icc-cpi.int/NR/rdonlyres/1FA7C4C6-DE5F-42B7-8B25-60AA962ED8B6/143594/030905_Policy_Paper.pdf). While this policy appears reasonable *in abstracto*, it may lead to significant negative repercussions *in concreto* (e.g., inability of the OTP to prove certain crimes committed by the "commanders-in-chief" in the absence of *res judicata* against other leaders or mid-level commanders, a too wide impunity-gap that States' authorities may be unable to tackle, a perception that the OTP policy is too heavily restricted and guided by States' policies to limit the budget and size of the OTP itself, thus infringing upon its independence and effectiveness).

commission of the crimes, will inevitably have a symbolic and only partially restitutive nature, due to the irreparable damage caused by atrocities like extermination, murder, rape, or torture. Legal concepts such as restitution, compensation, and rehabilitation (which includes guarantees of non repetition and may include satisfaction and "memorialization") will assist the judges while performing their decision-making duties, together with the factual representations and submissions made by victims or groups of victims who will apply to the Court for reparations. The experience of national jurisdictions of civil-law countries may provide the ICC with interesting ways and means to implement the statutory norms on reparations.

VICTIMS' PARTICIPATION AND ICC COURTROOM

The court rooms of the ad hoc International Criminal Tribunals for the former Yugoslavia and for Rwanda (ICTY and ICTR) have not been conceived to accommodate the presence of victims, since victims were not recognized as intervenient parties in the ad hoc Tribunals procedural law. To overcome this problem and – above all – to fulfill the requirements of the procedural law of the ICC, within which a precise role is attributed to victims, the Court-room of the ICC permanent premises should be designed in a different way, thus rectifying the mistake made so far in the interim headquarters of the Court in The Hague. The organization of the space in the courtroom may have a symbolic and important meaning to many victims, since the recognition of their role in the justice process and, consequently, their position in open Court will make them understand how an institution representing the international society recognizes and respects them. An effective access to victims or groups of victims to ICC proceedings shall in no way reduce the space and time allocated in such proceedings to its fundamental parties, the prosecution and the defense. But since the role of the prosecution is not that of bringing charges and winning a case, but is that of establishing the truth and searching and disclosing all incriminating and exonerating circumstances equally, it must be understood that the Prosecutor is not just a party in the proceedings. While the Prosecutor seems to play the role of party in an apparently adversarial framework, the goal of the Prosecutor is to be impartial and search for the truth. In this respect, the Prosecutor is the first defense counsel of the accused, since he/she is under the unconditioned duty to search and present exculpatory evidence in all cases such evidence is found. And if the Prosecutor fails, the judges "shall have the authority to request the submission of all evidence that it considers necessary for the determination of the truth."

The combined reading of these and many other provisions of the Rules of Procedure and Evidence make clear that the ICC proceedings are not simply adversarial, but they draw prominent inspiration from the civil-law systems. In those systems, Prosecutors are magistrates, who are members of the judiciary together with the judges. The ICC Prosecutor is an organ of the Court and a magistrate. Even though she appears to be a party to the proceedings, she is not – and she cannot be – an "advocate of the prosecution." The Prosecutor is, instead, an impartial player who has a functional role in investigating and prosecuting with the ultimate goal of achieving a judicial truth, namely the truth pertaining to the individual criminal responsibility in a concrete case under the law.

Victims have an inalienable right to know the truth. They are, therefore, not interested in convictions of innocent individuals, who have the right to acquittal. If the Prosecutor does not genuinely fulfill her duties, victims will act as guardians of the interest of justice and express their views and concerns in accordance with article 68.3 of the Statute. At the same time, the emotions, and often trauma, afflicting victims shall not produce uncontrolled interventions against the accused and consequent disruption of the proceedings. The power of the judges in regulating victims' interventions will avoid these situations, and the almost necessary presence of a legal representative will ensure that statements and questioning on behalf of victims will take place in respect of the Court procedure and the fair trial. The separation of victims from the accused in the courtroom and the lack of confronting positions (all parties face the judges, who are in control of the proceedings) will create a conducive environment for the search of the judicial truth.

PROCEDURE FOR THE APPLICATION OF VICTIMS TO APPEAR IN ICC PROCEEDINGS

Public information and outreach are crucial in ensuring that victims and groups of victims are aware of the possibility to participate in ICC proceedings. Definition of victims under rule 85 entitled reads as follows:

"For the purposes of the Statute and the Rules of Procedure and Evidence:

(a) 'Victims' means natural persons who have suffered harm as a result of the commission of any crime within the jurisdiction of the Court

(b) Victims may include organizations or institutions that have sustained direct harm to any of their property which is dedicated to religion, education, art or science or charitable purposes, and to their historic monuments, hospitals and other places and objects for humanitarian purposes."

It is up to the judges to assess whether a victim who applies to participate in a given ICC proceeding is a victim under rule 85. In its first seven years of practice, the Court has recognized that the crucial test for recognition of the procedural status of victim before the ICC is the nexus between the conduct for which the accused is brought before the Court (i.e., the charges) and the harm suffered by the victim, whether a survivor (e.g., a child soldier) or a family member of a murdered victim. The most critical issue for the applicant-victims is, therefore, to make sure that a link between their actual victimization ("the harm suffered") and the concrete situation or crime under investigation is established. Victims' applications are directed to the Court's registrar, who has the task under Rule 16.3 to maintain "a special register of victims who have expressed their intention to participate in relation to a specific case."

CONCLUSION: PRACTICAL CHALLENGES FOR ICC IN VICTIM SUPPORT AND ASSISTANCE

Some States' representatives and a few observers to the ICC decision-making process expressed the concern that the innovative role of the ICC in promoting the respect of victims' rights cannot imply the realization of a victims' support system at the international level in the framework of the Court: In their view, the limited resources of the ICC should not be directed towards the care of victims while the Court's fundamental aim is to fight impunity and thus contribute to the prevention and repression of crimes. This concern is having a true bearing on the budgetary allocations on and development of ICC structures such as the Victims and Witnesses Unit and the Victims Participation and Reparations Section within the Court's Registry. However, this concern should be addressed in the wider framework of the ICC system, and not confined to the Court as such. The ICC system comprises of the primary role of jurisdictions (and related-agencies) of Member States and the complementary role of ICC organs in protecting victims' rights. It goes without saying that the application of the principle of complementarity to victims' assistance would make possible for the ICC to concentrate only on situations in which victims may not have access to a remedy. In these situations, a key role that the ICC should be able to play is the one of coordination and, as appropriate, cooperation with international organizations and other entities that may assist victims.

Another role that the ICC plays, in the context of its outreach efforts, relates to the management of the expectations of victims and their communities. While explaining that victims have rights under the Rome Statute and international law, the ICC outreach programme may provide information on the necessity for victims to first approach national agencies, if available, and international organizations operating in the field to verify the availability of assistance as well as access to justice and procedures to obtain reparations. But once such avenues are exhausted, victims are entitled to find an answer to their questions before the ICC. And the Court itself, in the absence of available national programmes, should be able to recommend to relevant national and international institutions the action to be undertaken to fulfill the rights of victims.

REFERENCES TO THE INITIAL PRACTICE OF THE ICC

Trial Decisions on Victims' Participation: Katanga and Ngudjolo case, 22 Jan. 2010: www.icc-cpi.int/iccdocs/doc/doc810967.pdf – Lubanga case, 18 Jan. 2008, www.icc-cpi.int/iccdocs/doc/doc409168.PDF

Pre-Trial Decision on Victims' Participation: Kony et al. case, 10 Aug. 2007, www.iclklamberg.com/Caselaw/Uganda/PTCII/ICC-02-04–101_English. pdf – Lubanga case, 17 Jan. 2006, www.icc-cpi.int/iccdocs/doc/doc183441.PDF

Appeals Judgements on Certain Aspects of Victims' Participation: Lubanga Case, 11 July 2008, www2.icc-cpi.int/iccdocs/doc/doc529076.PDF ; 13 Feb. 2007, www.icc-cpi.int/iccdocs/doc/doc248155.PDF (with dissenting opinion of Judge Song)

Pre-Trial Decision on Protective Measures and Victims' Rights: Lubanga case, 10 Feb. 2006: http://145.7.218.139/iccdocs/doc/doc236260.PDF

Assembly of States Parties Web site on ICC permanent premises: www.icc-architectural-competition.com

ABOUT THE AUTHOR

David Donat Cattin (Ph.D., Law) is director of the International Law and Human Rights Programme at Parliamentarians for Global Action (www.pgaction.org), The Hague, Netherlands. He is also a lecturer of the Salzburg Law School on International Criminal Law at University of Salzburg (Austria) and a founding member of the Victims' Rights Working Group (1997), an informal group of NGOs and activists who played a significant role in ICC-related negotiations.

50 Nongovernmental Organizations and International Criminal Justice

Rosemary Barberet

INTRODUCTION: THE ROLE OF "CIVIL SOCIETY" AND THE HISTORY OF NGOS IN INTERNATIONAL CRIMINAL JUSTICE

Although it has long been recognized that citizens working together are effective pressure groups for social change, only recently have scholars researched the role of "transnational civil society": organized citizens who work for global social. In the study of international criminal justice, students are often introduced to the study of national, intergovernmental, or supranational bodies that enforce and interpret national and international law, but rarely to the work of nongovernmental organizations in the delivery of criminal justice-related services and the lobbying for policy changes. This chapter aims to fill that gap by presenting an overview of the work of nongovernmental organizations that is relevant to international criminal justice.

WHAT IS AN NGO?

NGO, an abbreviation for nongovernmental organization, is an international term used to denote formally registered organizations that are not part of the state or otherwise governmental apparatus nor the profit-making sector of the economy. They are commonly referred to as "civil society," and in various contexts are also called "nonprofit" or "voluntary" organizations. Of course, there are many such organizations in the world, and not all are directly relevant to international criminal justice. The civil society database of the UN Department of Economic and Social Affairs lists more than 13,000 organizations with international interests, and more than three thousand who have been granted consultative status with the United

Nations. Those NGOs that aim to influence international criminal justice policy because their main mission, aims, or activities are directed at policy or intervention arenas in international criminal justice are those that are of interest to this chapter. As examples, these include human rights organizations such as Amnesty International and prison reform organizations such as Penal Reform International. In both Vienna (the headquarters of the United Nations Office on Drugs and Crime, and the annual meeting place of the UN Commission on Crime Prevention and Criminal Justice) and New York, there is an Alliance of NGOs on Crime Prevention and Criminal Justice, which serves to coordinate the work of NGOs active in the area of international criminal justice. These Alliances are evidence that the NGO community, originally conceived as local, grassroots activism, is increasingly transnational in scope. Apart from activism at the United Nations, NGOs are formed at different levels. While some NGOs are only active at the local level, others are national in scope, regional, and international. When the problems that NGOs seek to prevent are transnational, it is not surprising to find NGOs that work at all levels.

HOW ARE NGOS RELEVANT TO ICJ?

NGOs are relevant to ICJ through their areas of expertise and the ways in which they use their expertise in their relations with external organizations. ICJ-oriented NGOs are those that are related to criminal justice improvement or reform, to the denouncement of human rights violations, to offender rehabilitation, victim support, and the prevention of crime or human rights violations. Human rights NGOs, such as Amnesty International or Human Rights Watch, focus all of their efforts on preventing, denouncing, and documenting human rights violations. Other large NGOs may have a broad mission, of which the international criminal justice component may only be a part. Save the Children, for example, works in the area of children's rights worldwide (see Van de Voorde and Barberet, Chapter 20), and devotes part of its energies to help children who are the victims of violence, abuse, neglect, and exploitation, including child soldiers and trafficked children. Soroptimist, an international organization of business and professional women who work towards the empowerment of women and gender equality, devotes a part of its activities to combating domestic and sexual violence worldwide, the trafficking of women, female infanticide, and female genital mutilation. Smaller NGOs often have more limited missions. The World Society of Victimology, whose membership includes victim assistance practitioners, academics, social workers, physicians, lawyers, and students, works to further research on victims and foster victim-oriented practices. Penal Reform International, an international NGO that works on penal and criminal justice reform, devotes all of its energies toward the reduced use of prisons as punishment, the abolition of the death penalty, fair and humane criminal justice systems, and the development of alternative custodial measures. The Web sites for these organizations are listed at the end of this chapter. In sum, these organizations are examples of how, by developing an area of expertise, NGOs can deliver services, provide information, and influence policy, as we shall see now.

NGOS AND THE UNITED NATIONS

Some NGOs choose to be active in the United Nations system. The participation of NGOs in the UN system varies greatly, but most NGOs whose work is relevant to international criminal justice apply for consultative status with the Economic and Social Council of the United Nations (ECOSOC). Currently, there are more than three thousand NGOs "in status" and among those more and more are from developing countries; however, there is no easy way to estimate how many of these NGOs tackle issues of international criminal justice, because while some NGOs tackle these issues exclusively, many NGOs tackle criminal justice issues along with other social issues.

NGOs are expected to support the mission and activities of the United Nations by providing input into decision-making. In other words, NGOs that receive consultative status are not supposed to be anti-United Nations. Every four years, NGOs must submit reports of what they have done to contribute to the work of the United Nations. Most NGOs attend and observe United Nations meetings and disseminate information, including research findings and their own fact-finding missions, to the United Nations Community. Some NGOs organize ancillary or parallel events alongside United Nations meetings, and still others actively advocate for certain policies or positions, often via specific wording in resolutions, declarations, and treaties. NGOs bear witness to violations of international law, and appeal to the implementation and enforcement of international law in their local communities. Still other NGOs partner with the UN in its operational role. In the 1970s, the United Nations asked the World Wide Fund for Nature for help in monitoring the CITES Convention (Convention on International Trade in Endangered Species of Wild Fauna and Flora), and in partnership they created TRAFFIC, a network of offices around the world that monitors compliance with CITES (Wapner, 2007: 260).

STRENGTHS AND LIMITATIONS OF NGOS

The work of NGOs is generally praised by the press and United Nations officials, and is considered key to good decision-making. This is because NGOs are often the only groups to bring expertise to the decision-making process. The diplomatic community, as well as many United Nations staff, are not trained in specific policy issues, nor are they given the resources to undertake detailed research before every decision is made. NGOs are also assumed to be the sounding board of civil society. As Wapner explains (2007: 254), "[t]here has always been a tension between the UN's state-centered character and its aspiration to represent 'We the peoples of the United Nations,' the opening words of the organization's Charter."

However, NGOs also have their critics. Some argue that NGOs are not really representative of civil society, but are rather interest groups that are as biased as some private lobbies could be. Others argue that most NGOs are based in the global North, and thus do not represent the developing countries of the world (see Smith, 2004: 313). The proliferation of NGOs suggests to many that NGOs are not truly effective, and cannot be counted on as voices of authority. The transparency procedures applied to NGOs are minimal: NGOs are really only scrutinized when they apply for consultative status.

CASE STUDY: NGOS AND THE INTERNATIONAL CRIMINAL COURT

One of the more successful examples of the effectiveness of nongovernmental organizations is the case of the NGO Coalition for an International Criminal Court (CICC), established in 1995. Many attribute the creation of the ICC to the pressure exercised by this Coalition. Cakmak (2009) has analyzed this process in detail. The Coalition for the ICC was present at the 1998 Rome Conference and helped create a more wide reaching institution than that originally proposed by the International Law Commission report of 1994. For example, it ensured that gender based violence would be taken seriously, and that victims and witnesses would be guaranteed safeguards. It also conducted a global ratification campaign that led to the rapid entry into force of the Rome Statute and thus the creation of the court. It continues to promote the court as well as to encourage its visibility and transparency. The Women's Initiative for Gender Justice, part of the CICC, produces a Gender Report Card on the International Criminal Court, keeping the ICC to its mission of mainstreaming gender issues throughout the structure and functioning of the court. NGOs help law enforcement and prosecution in training, investigating and gathering evidence. In September 2005 the

Women's Initiatives for Gender Justice conducted a review of twenty reports on Darfur specifically assessing the documentation of rape and other forms of sexual violence committed against women in this conflict. NGOs also help in identifying credible witnesses and assist victims during the court process. Finally, NGOs assist in the process of restorative justice and reconciliation. In 2008, Redress and African Rights conducted a study of the survivors of the Rwandan Genocide and postgenocide justice in Rwanda, to bring "lessons learned" to the International Criminal Court.

The CICC was founded with twenty-five NGOs. Today, there are more than two thousand member organizations (Cakmak, 2009). What is unusual about the CICC is that, as Cakmak explains, it is a principled and loosely structured network. Originally, members exchanged information and resources, and strategized to create this new institution. With time, the NGOs in the CICC created subgroups or caucuses according to themes or topics, such as Women's Initiatives for Gender Justice, Victims' Rights Working Group, and the Children's Caucus, among others. Today, the CICC works at "protecting the letter and spirit of the Rome Statute, raising awareness of the ICC at the national, regional and global level; monitoring and supporting the work of the Court; promoting ratification and implementation of the Court's founding treaty, the Rome Statute; monitoring and supporting the work of the Assembly of States Parties; facilitating involvement and capacity building of NGOs in the ICC process; and expanding and strengthening the Coalition's worldwide network" (Cakmak, 2009: 376). The CICC is inclusive and issue-oriented. In its diversity lies its strength. Issue orientation also means that NGOs can act as part of the CICC as well as independently, and that energies are not wasted created a new NGO but rather on formalizing and coordinating efforts that already exist in the global NGO community, around the continuing need for the International Criminal Court.

SUMMARY AND CONCLUSION

Nongovernmental organizations are a growing influence in international criminal justice, both through their relationship with the United Nations and as grassroots movements that are becoming increasingly transnational. Through these organizations, citizens organize and work together to promote social change and achieve global peace, justice, and security. Their work is different from that of intergovernmental organizations; ideally, the two complement each other, but it is also true that the conflict that ensues from different points of view serve to enhance the democratic process of global governance.

REFERENCES

Cakmak, C. (2009). Transnational Activism in World Politics and Effectiveness of a Loosely Organized Principled Global Network: The Case of the NGO Coalition for an International Criminal Court. *The International Journal of Human Rights*, 12, 373–93.

Smith, J. (2004). Transnational Processes and Movements. In D. Snow, S. Soule, & H. Kries (Eds.), *The Blackwell Companion to Social Movements*. Malden, MA: Blackwell.

Wapner, P. (2008). Civil Society. In T.G Weiss & S. Daws, S. (Eds.), *The Oxford Handbook on the United Nations*. Oxford: Oxford University Press.

WEB SITES

The Conference of NGOs in Consultative Relationship with the United Nations, http://www.ngocongo.org

New York Alliance of NGOs on Crime Prevention and Criminal Justice, www.cpcjalliance.org

NGO Branch, UN Department of Economic and Social Affairs www.un.org/esa/coordination/ngo

World Society of Victimology, www.worldsocietyofvictimology.org

Coalition for the International Criminal Court www.iccnow.org

Penal Reform International, www.penalreform.org

Amnesty International, www.amnesty.org

Human Rights Watch, www.hrw.org

Prerana, www.preranaatc.com

KARDS, http://humantrafficking.kardsafrica.org/joomla

ECPAT International, www.ecpat.net

Coalition Against the Trafficking of Women or Children, www.catwinternational.org

Gender Report Card (ICC), www.iccnow.org/documents/GRC09_web_version.pdf

Rwandan Genocide Study, www.iccnow.org/documents/RwandaSurvivors31Oct08.pdf

ABOUT THE AUTHOR

Rosemary Barberet is an associate professor in the Sociology Department of John Jay College of Criminal Justice where she teaches International Criminal Justice courses. Although trained in criminology in the United States (Ph.D., University of Maryland, 1994), she has spent most of her academic career in Europe (Spain and England). Her publications have dealt with victimology, crime indicators, and comparative methodology. From 2001–05 she chaired the International Division of the American Society of Criminology. Dr. Barberet has received the Herbert Bloch Award of the American Society of Criminology and the Rafael Salillas Award of the Sociedad Española de Investigación Criminológica. She currently represents the International Sociological Association at the United Nations.

51 Global and Regional Human Rights Commissions

José Luis Morín

INTRODUCTION

Aspiring to promote respect for human rights as expressed in the U.N. Charter of 1945, the United Nations created the U.N. Commission on Human Rights – now the Human Rights Council. Regional organizations – the Organization of American States (OAS), the Council of Europe, and the Organization of African Unity (now the African Union) – have founded similar quasijudicial entities that seek to provide address human rights violations in their respective parts of the world (Steiner, Alston, & Goodman, 2007). This chapter presents a brief overview of global and regional human rights commissions, their evolution, shortcomings, and achievements. It focuses on commissions that function as standing human rights entities of the United Nations or other regional authorities. It does not discuss commissions established for specific purposes, such as the Truth and Reconciliation Commission in South Africa.

THE UNITED NATIONS: FROM COMMISSION TO HUMAN RIGHTS COUNCIL

Pursuant to Article 68 of the U.N. Charter requiring that the Economic and Social Council (ECOSOC) create "commissions in economic and social fields and for the promotion of human rights," the United Nations Commission on Human Rights was established in 1946 as a "charter-based" or "non-treaty-based" human rights mechanism. By 1948, the U.N. Commission on Human Rights produced the Universal Declaration on Human Rights, adopted that same year by the U.N. General Assembly.

The U.N. Commission on Human Rights expanded its work over time beyond developing new international human rights instruments to engage in monitoring and securing compliance with human rights and playing a key role in many of the United Nations' human rights institutions, programs, and activities in coordination with the Office of the U.N. High Commissioner for Human Rights. The Commission investigated the human rights situation in numerous countries utilizing a variety of fact-finding approaches, including working groups, rapporteurs, observer delegations, special envoys, and representatives – as in the case of the 1967 Ad Hoc Working Group of Experts on southern Africa – and it issued findings annually and publicly. The Commission's work also integrated two complaint procedures to address human rights complaints – one which permits the public debate of human rights cases in accordance with ECOSOC Resolution 1235 (XLII) of 1967, and a second which authorized the Commission to conduct confidential investigations on complaints or "communications" it receives pursuant to ECOSOC Resolution 1503 (XLVIII) of 1970, commonly referred to as the 1503 Complaint Procedure (Buergenthal et al., 2002; Steiner, Alston, & Goodman, 2007).

Over the course of its existence, the U.N. Commission on Human Rights has been strongly criticized, often by Western nations that complained that the Commission's agenda was driven by states with disreputable human rights records (Fasulo, 2009; Ramcharan, 2007). An example often cited is the case of Libya, which was elected to chair the Commission in 2003 (Hanhimäki, 2008).

Dissatisfaction with the Commission prompted the passage of General Assembly resolution 60/251 of 15 March 2006, creating a forty-seven-member Council of Human Rights to replace the fifty-three-member Commission on Human Rights. The resolution – which passed overwhelmingly, with 170 of the U.N.'s 191 member states in favor and only four opposed (the United States, the Marshall Islands, Palau, and Israel) – calls for an equitable regional distribution of seats, with thirteen seats for Africa, thirteen for Asia, six for Europe, eight for Latin America and the Caribbean, and seven for Western Europe and other states (Hanhimäki, 2008).

In 2007, the Council adopted an "Institution-building package" to guide its work. This work plan includes a "Universal Periodic Review" mechanism to assess the human rights situations in all 192 U.N. member states by 2011; a new "Advisory Committee" to provide expertise and advice on thematic human rights issues; and an updated "Complaints Procedure" mechanism to improve upon the 1503 Complaint Procedure for individuals and organizations to file complaints in a manner that is more efficient and unbiased. The Human Rights Council is also continuing to avail itself of "Special Procedures" established by the previous Commission on Human

Rights that include the use of special rapporteurs for matters pertaining to particular countries or themes such as terrorism and torture or working groups to address issues such as arbitrary detentions and enforced or involuntary disappearances.

The Council, designed to pacify criticism of the Commission, has quickly drawn criticism of its own. As with the Commission, the Council's members sit as representatives of U.N. member states. As such, the criticism that the Council's membership consists of states that are serious human rights violators has resurfaced (Fasulo, 2009; Ramcharan, 2007). In a change of course from the Bush administration, which railed against the Human Rights Council particularly for its emphasis on Israel's treatment of Palestinians, the Obama administration has decided to work for change from within, allowing the United States to be voted in as a member of the Council in 2009 (MacFarquhar, 2009). In keeping with General Assembly resolution 60/251 of 2006, an assessment of the Council's work shall take place in five years, providing an opportunity to evaluate its effectiveness and function.

Among its achievements, the U.N. Charter-based human rights machinery has set standards for the human rights observance and enforcement. As one international human rights scholar notes, the Commission on Human Rights' "initial vision of an international bill of human rights – consisting of a declaration, one or more covenants, and measures of implementation – has inspired the human rights movement throughout the UN's history" (Ramcharan, 2007). Criticisms that its actions are too political or selective notwithstanding, the Human Rights Council's utility, like its predecessor, is that it serves as a vehicle for progress through the development of a substantial agenda and legal parameters for the promotion of human rights worldwide.

In contrast to the Human Rights Council, it should be noted that the U.N. human rights system also consists of "treaty-based" mechanisms for human rights oversight and enforcement provided under treaties ratified by member states. Part IV of the 1966 International Covenant on Civil and Political Rights, for example, establishes the Human Rights Committee, a body of independent experts that monitor the treaty's implementation. Under the First Optional Protocol to the International Covenant on Civil and Political Rights of 1996, the Human Rights Committee can also receive complaints concerning states that have ratified the Protocol. Other treaties contain similar individual complaint procedures, such as the Convention on the Elimination of All Forms of Discrimination Against Women, and some require periodic compliance reports, as with the Convention on the Rights of the Child (Bayefsky, 2002; Lewis-Anthony & Scheinin, 2004).

REGIONAL HUMAN RIGHTS COMMISSIONS

Presently, three regional human rights systems operate in the world today – the American, European, and the African. An Arab system is mostly inactive, and a system for Asia is being proposed. While a concern about "regional" versus "universalist" approaches has been raised, no significant conflict between regional systems and U.N. human rights scheme has occurred (Steiner, Alston, & Goodman, 2007). The following is a brief description of the three functioning systems.

Organization of American States: The Inter-American Commission on Human Rights

The Organization of American States (OAS) is a regional organization comprised of the thirty-five sovereign nations of the Americas. The Inter-American Commission on Human Rights was established in an amendment to the OAS Charter of 1948 which entered into force in 1970 and is guided by the American Declaration of the Rights and Duties of Man of 1948, a normative and authoritative instrument protecting fundamental rights, such as the right to life, the right to equality before the law, among others. It also plays a role in the procedures found in the 1969 American Convention on Human Rights.

The Inter-American Commission's quasijudicial functions include the ability to receive and render opinions on individual cases. In comparison with the U.N. Human Rights Council, its members are not governmental representatives but experts chosen by the OAS General Assembly. Petitioners before the Inter-American Commission may also request hearings, something not possible under the U.N. 1503 Complaint Procedure. Before the merits of a petition to the Inter-American Commission are heard, a cpetition undergoes an admissibility phase in which the petition may be rejected for not complying with admissibility rules. Although lacking the power to enforce its decisions, it can seek settlements and bring cases to the attention of the OAS General Assembly.

Under the American Convention on Human Rights, the Inter-American Commission can present cases to the Inter-American Court of Human Rights against a state that has ratified the Convention. In such cases, the Court can issue orders to enforce its rulings. Among its other responsibilities, the Inter-American Commission conducts country studies and on-site investigations of the human rights situation in various OAS member states (Buergenthal et al., 2002; Shelton, 2004; Steiner, Alston, & Goodman, 2007).

COUNCIL OF EUROPE: FROM EUROPEAN COMMISSION TO EUROPEAN COURT OF HUMAN RIGHTS

The Council of Europe, established in 1949, created a system for the protection of human rights that has adopted numerous human rights treaties, including the European Convention on Human Rights, signed in 1950 and entered into force in 1953. Article 19 of the European Convention originally provided for the creation of a European Commission of Human Rights and a European Court of Human Rights, but both were replaced by a permanent human rights court under Protocol No. 11 that entered into force in 1998. This change now allows individuals to submit complaints directly to the Court, which has ruled on more than ten thousand cases since its inception (European Court of Human Rights, 2009).

Prior to its elimination, the European Commission sought settlements, issued nonbinding opinions, or referred cases to the Court. The current European Court of Human Rights provides a more rigorous human rights enforcement mechanism for cases addressing individual and interstate complaints (Boyle, 2004; Buergenthal et al., 2002) and guarantees certain basic rights, such as right to life, freedom of expression, and the prohibition against right torture and arbitrary and unlawful detentions.

The African Union's African Commission on Human and Peoples' Rights

In 1981, the Organization of African Unity – now the African Union – adopted the African Charter on Human and Peoples' Rights (African Charter), which entered into force in 1986. In contrast to the European and American conventions on human rights, the African Charter has a distinct focus on duties as well as individual rights. For instance, it establishes a duty "to preserve and strengthen the national independence and territorial integrity" (Article 29 (5)), in addition to protecting individual liberty and security (Article 6). Africa's experience with colonialism is reflected in the document's adherence to securing the rights of all peoples to self-determination (Article 20). Two other important human rights instruments of the African human rights system are the African Charter on the Rights and Welfare of the Child of 1990 and the Protocol to the African Charter on Human and Peoples' Rights on the Rights of Women in Africa of 2003.

The African Charter calls for the creation of an African Commission on Human and Peoples' Rights to promote human rights and act in a quasijudicial capacity to address interstate and individual communications. The

African Commission also has the authority to refer cases to the African Court on Human Rights, established under the Protocol to the African Charter Protocol to the African Charter on Human and Peoples' Rights on the Establishment of an African Court on Human and Peoples' Rights, adopted in 1998. Under the Protocol, the African Commission retains an important role in hearing cases, as the Court could also transfer cases to the Commission for resolution (Steiner, Alston, & Goodman, 2007).

CONCLUSION

As imperfect and controversial they may be in certain respects and at certain times, global and regional human rights commissions have made significant contributions in setting human rights standards, as evidenced by the Universal Declaration on Human Rights. Human rights commissions provide many victims with a forum for redress and resolution of their cases, and they have proven effective in addressing some very crucial human rights questions, as in the case of *Tyrer v. United Kingdom*, 26 Eur. Ct. H.R. (ser. A) (1978), which held that the judicial corporal punishment inflicted on a juvenile violated the prohibition of torture, inhuman, or degrading treatment. Although human rights commissions may be limited in their enforcement capacity, in many instances they have provided a means for obtaining some relief for victims. Regional human rights commissions have been especially effective when given the authority to transfer cases to a court with enforcement powers, as in the case of *Velasquez Rodriguez Case* [Compensatory Damages], I.A. Court H.R., Series C: Decision and Judgments, No. 7 (1988), where the government of Honduras was ordered to pay monetary compensation in this case involving the issue of disappearances. Thus, global and regional human rights commissions can be a force for progress in the promotion and protection of human rights.

REFERENCES

Bayefsky, A. F. (2002). *How to Complain to the UN Human Rights Treaty System*. Ardsley, NY: Transnational Publishers.

Boyle, K. (2004). Council of Europe, OSCE, and European Union. In H. Hannum (Ed.). *Guide to International Human Rights Practice*, Fourth Edition. Ardsley, NY: Transnational Publishers, pp.143–70.

Buergenthal, T., D. Shelton,, & D. Stewart. (2002). *International Human Rights in a Nutshell*, Third Edition. St. Paul, MN: West Group.

European Court of Human Rights. (2009). *The European Court of Human Rights: Some Facts and Figures, 1959–2009*. Retrieved from http://www.echr.

coe.int/NR/rdonlyres/ACD46A0F-615A-48B9-89D6-8480AFCC29FD/0/
FactsAndFiguresEN.pdf.

Fasulo, L. (2009). *An Insider's Guide to the UN*, Second Edition. New Haven, CT:
Yale University Press.

Hanhimäki, J. M. (2008). *The United Nations: A Very Short Introduction*. Oxford:
Oxford University Press.

Lewis A., S. & M. Scheinin. (2004). Treaty-Based Procedures for Making Human
Rights Complaints within the UN System. In H. Hannum (Ed.), *Guide to
International Human Rights Practice, Fourth Edition*. Ardsley, NY: Transnational
Publishers, pp. 43–64.

MacFarquhar, N. (2009, May 13). U.S. Joins Rights Panel After a Vote at the U.N.
The New York Times, p. A5.

Ramcharan, B. G. (2007). Norms and Machinery. In T. G. Weiss & S. Daws (Eds.),
The Oxford Handbook on the United Nations. Oxford, Oxford University Press,
pp. 439–62.

Shelton, D. (2004). The Inter-American Human Rights System. In H. Hannum
(Ed.), *Guide to International Human Rights Practice*, Fourth Edition. Ardsley,
NY: Transnational Publishers, pp. 127–42.

Steiner, H. J., P. Alston, & R. Goodman. (2007). *International Human Rights in
Context: Law, Politics, Morals, Third Edition*. New York: Oxford University
Press.

WEB SITES

African (Banjul) Charter on Human and Peoples' Rights: www.africa-union.org/
official_documents/Treaties_%20Conventions_%20Protocols/Banjul%20
Charter.pdf

Inter-American Commission on Human Rights: http://www.cidh.oas.org/DefaultE.
htm

Organization of American States Web human rights page: www.oas.org/en/topics/
human_rights.asp

UN Human Rights Council: www2.ohchr.org/english/bodies/hrcouncil

U.N. human rights information and documents: www.ohchr.org/EN/Pages/
WelcomePage.aspx

ABOUT THE AUTHOR

José Luis Morín is professor in the Latin American and Latina/o Studies Department
at John Jay College of Criminal Justice (CUNY). He teaches in the areas of international and domestic criminal justice, civil rights, international human rights, and
Latin American and Latina/o studies. He has taught courses on international law
and indigenous rights at the University of Hawaii at Mānoa, and worked many years
as a civil rights and international human rights attorney.

52 The Truth and Reconciliation Commission in South Africa

Stephan Parmentier and Elmar Weitekamp

INTRODUCTION

Debate over what to do about previous gross and systematic violations of human rights often arise during times of transition, when societies are moving away from an autocratic regime toward more democratic forms of government. In the criminological literature, many of these acts are considered "political crimes," meaning crimes committed by people against the state, designed to protest, change, or oust the existing establishment, as well as crimes committed by the state against people to sanction the acts that threaten that same establishment (Parmentier, 2001). The problem is one of "dealing with the past" (Boraine, Levy, & Scheffer, 1997), "transitional justice" (Kritz, 1995), or "post-conflict justice" (Bassiouni, 2002). Over the last decades various transitional justice mechanisms have been developed to deal with the legacy of a dark past: (1) in many cases the violations or crimes were not dealt with at all, thus resulting in a situation of impunity or the incapacity of the judicial system to prosecute; (2) the violations and crimes have become the object of criminal prosecutions, by national courts, courts in a third country, hybrid courts, or international tribunals and courts; or (3) other mechanisms such as amnesty, lustration (i.e., government policies of limiting the participation in public office of civil servants and security personnel attached to the former regime) and truth commissions. Each of these may be used independently or as complementary mechanisms operating alongside others. The truth commission process has been described as a "third way," in other words, as a mechanism that lies between impunity and formal prosecution.

A truth commission is a nonjudicial body of enquiry with the following characteristics: (1) it is primarily concerned with the past but also formulates recommendations for the future; (2) it is not concentrating on one or more particular events but tries to sketch a global picture of the past; (3) its activities are limited to a specific period established beforehand and its conclusions are laid down in a report; and (4) it receives the support from the political authorities (Hayner, 2001). Truth commissions operate in a nonjudicial manner outside of court. They were created in Latin America in the 1980s and early 1990s (i.e., Argentina, Chile, and El Salvador) and later were adopted in other parts of the world as well (e.g., in East Timor and Sierra Leone). In recent years some truth commissions were established in mature democracies like the United States and Canada to deal with the legacy of racism directed toward African-Americans and indigenous peoples.

This chapter analyses one such truth commission, the one that operated in South Africa following the first democratic elections of 1994. We will take a closer look at its background, its mandate, and its institutional framework.

THE TRUTH AND RECONCILIATION COMMISSION IN SOUTH AFRICA

The Historical Background: A "Third Way"

The idea to set up a commission of enquiry was formulated in the fall of 1992, by Kader Asmal, a prominent intellectual and member of the African National Congress (ANC), with a view of investigating allegations of human rights violations in some of its training camps organized in neighboring African countries. When it became clear that the apartheid government wished to introduce far-reaching amnesty provisions for members of the outgoing elite, the ANC launched an appeal for a commission to investigate both its own abuses and those of the government. It was a strong and deliberate attempt to ensure that the serious human rights abuses of the past would not go unacknowledged and that some form of accountability be installed, though of a nonjudicial nature (Boraine, Levy, & Scheffer, 1997; Kritz, 1995).

While the Truth and Reconciliation Commission became the predominant institution to deal with the legacy of the apartheid regime after the 1994 democratic elections it was not the only institution to do so. After the elections a number of criminal trials were also instituted against high-ranking officials of the former regime, although most led to acquittals (Hayner, 2001). Some commentators have argued that the determination of the criminal courts to prosecute certain crimes of the past prompted many people to cooperate with the TRC and to appear before it. Thus, they would prefer public exposure and shame above the risk of being held liable in a criminal court.

The Mandate: Seeking Truth and Promoting Reconciliation

The TRC was set up with five tasks (art. 3,1 and 3,2): (1) to establish a picture of the gross human rights violations covered; (2) to facilitate the granting of amnesty for specific acts and under specific conditions; (3) to grant victims an opportunity to relate their own accounts and to recommend reparation measures for them; (4) to compile a comprehensive report; and (5) to make whatever recommendations in view of the overarching objective.

The two essential tasks were to seek truth and to promote reconciliation (Villa-Vicencio & Verwoerd, 2000). The Report distinguishes between four forms of "truth" (Report, vol. 1, 110–14): (1) factual or forensic truth, meaning the evidence obtained and corroborated through reliable procedures normally used in court; (2) personal and narrative truth, meaning the many stories that individuals told about their experiences under apartheid; (3) social or dialogue truth, established through interaction, discussion, and debate; and (4) healing and restorative truth, meaning the truth that places facts and their meaning within the context of human relationships. Also the concept of reconciliation was subdivided in four different levels (Report, vol. 1, 106–10; Bloomfield et al., 2003): (1) the intrapersonal level of coming to terms with painful truth, for example, after exhumations and reburials of beloved ones; (2) the interpersonal level of specific victims and perpetrators; (3) the community level, when addressing the internal conflicts inside and between local communities; and (4) the national level, by focusing on the role of the state and nonstate institutions. The Commission has tried to clarify the relationship between these various notions by consistently repeating that truth constituted the road to reconciliation. It also made the link with the notion of restorative justice, interpreted in the Report as "restoring civil and human dignity" for all South Africans (Report, vol. 1, 125–31; Parmentier, 2001). This restorative process was first of all directed to the victims, who were given extensive possibilities to tell their stories and who received recognition for their severe victimization, and also to the perpetrators, by trying to understand their motives and the social and political structures they operated in, without excusing the violations they committed.

The Institutional Framework: One Commission, Three Committees

The TRC was given authority to investigate a number of gross violations of human rights expressly mentioned in the Act (section 1(1)). These violations included the killing, abduction, torture, or severe ill-treatment of persons, in the period between March 1, 1960 and May 10, 1994. It investigated the violations of both parties – the former apartheid regime and the former "freedom fighters," including those committed in neighboring countries (like Mozambique and Zimbabwe) and in other parts of the world but attributable to one of the conflicting parties.

The Commission was composed of seventeen members, appointed by the president on the basis of their expertise in the field of democracy and human rights and after a public debate allowing public institutions and nongovernmental organizations to propose concrete names of possible commissioners. One of the unique features of the TRC lay in its interdisciplinary composition, as it was not limited to lawyers but also included medical doctors, educators, theologians and other professions, under the charismatic leadership of Desmond Tutu. While the Commission assumed its responsibility as a plenary body most of its actual work took place in three separate Committees.

Best known is the Human Rights Violations Committee (HRVC), entrusted with the investigative aspect (Report, vol. 1, 140–51). The Committee gathered more than 21,000 written statements from victims all over South Africa, relating to more than 37,000 violations of human rights. Among the most innovative aspects of its work, in comparison with previous truth commissions in other parts of the world, were the more than seventy-five public hearings organized by this Committee all over the country (Hayner, 2001: 32–49). The hearings took different forms. Most of them provided individual victims and offenders with a public forum to tell their individual stories and to increase their understanding of what had happened and why. Other hearings focused on specific events, such as mass killings, or on specific groups of society, such as women and children. Finally, the Committee held "institutional hearings" about specific sectors of society, such as the legal and medical professions, the media, and business, in order to hear their views about the crimes committed under the apartheid regime. Sometimes, the Committee used its legal powers of subpoena, search, and seizure, in order to oblige certain witnesses and perpetrators to be questioned, as well as to produce probative evidence. The combined results of all hearings were published in the five-volume Report of 1998, which, for the first time, detailed a specific part of South Africa's horrendous past and thus enabled the construction of a collective memory of mass victimization that could be shared by various sectors of society.

A unique feature of the TRC was its Amnesty Committee (AC), in charge of dealing with individual applications for amnesty and chaired by a magistrate (Report, vol. 1, 1998, pp 153–7). The "carrot" of amnesty was included to elicit information from offenders about political crimes that would otherwise have remained in the dark (Sarkin, 2004). Amnesty could only be granted under very strict conditions: (1) it was limited to political crimes committed within a specific period of reference; and (2) it required the full disclosure of all relevant facts. The South African version of amnesty thus differed substantially from amnesty provisions in other parts of the world, notably in Latin America, where amnesty was mostly introduced to serve specific groups, such as the military and the police, and came about by enacting "blanket" amnesties through legislation. The Amnesty Committee continued its work until 2003 and in that period dealt with more than 7,100 applications in total, of which a good 1,300 received full or partial amnesty (Report, vol. 6, 2003, p. 36; Sarkin, 2004). The decision to grant amnesty precluded any further criminal or civil action in court against the person concerned. Less clear is the situation of those who were denied amnesty and in some cases criminal investigations have been initiated.

Finally, the Reparation and Rehabilitation Committee (RRC) was to make recommendations on reparation and rehabilitation matters to the government (Report, vol. 5, 1998, pp. 170–95). It recommended measures at various levels: individual reparations; symbolic reparations, and legal and administrative matters; community rehabilitation programs; and institutional reforms. While it did not possess any legal authority to order the restitution of property, to impose community service or to organize programs for the reintegration of victims or offenders, it could grant urgent and interim reparations to some persons in need of medical, psychological, or material help. Since the end of the TRC many victims have urged the government to implement the recommendations and by working with victim support groups and NGOs to lobby government agencies and file complaints in courts. Very few concrete results have been achieved and the government has been extremely reluctant to put into effect any recommendations on reparation and rehabilitation, as it has argued that the country should concentrate on political stability and economic development instead.

CONCLUSION

The South African Truth and Reconciliation Commission has attracted worldwide attention for its dealing with the horrendous legacy of apartheid. As the result of a political compromise and in a context of a "negotiated transition" to democracy, the TRC was set up as a nonjudicial body with the objectives to seek the truth and to promote reconciliation outside of court. It displayed some unique features, such as the legal authority to grant amnesty on an individual basis, and its own decision to hold public hearings with a view of reaching out to communities, the nation, and the world.

The truth commission process was not completely detached from the criminal justice system in South Africa. First, it has been argued that the ongoing criminal trials of the mid-1990s were threatening enough to many South Africans to encourage them to cooperate with the TRC. It remains to be seen how the information obtained through the Commission's written submissions, public hearings, and amnesty proceedings may be used in criminal proceedings in the coming years.

On a more general level the South African TRC has provided an innovative model to deal with specific crimes of a very dark past. Some have argued that this model can be transferred to other countries and other contexts. Given the uniqueness of the South African case, however, this is subject to ongoing debate. It seems that every transitional justice experience is unique in its own right, although it is possible to draw important lessons from different experiences across the globe.

REFERENCES

Bassiouni, C. (Ed.). (2002). *Post-Conflict Justice*. New York: Transnational Publishers.
Boraine, A., J. Levy, & R. Scheffer, (Eds.). (1997). *Dealing with the Past: Truth and Reconciliation in South Africa*. Cape Town: Institute for Democracy in South Africa (idasa).
Bloomfield, D., T. Barnes, & L. Huyse, (Eds.). (2003). *Reconciliation After Violent Conflict: A Handbook*. Stockholm: International Idea.
Hayner, P. (2001). *Unspeakable Truths: Confronting State Terror and Atrocity*. New York: Routledge.
Kritz, N. (Ed.). (1995). *Transitional Justice: How Emerging Democracies Reckon with Former Regimes*, Vols. 1–3. Washington, D.C.: United States Institute of Peace.
Parmentier, S. (2001). The South African Truth and Reconciliation Commission: Towards Restorative Justice in the Field of Human Rights. In E. Fattah &

S. Parmentier (Eds.), *Victim Policies and Criminal Justice on the Road to Restorative Justice*. Leuven: Leuven University Press, pp. 401–28.

Sarkin, J. (2004). *Carrots and Sticks: The TRC and the South African Amnesty Process*. Antwerp/Oxford: Intersentia/Hart.

Truth and Reconciliation Commission of South Africa. (1998). *Report*. (5 Vols.). Cape Town: Juta & Co.

Truth and Reconciliation Commission of South Africa. (2003). *Report* (Vol. 6 & 7). Cape Town: Juta & Co.

Villa-Vicencio, C. & W. Verwoerd, (Eds.). (2000). *Looking Back, Reaching Forward: Reflections on the Truth and Reconciliation Commission of South Africa*. Cape Town: University of Cape Town Press.

WEB SITES

www.csvr.org.za (Centre for the Study of Violence and Reconciliation)
www.doj.gov.za/trc (Truth and Reconciliation Commission)
www.ictj.org (International Centre for Transitional Justice)
www.idea.int (International Institute for Democracy and Electoral Assistance)
www.truthcommission.org (Programme on Negotiation, Harvard Law School, and European Centre for Common Ground)
www.usip.org/library/truth.html (United States Institute of Peace)

ABOUT THE AUTHORS

Stephan Parmentier studied law, political science, and sociology at the Catholic University of Leuven (Belgium) and the University of Minnesota-Twin Cities (USA). He is currently a professor of Sociology of Crime, Law, and Human Rights at the Faculty of Law of the K.U. Leuven and served as the Academic Secretary of the Faculty and the Head of the Department of Criminal Law and Criminology. He has been a visiting professor and a visiting scholar at various universities in Europe, Australia, Africa, and the Americas. His research interests and publications relate to political crimes, transitional justice and human rights, and the administration of criminal justice.

Elmar Weitekamp holds the degrees of Master in Social Work in Mönchengladbach (1980), M.A. in Criminology (1982), and Ph.D. in Criminology (1989) at the University of Pennsylvania. He is currently a research professor of Victimology and Restorative Justice at the University of Tübingen. He serves as the co-director of the postgraduate course in Victimology, Victim Assistance, and Criminal Justice of the World Society of Victimology, and has been a visiting professor at the University of Melbourne (Australia). His research interests and publications relate to victimology, restorative justice, and juvenile gangs.

53 The Guatemalan Truth Commission

GENOCIDE THROUGH THE LENS OF TRANSITIONAL JUSTICE

Marcia Esparza

INTRODUCTION

More than thirty truth commissions have been set up throughout the world since the 1970s, in Latin America and Africa, in particular. Truth commissions are typically created either by presidential decrees, as they were in Chile and Peru, or through agreements negotiated between governments and guerrilla forces, as in Guatemala.

The overall purposes of truth commissions are to reach the truth about past atrocities, provide a safe forum for testimonies, write reports of their findings, reconcile opposing groups in war-torn societies, and make recommendations. Truth commissions seek to discover what really happened to people who were forcibly "disappeared," and to discover where people who were murdered are buried. They provide a safe forum in which victims, survivors, and sometimes perpetrators can publicly attest to violence, abuses, and human rights violations they have experienced or witnessed.

A standard characteristic of truth commissions is that they do not have the power to prosecute, or to grant perpetrators amnesty for their crimes, except in the case of the South African Truth Commission (1996–8). They seek to reconcile war-torn-fragmented societies and yield reports on their findings, which also contain recommendations for steps governments can take to prevent political violence from recurring. In Chile, for example, the Commission recommended that the state provide victims and families with special health programs recognizing and helping to heal their sufferings.

Using primary data collected from the victims of the massacres perpetrated against indigenous Mayans in Guatemala, this chapter aims to provide details of the Guatemalan Truth Commission in terms of its history and nature, the processes of reaching the truth and the recommendations of the memory of silence project.

GUATEMALA: ETERNAL SPRING, ETERNAL BLOODSHED

Guatemala borders the North Pacific Ocean. It is located between El Salvador and Mexico, and between Honduras and Belize in Central America, on the Gulf of Honduras in the Caribbean Sea.

Today, twenty-three different linguistic groups live mainly in the northwestern part of the country. Large sectors of the population eke out their livings in a subsistence economy, relying on the harvests of *milpas* (corn fields) on tiny plots of land. Indigenous people make up the majority of those whom the landed oligarchy use as cheap laborers, employing them as they have for centuries over a century as seasonal migrants who work in large coffee, sugar, and banana plantations located in the lowlands, or southern coastal areas. Guatemala is characterized by its precapitalist agrarian socioeconomic and political structure, as well as by extreme social polarization. Unlike other commissions, the Guatemalan Truth Commission traced the exclusion and exploitation of indigenous peoples back to colonial times (Grandin, 2005). It was unique in that it provided a comprehensive historical account of the sociopolitical economic structure that maintains indigenous peoples as slaves in coffee plantations.

Historical Background

In Guatemala, starting in the 1960s, rural indigenous communities organized a vibrant social movement demanding economic, political, cultural, and social rights. The movement threatened the power of the authoritarian government. In the late 1970s, heightening the conflict, sectors of the indigenous population supported a growing left-wing guerrilla movement called the National Revolutionary Unity of Guatemala or *Unidad Revolucionaria Nacional Guatemalteca*, (URNG). The government responded by launching bloody counterinsurgency campaigns, to quell the growing resistance. Under the rules of Generals Romeo Lucas Garcia (1978–82) and Efrain Rios Montt (June 1982 to August 1983), brutal campaigns of genocide were perpetrated against four Mayan groups: Maya-Q'anjob'al, Maya-Chuj, Maya-Ixil, Maya-K'ich'e, and Maya Achi.

In the 1990s, peace negotiations between the guerrillas, the Guatemalan government, and sectors of civil society gave rise to the Oslo Peace Accord of June 1994, which created the Guatemalan Truth Commission, called the

Commission to Clarify Past Human Rights Violations and Acts of Violence That Have Caused the Guatemalan People to Suffer (HCCG), *Comisión de Esclarecimiento Histórico*, (CEH). Its specific aims were (1) to clarify with objectivity and impartiality the human rights violations and acts of violence causing people suffering during the war, (2) to prepare a report of the findings of the investigation, and (3) to recommend ways the government could promote peace and reconciliation (CEH, 1999, Conclusions, pp. 47–69).

Negotiating Truth and Silences

Initially, the commission was mandated to work for only six months; then six more months were added. A staff of approximately two hundred people, assigned to fourteen offices across the country. German professor Christian Tomulschat, the Guatemalan teacher Otilia Lux de Coti, and Guatemalan lawyer, Alfredo Balsells Tojo, led the Commission. Chilean lawyer Jaime Esponda was head of the Investigative Unit. This unit was charged with determining whether abuses described in the testimonies the staff collected should be considered human rights abuses under international law.

The author of this chapter was assigned to conduct interviews and record testimonies in the Department of El Quiché, where half of the 669 massacres took place. As sources of the information they needed to help them clarify what crimes were committed and by whom, the Guatemalan Truth Commission gathered oral testimonies from survivors and victims.

One example of testimonies collected is this account the author gathered from a Catholic priest. He told her that civilians collaborating with the Guatemalan army, called Civil Defense Patrols (PACs), served as the "eyes" and "ears" of the military, controlling frequently traveled roads, checking villager's identification cards, and spying on neighbors, local groups, and associations. With the help of hooded guides, PACs often swept roads and hills searching for and rounding up villagers the army accused of being communists. These hunts often concluded with the public execution of the so-called communists, in gruesome spectacles in which their bodies were hacked to pieces. The priest told the author,

> At first, to avoid murdering family members and neighbors, some PAC members would strike the ground rather than their victims. To make them show their loyalty, the Army began forcing them to stain their machetes with blood every time when they hacked their victims (Interview, El Quiché, Guatemala, 1999).

The Guatemalan Truth Commission set in motion an extraordinary recollection of testimonies. Many victims and survivors had already organized grassroots organizations and the Truth Commission reached out to groups such as the Widows National Association or *Asociación de Viudas de Guatemala*, (CONAVIGUA) which had formed during the war to pressure the government to account for the whereabouts of relatives who had been "disappeared," and to provide reparations for their losses. The Commission interacted with 20,000 people, and received more than seven thousand testimonies (CEH, 1999, Vol. I, p. 33).

The Commission launched a nationwide media campaign calling on everyone who had information about human rights crimes to come forward. Often, field researchers had to walk, hike, ride horses, and even fly by helicopter to reach remote communities in the mountains, where testimonies were often collectively recorded as community members gathered to recollect their memories of the war. The Truth Commission's researchers' visits to communities were very important, since many didn't have the time and money to travel to the offices in the centers of their towns to give their testimony, even for one day. For thousands of these women, Commission's researchers were the only people they had met who would listen to them as they told of their horrific experiences.

In addition to direct oral testimonies, the Commission sought information from historical documents provided by the parties involved in the armed conflict – the government and its armed forces, the URNG guerillas, and other parties ginvolved in the war, including the United States. The Commission also used data the Catholic Church had collected during its own initiative, which was called the Recovery of Historical Memory Project (REMHI), conducted from 1995 to 1998 through its Human Rights Office (ODHAG).

"Guatemala: Memory of Silence" – A Final Report

"Guatemala: Memory of Silence" was the title of the final report. The Guatemalan Truth corroborated REMHI's report, "Guatemala Never Again" or *Guatemala Nunca Más*, which showed that the Guatemalan state had committed genocide against indigenous Mayan groups between 1981 and 1983.

Released to the public on February 25, 1999, "Guatemala: Memory of Silence" consisted of twelve volumes. It was submitted to the then United Nations Secretary-General Kofi Annan and many sectors of Guatemalan society, and the international community embraced it as the official, authoritative story of some of the darkest years the country had lived through during the last century.

"Guatemala: Memory of Silence" established that the Guatemalan government bore responsibility for ninety-three percent, and the URNG left-wing guerillas for only three percent, of all murders, disappearances, and torturing committed between 1962 and 1996. Eighty-three percent of all the victims of the conflict were identified as Mayan (CEH, 1999, Conclusions, p. 85). Testimony after testimony told of how the army slaughtered civilians the government falsely accused of being members of, or of supporting, the URNG. The following is an account the Commission collected in the Department of Huehuetenango, where an estimated 350 people were killed:

> On that morning soldiers from the army base #19 arrived in the Finca. First, they called all members of the community to a public meeting: women, children, men, young and old. They separated the men and locked them up in the courthouse. Then they rounded up the women and locked them up at another location. They killed the women first by burning them alive. Then they killed the children. Informants could see through a hole in the window. They watched the soldiers cut the children's stomachs with knives and grabbed their legs smashing their heads against heavy sticks. A few survivors escaped walking and crawling all night long until they reached the border with México. (Illustrative case #18, July 17, 1982. Massacre in San Francisco Nentón, CEH, 1999, Vol. VI, p. 345).

The Recommendations

The Truth Commission was responsible for recommending measures the state could take to "... preserve the memory of the victims, to foster a culture of mutual respect and observance of human rights, and to strengthen the democratic process" (CEH, 1999, Conclusions, p. 47). The CEH's recommendations "... [were] fundamentally designed to facilitate unity in Guatemala and banish the centuries-old divisions suffered" (CEH, 1999, Conclusions, p. 48). For example, the Commission recommended that a day of victims' remembrance be designated to safeguard victim's memories.

The Guatemalan Truth Commission accomplished two important goals. Firstly, it gave people who had not been heard the chance to tell about grievous wrongs Guatemalan soldiers and collaborators, and in some cases guerrillas, perpetrated against them and members of their families and communities. Secondly, it made these stories part of the official, permanent public record. People in Guatemala, and all over the world, could now read true accounts of what happened during the war.

Unfortunately, while the "Guatemala: Memory of Silence" accomplished some important goals, it fell short of its objective of bringing about reconciliation. Firstly, the government did little to disseminate the Truth Commission's findings among the populace. Secondly, the findings the government did disseminate were written mainly in Spanish, and only minimally in Mayan languages, though Mayans, for the most part, can barely read or write in Spanish. The most serious shortcoming is the fact that the report did not lead to even one perpetrator being held responsible for his crimes (see, Esparza et al. 2009).

CONCLUSION

Truth commissions are one of the mechanisms of transitional justice many countries use to shift away from an authoritarian, toward a more democratic, form of government. They rarely name individual perpetrators or try them in courts. More than twenty truth and reconciliation commissions have been set up throughout the world since the 1970s. The work of truth commissions is an important first step in uncovering human rights abuses and crimes against humanity, as established in the Universal Declaration of Human Rights and in the Geneva Convention protecting the rights of civilians and combatants involved in armed conflicts.

The Guatemalan Truth Commission concluded that the Guatemalan State had committed genocide against the Mayan population during the administrations of Generals Lucas Garcia and Efrain Rios Montt.

The Truth Commission was valuable in two ways. One was that it gave people who had not been heard the chance to tell about grievous wrongs Guatemalan soldiers and collaborators, and in some cases guerrillas, perpetrated against them and members of their families and communities. Another was that it made these stories part of the official, permanent public record. Among its shortcomings are two problems. One, the findings the government disseminated were written mainly in Spanish, though most Mayans can barely read or write in Spanish. More detrimentally, no perpetrator has yet been held responsible for his crimes. It is important to note that while survivors' testimonies have played a key role in exposing the dynamics of state violence, truth commissions are now recognized as limited (Daly, 2008) in their accounts of what moves people to become torturers, killers, or accomplices.

FURTHER IN SITU MATERIAL, READINGS, AND WEB SITES

For a visual understanding of the Guatemalan genocide, visit the Historical Memory Project's Archival Collection at the Lloyd Seal Library at John Jay College of Criminal Justice. This project's archival material includes ten photographs of the Guatemalan genocide by acclaimed photographer, Jonathan Moller.

REFERENCES

Commission for Historical Clarification (HCCG). (1999). *Guatemala, Memory of Silence – Conclusions and Recommendations.* Guatemala: Oficina de Servicios para Proyectos de las Naciones Unidas (UNOPS).

Comisión para el Esclarecimiento Histórico (CEH). (1999). *Guatemala: Memoria del Silencio* (Vols. 1–12). Guatemala: Oficina de Servicios para Proyectos de las Naciones Unidas (UNOPS).

Daly, E. (2008). Truth Skepticism: An inquiry into the Value of Truth in Times of Transition. *The International Journal of Transitional Justice*, 2(1), 23–41.

Esparza, M., D. Feierstein, & H. Huttenbach. (Eds.) (2009). *State Violence and Genocide in Latin America: The Cold War Years.* London: Routledge.

Grandin, G. (2005). The Instruction of Great Catastrophe: Truth Commissions, National History, and State Formation in Argentina, Chile, and Guatemala. *The American Historical Review.* Retrieved March 4, 2010 from www.history-cooperative.org/journals/ahr/110.1/grandin.html

Hayner, B. P. (1991). *Informe de la Comisión Nacional de Verdad y Reconciliación.* Santiago: Talleres de la Nación.

(2001). *Unspeakable Truths: Confronting State Terror and Atrocity: How Truth Commissions Around the World Are Challenging the Past and Shaping the Future.* New York: Routledge.

ABOUT THE AUTHOR

Marcia Esparza, Ph.D., is an associate professor in the Department of Criminal Justice at John Jay College and the Director of Historical Memory Project, (a documentation center that memorializes the history of state crime and violence in the Americas). From 1994 through 2000, she undertook field research in Guatemala. This research included working for the Guatemalan Truth Commission (officially named, the Commission to Clarify Past Human Rights Violations and Acts of Violence That Have Caused the Guatemalan People to Suffer (HCCG), or *Comisión para el Esclarecimiento Histórico*, (CEH). As an international consultant, Dr. Esparza recorded testimonies from war survivors and a few perpetrators and has presented her research in Athens, Greece and Granada, Spain.

PART VII

INTERNATIONAL COOPERATION
AND CRIMINAL JUSTICE

The growth in transnational crimes has resulted in an increasing need for international cooperation among police agencies and for new multilateral agreements regarding the arrest and prosecution of offenders. For many years, Interpol has embodied this cooperation, but many more such international organizations have been established in recent times. This is notably the case in the European Union. In 1999, the EU Council of Ministers established the European Police Office, or Europol, a fully-fledged, multipurpose policing agency. It performs an intelligence and information-clearing function supported by high-level information systems, linked to each member states' security and police institutions (see Chapter 56 by Connor Brady). Subsequently, the EU established Eurojust and the European Judicial Network, which are designed to assist day-to-day cooperation between member states and to simplify extradition processes. As Matti Joutsen explains (Chapter 57), this has substantially improved the speed and efficiency of dealing with cases that span national borders in the EU.

Other notable efforts to improve the policing of transnational cases include the establishment of ASEANAPOL and international protocols established by the World Customs Organization and the G7's Experts on Transnational Crime. However, as Rob Mawby reminds us (Chapter 54), the difficulties of coordinating the actions of different law enforcement entities in different countries should not be underestimated. Even data sharing among different police forces is greatly complicated by language difficulties and differences in computer technologies and recording systems. Additionally, each law enforcement agency has its own model of operations and its own organizational structures, which again might impede collaboration with other agencies. William McDonald in Chapter 58 echoes the theme that we should not expect too much, too quickly in improved consultation and cooperation. In addition to obstacles identified by Mawby, McDonald cites the lack of extradition agreements among certain states; differences in the legal definitions of crimes; asymmetry in the professionalism of the law enforcement agencies; corruption; and international and domestic politics.

There are some specific difficulties of coordinating the policing of borders between countries. Effective border policing performs a critical role in the control of transnational crimes such as human smuggling and drug trafficking (see Chapter 55 by Rob Guerette). In some countries, the military is given the responsibility of border policing. In others, such as the United States, border policing is performed by a distinct policing agency.

Finally, it is important to note that cooperation among nonlaw enforcement institutions will be needed to deal with certain crimes. For example in dealing with money laundering and international frauds, global cooperative efforts are needed by such institutions as the World Bank, the International Monetary Fund, the African Development Bank, the Asian Development Bank, and the Financial Action Task Force (FATF) (see Chapter 59 by Adam Graycar).

Improved capacities to deter, detect, and respond appropriately to transnational and international crimes will bring tangible improvements in the quality of life for millions of people around the world. It is vital that these fledgling efforts to improve global cooperation are nurtured and allowed to take wing.

54   World Policing Models

Rob Mawby

OVERVIEW

When members of the public travel abroad and experience crime and the response of the police in these other countries, they take with them a common sense notion of what "the police" means. They will often draw distinctions between their own society and these "other" systems. Teasing out the similarities and the differences between police systems and their components in different societies, explaining the differences, drawing examples of good practice that might be introduced elsewhere, and learning from experiences of bad practices – these are the key features of comparative police studies. While the difficulties surrounding such endeavors may be considerable, the potential benefits make the challenge worthwhile.

The nature of "the police" varies markedly between countries and over time. For example, the public police model that emerged in the United Kingdom and United States in the nineteenth century differed from the centralized, autocratic arm of state authority that preceded it on continental European (Chapman, 1970), and while the crossnational interchange of ideas in recent years has resulted in police structures and methods from one country being imported to others, there are still stark contrasts. This chapter, therefore, begins by offering a definition of the police that incorporates variations, before moving on to consider alternative models and recent trends.

DEFINITIONS

First, it is crucial to distinguish between "policing" as a process and "the police" as an organization. "Policing," a term we might apply to the process of preventing and detecting crime and maintaining order, is an activity that is engaged in by a growing number of agencies or individuals: members of the public, the private sector and locally based organizations like neighborhood watch (Bayley & Shearing, 1996). The police as an institution, in contrast, might be responsible for many other services that are only tenuously related to maintaining order or preventing crime.

When we consider police systems in different societies we mean by the police an agency that can be distinguished in terms of its legitimacy, its structure, and its function (Mawby, 1990). Legitimacy implies that the police are granted special authority by those in power, whether this is an elite within the society, an occupying force, or the community as a whole. Structure implies that the police is organized, with some degree of specialization and with a code of practice within which, for example, the extent to which use of force is legitimate is specified. However, the extent of organization or specialization, and the types of force considered appropriate, will vary. Finally, function implies that the role of the police is concentrated on the maintenance of law and order and the prevention and detection of offences, but there might be considerable differences in the balance between these, and in the extent to which other duties are assigned to the police.

ALTERNATIVE POLICE SYSTEMS

This section considers the police systems of a wide range of countries worldwide. This endeavor can, however, be approached in a number of different ways. One is to focus on countries separately and to identify the core features of their policing systems in the context of their social and political systems, subsequently classifying them according to a typology. An alternative approach is to identify different models that apply to groups of countries. For example, we might distinguish between Anglo-American policing, policing on Continental Europe, communist/postcommunist policing, colonial police and the type of policing that has emerged in the Far East. However, there are, arguably, as many differences between countries within a model as there are between alternative models, a point made forcefully by Anderson and Killingray (1991, 1992) in the context of a colonial police system. Equally, there are often variations within a country. For example, in Canada marked variations exist between the centralized RCMP and local urban and provincial police. Therefore, there is an attempt to distinguish between two broad models of policing: a control-dominated system and a community-oriented system.

A control-dominated system is one where the main function of the police is to maintain order, where the population generally fails to recognize the legitimacy of the state and its agents, the police. In such societies, the police may carry out a range of administrative tasks on behalf of the state, but rarely provide a public service that addresses the welfare needs of the community. The police is, consequently, generally organized and managed centrally and has many paramilitary qualities. In some cases, the distinction between police and military is negligible.

In complete contrast, a community-oriented system is one where the main function of the police is to provide a public service that addresses the wider needs of the community. Maintaining order is important, but the emphasis is more on crime as symptomatic of community problems than an affront to authority. Such a model assumes that the police are accorded considerable legitimacy by local communities. The police are consequently generally organized and managed locally and barriers between police and public are minimized. Community policing and problem-oriented policing typify this approach.

The control-dominated system can be identified with traditional policing on Continental Europe, the colonies established by Britain and its European neighbors, and Communist Europe. Raymond Fosdick, for example, who worked as an administrator with the New York Police Department, toured Europe at the beginning of the twentieth century. His text, published in 1915 and subsequently reissued (Fosdick, 1969), contrasted the centralized, militaristic, control-oriented police systems he found there with the situation in England and the USA. This notion of a "Police State" (Chapman, 1970) formed the basis for the development of policing in communist Russia and subsequently, its satellites in Eastern Europe. This was characterized by: a centralized and militaristic uniformed police subordinate to the secret police; an emphasis upon maintaining political order rather than tackling conventional crime; and a close link between police and communist party, with minimal public or legal accountability. The other police system that has been consistently recognized in the literature as control-dominated is the colonial model. For example, the British government allegedly created a police system for its empire that was appropriate for the control of a subjugated population where the needs of economic imperialism required a politically controlled paramilitary force prioritizing public order (Cole, 1999). The model it used was the one first established for Ireland where the police could not rely on public consent. Colonial police may be characterized as: militaristic (e.g., armed and living as units in barracks) and, in many cases, centralized; prioritizing public order tasks; and deriving their legitimacy from their colonial masters rather than the indigenous population. Additionally, given the difficulties occupying powers have had in locally recruiting loyal and reliable police officers, a common tactic was to recruit from either indigenous minorities or from other colonies, on the basis that such groups would be less likely to form allegiances with local people against the interests of the occupying power.

While identifying a control-dominated model may be useful, it should not blind us to the fact that most countries associated with it differ in a number of respects. For example, although British colonial authority was centralized in London, within different countries the police system was often regionally based; and officers were not always issued with firearms. On Continental Europe, there were also considerable variations, with, for example, the Dutch system neither overtly militaristic nor excessively centralized, and although countries such as France, Spain, and Italy traditionally had control-dominated police systems, in each case the maintenance of at least two police forces allowed the rulers to ensure that no one institution achieved sufficient power to threaten government.

The task of assigning specific police systems to a community-oriented model is even more difficult. Although this may be the type of democratic policing that many of us aspire to, it is difficult to nominate any one country as even approaching achieving it (Brogden, 1999; Mawby, 1990). In England and Wales, for example, often eulogized as the home of "community policing," modern systems of policing emerged at least in part as a means of maintaining order in the midst of working class protest, a point revisited when Margaret Thatcher's government used the police to break the miners strike in the early 1980s. And in many cases police were recruited from rural areas to work in the cities, undermining the claim that they were local citizens in uniform. In the USA, where police systems have been traditionally locally based, personnel have been recruited locally, and officers have engaged in a wide range of "noncrime" responsibilities, the image of the police as a militaristic body charged with fighting the "war" against crime is equally pervasive. Elsewhere, Bayley's (1976) early presentation of the Japanese police as community-based and welfare-oriented has been questioned (Leishman, 1999; Miyazawa, 1992). It may, therefore, be that the key strength of specifying a community-oriented model is as an ideal type, in the Weberian sense, so as to better evaluate police systems and changes within them.

RECENT TRENDS

While traditionally, the main generators of change have been conquest and migration (Mawby, 1990), more recently two broad generators of change can be identified: external influence and internal pressure.

External influence is particularly important in postmodern societies where similar influences are prevalent across national boundaries and where examples of innovative developments in one society are readily available as examples of best practice elsewhere. The expansion of private policing is a case in point (Bayley & Shearing, 1996). Formal pacts add a further impetus to change. For example, the emergence and expansion of the European Union has involved greater crossborder cooperation and, consequently, increased pressure toward the harmonization of policy. Most recently, Europol was ratified in 1999 as the EU organization for cross-border coordination between national law-enforcement agencies, providing collation, analysis and dissemination of information, and a European Police College (CEPOL) was established in 2001. Such initiatives may lead to increased cooperation, but national interests may prevent more radical change, as illustrated by conflicts over drug policies. A further source of external pressure involves postwar reconstruction. Here Fairchild (1988) has detailed the transformation of the (West) German police under allied occupation.

Internal pressures to change the structure and functions of the police are also evident, but it is sometimes difficult to identify any consistent pattern. For example, in countries such as Sweden and the Netherlands the police have become more centralized; in contrast, the traditionally centralized French system has diversified to allow the addition of local police bodies. Internal changes may, on the other hand, be predicated by regime change. This is particularly well illustrated in the case of former Eastern Bloc countries and postcolonial societies. In each case, the transformation of the traditionally control-dominated police into a community-oriented police was commonly advocated by aspiring leaders. However, in the former case a perceived threat to law and order led to a dismantling of police reform agendas (Mawby, 1999), with subsequent reforms less radical than had been anticipated (Beck, Chistyakova, & Robertson, 2006), while in the case of postcolonial societies, new governments also sometimes retained old police systems in order to establish and assert their authority (Anderson & Killingray, 1992). South Africa provides an excellent recent example of the difficulties of enacting reform (Brogden & Shearing, 1993).

In many cases, of course, internal pressures for reform may combine with external influences. For example, both the USA and many Western European countries have been influential in advising former Eastern Bloc counties on reform agendas, in the former case including the funding of a police college in Budapest. However, as in the case of South Korea (Lee, 1990), the pressure toward community-oriented policing might be outweighed by foreign policy concerns, be these political or international crime related. This point has current resonance in the context of Iraq (Pino & Wiatrowski, 2006).

SUMMARY

This chapter provides an introduction to policing in different societies, starting with a discussion of how "the police" is defined. It then considers alternative policing systems, identifying two models: control-dominated and community-oriented (Sullivan & Haberfeld, 2005). Although there are numerous examples of the former, the latter is more a target than a reality. This leads into a discussion of recent changes in former colonial and communist societies.

Inevitably, we can here provide only a broad sweep of policing systems across the globe and there are areas and sociopolitical systems missing from the list. What we have attempted to do is to raise questions concerning the relationship between policing and the wider context within which it takes place.

REFERENCES

Anderson, D. M. and D. Killingray. (Eds.) (1991). *Policing the Empire.* Manchester: Manchester University Press.

Anderson, D. M. and D. Killingray. (Eds.) (1992). *Policing and Decolonisation.* Manchester: Manchester University Press.

Bayley, D. H. (1976). *Forces of Order: Police Behaviour in Japan and the United States.* Berkeley, CA: University of California Press.

Bayley, D. & C. Shearing. (1996). The Future of Policing. *Law and Society Review,* 30(3), 585–606.

Beck, A., Y. Chistyakova, & A. Robertson. (2006) *Police Reform in Post-Soviet Societies.* Abingdon: Routledge.

Brogden, M. (1999). Community Policing as Cherry Pie. In R. Mawby (Ed.), *Policing Across the World: Issues for the Twenty-First Century.* London: UCL Press, pp. 167–86.

Brogden, M. & C. Shearing (1993). *Policing for a New South Africa.* London: Routledge.

Chapman, B. (1970). *Police State.* London: Pall Mall Press.

Cole, B. (1999). Post-Colonial Systems. In R. Mawby (Ed.), *Policing Across the World: Issues for the Twenty-First Century.* London: UCL Press, pp. 88–108.

Fairchild, E. S. (1988) *German Police.* Springfield, MA: Charles C.Thomas.

Fosdick, R. B. (1969). *European Police Systems.* Second Edition. Montclair, NJ: Patterson Smith.

Lee, S. Y. (1990). Morning Calm, Rising Sun: National Character and Policing in South Korea and in Japan. *Police Studies*, 13, 91–110.

Leishman, F. (1999). Policing in Japan: East Asian Archetype?, In R. Mawby (Ed.), *Policing Across the World: Issues for the Twenty-First Century*. London: UCL Press, pp. 109–25.

Mawby, R. I. (1990) *Comparative Policing Issues: The British and American Experience in International Perspective*. London: Routledge.

(1999). The Changing Face of Policing in Central and Eastern Europe. *International Journal of Police Science and Management*, 2(3), 199–216.

Miyazawa, S. (1992). Policing *in Japan: A Study on Making Crime*. New York: State University of New York Press.

Pino, N. & M. D. Wiatrowski (2006). *Democratic Policing in Transitional and Developing Countries*. Aldershot: Ashgate.

Sullivan, L. E. & M. R. Haberfeld (2005). *Encyclopaedia of Law Enforcement: Volume 3 International*. Thousand Oaks, CA: Sage.

ABOUT THE AUTHOR

Rob Mawby is Visiting Professor of Criminology and Criminal Justice at the University of Gloucestershire, England. His research interests cover comparative policing, victimology, crime reduction, and tourism and crime. He is the editor of *Crime Prevention and Community Safety: An International Journal* and is the author of eight books and more than one hundred articles. Outside academia he has worked with police and other criminal justice agencies in a variety of capacities, and was a member of police science subcommittee (2004–7) of the European Police College (CEPOL).

55 Crossborder Policing

Rob T. Guerette

INTRODUCTION

One of the primary functions of national governments is to provide security for its people. Since the earliest times this has meant protecting against crossborder invasions and infiltrations from other governments or individuals who are believed to threaten the national order or social structure (Rotberg, 2003). Establishing national security is necessary so that other government services can be delivered. These include systems for regulating the norms and mores of the society generally, as well as establishing systematic means of managing disputes, establishing and enforcing legal codes, and facilitating economic markets, among others. The ability of governments to ensure the security of the nation state also helps to promote the sovereignty of the nation and demonstrates the competence of political leaders.

Though border guards were originally established to defend against incursion from other countries, increasingly, their role has shifted toward managing what have been called "nontraditional" or "critical" security threats, such as smuggling and trafficking (Farer, 1999). To secure nation states from external threats most countries have established police organizations that are responsible for managing border areas.

THE NATURE OF CROSSBORDER POLICING[1]

In some nations, the military is given the responsibility of border policing. In others, such as the United States and the European Union, border

[1] The terms "border" policing and "crossborder" policing are used interchangeably throughout this chapter. As used here, the reference is to any policing activity that is directed toward detecting or preventing crimes and other illicit activities that are carried out across nation state boundaries.

policing is performed by a distinct policing agency. Sometimes referred to as the "border guard," the primary role of these agencies is to enforce laws against illegal immigration, though they are also responsible for countering drug smuggling, human smuggling or trafficking, and safeguarding against terrorism. Policing borders presents more difficulty for destination countries compared to interior policing because nations lack authority to comprehensively address transnational crimes that originate in other countries.[2] Because of this, border police must often rely on cooperation from governments in origin and transit countries.[3]

In some ways border police units are hybrid forms of policing agencies in that they operate similar to local level police organizations yet they derive their authority from the national government rather than the local municipality where they operate. They are similar because, like local police, border police engage in routine patrols and respond to calls for assistance. They differ in that border police enforce national or federal laws such as those governing immigration and the movement of illicit goods rather than laws against conventional crimes such as robbery, assault, or burglary which are the responsibility of local level police agencies. The extent to which this is true, however, varies from country to country and largely depends on whether securing the border is the responsibility of the military or a separate border-policing agency.

During times of crisis, border police groups are sometimes used to support the nations' military against external threats. When not in times of war or international conflict, the role of border police focuses more on preventing, detecting, and responding to the illicit movement of people and products across their national borders. Most border policing agencies have increasingly relied on developing technology to detect unauthorized activity and to secure the nation state (Andreas, 2001). These technological advancements include the use of underground motion sensors, remote surveillance cameras, and real-time satellite surveillance systems, among others.

OVERVIEW OF BORDER POLICING IN THE UNITED STATES AND THE EUROPEAN UNION

There is considerable similarity across the various border police agencies in terms of their purpose and operational practice. However, many border

---

[2] A "destination" country is one which goods or people are smuggled into as the final destination.

[3] An "origin" country is one where goods or people originate. A "transit" country is one that serves as a transfer point between origin and destination countries.

police agencies have their own distinctive characteristics and qualities that stem from the historical geopolitical context within which the agency was founded. Some agencies have evolved into their current arrangement in response to changing conditions brought about by globalization. The following provides a brief overview of border policing in just a few places around the world.

United States Border Policing

There are three primary agencies responsible for securing the borders of the United States all which operate within the Department of Homeland Security: the U.S. Border Patrol, Immigration and Customs Enforcement, and the U.S. Coast Guard.

The primary role of the U.S. Border Patrol is to secure the nearly six thousand miles of U.S. land border between the points of entry and two thousand miles of water border surrounding Florida and Puerto Rico. The USBP carries out its mission through several operational strategies, including routine patrol and surveillance of international borders, tracking of unauthorized migrants and smugglers; vehicle inspections at traffic checkpoints; inspection of transportation lines entering the country; helicopter patrols of remote border areas, marine patrol along bodies of water and bike patrol within border towns and cities. The Border Patrol also relies on technology to monitor borders including infrared night-vision devices, seismic ground sensors, CCTV systems, modern computer information processing systems, and unmanned aerial aircraft.

The U.S. Immigration and Customs Enforcement (ICE) agency is responsible for monitoring the flow of people and products coming into the U.S. at the nation's points of entry. These include those positioned in airports, land based entrances along roadways, and maritime ports around the country. Working in collaboration with the USBP and other government agencies, ICE is responsible for enforcing a broad range of federal statutes which involve matters of visa security, illegal arms trafficking, document and identity fraud, drug trafficking, child pornography and sex tourism, immigration and customs fraud, intellectual property rights violations, financial crime, and human smuggling and trafficking, among others.

The U.S. Coast Guard (USCG) is responsible for monitoring the U.S. border waterways. Operating under the auspices of the U.S. Department of Homeland Security, the USCG is divided into three operational units: aviation forces, boat forces (vessels less than sixty-five feet in length), and cutter forces (vessels more than sixty-five feet in length). The USCG undertakes a variety of tasks but those relevant to border policing center mostly on the interdiction of migrants and narcotics smugglers while they are attempting entry into the country, environmental protection, securing of the nation's maritime ports against crime and terrorist activity, and interdiction of other nation's fishing vessels within U.S. protected zones.

The European Union

The borders of the European Union are operationally secured by the individual border police agencies of the external member states of the Union. An organization called Frontex which derives from the French, meaning "external borders" is responsible for coordination of border security measures of the individual member nations. Formally, Frontex was known as the European Agency for the Management of Operational Cooperation at the External Borders of the Member States of the European Union. The headquarters of Frontex is located in Warsaw, Poland. Frontex is a young agency that was established by EU Council Regulation and became operational in October of 2005.

Another agency with responsibility for securing EU borders is Europol. Europol stands for the "European Law Enforcement Organisation" which facilitates cooperation of the policing authorities in the EU member states to prevent transnational crimes such as terrorism, drug, and human trafficking. Unlike the other border police agencies, however, Europol's responsibility is to gather and disseminate intelligence of transnational crime. The agency does not conduct policing operations.

Each of the EU member nations maintains their own agencies responsible for customs and border security. They operate like most border security forces in the sense that they patrol border areas and regulate flows of people and products that come into the country and the European Union. While each of the member states maintains their own sovereignty, they must follow the rules and regulations of the European Union as a requisite for membership. The Schengen Agreement provided for the removal of systematic border controls between participating countries of the European Union. This agreement liberalized the requirements for travel between the EU member states, while security and regulatory controls along the external borders of the EU have been strengthened.

One of the most visible developments in EU border policing involves securing the southern borders. The Spanish government has created a surveillance system of its maritime border along the African straights using the latest in available technology. Named SIVE, which stands for "External

Surveillance Integrated System," the early warning system pulls together data received from sensors deployed on the ground, in aircraft, in boats and on satellites, to produce real-time graphical displays of the border zone. There are plans to implement a similar system, labeled EUROSUR (European Border Surveillance System), to monitor the entire border region of the European Union.

CHALLENGES AND CRITICISMS OF CROSSBORDER POLICING

Several challenges face crossborder policing. First, jurisdictional issues often limit the ability of border police to fully address transnational crime issues which originate outside of their jurisdiction where they have no legal authority. As a consequence, they must rely on cooperation with neighboring countries which often have limited resources or lack the incentive to provide meaningful assistance (Nadelmann, 1993). Transnational crime groups take advantage of this jurisdictional divide in carrying out their illicit business (Naim, 2005). Second, many border areas are comprised of vast and diverse terrain that makes it difficult to comprehensively police. Agencies must focus their limited resources on known high traffic areas, which mean many places along border areas go unmonitored. Third, technological advancements, such as the Internet and other forms of communication, have given unprecedented abilities to smugglers, traffickers, and terrorists to conduct their business (Battacharyya, 2005; Naim, 2005). This assists them in effectively circumventing border security measures.

Criticisms of border policing in any country can be divided into two categories: those that address the function and those that address the process. The most frequent criticism of the function of border policing concerns the exclusion of migrants from opportunities in destination countries. Some argue that preventing individuals from migrating freely in search of better living conditions violates intrinsic human rights. Others see it as an intrinsic right of nations to safeguard their borders from products and people entering without permission.

The most common process criticism of border policing concerns the treatment of migrants by border police. Agents are frequently criticized for using excessive force against migrants (King, 2004; Phillips, Rodriguez and Hagan, 2002). Though it is uncertain whether excessive force among border police is greater than among police generally, reports of its occurrence are common. Moreover, the process of border policing is sometimes cited as ineffective in distinguishing refugees with legitimate claims of political asylum from illegal immigrants. A related concern stems from ever increasing

Table 55.1. Challenges and criticisms of crossborder policing

Challenges	Nature of the problem/issue
Legal jurisdiction	• Limits police powers to within own country. • Unable to address transnational crime groups at their base of operations/origins (i.e., in other countries).
Vast and diverse terrain	• Limited resources means unable to police all border areas. • Must focus on known high traffic corridors.
Technology	• Allows transnational crime groups to rapidly access information, communicate, and orchestrate finances. • Facilitates circumvention of border security measures.
Criticisms	
Blocking opportunities	• Opportunities for gainful employment, access to healthcare, and dignified living conditions are argued to be universal human rights. Blocking access to these violates these rights as well as the right to freedom of movement.
Treatment of migrants	• Securing borders leads migrants to evermore treacherous methods of gaining entry resulting in death and harm to migrants. Security is said to cause death of migrants. • Mistreatment of migrants by border police is at times criminal. Border police may fail to recognize migrants' legitimate claims of asylum. • Migrants are commonly victimized and exploited by others during their migration.

dangers that migrants undertake in the aftermath of heightened border enforcement campaigns. Many border watchers criticize governments for displacing migrants to routes that are more remote and perilous resulting in greater fatalities among migrants. In response, some governments have stepped up life saving operations along border areas. The U.S. Border Patrol, for instance, adopted the Border Safety Initiative (BSI) to reduce the number of migrant deaths along the U.S. and Mexico border (Table 55.1).

SUMMARY

The agencies responsible for securing borders use a variety of techniques including physical patrols and tracking and have increasingly employed technological innovations such as satellite surveillance and electronic monitoring systems. Border policing around the world has become more important in light of concerns about terrorism and greater immigration as global resources have been concentrated in certain regions of the world. Criticisms of border policing stem from the exclusion of individuals from opportunities in destination countries and the manner in which apprehended immigrants are treated. The greatest challenge of border policing involves finding ways to competently secure national borders while also being responsive to individual rights.

REFERENCES

Andreas, P. (2001). *Border Games: Policing the U.S-Mexico Divide*. Ithaca, NY: Cornell University Press.
Bhattacharyya, G. (2005). *Traffick: The Illicit Movement of People and Things*. Ann Arbor, MI: Pluto Press.
Farer, T. (Ed.) (1999). *Transnational Crime in the Americas: An Inter-American Dialogue Book*. New York, NY: Routledge.
King, L. (2004, September 29). The World: 5 in Israeli Border Police Charged with Abuse. *Los Angeles Times*, P. 3.
Nadelmann, E. A. (1993). *Cops Across Borders: The Internationalization of U.S. Criminal Law Enforcement*. University Park, PA: Penn State Press.
Naím, M. (2005). *Illicit: How Smugglers, Traffickers and Copycats Are Hijacking the Global Economy*. New York, NY: Doubleday.
Phillips, S., N. Rodriguez, & J. Hagan, (2002). Brutality at the Border? Use of Force in the Arrest of Immigrants in the United States. *International Journal of the Sociology of Law*, 30(4), 285–306.
Rotberg, R. I. (2003). *When States Fail: Causes and Consequences*. Princeton, NJ: Princeton University Press.

WEB SITES

Frontex Main Site: www.frontex.europa.eu
U.S. Customs and Border Protection Main Site: www.cbp.gov
U.S. Coast Guard Main Site: www.uscg.mil
Europol Main Site: www.europol.europa.eu

ABOUT THE AUTHOR

Rob T. Guerette is a crime scientist with a research interest in transnational crime and national security issues, situational crime prevention, and problem-oriented policing. He is an associate professor of criminal justice in the School of International and Public Affairs at Florida International University. He holds a doctorate from Rutgers University-Newark and was a fellow at the Eagleton Institute of Politics, Rutgers University-New Brunswick.

56 Challenge and Transition

POLICING DEVELOPMENTS IN THE EUROPEAN CRIMINAL JUSTICE SYSTEM

Conor Brady

EVOLUTION OF THE NEW EUROPE

A description of current and recent developments in European policing necessitates, by way of preface, some outline of the political structures that are evolving in the EU. It was Henry Kissinger who posed the question – when you want to "phone Europe, who do you call?" That was more than thirty years ago. Europe – or the European Union, to be exact – was then a very much smaller place. It comprised nine countries with a population of less than two hundred million using four major languages. Today, the European Union is twenty-seven countries, with more than six hundred million people with twenty-three official languages. How can such a disparate collection of peoples and nations, run a criminal justice system or operate effective policing structures? How can it operate to enforce criminal law across frontiers that have existed in some cases for one thousand years?

Three times more than one hundred years, the nations of Europe went to war against one another and scores of millions of people died, great cities were razed to the ground, whole countrysides were left a wasteland. After the devastation of World War II, a number of far-seeing political leaders, principally Maurice Schumann and Jean Monnet, resolved that Europe would never go to war against itself again. They believed that the best way to ensure this was to build a Europe where resources were held in common, where prosperity of one would be the prosperity of all.

In 1956 the European Coal and Steel Community was created, putting France's and Germany's heavy industry into the common ownership of the two countries. There would no longer be any reason for a war between the states since they were now partners.

In 1960, the European Economic Community grew from the ECSC. In the Treaty of Rome, six countries came together to form a common market and a free trade area. They were Germany, France, Italy, Belgium, the Netherlands, and Luxembourg.

In time, the six became nine, when Britain, Ireland, and Denmark joined. Then the nine became the fifteen, when they were joined by Spain, Portugal, Greece, Sweden, Finland, and Austria. The fifteen became the twenty-five, in 2004 with new members Poland, the Czech Republic, Hungary, Latvia, Estonia, Lithuania, Malta, Slovenia, Slovakia, and Cyprus. In 2007 Bulgaria and Romania joined the Union, bringing membership to twenty-seven.

As the economies grew and became more closely integrated, it became clear that there was a need for parallel harmonization in social policies, in education, health care, human rights, law – and, in the latter case, for policing, for criminal justice and for judicial procedure (Glavey, 2000).

In the Treaty of Maastricht in 1992 and the Treaty of Amsterdam 1996, the European Communities became the European Union. By then, the Communities had a European parliament, elected directly by the people: a Commission – which is, in effect, the executive; a Council of Ministers, which represented the political oversight of the Community. The Council of Europe had also afforded Europeans a court of final appeal, to which any citizen or litigant could turn if he or she believed that local, domestic law was in conflict with one's rights under the European Convention on Human Rights.

In 2004, the heads of governments of the EU states agreed on a new draft constitution for the Union. This has yet to be ratified by the member-states. Some have mistakenly begun to see this process creating a United States of Europe. This is to misunderstand the reality. Europe had no single government, no army. Yet the EU has recognized that if there is common economy there has to be a harmonization in other areas. If borders and frontiers are abolished, economic activity will spread. But so also will criminal activity.

THE "THREE PILLARS" OF THE EUROPEAN UNION

The EU is described as being supported by three distinct "pillars."

The first is the economic pillar. Without a doubt, this has been an extraordinary success. The EU has created an economic zone that exceeds the US in GDP. It has created a free market in goods and services. It achieved harmonization of key economic policies. It now uses a common currency, the Euro. The term "free market" is generally preferred by commentators in European media.

The second pillar deals with foreign policy and defense. It is a crucially important area for the future development of the Union. But it does not touch directly on the subject of this paper.

The third pillar seeks to establish an "area of freedom, security and justice" within the EU. The development of an EU policy on Justice and Home Affairs began with the Treaty of Maastricht which came into operation in late 1993. It could be said that flesh and blood were added to the bones of the Maastricht Treaty in the Tampere declarations of October 1999 and brought to life in the (Second) Treaty of Amsterdam, also in 1997 (Swallow, 1994). It was clear that an effective and efficient policing and criminal justice system could not operate across the Union without significantly overhauling existing linkages and structures. The countries of the EU, heretofore, had a liaison system that operated through Interpol at its headquarters at Lyon, France.

For many years, at political level, the EU had a loose and somewhat informal forum for cooperation on issues of justice, home affairs, law enforcement, and crime. This was the Trevi Group, established in 1976. In 1984 it took the form of regular meetings between EU Ministers for Justice. (In the aftermath of the 2004 terrorist bombings in Madrid, however, a EU antiterrorist coordinator, Mr. Gjis De Vries, was appointed.). But until 1999 there was no police or law-enforcement system, specific to the EU. A police officer in one part of the Union who wanted information from another, was in exactly the same position as an officer calling from an African or a South American police service. Operationally, the Schengen accords proved very inadequate, leaving police officers on the ground frustrated.

In developing new structures for policing and law enforcement, the EU has had to advance slowly, sensitively, and with a constant awareness of the necessity of balancing efficiency and effectiveness against individual freedoms and rights. Thus, it was decided that in addition to the development of new policing and judicial linkages, there should also be a new European Charter of Fundamental Rights in order to underpin personal freedoms. The Charter was signed into law in October 2000 (Walsh, 2000).

In 1992, under the terms of the Maastricht Treaty, the EU established the first specifically law-enforcement agency of the Union. From 1992 to 1994 it remained largely an idea on paper but in 1994 it became a reality as the Europol Drugs Unit (EDU.)

THE SETTING UP OF EUROPOL

In 1995, the EU Council of Ministers provided for the establishment of the European Police Office or Europol. By 1999, Europol was up and running as a fully-fledged, multipurpose policing agency. Europol is located at The Hague, in the Netherlands, and each country of the union has officers on permanent attachment there. They are essentially an intelligence and information-clearing operation and are supported by high-level information systems, linked to each member states' security and police institutions.

Europol's priorities are:

- Illegal drugs and narcotics and linked criminal activity
- Terrorism and terrorist activities
- Human Trafficking
- Money Laundering
- Forgery, counterfeiting, and fraud (the organization has a special mission to protect the integrity of the Euro)
- The control and transporting of nuclear and other hazardous materials.

The development of this new policing instrument, however, has to be seen in the context of other, linked initiatives. In 1995, the EU promulgated what has become known as the Schengen Area, an initiative named from the city in which it was agreed. Some EU countries were "foot dragging" but the impetus for Schengen came from within the main EU states – even if it was not shared or supported by all members.) The Schengen Area defines a single border around the EU; it has common rules on visas, on asylum seekers, on border checks and on the movement of persons. The border in part runs inside Europe – along the English Channel, to be precise, and currently, to some extent, between EU member states in Central and Eastern Europe. A further development was the advent of the Schengen Information System which shares information across the EU on persons and objects that may be of interest in issues of public security.

A principal instrument of Schengen is the Sirene system of linked databases, operating in each state and providing detailed information on travel and movement in and out of and within the Union. Other initiatives included the establishment of EURODAC, an EU-wide fingerprinting database.

A European Police Chiefs Operational Task Force was established. This now meets regularly to define and agree action on operational issues across the Union. A European Police College – CEPOL – was established. This is a network of European Police Colleges that share expertise, serving the needs of law-enforcement agencies right across the Union.

A network of prosecutors, magistrates, and police investigators called EUROJUST was created. This enables investigating magistrates and prosecutors to work together across national boundaries in the investigation and prosecution of serious and organized crime.

It is important to understand that this is a system of networks or linkages that aims to improve efficiency among 120 police agencies across Europe. The structures are horizontal rather than vertical. They have secretariat services in one or other of the EU capitals, but they do not operate on a central, controlling basis.

DIFFERENT SYSTEMS WITH COMMON VALUES

Different countries have their own traditions, culture, and languages, and each has its own value system in relation to crime, law-enforcement, and criminal justice. For example, two quite different trial models operate in the Union: common law and the roman law.

Yet there are some values held in common. No state of the Union operates the death penalty. The principle of judicial review – the right of appeal, if necessary to the EU courts, is guaranteed. Due process is guaranteed – although some states, including Ireland, do retain the right, in certain circumstances, to operate military courts, rather than civil courts, where there is a threat to state security.

It is difficult to make an assessment of how the EU police and security services are effective against terrorist organizations and networks. The Madrid bombings represented a significant success for the terrorists. The London bombings of July 7th 2005 were also a success for terrorists although investigations indicate that the plot was virtually all "home grown" within the United Kingdom.

One also has to ask, what do Europeans actually want in their policing services? Generally, in Europe it is not easy to sell the concept of "zero tolerance." It is not a place in which one could as easily mobilize the sort of measures that the United States has put together in the "Homeland Defense" plan. Its cultural and historic inheritance is different. To strengthen policing systems in this climate is a difficult calculation. The most obvious gap in EU policing has been the lack of an operational, on-the-ground, unit or force that can discharge the same functions as the FBI does in the United States. However, in 2004 the gap was somewhat fulfilled by the establishment of Joint Investigation Teams (JITs) that operate along with officers from Europol, with what would be roughly equivalent to a federal authority. However, each state of the EU has had to pass legislation to enable officers from other jurisdictions to operate within their territory.

Linked to this development is the introduction of the European Arrest Warrant (EAW), which has been effective since January 1, 2004. Each state of the Union operates its own extradition systems and they vary greatly in complexity and emphasis. With the EWA, one judicial system will effectively surrender its authority to the other, recognizing its decisions as if they were its own. Nonetheless, there will be a court decision in every instance before an accused person can be taken from the jurisdiction. An EWA cannot be issued for investigative detention and it will apply to a list of schedule offences including murder, rape, drugs trafficking, and terrorism.

POSSIBLE FUTURE DEVELOPMENTS

Will the development of the EU's criminal justice and policing systems go further? It is difficult to say. There is division on the possibility of creating a EU-wide prosecutor service. Some take the view that if people are to be prosecuted it should be by their own countries and not by some vague, anonymous authority known as "Europe." There is also division over what is known as the "approximation" of European criminal law – that is effectively to harmonize offences, sentencing policy, and so on right across the Union. Some argue that this would be a good thing, bringing consistency. Others say, no, and argue that each country should define its own priorities.

SUMMARY AND CONCLUSIONS

Innovation and reform in the EU's policing and criminal justice systems are still taking place. They are being developed in parallel with Europe's increasing political, economic and social cohesion. It is a changing picture.

The "third pillar" of the EU, dealing with issues of "freedom, justice and security," is still under construction. Europol and other elements of the criminal justice system are now playing an increasing role in liaison with national law enforcement agencies across the Union's twenty-five member states.

EU states will have to decide to what extent they are prepared to accept the harmonization of criminal justice structures, perhaps at the expense of traditional national values. Certain EU states have more recently begun to question the speed and the depth of the European integration process. The Irish, by referendum, initially rejected the Treaty of Lisbon but accepted it in a second referendum late in 2009. Other European parliaments or leaders have hesitated over the Treaty, but by the end of 2009 it had passed all hurdles and was due to come into effect. Whether this more cautious attitude will spill over into the development of the Union's "third pillar" remains to be seen.

REFERENCES

Glavey, F. (2000). *Accountability, the Right to Privacy and Third Pillar Arrangements. Co-Operation Against Crime in the European Union.* Institute of European Affairs.

Swallow, P. (1994). *The Maastricht Treaty's Third Pillar.* UK: University of South-hampton.

Walsh, D. (2000). *How the Third Pillar Works.* Dublin: Institute of European Affairs.

ABOUT THE AUTHOR

Conor Brady is Editor Emeritus of *The Irish Times* newspaper based in Dublin. He is author of "Guardians of the Peace," a history of Irish policing. From 2002 to 2004 he was a visiting professor at John Jay College of Criminal Justice, City University of New York. In 2006 he was appointed by the president of Ireland as one of three Commissioners of the Garda Siochana Ombudsman Commission, Ireland's independent police oversight body.

57 The European Union and Judicial Cooperation

Matti Joutsen

GENERAL OVERVIEW

Traditionally, each country around the world makes its own decisions on law and policy. Even in the modern world, where the emphasis is on international cooperation, it is the national government that sets the policy, the national legislature that enacts the law, and the national courts that have the final say on what is lawful and what is not.

The European Union is an exception to this rule, and represents a unique form of international cooperation. A total of twenty-seven European countries have joined together to form an intergovernmental structure. Many important policy questions that have crossborder implications are decided by these "member states" acting together. Once such a decision is taken by the European Union, each national legislature must adapt its laws accordingly. The decisions concern not only police and judicial cooperation, but also for example migration and border control, taxation, the economy, consumer affairs, industry, agriculture, and so on.

Police and judicial cooperation in the European Union consists primarily of measures designed to ensure that offenders cannot take advantage of differences in national law and national jurisdiction, and that they can and will be brought to justice no matter where they commit their offence. Since September 11, 2001 in particular, the reality and the threat of terrorism have led to increased attention being paid to cooperation in criminal justice and in the management of borders.

KEY CONCEPTS

The "third pillar." The European Union was originally known as the "European Communities" (or, more popularly, as the "Common Market").

The Common Market was designed to make it possible for persons, products, services and capital to move freely from one member state to the next. Such freedom of movement obviously helps economic growth, but it also opens up new opportunities for crime, and new possibilities for offenders to slip from one country to another, trying to evade justice. It also opened up special questions of foreign policy and security policy, questions that have to be decided in the same way throughout the Common Market.

The response to this need was the 1992 Maastricht Treaty, which gave the European Union certain powers in three sectors, known as "pillars": internal trade (the first pillar), foreign policy and security policy (the second pillar) and cooperation in justice and home affairs (the third pillar).

The principle of subsidiarity. Not all questions relating to law enforcement and criminal justice (or, for that matter, foreign policy and security policy) are decided by the European Union. Most questions continue to be decided by the individual member states. Each member state continues to draft its own laws, and has its own law enforcement arrangements and criminal justice system. According to what is known as the subsidiarity principle, the European Union is competent to act in two cases: The fundamental treaties explicitly empower the European Union to do so, or the matter is an important one, and the objectives sought cannot be achieved by each member state acting on its own. A good example of this is trafficking in persons. If each country could decide on its own how to police its borders and how to respond to trafficking in persons, traffickers will be quick to find out into which country is the easiest to smuggle persons. And once persons are smuggled into one EU member state, it is very easy to cross the borders into any of the others. Following this reasoning, the subject is something that must be considered by the European Union as a whole.

The basic institutions. Decisions in the European Union are made by four institutions: the Council of Ministers, the Commission, the European Parliament, and the European Court. In police and judicial cooperation, the Council of Ministers and the Commission are the most important bodies. Usually, it is the Commission that proposes decisions, although also a member state can do so. The decisions are prepared in working groups with representatives from the different member states, and are adopted by the Council of Ministers. When deciding on police and judicial cooperation, this Council consists of the ministers of justice and internal affairs of each member state. (These ministers hold a Cabinet level position, and their functions are broadly comparable to those of the U.S. Attorney General and the Secretary of Homeland Security.) The European Parliament is consulted, but its views are not binding.

The acquis communautaire. The most important types of decisions adopted by the European Union on police and judicial cooperation are called framework decisions. These establish a certain goal, such as the criminalization of certain conduct (e.g., participation in a criminal organization), or the establishment of certain procedures for crossborder cooperation (such as for the extradition of offenders). It is then up to each member state to change its own legislation in order to achieve the goals that had been set. The framework decisions, together for example with the treaties, as well as the judgments of the European Court, form part of what is known as the "acquis communautaire" of the European Union, the body of law that also countries joining the EU must accept.

The requirement of consensus. When the Maastricht Treaty was adopted, the member states were so protective of their law enforcement and criminal justice system that they decided that European Union decisions on police and judicial cooperation must be made by consensus. This proved to be a considerable stumbling block to greater cooperation; even a single dissenting member state can block agreement. Given that the different countries have quite different laws and priorities, this requirement for consensus has led to very difficult negotiations, and the decisions themselves have become increasingly complex, and more difficult to understand.

Mutual recognition. According to traditional judicial cooperation, each country has enormous discretion in deciding whether or not to recognize and enforce a decision given by a foreign court. The process is long and complex, and there are many grounds on which a country may (and, in some cases, must) refuse to enforce a foreign judgment.

As noted later in this chapter, the European Union member states have adopted the principle of mutual recognition. According to this principle, the courts of one member state must recognize a judgment or decision made by a court in another member state, and enforce it accordingly, with a minimum of formalities. For example, if the court in one country issues an arrest warrant, courts in any other member states of the European Union must be prepared to enforce the arrest warrant.

The Lisbon Treaty. In order to simplify decision-making (and at the same time make it more transparent and democratic by giving the European Parliament a greater role), the new Lisbon Treaty that entered into force in December, 2009 fundamentally changes the way decisions are made. From the point of view of police and judicial cooperation, the most important change will be that decisions no longer have to be made by consensus, but by a "qualified majority." Proposals for decisions are to be made primarily by the Commission, although also one-fourth of all member states, acting together, can make a proposal for a decision. The European Parliament will be more closely involved in the negotiations over the contents of decisions.

THE EVOLUTION OF JUDICIAL COOPERATION IN THE EUROPEAN UNION

All of the member states of the European Union are also members of a larger intergovernmental organization, the Council of Europe. (Note the potential for confusion in terminology: the Council of Europe is not the same as the European Council!) The Council of Europe has adopted a large number of conventions, recommendations, and resolutions on judicial cooperation, including an extradition treaty and a mutual legal assistance treaty, as well as the European Convention on Human Rights. The conventions in particular have been enormously influential in judicial cooperation worldwide.

As already noted, the dynamics of the internal market led to the member states deciding, in the Maastricht Treaty, that the European Union should deal also with police and judicial cooperation. With its new mandate, the European Union started working on a number of proposals. It started drafting its own treaties to update and supplement the Council of Europe treaties. This work led to extradition treaties adopted in 1995 and 1996, and to a mutual legal assistance treaty adopted in 2000. Decisions were also soon taken that required the member states to criminalize, for example, certain racist and xenophobic conduct, trafficking in human beings, and the sexual exploitation of children.

In 1997, the European Union decided on a set of measures (an "action plan") for responding to organized crime. The action plan called for the criminalization of money laundering and participation in a criminal organization, more effective measures for the tracing of assets, and the identification of best practice in mutual assistance. A system for mutual evaluation was set up, by which teams of experts from different countries would assess how effectively each member state was dealing with a certain issue, such as extradition or mutual legal assistance. The action plan also led to the establishment of what is known as the European Judicial Network, which allows the practitioners responsible for extradition and mutual legal assistance to be in direct contact with their counterparts in other countries (instead of, as is the usual case elsewhere in the world, going through diplomatic channels). Many of the measures called for in the action plan were adopted in less than three years – an impressive achievement in international cooperation.

One of the debates in the EU has been over how to overcome the differences in the laws, procedures, and practices of the many member states. For example, the definition even of basic types of crime, and the rights given to suspects and defendants, can vary considerably. Some have argued for harmonization of laws: They say that the laws defining the main forms of crossborder crime, as well as the basic elements of criminal procedure, should be the same in all EU member states. Others, in turn, have argued instead for mutual recognition of decisions and judgments: They say that the courts and other authorities of each member state should be required to accept as such, and be prepared to enforce, decisions taken in other member states.

In 1999, the European Union decided that the basis for cooperation should be mutual recognition. However, work would continue on harmonization of key areas of legislation, such as the prevention and control of money laundering. At the same time, the European Union decided to establish a central body for cooperation among prosecutors and investigating magistrates, to be called Eurojust. Eurojust works essentially in the same way as Europol works for law enforcement cooperation.

Two years later, this work on legal integration was hastened by the impact of the terrorist attacks in New York and Washington, D.C. on September 11, 2001. The attacks led to the adoption of an EU decision harmonizing domestic legislation that defines terrorist crimes. Furthermore, only three months after the attacks, the European Union adopted its first decision on mutual recognition, the so-called EU arrest warrant. This decision replaced extradition proceedings entirely with a much more rapid procedure for the surrender of fugitives. Soon after, a decision was adopted on the mutual recognition of orders on the freezing of assets and evidence. As a result of these two decisions, once a court in any EU member state orders the arrest of a certain suspect or convicted offender, and the freezing of his or her accounts, the courts in any and all other member states can enforce these immediately.

Subsequently, the principle of mutual recognition was extended for example to the obtaining of evidence, and to financial penalties (fines) and confiscation orders.

One more consequence of the terrorist attack was that the EU decided to supplement the existing patchwork of bilateral treaties that the member states have with the United States, with more general and updated EU–US treaties on extradition and mutual legal assistance.

At the end of 2009, the European Union decided on further work on police and judicial cooperation, in the form of the so-called Stockholm Program. Between 2010 and 2014, decisions can be expected on ways to overcome crossborder problems connected with, for example, minimum standards for dealing with suspects and defendants, the use of pretrial detention, the gathering of evidence, and the protection of victims and witnesses. A separate focus will be the prevention and investigation of cybercrime. In respect of terrorism, the priority areas for further work include the countering of radicalization in vulnerable populations, greater surveillance of the use of the Internet for terrorist purposes, and combating the financing of terrorism.

CONCLUSIONS

The European Union has transformed the European debate on criminal policy. Many key debates which had previously been conducted on the national level have now moved to the European Union level, and European Union decisions have considerable influence on national law, policy, and practice. Agreement has been reached on the minimum requirements when criminalizing a number of different offences (such as racism and xenophobia, trafficking in human beings and sexual exploitation of children, terrorism, and participation in a criminal organization). International cooperation in criminal matters has been smoothed by the establishment of Eurojust and the European Judicial Network, and by a fairly rigorous system for mutual evaluation of the day-to-day practice in international cooperation. Conventions have been adopted in order to simplify extradition and mutual assistance. The growing scope of mutual recognition has made the enforcement of court decisions and judgments much more rapid and effective.

REFERENCES

Cullen, P. J. & W. C. Gilmore. (1998). Crime Sans Frontières: International and European Legal Approaches. *Hume Papers on Public Policy*, Vol. 6 (1&2), Edinburg, UK: Edinburgh University Press.

De Ruyver, B. G. Vermeulen, & T. V. Beken. (2002). *Strategies of the EU and the US in Combating Transnational Organized Crime.* Institute for International Research on Criminal Policy, Antwerp.

Fletcher, M., R. Lööf & B. Gilmore. (2008). *EU Criminal Law and Justice.* Cheltenham, UK: Elgar European Law Series.

Guild, E. & F. Geyer. (2008). *Security Versus Justice? Police and Judicial Cooperation in the European Union.* Aldershot: Ashgate.

McDonald, W. F. (Ed.) (1997). *Crime and Law Enforcement in the Global Village.* Cincinnati, OH: Academy of Criminal Justice Sciences and Anderson Publishing.

Mitsilegas, V. (2009). *EU Criminal Law.* Oxford: Hart Publishing.

Peers, S. (2000). *EU Justice and Home Affairs Law.* Harlow, England: Longman and Pearson Education Limited.

WEB SITES

Acquis of the European Union in the field of Justice and Home Affairs (Title IV
    of the TEC and title VI of the TEU), available at http://europa.eu.int/comm/
    justice_home/acquis_en.htm

ABOUT THE AUTHOR

Dr. Matti Joutsen is Director of International Affairs at the Ministry of Justice
of Finland. He has served as a criminologist, as a judge, and as Director of the
European regional institute in the United Nations network for crime prevention
and criminal justice. He is an active participant in the work of the European Union,
the Council of Europe and the United Nations, and was heavily involved in the
drafting of the UN Convention against Transnational Organized Crime.

58 The Longer Arm of the Law

THE GROWTH AND LIMITS OF INTERNATIONAL LAW ENFORCEMENT AND CRIMINAL JUSTICE COOPERATION

William F. McDonald

THE NATURE OF THE PROBLEM

Old Roots, New Growth

The problems of criminals fleeing abroad to avoid prosecution or committing crimes that crosspolitical borders have existed since ancient times. Smuggling may be the world's second oldest profession. Agreements among states to return fugitives have been recorded since ancient Egypt. In today's world of porous borders the possibilities for transnational crime and fugitivity have multiplied a thousandfold.

As of the twenty-first century nation states are expanding institutions of international cooperation in law enforcement and criminal justice matters. Compared to the beginning of the nineteenth century when international cooperation was virtually nonexistent and the prevailing assumption was that "the courts of no country enforce the laws of another country,"[1] today's world is strikingly different. A web of bilateral, regional, and international agreements, conventions (treaties) and institutions addressing transnational crime and criminals are proliferating (Andreas & Nadelmann, 2006).

This chapter traces these developments and identifies gaps that remain in the canopy of international law enforcement and criminal justice. These developments began slowly in the nineteenth century, took off after World War II, and accelerated in the 1990s.

Formerly criminologists dealt with crime in other countries under the rubric of "comparative criminology." Interrelatedness as such became a

---

[1] A principle of international law invoked by Chief Justice Marshall. 23 U.S. (10 Wheat.) 66, 123 (1825).

focus of criminological concern in 1974 with the phrase, "transnational crime," which is not a legally-defined crime but rather refers to criminal activities, transactions, or schemes that violate the laws of more than one country or have a direct impact on a foreign country (Mueller, 1999). In 1996 the National Institute of Justice (NIJ) established its International Center for the study of crime and justice. At the national policy level, transnational crime became a focal concern for the first time when President Clinton targeted it as a threat to national security (U.S. President Clinton, 1995). The State Department had become a player in the formulation of American crime policy (Winer, 1997).

THE EVOLUTION OF INTERNATIONAL AGREEMENTS TO COOPERATE

From Conflict to Cooperation

In the nineteenth century legal theorists began rethinking the relationship between crime, courts, and foreign states. The new thinking reflected political, economic, and technological changes in the world. Domestically, the nation state had established modern police agencies to promote law and order at home. Internationally, states had realized that it was in their self-interest to cooperate in the suppression of transnational crime. This was not always the case.

For example, prior to the seventeenth century, piracy had been officially authorized, albeit with some restrictions by states. Known as "privateering" it was a means of harassing enemies and obtaining resources. The high seas were regarded as a no-man's-land. However, by the eighteenth century the volume of international trade among Western states was increasing. Norms regarding international relations began to change. Doing business with one another came to be regarded as more valuable than stealing from one another.

It was not just economic or state interests that stimulated the development of what Nadelmann (1990) calls "global prohibition regimes." The latter are norms that prohibit, in both international law and domestic criminal laws, certain acts by either state or nonstate actors. The regimes against slavery; against international trafficking of women for prostitution; and against trafficking of controlled psychoactive substances were all driven by moral concerns of particular individuals – who Nadelmann characterizes as "moral entrepreneurs," or in other words, people with the urge to remake the world according to their personal, absolutist ethic.

Extradition and Judicial Cooperation

As governments replaced self-help methods of bringing criminals to justice, they also became interested in extraditing criminals and in having fugitives punished. Formerly, only fugitives who were a threat to the state aroused much governmental effort. Pirates, vagabonds, conspirators, embezzlers, counterfeiters, and assassins had been the focus of most of the minimal efforts by European states prior to the nineteenth century (Joutsen, 2005).

By the twentieth century many states had signed bilateral agreements (treaties) to extradite fugitives for common crimes. Some states even agreed to assist one another with the judicial process related to criminal matters. Known as "mutual legal assistance treaties" (MLATs), these latter agreements broke with the tradition whereby the courts of one state did not help enforce the laws of another state. With MLATs the law enforcement and judicial systems of one state perform certain tasks – such as by taking testimony from witnesses or collecting physical evidence or checking records – needed for the investigation and prosecution of a case in foreign state. MLATs have since become widely accepted and broadened in scope (Joutsen, 2005).

International cooperation in criminal matters increased as the twentieth century closed. In addition to extradition and judicial assistance, there are agreements dealing with related matters: the transfer of proceedings from the state where the offense occurred to another state for trial under the latter's legal system; the recognition of judgments – including imprisonment, fines, and others, and the transfer of prisoners (Joutsen, 2005: 269).

Also noteworthy is the appearance of several multilateral conventions on cooperation with respect to specific forms of crime such as the UN Conventions against Drugs (1961, 1971, 1988); Transnational Organized Crime (2000); Corruption (2003). The Protocol against Human Trafficking (2000) represented the culmination of more than a century of diverse initiatives by reformers to achieve international cooperation against "white slavery," the trafficking of women for sexual exploitation.[2]

In addition, international and regional institutions of law enforcement and judicial cooperation have proliferated (e.g., Interpol, Europol, Eurojust, the World Customs Organization; the G7's Experts on Transnational Crime; ASEAN Chiefs of Police – ASEANAPOL). Many countries are now

---

[2] The phrase "white slavery" originated in the late 1800s to both distinguish the campaign from the one black slavery yet convey the same high moral purpose.

posting police liaison officers at foreign embassies. International joint task forces of police and prosecutors are commonplace. The cumbersome old system of *letters rogatory* (formal diplomatic letters of request between states) for obtaining legal assistance in criminal matters from another state is being replaced by agreements allowing direct communication among law enforcement agencies.

THE GROWTH OF LAW ENFORCEMENT COOPERATION

Political Versus Common Crime

Today's system of international police cooperation grew out of nineteenth century European initiatives. Two kinds of cooperation occurred: cooperation against common crime ("low policing") and the more notorious cooperation against political crime and threats against the state ("high policing"). After years of political agitations, the Italian government convened the International Anti-Anarchist Conference in Rome in 1898. The fifty-four delegates were unwilling to create an international police agency but did agree to exchange information and improve the Bertillonage system of identification.[3] They also agreed to allow officials who were tracking anarchists to bypass diplomatic channels and to communicate directly by telephone or telegraph.

In St. Petersburg in 1904, ten European states signed a secret protocol that regularized the cooperative arrangements agreed to in Rome. Jensen (1981) argues that these two conferences laid the groundwork for future cooperation against nonpolitical crime, or what eventually became Interpol. By the early 1900s the need for multilateral police cooperation against common crime had been widely recognized. International meetings were convened in Europe (in 1909, 1911, 1914, 1923) and the Americas (United States in 1893, 1922, and Latin America in 1901, 1905, 1910, 1920). The American initiatives never produced any viable operational structure (Deflem, 2002).

The International Criminal Police Organization: Interpol

The First International Congress of Judicial Police that met in Monaco in 1914 on the eve of World War I was intended to create structures that would facilitate transnational police efforts against common criminals.

---

[3] This anthropometric system was based on measurements of eleven features of the human body. It was used until 1903 when two inmates in the same prison were found to have identical measurements. Thereafter, it was replaced by fingerprints (McPhee, 2008).

The participants endorsed several proposals that were never implemented because of the war. In 1923 the International Police Congress was convened in Vienna. The 131 attendees, mostly European police officials, created the International Criminal Police Commission (ICPC). After World War II, the ICPC was revived; re-located to France; and in 1956 renamed, International Criminal Police Organization (ICPO) – Interpol. It gradually came to be recognized as an international organization – participating in UN and Council of Europe business, being mentioned in treaties and being acknowledged in legal instruments of various governments (Anderson, 1989).

By the early 1970s, Interpol was regarded as unresponsive to the regional needs of Europe (Fijnaut, 1987: 38). The creation of a European alternative to Interpol was probably an inevitable outcome of European economic integration, but it was hastened by the terrorism of the early 1970s. In 1975 the ministers of internal affairs meeting in Rome established a body called "TREVI" to promote cooperation in the fight against terrorism. In 1986 they expanded its remit to include international crime. A year earlier the Benelux countries signed the Schengen Agreement by which they formalized police cooperation amongst themselves. In 1995 the Council of the European Union drafted a convention for an organization called the European Police Office (Europol) that went into effect in 1998 and was joined by a companion prosecutorial institution (Eurojust) in 2000 (Council of the European Union, 2002).

The United States did not officially participate in the European conferences leading to the establishment of the ICPC; nor did it have much to do with ICPC prior to World War II or afterwards (Deflem, 2002). In 1962 the United States officially established a National Central Bureau of Interpol but until 1990 its function was *de minimus*. FBI Director, J. Edgar Hoover, preferred to rely upon Americas' well-developed system of legal *attachés* (Legats) and the FBI's extensive contacts with foreign agencies (Andreas & Nadelmann, 2006).

GAPS IN THE CANOPY

While there has been progress in the building of the law enforcement and criminal justice systems for the global society, the job is far from complete. There are gaps (McDonald, 2007). This happens for a variety of reasons: the lack of extradition agreements among certain states; differences in the legal definitions of crimes; asymmetry in the professionalism of the law enforcement agencies; corruption; and international and domestic politics.

Even if states have extradition agreements between them, they sometimes refuse to extradite because of: the nonextradition of nationals; the "political

offense" exception; the low quality of fairness or humaneness of the requesting country's criminal justice system especially its use of capital punishment; and, the potentially destabilizing domestic political ramifications of
cooperating with certain foreign powers (such as the United States).

According to a customary rule of international law, states are expected
to extradite or prosecute (*aut dedere aut judicare*). Prosecutions by one state
on behalf of another state are called "vicarious" or "foreign" prosecutions.
They seldom occurred – often because of cost or lack of interest. Since the
1980s, however, they have become important to American local criminal
justice systems in dealing with criminals who flee to Mexico.

When extradition treaties did not exist or were inadequate to accomplish
the rendition (the forcible transfer of a person from one state to another)
of a fugitive, other methods have been used. Fugitives have been legally
deported or "pushed over the border" by informal agreements. Fugitives
have been lured home or to a third country where extradition can be
arranged. Others have been kidnapped and returned by bounty hunters or
foreign agents hired by aggrieved victims or by law enforcement officials.

Irregular rendition

In 1985, U.S. Drug Enforcement Administration (DEA) agent, Enrique Camerena
was tortured to death by drug lords in Mexico. He was kept alive during the
torture by a Mexican doctor, Alvarez-Machain. When Mexican police authorities
failed to pursue the case, the DEA paid bounty hunters to have Alvarez-Machain
kidnapped and brought to the United States to stand trial. Mexico protested the
violation of its sovereignty (Zagaris & Peralta, 1997).

Since 9/11 and even before, the CIA has engaged in "extraordinary ren-
ditions" whereby it allegedly snatched suspected terrorists in foreign countries (allegedly with the consent of the host state) and flew them to third
countries (often their homelands known for human rights abuses) where
they have been turned over to the government for questioning. Critics have
dubbed this practice "torture outsourcing." Supporters argue that it is a
risky but necessary tool (Byman, 2005).

CONCLUSION

The process of establishing formal social control over geographic territories
defined by national political boundaries was largely achieved by Western
governments during the eighteenth and nineteenth centuries. By 1900,

victims of crime in those societies could expect the assistance of professional police and prosecutors in bringing their victimizers to justice but this
was not so if their victimizer fled to another country. Extending the reach of
national law enforcement agencies beyond national boundaries, and creating regional and international institutions of law enforcement and criminal
justice that span those boundaries is a project that is well underway but far
from being perfected.

REFERENCES

Anderson, M. (1989). *Policing the World: Interpol and the Politics of International
    Police Co-Operation*. Oxford: Clarendon Press.
Andreas, P. & E. Nadelmann. (2006). *Policing the Globe: Criminalization and Crime
    Control in International Relations*. New York: Oxford University Press.
Byman, D. (2005, April 17). Reject the Abuses, Retain the Tactic. *Washington Post*,
    Sec. B, p. 1.
Council of the European Union (Justice and Home Affairs). (2002, June 3). *Council
    Decision of 28 February. 2002 Setting up Eurojust with a View to Reinforcing the
    Fight Against Serious Crime. Retrieved from* http://ec.europa.eu/justice_home/
    doc_centre/criminal/doc_criminal_intro_en.htm
Deflem, M. (2002). *Policing world society: Historical Foundations of International
    Police Cooperation*. New York, NY: Oxford University Press.
Fijnaut, C. (1987). The Internationalization of Criminal Investigation in Western
    Europe. In C. Fijnaut, C. & R. Hermans (Eds.). *Police Cooperation in
    Europe: Lectures at the International Symposium on Surveillance*. Lochem: Van
    den Brink. 32–56.
Jensen, R. B. (1981, April). The International Anti-Anarchist Conference of 1898
    and the Origins of Interpol. *Journal of Contemporary History*, 16, 323–47.
Joutsen, M. (2005). International Instruments of Cooperation in Responding to
    Transnational Crime. In P. L. Reichel (Ed.). *Handbook of Transnational Crime
    & Justice* (pp. 255–73). Thousand Oaks, CA: Sage Publications.
McDonald, W. F. (2007). When States Do Not Extradite: Gaps in the Global Web of
    Formal Social Control. In S. Shoham, O. Beck, & M. Kett, (Eds.), *International
    Handbook of Penology and Criminal Justice*. Boca Raton, FL: CRC Press, pp.
    503–30.
Mueller, G. O. (1999). Responding to the Challenge of Transnational Crime. In P.
    Williams (Ed.), *Transnational Crime*. Milan, Italy: ISPAC.
Nadelmann, E. A. (1990). Global Prohibition Regimes: The Evolution of Norms in
    International Society. *International Organization*, 44(4), 479–526.
U.S. President Clinton, W. J. (1995, October 22). *Address to the General Assembly of the
    United Nations*. Retrieved June 14, 2005, from the White House Web site www.
    pub.whitehouse.gov/uries/I2R?urn:pdi://oma.eop.gov.us/1995/10/23/3.text.1.
Winer, J. M. (1997). International Crime in the New Geopolitics: A Core Threat
    to Democracy. In W. F. McDonald (Ed.), *Crime and Law Enforcement in the
    Global Village*. Cincinnati, OH: Anderson, pp. 41–64.

ABOUT THE AUTHOR

William F. McDonald is a professor of sociology, and co–director, Institute of
Criminal Law and Procedure, Georgetown University. He received a D.Crim. from
the University of California, Berkeley; a M.Ed. Boston College and a B.A. from the
University of Notre Dame. He has taught criminology, criminal justice, research
methods and statistics, and comparative criminal justice systems. His published
work include books on immigration and crime, the globalization of law enforcement; the victim; the prosecutor; and the defense counsel; plea bargaining; fifty
authored and co-authored monographs, journals and articles on sentencing; police-
prosecutor relationships; illegal immigration; pretrial release; drug law enforcement;
victimology and comparative criminal justice.

59 International Cooperation to Combat Money Laundering

Adam Graycar

MONEY LAUNDERING

Money laundering is a process that turns "dirty money" into "clean money." The proceeds of crime – dirty money – are disguised to hide their illicit origins, and then the money is integrated into the legitimate economy. The process washes dirty money until it appears to be clean. Often, but not always, the cleaning of dirty money involves moving it across national borders and integrating it into another economy.

Criminals disguise the illegal origins of their wealth, and terrorist organizations try to conceal the destination and the purpose for which the money has been collected. Money laundering plays a part in corruption as corrupt public officials need to hide the kickbacks they receive and the public funds they may have misappropriated. Organized criminal groups have substantial proceeds from drug trafficking and commodity smuggling. Together, these activities have profound social consequences and require cooperative international activity to combat them.

There is a great deal of international and national activity to counter financial crime and money laundering. Legislation exits in most countries to criminalize money laundering and the associated activities such as opening accounts in false names. Law enforcement agencies have investigated and prosecuted those accused of money laundering and prison sentences have been imposed. Money laundering is certainly big business and is significant for many economies. In its Global Anti-Money Laundering Survey 2007, KPMG opens with these words: "Estimated money laundering flows are reported to be in excess of US$1 trillion being laundered every year by drug dealers, arms traffickers and other criminals" (KPMG, 2007: 4).

There are both domestic and international cooperative efforts to combat money laundering. The US Money Laundering Threat Assessment (2005) offers a detailed analysis of thirteen money laundering methods, ranging from well-established techniques for integrating dirty money into the financial system to modern innovations that exploit global payment networks, as well as the Internet. The methods the report describes in detail are Banking; Money Services Businesses (Money Transmitters, Check Cashers, Currency Exchangers, Money Orders, Stored Value Cards); Online Payment Systems; Informal Value Transfer Systems; Bulk-Cash Smuggling; Trade-Based Money Laundering; Insurance Companies; Shell Companies and Trusts; and Casinos.

GLOBAL COOPERATIVE EFFORTS

There are numerous international agencies and collaborative networks that toil actively against money laundering and which have striven for uniform standards and cooperative development. Among them are the World Bank, the International Monetary Fund, the African Development Bank, the Asian Development Bank, Interpol, the United Nations Global Program against Money Laundering, and the Financial Action Task Force (FATF). Details on all of these can be found on their Web sites. In addition several United Nations conventions have money laundering as the key.

United Nations

The 1988 United Nations Convention against the Illicit Traffic in Narcotic Drugs and Psychotropic Substances was the first international convention that criminalized money laundering. It contained legal instruments for nations to use. The International Convention for the Suppression of the Financing of Terrorism came into force in April 2002. This requires member states to take measures to protect their financial systems from being misused by persons planning or engaged in terrorist activities. This was followed by two other UN conventions, the UN Convention Against Transnational Organized Crime in 2003, and in 2005 by the United Nations Convention Against Corruption (UNCAC).

Together, these conventions require explicit commitments against money laundering. States are to develop domestic regulatory and supervisory regimes for banks and nonbank financial institutions as well as mechanisms to deter and detect all forms of money laundering. States are also to emphasize requirements for customer identification, record keeping, and the reporting of suspicious transactions and develop an ability to cooperate and exchange information at the national and international levels. State parties, the UNCAC Convention says, shall endeavor to develop and promote global, regional, subregional, and bilateral cooperation among judicial, law enforcement, and financial regulatory authorities in order to combat money laundering.

These form the UN's Global Program against Money Laundering, Proceeds of Crime, and the Financing of Terrorism. The objective is for all states to adopt legislation for the legal instruments against money laundering and to counter the financing of terrorism. Through technical assistance programs the UN helps equip states with the knowledge, means, and expertise to lay in place legal frameworks, as well as to investigate and prosecute complex financial crimes. This is backed by information exchange and mutual legal assistance.

The Financial Action Task Force (FATF)

To complement the work of the United Nations, the FATF is a policy-making body that works to bring about national reforms and to generate the political will to counter money laundering. An intergovernmental body, the FATF was established in July 1989 by a Group of Seven (G-7) Summit in Paris, initially to examine and develop measures to combat money laundering. At that time the FATF comprised fifteen jurisdictions, plus an international organization. It now comprises thirty-four members.

Its role is clearly summarized on its Web site (www.fatf-gafi.org): "The FATF monitors members' progress in implementing necessary measures, reviews money laundering and terrorist financing techniques and countermeasures, and promotes the adoption and implementation of appropriate measures globally. In performing these activities, the FATF collaborates with other international bodies involved in combating money laundering and the financing of terrorism."

The four essential objectives of the FATF are to:

- Revise and clarify the global standards and measures for combating money laundering and terrorist financing.
- Promote global implementation of the standards.
- Identify and respond to new money laundering and terrorist financing threats.
- Engage with stakeholders and partners throughout the world.

The FATF has established the international standards for combating money laundering and terrorist financing, in what are known as the 40+9 Recommendations – that is forty initial recommendations plus nine special recommendations to deal with terrorist financing.

The forty recommendations were initially developed in 1990, revised in 1996, and thoroughly reviewed in 2003. The FATF Web site has extensive discussion on the forty recommendations and the methodologies for implementing and evaluating them. The recommendations are very comprehensive, and are grouped as follows.

The first three of the forty recommendations relate to legal issues and legal systems and cover the scope of the criminal offence of money laundering and provisional measures and confiscation.

The bulk of the recommendations relate to measures to be taken by financial institutions and nonfinancial businesses and professions to prevent money laundering and terrorist financing. These cover:

- Customer due diligence and record-keeping
- Reporting of suspicious transactions and compliance
- Other measures to deter money laundering and terrorist financing
- Measures to be taken with respect to countries that do not or insufficiently comply with the FATF Recommendations
- Regulation and supervision.

The remaining recommendations relate to institutional and other measures necessary in systems for combating money laundering and terrorist financing. They cover:

- Competent authorities, their powers and resources
- Transparency of legal persons and arrangements
- International cooperation
- Mutual legal assistance and extradition
- Other forms of cooperation.

The FATF standards have been endorsed directly by 180 jurisdictions around the world, as well as by the Boards of the International Monetary Fund and the World Bank. In addition, the United Nations Security Council in its Resolution 1617 of July 2005 stated that it "strongly urges all Member States to implement the comprehensive international standards embodied in the FATF Forty Recommendations on Money Laundering and the FATF Nine Special Recommendations on Terrorist Financing."

The FATF works to generate the necessary political will to bring about national legislative and regulatory reforms in the areas addressed by the 40+9 Recommendations.

Following the terror attacks of September 11, 2001, nine special recommendations were developed by FATF. These cover topics such as criminalizing the financing of terrorism and associated money laundering; freezing and confiscating terrorist assets; reporting suspicious transactions related to terrorism; international cooperation; and several recommendations on the movement of money and special remittances through wire transfers and cash couriers. There is also a recommendation on nonprofit organizations.

Nonprofit organizations are particularly vulnerable to terrorist organizations posing as legitimate entities, and can be used as conduits for terrorist financing, and to conceal or obscure the clandestine diversion to terrorist organizations of funds intended for legitimate purposes. We can, therefore, see the issue is broader than banks and financial institutions alone.

ENFORCEMENT

The UN and the FATF are mostly concerned with developing positions and instruments for use by various countries. Enforcement has been both country-based, and when cooperation has been required, a prominent role has been played by Interpol which would provide information on money laundering activities to national law enforcement agencies. Interpol was formed in 1923 to facilitate police to police cooperation on a global scale. Noting that the breach of customs controls are crucial elements in money laundering, The World Customs Organization has since 1952 been working on harmonization of customs procedures and the provision of information to its members about the movement of illicit money and goods.

There are many players, the UN and its constituent parts, the FATF, Interpol, and World Customs Organization, plus many more operators such as International Monetary Fund (IMF), Commonwealth Secretariat, Organization for Security and Cooperation in Europe (OSCE), Asian Development Bank (ADB), UN Counter-Terrorism Executive Directorate (CTED), UN Counter-Terrorism Implementation Task Force (CTITF), regional development banks, European Union, United Nations Commission on International Trade Law (UNCITRAL), as well as the US Department of Justice (OPDAT), US Department of Treasury – Office of Technical Assistance (OTA), Inter-American Drug Abuse Control Commission of the Organisation of American States (OAS/CICAD), FATF-style regional bodies, and a number of individual country technical assistance providers. The one that gets closest to actual enforcement is the Egmont Group of Financial Intelligence Units.

Most countries have created Financial Intelligence Units (FIUs), and they operate in a wide range of different systems, and use different methods. These are the people who analyze financial intelligence, and if there is sufficient evidence of unlawful activity they then pass the information on to a prosecuting authority. Formed in 1995, The Egmont Group of Financial Intelligence Units is an informal international gathering of 116 national financial intelligence units. These FIUs meet regularly to find ways to cooperate, especially in the areas of information exchange, training, and the sharing of expertise.

While the international conventions specify the mandatory reporting of suspicious transactions to the national authorities there have not been any accepted standards or formats. The Egmont Group has provided support. In some countries, the FIU follows a police model, such as the NCIS in the United Kingdom. In these situations, suspicious transactions are reported directly to a law enforcement body for investigation. More commonly, and especially in Europe, there is a judicial model, where the office of the public prosecutor takes on the task of investigating. In other countries there is a hybrid model, where the FIU is a specifically designated administrate agency, which plays a reporting role and works with police, prosecutors, and the private sector. This model prevails in Australia (AUSTRAC – the head of which was, until 2009, Chair of the Egmont Group) and the United States (FinCEN). The Egmont Group has a formal relationship with the FATF, and in 2002 was accorded observer status at FATF meetings.

CONCLUSION

International cooperation is essential for combating money laundering. International conventions are based on the premise that if crime crosses borders, so too must law enforcement. Terrorists, criminals, drug dealers, traffickers in people and others who undo the works of civil society take advantage of the open borders, the free markets, and the technological advances that shape modern society.

Responses to money laundering are different to responses to volume crimes such as robbery, motor vehicle theft, burglary, assault, larceny, and even homicide. Two things stand out.

First, legal and illegal activities have the same *modus operandi*. Money from legal sources is converted in the same sorts of ways and into the same sorts of assets as is money from illegal sources. The challenge for enforcers is to regulate and investigate so as not to impede or taint the movement of legitimate capital. Responding to volume crime does not pose this dilemma for law enforcement.

Second, many of the agencies described above which work to combat money laundering do not deal in actual enforcement. The United Nations, the FATF, and the Egmont Group as well as the plethora of other agencies, are all framework constructors and information sharers. Much of the understanding of combating money laundering lies in understanding the problem, why it is a problem, and how regulatory arrangements are circumvented, rather than doing what needs to be done to investigate and prosecute. However, the very international nature of the problem requires international cooperation. Learning about this is a necessary first step in combating money laundering.

REFERENCES

Australian Institute of Criminology. (2009). Charges and Offences of Money Laundering. *Transnational Crime Brief*, No 4, Canberra. Australian Institute of Criminology. Retrieved from www.aic.gov.au/publications/tcb/tcb004.pdf

Financial Action Task Force (FATF). (2006). *Trade Based Money Laundering. Retrieved from* www.fatf-gafi.org/dataoecd/60/25/37038272.pdf

Financial Action Task Force (FATF). (2008). *FATF Annual Report 2007–2008. Retrieved from* http://www.fatf-gafi.org/dataoecd/58/0/41141361.pdf

Financial Crimes Enforcement Network. (2007). *Civil Money PenaltiesAssessed Against American Express Bank*. International and American Express Travel Related Services Company, Inc. Media release 6 August. Retrieved from www.fincen.gov/aebi_joint_release.pdf

Gilmore, W. C. (2004). *Dirty Money: The Evolution of International Measures to Counter Money Laundering and the Financing of Terrorism*. France: Council of Europe Publishing.

KPMG. (2007). *Global Anti–Money Laundering Survey 2007 – How Banks Are Facing Up to the Challenge. Retrieved from* www.kpmg.com/SiteCollectionDocuments/Global%20Anti-money%20laundering%20survey%202007.pdf

Levi, M. & P. Reuter. (2006). Money Laundering. In M Tonry (Ed.). *Crime and Justice: A Review of Research*, Vol. 34. Chicago: University of Chicago Press, pp. 289–375.

US Department of Justice. (2005). *U. S. Money Laundering Threat Assessment*. Retrieved from www.usdoj.gov/dea/pubs/pressrel/011106.pdf

World Bank. (2003). *Anti-Money Laundering and Combating the Financing of Terrorism*, Washington, World Bank, Working Paper number 27185 www-wds.worldbank.org/external/default/WDSContentServer/WDSP/IB/2003/11/12/000160016_20031112164246/Rendered/PDF/271850Anti1mon1entral010West0Africa.pdf

UNITED NATIONS CONVENTIONS

United Nations Convention against Illicit Traffic In Narcotic Drugs And Psychotropic Substances, 1988
www.unodc.org/pdf/convention_1988_en.pdf

United Nations Convention Against Transnational Organized Crime And The Protocols Thereto, 2004

www.unodc.org/documents/treaties/UNTOC/Publications/TOC%20Convention/
    TOCebook-e.pdf
United Nations Convention Against Corruption 2004 www.unodc.org/documents/
    treaties/UNCAC/Publications/Convention/08–50026_E.pdf
Various international conventions and multilateral conventions can be found at http://
    treaties.un.org/Pages/DB.aspx?path=DB/studies/page2_en.xml&menu=
    MTDSG

WEB SITES

Australian Institute of Criminology www.aic.gov.au
Australian Transaction Reports and Analysis Centre (AUSTRAC) www.austrac.
    gov.au
The Egmont Group www.egmontgroup.org
Financial Action Task Force (FATF) www.fatf-gafi.org
International Monetary Fund www.imf.org
United Nations International Money Laundering Information Network (IMoLIN)
    www.imolin.org
United Nations Office of Drugs and Crime (UNODC) www.unodc.org/unodc/en/
    money-laundering/index.html
World Bank www.worldbank.org

ABOUT THE AUTHOR

Dr. Adam Graycar has worked at senior levels of government, and has also been
the Director of the Australian Institute of Criminology and Dean of the School of
Criminal Justice at Rutgers, the State University on New Jersey. He is now a professor at the Australian National University.

PART VIII

INTERNATIONAL RESEARCH
AND CRIME STATISTICS

A fundamental requirement of science is measurement. Without measurement there is no possibility of advancing understanding about the phenomena in question, beyond anecdotal and impressionistic accounts and testing and developing theories to build the discipline. In criminology and criminal justice a great deal of effort has been devoted to developing reliable measures of crime, as well as comprehensive measures of criminal justice processes and outcomes.

At the national level, there now exist three main sources of data about crime: (1) official crime reports based on police records; (2) crime victimization surveys; and (3) self-reports of criminal offending. These data sources each have their strengths and limitations, which make them suitable for use in different contexts and for different purposes. Concerning the first of these sources, for many years some countries have published routine compilations of police records of crime, which are used as social indicators as well as to measure the workload of the criminal justice system. An excellent example is the Uniform Crime Reports (UCR), an assemblage of crimes reported to the thousands of independent law enforcement agencies in the United States. Because police records do not include the substantial numbers of crimes not reported by victims, some countries have more recently begun to conduct victimization surveys of sample of the general population. The best known of these surveys is the National

Crime Victimization Survey (NCVS) conducted each year with thousands of households throughout the United States. Chapter 60 by Steven Block and Mike Maxfield describes both the UCR and NCVS. Until recently, self-report surveys of offending crime have mostly been used in research studies, but a national-level self-report survey, the Offending Crime and Justice Survey, has now been initiated in the United Kingdom.

The difficulties of compiling reliable measures of crime at the national level are multiplied many times when these measures are developed for use at the international level. A fundamental problem is the lack of international agreement over definitions of crime. However, a variety of different data sources are available, which if carefully interpreted, can assist international comparisons of crime (see Chapter 62 by Marcelo Aebi for a discussion of the difficulties of international comparisons). Principal among these data sources are the International Criminal Police Organization's (Interpol) International Crime Statistics; the United Nations (UN) Surveys on Crime Trends and the Operations of Criminal Justice Systems; The European Sourcebook on Crime and Criminal Justice Statistics; and the World Health Organization's (WHO) data on homicide and purposely-inflicted injuries.

Two extremely innovative and important cross-national surveys of crime have also been created, the International Crime Victim Survey (ICVS), described in Chapter 62 by Jan van Dijk, and the International Self Reports of Delinquency (Chapter 63 by Ni He and Ineke Haen Marshall). These have produced valuable findings, but there is still a great deal of research to be done in developing comparative measures. This need for comparative measures presents many opportunities for creative research, including research that is qualitative in nature (see Chapter 64 by Gregory Howard, Martin Gottchek, and Graeme Newman).

60 The U.S. Uniform Crime Reports and the National Crime Victimization Survey

Steven Block and Michael G. Maxfield

INTRODUCTION

Measuring national crime rates reflects two fundamental activities of government: to protect public safety and to document social indicators. Governments report data on crime in the same way that national statistics are collected for population, employment, education, income, consumer prices, and birth and mortality rates, along with countless other measures. Just as consumer prices are measured by an index that reflects the sorts of things people routinely purchase, an index of national crime is measured.

This chapter describes two national measures of crime in the United States. Uniform Crime Reports (UCR) are police-collected measures of crime compiled by the thousands of independent law enforcement agencies throughout the country. Largely because police-based measures have built in limits, victim-based measures of crime have been collected for more than thirty-five years. Each measures slightly different dimensions of crime.

UNIFORM CRIME REPORTS: CRIMES KNOWN TO POLICE

Begun in 1929, the Uniform Crime Reports, administered by the Federal Bureau of Investigation (FBI), serve several purposes. First, they provide national estimates of serious crime in the U.S. each year. Second, UCR data estimate annual arrests for serious crime and a variety of lesser offenses. Third, UCR data are reported for individual law enforcement agencies, in addition to totals for each state and the nation, which facilitates analysis below the national level. Fourth, the relatively long time period for UCR data makes it possible to examine short- and long-term trends in crime. Fifth, detailed data on individual homicide incidents have been reported since 1976; this makes it possible to examine features of individual victims, offenders, and homicide characteristics.

These basic goals are embodied in the *uniform* part of the UCR name – the data series was begun to provide consistent records of crime across law enforcement agencies. This is important because criminal justice in the United States is a highly decentralized endeavor. Each state maintains its own system of courts, and within states most municipalities and counties maintain their own law enforcement agencies. In 2007, about 13,500 agencies reported summary UCR data (FBI, 2008).

Types of UCR Data

UCR Part 1 offenses are commonly referred to as "crimes known to police," which means these numbers reflect crimes reported to police, recorded by police, and reported to the FBI. The UCR also presents totals of persons arrested for a variety of other Part 2 offenses. These include less serious assaults, drug offenses, fraud, public order offenses, weapons violations, and juvenile status offenses. These crimes are tabulated only if someone is arrested because such offenses are often not reported to police and thus difficult to estimate.

UCR Part 1 and Part 2 offenses are reported as summary-based data. This means that data are available as summary totals for each reporting jurisdiction – city, county, zero-population agency, and aggregations of these. Summary-based data are useful for obtaining national- and subnational level estimates of crime, but cannot be used to analyze individual incidents or groups of incidents. For example, total reported Part 1 offenses are available for Chicago (and other cities with a population of 10,000 or more) for each reporting year. But no information is available about any of the individual incidents that were reported in Chicago, or about any of the individual people arrested in Chicago.

In contrast, incident-level data are available for all homicides reported to the UCR program. Known as Supplementary Homicide Reports (SHR), these data provide information about individual homicide incidents, such as characteristics of victims and offenders (if known), weapon used, and other features of homicide incidents. This means that researchers can analyze data about each homicide incident.

One other feature of UCR data that is important in national-level analysis is nonparticipation by some law enforcement agencies. Participation in the UCR is voluntary. In an effort to adjust for non-participating agencies, the FBI estimates state and national totals for index offenses. Table 60.1

Table 60.1. Uniform crime report index crimes reported and estimated in 2007

	Crimes reported by		
	Participating total agencies (13,468)	Estimated crimes	Percent estimated
Violent			
Murder & non-negligent Manslaughter	15,707	16,929	7
Forcible rape	78,669	90,427	13
Robbery	422,184	445,125	5
Aggravated assault	789,254	855,856	8
Property			
Burglary	1,989,593	2,179,140	9
Larceny-theft	5,970,603	6,568,672	9
Motor vehicle theft	1,028,723	1,095,769	6

Source: FBI (2008).

shows 2007 index crime totals from the 13,468 participating agencies only and 2007 totals that include FBI estimates to compensate for nonparticipating agencies:

Limits of UCR Data

Counts of UCR offenses do not include certain types of crime in all cases and provide selective data in other instances. Most prominent in the first group are crimes not reported to police. Research has found that personal crimes not involving injury and property crimes involving small monetary losses are frequently not reported to police.

A source of inconsistency across reporting agencies stems from the fact that crime definitions vary in different states (Maltz, 1999). These differences present reliability problems that should be considered in making comparisons in crime levels or rates across jurisdictions. However, research focusing on national-level crime rates, especially trends over time, would be less affected by variation in crossjurisdictional practices.

NATIONAL CRIME VICTIMIZATION SURVEY (NCVS)

The NCVS is an alternate measure of national-level crime based on interviews with residents in a large nationally representative sample of U.S. households (see Table 60.2 for a comparative account of UCR and NCVS). Regular national crime surveys were first conducted in 1972 in an effort

Table 60.2 Comparison of UCR and NCVS

Uniform Crime Reports	National Crime Victimization Survey
• Count serious crimes known to police, and arrests for other crimes. • Collected by thousands of local and state law enforcement agencies in the US; reported to the FBI, usually through state-level agencies. • Participation in the UCR is voluntary, though many states require participation; over 90 percent of agencies participate. • Except for homicide, UCR data are summary-based – data are available at the agency level. Incident-based homicide data are available, providing details on each homicide incident. • Some variation in definitions and collection procedures exist across agencies; cross-agency comparisons must be made with caution. • Produces summary-based data that can be used to estimate national, state, and local crime rates. • Best for assessing long term trends, nationwide and within individual agencies. • Do not include crimes not reported to police	• Counts personal and household victimizations, including crimes not reported to police. • Is based on a large nationally representative sample of households. • Household representatives are interviewed twice each year to increase the accuracy of recall and crime estimates. • Permits analysis of individual incident details. • Uses more uniform collection procedures. • Produces incident-based data that can be used to estimate national-level victimization rates, but not local rates. • Best for measuring crimes less often reported to police. • Does not count commercial victimizations, or victimization of children under age twelve.

to measure crime and support analysis in ways that are not possible with summary-based police data. The NCVS is administered by the Bureau of Justice Statistics; interviews are conducted by the Census Bureau.

One of the chief differences between survey-based measures of victimization and police-based counts of crime is that surveys include crimes not reported to police. Victimization surveys made it possible to measure the so-called dark figure of unreported crime. The NCVS has evolved into its current form to become the world's longest-running annual victimization survey.

Overview of NCVS Procedures

The NCVS is a household-based sample. Using a complex multistage cluster design, a nationally representative sample of about 38,000 households is drawn yielding interviews with about 70,000 individuals (Rand, 2007). Households are retained in the NCVS sample for three years; individuals in the sampled households are interviewed twice each year, usually by telephone.

These basic procedures reflect the primary purpose of the NCVS – to estimate national levels of victimization. Because some crimes are relatively rare, a large sample is drawn so that adequate numbers of victims will be selected. In each interview respondents are asked about incidents for the previous six months. People are interviewed every six months to minimize the recall period between interviews, and thus increase the accuracy of annual estimates.

The NCVS has been conducted largely in its present form since 1972 and, therefore, offers a long, uniform series that can be used to trace patterns of change in victimization. A major redesign of questions to screen for possible victimization was implemented in 1993. Screening questions became more explicit in an effort to detect violent offenses, especially sexual assaults and crimes involving intimate partners or family members.

In addition, the NCVS has occasionally served as a research platform. This means questions, or batteries of questions, are temporarily added to supplement standard items. For example, in 1999 all NCVS respondents answered a series of questions about their contacts with police, including traffic stops (Langan et al., 2001). Other national crime surveys, most notably the British Crime Survey, have been more extensively used as platforms for research on specific crime and justice questions.

Limits of NCVS Data

Although the NCVS offers better estimates of certain offenses, survey data are deficient in important ways. Some limits are due to NCVS sample and survey design; others are consequences of survey methods in general.

Because the NCVS uses a household-based sample, individuals not living in households are excluded. Homeless persons are obvious examples. Another consequence of the household-based sample design is that the NCVS does not count commercial victimizations such as burglary of a business. Finally, the NCVS does not collect information about victimizations of individuals under age twelve. This excludes child abuse, assaults, and theft of personal property that targets young children.

Other problems stem from difficulties of collecting information about crime by interviewing victims. People tend to forget distant events or things they might view as minor problems. Although NCVS interviews are conducted every six months, respondents might forget some incidents that occurred between interviews. This is more likely to be true for minor incidents or individuals victimized more than once; in the latter case, victims may not be able to distinguish individual incidents.

Collecting data through surveys also tends to underestimate sensitive events or conditions – things people might be embarrassed to talk about (Cantor & Lynch, 2000). Domestic violence and sexual assaults are examples of incidents that are difficult to measure in general purpose crime surveys. Other general purpose surveys, such as the British Crime Survey (Mirrlees-Black, 1999) and specialized efforts like the National Violence Against Women Survey (Tjaden & Thoennes, 2000), have revealed higher rates for sexual offenses and intimate-partner violence compared to those estimated by the NCVS.

SUMMARY AND CONCLUSION

The U.S. experience illustrates that developing data series to count crime at the national level is complex. Obtaining reasonable counts of crime requires multiple approaches. Efforts in other countries such as the Offending, Crime and Justice Survey (OCJS) and the International Crime Victims Survey (ICVS) offer lessons for developing crime data series. A recent publication by the U.S. National Research Council (2008) recommends changes to the NCVS to improve response rates and produce subnational estimates. Others have described police data and crime surveys in England (Hough & Maxfield, 2007). Agencies interested in conducting their own surveys can learn from a guide designed for U.S. police departments (Weisel, 1999).

REFERENCES

Cantor, D., & J. P. Lynch. (2000). Self-Report Surveys as Measures of Crime and Criminal Victimization. In D. Duffee (Ed.), *Measurement and Analysis of Crime and Justice*, Vol. 4). Washington, D.C.: U.S. Department of Justice, Office of Justice Programs, National Institute of Justice.

Federal Bureau of Investigation. (2008). *Crime in the United States 2007*. U.S. Department of Justice, Federal Bureau of Investigation. Retrieved August 2, 2009, from http://www.fbi.gov/ucr/cius2007

Hough, M., & M. Maxfield, (Eds.). (2007). *Surveying Crime in the 21st Century*. Crime Prevention Studies (Volume 22). Monsey, NY: Criminal Justice Press.

Langan, P. A., Greenfeld, L. A., Smith, S. K., Durose, M. R., & Levin, D. J. (2001, February). *Contacts Between Police and the Public: Findings from the 1999 National Survey*. Washington, D.C. U.S. Department of Justice, Office of Justice Programs, Bureau of Justice Statistics.

Maltz, M. D. (1999, September). *Bridging Gaps: Estimating Crime Rates from Police Data*. A discussion paper from the BJS Fellows Program. Washington, D.C.: U.S. Department of Justice, Office of Justice Programs, Bureau of Justice Statistics.

Mirrlees-Black, C. (1999). *Domestic Violence: Findings from a New British Crime Survey Self-Completion Questionnaire*. London: Home Office Research, Development, and Statistics Directorate.

National Research Council. (2008). *Surveying Victims: Options for Conducting the National Crime Victimization Survey*. In R. M. Groves & D. L. Cork, (Eds.) [Panel to review the programs of the Bureau of Justice Statistics. Committee on National Statistics and Committee on Law and Justice, Division of Behavioral and Social Sciences]. Washington, D.C.: National Academy Press.

Rand, M. R. (2007). The National Crime Victimization Survey at 34. In M. Hough & M. Maxfield (Eds.), *Surveying Crime in the 21st Century*. Crime Prevention Studies, Volume 22. Monsey, NY: Criminal Justice Press, pp. 145–63.

Tjaden, P. & N. Thoennes. (2000, November). *Full Report of the Prevalence, Incidence, and Consequences of Violence Against Women*. Washington, D.C.: U.S. Department of Justice, Office of Justice Programs, National Institute of Justice.

Weisel, D. (1999, October). *Conducting Community Surveys: A Practical Guide for Law Enforcement Agencies*. Washington, D.C.: U.S. Department of Justice, Office of Justice Programs, Bureau of Justice Statistics, and Office of Community Oriented Police Services.

WEB SITES

Published tabulations for the UCR and NCVS can be obtained from Web sites maintained by the Bureau of Justice Statistics: http://www.ojp.usdoj.gov/bjs/cvict.htm

Original data files for the UCR, NCVS, Supplementary Homicide Reports, and the National Incident-Based Reporting System can be obtained from the National Archive of Criminal Justice Data: http://www.icpsr.umich.edu/NACJD/index.html

ABOUT THE AUTHORS

Steven Block is a graduate student in the School of Criminal Justice at Rutgers University, Newark. His primary research interests include crime data, crime prevention, and the role of morality in law. He has worked on research projects involving prisoner re-entry, at-risk youth education, and motor vehicle theft. Steven has taught several sociology and criminal justice courses at Fordham University, Kean University, and Rutgers University.

Michael G. Maxfield is a professor of Criminal Justice at John Jay College of Criminal Justice. He is the author of numerous articles and books on a variety of topics – victimization, policing, homicide, community corrections, and long-term consequences of child abuse and neglect. He is the coauthor (with Earl Babbie) of the textbook, *Research Methods for Criminal Justice and Criminology*, now in its fifth edition. Professor Maxfield serves as editor of *The Journal of Research in Crime and Delinquency*. Professor Maxfield received his Ph.D. in political science from Northwestern University.

61 Highlights of the International Crime Victims Survey

Jan van Dijk

BACKGROUND TO THE INTERNATIONAL CRIME VICTIM SURVEYS

Over the past three decades an increasing number of countries have undertaken "victimization surveys" among the general population about experiences of crime. These surveys provide a source of data on crime independent of crime statistics recorded by police (Maxfied, Hough, & Mayhew, 2007). They also provide important additional information on crime including rates of reporting crimes to the police, victims' experiences with the police, fear of crime, and the use of crime prevention measures. If the research methodology used is standardized, the surveys also offer a new opportunity for the collection of crime statistics, which can be used for comparative purposes. This allows crime problems to be analyzed from a truly international perspective (Kury, 2001).

The first International Crime Victims Surveys (ICVS) took place in 1989 in a dozen countries. It has since been repeated four times in 1992, 1996, 2000, and 2005. Since its initiation, surveys have been carried out one or more times in seventy-eight countries including all twenty-seven Member states of the European Union, Australia, Canada, Japan, and The United States of America (van Dijk, van Kesteren, & Smit, 2007). More than 320,000 citizens have been interviewed to date in the course of the ICVS with the same questionnaire, translated into thirty or more languages. This process has resulted in a body of victim survey data across a variety of countries covering a period of twenty years. The full dataset is available for secondary analyses (ICVS, 2005).

METHODOLOGY

The ICVS targets samples of households in which only one respondent is selected aged sixteen or above. National samples include at least 2,000 respondents who are generally interviewed with the CATI (Computer Assisted Telephone Interview) technique. In the countries where this method is not applicable because of insufficient distribution of telephones, face-to-face interviews are conducted in the main cities, generally with samples of 1,000 to 1,500 respondents. Compared to the national surveys in the USA and England/Wales the ICVS uses relatively small sample sizes to keep costs at a minimum. Prevalence rates of victimization are published with their margins of error at the 90 percent confidence level.

The questionnaire includes sections on ten types of "conventional" crime, of which each question provides a standard definition. The ICVS provides an overall measure of victimization in the previous year by any of the eleven "conventional" crimes included in the questionnaire. Among the "conventional" crimes, some are "household crimes," in other words, those which can be seen as affecting the household at large, and respondents report on all incidents known to them. A first group of household crimes deals with the vehicles owned by the respondent or his or her household:

§ Theft of car
§ Theft from car
§ Theft of bicycle
§ Theft of motorcycle.

A second group refers to breaking and entering at the home address:

§ Burglary
§ Attempted burglary.

A third group of crimes refers to victimization experienced by the respondent personally:

§ Robbery
§ Theft of personal property
§ Assaults and threats
§ Sexual incidents (in the first rounds this question was only put to female respondents).

As said, the ICVS tries to measure crime, independently of police administrative records. Indeed, one of the most important findings of the ICVS deals with the reporting of victimizations by victims to the police and their reasons for nonreporting crimes, thus to provide comparative information on why police statistics often do not reflect the full crime picture. Those who have reported a victimization to the police are asked to assess the way the police has handled their report. Furthermore, all respondents are asked to assess the performance of the police in preventing and controlling crime in their areas, perceptions of crime threats, reception of victim support, and use of common crime prevention measures.

SOME MAJOR FINDINGS ON LEVELS OF CRIME

The results of the ICVS 1996–2005 shows that, on average, approximately 25 percent of citizens, living in urban areas suffered at least one form of victimization over the twelve months preceding the interview. In Africa and Latin America significantly higher levels of victimization were observed (33 percent and 34 percent, respectively).

Globally, over a five-year period, two out of three inhabitants of big cities were victimized by crime at least once. Criminal victimization has evidently become a statistically normal feature of urban life across countries of both the developed and developing world. Almost no citizens anywhere in the world can feel immune from these threats to their personal security.

Figure 61.1 shows one-year victimization rates for any of the ten crimes included in the ICVS for the countries participating in the ICVS 2004/2005. Surveys in the fifteen original member states of the European Union were funded by the European Commission under the name EU/ICS. In most of the surveys carried out in 2004/2005 booster samples of 1,000 were drawn from the capital cities. This allows the calculation of special capital city rates.

Figure 61.1 confirms that levels of victimization by common crime are universally higher among capital city populations than among national populations, with Lisbon as the only exception to this rule. The mean victimization rate of the participating cities is 21.7 percent, whereas the mean national rate was 15.7 percent. In almost all countries, risks to be criminally victimized are a quarter to a third higher for capital city inhabitants than for others. Differences between the ten top countries and the ten at the bottom are statistically significant at the 90 percent confidence level.

The ranking of cities in terms of crime puts Phnom Phen (Cambodia) and Maputo (Mozambique) on top. Relatively high rates are also found in London, Buenos Aires. Tallin, Amsterdam, Reykjavik, Belfast, Dublin, and Johannesburg. Victimization rates near the global city average of 21.7 percent are found in New York, Copenhagen, Stockholm, Sao Paulo, and Oslo. The five safest capital cities of those participating are Hong Kong, Lisbon, Budapest, Athens, and Madrid.

High crime countries include, as said, both relatively affluent countries (Ireland, Denmark, and Iceland) and some of the least affluent (New

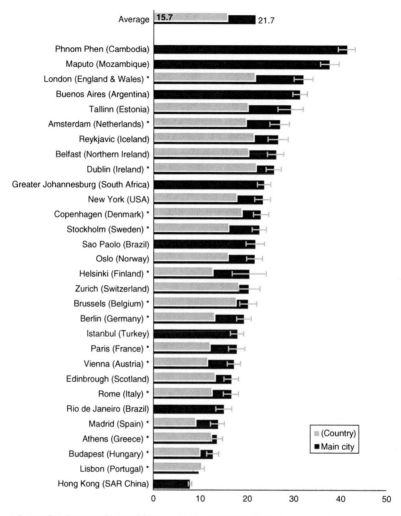

Figure 61.1. Overall victimization for ten crimes; one year prevalence rates (percentages) of capital cities and national populations in twenty-eight countries.
Source: ICVS, 2005.

Zealand, Estonia, and Mexico). The category of low crime countries is equally diverse. It includes both relatively affluent countries, such as Austria, and less prosperous ones, such as Hungary, Spain, and Portugal. Among the participating countries, levels of common crime seem to be neither associated with poverty nor with wealth. Macro factors known to be consistently associated with levels of common crime are urbanization and the proportion of young adolescents in the population. Together, these factors can explain some of the variation in overall levels of crime across countries.

The crime category of assault and threat is defined in the ICVS as personal attacks or threats, either by a stranger or a relative or friend, without the purpose of stealing. Although physical consequences may be minor in most cases, it may well have important emotional repercussions for victims. Assaults on women are more likely to be domestic in nature than assaults on men. In one third of the cases of violence against women, the offender was known at least by name to the victim. In one of five of the cases the crime was committed in the victim's own home. The level of violence against women across countries is inversely related to the position of women in society, with most developing countries showing much higher rates (van Dijk, 2008).

VICTIM EMPOWERMENT: POLICE RESPONSES AND VICTIM SUPPORT

Reporting to the Police

The ICVS shows that victims in Western Europe, North America (United States and Canada), and Oceania (Australia and New Zealand) are more likely to report their victimization to the police than those in other regions (see Figure 61.2). The picture of regional reporting rates is the reverse of that of victimization rates. In the regions where more crimes occur, fewer of those crimes are reported to the police. This general pattern introduces a fatal flaw into international police figures of crime by systematically deflating crime in developing countries.

In general, burglary is the most frequently reported crime (apart from car theft, which is almost universally reported). Burglary was most frequently reported in Western Europe, North America, and Australia. Important factors determining reporting are insurance coverage (the requirement for making a claim for compensation being dependent on reporting the incident to the police) and the ease of reporting (determined by factors such as access to the local police, availability of telephones, etc.).

Robbery was also frequently reported in Western Europe, but much less in the remaining regions, with a minimum in Latin America, where only one victim of robbery out of five reported to the police. In places where robberies are rampant victims are less likely to report. In the case of robberies reporting seems to be dependent on confidence in the police. Those refraining from reporting often have no trust in their local police. This is

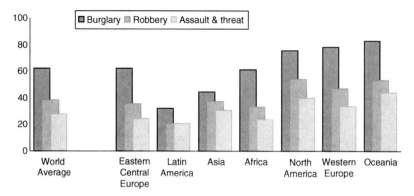

Figure 61.2. Percentage of assaults, robberies and burglaries, respectively, reported to the police, by region.
Source: ICVS, 2005.

born out by the finding that more than 50 percent of the Latin American victims of robbery who did not report to the police said they did so because "the police would not do anything" and approximately 25 percent said that they feared or disliked the police.

Finally, assaults and threats were the least frequently reported crime. Globally less than half of violence victims report to the police. Less than one in three of the female victims of threat and assault had filed a complaint with the police. Reporting rates are again lowest in Africa, Latin America, Eastern Europe, and Asia (one in five). As a general rule, the most vulnerable categories of victims – such as women in developing countries – are the least likely to seek assistance from the police, and thus those most in need of such empowering services are least likely to receive it.

Victim Satisfaction and Trust Levels

Among those who reported, less than half were satisfied with the way the police dealt with their case. Those least satisfied were the respondents from Africa, Asia, Latin America, and Central-Eastern Europe. Only in Western Europe, North America, and Australia more than 60 percent of victims who reported to the police positively evaluated the treatment received. The most common reason for dissatisfaction was that the police "did not do enough" or "were not interested." Around 10 percent said the police had been impolite or incorrect. This reason was given most often by victims of violence against women, especially by those from Latin America. Another common complaint is that the police failed to provide information about the case.

A special section of the ICVS deals with the assessment of police performance by respondents. The results suggest that in many developing countries the public remains skeptical about the capacity of the police to control local crime. At the country-level, lack of trust in the police appears to be strongly related to low rates of reporting of crimes to the police.

Ironically, then, low levels of police recorded crime in a country should not necessarily be seen as a good sign. Rather than as evidence for low levels of crime, low police figures may actually point to poor performance of the police and a resulting low trust level among the public, limiting the proportion of crimes reported to the police.

Victim Support Services

Victims of more serious crimes who had reported to the police were specifically asked whether they had received support from a specialized agency. In most countries, few victims had received such help. The figures are variable across offence type. Of those who reported burglaries to the police, 4 percent had received help. The level of support was the highest in the Western European countries, especially in United Kingdom, Sweden, Denmark, and the Netherlands where victim support for such victims is indeed institutionally most developed.

Approximately 16 percent of women victims of sexual offences who had reported to the police had received specialized support in North America, Western Europe, and Africa. Elsewhere the percentages were lower. In all regions only very few percentages of male victims of assaults had received specialized help (4 percent).

STRENGTHS AND WEAKNESSES OF THE ICVS

The ICVS has over the years proven to be a reliable source of information on the level and trends of crimes, which directly affect ordinary citizens on a large scale (so-called volume crime) (Lynch, 2006). It has over the years also improved its measurement of street level corruption and of sexual violence, although for the latter type of crime the use of specialized survey instruments such as the International Violence Against Women Survey (IVAWS) seems preferable (Johnson, Ollus, & Nevala, 2007). No information is provided by the ICVS on the most serious violent crimes such as homicides and kidnappings, or on crimes victimizing businesses or society at large (racketeering, grand corruption, environmental pollution). In these areas, ICVS data must be supplemented by data on police-recorded crimes or from other sources. Within Europe, the European Sourcebook has become an important source of international information on crime and justice (Aebi et al., 2006). Global information on homicides and on convictions for human trafficking can be consulted at the Web site of UNODC (www.unodc.org/statistics). A comprehensive overview of available international data on crime and justice is given in van Dijk (2008).

THE WAY AHEAD

By disclosing important aspects of crime and victimization at the international level, the ICVS has become an indispensable source of information for researchers, policy makers, and the international community. It is expected that in the future the ICVS will become even a more solid source of data, due to the fact that a greater number of countries will be included and that those who have already participated will continue to do so, thus reinforcing the longitudinal series. In this respect the decision of the European Commission to fund the execution of a revised version of the ICVS in all member states of the European Union is a major breakthrough. In 2010 the survey was executed in six European countries and Canada with the special aim of pilot testing promising new techniques of Internet-based interviewing. A fully-fledged repeat of the survey in all twenty-seven member states of the European Union with sample sizes of 8,000 per country is scheduled for 2013.

REFERENCES

Aebi, M. F., K. Aromaa, B. Aubusson de Cavarlay, G. Barclay, B. Gruszczynska, H. von Hofer, V. Hysi, J.-M. Jehle, M. Killias, P. Smit, & C. Tavares. (2006). *European Sourcebook of Crime and Criminal Justice Statistics 2006*. Den Haag: Home Office, Swiss Federal Statistical Office, Cesdip, Boom Juridische uitgevers, Wetenschappelijk Onderzoek- en Documentatiecentrum. Also available online at: www.europeansourcebook.org

International Crime Victims Survey, database and codebook (http://rechten.uvt.nl/icvs)

Johnson, H., N. Ollus, & S. Nevala. (2007). *Violence Against Women: An International Perspective*. Springer Press.

Kury, H. (Ed.) (2001). International Comparison of Crime and Victimization : The ICVS, de Sitter, Canada.

Lynch, J. P. (2006). Problems and Promises of Victimization Surveys for Cross-National research. *Crime and Justice*, Vol. 34. Chicago: University of Chicago Press.

Maxfield, M. M. Hough, & P. Mayhew. (2007). Surveying Crime in the 21st Century: Summary and Recommendations. In M. Hough & M. Maxfield (Eds.), *Surveying Crime in the 21st Century*. Monsey: Criminal Justice Press.

van Dijk, J. J. M (2008). *The World of Crime; Breaking the Silence on Problems of Crime, Justice and Development Across the World.* Thousand Oaks: SAGE.

van Dijk, J. J. M, J. van Kesteren, & P. Smit, (2007). *Criminal Victimisation in an International Perspective: Key findings from the 2004–2005 ICVS and EU ICS.* The Hague: Ministry of Justice/WODC (www. WODC.nl/publicaties)

ABOUT THE AUTHOR

Professor Jan J. M. van Dijk, Pieter van Vollenhoven Chair in Victimology, Human Security and Safety, was born in Amsterdam, the Netherlands in 1947. He received a Ph.D. in criminology from Nijmegen University in 1977. He initiated the International Crime Victim Surveys in 1988 and acted as president of the World Society of Victimology between 1997 and 2000. He received the Stephen Schafer award from the National Organization of Victim Assistance (NOVA) for his life-long contributions to victimological research and received an honorary doctorate from Tirunelveli University in India specifically for his promotion of ICVS in developing countries. In 2008, he received the Sellin-Glueck Award of the American Society of Criminology.

62 Crossnational Comparisons Based on Official Statistics of Crime

Marcelo F. Aebi

INTRODUCTION

Crossnational comparisons of crime are usually based in two main types of sources: crime statistics and crime surveys. Provided they use the same questionnaire and the same methodology, crime surveys constitute the best source for comparisons. Comparisons based on surveys are described in other sections of this book. This chapter is devoted to crossnational comparisons based on official statistics, which include police, prosecution, conviction, and correctional statistics. Because these statistics measure the reaction to crime and not crime itself, comparisons based on them are usually called comparisons of recorded crime.

BACKGROUND INFORMATION

Theoretically, official statistics allow researchers to compare offences, suspects, and offenders throughout the criminal justice system – from suspects known to the police to offenders imprisoned – as well as sanctions and measures imposed in different countries. However, in practice, such comparisons are often methodologically inappropriate because official statistics are constructed in a different way in each country. This means that, in most cases, crossnational differences in recorded crime rates do not reflect actual differences in the levels of crime.

The main sources for crossnational comparisons of recorded-crime are indicated in another section of this book. We have illustrated this chapter with examples from the *European Sourcebook of Crime and Criminal Justice Statistics*, the *American Sourcebook of Criminal Justice Statistics*, the *United Nations Surveys on Crime Trends and the Operations of Criminal*

Justice Systems (UNCTS), and the *Council of Europe Annual Penal Statistics* (SPACE I). The *European Sourcebook* was the first collection to include, in 1999, a methodological section on the statistical counting rules applied in each country. That section was later included in the UNCTS. Since the 2004 annual survey, SPACE I also includes a methodological section with information on the categories of persons included in the total number of prisoners in each country.

DISCUSSION OF MAJOR CONCEPTS

Difficulties in crossnational comparisons based on official statistics are due to four types of factors: legal, statistical, criminal policy, and substantive. The influence of these factors varies from country to country, hence introducing artificial differences in the levels of recorded crime.

- Legal factors refer to the influence of the legal definitions of offences adopted in each country and to the characteristics of its legal process.
- Statistical factors refer to the way in which crime statistics are elaborated. In that context we define the statistical counting rules as the rules applied in each country to count the offences that will be included in official statistics.
- Criminal policy factors relate to the crime and crime prevention policies applied in a country.
- Substantive factors refer to the actual levels of crime in each country – which are in fact the ones that the researcher is trying to compare – as well as to the propensity to report offences by the population and the propensity to record offences by the police or other recording authorities.

As a consequence, before comparing crime rates, researchers must compare the way in which official statistics are produced in each of the countries included in their analysis. In order to facilitate that task, we enumerate hereafter the main topics that must be checked when conducting such methodological comparison. These topics illustrate the concrete ways in which the four factors mentioned above introduce distortions in national crime rates.

- *Offence type*
  Most countries have two main categories of offences: crimes and misdemeanors. Usually – but not always – both are presented in separate police statistics and, typically, the ones used for crossnational

comparisons are the ones that include only crimes. Nevertheless, the criteria applied to distinguish crimes from misdemeanors vary across countries and across time. For example, some countries consider traffic offences as misdemeanors and others – like Finland since October 1999 – as crimes.

- *Definitions of offences*
  Crossnational differences can be produced not only by a different legal definition of an offence, but also by an inappropriate translation to or from a foreign language. Sometimes researchers translate foreign concepts as synonyms of concepts that exist in their own legal system, when indeed the term is similar but the concept is quite different. For example, the distinction between theft, robbery, and theft without violence is not always straightforward. In particular, robbery is considered a violent crime in common law countries and a crime against property in civil law countries. Thus, the recent worldwide increase in mobile phone thefts is reflected under different headings in different countries.

- *Subcategories included in each offence*
  In the *American Sourcebook*, figures for murder and nonnegligent manslaughter exclude assaults to kill; but other countries include this category in their figures. Such kind of differences exists for almost all offences. For example, according to the rules of each country, rape may or may not include violent intramarital intercourse, sexual intercourse with force – or without force – with a minor or a helpless person, homosexual rape, and incest.

- *Attempts*
  In Scotland or the Netherlands, attempts usually represent more than 80 percent of the total number of intentional homicides registered in police statistics; while in Ireland or Lithuania, they usually represent less than 10 percent of them. Thus, crime rates are affected not only by the inclusion or exclusion of attempts, but also by the rules applied in each country to classify offences as attempts. As a consequence, only completed homicides can be used for crossnational comparisons.

- *Time of data recording for statistical purposes*
  In some countries, data are recorded in police statistics when the offence is reported to the police (input statistics); in others data are recorded when the police have completed the investigation (output statistics); in between these extremes, some countries record data at an intermediate stage of the police investigation (intermediate statistics). Recent research has shown that, since the number of offences

registered by official measures of crime decreases as the criminal process advances, countries using input statistics tend to present higher crime rates than countries using output statistics.

- *Counting unit*
  As official statistics usually inform about the number of offences as well as the number of offenders, it would seem logical to presume that they use, respectively, the offence and the offender as their counting units. However, that is not necessarily true. For example, in the case of homicides, many countries use the victim as the counting unit.

- *Principal offence rule*
  If in the course of theft an offender also produces damages to the property and tries to kill a person, official statistics of countries applying a principal offence rule will show only one – the most serious – offence (i.e., attempted homicide), while in countries where there is no such rule, each offence (attempted homicide, damages to the property, and theft) will be counted separately.

- *Serial offences*
  Offences of the same kind committed by the same person during a certain time can be counted in different ways. For example, if a woman reports to the police that her partner has beaten her twenty-four times during the last twelve months, Germany will count only one offence, but Sweden will count twenty-four offences.

- *Multiple offenders*
  In some countries, the number of offenders engaged in an offence can play a role on the number of offences recorded. Thus, if a gang of five young people attacks one person, most countries will count one offence, but some will count five.

- *Categories of persons included in the total number of offenders*
  In their police statistics, some countries include minors and others exclude them; moreover the lower and upper limits to be considered a minor vary across countries. In correctional statistics, differences arise from the inclusion or exclusion of the following categories in the total number of prisoners: pre-trial detainees, persons held in facilities that do not depend on the prison administration (e.g., police stations), persons held in units for juvenile offenders, persons held in institutions for drug-addicted offenders, offenders with psychological disorders, asylum seekers or illegal aliens held for administrative reasons, and offenders serving their sentence under electronic monitoring. For example, in 2007, the prison population rate of the Netherlands was 113 prisoners per 100,000 inhabitants – one of the

highest in Western Europe – because the country included most of the preceding categories in its statistics. When such categories are excluded from the figures of all countries, the rate of the Netherlands goes down to seventy-two prisoners per 100,000 inhabitants and is among the lowest in Western Europe.

- *Opportunity and legality principle*
  Some countries apply the opportunity principle, which consists in giving the prosecution authorities discretionary powers that allow them to refrain from prosecution for some offences and under certain conditions, or to apply diversion measures or alternatives to prosecution. Other countries apply the legality principle, which forces the prosecuting authorities to prosecute whenever an offence has been committed and there is a suspect. Thus, the application of the legality principle increases the number of cases included in court statistics as well as the number of nonguilty sentences.
- *Reporting rates*
  Victimization surveys have shown that the rate of offences reported to the police varies across countries and across time. For example, according to the ICVS, between 1989 and 2005, the rate of assaults and threats reported to the police increased in Scotland but decreased in England and Wales.
- *Recording rates*
  The few empirical studies available on this topic suggest that the percentage of reported offences that are effectively recorded by the police can vary according to the offence. In particular, property offences are registered far more frequently than personal offences.
- *Changes in legal, statistical, or criminal policy factors*
  These changes modify the time series for an offence in such a way that sometimes it is impossible to establish the evolution of the offence during the period studied. An example of changes in legal factors can be found in Spain, a country that in 2004 introduced a new law on domestic violence that modified the criminal code transforming most misdemeanors in crimes. As a consequence, figures before and after 2004 are no longer comparable. As far as statistical factors are concerned, it is well known that a modification of data recording methods – such as the introduction of a new statistical system – generally introduces artificial changes in crime rates. For example, a zero tolerance policy should lead, at least in the short term, to an increase in the number of offences recorded by the police, because each minor offence will be included in the statistics.

In sum, for a comparative criminologist, it is essential to have a deep knowledge of all the preceding factors in order to apply, whenever possible, some corrections to the official crime rates. For example, if one country includes misdemeanors in its crime statistics and others do not, the researcher can subtract – if data are available – the number of misdemeanors from the total number of offences of the first country. However, in many cases, detailed information is not provided and, as a consequence, it is impossible to establish the exact influence of some of the rules applied to produce crime statistics.

SUMMARY AND CONCLUSION

As a rule, the main part of the differences in recorded crime rates across countries can be explained by differences in how offences are defined, collected, and archived. It would be a mistake to assume that such differences are real – in other words, that they reflect actual differences in the level of crime from one country. The researcher must keep in mind that, in this particular context, the form is more important than the substance.

In order to perform crossnational comparisons, the researcher needs to obtain information from each country on the legal, statistical, criminal policy, and substantial factors discussed in this chapter. However, only in exceptional cases will it be possible to obtain all the information required and adapt the data accordingly. Apart from those exceptional cases, a few kinds of comparisons are still possible. Thus, it is reasonable to study completed intentional homicide – excluding attempts – by combining official statistics with data from the World Health Organization Mortality Database. It is also feasible to study crime trends because in that case the researcher only needs to obtain information on changes in the factors discussed above. Finally, one interesting technique in order to improve crossnational comparisons consists in using data from victimization surveys to weight the number of offences recorded by the police according to their reporting rates.

As a consequence we can conclude that, with completed intentional homicide as a noteworthy exception, official statistics are usually inadequate for comparisons of crime levels across countries; but they can be useful for the study of crime trends.

RECOMMENDED READINGS

Aebi, M. F. (Ed.). (2004). Crime Trends in Western and Eastern European Countries. *European Journal on Criminal Policy and Research,* 10 (2–3) [Special issue].

Aebi, M. F. (2010). Methodological Issues in the Comparison of Police Recorded Crime Rates. In Shoham S., Knepper P. & Kett M. (Eds.). *International Handbook of Criminology*. London: Routledge, pp. 209–26.

Aebi, M. F., K. Aromaa, B. Aubusson de Cavarlay, G. Barclay, (2006). *European Sourcebook of Crime and Criminal Justice Statistics – 2006*. Third Edition. The Hague: WODC. Available online: www.europeansourcebook.org/esb3_Full. pdf

Aromaa, K. & M. Heiskanen (Eds.) (2008). *Crime and Criminal Justice Systems in Europe and North America 1995–2004*. HEUNI Publication Series No. 55. Helsinki: HEUNI. Available online: www.heuni.fi/43087.htm

Aromaa, K., S. Leppä, S. Nevala, & N. Ollus, (Eds.). (2003). *Crime and Criminal Justice Systems in Europe and North America, 1995–1997: Report on the Sixth United Nations Survey on Crime Trends and Criminal Justice Systems*. Helsinki: HEUNI. Available online: www.heuni.fi/21730.htm

Farrington, D. P., P. A. Langan, & M. Tonry (Eds.) (2004) *Cross-National Studies in Crime and Justice*, Washington: Bureau of Justice Statistics, U.S. Department of Justice. Available online: www.ojp.usdoj.gov/bjs/pub/pdf/cnscj.pdf

Killias, M. (Ed.) (2000). Crime Trends in Europe. *European Journal on Criminal Policy and Research*, 8 (1) [Special issue].

Kury, H. (Ed.) (2002). International Comparison of Crime and Victimization: The ICVS. *International Journal of Comparative Criminology*, 2 (1) [Special issue].

Robert, P. (Ed.) (2009). *Comparing Crime Data in Europe: Official Crime Statistics and Survey Based Data*. Brussels: VUBPRESS Brussels University Press.

Wade, M. & J. M. Jehle (Eds.) (2008). Prosecution and Diversion within Criminal Justice Systems in Europe. *European Journal on Criminal Policy and Research*, 14(2–3) [Special issue].

ABOUT THE AUTHOR

Marcelo F. Aebi is a professor of criminology at the University of Lausanne, Switzerland, and at the Autonomous University of Barcelona, Spain. He has been a visiting fellow at the Rutgers School of Criminal Justice (New Jersey, USA) and at the Max Planck Institute for Foreign and International Criminal Law (Freiburg, Germany), and professor at the Andalusian Institute of Criminology of the University of Seville (Spain). He is also scientific expert at the Council of Europe, the European Commission, and the United Nations Office on Drugs and Crime, as well as Executive Secretary of the European Society of Criminology.

63 The International Self-Report Delinquency Study (ISRD)

Ni He and Ineke Haen Marshall

BACKGROUND

The self-report method has gained widespread use among researchers, both in the United States and abroad (Junger-Tas & Marshall, 1999; Klein, 1989). The International Self-Report Delinquency Study (ISRD) is a large internationally collaborative self-report study of delinquency, victimization, and substance use of twelve to fifteen year old pupils in grades seven, eight, and nine. The ISRD project was developed to respond to the need for standardized, internationally comparable data on youth crime. International comparisons of survey data may only be made if all countries use the same (translated) questionnaires, and use comparable methods in questionnaire administration, sample selection, and data coding. The first ISRD study (1991–2) pioneered the use of standardized international self-report methodology on youth in thirteen countries (Junger-Tas et al., 2003). Fifteen years later, the study was repeated, this time with a larger number of countries and an expanded questionnaire (ISRD-2) (Junger-Tas et al., 2010). A third and larger ISRD study is planned for 2011–12. This chapter discusses the ISRD-2.

ISRD-2

The main objectives of the project are to study crossnational variability as well as international trends in juvenile delinquency, substance use and victimization over time; to improve standardized self-report methodology for comparative purposes, and to generally advance comparative criminological research beyond the constraints of officially recorded crime. Official crime rates do not lead to valid international comparison, due to variations

478

in crime definitions and in prosecution policies. Moreover, unlike official data, self-reports provide background information needed to test criminological theory (Junger-Tas & Marshall, 1999). The ISRD-2 aims to estimate the prevalence and incidence of youthful offending, substance use and victimization, as well as to examine the correlates of youth crime and to test different explanations of crime in thirty-one countries. The study also collects city- and country-level indicators.

METHODOLOGY

The ISRD has an explicitly comparative design. The standardization of methodology demands that all countries adopt the core ISRD-2 module and survey procedures, comparable sampling designs, and coordinated data management and analysis. That is a challenge, since ISRD-2 includes considerably more countries (thirty-one) than ISRD-1, in particular countries from Eastern and Central Europe, including Armenia, Aruba, Austria, Belgium, Bosnia-Herzegovina, Canada, Czech Republic, Cyprus, Denmark, Estonia, Finland, France, Germany, Hungary, Iceland, Italy, Ireland, Lithuania, the Netherlands, Netherlands Antilles, Norway, Poland, Portugal, Russia, Slovenia, Spain, Suriname, Sweden, Switzerland, United States, and Venezuela. A selection of countries was not based on a random sampling of the nations in the world, but on the shared interest from researchers working in universities, research institutes, and government agencies in these countries (Junger-Tas et al., 2010). The main focus of the ISRD is on Europe, although a number of non-European countries also have participated. ISRD-3 (planned for 2011–12) will expand the countries to include China, Turkey, and Mexico among others.

Questionnaire

The questionnaire was collectively produced by the participants in a number of workshops. ISRD-2 has a modular construction of the survey instrument, in other words, a core module with additional modules of questions to fit individual countries' interests. Most of the questions are closed-ended, often with an "other" open-ended response possibility. Questions focus on social demographic background information (including immigration status), family, neighborhood, school, leisure activities, and friends. There are also questions about major life events, attitudes toward violence, and (low) self-control. Questions are mostly drawn from social control and opportunity theories. A major part of the survey consists of questions about twelve different types of delinquency including carrying weapons, group fights, assaults, extortion, snatching, vandalism, shoplifting, bike thefts, thefts from car, car thefts, burglary, drug dealing (life time and last year prevalence and frequency, co-offending, and social response), substance use (drugs and alcohol), as well as victimization (including bullying). Questions on substance use (alcohol and drugs) are asked, but are not treated as measures of delinquency. A total of sixty-seven questions are included in the core module of the ISRD-2. The ISRD questionnaire is in the English language; each country translated the questionnaire as needed. The questionnaires were usually completed in a classroom setting, using pencil and paper. A few countries (e.g., Switzerland) used computerized administration instead (Junger-Tas et al., 2010).

Sampling

The ISRD-2 project is a school-based study, with random samples drawn either at the city level or at the national level. Most of the countries (twenty-two) used city-based sampling, averaging about seven hundred students from a large city or metropolitan area, seven hundred from a medium size city and seven hundred from a cluster of small towns, for a total sample size per country of about 2,100. A total of 44,962 surveys were collected in the city-based sample. For a variety of practical and theoretical reasons, nine countries opted for national samples instead, resulting in 22,921 completed questionnaires. Clearly, city-based and national samples have different advantages and disadvantages and may, strictly speaking, not be directly compared. In order to maximize comparability with the city-based samples, the countries with a national sample tried to oversample – although not always successfully – at least seven hundred youth from one large or medium city. Thus it is important to note that international comparisons of ISRD-2 prevalence rates should be limited to only those respondents who live in large or medium cities (sixty-two cities; n = 43,968; see Figure 63.1 below). A total of 67,883 students completed the questionnaire between 2005 and 2007.

The ISRD-2 project uses as the primary sampling unit seventh, eighth, and ninth grade classrooms (paralleling twelve- to fifteen-year-old students), stratified by school type. Most participating countries took great pains to randomly sample schools in the selected cities, followed by a random selection of classes within these schools, resulting in a fair representation of the school attending population in grade seven to nine.

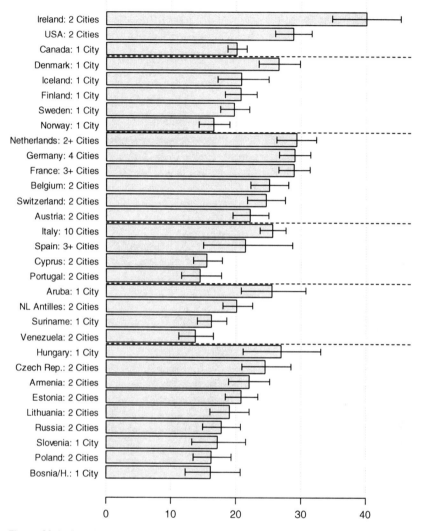

Figure 63.1. Prevalence rates in % (last year) of total self-reported delinquency (Enzmann et al., 2010)

Data Standardization

In order to ensure that the survey results were treated similarly by all research teams, data were entered by using the EpiData software. Standardized syntax was used to transfer data from EpiData to SPSS for each country, and to create all variables (define, code, and check for out of bound questionnaire responses) included in the core ISRD-2 questionnaire. The result of this exercise created thirty-one SPSS data sets with identical variable names and coding, which were then merged into one master file.

FINDINGS

Simultaneous analysis of the pooled data collected in thirty-one countries, 128 cities and towns, and 1,375 schools presents many challenges (e.g., weighing, cluster effects, multilevel analysis). As an important general analytic strategy, the initial ISRD analysis uses country clustering, which greatly facilitates describing a large number of countries simultaneously. Six county clusters are used: Anglo-Saxon countries (Canada, Ireland, USA), Northern European countries (Denmark, Finland, Iceland, Norway, Sweden), Western European countries (Austria, Belgium, France, Germany, Netherlands, Switzerland), Mediterranean countries (Cyprus, Italy, Spain, Portugal), Latin America (Aruba, Netherlands Antilles, Suriname, Venezuela), and Eastern and Central European countries (the postsocialist countries of Armenia, Bosnia-Herzegovina, Czech Republic, Estonia, Hungary, Lithuania, Poland, Russia, and Slovenia). This clustering is based on Saint-Arnaud and Bernard (2003) and Lappi-Seppälä (2007).

It is too early to report substantive findings, but preliminary analysis of the results (Enzmann et al., 2010; Junger-Tas et al., 2010) shows that significant differences in level and type of offending are found between country clusters, with the Western European and Anglo-Saxon cities generally (but not always) scoring highest, followed by Northern Europe, Latin American, and Mediterranean cities, with postsocialist cities at the bottom. Figure 63.1 below shows the main findings with regard to total prevalence rates. Remember that these rates are based on comparisons of data from the sixty-two large and medium sized cities only. In order to increase ease of interpretation, the rates are shown with the 95 percent confidence intervals, which may be used to estimate the significance of the differences between the countries. The dashed lines in the figures indicate the country clusters discussed above. The sequence of country clusters in Figure 63.1 follows the expanded scheme of Saint-Arnauld and Bernard (2003) (i.e., Anglo-Saxon, Northern Europe, Eastern Europe, Mediterranean, Latin America, and the Eastern and Central European clusters); within each country cluster, countries are ranked in declining overall delinquency prevalence. Furthermore, comparisons of ISRD-2 offending and victimization rates with those of the other two main sources of internationally available crime statistics (i.e., International Crime Victimization Survey and European Sourcebook data) suggest a moderate level of support for a convergence of different measures (Enzmann et al., 2010). In other words, the ISRD-2 results are quite compatible with other internationally available crime data.

The results for the U.S. component of the ISRD-2 have been reported elsewhere and are generally in line with theoretical expectations derived from social bonding, self-control, social disorganization, and lifestyle theories (He & Marshall, 2009; Marshall & He, 2010).

CHALLENGES

A project such as the ISRD faces tremendous challenges. Three are worthy of mentioning. First, it is hard to obtain enough funds to do this type of project. The ISRD is not funded by a central funding agency; each country had to obtain its own funding (with the exception of six Central and Eastern European countries which were funded by the EU). It is encouraging, however, that most countries were able to complete the study with a very modest budget, because of researchers' dedication and willingness to donate their time and skills. Second, working with a large number of foreign collaborators (more than one hundred) creates many problems related to language, cultural misunderstandings, and logistic and practical issues (e.g., organizing meetings, standardization of sampling, data collection, and coding). Fortunately, regular workshops (about twice yearly, starting in 2003) succeeded in building an enthusiast international research team, which – guided by the small (six member) ISRD Steering Committee – helped to overcome many of these obstacles. An important tool was the agreed-upon research protocol, including use of standardized sampling design (which could be adjusted to the local situation by the Survey Manager), and standardized data coding and entry (EPIDATA). Third, most countries faced some problems with regard to executing the classroom-based sample plan. Often, needed data were not available (e.g., lists of classrooms and schools), permission was not granted by the authorities, or parental consent was not given or severely limited the response rates. Each country prepared a technical report documenting how these problems were solved.

CONCLUSIONS

The ISRD-2 study offers the benefits of both standardized methodology and flexibility of culture-specific investigations. It appears that so-called flexible standardization (Junger-Tas et al., 2010) may be the most realistic approach to comparative survey research. Like all matters international, reasonable compromises are often the better solution. Experiences with ISRD-1 and ISRD-2 have shown that it is possible to assess both the convergence and the divergence of self-reported delinquency in a large number of nations and to acquire more knowledge about the correlates of crime. The first two sweeps of the ISRD study have paved the way for repeated studies in the future (comparable to the ICVS), which will allow the measurement of international trends in youth delinquency over time.

REFERENCES

Enzmann, D., I. H. Marshall, M. Killias, J. Junger-Tas, M. Steketee, & B. Gruszczynska, (2010). Self-Reported Youth Delinquency in Europe and Beyond: First Results of the Second International Self-Report Delinquency (ISRD) Study in the Context of Police and Victimization Data. *European Journal of Criminology*, 7 (2).

Esping-Andersen, G. (1990). *The Three Worlds of Welfare Capitalism*. Princeton, NJ: Princeton University Press.

He, N. & I. H. Marshall. (2009). *A Multi-City Assessment of Juvenile Delinquency in the U.S.: A Continuation and Expansion of the International Self-Report Delinquency Study (ISRD)*. NIJ Final Report (2006IJCX0045) submitted to the National Institute of Justice, the U.S. Department of Justice.

Junger-Tas, J. & I. H. Marshall. (1999). The Self-Report Methodology in Crime Research. In M. Tonry (Ed.), *Crime and Justice: A Review of Research*, Vol. 25. Chicago: University of Chicago Press, pp. 291–367.

Junger-Tas, J., I. H. Marshall, D. Enzmann, M. W. Killias, M. Steketee, & B. Gruszcynska, (2010). *Juvenile Delinquency in Europe and Beyond: Results of the Second International Self-Report Delinquency Study*. Berlin, New York: Springer.

Junger-Tas, J., Marshall, & D. Ribeaud, with the collaboration of M. W. Killias, G. J. Terlouw, N. Bruining, M. Born, N. He, C. Marshall, & U. Gatti, (2003). *Delinquency in an International Perspective: The International Self-Reported Delinquency Study*. Amsterdam, the Netherlands: Kugler Publications.

Junger-Tas, J., G. J. Terlouw, & M. W. Klein. (1994). *Delinquent Behaviour Among Young People in the Western World: First Results of the International Self-Report Delinquency Study*. Amsterdam, the Netherlands: Kugler Publications.

Klein, M. W. (1989). *Cross-National Research in Self-Reported Crime and Delinquency*. Los Angeles: Kluwer Academic Publishers.

Lappi-Seppälä, T. (2007). Penal Policy and Prisoner Rates in Scandinavia. In K. Nuotio (Ed.), *Festschrift in Honour of Raimo Lahti*. Helsinki: University of Helsinki, Forum Iuris, Publications of the Faculty of Law, pp. 265–306.

Marshall, I. H. & N. He. (2010). The USA. In Enzmann, D., Gruszczynska, B. Junger-Tas, J., Killias, M., Marshall, I. H., & Steketee, M. (Eds.), *Juvenile Delinquency in Europe and Beyond: Results of the Second International Self-report Delinquency Study* (Chapter 10). Berlin, New York: Springer.

WEB SITE

The complete questionnaire may be found at Web site http://webapp5.rrz.uni-hamburg.de/ISRD/JDEB

ABOUT THE AUTHORS

Dr. Ni He is an associate professor of Criminal Justice in the College of Criminal Justice, Northeastern University (Boston, MA). He received his law degree (LL.B.) from Xiamen University (PRC) in 1988 and his Ph.D. in criminal justice from the University of Nebraska-Omaha (USA) in 1997. Dr. He's primary teaching and research interests include comparative criminology, criminal justice, and quantitative methodology. He was a co-principal investigator (with Dr. Ineke Haen Marshall) for the U.S. portion of the thirty-one-nation International Self-report Delinquency Study funded by the National Institute of Justice, U.S. Department of Justice (2006–2008). More recently Professor He and Professor Lanying Li (School of Law, Xiamen University) were awarded a joint international grant from the MacArthur Foundation (2009–11) to study Chinese criminal courts in Fujian Province. Dr. He's scholarship can be found in a variety of refereed professional journals. He is the author of *Reinventing the Wheel: Marx, Durkheim and Comparative Criminology* (1999) and *Policing in Finland* (2006).

Dr. Ineke Haen Marshall has a joint appointment in sociology and criminal justice at Northeastern University. She received her M.A. in Sociology from Tilburg University (Netherlands) and her Ph.D. degree from Bowling Green State University. She specializes in the study of comparative criminology, ethnicity and crime, self-report methodology, juvenile delinquency, and criminal careers. She is a member of the Steering Committee of the International Self-Report Study of Delinquency (ISRD-2) and co-author of *Delinquency in an International Perspective: The International Self-Report Delinquency Study* (2003) and *Juvenile Delinquency in Europe and Beyond: Results of the Second International Self-report Delinquency Study* (2010).

64 Criminology, Method, and Qualitative Comparative Analysis

Gregory J. Howard, Martin Gottschalk,
and Graeme R. Newman

INTRODUCTION

Whether it is news that ships have been pirated off Somali and Sweden, or word that Scottish authorities have released a notorious prisoner on grounds of compassion, those interested in the practice of comparative criminology can find significant fodder for their investigations in various news sources. For example, *The New York Times* reported on a brazen bank robbery in Baghdad in which nine culprits made off with $4.3 million in two get away cars after executing eight bank guards (Nordland & Mohammed, 2009). The robbers neglected the presence of security cameras and the time of the rising sun, so they were caught on videotape and observed by witnesses as they fled the scene of the crime. After a brief trial, four of the defendants were convicted and sentenced to death while one defendant was acquitted. Four other defendants, the suspected ring leaders with ties to the Shiite political elite, are still on the run. Intrigue is added to the case since many of the robbers were also bodyguards to Iraq's Vice President Adel Abdul Mahdi. News reporters Nordland and Mohammed (2009: A1) observed that the case "resonat[es] loudly for what it says about high-level corruption and the uneven application of law in Iraq." For a comparative criminologist, other questions might also be raised by this story: How does the legitimacy of the judicial process affect the standing of the government in the eyes of the public? How are CCTV and other surveillance practices integrated into the ordinary police practices of various nations? How does social reaction to robbery vary between societies? Whatever questions they might ask, our primary contention in this chapter is that criminologists engaged in comparative inquiry employ particular methods in order to produce more defensible understandings of crime and justice.

The practice of comparative criminology allows an investigator to determine whether a theory developed to account for crime and justice in one society can be generalized to other societies. To the extent that the theory falls short, the comparative researcher might be able to refine the explanation for the criminal behavior. A comparative criminologist might also question the relative effectiveness of various crime control strategies. Do innovations in social control practices like community policing work well in all societies? Finally, learning that a legal reform in one nation had the unintentional consequence of encouraging discrimination toward an ethnic minority population, a criminologist might deliver a critical sting and challenge that legal reform should it be proposed in her or his native land (Howard, Newman, & Pridemore, 2000).

This chapter will unfold in the following manner. First, drawing on the illustrious definition provided by Edwin Sutherland and Donald Cressey ([1924] 1960), the project of criminology will be unpacked. Second, attention will be directed toward the concept of comparative method, especially as it has been articulated by Charles Ragin (1987). Third, an application of Ragin's qualitative comparative analysis to the explanation of revolutions in Latin America will be described. Finally, the chapter will conclude with a summary of what has been learned about comparative criminology.

CRIMINOLOGY AND THE COMPARATIVE METHOD

While there is considerable debate about the nature of criminology, one of the more famous declarations of the criminological project was offered by Sutherland and Cressey ([1924] 1960). According to these luminaries:

> Criminology is the body of knowledge regarding crime as a social phenomenon. It includes within its scope the processes of making laws, of breaking laws, and of reacting toward the breaking of laws .... The objective of criminology is the development of a body of general and verified principles and of other types of knowledge regarding this process of law, crime, and treatment or prevention (Sutherland & Cressey, 1960: 3).

On this view, a criminologist understands crime to be inherently social in that only some acts are deemed offensive by a collectivity through its political process. Of the limited number of acts declared criminal, some folks will persist in carrying them out; however, only a portion of these criminal trespasses will yield a social reaction in the form of an arrest or punishment. The aim of a criminologist, therefore, is to explain how criminal laws are fashioned, how some people violate these laws, and how crime control authorities sanction some of these violations. In short, law creation, criminal behavior, and social control can be called the primary dependent variables of criminology, or the social phenomena that a criminologist wishes to explain. In undertaking such an explanation, a criminologist typically employs theory. A theoretical perspective provides a criminologist with a variety of independent variables, or a set of factors that might account for the dependent variable. The promise of a comparative method is that it can guide a criminologist as she or he tries to unravel the relationship between a dependent variable and some set of independent variables (Howard, Newman, & Pridemore, 2000).

Since comparative work in criminology has been informed by developments in sociology, it might be helpful to make a brief tour of that discipline. Émile Durkheim ([1895] 1982: 157), who famously declared that "comparative sociology is ... sociology itself," insisted that a comparative analysis should examine co-variation among social facts in various species of society. In other words, he maintained that social studies should search for an association between some dependent variable (e.g., social fact "y," say crime) and some independent variable (e.g., social fact "x," say income inequality) in various types of societies. For Durkheim, the comparative method was essentially a variable based enterprise in that it relied upon statistical analysis. On the other hand, Max Weber (1949) adopted a case-based pursuit that stressed historical detail. Specifying an "ideal type" or an "ideal typical developmental sequence," a social researcher might compare actual events in a particular historical setting to this logically derived imaginative statement in order to reveal the special causal factors at work in a situated society. While Weber's comparative method sought social explanations for historically unique phenomena, Durkheim's comparative method pursued social explanations for universal phenomena (Kapsis, 1977). Although these two classical theorists' approaches to comparative method differed with respect to technique and theoretical objective, they agreed that the aim of the comparative method was to develop social explanations. Similarly, comparative criminology accounts for the relationship between a dependent variable, like law creation, criminal behavior, or social reaction, and an independent variable by claiming there is a special social characteristic at work (e.g., the society is democratic or religiously tolerant). Thus, "whenever an investigator's explanation makes explicit use of societal or systems level similarities or difference, he/she is engaging in comparative sociology" (Ragin, 1981: 107).

Although Durkheim's variable-based and Weber's case-based comparative methods have found wide application in criminology, Ragin (1987) has identified a number of shortcomings with each approach and has developed a hybrid technique that he calls "qualitative comparative analysis." While variable-based methods split cases into parts, making it difficult to understand cases as historically unique wholes and to identify multiple or conjunctional causes for phenomena, case-based methods suffer from an embarrassment of richness as the historical complexity of a case makes it tough to examine more than a handful of cases at a time and to offer generalized explanations for social phenomena. With qualitative comparative analysis, Ragin (1987: x) retains the advantages of a case-based strategy in that it can specify how "different conditions combine in different and sometimes contradictory ways to produce the same or similar outcomes" and he provides a means by which researchers can study hundreds of cases simultaneously, making it possible to arrive at general theoretical claims. The key to Ragin's (1987: 84) method is the comparison of "wholes as configurations of parts" through the use of Boolean algebra. The basic method uses dichotomous dependent and independent variables, although more sophisticated techniques such as fuzzy sets and multivalue qualitative analysis permit the use of variables with more than two categories. For each case "the typical Boolean-based comparative analysis addresses the presence/absence of conditions under which a certain outcome is obtained (that is, is true)" (Ragin, 1987: 86). An analysis proceeds by first constructing a "truth table" to summarize the data and then by applying the logical techniques of Boolean algebra to the data in order to work "from the bottom up, simplifying complexity in a methodical, stepwise manner" (Ragin, 1987: 101).

Ragin's qualitative comparative analysis is not without shortcomings. First, its dependence on dichotomous variables requires that a researcher divide the world into the presence or absence of theoretically meaningful features, although the complexity of the world sometimes makes this all or nothing rendering difficult to defend. Techniques have been developed to overcome the shortcomings of dichotomous variables, but the use of fuzzy sets and multivalue variables raises other challenges. Second, because Ragin's method stresses the combination of conditions that leads to an outcome of interest, it is not suitable for identifying the unique contribution of a particular variable to that outcome, holding constant the influence of other relevant variables. Finally, although there have been efforts to improve the ability of qualitative comparative analysis to consider the temporal aspects of variables, the method has some difficulty accounting for social change.

Table 64.1. Truth table representing presence/absence of social revolution in selected Latin American cases

Cases	Guerrilla attempt	Peasant support	Guerrilla military strength	Dictatorial regime	Regime loses US support	Social revolution
Cuba, 1956–59	1	1	1	1	1	1
Nicaragua, 1971–79	1	1	1	1	1	1
Guatemala, 1975–88	1	1	1	0	1	0
Venezuela, 1960s	1	1	1	0	0	0
Argentina, 1958–63	1	0	0	0	0	0

Source: Adapted from Wickham-Crowley (1991: 88).

Using qualitative comparative analysis, Wickham-Crowley (1991: 87) examined twenty-eight Latin American cases of social revolution since 1956 to answer this question: "Why did some revolutionary guerrilla movements succeed in coming to power over the last third of a century, in Cuba and later in Nicaragua, while their contemporaries and imitators failed to do so?" Five conditions favorable to social revolutions (i.e., a substantial attempt at guerilla warfare, peasant support for the insurgency, appreciable guerrilla military strength, a dictatorial regime, and the withdrawal of support for the regime by the United States government) were identified. For each of the twenty-eight cases in his analysis, Wickham-Crowley represented the presence (indicated with a 1) or absence (indicated with a 0) of social revolution as well as the presence or absence of the five explanatory conditions in a truth table (see Table 64.1 for data on five of Wickham-Crowley's cases). As Table 64.1 demonstrates, social revolutions were successful in Latin America only in those cases (i.e., Cuba and Nicaragua) where each of the five conditions was present. If any one of those conditions was absent (e.g., Guatemala, Venezuela, and Argentina), a substantial attempt at guerilla warfare did not succeed in overthrowing a regime. Clearly, these data show that a singular combination of conditions is associated with fruitful social revolution. On the other hand, these data show that several different combinations of the five conditions can lead to a failed social revolution. As this study demonstrates, qualitative comparative analysis permits one to scrutinize more cases than is possible with a traditional case-based approach, and the richness of the historical cases can be probed with data minimization strategies for combinations of conditions that are associated with the presence or absence of a particular outcome (see Miethe & Drass

[1999] for an application of qualitative comparative analysis to instrumental and expressive homicides in the United States).

The applicability of the qualitative comparative method to criminology should be apparent. A criminologist would articulate an outcome for which she or he seeks an explanation (e.g., the presence or absence of the death penalty). The criminologist would then nominate the conditions thought to be associated with the outcome by considering hypotheses in the extant literature. Equipped with a set of theoretically informed dependent and independent variables, and a sense of the relationships between them, a criminologist would then examine historically situated cases. Using the procedures of Boolean algebra to simplify the complexity of the world in a theoretically defensible fashion, qualitative comparative analysis would permit a criminologist to advance elegantly the "dialogue of ideas and evidence in social research" (Ragin, 1987: xv).

CONCLUSION

This chapter has briefly discussed comparative criminology. After identifying several reasons for pursuing comparative inquiry, the chapter defined the criminological project and then discussed comparative method. While there are different comparative methods, common to this form of inquiry is the use of societal characteristics to explain relationships between dependent and independent variables. The chapter focused on Ragin's (1987: 168) qualitative comparative analysis since its synthesis of variable-based and case-based approaches to social inquiry "allows investigators both to digest many cases and to assess causal complexity." After reviewing a specific application of qualitative comparative analysis, the chapter concluded by suggesting that Ragin's comparative analysis might promote the "dialogue of ideas and evidence" in criminology.

REFERENCES

Durkheim, É. ([1895] 1982). *The Rules of Sociological Method*. Translated by W. D. Halls. New York: The Free Press.

Howard, G. J., G. Newman, & W. A. Pridemore. (2000). Theory, Method, and Data in Comparative Criminology. In D. Duffee (Ed.), *Criminal Justice 2000: Measurement and Analysis of Crime and Justice*, Vol. 4. Washington, DC: National Institute of Justice, pp. 139–211.

Kapsis, R. E. (1977). Weber, Durkheim, and the Comparative Method. *Journal of the History of the Behavioral Sciences*, 13, 354–68.

Miethe, T. D. & K. A. Drass. (1999). Exploring the Social Context of Instrumental and Expressive Homicides: An Application of Qualitative Comparative Analysis. *Journal of Quantitative Criminology*, 15, 1–21.

Nordland, R. & R. Mohammed. (2009, Sepetmber 9). In Bank Killings, Highs and Lows of Iraq Justice. *The New York Times*. Retrieved September 3, 2009, from http://www.nytimes.com/2009/09/03/world/middleeast/03iraq.html?ref=world.

Ragin, C. C. (1981). Comparative Sociology and the Comparative Method. *International Journal of Comparative Sociology*, 22, 102–20.

    (1987). *The Comparative Method: Moving Beyond Qualitative and Quantitative Strategies*. Berkeley, CA: University of California Press.

Sutherland, E. H. & D. R. Cressey. ([1924] 1960). *Principles of Criminology*, Sixth Edition. Chicago: J. B. Lippincott.

Weber, M. (1949). *The Methodology of the Social Sciences*. Translated by E. A. Shils & H. A. Finch. New York: The Free Press.

Wickham-Crowley, T. P. (1991). A Qualitative Comparative Approach to Latin American Revolutions. *International Journal of Comparative Sociology*, 32, 82–109.

ABOUT THE AUTHORS

Gregory J. Howard is an associate professor of sociology at Western Michigan University.

Martin Gottschalk is an associate professor of criminal justice studies at the University of North Dakota.

Graeme Newman is Distinguished Teaching Professor of Criminal Justice at the State University of New York at Albany.

PART IX

INTERNATIONAL RESEARCH RESOURCES

The information revolution of the past twenty years has helped to create and disseminate vast stores of data on every imaginable topic. While this has benefited every field of research, it may have particularly helped those studying crime occurring in distant parts of the world. From the relative comfort of their offices these researchers can travel to the far reaches of the planet at the click of a keyboard and gather critical items of information about crimes committed, offenders arrested, and punishments administered. On a personal note, this almost makes me wish that I was starting my research career now, rather than twenty years ago when, as a young student, I had to traverse half the Indian subcontinent, from my university in Madras (now Chennai) to the Tata Institute of Social Sciences Library in Bombay (now Mumbai) to compile the literature review for my research on women policing.

No doubt the Tata Institute Library still holds a vast store of books, journals, government reports, and newspapers, which are all of great value for researchers. There is also no doubt that the library, just as all other research libraries, has been transformed by the Internet, which provides electronic access to many of the paper materials held on their shelves. Even in the libraries themselves it is easy to see the results of this revolution. Rarely do students and professors wander among the stacks, searching for that elusive book or journal. Instead, they will be found interrogating the library computers, which have grown exponentially in number from the time, less than twenty years ago, when they held access only to the library catalogue.

While the libraries of modern educational institutions strive to expand their collections and to find ways to connect to new e-sources, it is of little use if they cannot help their users to find the information they need. The multidisciplinary nature of international crime and justice makes it practically impossible to provide students and researchers with a definitive list of resources. However, Maria Kirakova, a librarian at John Jay College of Criminal Justice, lists the best of these resources and provides a guide to accessing them (Chapter 65). Her work shows how the new electronic world of libraries still depends on the knowledge and energy of well-trained librarians to make their resources accessible.

The need for human links, as well as electronic coordination, was recognized by the founders of the World Criminal Justice Library Network (WCJLN). This organization consists of a group of librarians and information specialists drawn from more than thirty countries, who work in universities and colleges and in government and nongovernment organizations and research institutes (see Chapter 66 by John Myrtle and Phyllis Schultze). They are of great help to one another, when a researcher cannot gain access to an important paper published in another country – something that occurs with great regularity. To fulfill its purpose, the Network does not rely simply on electronic communications among the members, but the bonds between them are cemented at biannual meetings, held in different parts of the world, where matters of mutual concern are discussed and developed. Librarians, like everyone else, are much more likely to help one another when they personally know and like one another. Perhaps there is a wider lesson here for the field of international crime and justice.

65 International Criminal Justice

PRINTED AND ELECTRONIC MEDIA, JOURNALS, AND PROFESSIONAL ASSOCIATIONS

Maria Kiriakova

INTRODUCTION

International criminal justice is a relatively new field of study and despite the fact that it is closely related to the field of comparative criminal justice, it also includes components from such academic disciplines as politics and economics, sociology and anthropology, computer and information science, law and public administration, gender studies and linguistics, and many others. The multidisciplinary nature of the field makes it practically impossible to provide the researcher with a definite list of resources. This chapter provides a vast array of library resources that could assist in international crime and justice research.

LOOKING FOR INFORMATION

Depending on your research topic, you may be able to locate reliable information sources right away; however, some topics will require more time to dig for information. Don't be nervous – there are always librarians who will assist you with the library research. Nowadays, librarians can be reached not only in person but also by phone, e-mail, through chat and tweets.

Where to look for information will depend on the nature of the research question and most of all on the currency of the topic and its interest to the public. Today, the Internet is the first source of information. But don't forget that books still have a value if you are looking for an in-depth treatment of a subject. If you find an article or a book that are perfect for your topic, check their reference or additional readings lists – it will contain other useful sources of information related to your research. Then run a search in the library online catalog or other bibliographic databases to see where and how these materials can be accessed.

INTERNET SEARCH VERSUS LIBRARY RESOURCES SEARCH

So far, there is no universal search tool that would provide you with all the possible materials available on your topic – books or dissertations, government or agency reports, journal articles or conference proceedings, just to name a few. Internet browsing in combination with searching specialized library databases will equip you with well-balanced results.

There is nothing wrong with going to the Internet first, especially when choosing search tools that are aimed at research such as Google Scholar (www.google.scholar.com) or Scirus (www.scirus.com), for example. These search engines will provide you with an option to link the search results to databases and full-text resources of the libraries with which you are affiliated.

If you already have a specific citation (information about a certain book or an article), it is advisable to go directly to your library's Web site and locate materials either through the library online catalog or its databases. Academic libraries are experimenting now with federated search mechanisms that will search across multiple specialized databases, library catalogs, digital repositories, and even the Internet. This search method is not fault-proof yet, so it is a good practice to go to selected databases individually for more thorough research.

Most library online catalogs provide information about their collections available in a variety of formats – print, electronic, microform, audio, visual, etc. In addition to author and title searches, library holdings in the catalog can be broadly browsed by keywords and more narrowly by subject terms. Although government and organizational reports can also be found through regular Internet search, librarians monitor what valuable free online information is available in the mission areas of their institutions and keep links to such materials in the library catalogs.

Always read the full description of a record in the catalog: see where print copies of the books are located in the library, look for the links for the electronic copies for books, government and agency reports, and check the subject terms hotlinks for similar items on the same topic. Although libraries keep records of their electronic books in their online catalogs, some researchers prefer going to individual collections of e-books like ebrary, myLibrary, or netLibrary.

SELECTED INTERNET RESOURCES

Below is a list of some useful Web sites and homepages of criminal justice research and policy agencies which can guide you to a range of international resources, as well as hard to find statistical data.

BJS, Bureau of Justice Statistics (http://bjs.ojp.usdoj.gov) – is the major source of criminal justice statistics for the USA. International statistics will be added soon according to the site.

CIA World Factbook (www.cia.gov/cia/publications/factbook) – is updated weekly; it contains data about countries of the world with a special section on the country's involvement in transnational issues.

Eurojust (www.eurojust.europa.eu) – is a judicial cooperation body created to help provide safety within an area of freedom, security, and justice in the European Union. The "Useful Links" tab on the menu bar will link you to such important resources as Eur-Lex (http://eur-lex.europa.eu), a free database of EU law; European Law Enforcement Agency Europol (www.europol.europa.eu) and POLIS (http://polis.osce.org), Policing On-Line Information System of the Organization of Security, and Co-Operation in Europe, OSCE.

European Sourcebook of Crime and Criminal Justice Statistics (www.europeansourcebook.org) – whose third edition covers the data up-to-2003, and whose fourth edition should be coming out soon.

HEUNI (www.heuni.fi) – is the official Web site for the *European Institute for Crime Prevention and Control*. Access to the specialized studies, reports, and statistics.

Home Office, United Kingdom (www.homeoffice.gov.uk) – provides crime statistics from the United Kingdom, as well as links to international data (www.crimereduction.homeoffice.gov.uk/sta_index.htm# International).

Human Rights Watch (www.hrw.org) – reports about the violations of human rights in individual countries and an annual world status report.

INCB (www.incb.org) – *International Narcotics Control Board* is the independent and quasijudicial monitoring body for the implementation of the United Nations international drug control conventions.

International Association of Chiefs of Police (www.theiacp.org) – is the world's oldest and largest nonprofit membership organization of police executives with members in eighty-nine countries.

International Centre for Criminal Law Reform and Criminal Justice Policy (www.icclr.law.ubc.ca) – provides advice, information, research, and proposals for policy development and legislation.

International Center for the Prevention of Crime (www.crime-prevention-intl.org) – promotes research-based policies and practices that work to prevent crime and build community safety.

International Centre for Prison Studies (www.kcl.ac.uk/schools/law/research/icps) – provides statistics on prison systems and conditions, as well as incarceration rates in more than two hundred countries.

International Policing Expertise Platform (www.ipep.info) – is a clearing-house for current criminal justice information.

International Victimology Web site (INTERVICT) (www.victimology.nl) – provides information about current victimology research and encourages international exchange of expertise and experience.

Interpol (www.interpol.int) – is the international police organization that facilitates crossborder criminal police cooperation; links to the departments of Justice throughout the world.

National Criminal Justice Reference Service (NCJRS) (www.ncjrs.org) – covers all aspects of law enforcement and criminal justice; its topic coverage ranges from preliminary research to detailed descriptions of successful programs.

Transparency International (www.transparency.org) – is a politically nonpartisan organization that raises awareness about corruption on a global level.

UNICRI (www.unicri.it) – *the United Nations Interregional Crime and Justice Research Institute* assists intergovernmental, governmental and non-governmental organizations in formulating and implementing improved policies in the field of crime prevention and criminal justice.

UNODC (www.unodc.org) – the site map of the United Nations Office on Drugs and Crime serves as the major gateway to information and UN publications on international efforts. (United Nations Surveys on Crime Trends and the Operations of Criminal Justice Systems, CTS) is available under Resources/Data analysis link from the side menu.

UNICRI and *UNODC* are part of *the United Nations Crime Prevention and Criminal Justice Programme Network* (PNI). (www.unicri.it/wwk/related/pni/institutes.php) and (www.unodc.org/unodc/en/commissions/CCPCJ/institutes.html)

WODC (http://english.wodc.nl) – WODC (the Dutch abbreviation for Wetenschappelijk Onderzoek- en Documentatiecentrum, in English: Research and Documentation Centre) may be described as an international criminal justice knowledge centre.

SCHOLARLY ARTICLES AND SPECIALIZED LIBRARY DATABASES

There are many scholarly journals published today that include articles on international criminal justice. Where to look for scholarly articles? Despite the fact that the academic world has changed drastically in the last decade and made research more open and accessible thanks to the Internet, scholarly articles are still a commodity and are available in many instances only in the commercial bibliographic databases, in other words through the library, where you have to be identified as a legitimate user. Keep in mind that databases can contain more than articles, so analyze the results of your search and mark off the search box to include only scholarly (peer-reviewed) articles in the search. Here are just some examples of useful databases or aggregators (check your library holdings for accessibility):

Criminal Justice Abstracts – is an excellent source of scholarly articles, books, chapters in books, government reports, and dissertations. Some international publications are included with in-depth abstracts in English. The same platform allows having access to other CSA databases: Sociological Abstracts and Worldwide Political Abstracts.

Criminal Justice Periodicals Index – provides information from practitioners' point of view; includes police and other law enforcement professional, or trade, publications, as well as scholarly journals.

EBSCOhost – provides more than a hundred specialized databases covering practically all areas of knowledge. The search can be performed either in an individual database or in multiple databases simultaneously. Databases that you might find useful are Academic Search, MasterFILE, International Political Science Abstracts, International Security & Counterterrorism Reference Center, Middle Eastern & Central Asian Studies, Military & Government Collection, National Criminal Justice Reference Service Abstracts, Newspaper Source, Peace Research Abstracts, SocIndex, Urban Studies Abstracts, Violence & Abuse Abstracts.

Hein Online – is the world's largest image-based legal research database. Publications are organized into separate sets based on the U.S. or international focus (for example, European Center for Minority Issues, Foreign & International Law Resources Database, Treaties and Agreements Library, United Nations Law Collection, World Trials Library) and available in full-text access cover-to-cover.

Ingenta library gateway – is a searchable database of more than eleven million citations from more than 20,000 journals. It offers online access to selected electronic journals based on institutional subscriptions as well as current awareness service.

Jane's – is the ultimate source for information on the subjects of defense, geopolitics, weapons systems, and security.

JSTOR – is a collection of complete runs of hundreds of academic journals in full-text except for the current issues (last two to five years depending on the copyright agreements between the JSTOR and the publishers).

Justus – is a full-text online legal library of UK, Irish and European Union case law.

LexisNexis – the Legal Research part of LexisNexis Academic has access to a vast collection of law reviews. The news part allows searching for newspaper and magazine articles in English and some other languages. LexisNexis Statistical provides data from state and federal government reports, private sector sources, and international intergovernmental organizations.

NCJRS Library/Abstracts – (also available through EBSCOhost). Free database of criminal justice literature from around the world. Excellent thesaurus of criminal justice terms.

Project MUSE – online database of more than two hundred journals in humanities and social sciences from nonprofit publishers.

ProQuest – includes citations and full-text articles in academic and professional disciplines, for example, business, economics, gender studies, health, literature, management, political science; as well as news and general interest items.

SAGE Criminology Collection – allows searching for articles in twenty-four criminal justice journals.

Social Sciences Full Text – indexes more than 415 English-language periodicals in anthropology, criminology, economics, law, geography, policy studies, psychology, sociology, social work, and urban studies.

Westlaw – mostly used by legal professionals, it provides full-text of state and federal cases, law reviews, and access to news and legal reference sources in English and other languages.

WorldLII (*www.worldlii.org*) – the World Legal Information Institute (WorldLII) collects legal materials on international level and provides free access to them through its Web site.

WorldCat (*http://worldcat.org*) – free online database that will search for books, articles, and other materials available in the print and electronic collections of the libraries worldwide. Check if your library is a member of this network.

SEARCH TECHNIQUES

One of the most challenging aspects of every research project is the ability to formulate the topic and then describe it in simple terms. The selection of search terms, or keywords, as well as the way they are presented to the online system can either advance or obstruct the search.

Your keyword might be a simple significant word (such as terrorism or apartheid) or a phrase ("trafficking in small arms," "shootings by police," or "shooting of police," for example). It is recommended by the majority of the databases to put double quotes (" ") around phrases to keep the search as exact as possible.

As a rule, online databases will provide the searchers with a thesaurus or a list of controlled subject terms, or descriptors. Using subject terms requires practice and knowledge of the topic. For a novice researcher, it is more beneficial to start with a keyword search. When going through the results select the most relevant records and open them in full view where so subject terms will be displayed as hotlinks. Decide if you would like to see more records that use only these subject headings. Browsing through a thesaurus helps to identify more specific terms that might apply to your topic.

PROFESSIONAL ASSOCIATIONS

Below is a list of some criminal justice associations and professional organizations with an international flavor and with the membership available to the students.

Academy of Criminal Justice Sciences, ACJS (www.acjs.org).
American Anthropological Association (www.aaanet.org).
American Political Science Association (www.apsanet.org).
American Society of Criminology, ASC (www.asc41.com) has an International Division (www.internationalcriminology.com).
American Society of International Law (www.asil.org).
American Sociological Association (www.asanet.org).
Amnesty International (www.amnestyusa.org/index.html).
Australian and New Zealand Society of Criminology (www.anzsoc.org).
British Society of Criminology (www.britsoccrim.org).
Canadian Society of Criminology (www.crimsociety.wlu.ca).
Criminological and Victimological Society of Southern Africa (www.crimsa.ac.za).
European Society of Criminology (www.esc-eurocrim.org).
Human Rights Watch (www.hrw.org).
International Association for the Study of Organized Crime (www.iasoc.net).
International Sociological Association (www.isa-sociology.org).
International Studies Association (www.isanet.org).
Mexican Society of Criminology (www.somecrimnlen.es.tl).
Pakistan Society of Criminology (www.pakistansocietyofcriminology.com).
Sociologists Without Borders (www.sociologistswithoutborders.org).
South Asian Society of Criminology and Victimology (users4.jabry.com/sascv/default.html).
World Society of Victimology (www.worldsocietyofvictimology.org).

LIST OF JOURNALS FOR THE STUDY OF INTERNATIONAL CRIME AND L JUSTICE

The list below is not exhaustive, but rather can be used as a starting point. Searching bibliographic databases will help identify key journals in particular topics. The WCJLN (World Criminal Justice Electronic Library Network) Web site (*http://andromeda.rutgers.edu/~wcjlen/WCJ/*) includes a comprehensive list of journals as well.

African Journal of Criminology and Justice Studies
Asian Journal of Criminology
American Journal of Comparative Law
Australian and New Zealand Journal of Criminology
British Journal of Criminology
Canadian Journal of Criminology and Criminal Justice
Crime & Justice International
Crime, Law and Social Change
Criminology: An Interdisciplinary Journal
European Journal of Crime, Criminal Law, and Criminal Justice
European Journal of Criminology
European Journal on Criminal Policy and Research
Howard Journal of Criminal Justice
Indian Journal of Criminology
International Journal of Criminal Justice Sciences
International Criminal Justice Review
International Criminal Law Review
International Criminal Police Review (Interpol)
International E-journal of Criminal Sciences
International Journal of Comparative and Applied Criminal Justice
International Journal of Comparative Criminology
International Journal of Comparative Sociology
International Journal of Drug Policy
International Journal of Law and Psychiatry
International Journal of Offender Therapy and Comparative Criminology
International Journal of Police Science and Management
International Journal of Social Inquiry
International Journal of the Sociology of Law
International Review of Victimology
International Security
Journal of Scandinavian Studies in Criminology and Crime Prevention
Journal of International Criminal Justice

Pakistan Journal of Criminology
Police Practice & Research: An International Journal
Policing: An International Journal of Police Strategies & Management
Prison Service Journal
Revue de Droit Penal et de Criminologie
Studies in Conflict & Terrorism

ABOUT THE AUTHOR

Assistant Professor Maria Kiriakova is a reference and collection development librarian at John Jay College of Criminal Justice, City University of New York. She has contributed articles to various reference books in the area of criminal justice such as *Encyclopedia of Crime and Punishment* and *Encyclopedia of Law Enforcement*.

66 World Criminal Justice Library Network

John Myrtle and Phyllis A. Schultze

INTRODUCTION

The World Criminal Justice Library Network (WCJLN) is a group of librarians and information specialists with members from more than thirty countries, representing academic institutions, government and nongovernment organizations, research institutes, together with individual scholars. The Network was established at a meeting at Rutgers University, Newark, NJ, in April 1991 and has grown to be an influential contributor to communications and the dissemination of information in the field of criminology and criminal justice. This paper provides background to the establishment of the Network, a description of its services, and an outline of the development of its services.

ANTECEDENTS

A number of the individuals and agencies involved in the establishment of the World Criminal Justice Library Network had previously been involved with the United Nations Criminal Justice Information Network (UNCJIN). UNCJIN, formally established in March 1989, was an initiative of the United Nations Crime Prevention and Criminal Justice Branch, Vienna, and its affiliate United Nations research institutes.

UNCJIN had two main aims: first, to facilitate the sending and exchange of information between members, and the exchange of information with members of other networks, and second, to provide data from a variety of databases, including United Nations surveys of crime trends, crime victims surveys, and other information such as legislation. From the early stages of the network it was recognized that a wider range of affiliates would enhance its effectiveness. While most of the UNCJIN members employed librarians or information specialists, they were often dependant on specialist criminological libraries and information services within agencies or universities not directly affiliated to UNCJIN. By 1990, it had become clear that communications and dissemination of information for practitioners, teachers, and students within the field of criminology would be enhanced if a network was established that not only utilized the resources of UNCJIN but also the resources of other criminology libraries and librarians.

ESTABLISHMENT OF THE WORLD CRIMINAL JUSTICE LIBRARY NETWORK

The specific idea of establishing a network of criminal justice librarians and information specialists was the brainchild of Professor Ronald Clarke, then Dean of the School of Criminal Justice at Rutgers University, Newark, NJ, and Professor Graeme Newman, a distinguished professor in the School of Criminal Justice at the State University of New York at Albany, NY. Prior to his appointment to Rutgers University, Professor Clarke had been head of the Criminal Justice Research Department of the British Home Office.

Professor Newman, an Australian-born academic, had worked for an extended period within the United Nations and when he moved on to teaching work in American universities he maintained links with United Nations agencies. Newman has been a visionary and pioneer in recognizing the importance of electronic communications and technological innovation for enhancing the sharing of information for both information professionals and practitioners. He was instrumental in the establishment of the United Nations Criminal Justice Information Network and was the founding coordinator of UNCJIN. Clarke and Newman recognized that with the growing globalization of crime and criminal justice issues, they should bring together librarians and information specialists in the field of criminology and exploit their expertise. To that end they convened a meeting of these librarians for April 1991 at Rutgers University.

It was significant that Rutgers University was chosen as the venue for the initial meeting because their Don M. Gottfredson Criminal Justice Library had developed to be the leading academic information provider in the field of criminology in the United States, its reputation built around:

- a strong service ethic, for the benefit of teachers, students, and practitioners;
- building one of the world's leading library-based collections in the field of criminology and criminal justice;

- their contribution to the development of Criminal Justice Abstracts as a leading reference database in the field.

The gathering of librarians at Rutgers was meeting in a period that pre-dated the pervasive impact of the Internet and e-mail. The immediacy of a face-to-face meeting was critical in assessing the need for a worldwide network of librarians and information specialists, and identifying issues of importance and priorities for the network. Participants at this foundation meeting responded with enthusiasm; acknowledging the opportunity being offered by UNCJIN as a means of electronic communication; agreeing to exchange publications, accessions lists, and other paper-based informa-tion. A steering committee for the network was established with Graeme R. Newman and the Rutgers Criminal Justice Librarian, Phyllis A. Schultze, as co-chairs. The steering committee would implement the decisions from the meeting, and initiate planning for future meetings. As a starting point, it was agreed that members would meet every second year in different centers and countries.

A diverse range of libraries and agencies were involved in the initial meeting. In addition to the Rutgers Criminal Justice Library, the prominent contributors included:

- Australian Institute of Criminology (J. V. Barry Library); the Institute, an Australian government agency affiliated to the United Nations Crime Prevention and Criminal Justice Branch and foundation member of UNCJIN, was established in 1973 with a focus on research, training and information work. The Institute publications include the series *Trends & Issues in Crime and Criminal Justice* and the library produces a reference database, *CINCH, the Australian Criminology Database* with information on Australian criminal justice subject matter.
- Institute of Criminology, Cambridge University (Radzinowicz Library); the library was founded in 1960 and named after Sir Leon Radzinowicz, the first Director of the Institute (from 1959 to 1972). The library houses the most comprehensive criminology collection in the United Kingdom and is internationally recognized as a world-class criminal justice resource.
- Institute of Criminology, University of Tuebingen; in close cooperation with the Tuebingen University Library, since 1969 the Institute of Criminology is responsible for the German national criminology library (Bibliotheksschwerpunkt Kriminologie). Together with a range of services, the library has developed the *KrimDok* database with references to more than 100,000 documents (German and foreign

monographs and articles). Access to the database is free of charge through the Institute's Web site.

- National Criminal Justice Reference Service (NCJRS); NCJRS was created in 1972 by the National Institute of Justice, within the US Department of Justice, to provide information for Department of Justice agencies. Since then the NCJRS network has been extended and provides indexes, abstracts, and documents in many areas of criminology and criminal justice. The free *NCJRS Database* indexes journal articles, books, and research reports on criminology and criminal justice back to 1970.

Following the initial 1991 meeting, the members of the World Criminal Justice Library Network met again two years later in Siracusa, Sicily. A significant feature of the Siracusa meeting was demonstrations of e-mail and Internet services by Graeme Newman. At this stage the majority of WCJLN members did not have access to such services. Throughout the 1990s the Network widened and communications became more sophisticated as member libraries and agencies embraced Internet and e-mail services and developed Web sites. The Network was also enhanced by the development of a WCJLN Web site hosted at Rutgers University and managed by the Librarian at the Rutgers School of Criminal Justice. Another important feature was the introduction of an electronic discussion list (WCJLN-L) for the Network; it has been managed by Dennis Benamatti and hosted in the United States, initially by Marist College, then Sacred Heart University, and currently by John Jay College, New York.

The Web site, entitled *The World Criminal Justice Library Electronic Network*, benefits Network members as well as students and academics researching international criminal justice topics. For members there is a directory of WCJLN member libraries; in addition, there are features such as links to online library catalogs, statistical resources, general reference sources, bibliographies, online periodicals, online databases, and information on forthcoming conferences.

The links to the online catalogs of major criminal justice libraries is an important feature of the Web site. These catalogs include those for the Australian Institute of Criminology, the Institute of Criminology at Cambridge, the US National Institute of Corrections, the Rutgers Law Library Catalog at Newark (incorporating the Criminal Justice Library holdings), as well as several other noteworthy collections.

As well as listing library holdings, some of the catalogs also provide links to full-text documents or abstracts of materials contained in their collection. For example, the library of the California Police Officer Standards and Training Center (POST Library) contains abstracts of periodical literature, abstracts and full-text of some of the POST Command Papers. The Australian Institute of Criminology provides links to a number of bibliographies, a listing of online journals and reports, and other database and online resources. The Library of the National Institute of Corrections (Robert J. Kutak Memorial Library) regularly abstracts unpublished materials; in addition a link is provided to the full-text for most documents. Library items include research reports, program evaluations, journal articles, monographs and published books.

Another feature of the WCJLN Web site is the links it provides to online periodicals. An increasing number of periodicals are providing access to at least an abstract of their articles, and in some cases, access to the full-text of the publication. Some of these are Web-based only, with no print edition available. Some examples of journals that are published full-text on the Web include the *Western Criminology Review*, the *Journal of Criminal Justice and Popular Culture*, the *Drug Court Review*, the *Internet Journal of Criminology*, and the *FBI Law Enforcement Bulletin*.

One feature of the WCJLN is the wide range of libraries represented. Some are from well-resourced government agencies or are affiliated with large university libraries. Other members work in smaller libraries and are quite isolated from other criminal justice librarians. For these people, in particular, the biennial meetings of the Network have provided an important opportunity to make contact with fellow professionals and discuss relevant issues. Ivanka Sket, Information Specialist with the Institute of Criminology at the Faculty of Law, Slovenia, was an early member of WCJLN with responsibility for a small academic library. She summed up the importance of the Network's meetings in the following way:

> I ... remember all the conferences held in the past, which gave us the wonderful opportunity to get to know each other, to follow new advances in criminal justice information, to learn what was new in terms of technical progress in information sciences, to see how other criminal justice libraries work, how they are organized and to enjoy a rich exchange of information and experience between librarians, information specialists and all other professionals working in the criminal justice area.

At some of the meetings of the Network, the agency responsible for organizing the meeting has used the opportunity to sponsor a librarian who would not normally be able to attend the meetings or even regularly contribute to the Network. As a consequence, the librarian from the United Nations African Institute for the Prevention of Crime and the Treatment of

Offenders (UNAFRI), based in Kampala, Uganda, was able to attend several of the meetings. Similarly, librarians from the University of South Pacific and from Papua New Guinea's Department of Justice were sponsored to attend the 2003 Canberra meeting in Australia.

As valuable as the meetings of the Network are for members, there are two limitations; first, that only a minority of members are able to attend, and second, the infrequency of meetings. For these reasons, the Network's electronic discussion list is a valuable communication tool. Members have found a wide variety of applications for the discussion list, such as making requests for information about publications, forwarding lists of new library accessions, communicating information about new publications or coming events, or advising of changes in library personnel. WCJLN-L is a closed and unmoderated list. Requests for access are evaluated before membership is approved.

A particular strength of the World Criminal Justice Library Network is that it has encouraged the growth of regional networks or meetings of criminal justice librarians. Prior to the establishment of the WCJLN, the Australian Institute of Criminology had been involved with regional meetings, organizing conferences for librarians in the criminal justice system, held every second year (from 1977 to 1992). New Zealand librarians regularly attended these conferences and the 1992 conference was attended by the Rutgers librarian and librarians from the Barcelona Police College. In addition, at various times regional meetings of members from European countries have been convened, such as meetings of criminal justice librarians from Nordic countries.

It is a sign of the strength of the WCJLN that it is not just recognized for the quality of its databases and library collections. As an example, librarians and information specialists within the Network have been called upon to undertake important roles within the field of criminal justice. Examples include: working as advisor and reviewer for the Campbell Collaboration; making presentations to international criminal justice symposia; creating and managing knowledge platforms; and providing online access to vital government reports.

CONCLUSION

Sir Leon Radzinowicz, founding director of the Institute of Criminology at Cambridge University, wrote in his memoirs of the establishment of the Institute's Library:

> At the first meeting on the Advisory Council of the Institute in 1961, Lord Nathan emphatically stated that "the creation of a Library was regarded

as of the first importance by the Wolfson Foundation" [a benefactor offering generous financial support to the Institute]. And Lady Wootton reinforced it by "expressing the hope that the library would be made available to scholars from all over the world."

Nearly fifty years on, the members of that Advisory Council are likely to have viewed with satisfaction the developments in technology that would now enable the catalog of a library such as the Radzinowicz Library to be searched from different parts of the globe. In addition, they would be encouraged by the cooperative spirit that enables the Institute's librarians to be active contributors to the World Criminal Justice Library Network.

Two decades ago, the founding members of the World Criminal Justice Library Network at the initial meeting at Rutgers University resolved that the new network would have two principle objectives:

1. to develop specific ways of sharing services and criminal justice information on a global scale; and
2. to enhance communications among WCJLN members.

There is no doubting the progress in achieving these ends; the energy and commitment of members, together with unforeseen progress in technological innovation, has meant that the World Criminal Justice Library Network has significantly advanced the dissemination of criminal justice information worldwide.

APPENDIX

Meetings of the World Criminal Justice Library Network

1. Foundation meeting (1991) Newark, NJ, USA
2. Second meeting (1993) Siracusa, Italy
3. Third meeting (1995) Villingen-Schwenningen, Germany
4. Fourth meeting (1997) Washington, DC, USA
5. Fifth meeting (1999) Helsinki, Finland
6. Sixth meeting (2001) Zutphen, the Netherlands
7. Seventh meeting (2003) Canberra, Australia
8. Eighth meeting (2004) Ljubljana, Slovenia
9. Ninth meeting (2006) Montreal, Canada
10. Tenth meeting (2008) Solna, Sweden

ABOUT THE AUTHORS

John Myrtle is an associate investigator in the ARC Centre of Excellence in Policing and Security, Griffith University, Australia. He was formerly Principal Librarian, J V Barry Library, Australian Institute of Criminology; a member of the Scientific Commission, International Society of Criminology; and a founder member of the World Criminal Justice Library Network.

Phyllis A. Schultze is the director of the Rutgers University Don M. Gottfredson Library of Criminal Justice. She is co-author of *Researching a Problem* (Office of Community Oriented Policing Services, 2005) and *Criminal Justice Information: How to Find It, How to Use It* (Oryx Press, 1998) and served on the editorial board for the Encyclopedia of Crime and Punishment (Sage, 2002). Schultze earned a bachelor's degree from Calvin College and a master's in library science from Rutgers University. She serves as co-chair of the World Criminal Justice Library Network and is a member of the American Society of Criminology and the Academy of Criminal Justice Sciences.

MAURITANIA
SENEGAL
MALI
NIGER
GAMBIA
GUINEA
BISSAU
GUINEA
BURKINA FASO
BENIN
SIERRA
LEONE
IVORY
COAST
GHANA
NIGERIA
ATLANTIC
OCEAN
LIBERIA
TOGO

0   150   300 miles
0   150 300 km

GREENLAND
(DENMARK)
ARCTIC
Arctic Circle

U.S.
CANADA
ICELAND
UNITED KINGDOM
IRELAND
FRANCE

UNITED STATES
NORTH
ATLANTIC
PORTUGAL   SPAIN

NORTH PACIFIC
OCEAN
MOROCCO
Tropic of Cancer
MEXICO
OCEAN
WESTERN
SAHARA
HAWAIIAN ISLANDS
U.S.
MAURITANIA MALI

CAPE
VERDE
GUYANA
SURINAME
COLOMBIA
FRENCH GUIANA
(Fr.)
Equator
ECUADOR
VENEZUELA

WESTERN
SAMOA
PERU
BRAZIL
SOUTH

BOLIVIA
ATLANTIC
TONGA
PARAGUAY
OCEAN
Tropic of Capricorn

0   150   300 miles
0   300   600 km
U.S.
CHILE
URUGUAY

THE
BAHAMAS
SOUTH

MEXICO
CUBA
DOMINICAN
REP.
PACIFIC

BELIZE
JAMAICA
HAITI
PUERTO
RICO
ANTIGUA &
BARBUDA
OCEAN

GUATEMALA
HONDURAS
ST. KITTS & NEVIS
GUADELOUPE
DOMINICA

EL
SALVADOR
NICARAGUA
MARTINIQUE
ST. LUCIA
ST. VINCENT & THE GRENADINES
BARBADOS
GRENADA

COSTA RICA
PANAMA
TRINIDAD & TOBAGO
COLOMBIA
VENEZUELA

Projection: Robinson

NORWAY SWEDEN ESTONIA
DENMARK NORTH SEA LATVIA RUSSIA
RUSSIA LITHUANIA
NETHER- BELARUS
LANDS POLAND
GERMANY
BELGIUM CZECH UKRAINE
LUXEMBOURG REPUBLIC
LIECHTENSTEIN SLOVAKIA MOLDOVA
SWITZERLAND AUSTRIA HUNGARY
SLOVENIA ROMANIA
FRANCE CROATIA
MONACO BOSNIA SERBIA BLACK SEA
SAN HERZEGOVINA
MARINO MONTE- BULGARIA
ITALY NEGRO
MACEDONIA
ALBANIA
GREECE
MEDITERRANEAN SEA TURKEY
ALGERIA TUNISIA MALTA

0 100 200 miles
0 200 400 km

OCEAN
NORWAY
FINLAND
RUSSIA
KAZAKSTAN
MONGOLIA
NORTH
KOREA
TURKEY UZBEKISTAN KYRGYZSTAN NORTH JAPAN PACIFIC
TURKMENISTAN TAJIKISTAN SOUTH OCEAN
TUNISIA CYPRUS SYRIA CHINA KOREA
LEBANON AFGHANISTAN
ALGERIA ISRAEL IRAQ IRAN
LIBYA JORDAN KUWAIT PAKISTAN NEPAL BHUTAN Tropic of Cancer
EGYPT BAHRAIN
QATAR UNITED MYANMAR
NIGER ERITREA SAUDI ARAB BANGLA- (BURMA) TAIWAN
CHAD ARABIA EMIRATES DESH
NIGERIA SUDAN YEMEN OMAN INDIA LAOS
CAMEROON DJIBOUTI THAILAND VIETNAM PHILIPPINES
CENTRAL ETHIOPIA CAMBODIA MARSHALL
EQUATORIAL AFRICAN REP SOMALIA (KAMPUCHEA) ISLANDS
GUINEA UGANDA KENYA MALDIVES SRI BRUNEI PALAU FEDERATED STATES OF
GABON DEM. REP. RWANDA LANKA MALAYSIA MICRONESIA Equator
SAO TOME OF BURUNDI SINGAPORE NAURU KIRIBATI
& PRINCIPE CONGO TANZANIA SEYCHELLES INDONESIA SOLOMON
ANGOLA MALAWI PAPUA TUVALU
ZAMBIA COMOROS EAST TIMOR NEW GUINEA
ZIMBABWE MADAGASCAR VANUATU FIJI
NAMIBIA BOTS- MAURITIUS
WANA AUSTRALIA Tropic of Capricorn
SOUTH SWAZILAND
AFRICA LESOTHO
NEW
ZEALAND
SOUTHERN OCEAN

INDIAN OCEAN

ANTARCTICA

0 1000 2000 3000 miles
0 1000 2000 3000 4000 5000 km

0 100 200 miles
0 100 200 km
RUSSIA
CASPIAN
BLACK SEA GEORGIA SEA
ARMENIA AZERBAIJAN
TURKEY
AZERBAIJAN
IRAN

Index

CPSIA information can be obtained at www.ICGtesting.com
Printed in the USA
BVOW070351260213

314206BV00002B/91/P

9 780521 144490